THE STORY OF YOUR LIFE

A history of *The Sporting Life* newspaper (1859-1998)

To Gus & his cats

With best wishes

Jamie Campbell

January 2017

"As a humble disciple of an able teacher, I fearlessly claim for my penny sporting guide a range of information and a profundity of knowledge which it would be difficult to surpass."
– Charles Dickens, *All The Year Round*, 16 December 1865.

"Many of the more important improvements made in the presentation and conduct of racing have been, to a great extent, the result of persistent press criticism of abuses and shortcomings."
– Eric Rickman, *Come Racing With Me*, 1951.

"Without newspapers to stimulate interest in betting and encourage readers to take sides about horses, men and issues, racing would wither away."
– 'Jack Logan', *The Sporting Life*, 8 December 1978.

"Of course I read *The Sporting Life*."
– Queen Elizabeth, the Queen Mother, 1987

THE STORY OF YOUR LIFE

A history of
The Sporting Life
newspaper (1859-1998)

James Lambie

Matador
5 Weir Road
Kibworth Beauchamp
Leicester LE8 0LQ, UK
Tel: (+44) 116 279 2277
Email: books@troubador.co.uk
Web: www.troubador.co.uk/matador

ISBN 978 1848762 916

British Library Cataloguing in Publication Data.
A catalogue record for this book is available from the British Library.

Typeset in 11pt Book Sabon by Troubador Publishing Ltd, Leicester, UK
Printed in the UK by TJ International, Padstow, Cornwall

Matador is an imprint of Troubador Publishing Ltd

ACKNOWLEDGEMENTS

The list is a long one, but first and foremost thanks are due to James de Wesselow of *Raceform*, Alan Byrne of the *Racing Post* and that paper's proprietors, FL Partners, for granting copyright clearance for all *Sporting Life* material used in this book. Similarly, I am indebted to the British Library Board for allowing me to reproduce editorial material and illustrations gleaned from that national treasure house for historical research, the Newspaper Library in Colindale, and also to *The Times*, *Daily Telegraph*, *Daily Express* and *The Herald*, for permission to quote from their newspapers, and to all the *Life's* former editors and journalists who, with one exception, gave up their time to be interviewed. Special thanks to Tony Morris who cast a dilatory but expert eye over the tome and corrected some embarrassing errors; to Sir Mark Prescott for the photos of Master McGrath (previously unpublished), and Mick the Miller; to Alec Russell for his invaluable photographic help and to Paddy Finlason (Thoroughbred Advertising), Melanie Knight (Mirrorpix), Elaine Penn (University of Westminster), Richard Prior (Getty Images), Jeremy Smith (London Metropolitan Archives) and Sarah Williams (Museum of London) for supplying some of the excellent photos used in this book. Others who deserve an honourable mention are Christopher Martin-Jenkins MBE for his guidance on cricket matters; Toby Brotherton and Sean Morrill for their critical appraisal; Mick Connaughton and Bryan Pugh for their proof reading, and Bob Menzies and Lucinda Elrick for their help on the IT front. Complete strangers also willingly gave their time to answer my queries, in particular, David Golton of Flora, sponsors of the London Marathon. The Office for National Statistics kindly supplied their Composite Price Index which gives a guide to the value of money in past years compared to the present day, while the Audit Bureau of Circulations was no less helpful in allowing me to use their figures to chart the rise and fall of the *Life* and its contemporaries over the years. Many thanks to the British Library staff for digging out hundreds of volumes and reels of microfilm essential to my research, and also to the staff at the National Archives and the Guildhall Library. Finally, I owe many pints of best bitter to Tim Martin-Jenkins and Mick Connaughton for allowing me to take up squatter's rights at their flats during my bi-annual, month-long research trips to London. Without their generosity and, in the latter case, gritted-teeth tolerance, this book could not have been written.

Picture Acknowledgements: © London Metropolitan Archives: front cover, 4, 5, 14; British Library Board: 2, 6, 7, 8a, 10b, 11, 15, 16, 20; British Library/Racing Post: 3, 9, 10a, 21, 27, 28, 29, 32, 33, 34a, 37, 38; Getty Images: 23, 31, 34b, 35, 40, 41, 43, 51; Author's collection: 1, 8b, 12a, 13, 18, 19, 22, 24, 30, 45, 46a, 47; Racing Post: 44, 48, 50; Sir Mark Prescott's collection: 12b, 36; Museum of London picture library 26a; University of Westminster Archives: 26b; Thoroughbred Advertising: 39a,b,c,d; Wikipedia: 17, 25; Mirrorpix: 42; Ed Byrne: 46b; Phil Smith: 49.

Every attempt has been made to trace the copyright holders of the photos in the author's collection, but some remain unaccredited. We would be grateful if the relevant people contact us.

Note: The Composite Price Index gives only an approximate guide to the value of the £ in past years compared to today; as such I have used a very rough average to cover the years 1820-58 of £1 being equivalent to £85 today. From 1859 to 1914 a £1 bet on a horse would be equivalent to staking, perhaps, £90 today. The war years (First and Second) and their immediate aftermath saw dramatic falls in the value of the £ to around £35 in the early 1920s and again in the mid '40s. Over the last 40 years or so consumer prices have soared as illustrated by the price of the *Sporting Life* (10p in 1974; £1 in 1998 = a 900% increase in 24 years) and the £ of yesteryear can be more accurately compared by using the CPI which is compiled from various retail price indexes.

CONTENTS

— Part One – 'The Early Years' (1859-1874) —

— Part Two – The Uncertain Years (1875-1918) —

Fred Archer, champion jockey for 13 seasons, commits suicide – his career and weight problems – how the *Life* broke the news – his involvement in a jockeys' ring – his death clears the way for a Jockey Club purge – Lord Ailesbury is warned off – Blake dismisses the story in four lines – Lord Durham accuses Sir George Chetwynd and his jockey, Charlie Wood, of fixing races – Wood sues, is awarded a farthing damages, and is warned off – Chetwynd sets his damages at £20,000 – the *Life* devotes 34 columns to the 12-day hearing – Chetwynd also awarded a farthing damages – he resigns from the Jockey Club – postscripts.

— Part Three – 'The Golden Years' (1919-1998) —

ILLUSTRATIONS

Front cover: Winning punters celebrate outside the *Life's* offices in Fleet Street

PART ONE

THE EARLY YEARS

(1859-74)

The Sporting Life is well advertised in Clare Market behind the Law Courts in the Strand.

INTRODUCTION

P ART NARRATIVE, part reportage, this book tells the story of *The Sporting Life*, the most famous of all sporting newspapers, through the campaigns it waged, the events it covered, and the journalists who wrote for it. Particular prominence has been given to horseracing, which formed the core of its contents, but numerous other sports and pastimes were chronicled in its kaleidoscopic columns and as such they have their place in these spindrift pages.

Launched on 24 March 1859, the paper appeared just in time to herald in the dawn of international competition when an English cricket XI embarked upon their first overseas tour (to North America *not* Australia). The following year, what is generally regarded as the first fight for the heavyweight championship of the world took place (illegally) in a field on the Hampshire-Surrey border. A special edition devoted to that famous mill between the English champion, Tom Sayers, and the Irish-American, Jack Heenan, resulted in the infant bi-weekly eclipsing the sales of its chief rival, *Bell's Life in London*, to establish itself, through its cheapness and the quality of its journalism, as the favourite sports paper of the people.

Its readership encompassed all sections of society and included the greatest wordsmith of his time, Charles Dickens, who described himself as "a humble disciple of an able teacher ... [*which*] is served up to me every Wednesday and Saturday at the moderate price of one penny, and I am advised, admonished, warned and instructed, with a vigour, prescience and versatility perfectly astonishing to myself."[1] The appeal of the paper was just as strong more than a century later when Queen Elizabeth, the Queen Mother, was asked in a television interview whether she read 'Racing's Greatest Daily'. "Of course I read the *Sporting Life*," she smiled sweetly.

Queen Victoria would not have been amused to find the racing-man's bible on her breakfast table, but it was during her imperial reign that England exported sport to the world, and the *Life* was there to record history in the making.

It was in the back room of a London pub in 1863 that the newly formed Football Association hammered out a unified set of rules for what the paper chose to describe as an "exciting and health promoting winter pastime" – a pastime that became a pandemic which swept the globe.

Similarly, rugby did not have a common code until the RFU was established in 1871 – a year that saw the first of the home internationals played and the inauguration of the FA Cup competition – while in 1877 proponents of the new game of lawn tennis staged their first championship tournament at the All-England Croquet Club in Wimbledon.

Other less orthodox pursuits were given space in the paper's all-embracing pages. Prominent among them were the ratting contests in which terriers were matched against each other and the clock as they demolished seething packs of the vilified rodents. More refined were the songbird singing competitions in which captive larks and finches gained marks for the sweet poetry of their trills and 'tug-wizzeys'. These and other long-forgotten pursuits such as bottle-carrying and clog dancing were part of the social fabric of England recorded by a band of largely anonymous journalists – many of them freelance penny-a-liners – who wrote under the ubiquitous byline of 'Our Special Correspondent' and took their identity with them to the grave.

By contrast, the men who gave the *Life* its literary clout during its early years were celebrated exponents of their art. Harry Feist, the first and greatest of the paper's widely diverse collection of editors, had what can only be described as a genius for his calling. His leader writer, Henry Hall Dixon, is still well known for the books he wrote under the signature of 'The Druid', and his Special Commissioner, Fred Taylor, had been one of the 'noble six hundred' who rode into the valley of death at Balaclava.

Poor Dillon, the *Life's* first French correspondent, did not last long but earned a sort of immortality when he was killed in a duel with a Parisian aristocrat, while Bob Watson, an all-round sports reporter and referee, was closely associated with the last of the great bareknuckle prizefighters and was also responsible for setting Matthew Webb on the road to worldwide fame as the first man to swim the English Channel.

Later on, there was the scholarly style of the campaigning columnist, Theodore Cook, an Olympic fencer who was knighted for his services to sport. Not so honoured was the paper's German-born bloodstock correspondent, Friedrich Becker, who was interned on the Isle of Man during the First World War.

The interwar years saw the racing driver, Tommy Wisdom, join the team and for three decades he laced his graphic reports from the world's Grand Prix circuits with a frisson of excitement that could only come from one who regularly competed against the best at Brooklands, Le Mans and in many Monte Carlo rallies.

In an altogether different world, the ancient game of golf was described as never before by the lyrical pen of Henry Longhurst, and later still the angst-ridden Jeffrey Bernard entertained readers between his numerous 'indispositions' for 12 alcohol-hazed months before one drunken episode too many earned him his P45.

These men, together with many other gifted reporters and columnists, helped to make the *Life* a publication of world renown, yet in the entire history of Fleet Street it is doubtful whether any paper had such a disastrous start or suffered a more ignoble end – stabbed in the back by its own proprietor.

Its initial misfortunes were self-inflicted and humiliating. Not only did it miss the deadline for its first number to appear a day late, but it was just a few weeks old when it lost a costly court case and was forced to change its title (to its lasting benefit).

During its first few years two of its publishers were sacked for misconduct, its manager did a runner to escape his creditors, and its proprietor and editor were made bankrupt.

Towards the end of the nineteenth century the paper almost went under in the face of strong competition at a time when its lead column suffered from the bizarre ramblings of one eccentric editor and the apathetic attitude of another. It endured the rabid attacks of the Anti-Gambling League and struggled on when parliamentary legislation cut off the valuable revenue it received from its principal advertisers – bookmakers and tipsters.

It was the voice of racing throughout two world wars; it weathered the general strike of 1926, the national newspaper strike of 1955 and a welter of internal disputes and industrial sabotage instituted by the print unions in the 1970s and '80s. It even survived the ravages of its one-time proprietor, Robert Maxwell, who issued dismissal notices (subsequently suspended) to the entire staff as he plundered their pension fund, but it finally succumbed to the incompetence of its management and the cut-throat policies of the commercial world.

On Tuesday, 12 May 1998, after 139 years and 36,910 numbers, the *Sporting Life* rolled off the presses for the last time and part of Britain's sporting heritage died with it. So it was that the prophetic words of its long-time editor, A B Clements, came to pass.

IN THE BEGINNING

"NOTHING IS IMMUTABLE," warned Ben Clements in an editorial he wrote for the centenary issue of the *Sporting Life* on Grand National day 1959. "We can glory in the past, but the power and responsibility are with the present holders of office; and if they are weak, they will fail." The word 'weak' is hardly an adequate description of those who held office at the *Life* during its final years and the hard-nosed editor, who had no time for anyone he felt was less than worthy of his paper, would assuredly have used a more fitting epithet had he been able to foresee the future. But 'Clem' had long since passed on by the time the gravediggers got to work.

As it was, he blithely concluded: "And so, as we approach our hundredth birthday, we give an undertaking to forget it. We do not covet the titles of 'Elder Statesmen' or 'Grand Veterans'. We are pledged faithfully to record the happenings of yesterday; but we are dedicated to today and the wonderful times to come."

And there were, indeed, wonderful times to come, but they were merely the final chapters in the rich and fascinating history of a paper that first appeared on the streets of London and the world beyond on Thursday, 24 March 1859. That year was a significant one in many ways. By an uncanny twist of fate it saw Edwin Drake drill the world's first oil well at Titusville, Pennsylvania – what gushed out of the ground that day was the seminal power of the petrodollar that was to play a major role in sealing the fate of the *Life* 139 years later.

Closer to home on the literary front, the year had started with *The Times* publishing a series of letters dispatched from 'the Dark Continent' by Dr David Livingstone. Charles Dickens penned another best seller in *A Tale of Two Cities*, while Darwin outraged the clergy with his *On the Origin of Species* and Florence Nightingale's *Notes on Nursing* reminded hospital authorities that "the greater part of nursing consists in cleanliness" – a message that seems to have got lost somewhere down the line.

The London of the time was a gaslit city; dank, dangerous and hung heavy with fog in winter; dusty, stinking and stifling in summer; rat-infested all year round. A city where the masses lived in squalor and abject poverty, while the sons of the 'upper ten thousand' frequented the all-night gambling hells and whorehouses of the West End, squandering their wealth and health as if there was no tomorrow.

At the other end of town unemployed labourers sought out dockside opium dens to ease their troubled minds while, as in any great city where there is such a yawning divide between rich and poor, prostitution was rife.* Income tax was nine-pence in the pound and public executions were still drawing crowds to the gallows outside Newgate prison in the shadow of St Paul's Cathedral.

No comets appeared in the heavens that March, but the augurs of ancient Rome would have seen the portents of some great event in the shower of fish – "small and very lively" – that fell from the sky on the valley of Aberdare in Wales. In the same week as *The Times* reported this piscatorial phenomenon, advertisements in lesser journals announced the forthcoming publication of a new sporting paper costing just one penny.

Rumours that such a publication was being planned had been in circulation for some time and

---

* Police records of the time show there were 2,825 brothels to cater for a population of some three million. Of 8,600 full-time prostitutes, 921 were categorised as: "well-dressed, living in brothels; 2,616 well-dressed walking the streets, and 5,063 infested lowly neighbourhoods."[1]

there was much speculation in the well-patronised hostelries of Fleet Street as to who was behind it. To bring out a paper that would be in competition with the long-established *Bell's Life in London* was a bold move for anyone to take, and to price it at a penny (38p) seemed financial suicide. The production costs alone would be formidable, but when the title of the paper became known, it appeared it was to be an offshoot of *Bell's Life* which, even at the price of five-pence, was required reading for any true 'turfite' as a follower of racing was called. The launch advert was short and to the point:

> *Penny Bell's Life and Sporting News.* New, full-sized, weekly paper will appear on Wednesday, March 23. A liberal allowance to the trade. As there will be an enormous circulation, orders must be sent immediately. Office: 1 Crane Court, Fleet Street. Bills on application.[2]

It was rightly assumed that the penny paper was being aimed at a lower class of reader than those who bought *Bell's Life,* which not only catered for the sportsman but also carried pages of foreign, domestic and parliamentary news, stock market reports and columns on police, military and naval intelligence. Published on a Sunday, its eight tightly-packed pages were often so overloaded with general news, that a two-page 'gratuitous' sports supplement (yes, even then!) had to be added.

In addition to *Bell's Life,* there was the *Racing Times*, which was devoted solely to the Turf. This weekly quarto had been launched in 1851 when the working-man's interest in racing had been fanned by the rapid growth of list houses (betting shops) in London. That these two papers were sufficient to satisfy the needs of the sporting public seemed to be confirmed when the *Racing Telegraph*, brought out in opposition to the *Racing Times* in 1852, folded after just 14 months.

At the time, racing received scant coverage in the national press which confined itself almost entirely to the main meetings of the year. Reports on smaller meetings appeared, if at all, only in provincial papers local to the races or in leather-bound monthly or quarterly book-sized publications which, at 2s 6d (£10.60) or more a copy, were well beyond the pocket and often the comprehension of the ordinary punter. Because the journalists of the day "were determined to appear scholar-like, feeling perfectly safe with the scholarship of their readers,"[3] they peppered their articles with Latin, French and even Greek phrases together with quotes from 'the immortal Cicero'.

The Sporting Magazine was, for instance, first published in 1792 to "woo the votaries of Dian and the frequenters of Newmarket" with information and "lyric compositions of the sylvan, rustic and Anacreontic kind". The first publication to carry regular articles on racing, it advertised itself as a "Monthly Calendar of the Transactions of The Turf, The Chase, and every other Diversion Interesting to the Man of Pleasure, Enterprise & Spirit."

In 1821 the magazine introduced the public to the initially anonymous writings of Charles James Apperley, an immodest, sycophantic scribe who once held the belief that "to write for a sporting paper is no job for a gentleman," but, cosseted by a salary of £1,500 (£127,500) a year, it was not long before he boasted "no one but a gentleman is qualified for the position."[4]

Apperley's authoritative articles on foxhunting and the mail and stagecoaches that plied the highroads of England quickly acquired a following that increased when he extended his coverage to the Turf and began to write under the signature of 'Nimrod'. But fame led to extravagance and he was soon complaining that his expenses did not cover his costs which included the upkeep of five hunters and attendant grooms. Embarrassed by mounting debts, he decamped to France from where he posted off his best-known essays on *The Chase, The Road* and *The Turf* to the *Quarterly Review* (1809).

Together with Whyte-Melville (his replacement on the *Sporting Magazine*) and R S Surtees, who was to launch the *New Sporting Magazine* (1831) to rival the original, Apperley led a select few who wrote for the upper classes on racing and hunting.

The daily press such as the *Morning Chronicle* (1769), *Morning Post* (1772), *Morning Herald* (1780), *The Times* (1785) and the *Morning Advertiser* (1794), relied on freelance contributors or took their reports from the sporting news agency run by William Ruff whose son (also William) founded the famous *Ruff's Guide to the Turf* in 1842.

Some Sunday papers also covered sport; *Bell's Weekly Dispatch* (1801), in particular, gave prizefighting more space than most during the Regency period (1811-20) when pugilism enjoyed a revival under the patronage of the future king, George IV.

Pierce Egan, who wrote for the *Dispatch*, can be regarded as the father of modern sports journalism. In contrast to Apperley and his ilk, he wrote for the masses in a colourful style that appealed to followers of the noble art. The 'claret' (blood) always flowed freely through his PR (prize ring) reports as the 'mawleys' (fists) flew, the 'ivories' (teeth) rattled and the 'optics' (eyes) swelled and closed. But it was with his novel, *Life in London*, that Egan hit the big time. Published in monthly instalments and illustrated by the savagely brilliant caricaturist, George Cruikshank, it featured "the Day and Night scenes of Jerry Hawthorne Esq. and his elegant friend Corinthian Tom, accompanied by Bob Logic, the Oxonian, in their Rambles and Sprees throughout the Metropolis."

The public could not get enough of the raffish adventures of Tom and Jerry (Egan, as 'Bob Logic', was the narrator). A play followed and then on 13 January 1822, Egan launched a Sunday paper, *Life in London*, containing general news and sport. Seven weeks later a London printer, Robert Bell, unashamedly stole Egan's title and attached his own name to it. *Bell's Life in London*, which carried the appendage '*and Sporting Chronicle*', was not only the same price (7d = £2.50) as its rival, but offered similar reading "Combining with the News of the Week a rich Repository of Fashion, Wit and Humour and interesting Incidents of High and Low Life."

Such blatant plagiarism was not uncommon in the cut-throat world of Fleet Street and, in the inevitable slanging match that followed, Bell predicted *Life in London* would soon "shrink into nothingness". This duly came about a few months later when he bought out Egan and incorporated *Life in London* into his own paper. Undaunted, Egan was back two years later with *Pierce Egan's Life in London and Sporting Guide*. In a front-page 'Address to the Sporting World', he left his rival in no doubt he had a fight on his hands as he declared with block-capital emphasis:

I only request a 'clear stage' and FAIR PLAY that I may have an opportunity of supporting the principles of my King and the honour of my country; upholding the cornerstones of the English nation – humanity of heart – generosity of disposition – firmness of mind – and courage of soul. To support these native characteristics of Britons has long been my aim and I shall never lose sight of them but with my life.

Leaving aside the fact that George IV had no principles, it was no contest. The weight of Egan's name and the vitality of his paper soon won over readers from *Bell's Life* and within six months Bell had thrown in the towel and sold his paper to William Clement, the proprietor of *The Observer* (1791).

Egan had his revenge, but it was a Pyrrhic victory because, with newspaper taxes at their peak, production costs were extortionate and three years later he was forced to put his paper up for auction when it was bought by Clement and absorbed into *Bell's Life*.

Such then is the contorted early history of a paper which, once firmly established, saw off its less substantial rivals as its circulation gradually increased from 3,000 until it topped the 29,000 mark in 1859. It was then that another unprincipled publisher, George William Maddick, took a leaf out of Robert Bell's book (namely, the title page), and launched the *Penny Bell's Life and Sporting News*, which, in a few short, litigious weeks, was to transform itself into *The Sporting Life*.

THE PENNY PRESS

THE *PENNY BELL'S LIFE* was born at a time when the English nation had become obsessed with sport in all its forms. In an era of sexual repression and dire warnings that 'the follies of youth' could result in "spermatorrhoea, impotency, depression, blindness and eventually complete physical degeneration,"[1] the doctrine that a healthy body equalled a healthy mind was pounded out with a missionary zeal.

The Victorians' passion for physical recreation was matched only by their love of financial speculation whether it be betting on horses or investing in railway shares. The compulsion was to be found in all sections of society and it provided the basis for the remarkable success the penny paper achieved in its formative years despite a succession of disasters that would have destroyed a more orthodox journal.

There could not have been a better time to launch a sports paper. Its arrival coincided with a series of high-profile events that enabled it to tap into a rich vein of national pride that stemmed from the country's faith in the invincibility of its sportsmen. There were no better jockeys, cricketers, runners, oarsmen or swimmers. "They even taught us Swiss how to climb our own mountains and make a sport of it," complained Jung.

It was also an exciting time in journalism as the newspaper trade was being borne along on a tide of inventions brought in by the industrial revolution. Up to the 1840s news of events had been relayed to the printing houses of London by mail coach, carrier pigeon or mounted courier. On Derby day "Londoners used to crowd Waterloo Bridge and the Strand to see the courier of *Bell's Life* or the *Globe* ride home carrying the names of the winners in a sealed pouch slung round his neck."[2]

Carrier pigeons were faster but not so reliable as they were vulnerable to attack from their natural enemies (hawks, etc) in the air and from 'lovers of the trigger' on the ground. These winged messengers could cover the 55 miles from Goodwood to London in 75 minutes provided they weren't "picked off on race days by gunners, who were anxious to read the little billet on their leg … We have heard of them coming from Epsom with an entry list printed on tissue paper tied to each leg, so as to balance them."[3]

The best birds were the Antwerp-bred pigeons used by the Rothschild bankers on the Continent. William Clement shrewdly obtained a few of the coveted 'Antwerps' and bred a colony of them on the roof of the *Bell's Life* building in the Strand:

> This helped make *Bell's Life* the power it became in the country and old Ned Smith, who had control of the 170 Strand pigeon loft, used to declare that the only pigeons worth having were the Rothschilds' and his own … After a Derby, hundreds were thrown off in front of the grandstand and for Newmarket, Lambourn, Wantage, Goodwood, Ilsley and suchlike comparatively short flights the messages were safe, but they failed to reach Malton when Cotherstone won the [*1843*] Derby.[4]

The big breakthrough in the transmission of news came with the development of the electric telegraph which was initially installed as a safety device to control the running of trains on the country's rapidly expanding railway network. The telegraph was soon adapted for commercial purposes and in 1847 it was used to relay the Queen's speech to parliament to the provincial press, but its transmission to some northern cities was hardly an unqualified success. The 730-word text had to be sent through two intermediate stations at Normanton and Derby, and with attendant hitches it took five hours to reach Leeds.

A speedier service was provided by the seabed cable laid between Dover and Calais in 1851, a link that induced a former German bank clerk, Julius Reuter, to move his recently established continental news agency to London.

Meanwhile, advances in the printing industry had brought about radical changes in Fleet Street. At the beginning of the century, newspapers were produced on hand-operated wooden presses, but in 1814 *The Times* stole a march on its rivals by installing a steam-driven cylinder press that could produce 1,100 copies an hour. Not only did the new technology make production cheaper and more efficient, but further innovations such as the rotary press, stereotype plates, mechanical typecasting and typesetting and automatic ink-feeds, were to revolutionise the industry as the century progressed.

Together with a rapidly developing society and a wider and faster distribution system provided by the railways, newspapers entered the age of mass circulation despite still being heavily taxed. This 'tax on knowledge' was initially designed by crown and parliament to curb the growing power of the press. Introduced in 1712 by Robert Harley, chief minister to Queen Anne, the Newspaper Stamp Act imposed a duty of a penny on each published news-sheet while a shilling tax was levied on each advertisement. These taxes were steadily increased until stamp duty was 4d and the tax on adverts 3s 6d, which, together with a duty on newsprint, imposed a huge burden on the industry and forced the price of *The Times* up to 7d in the 1820s when a bottle of gin could be bought for a shilling.

During the following decade the taxes were reduced and eventually pressure from such Liberal reformers as the free-trader Richard Cobden brought about their abolition. When Cobden addressed the subject of stamp duty in 1850 he declared: "So long as this penny lasts there can be no daily press for the middle or working class; who below the rank of a merchant or a wholesale dealer can afford to take in a daily paper at five-pence?"[5]

It was left to William Gladstone to grasp the nettle when, as Chancellor of the Exchequer in 1853, he did away with the tax on advertisements and two years later abolished stamp duty. He completed the hat trick by scrapping the tax on newsprint during his second term as Chancellor in 1861. These moves paved the way for a veritable explosion in the newspaper industry marking, as it did, the birth of the 'penny press'.

The *Daily Telegraph* led the way when it hit the streets on 29 June 1855. Initially priced at 2d, it had a shaky start but "after an infancy cradled in debt and difficulty,"[6] it was taken over as a bad debt by its printer, Joseph Moses Levy (later Lord Burnham), who had recently acquired the *Sunday Times*. Levy at once halved the price of the *Telegraph* which, under his management and with its rivals selling at 5d, soon overtook *The Times* in terms of circulation.

Up to this period there had been only one daily paper published outside London – Liverpool's *Northern Daily Times* (1853) – but the removal of the stamp duty saw the bi-weekly *Scotsman* (1817) and the *Manchester Guardian* (1821) convert to daily status. In the same year the *Liverpool Daily Post* and the *Sheffield Daily Telegraph* were born along with 15 other provincial newspapers.

It was into this heady environment of free enterprise and vibrant journalism that the *Sporting Life*, under its temporary alias of the *Penny Bell's Life*, launched itself four years later. The paper was founded by a motley consortium headed by two decidedly chancy printer-publishers, George Maddick and William Strange. Maddick had been behind the short-lived *Racing Telegraph* that was brought out to rival the *Racing Times* in 1852, while he also founded the more durable *Court Circular* in 1856.

The latter publication, which described itself as 'A Journal of Fashion, Literature, Science and Art,' provided a perfect example of its proprietor's readiness to cash in on a well-known title in order to lure in readers and the trade.

His *Court Circular* had nothing to do with the daily communiqué that announces the agenda of the royal family, but the 'borrowed' title served its purpose since "it caught on wonderfully with advertisers, but one is bound to admit that George Maddick knew a good deal more about Wine Office Court than he did the Court of St James's."[7]*

William Strange also had an eye for the main chance and had made a killing a few years earlier when he published the unclaimed dividend books of the Bank of England, which sold 30,000 copies in two years. At 57, he was 22 years older than his business partner and, well aware of the gamble they were about to undertake, he was happy to let Maddick act as the promoter of the new paper.

The two men had the backing of a couple of enthusiastic youngsters who had sunk all they could beg or borrow into the venture. William Henry Stephens was the son of a popular actor of the same name who was, conveniently, on a three-year tour of America at the time. His qualifications for taking the position of manager of the new journal are not known, but he was probably talked into it by his friend, Henry Mort Feist, who also came from a theatrical background and was the driving force behind the whole enterprise.

Feist, the self-appointed editor, was just 22, yet he was able to give the paper the authority and integrity it needed to sell itself to the public. Not only did he possess a wisdom far beyond his years, but he was a gifted writer with an insatiable appetite for work and a thorough knowledge of racing and other sports. He was, in fact, born to the job.

A tall, handsome, intelligent-looking youth with a pale, grave face and sad eyes that disguised a quick wit and a lively, amiable nature, he was the son of Charles Feist, a Yorkshireman, who had moved to London in 1813 to study law.

Feist senior soon found work in a solicitor's office was not for him and opted instead for the Bohemian existence of a travelling actor. He joined a celebrated company of comedians and went on tour for five years before marriage and parental responsibilities forced him to settle down.

He became the proprietor of a school in the Norfolk town of Swaffham where he taught for seven years before he moved on to fill a similar post in Newmarket for a further 14 years. It was here, where many of his pupils came from racing families, that he began to chronicle the romance of the Turf. He had already shown he had a way with words with three volumes of poetry to his name and had also written several textbooks which became standard works in schools throughout England.

Through his friendship with John Chapman, a theatrical producer and managing editor of the *Sunday Times*, he was taken on as Newmarket correspondent for that paper. Writing under the *nom de plume* of 'Judex'†, his articles were so well received that efforts were soon being made to entice him to London. For a long time he held back, but in 1842 he finally relented and became editor of the *Sunday Times'* Turf department.

Harry Feist was thus brought up on a diet of racing and journalism and it was as a callow youth

---

* Wine Office Court, situated just off Fleet Street, became the home of the London Press Club, which Maddick frequented in his later years.

† *Noms de plume* were originally used by writers to protect themselves from prosecution and possible torture. In the seventeenth century, branding and the cutting off of ears were the standard penalties imposed on recalcitrant scribes who dared criticise the crown, the clergy or parliament.

Harry Feist, 'Augur' and founding editor of the *Life*: "The influence of his pen was felt far beyond the range attained by other sporting writers." – *SL* 19-12-1874

of 15 that he started to write an occasional article for the *Racing Times* under the pseudonym of 'Augur'. It was an apposite signature. Not only did it convey the ability to foretell future events as did the augurs of ancient Rome who studied the flight of birds – rather than the form book – to arrive at their predictions, but, more pertinently, it was the name of a horse he fancied for the 1852 Derby.

In January that year the tyro tipster's 'letter' to the editor of the *Racing Times* began:

> I send you a few more observations which I trust will prove serviceable to your numerous readers. For the Derby I still prefer Augur and Chief Baron Nicholson, but would advise an investment on Elcot; he will see a much shorter price.

It was no fairytale start, but nor was it a bad one. Feist had found the right line of form – the trouble was he went for the wrong horse. Augur, a 30-1 chance, could finish only seventh to the 25-1 winner, Daniel O'Rourke, a horse he had beaten narrowly when winning the Champagne Stakes at Doncaster the previous year. Chief Baron Nicholson, at 40-1, was a worthy third only a length behind the winner, but Elcot did *not* 'see a much shorter price' and ran like the 100-1 chance he was.

The following year, young Feist witnessed his first Derby when, to sample the carnival atmosphere of the occasion, he joined the throng of Cockney revellers on the road to Epsom as he walked the 13 miles from his home in Norwood, south London. It was well worth the hike for he saw a memorable winner in the John Scott-trained West Australian, who went on to become the first horse to complete the combination of victories that became known as the Triple Crown – the Two Thousand Guineas, Derby and St Leger.

When Charles Feist died in 1856, Harry had his indentures as an apprentice engraver cancelled and went to assist his elder brother Albert, who had succeeded their father at the *Sunday Times*. He was, therefore, no raw novice when he became editor of George Maddick's new publication, but while his appointment was an inspired one, the decision to call the paper the *Penny Bell's Life and Sporting News* most assuredly was not. The convoluted and deliberately misleading title was designed to attract readers by implying it was a sister paper to *Bell's Life* selling at a fifth of its price.

Feist had urged Maddick to choose a title more worthy of a new and vigorous paper, but he was overruled. The decision to stick with the (un)original title was to cost the proprietors dear, but there were more pressing problems on the first day of publication as a small staff worked feverishly through Tuesday night in order to bring out the paper in time to catch the early morning trains.

History does not record the precise nature of the trouble, but there is a strong suspicion that few, if any, dummy runs had taken place before the launch. Plans were being made on the hoof and consequently the paper had the worst possible start any newspaper could have – it missed the deadline for its first number!

THE BATTLE OF THE BELLS

WHEN THE 'penny imitator', as it was predictably dubbed, finally appeared on the streets with its dateline altered from Wednesday to Thursday, March 24, 1859, it was seen that the words 'Bell's Life' were the most prominent part of its title. The famous name dominated an elaborate, banner-like design that featured a montage of the principal sports and pastimes covered by the paper, namely: racing, cricket, prizefighting, pedestrianism (foot racing), aquatics, hunting, shooting and fishing.

It was also evident there had been a major rethink since the paper first advertised itself as a 'full-sized weekly' since it was now stated it would be published *twice* a week, on Wednesdays and Saturdays, at No. 1 Crane Court, Fleet Street, in the parish of St Dunstan-in-the-West in the City of London. A secluded little yard tucked away off the north-west side of 'The Street', Crane Court had proved to be quite a nursery for famous journals having seen the birth of *Punch* magazine in 1841 and the *Illustrated London News* (1842) amongst others.

The newcomer to the crèche was a six-column broadsheet, which ran to four pages of 8pt inky condensed type. In its first number, small engravings (headpieces) depicting the sport that was being covered, topped the relevant columns. This opened up the paper and made it easy on the eye, but because there was 'pressure on space' from the start the experiment was never repeated; instead the prevailing trend of cramming the maximum amount of text into the space available became the norm. Each column contained some 2,400 words, which may have represented value for money, but also made for loose journalism, closely packed pages and strained eyes for readers by gas or candlelight.

The front page carried an introductory address; the fixture list of race meetings for 1859; a report of the previous week's racing at Warwick; a summary of the past shooting season; a 'Training Intelligence' column with reports from some of the main racing centres, and a 'Turf Market' review that noted significant betting moves on forthcoming feature races.

There were also two race-preview articles by the paper's principal columnists who wrote under pen names that honoured former 'cracks' of the Turf. In this instance the names adopted were 'Voltigeur', the winner of the 1850 Derby and St Leger, and 'Birdcatcher', a celebrated Irish racehorse and stallion. 'Voltigeur', one of the many pseudonyms used by Harry Feist during the course of his career, betrayed his thespian roots as he introduced himself in a style heavily redolent of the time:

As the manager of a theatre steps before his proscenium on the inauguration of a season and claims indulgence and appreciation for the labours he intends to expend for the delectation of his patrons, so does 'Voltigeur' come before the public with a prefatory explanation of his intentions and claims to the suffrages of his readers.

Thankfully, the erudite editor soon settled for less pretentious prose as he candidly admitted he was "no gifted soothsayer, but rather a literary 'tout' whose talismen are *Ruff's Guide, Feist's Book* and his own hard-earned experience of stable practices."

---

* In 1857, Albert Feist launched *Feist's Racing Record*, a monthly form book costing 2d. At the same time he was also writing for the *Daily Telegraph* under the signature of 'Hotspur', a pseudonym he first used when he was a regular contributor to the *Racing Times*. Young Harry, it should be added, had gained his 'hard-earned experience' by working in a racing stable during his school holidays.

'Birdcatcher', whose article was datelined 'Epsom, March 21', announced:

It is my good fortune to be placed in a position which enables me to secure the most genuine and reliable information from both British and Continental racing establishments, and I have little doubt that your readers will rapidly perceive the authentic nature of my lucubrations.

Mysteriously, after this initial offering, Birdcatcher's signature disappeared from the pages of the *Life* forever, so it was with limited 'lucubrations', much 'prefatory explanation' and an undisguised determination to become a motive force in the predominant sport of the day, that the new journal set forth to inform, entertain and improve the lot of its readers.

Feist, obviously keen to create an impression from the start, sketched a decidedly controversial summary of the current state of racing in his editorial address, which took up a full column and did not flatter the sport. Among other things, he maintained:

Racehorses have fallen into the hands of speculators who keep them, as Lord Derby vigorously and correctly expressed it, purely as 'instruments of gaming' ... Many of the racing establishments in England at the present moment are subjected to the despotism of large speculators who pull the wires as they please and reduce the trainer to a nefarious puppet.

Why should this unpleasant fact be glossed over? It has long been the error, or rather venial vice, of racing journalists to mislead the public on this score and, in mistaken zeal for the welfare of 'our Isthmian Games', to hush up an abuse which can only be crushed by remorseless exposure.

A racing journalist should be the advocate of the sport and not the obstinate champion of its adherents. It is a matter of utter indifference to us if we offend a certain body of speculators. We have firmly resolved to do our duty as an exponent of pastimes honourably and honestly pursued, and not a single abuse shall escape us in the independent and determined policy it is our intention to inaugurate.

The word 'speculators' could apply equally to gamblers or bookmakers and Feist certainly had the latter in mind as he went on to elaborate:

Since bookmaking has become a science, the Turf has almost daily displayed a corresponding decline ... Legitimately and honourably pursued, the calling of bookmaker is neither discreditable nor objectionable. But when the bookmaker sets aside the common principles of honesty to compass his designs – when he bids enormous prices for animals on purpose to prevent their upsetting his wagering calculations – when he corrupts jockeys and buys up trainers – when he bets on the London pavement in direct defiance of the law, he not only disgraces horse racing, but violates the regulations of our social existence...*

We openly declare that the recklessness of bookmakers and their indifference to moral rectitude is the chief cause of the Turf being regarded by the general public with a cautious suspicion ... 'Flash betting', the 'milking' and 'faking' of horses are grand evils which have sprung from the present unscrupulous bookmaking system and it shall be our mission to castigate all offenders on the detection of every deviation from honesty.

---

* This was not strictly true; it was not until 1867 that street betting was outlawed in London, while a general law prohibiting it throughout the country did not came into force until 1906.

This was all good fighting talk and if it didn't exactly have the wicked bookmakers quaking in their boots, it certainly helped to sell the paper. In its third issue on March 30, under a front-page item headed 'Our Success', a paean of self-praise incorporating block capitals for emphasis, proclaimed:

> The success which we have obtained constitutes no secondary event in the history of journalism in this country. To have issued a paper which, in its first week, has obtained A SALE LARGER THAN ANY OTHER SPORTING JOURNAL IN THE WORLD is an achievement of no common order.
>
> Our most sanguine expectations have been more than realised; indeed, it was impossible to have calculated upon so extraordinary a triumph – a triumph which can only be sustained by the most strenuous exertions on our part. From every quarter of the United Kingdom we have received the most flattering assurances of support and when our arrangements are concluded this paper will be the most complete journal of its kind ever published ... in a few weeks we shall be able to supply with punctuality a HUNDRED THOUSAND of each edition.

The fact that the paper was such an immediate hit with the public stirred up a hornets' nest of jealous indignation in the offices of *Bell's Life* a few blocks away at 170 Strand. The first indication of the impending storm came on April 9 when, without explanation, the new journal dropped its flourishing masthead and replaced it with a more orthodox '*Penny Bell's Life*' set in 108pt Old English Gothic with '*and Sporting News*' appended as a sub-title in reduced type.

Confirmation that 'the battle of the Bells' was about to begin appeared in the next number four days later when a leading article in the penny paper mischievously played upon its rival's motto '*Nunquam dormio*' (We never sleep). It taunted:

> When Mein Herr Rip Van Winkle awoke from his protracted somnolency he was astounded to perceive the utter transformation things had undergone and the poor dumpkopf was totally ignorant of the fact that, while he had lain in a state of coma, the world, and all things of the world, had been true to their traditions of progress.
>
> Certain newspapers are, unfortunately, in the predicament of the bewildered Rip; they have enjoyed long and uninterrupted repose and have suddenly been aroused to the awkward fact that they are half a century behind the era of advancement.
>
> The *Penny Bell's Life* may have to endure for some time the spleen of the Rip Van Winkles of the sporting press, but ultimately the good old gentlemen will become more genial and their offended dignity will subside when they perceive that the generation which has sprung up during their slumber means them no harm.
>
> Seriously, we are in the unpleasant position of being misunderstood and misrepresented and people whose integrity, enterprise and industry we have been taught to respect from our infancy are turning upon us as though we were incipient cut-throats.
>
> When the daily penny press originated it encountered precisely the same tone of feeling from the dear journals that we are now experiencing at the hands of our high-priced sporting contemporaries. Persons connected with the *Times, Daily News, cum multis aliis*, sneered at the sheets of the pennies and put a limit of a few weeks upon their existence. How completely the calculations have been at fault it needs no declaration from us to prove.
>
> That the success of the penny daily press was but the foreshadowing of a parallel prosperity in our

own case, we have ample reason to believe. We have already called into existence a fresh class of readers to whom a penny is little consideration, but who cannot patronise papers which cost five times that amount.

At this point, by a timely coincidence that had more to do with journalistic licence than the sudden arrival of a writ, the leader announced:

> Since the few foregoing remarks were written, we have received a notice of injunction from the proprietors of *Bell's Life in London* to restrain us from using our present title … Our readers already know too much of our principles to believe that we should quietly succumb to the machinations of frantic monopolists and we have resolved to spare no pains to give a full exposure in court to a shameful attempt to malign the reputation of our journal.

So it was that just four weeks after the launch of the 'penny imitator', 'The Great Injunction Case' was heard in Chancery before vice-chancellor Sir John Stuart on Thursday April 21. It was billed as: "Charles and George William Clement v. George Maddick. Counsel for the plaintiffs Mr Malins QC and Mr J H Palmer; Mr Bacon QC and Mr Karslake for the defendant."

The plaintiffs were the sons of William Clement whose journalistic ventures had made him a rich man long before he died in 1852. Their counsel, Richard Malins, had been looking forward to taking the case. Renowned for his eloquence, he could see it would give him a free rein in that department.

In his opening address, the portly barrister adopted his usual attacking stance as he adjusted his monocle and fixed the vice-chancellor with a challenging stare which implied he was holding all the aces, as, indeed, he was. He pointed out that for upwards of 30 years his clients' newspaper had "from habit and common parlance" been called *Bell's Life* and that letters addressed to 'The Editor, *Bell's Life*, London' or '*Bell's Life*, Fleet Street' always found their way to the paper's offices at 170 Strand.

In addition, cheques were invariably made payable to '*Bell's Life*', and it had long been the practice of those engaged in sporting wagers to make the proprietors of the paper stakeholders. From £8,000 to £10,000 a year (£720,000 to £900,000) passed through their hands in this way and a considerable portion of that sum was sent to them through the post. Furthermore, articles taken from the newspaper and published abroad or in other papers in Britain were acknowledged by the short style of '*Bell's Life*'.

The plaintiffs, Malins said, claimed they had acquired an exclusive right to the title of Bell's Life, and the use of that name by the defendant was calculated to depreciate the sale and profits of their newspaper and cause serious loss and inconvenience to them in the number of misdirected deliveries that would constantly occur in correspondence and remittances sent to them. Evidence in the form of letters was then produced to show that numerous applications had been made to the *Bell's Life* office for the *Penny Bell's Life*.

The gloves were certainly off as the redoubtable QC pressed home his attack by asserting that the inferiority of the penny paper to that of his clients' would bring their newspaper into disrepute: "The practice of palming off one man's goods as the property of another is a gross fraud," he boomed. "Mr Maddick, being the proprietor and publisher of this paper, is committing a wrong upon the plaintiffs as if he were, day by day, putting his hands in their pockets and robbing them of their money."

In the face of such an onslaught Maddick's defence was virtually non-existent and his claim that,

"I assumed and used the name and style of the *Penny Bell's Life and Sporting News* merely for the purpose of conveying, in the readiest way, the information that my paper was intended to contain sporting subjects," was risible.

At this juncture Sir John Stuart, obviously seeking an early settlement to what was an indefensible case, offered a gentle hint by remarking: "If both parties are determined to stand upon their utmost rights, of course it is my duty to do the best I can for them; but I should think that the intervention of a little good sense might set the matter right." He then asked Maddick's brief: "Is there any case of a *Penny Times*?"

Edward Karslake, like Malins, was seldom lost for words but on this occasion he was struggling as he replied weakly: "There was the *Penny Pickwick* and the *Pickwick Papers*. The *Penny Pickwick* is the real Pickwick."

Sir John, as befitting a canny, West-Highland Scot from Ballachulish, had no time for pointless and expensive litigation. He paused a few seconds to ponder this response before he dropped an even bigger hint to the defendant: "Of course it will be a great deal more than a penny affair if you will go on. You *may* go on if you like."

And go on they did. It transpired that Maddick had tried to circumvent the injunction by transferring the ownership of his paper to the manager, William Stephens, and a fellow associate, Richard Robinson. This desperate ploy only provided a stay of execution as the case had to be adjourned until the following Wednesday so the bill of injunction could be amended to include the two new 'proprietors' as co-defendants.

On the Saturday, the beleaguered 'penny' prepared its readers for a change of title with the front-page notice:

> Pending the proceedings against us in Chancery, we beg to remind our readers that even if it were possible that the injunction could be granted, it would only have the effect of causing us to relinquish a single word of our present title. This is the only change which can be effected. The paper will undergo no other alteration in character or matter.

The next day, *Bell's Life* strenuously denied its injunction had been designed to crush its rival or to interfere with *fair* competition as it declared:

> Free trade is now the order of the day and we should be 'frantic monopolists' indeed were we now to depart from those liberal principles which we have always advocated. To any party honestly desirous of establishing a sporting newspaper, there would be no difficulty in finding an appropriate name for it without invading the rights of any journal already in existence. For example, what would more clearly indicate the character of such a periodical than to call it the *Penny Sporting Chronicle*, the *Penny Sporting News* or the *Penny Sporting Record*, in fact, any other suitable heading might easily be framed by a very moderate exercise of the inventive faculties.

When the case resumed, Sir John Stuart addressed Maddick's leading counsel, James Bacon, as he referred to the change made to the masthead of the paper on April 9: "The title seems to have been altered a little pending the litigation," he observed dryly. "It's a pity you had not altered it a little more. Had you not better go further now and alter the title to satisfy the plaintiffs?"

Bacon, as was his wont, had listened to the proceedings in a semi-recumbent position, eyes half-closed, legs crossed and stretched out in front of him. He only stirred to take an occasional pinch of snuff or make a witty, *sotto voce* remark to a colleague behind him, but now he acknowledged the vice-chancellor's point with a slow, cynical smile.

Unable to apply his usual solid arguments to the case, he still gave it his best shot as he pointed out there were numerous instances of papers 'borrowing' part of their titles from established journals. "The principles are clear," he insisted. "There are the *Sunday Times* and the *Weekly Times* and there was for many years the *New Times*, and there are many other newspapers which anybody is likely to imitate, for imitation is no fraud."

But by now Sir John was tired of the whole charade: "Why not strike out the words 'Bell's Life' from your paper and give it some other name?" he snapped at the unhappy Bacon. It was obvious, as it had been from the start, what the outcome would be and in giving judgement the vice-chancellor ruled that if it was clear the defendants could not publish a paper called *Bell's Life*, it followed they could not publish a *Penny Bell's Life*, which was nothing more than a *Bell's Life* for a penny. The plaintiffs were therefore entitled to their injunction with costs.

The case, having taken up almost two full days, cost Maddick and his backers a pretty penny indeed as Stuart had so judiciously but vainly tried to warn them. It was ironic that the founders of what was to become a national institution had to lose a court case and a great deal of money in order to arrive at a title that became famous throughout the world. But so it was that on Saturday, 30 April 1859, the simple, all-embracing title of *The Sporting Life* made its appearance. On the front page a brief announcement stated:

> Our journal is this week published under a fresh title according to the decision of Vice-Chancellor Sir John Stuart. The Paper will, however, undergo no other alteration.

Accompanying this notice a defiant leader headed 'The Story of Our Lives' declared:

> Shakespeare said: 'What's in a name? A rose by any other name would smell as sweet'. And we trust that the loss of our bare name and title will not be misapprehended as a loss of any of our attributes. It was rightly said in court, during the proceedings of the injunction, that our paper has already attained a wide celebrity, and to believe that this could be attained by anything but considerable intrinsic merit would be blinking the truth.

The article went on to credit the Clement brothers with having shown "no ungenerous exultation at our temporary discomfiture," a remark that proved well wide of the mark when *Bell's Life* appeared the following day. In explaining the importance of defending its title, the old paper claimed (rather prophetically in the past tense):

> Our name was valuable, *Bell's Life* was known everywhere. It was familiar as a Household Word with thousands and thousands in the United Kingdom, on the Continent and in America; it was the symbol of England to the sailor and the soldier in all those distant regions where the service of their country required their presence; it renewed their recollections of the sports and the freedom of home. It was precisely for this reason that its name was to be stolen. That has been done, and not by a rival – for in no sense does it deserve that title – but a mere mimic has committed this act of plagiaristic petty larceny in order to benefit itself at the expense of ourselves and the public.

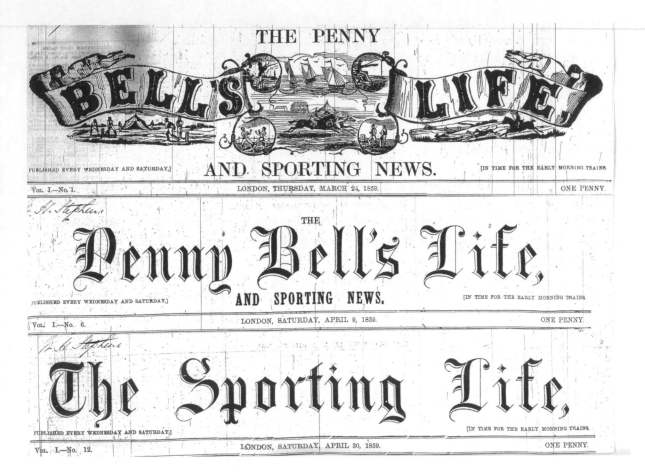

How Sir John Stuart and the Clement brothers transformed the *Penny Bell's Life* masthead into *The Sporting Life* in the space of six weeks.

Within three decades of this 'act of plagiaristic petty larceny' the 'mere mimic' was to swallow up *Bell's Life*, but first it had to survive the fall-out of the injunction case as the action moved on to the Bankruptcy Court and then returned to Chancery before finally winding up in the Court of Appeal. This was Fleet Street writing its own story; a story of financial ruin and personal tragedy of true Dickensian proportions.

BANKRUPT AND BEETON

THERE WERE four main players in the drama that unfolded in the wake of the Great Injunction Case. In order of appearance they were, John George Shipley, a painfully naive West End saddler who was sadly miscast as the knight in shining armour riding to the rescue of the *Sporting Life*. Hopelessly out of his depth among the wheeler-dealers of Fleet Street, he was duly plucked like a pigeon.

Complicit in his fate was John Hutton, the dry-as-dust proprietor of the *Weekly Times* – 'A London Newspaper of History, Politics, Literature, Science and Art' – and a shallow opportunist who preferred to let others take the risks of newspaper management while he reaped the profits of their labours.

Hutton was in league with – and tool of – the villain of the piece, William McMurray, a manipulative Cheapside paper merchant who specialised in intricate financial deals that were designed to line his pockets at the expense of any innocent who fell into his clutches.

Lastly, there was Samuel Orchart Beeton, a charismatic Cockney publisher who shone out as the tragic-hero of the production as he fought for control of the *Life* while he helped to restore its dissipated fortunes. Just when he appeared to have the fruits of victory in his grasp they were snatched from him in the final act.

There was also a strong supporting cast featuring Sir John Stuart, Richard Malins, Bacon and Karslake, who all returned to take another bow in Chancery, while, crucially, a cameo role was given to Lord Justice Sir James Knight-Bruce who, in the dotage of his 74th year to heaven, had the task of unravelling the machinations of the rival parties.

Ironically, the only true thespians, Harry Feist and William Stephens, were limited to walk-on parts or, to be more exact in the case of the latter, a walk-off part which saw him exit stage left to flee north o'er the border pursued by a pack of angry creditors.*

Feist, to his credit (which, in monetary terms, was nil), stayed at his post to settle what debts he could after he was made bankrupt in 1861.

The curtain rose on what was to prove a long and complex legal battle, on Derby Day, Wednesday, 1 June 1859. The scene was the deserted editorial floor of the *Life's* Crane Court offices. There was much evidence of packed portmanteaux around a subs' desk still strewn with the debris of a hectic night's work. Amongst the litter lay a discarded page proof that carried 'Sentinel's' summing up of the big race (he went for Musjid, the well-backed 9-4 winner) and an 'Important Notice to Subscribers and the Trade':

> The large and weekly increasing demand for *The Sporting Life* has rendered it imperative upon the proprietors to remove at once to more commodious offices than Crane Court could afford and they are happy to announce that they have just concluded the purchase of the lease of the premises, until very recently occupied by the *Illustrated Times*, at No. 148 Fleet Street, where in future *The Sporting Life* will be published, and where also communications for the Editor should be addressed.

The paper's new offices had been leased by John Shipley, who had recently launched himself into

---

* At his bankruptcy examination in 1861 Stephens explained: "I came to Scotland for sequestration partly in order to avoid exposure in London and partly because I understood that the matter could be carried through more cheaply in Scotland and this was important to me as my father had refused to make any advances for the purpose unless I came to this country."[1] Bailed out by his father, Stephens settled with his creditors for a fraction of what they were owed and obtained his discharge before the year was out.

the newspaper business with reckless abandon. In addition to buying out Maddick's share in the *Life*, he had also taken over the *Court Circular* and acquired various other titles at greatly inflated prices including the racing weekly, the *Eclipse and Sporting Calendar*, which was to share the Fleet Street offices with the *Life*.

Described as "a nice, clean-made, eleven-stone man, fit for anything under the sun, with a handsome face which did not tell of more than 36 or 37 summers, but whose light whiskers accorded ill with a premature grey head,"[2] Shipley knew little or nothing of the newspaper world and would have done better to stick to his own trade.

He had inherited a thriving business on the death of his father and the advertisements the *Life* carried for his Regent Street premises showed he was not short of wealthy patrons since he was referred to as a "Saddlery, Harness, Horse Clothing, Whip, Bit and Spur Manufacturer to the Royal Family, the Court of Russia, Prussia, Naples, Tuscany &c. Her Majesty's Cavalry and the Indian Army".

Enough to be going on with, one would have thought! What induced a respectable saddler to plunge headlong into the sea of sharks that was Fleet Street remains a mystery, but it was to prove his undoing – not that the streetwise Maddick and Strange were to fare any better with their post-*Life* ventures as a paper trail of costly flops was to show.

Strange, now witheringly described as "a discharged servant of the proprietors of the *Sporting Life*,"[3] wasted no time in bringing out a rival paper in the *Penny Sporting Times*. The bi-weekly lasted barely a month before the money ran out and the bailiffs were called in after its principal backer, a certain Mr White, had "absconded to avoid his creditors and the printers became clamorous for payment pleading to Strange 'the old scoundrel White has gone away – what are we to do?'"[4]

Strange did the decent thing and paid the men out of his own pocket, but there was no one to bail him out when he presented himself at the Bankruptcy Court in March 1860. It was not his first visit to the Basinghall Street cleaners; during his examination it emerged he had been made bankrupt in 1831 and insolvent in 1854. He also admitted he had been jailed for libel, but not, he vigorously protested, for selling pornographic prints as his creditor had implied.

Meanwhile, Maddick, who had escaped bankruptcy by the skin of his teeth and the sale of his papers, stayed on at his Crane Court offices to bring out *The Shareholder*, a financial weekly that folded within three months. Undeterred, he then reverted to the tried and trusted Turf and theatrical market with the *Sporting Telegraph and Daily Record of Music and Drama*, but this snappy little title lasted no longer than its predecessor, the *Racing Telegraph*, and it was taken over by the *Sporting Life* on Grand National day 1861.

The *Life* did not deem the acquisition of its first scalp worthy of mention save for inserting the line 'with which is incorporated *The Sporting Telegraph*' under its title, but a parting 'To Our Readers' announcement in the *Telegraph* included a so-called 'prospectus' of the *Life* which amounted to three-quarters of a column of waffle, probably penned by John Hutton who had recently bought the paper from Maddick and had also become joint-proprietor with Shipley in the *Life* and the *Eclipse*.

To secure these deals Hutton had borrowed £2,000 from William McMurray, who had advanced a similar sum to Shipley to enable him to pay off some of his mounting debts. By this means McMurray acquired a legal claim on both men's shares in the papers. It seemed he was as much a loan-shark as he was a paper-maker, and from this point on the Shylock of Fleet Street wove a tangled web of moieties and mortgages, loans and liens that was to confound the best judicial brains in the business – or one of them, at least!

It was not long before Shipley's ruinous flirtation with Fleet Street had run its course and, in February 1861, he too was declared bankrupt with debts of £12,282 (£1.1m). Of his 132 creditors, by far the largest was the *Life's* paper merchant, Wm McMurray who therefore became the principal assignee of the sequestered estate. His job was to value and realise its assets and distribute the cash to the creditors. It was a task the scheming Scot undertook with an enthusiastic bias towards his own interests.

He accordingly assessed the jewel in Shipley's battered crown (his half-share in the *Life* and the *Eclipse*) to be worth £1,500 (£135,000) and a few days later he informed his fellow assignees he had sold the share to John Hutton for that sum. What's more, he had the gall to tell them: "If such a share had been put up for sale by public auction I am quite sure it would not have realised anything like that sum."

He was quite right of course – it would have made much more. Just two weeks later, on 1 March 1861, with Hutton's 'authority' ('connivance' would have been a better word) he secretly resold the same share to Sam Beeton for £4,325 (£389,250). In one stroke McMurray had not only recouped what he had been owed by Shipley, but he still held Hutton's mortgaged half-share in the papers.

Not that Beeton was complaining. For him, acquiring Shipley's share was the first step on the road to outright ownership as he had already agreed with McMurray to buy the papers for £8,000 and pay an additional £650 for the leasehold of the offices.

At 30, Sam Beeton was riding the crest of a wave. By an extraordinary coincidence he had made his fortune at 148 Fleet Street nine years earlier by the simple expedient of being in the right place at the right time. Fresh out a seven-year apprenticeship at McMurray's paper works, he had gone into partnership with Charles H Clarke who was in the process of bringing out a pirated edition of *Uncle Tom's Cabin* – Harriet Beecher Stowe's celebrated saga of Negro slavery in America.

At first the book attracted little interest, but when its price was cut from 2s 6d to 1s (£10.60 to £4.25), sales took off and the demand for it quickly outstripped production. Larger premises were found at 148 Fleet Street, and by running 17 presses around the clock the partners were able to turn out 150,000 copies in the first few months.

The book, which reputedly acted as a catalyst for the American civil war, soon broke all records as a bestseller and since there was no copyright agreement between Britain and America at the time, all profits from its sale in the UK went to the publishers.

With his share of the proceeds Beeton was able to start up on his own and in 1855 he launched the *Boy's Own Magazine* which proved an instant success. The following year he made another inspired move when he married Isabella Mayson, the attractive stepdaughter of Henry Dorling, an Epsom printer who was, more to the point, clerk of the course and manager of the famous Surrey racecourse.

The two families had known each other for many years and ties had been strengthened when Beeton's father became responsible for instituting two races at Epsom that were to become almost as popular with the public as the Derby and the Oaks.

Samuel Powell Beeton was the landlord and resident bookmaker at The Dolphin in Milk Street close by Mary-le-Bow church of Bow Bells fame. The hostelry was so famous for the betting that was carried on there, it was known as 'the Tattersalls of the East End'. In fact, business was so good in sporting taverns generally that, in 1846, Beeton organised a collection among his fellow publicans cum bookmakers to sponsor the first running of the Great Metropolitan Handicap at the Epsom spring meeting that year.

The £300 (£25,500) raised by the 'Licensed Victuallers of London' attracted a field of 29 runners and the race proved such a success that the publicans boosted their contribution to £500 (£42,500) the following year, and in 1851, when Beeton extended his subscription list to include the sporting taverns of the suburbs, another new race, the City and Suburban Handicap, was added to the spring fixture.

Unfortunately for Epsom, the generosity of the innkeepers dried up when the Betting Houses Act

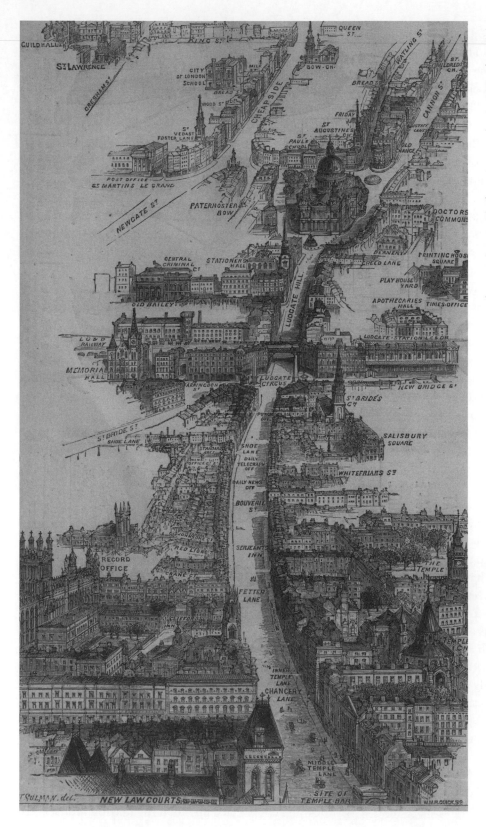

A late 19th century map of Fleet Street, Ludgate Hill and Cheapside. Towards the bottom, between the Record Office and Fetter Lane, is Crane Court where the *Sporting Life* was born, a little further down 'The Street' on the left opposite the *Daily News,* is No. 148, the home of the *Life* for 60 years, while at the top of the map almost opposite Bow Church is Milk Street where Samuel Powell Beeton ran The Dolphin tavern, 'the Tattersalls of the East End'.

of 1853 outlawed gambling in public houses, but the 'City and Sub' and the 'Great Met' continued to flourish under the management of the Dorling family.

Sam Beeton jnr had only a passing interest in racing at this time, but his wife had been brought up with the roar of the Derby-day crowd ringing in her ears and, ever the business woman, it is quite possible she persuaded her husband that the cash-strapped *Sporting Life* would be a sound investment.

It was while Beeton was haggling with McMurray over a price for the paper that Mrs B quietly slipped into the pages of culinary history as she worked on her monthly journal, the *Book of Household Management* which, when its 24 instalments were published as a single volume in 1861, was to spawn a whole library of Mrs Beeton cookery books that would bestow on the author a worldwide celebrity that endures to this day.

It seemed the Beetons could do no wrong; everything they touched turned to gold, but there was little time to celebrate. The Victorian work-ethic demanded total commitment and Sam was toiling day and night publishing a growing number of titles from his offices at 248 Strand where his talented wife edited the *Englishwoman's Domestic Magazine* – the first woman's journal to achieve anything like a mass sale with a monthly circulation approaching 60,000.

The *Life* was soon carrying full-column adverts for S O Beeton's publications. The contents of each issue of *Boy's Own Magazine* was listed alongside a wide range of 'Beeton's Penny Books' and an equally eclectic selection of 'Beeton's Shilling Series', and every year the latest edition of *Beeton's Christmas Annual* was proclaimed to be "Better than ever".

It was obvious the hard-worked publisher was going to need assistance if he was to re-establish the *Life* on a sound financial footing. Since John Hutton had no interest in taking any part in the management of the paper and Harry Feist was more often out of the office than in, Beeton brought in his brother-in-law, Edward Jonathan Dorling, to act as managing editor and take over the role of publisher after Frederick Kelly went the way of William Strange when he was dismissed in April 1861.

Kelly's crime had been to use his position with the *Life* to embark on a little private venture of his own, which he brazenly advertised in the paper:

To The Sporting Public – F G Kelly, Publisher of the *Sporting Life*, begs to inform his friends and the public that he executes Commissions on all events throughout the season. 5 per cent on winnings. Address F G Kelly, 148 Fleet Street.

This misguided enterprise was brought to an abrupt halt the following week when an equally brief notice announced:

The Proprietors of the *Sporting Life* beg to inform their readers that the advertisement of their late publisher to execute commissions was inserted without their knowledge and they cannot be responsible for any monies sent to the office for such a purpose.

The sacking of two publishers in as many years hardly reflected well on the paper, but in Dorling it finally gained a man who was a force for the good. Bella Beeton's stepbrother was just 22, but his appointment was no mere act of nepotism. Described as "a charming man, kindly and tactful and well-liked by everyone with whom he came in contact,"[5] he was to contribute a great deal to the success of the *Life* in the coming years.

Sam Beeton, meanwhile, completed his purchase of the *Life* and *Eclipse* in May when McMurray informed him he had settled with his co-assignees in Shipley's estate and could now sell Hutton's mortgaged half-share to him. But, as with the first sale, it was not a simple cash transaction. In keeping with the complex nature of the whole business, it involved bills of exchange payable over various dates at a modest rate of interest.

So far, so good. The *Life* flourished under its new management and, with the repeal of the duty on newsprint in 1861 and an increase in sales and advertising revenue, it soon became a goldmine. Then, in July 1862, Beeton received a request from Hutton for an account of his profits in the paper.

Beeton was, to put it mildly, taken aback. The last dealings he had with Hutton had been four months earlier when he struck him off the 'free list' of complimentary copies. When Hutton protested, Beeton relented, and in a letter to his former partner he informed him: "You shall have a copy in future, but at the same time you cannot look on it as a right on account of your having been a proprietor of the *Sporting Life*."

Now he wrote to Hutton demanding an explanation for "a most extraordinary application" and at the same time informed McMurray of the situation. He then took the precaution of registering himself as the sole proprietor of the papers at the Inland Revenue office in Somerset House – something he should have done 16 months earlier when, as he claimed to believe, he had acquired outright ownership.

In September, McMurray returned Beeton's bills of exchange for the second share, claiming: "Mr Hutton will not give the consent necessary on his part to such a sale." He also threatened to take legal action unless Hutton's partnership in the papers was restored. Beeton now knew where he stood. He refused to alter the registration and the following month Hutton duly served him with a writ:

> Take notice that the partnership existing between you and myself in the *Sporting Life*, the *Eclipse* and *Sporting Telegraph* newspapers is dissolved from and after this day; and I hereby require you not to do any act in the management of the said papers whereby I, as one of the joint proprietors thereof, may be made liable; and I shall forthwith take such proceedings as I may be advised for the winding up of the said 'joint business'.

A lawsuit inevitably followed and it must have been with a sinking heart that Sir John Stuart saw the name of the *Sporting Life* crop up in his court in the summer of 1863. This time there was no simple, cut and dried case to give judgement on but one that tested his much-vaunted faculties to the limit.

In 'Hutton v Beeton', Hutton pleaded he was entitled to a share in the newspapers; that the partnership with Beeton should be dissolved; the assets realised and a receiver be appointed to carry on the business. Beeton filed a cross-bill requesting that McMurray be ordered to fulfil his agreement for the sale of the papers.

To add to the confusion of claim and counter-claim, it became clear from early on in the proceedings that someone was telling 'porkies' – large ones. In their respective affidavits, each man maintained that various statements made by the other party were either "wholly untrue" or "totally incorrect".

In his suit Beeton alleged that, as a result of the increased value of the newspapers due to his management, the defendants had "concocted a scheme to deprive me of the property which he [*McMurray*] had sold to me."[*]

McMurray, for his part, stated: "I soon discovered that Mr Beeton had wholly deceived me and

---

[*] In support of this claim, Edward Dorling stated in his affidavit that from 1 July 1861 to the end of March 1862, the circulation of the *Sporting Life* had gone up from 41,500 to 62,000 copies and the average value of advertisements had risen even more dramatically from £5 to £35 (£450 to £3,150).

had misrepresented his pecuniary circumstances, and he was obliged to and did apply to me for assistance to prevent his stopping payment and bankruptcy – I renewed his bills and assisted him with money from time to time ... He has not paid to me or to Mr Hutton one shilling on account of the alleged purchase of the second half of the said newspapers and property."

There was, evidently, another side to this tarnished coin and for the best part of a week Sir John Stuart heard the conflicting arguments of the litigants and their counsels. Finally, in what he described as "a case of singular difficulty not lessened by the number of days the hearing has occupied," he came down wholly on the side of Beeton.

He found McMurray had entered into the transaction of 1 March 1861 with full powers as a mortgagee of Hutton; that all three parties regarded the first contract as inchoate and ultimately Beeton was to have the whole of the papers. It appeared to be a resounding victory for Beeton, especially when it was followed up later that year by a short notice in the *Life* on 3 November 1863:

> We have much pleasure in announcing that yesterday Vice-Chancellor Sir John Stuart confirmed the judgement which he delivered on July 27 last in the suits in Chancery, which have been pending for some time respecting the ownership of *The Sporting Life*. The effect of his decision is to establish the proprietorship and management under which this journal has been conducted since March 1861. Our readers may be certain that we shall continue with greater zeal than ever to render *The Sporting Life* the faithful and impartial organ of sport in all its branches.

Beeton, meanwhile, had been appointed the receiver in the papers pending an appeal by Hutton and McMurray, which came before Lord Justice Sir James Knight-Bruce in a series of hearings during the summer of 1864. As in the previous case, Beeton was represented by Richard Malins and Edward Karslake, while the Attorney-General Sir Hugh Cairns, and James Bacon appeared for Hutton. McMurray's barrister took little part in the cut and thrust debate which raged between the chief protagonists for five days.

From the outset, Cairns tore into various aspects of Sir John Stuart's judgement. He claimed Hutton's interest in the papers had been ignored and that the vice-chancellor had been led astray by "the eloquent harangue of Mr Malins and the sonorous declarations of Mr Karslake, both of whom raised a cloud of dust which had influenced his Honour to make a decree that could only be reconciled in the supposition that the case was made out in Mr Beeton's bill."

This argument found favour with Knight-Bruce, who remarked: "The vice-chancellor seems to have treated Mr Hutton as little more than an automaton."

Karslake responded by declaring Hutton was precisely that and was no more than the tool of McMurray. Hutton, he asserted, had given his assent to the sale by implication, if not actually. He could not stand by and see Beeton exercise the rights of sole proprietor and wait until the tide had turned and, when the property had become valuable, then claim a share of the spoils on the ground that he had not given his consent to the sale.

Bacon, on the other hand, argued that Hutton had only agreed to Beeton managing the papers; believing that if left to him and Dorling it would be better for all parties.

By the fifth day the only thing that was certain was that all parties were visibly wilting under the relentless barrage of spurious arguments and affidavits (18 on behalf of Beeton, 12 for Hutton, none for McMurray) put up by both sides. And no one was wilting more than the Lord Justice who was feeling the full weight of his three score years and thirteen. On the final day of the hearing he came out with the profound statement: "There are three parties here engaged – Mr Beeton, Mr Hutton and Mr McMurray – and I must admit that I have little or no admiration for any of them."

In summing up, he declared that Beeton had no proof to support his claim on Hutton's share and his bill should be dismissed with costs awarded to Hutton. The subsequent decree completely overturned the original judgement as Cairns dictated the final terms which were harsh and unconditional.

Neither Beeton nor Dorling would be allowed to set up a rival publication to the *Sporting Life*, nor induce any of its staff to leave it or any customer to withdraw their support from the paper. Instead they had to undertake to strive for its success and give Hutton and McMurray all reasonable access to the accounts. The Attorney-General might as well have ordered them to sell their souls to McMurray!

Beeton, who was always up for a fight, immediately announced his intention to appeal to the House of Lords. In the meantime, McMurray's nephew, William McFarlane, was appointed the receiver in the papers, but before Beeton's appeal could be heard he was hit by a tragedy which knocked all the stuffing out of him.

In February 1865, his beloved Bella died from puerperal fever a few days after giving birth to their fourth child. She was just 28. Beeton was used to coping with grief. His first child had died in infancy in 1857; his second when three years old in 1862; his half-sister in 1863 and his stepmother in 1864, but to lose his soul mate, business partner and anchor of his hectic, chaotic life, took him into a new realm of despair he never could have imagined. Shortly afterwards, he expressed his pain in a letter to a favourite uncle:

> To tell you all – my agony is excessive, but I have hours of calm and quiet which refresh me and enable me to meet the dreadful grief that well nigh overpowers me and renders me unable to move or stir. But I hope to conquer at last, and will strive with all the courage I have and can receive by appeals to her good spirit and to the All-Ruler, to live a good life, honest and pure, to hold the love and respect of good men, and not to lose my own self-respect. In doing this, and in trying to bring up my two little ones, I shall obtain, I think, some comfort.[6]

With his new perspective on life, wrangles over the ownership of a penny paper paled into insignificance. He withdrew his appeal to the Lords and, after reaching an agreement with Hutton and McMurray over his share in the papers, he severed all connections with the *Sporting Life* in December 1865. In the same month as Beeton took his leave, the work he had put into helping mould the *Life* into the paper it had become was recognised and applauded by no less an authority than Charles Dickens. Writing in his magazine, *All The Year Round*, the great man paid his tribute under the clever heading 'The Rough's Guide':

> My sporting information is derived from sources altogether distinct from that Guide to the Turf which is issued periodically by the ingenious Mr Ruff. It is served up to me every Wednesday and Saturday at the moderate charge of one penny, and I am advised, admonished, warned and instructed, with a vigour, prescience and versatility perfectly astonishing to myself.
>
> Carping critics say that my guide is the favourite organ of the roughs and that it is to be found in the parlours of pugilism, and in houses where out-door betting men and fraudulent 'welshers' chiefly congregate. The same objection would apply to the air we breathe and the bread we eat.

As a humble disciple of an able teacher, I fearlessly claim for my penny sporting guide a range of information and a profundity of knowledge which it would be difficult to surpass. What is it to me if the rough share my partiality for vigorous Saxon, or be delighted as I am with words and phrases it requires natural aptitude and a special education to understand?

Find me a newspaper in which races, fights, hunts, coursing meetings, advertisements, answers to and letters from correspondents are more thoroughly in accordance with what we have ever been taught to consider good sporting taste and I will admit that what is sauce for the rough is not sauce for the clean-shirted turfite; but, till then, pardon me if I hold my original views and maintain the excellence of my organ as an astute mentor and a just judge.

Dickens went on to give what the paper in question described as "an entertaining, ingenious and most flattering criticism on the *Sporting Life*," which Beeton must have read with a mixture of pride and profound regret.

And the fates had not finished with him. As had been indicated in court, his finances were already in a parlous state before legal costs added an extra burden to them (an overstretched business was one cause and, perhaps, also gambling debts as he had become "deeply devoted to the pleasures of the racetrack"[7] since his involvement with the *Life*).

The final straw came with the overnight collapse of London's largest discount house, Overend-Gurney, in May 1866. *The Times* described the crash as a national calamity, which was no exaggeration since the bank's liabilities amounted to £11m (£1bn). Thousands were ruined and it certainly finished off Beeton who was left with no option but to hand over his business to a rival publishing firm and work for them as a salaried editor.

Two years later, deeply wounded by the slings and arrows of outrageous fortune, he implied that his father-in-law, Henry Dorling, was a sleeping partner in the *Life* and had sold him out when he most needed help. In a souvenir publication for the 1868 Derby entitled *London's Great Outing: The Derby Carnival*, he wrote:

> The Clerk of the Course has studied too closely for one and twenty years the art of filling his pockets from every available source, and is too fond of the red gold not to have made everything that he had any control over quite easy to purchase. Ready, ay, ready to sell anybody or anything, that's the family motto.

The bitterness of the betrayal lingered with Beeton for the rest of his days which were typically turbulent and all too short. More court cases and reverses followed before, broken in health but not in spirit, he died in a Richmond (Surrey) sanatorium on 6 June 1877.* He was 46.

The *Sporting Life*, then owned by William McFarlane (John Hutton having died two years earlier), did not record his passing.

---

* The death certificate gives the cause as 'phthisis' (a wasting disease such as tuberculosis), but in her impressively researched book, *The Short Life & Long Times of Mrs Beeton*, Kathryn Hughes makes out a strong case for Beeton having died of tertiary syphilis, an infection that would also have accounted for the early deaths of his first two sickly children.

BETTING IN BRIDE LANE

CHARLES DICKENS was not the only admirer of the paper that supplied him with a 'profundity of knowledge at the moderate charge of one penny'. From the start, the *Life* was borne along on the tide of goodwill it had generated among its readers as it campaigned for the elimination of outdated practices that not only invited corruption, but were openly sanctioned by the Jockey Club.

At the time, the Rules of Racing (66 in number) catered for the interests of the racehorse owner at the expense of the punter. It was, for instance, quite in order for an owner who had two (or more) runners in a race, to declare to win with one horse and instruct the jockey riding the other to stop it from winning even though it might have been heavily backed by the public.

Owners could also scratch their horse from a race if they had been forestalled in the market; i.e. if it had been backed at better odds than they were able to obtain, while they were allowed to adopt fictitious names provided they registered their *nom de course* with Weatherbys, the Jockey Club's secretariat.

Such rules provided unscrupulous owners with a cheat's charter which they were not slow to employ in their constant battle to outwit bookmakers. The latter, for their part, were more than a match for any chicanery and ruthlessly exploited a wide range of retaliatory options open to them; bribery being the most effective weapon in their armoury.

Stable lads, forever on the bottom rung of racing's financial ladder, were the softest targets. Many were prepared to sell inside information for a fiver (£450) – the equivalent of a year's wages for a first-season apprentice – even though exposure would result in instant dismissal, blacklisting and often jail.* It would cost more to have a horse nobbled or to bribe a jockey to lose a race, but such measures were only resorted to in extreme cases. More often than not, individual bookmakers would form an alliance with an owner for their mutual benefit.

All the big betting owners had their own agents acting for them. These men were made privy to stable secrets and if a horse went lame before a race for which it had been backed, they could lay it off to other bookmakers and the public in order to recoup the owner's stake and line their own pockets before news of the injury leaked out.

For every principled owner who would scratch his horse in such circumstances, there was another who would enter a horse he had no intention of running – his sole purpose being to milk the public by using the services of a bookmaker to lay the horse for as much money as possible before the market began to smell a 'dead 'un', as such horses were cynically, and sometimes not inaccurately, called. Certain layers became so notorious for feeding off the corpses of these 'stiffs' that in 1869 the *Life* noted:

---

* In 1865, George Bollen, an apprentice employed by the Danebury trainer John Day, was sentenced to two months hard labour in Dorchester jail after being found guilty of "giving information to some betting men on the merits of particular racehorses". Bollen received little sympathy from the *Life* which remarked: "An apprentice who is guilty of such gross misconduct is as reprehensible as a common thief, inasmuch as he steals something by which his master is not only injured, but the supporters of the stable are also seriously discouraged ... It is, however, unfortunate that in these cases the more reprehensible parties escape scot-free like the clique who have suborned Bollen and degraded and ruined the boy by leading him into a course which has terminated in misery and a common prison."

There is a very considerable band of bookmakers who, from their successful onslaughts on 'dead 'uns', have been aptly christened 'the undertakers' and when these are seen to be betting eagerly against favourites it is generally considered a fatal case.

Racing was, in effect, riddled with cunning owners, crooked bookmakers, conniving trainers, corrupt jockeys and all the assorted detritus – card-sharpers, thimble-riggers, pick-pockets, welshers,* etc – that operated on the peripheries of the betting ring, while the woefully ignorant and ill-informed punter was ripped off on all sides.

There was, therefore, a great need for an innovative and forceful newspaper that would stand up for the rights of the public by exposing abuses and corruption within the sport. At a very basic level the *Life's* 'Answers to Correspondents' column,† which dealt mainly with sporting and betting queries, attempted to keep readers on the straight and narrow by advising them in a terse, no-nonsense style.

For example, 'W.W.S.' was told: "Your good sense, if you have any, should answer you in the negative;" 'W.H.T.' learnt: "The simple answer is that you have been done;" 'Nemesis' was scolded: "Serves you right. Why make such a foolish undertaking?" as was 'Censorious': "You really are what your signature implies. The party you allude to is above suspicion;" 'A.B.' was cryptically informed: "1). 37 years, 7ft 6in, weight 500lb. His parents were rather tall. 2). The Life Guards;" while 'W.J.K.' was instructed: "Have nothing to do with such fellows, go to your family physician at once."

On a broader front, a few of the *Life's* early crusades brought about almost immediate reforms, while others were ignored or acted upon in the Jockey Club's own good time, but its longest-running campaign was aimed not at the Turf authorities but at the State legislature that had imposed a set of class-biased betting laws on the country in 1853.

To accompany the paper's first major news story, which was centred on the betting that was taking place in nearby Bride Lane, a leading article proposed all betting should be legalised by licensing bookmakers and betting shops. This was a simple solution to the existing unregulated free-for-all. It would have saved the police and the courts much valuable time and money in pursuing petty prosecutions; prevented widespread police corruption; given the Treasury a ready source of income and, in all probability, provided racing with a fair slice of the cake sooner rather than later – 102 years later, to be precise!

But the politicians of the Victorian era were no more receptive to sound advice than their latter-day counterparts and they predictably cocked a deaf 'un to the wise counsel of the penny journal. As a result, the laws on betting remained in a muddled and farcical state until the Betting and Gaming Act of 1960 finally legalised all forms of betting.

Bookmakers did not come into existence until the end of the eighteenth century when the growing popularity of the early classics – the St Leger (1776), the Oaks (1779) and the Derby (1780) – began to attract bigger fields and races in general became more competitive. Before then betting had been

---

* The term to 'welsh' or 'welch' on a bet came into common use with the advent of bookmakers at the end of the eighteenth century, but its origin is uncertain. The *Life's* long-time correspondent (1916-1971) Jack Fairfax-Blakeborough maintained it came from David Welch, a pioneer bookmaker in London who was notorious for not settling winning bets; others believe it owes its origin to George IV who, when Prince of Wales, consistently failed to honour his gambling debts, while still more claim it comes from the racist nursery rhyme 'Taffy was a Welshman, Taffy was a thief'.

† This small but important column eventually evolved into the 'Green Seal Service' in 1967 when the paper acted as an independent arbitrator in betting disputes.

conducted on a one-to-one basis between the racehorse owners themselves or the landed gentry who would gamble vast sums on privately arranged matches and sweepstakes.

Bets would be made either at a specified rendezvous point in the town staging the race meeting or at a betting post sited on the course. On-course business was generally carried out on horseback with the participating parties forming a circle from which they would take it in turn to ride into the centre of the 'betting ring' and declare which horses they wanted to back or were prepared to lay.

It was a betting exchange conducted from the saddle as opposed to the Internet. Cash was not involved; all transactions were recorded in private betting books to be settled at a later date – Monday being the official settling day.

The chance of seeing the 'nobs' backing their fancies for large sums was one of the spectacles of any race day and always attracted a motley crowd of onlookers, and it was from this milling throng that the bookmaker emerged. He invariably came from the lower classes and would have started out as a backer in the taverns of London – the Mecca for betting men – in order to build up sufficient capital to set up in business.

Originally, off-course betting had been confined to exclusive gentlemen's clubs, but towards the end of the eighteenth century it entered a new era when the auctioneer, Richard Tattersall, set aside a room in his range of offices and stables at Hyde Park Corner for the use of the Jockey Club. Membership was by annual subscription and the room's select clientele was soon extended to include a few representatives from the emerging breed of bookmakers, assorted politicians* and some of the young bucks of the day who had large family estates and sizeable fortunes to squander before they drank themselves into an early and dishonourable grave.

By the time Tattersall's grandson, also Richard, took over the business in 1810, his family's name had become as famous for the betting that went on in its subscription room as for the horse and hound sales the firm held twice a week at 'the Corner'.

Although young Dick disapproved of heavy gambling and had an even greater dislike for the rabble of bookmakers who were attracted to his premises like vultures to carrion, he knew he could not afford to alienate his customers, so when he built a grand, new betting emporium in 1815, he had the notice 'Messrs Tattersalls trust Gentlemen will not encourage dog-stealers who frequent this yard' posted on the entrance gate.[1]

The intended slight did not deter the 'dog-stealers' who removed the sign in an indignant protest the following day and continued to conduct their business with men who, like themselves, were not favoured with membership of the subscription room.

In order to attract the additional custom of Tattersalls' 'gentlemen', the layers offered a point or two over the odds available in the inner sanctum, and in this way the fortunes of not a few were made. The most famous of them was William Davies (or Davis), the 'Leviathan of the Turf', who joined the crowd of 'pencillers' operating in the yard outside the room soon after he had established himself as London's foremost bookmaker.

Trading under the slogan 'Punctual payment with a pleasant courtesy of words', he had initially set himself up at the Durham Arms in Serle Street off the Strand from where many of his clients had cause to visit the bankruptcy courts in adjoining Carey Street. Davies nearly joined them in 1845 after

---

* Prime Ministers such as Palmerston, Derby and Rosebery were prominent patrons of the Turf during the latter half of the nineteenth century and betting at Tattersalls was often brought to a halt as the politicians left *en masse* to attend debates in parliament.

he had to pay out seven crisp £1,000 notes (£595,000) to Charles Greville who had backed his horse, Alarm, at 7-1 to win the Cambridgeshire.

The publicity generated by the bet was enormous. The landlady of the Durham Arms soon made enough money from the increased trade her on-site bookmaker brought in to retire, while Davies, his name made as a 'safe man' and a fearless layer, took on extra clerks and posted up more lists (of odds and horses) at the Coach and Horses in Piccadilly and in Joe Barr's hostelry in Long Acre, a street renowned for its sporting taverns.

For the first time, the working man became hooked on racing in a big way and "an epidemic of gambling was declared to have attacked even the poorest class who were being offered facilities for risking their hard-earned sixpences and shillings."[2] It was not long before list-betting overflowed from the comparative security of the pubs into seedy back rooms, rented for a few shillings a week by every fly-by-night who could steal or scrape together the necessary cash to set up in business.

> From 1850 to the end of 1853 the 'listers' were in their glory; and at one period about four hundred betting houses were open in London alone, of which, perhaps, ten were solvent. Among these proprietors, Mr Davies never laid the odds to less than £1 [£85]; one or two others adopted 10s as their limit, and some 5s, while not a few would do the odds for a lad at 6d [£2.25].[3]

Welshers flourished as never before and when, following a series of scandals, a man named Dwyer, who ran a cigar store cum betting shop in St Martin's Lane, decamped with some £25,000 (£2.12m) of the public's money after the 1851 Chester Cup, it was obvious that something had to be done. But legislation to stamp out such rampant swindles was slow in coming, and when it finally arrived it was of the half-baked variety.

In the summer of 1853 the Attorney-General, Sir Alexander Cockburn, brought in a bill for the suppression of list houses. In introducing it he declared there was "not a prison or a house of correction in London which did not, every day, furnish abundant and conclusive testimony of the vast number of youths who were led into crime by the temptation of these establishments."[4]

Such was the urgency of the situation, the bill was rushed through parliament with hardly a murmur of dissent and within six weeks it had become law. Anyone keeping or assisting to keep any house, office, room or *place* for the purpose of betting, was subject to a fine of £100 (£8,500) or six months' imprisonment.

The word 'place' was open to a wide interpretation and was to give rise to innumerable legal wrangles over the coming years. Moreover, the Act did not extend to Tattersalls or other exclusive clubs since it was argued that their members bet amongst themselves as opposed to bookmakers who bet with all comers. This totally fallacious distinction ignored the fact that many bookmakers operated in these establishments; but it was felt that while the rich were capable of looking after themselves, the poor needed protecting from themselves – and from the bookies!

The Act was thus flawed in the very first principle of justice in that it enshrined one law for the rich and another for the poor; in this case the ordinary working man who, being excluded from West End clubs by reason of finance and social standing, was obliged to turn to the bookmakers who had been forced out onto the streets or who plied their trade on patches of waste ground where they displayed their lists on portable stands or hung them around their necks.

While there was no specific law against street betting at the time, these bookmakers lived a precarious and peripatetic existence as they constituted what was termed 'a common nuisance' due to the unsavoury mob who, as gulls follow a trawler, latched onto them in the hope of picking up some tips or loose change from winning punters.

The situation is perfectly illustrated by the protracted dispute that surrounded the betting that was taking place in Bride Lane; a narrow, dog-legged passage barely 80 yards long, running from the bottom end of Fleet Street into what is now New Bridge Street. At its Fleet Street end the lane squeezes between the Punch Tavern and the back of St Bride's church which stands on a site where Christians have gathered to worship for 1,500 years. The local parishioners were none too happy, therefore, when a large crowd of 'betting men' – estimated to be between 250 and 500 – began to do business on their back doorstep in a raucous rabble.

On 30 March 1859, the *Life* reported that a deputation from the parish of St Bride's had waited upon the Lord Mayor to call his attention to "the annoyance and inconveniences to which the inhabitants of Bride Lane, with some portions of Bridge Street and Fleet Street, are exposed in consequence of the congregation there of crowds of men for betting purposes."

The deputation was led by a vestry clerk named Attwood Smith who informed the Mayor that shopkeepers in the area suffered "most seriously in their trade since their customers are frequently afraid to pass through such a crowd." He added: "The evil has now reached to such a height that we are now here to ask your lordship whether there is any law which will meet the case and if so, whether your lordship will undertake to put that law into force."

His lordship replied, none too helpfully: "If you show me such a law I will be obliged to you." Smith duly obliged by citing the law of obstruction, but this failed to impress the Mayor who advised the deputation to take their case to the magistrates as Bride Lane was outside his jurisdiction.

Not to be put off by this rather important point, a tradesman chipped in to say: "We are often taken away from our business, my lord, to ask these men if they will move on. Sometimes they do so, to come back again directly; but at other times they load us with abuse if they see that there is no policeman near. It would be a serious inconvenience to us even if they were all gentlemen, but when you take into consideration that they are a mixture of the lowest of the low, your lordship will see how very serious is the inconvenience, to say the least of it, to which we are exposed."

The Mayor no doubt tut-tutted in sympathy and, having heard further evidence from the deputation, promised that "if anything can be done, it shall be done."

In an editorial that accompanied this report, the opening paragraph holds as true today as when it was first written:

Hasty legislation is one of the curses of the political history of this country. Measures are introduced into Parliament by ambitious underlings who, anxious for distinction, are too indolent and indifferent to weigh matters efficiently, or to consider what will be the effects of their interference with ancient liberties.

The Bill which was framed to suppress Betting Houses is precisely of this nature … shallow people imagined that betting on horse racing was easily repressed, but persons actively connected with the Turf knew that such an enactment would be thoroughly and ludicrously inoperative, if not utterly abortive. It is perfectly absurd to attempt to put down betting by any legislative process for the wagering propensity will forever remain an ineradicable one with all Englishmen…

The manner in which betting houses and their occupants were dealt with by the police constitutes a disgraceful chapter in the many outrageous chronicles of the London constabulary force. Stalwart ruffians descended upon inoffensive persons who were engaged in making friendly bets and, without more ado, dragged their victims from their convivial cups before a magistrate.

The mere possession of a betting card or fragmentary racing document was converted into material for a conviction, and imaginary offenders had their private letters turned from their pockets and subjected to the prying scrutiny of Sir Richard Mayne's sneaking spies.* Men who were merely engaging in a speculative transaction as honest and legitimate as any Stock Exchange business, were hunted from house to house and finally treated as burglars or coiners…

We do not come forward to defend the betting houses system as it existed because it was notorious that every vagabond and needy villain had recourse to the establishment of betting offices on purpose to plunder the public. But had those offices been licensed and had Government demanded that so much money should be deposited by the proprietors in the Exchequer as a security, then the system could not have been pernicious.

This lucid reasoning (almost certainly penned by Harry Feist whose father had been a staunch advocate for the legalisation of betting) helped to establish the reputation of the *Life* in its first few, all-important weeks, but it could not redress the inequitable laws the legislature had imposed on the working classes, and over the next 100 years the paper was to report countless prosecutions under the 1853 Act.

Meanwhile, the parishioners of St Bride's stepped up their campaign against the Bride Lane speculators. In its original article on the subject, the *Life* had been staunch in its defence of the 'betting men', but by April 1861 it was markedly more sympathetic to the cause of the vestrymen as it attacked "the beery, gin-and-bitters-drinking rapscallions who muster daily in Bride Lane and elsewhere". With magnificent rhetoric it asserted:

They are a reproach upon the Turf; they are living libels on the national pastime – low, greasy vagabonds, who glare with dull, fish-like eyes into handicap books one part of the day and prowl about newspaper offices during the afternoon waiting for 'th tissher' as they term Mr. Wright's telegrams.†

It is these fellows who have brought disgrace upon the great body of metropolitan speculators. They are the 'cadgers' who haunt the spots where decent and honest men – turned into the streets by the iniquitous and short-sighted policy which resulted in the Suppression of Betting Houses Act – call to invest money on a horse race. They are the 'leery' parasites of successful bettors who hang about in the hope of 'picking up a trifle' from those who have won.

Despite this crushing condemnation of the cadgers, the *Life* maintained an embarrassingly naive

---

* Sir Richard Mayne was Chief Commissioner of the Metropolitan police.

† In 1853 William Wright, in partnership with Albert Feist, succeeded William Ruff in supplying newspapers and West End clubs with a results service known as 'racing expresses'. In a report on Wright's death in October 1859, the *Life* recorded that as well as race results, he had supplied, "frequent and rapid reports of the betting and other transactions from the race meetings throughout the United Kingdom. He organised an extensive staff, enlarged his arrangements, and trained a little colony of pigeons at Chichester and Windsor to accelerate the Goodwood and Ascot expresses and hence arose Wright's tissues now so familiar to racing men. On many occasions, races (several Cambridgeshires included) at Newmarket have been run, expressed to the telegraph office at Newmarket, sent to London, manifolded, and out for delivery, all within the short space of ten minutes." (News sent by carrier pigeon was written on tissue paper and the term 'tissue', through its adoption and adaptation by the newspaper trade, is still used today to describe the bookmakers' early betting forecasts on the day's races).

defence of the 'scrupulously honest' bookmakers throughout the Bride Lane saga – a blind bias that was to backfire in spectacular fashion as instanced by this particular article which went on to relate:

> A certain speculator, who made a book in the vicinity of Oxford Street, after being systematically hunted and persecuted, hit upon the happy idea of conducting his business in Hyde Park, where he justly concluded that no one would have the power to order him to 'move on'. In this resolution he displayed much shrewdness and in the racing months the casual frequenter in Hyde Park will perceive, under a clump of trees, a ring of men which, in the distance, looks exactly like one formed for a prize fight.
>
> On approaching the assemblage closely it will be found that, so far from having any pugnacious inclinations, the crowd of people are quietly watching the movements and remarks of a dapper little man who writes with electric rapidity something in a little book. This is the 'Park Leviathan'. It is he who attracts the crowd and, to his credit, people from all parts of the metropolis make pilgrimage to Hyde Park to deal with him because he meets all his engagements with the utmost promptitude.*

Eventually, the vestrymen succeeded in getting the authorities to act and that summer four bookmakers were served with a summons, the gist of which was that they did "induce the assembling of divers large numbers of persons in Bride Lane whereby the said public thoroughfare was greatly impeded and the free use, passage and enjoyment thereof by Her Majesty's liege subjects greatly hindered to the common nuisance of the said liege subjects of our Lady the Queen."

In August 1861, Messrs Newcome, Pouter, Wales and Skeratt appeared before Alderman Hale at the Guildhall. They were not there for long. Hale informed them of a law that: "prohibited tradesmen from obstructing the thoroughfares; and costermongers, even while getting an honest living, have been fined for obstructing the streets with their barrows; and in some instances girls with baskets of fruit on their arms have paid the penalty for such offences."

Plainly the defendants would have to answer the charge of obstruction. The matter, having taken two and a half years to reach the courts following the initial deputation to the Lord Mayor, was now rushed through with indecent haste. Just one week later the 'Bride Lane Four' were on trial at the Old Bailey.

It was a walkover for the vestrymen, particularly after it emerged that there was a school in Bride Lane and the children had to force their way through the throng of bookmakers and punters as they left at midday for dinner and returned at two, "just the time when the metallics are in full circulation".

The four bookmakers were bound over to keep the peace as the *Life* noted: "The proceedings were listened to with very great interest by a large number of the betting fraternity, many of whom appeared much chopfallen at the result." A week later, the paper wrapped up the story as it remarked:

---

* This remained true only until Catch 'em Alive landed a gamble in the 1863 Cambridgeshire after which the celebrated 'Park Leviathan' did a runner although he did not disappear for long. Less than a year later the *Life* gave the welshing bookmaker a less complimentary write-up as it reported: "Russell has returned. The well-known, jack-booted, Hyde Park Ranger has once more taken up his abode in Bird Street, Oxford Street, and resumed his normal condition behind the beer house bar. He no longer carries on business beneath a friendly tree in the Park and fears perhaps its proximity to the Serpentine and the dangers of compulsory immersion ... Gentlemen who had backed Catch 'em Alive with Mr Russell were ingenuous enough to imagine that he would return the staked money if nothing else, but they were under a delusion ... it reads like an act of gigantic impudence for a man, within the short period of twelve months, to return to his old haunts and commence bookmaking 'just as if nothing had occurred'."

The recent prosecution at the Old Bailey has produced the desired effect. Mr Newcome, indeed, is to be found in the locality, but the usual crowd has migrated to 'the ruins' in Farringdon Road and 'the lane' is at last as empty and tranquil as the veriest lover of peace and quietness can desire.

'The ruins', a large piece of waste ground opposite Farringdon Station, were just half a mile from Bride Lane and seemed to offer an ideal sanctuary for the uprooted speculators. Shelter from the elements could be found under the railway arches, while the crowds that assembled there caused no inconvenience to the general public.

The site became so popular that within a few years about 100 bookmakers congregated there "to give the locality quite the appearance of a fair,"[5] but, almost inevitably, protests from the anti-betting brigade dogged their heels. In October 1865 a petition against the 'betting men' was presented to the Court of Common Council. In reporting the matter, the *City Press* was indignant that "land belonging to the City should be devoted to so illegal and demoralising a purpose" as it attacked the layers "who live by their wits, or by something worse, and who infest society". The paper demanded that:

…these persons should be dealt with as trespassers, driven away from the post where they entrap their victims and, to prevent them from again occupying the land, it would be well if the Corporation authorities did as other freeholders do; place a high fence around it and hoard it in.

The *Life* responded by describing 'the ruins' as an unsavoury spot that "has been, for many years, a lasting disgrace to the City of London, simply from its disuse and from being made the receptacle for dead cats and the offal of Saffron Hill." And in defence of the bookmakers, it pondered provocatively:

Perhaps the City authorities have never thought that the family of the Rothschilds, to whom they owe so much of their distinction, are nearly all, more or less, 'betting men' if by that term be implied persons who devote time and money to speculation on horse racing and whom, we are now informed, are 'pests to society'.

The *City Press*, however, had the ear of the Corporation and within a week 'No Trespass' signs were posted on the site as the *Life* reported:

In consequence of this severe measure, some of the principal speculators have shifted their quarters, while others still hang about the old spot and carry on a species of peripatetic trade with their old constituents as the police keep moving them on whenever they choose. We hear that the 'quiet' piece of ground in front of the Sadler's Wells Theatre was largely patronised on Saturday morning by the betting fraternity, but that the minions of Sir Richard Mayne soon effected an unceremonious clearance.

This pattern was to be repeated time and again. No sooner had the police cleared one area than the persecuted pencillers and their followers moved on to another site. Fleet Street was especially popular with the nomadic tribe since many printers and journalists were inveterate punters and the *Life*, itself, acted as a magnet to betting men.

The 'tissue', or large poster, in its front window displayed the latest information on the probable runners at the day's main meeting and also the results as soon as they came in on the telegraph. In fact, the crowds that gathered outside No. 148 to await the outcome of a big race caused far greater inconvenience to 'Her Majesty's liege subjects' than the Bride Lane bookmakers ever did.

It was no surprise, therefore, that the *Life* received a rap over the knuckles when the passing of the Metropolitan Streets Act made it an offence of obstruction for three or more people to meet for the purpose of betting on a street in London. The Act came into force on 1 November 1867, and the following day the paper reported:

> The new Act for the regulation of metropolitan street traffic set in yesterday with remarkable severity and its most satisfactory and wholesome operation was to sweep away the ragamuffins and desperate welshers who followed in the track of the respectable bookmakers at the Arches in Farringdon Street … Later in the day a bland inspector of the City police called in upon us and informed our publisher that the 'tissue' of arrivals and results which we are in the habit of exhibiting in our window in Fleet Street must be withdrawn, otherwise legal proceedings would be taken under the Nuisances Act. By

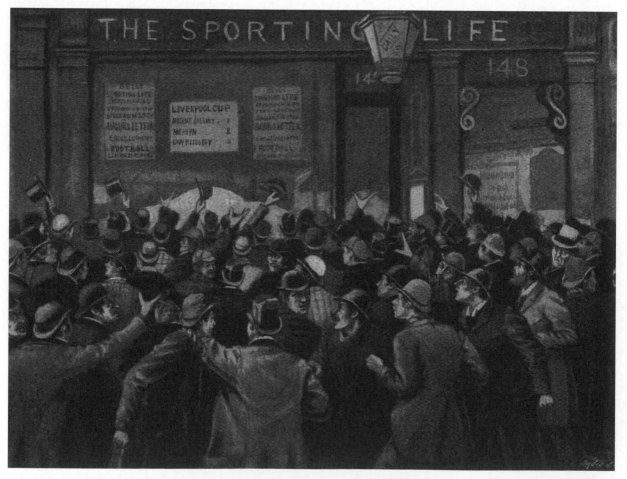

Another piece of abortive legislation! – the Metropolitan Streets Act did not stop crowds from gathering outside the *Life*'s offices to await the 'tissue' of big-race results being posted up in the front window – here they celebrate the victory of the 3-1 favourite, Madame d'Albany in the 1891 Liverpool Autumn Cup.

the same rule, the authorities might order the tradesmen all up Fleet Street to withdraw their goods from their windows, as they attract loungers and other 'obstructives' on the pavement.

We question the right of the police to enforce the removal of the 'tissue', but, as there must be concessions to public convenience in great cities, we are bound to act in unison with our sporting neighbours and contemporaries and abandon the display of the 'flimsy' which has so long been the familiar informant of the London sporting public.

Nevertheless we shall at all times exhibit the result of the great event of the day with the usual despatch which has invariably made us the first to communicate such important intelligence.

Nor were the ever-resourceful bookmakers to be outdone. After being driven out of Bride Lane, banished from Hyde Park (in 1866) and evicted from 'the ruins', they had returned to the Fleet Street area to open up 'pantile clubs', which were little more than roofed-in back yards where, on the payment of a nominal subscription, 'members' were proposed, seconded and elected all within a few minutes.

The Alliance Club in Whitefriars Street, opposite the *Life's* offices, was one of the busiest of these poor men's Tattersalls, which were tolerated because of the bungs the bookmakers paid to the local 'plod' who grew "as obese as septuagenarian Aldermen"[6] on their takings. This happy arrangement lasted until November 1872, when a new Lord Mayor, Sir Sydney Waterlow, declared his number one priority was to rid the City of 'betting men' (except, of course, those who gambled on the Stock Exchange).

Within days of his inauguration, the headline 'Great Capture of Bookmakers in the City' showed that Waterlow was a man of his word. The Shrewsbury Cup was the big race of the day and the clubs were busy with lunchtime customers when it was reported:

Shortly before one o'clock a number of closed four-wheelers and hansom cabs drove down Whitefriars Street and, as if by pre-concerted signal, a posse of City police, about thirty in number, darted out of the vehicles and instantaneously dashed for the entrance of the Club; a strong body entering while a powerful detachment kept guard at any place of probable egress or escape.

It is needless to mention that a panic ensued among the members present who were about three hundred strong, and wild attempts were made on the part of some individuals to escape. One operator, it is believed, did vault almost as dextrously as Lulu,* through a skylight and so got clear off. Others … commenced to destroy their papers and documents and threw them about the place in the wildest confusion…

Such a formidable display in the chief metropolitan thoroughfare created great excitement in the neighbourhood. The uninitiated might have imagined that a raid was being made upon a body of desperate Fenians, rather than upon a few scores of men who were committing no graver offence than betting and whose only weapons or instruments were a book and pencil!

A simultaneous raid had been made on the Exchange Club in nearby Blackfriars and, for once, the punters at both clubs got the better of the layers as they were released, while the bookmakers were marched off to be charged at the Fleet Street nick. The raids triggered a bitter attack on Gladstone's administration by the *Life* which declared:

---

* Lulu was a scantily clad acrobat whose vaudeville performances were all the rage at the time.

There has never been a moment when a Government was so unpopular, and even detested, as that which now holds the seal of office under a factitious profession of 'Liberalism'. Every new measure seems pointed against the comforts, the conveniences, the pleasures and the profits of the lower or middle classes until people ask themselves if our boasted freedom be not a myth and the refrain that 'Britons never, never shall be slaves,' a wild delusion on the part of the patriotic lyricist.

One half of the blunders committed by our rulers is attributable to their ignorance of the classes for whom they legislate, or an absolutely impertinent pretension of paternal solicitude for public virtue and welfare ... It is hypocritical cant to acknowledge betting in the West End of London and crush it when pursued east of Temple Bar.

The new Lord Mayor has started his official career with a proceeding which will render him intensely unpopular ... indeed, the ground on which the Alliance Club stands has already been derisively styled the 'field of Waterlow' in commemoration of the recent raid ... Surely the Lord Mayor, in his ten years' magisterial experience, must have known many cases of men ruined by commercial gambling and heard of thousands of people wrecked by bubble companies and fraudulent schemes and, to be consistent, he might well order the police to make raids in Capel Court and Lombard Street.*

The time has arrived when we must demand the recognition of Turf speculation in whatever class of people, as one of the legitimate sources for the investment of money.

In all some 60 bookmakers were arrested, while 118 betting books and one carrier pigeon were seized and at least one layer learnt to his cost who his true friends were as:

…several operators, in the first alarm of the raid, contrived to send their money out of the Club by trusty friends who were permitted to depart. One bookmaker is said to have been the victim of misplaced confidence. He entrusted two individuals to remove £200 each and they were so faithful to their trust, they have never been seen or heard of since!

When the bookmakers were arraigned before the magistrates at Mansion House the following week only a few were prosecuted, which, the *Life* asserted, was adding insult to injury as, after being "surrounded and captured like so many brigands," they were told "they were at liberty to go about their business and, we will add, left the court without the slightest stain upon their characters". The paper also poured scorn on the "mean and undignified" method of entrapment used by the police whose first witness was…

Watkins, formerly a railway clerk or porter, but now and for three months, one of the City policemen. He informed the Lord Mayor that Inspector Bailey had given him £14 or £15 to commit, what they afterwards seek to prove, an illegal act – converting one of their constables, *pro tem*, into a 'betting man'.

The next witness called to justify the action of the first corporate city in the world, was a worthy named Richardson, a 'young man, bred a carpenter', but to all intents and purposes a hired eavesdropper, spy or common informer ... Upon such a thing as this, shirking his own honest trade and skulking about the slums of London, the legal advisers of the Corporation depend for incriminating testimony in an important prosecution!...

---

* Capel Court was as famous for its stockbrokers as Lombard Street was for its banks.

It has always been regarded as an opprobrium upon any prosecution to lead men into acts or offences for the purpose of ensuring their conviction. Probably after this, the ex-carpenter Richardson will be employed to parade the City with a smart silk handkerchief dangling from his tailcoat pocket after the manner of Fagan, to tempt pavement 'Arabs' to try their fingers at a little initiatory felony.

But, however tainted, the evidence was enough to convict four bookmakers who were each fined £50 (£4,500) for being in breach of the Betting Act as "money was paid and received in advance," the illogicality of which induced Harry Feist to comment:

> Why it is illegal to stake money I am at a loss to understand as the deposit … shows that the backer is well prepared to meet his engagements while, on the other hand, the conventional settling at Tattersalls may be a mere myth and delayed until estates are disposed of and timber cut down.

When Sir Sydney Waterlow relinquished his office a year later with the valedictory boast that he had done much to suppress "that lamentable evil, betting," Feist had the collapsed Overend-Gurney bank in mind as he replied:

> Good, my lord, but pray don't you think there was a very wide field before you in the City had you taken up your civic sword to cleanse and purify? Are there not sham companies, fraudulent financial firms and semi-broken banks by whom hundreds are daily plundered, that might have been looked after as well as the handful of men speculating with their own money, in a mild manner, on a few horse races?
>
> What about the stockbroker, Mr Christian, who was convicted for robbing a lady of hundreds the other day? Is there any raid to be made on the stockbrokers, and will anything be done with the Coal Exchange where the merchants are in conspiracy to keep the poor without their winter's fire?

Answer came there none.

SCRIBES AND TOUTS

I N THE late autumn of 1862 the *Sporting Life* was deprived of the services of its French correspondent in somewhat unusual circumstances. On November 1, the paper announced:

> A duel has lately been fought near Paris with fatal results, and the *Sporting Life* has lost, in the fallen man, a very valued correspondent.

The 'fallen man' was H L Dillon, the editor of *Le Sport*, who, a few months earlier, had written a leading article for the *Life* on the institution of France's first international race, the 100,000fr Grand Prix de Paris, which he and Napoleon III's half-brother, the Duc de Morny, had been instrumental in setting up.

As a result of carrying out his normal journalistic duties, the 32-year-old son of an English parson had, quite literally, crossed swords with Ludovic, the Duc de Gramont-Caderousse, a former attaché at the French Embassy in London and a renowned hell-raiser among the Parisian *demi-monde*. In addition to being a high-stakes gambler, the Duke was also a gentleman rider who believed that amateurs should participate solely for the love of the sport and be above accepting any financial reward for their services.

This was not generally the case with the top British amateurs who made a handsome living from 'presents' and 'travelling expenses'. These shamateurs generated as much resentment among the true amateurs, who were normally less talented but wealthier than their counterparts, as they did among the professionals whose rides they were poaching. It was this contentious issue that provided the basis for the fatal duel.

In the summer of 1862, Gramont-Caderousse had objected to the status of Tommy Pickernell, a leading English amateur, when they came up against each other in a race at Châlons in France and the dispute had resurfaced during the Baden-Baden meeting in Germany that autumn.

Pickernell, who rode under the pseudonym of 'Mr Thomas', had won the 1860 Grand National on Anatis and was to ride two more 'National' winners in The Lamb (1871) and Pathfinder (1875), but long before he achieved such lasting fame the demand for his services had created ill-feeling as far afield as Tasmania, where he went as a 19-year-old in 1852 to study sheep farming.

Tasmanian sheep were not the only ones to be fleeced by Pickernell during his stay 'down under'. His success in the saddle, which included winning six of the seven races at Hobart one day in 1855, resulted in the leading local jockey, David Richardson, writing to the press on behalf of his colleagues.

The aggrieved Richardson complained that 'Mr Thomas', "by offering his services gratuitously to the proprietors of racehorses is depriving poor men – and some of them with large families – of their usual and legitimate and only means of subsistence."[1]

When Pickernell's status was challenged in France, Dillon, who had "on various occasions made not exactly complimentary remarks about French amateur riders in general and Caderousse in particular,"[2] wrote an article in support of his compatriot and criticised the Duke for his unsporting action.

The *Life* recounted that the irate Duke had sent a stinging reply to *Le Sport* but, because "his letter was couched in too warm terms," it was rejected and appeared instead in a minor Belgian paper, the *Journal des Haras*:

From the day that note was printed, it would seem that Mr Dillon had determined to bring about an encounter … [but] de Gramont declined to meet him for the reason, he said, that the gentleman did not move in the same rank of society as himself and that he would not bring himself down, for any purpose, to the level of a writer.

The Duke's haughty sentiments soon changed when Dillon inflamed the situation still further by putting it about that his rival "would take good care not to go to Chantilly races" while he was there; a jibe that provoked the affronted nobleman to "act in such a manner as to render an encounter inevitable".

There had then been a dispute over the choice of weapons. Dillon, "who never had a sword in his hand until three days before the duel," understandably opted for pistols, but the Duke insisted on rapiers. Ultimately, Dillon, as the challenger, agreed to his opponent's demands and immediately embarked upon a crash course in fencing. It did him no good for the Duke was a seasoned duellist. He bore the barely-healed scars of two such épée-encounters over the previous two years and the account of his latest dalliance with death was but brief although it lacked nothing in anatomical detail.

The *Life* reported that the two men had met in the forest of St Germain near Maisons-Laffitte outside Paris:

The choice of position fell to M de Gramont; he took the least favourable, having the rain and wind against him. After three passes, Mr Dillon, as if seized with a sudden giddiness, threw himself forward with all the ardour of inexperienced courage upon M de Gramont.

The fight was at the height of its fury. The Duke at the same moment made a lunge, and his sword entered the right breast of his adversary, penetrating seven inches in depth, between the fifth and sixth ribs. Mr Dillon sank to the ground without uttering a word and died … The news of Mr Dillon's death was received by all who knew him with sorrowing sympathy, especially by those connected with the Parisian Press who could best appreciate the goodness of his heart and his obliging disposition.

His knowledge of horses and Turf subjects generally, was recognised by all and the Jockey Club held his opinion in high esteem … friends of the unfortunate gentleman intend prosecuting the principal and his seconds for homicide, *par imprudence*, and have laid their damages at £2,000.* Mr Dillon left a mother and a sister who were dependant on him for support, and we believe a subscription is being raised for them in Paris.

The death of the *Life's* worthy but rash correspondent was something Harry Feist could have done without. From the start he had been at pains to enlist the best and most informed writers for his paper and he appeared to have pulled off a major coup when, shortly after the 'Great Injunction Case', he persuaded the chief racing correspondent for *Bell's Life*, John Frederick Verrall who wrote under the name of 'Sentinel', to join his team.

Verrall had made his name through his *Racing Indicator* (1853), a small, over-priced (at 2s 6d = £10.60) tipster's circular that was, nevertheless, regarded as a valuable guide by many turfites. He had

---

* Dillon's mother duly obtained an order in the Court of Versailles that required Gramont-Caderousse to pay her an annuity of 3,600fr. (£144 = £12,960), but the Duke did not have to pay her for long. Three years later his wild excesses caught up with him and, stricken with consumption, he died at the age of 31.

been with *Bell's Life* for barely a year and he did not stay with his new paper for much longer. In August 1860, he moved on to carve out a lucrative career for himself as a clerk of the course and handicapper at numerous southern tracks including his home town of Lewes as well as Abington, Alexandra Park, Bromley, Canterbury, Croydon, Egham, Hungerford, Reading and Tonbridge (all long since defunct), while he also acted as a commission agent.

With Verrall's departure, Feist took the opportunity to ensure his paper had a high-profile correspondent who could be relied upon not to up-roots and depart as soon as a more tempting offer came along. There was only one man he could trust with the job, and that was himself. In a fine piece of propaganda, he added an editorial postscript to his preview of the 1860 Ebor meeting at York:

> The above is from the pen of 'Augur', late chief contributor to the *Morning Advertiser*, whose great successes have induced the proprietors of this journal to enter into an arrangement which will, for the future, confine his vaticinations to the *Sporting Life*.

As well as bestowing his Augur signature upon the *Life* in perpetuity, having already discarded another of his pen names ('Voltigeur') into some literary limbo, Feist wrote a schizophrenic letter of introduction 'To the editor of the *Sporting Life*' (i.e. himself) for the benefit of his readers.

This smoke and mirrors ploy was typical of the time, and while it was unusual for the editor of one paper to be writing for another (his stint as 'Augur of the *Advertiser*' had lasted just a few months), it paid to have as many irons in the fire as possible in the uncertain world of Victorian journalism and Feist soon found a replacement for the *Advertiser* when he donned his brother's mantle of 'Hotspur' on the *Daily Telegraph*.

He also wrote for several provincials – the *Newcastle Chronicle* (as 'Underhand') and the *Doncaster Gazette* ('Caractacus') to name but two – in his time, but his sights were always firmly fixed on establishing *his* paper as the best in 'The Street' for this was how he saw the *Life*, no matter whose name was on the newspaper register at Somerset House.

Competition was fierce and the chance of doing down a rival was seldom missed at a time when accuracy in racing journalism left a lot to be desired. One early attack was on the *Manchester Guardian* which, in 1859, had just taken on its first racing reporter. In an article larded with sarcasm, the *Life* remarked:

> We are lost in admiration for the enterprise of our spirited contemporary of the cotton metropolis, but we cannot help suggesting that a racing correspondent should know a little of the subject he has trust of … The writer states that the Trial Stakes at Northampton has quite settled any chance that Shafto, Indifference, King-At-Arms, Donati, &c. may have once had for the Derby. Indeed! Are Shafto, Indifference and King-At-Arms really 'eliminated'?
>
> Considering that none of those horses was entered in the Derby, their pretensions to the 'Blue Ribbon' of the Turf must have been settled some time since.

A whole catalogue of errors was then listed before the *coup de grâce* was administered with withering contempt:

> At the conclusion of his article he asserts that the meeting at Croxton Park was 'only remarkable for the defeat of Zuyder Zee'. Dear me! How sadly the sporting papers have been misinformed for they

stated that, so far from being beaten, Zuyder Zee won the Granby Handicap! We have merely pointed out a few trivial discrepancies which were, perhaps, scarcely worth rectifying.

Ouch! The mauling inflicted on the hapless hack may well have been merited but, as so often happens in such cases, nemesis was waiting just around the corner to club the caustic critic over the head with a salutary reminder that no one is infallible. In its very next number the *Life's* usual report on the business at Tattersalls commented:

The room was somewhat thinly attended and the subscribers devoted their time to the discussion of the recent death of Sir Charles Monck. Sir Charles was an eccentric but a popular patron of the turf withal, and he had his share of good fortune. By his death Gamester, who held a prominent position in the betting, is disqualified for the Derby, Harefoot for the Great Northern and several other animals for important engagements.*

Four days later, the words 'glass houses' and 'stones' came to mind when the front page carried the apology:

Sir Charles Monck – We sincerely regret having caught up the rumour of the death of the above sportsman and gentleman. The report having prevailed in quarters usually entitled to credence, we unwittingly allowed ourselves to be the vehicle for the publication of that which happily proved a mere *canard*.

Not that such blunders inhibited the *Life* in any way, although Feist got more than he bargained for that summer when he asked George Caldwell, the English correspondent for the New York sporting and theatrical weekly, *Wilkes' Spirit of the Times*, to write for the paper.

Caldwell, or 'George the Fifth' as his colleagues suggestively dubbed him, was a typically industrious scribe who used the *nom de plume* of 'Censor' when he wrote for his American paper and the *Life*, and 'Childers' when writing for *Bell's Life* and *The Field*. His 'Censor' alias suited him well since he had a particularly keen instinct for the jugular as he demonstrated in the series of open letters he wrote for the *Life*.

The first to fall victim to his lance-like pen was Apsley Pellatt who, during his term as MP for Southwark (1852-57), had attempted to tackle the thorny problem of tipsters' adverts in the press by having a draconian clause inserted in the Betting Bill of 1853. It had proposed:

That every person who shall by any bill, placard or writing, or by advertisement, notice, or intimation of any kind in any newspaper, offer to give information as to the result of any race, fight or game thereafter to be run or determined; and any editor or proprietor of any newspaper inserting … such advertisement, notice or intimation … shall, upon summary conviction … pay a sum not exceeding £20 [£1,700] or … be imprisoned in the common gaol or house of correction, with or without hard labour, for any period not exceeding one calendar month.

* Under the Rules of Racing all entries became void upon the death of their nominator. This archaic rule was to eliminate some top class horses from the classics before it was finally repealed in 1929. Gamester, it should be added, went on to win the Ascot Derby and the St Leger among other races.

Had this wide-ranging clause been incorporated into what was an already flawed bill it would have crippled the sporting press, but on this occasion the Home Secretary, Lord Palmerston, persuaded Pellatt to withdraw his amendment in the interests of speeding the passage of the bill through parliament.

Caldwell, however, did not forget the damage that had been intended and when Pellatt failed to regain his seat in the general election of 1859, the sporting scribe cast aside such honourable Victorian scruples as not kicking a man when he was down and instead put the boot in with undisguised relish: "You are ignorant and therefore not fit for a representative of the people," he snarled at the former MP.

Your feelings are un-English and your mind, unbiased by the generous influences of manly pursuits, renders you distasteful to Englishmen; you are obviously one of those tyrannic and superficial meddlers whose presence in a legislative assembly only gives dissatisfaction to the lower classes of the people, while your deficiency of perception causes you to suggest measures which bring the House of Commons into contempt throughout the civilised world ... your public career has aroused a detestation in me which would not render it safe for your personal comfort were we to meet in a free arena.

Fighting talk indeed! And 'Censor' was not finished. He taunted Pellatt by reminding him of his proposed legislation.

Did you imagine that this fortunately abortive attempt at gagging the Press and interfering with the peoples' modes of diversion would be passively permitted to sink into oblivion? If you did, you were egregiously deluded. A circular was sent – at the expense, I believe, of some influential racing men – to every voter in Southwark detailing your conduct in this detestable Betting Act business and to these circumstances your happy defeat may be ascribed.

Predictably, the Jockey Club did not escape the censure of 'Censor'. During the 1859 Guineas meeting, reporters were banned from the Newmarket weighing room on the grounds that their presence interfered with the duty of the officials. The fact that there was no such thing as a pressroom on the course did not concern the authorities who were determined to preserve the pristine exclusiveness of the meeting by making it as inhospitable as possible for the hoi polloi and members of the Fourth Estate.

There were just three ancient buildings on the Rowley Mile course; the weighing room, a jockeys' changing room, and a small stand reserved for members of the Jockey Club and Tattersalls' subscription rooms. At least four winning posts were dotted along the course at various points and the judge's box was a rickety affair on wheels pulled from one post to the other by a long-suffering donkey. Because many spectators were mounted it mattered little to them where a race finished or whether they had access to the stand. Bookmakers conducted their business from flys (two-wheeled carriages), while journalists wrote their reports in hired broughams (four-wheeled coaches).

Caldwell doubtlessly waited until he got back to the comfort of the Rutland Arms before he penned his letter to the Jockey Club:

Newmarket Heath, at the present moment, presents a spectacle which I blush to behold or even speak of. That spot over which you have supreme control, is the only one in England where the representatives of the Press are purposely thwarted in their duties, and the public might thereby suffer materially were it not that the reporters, who are, in reality, the representatives not of the Press but of the people, defy all obstructions and undergo unspeakable hardship in their zeal and determination to afford the public every information....

With the selfish and specious object of facilitating the meaner duties of your officials, you perpetrated the unparalleled act of shutting out the Press, forcing one to regard you as the Louis Napoleons of the Turf ... No other society of English gentlemen would be guilty of such an act...

Racing at Newmarket is not as it used to be, and yet you endeavour to keep up its pristine exclusiveness. The Heath is not supported by a few noblemen as of old, but by the general public who, by their subscriptions to the ring, absolutely support 'the meetings at headquarters' as the reporters term the Newmarket gatherings. Yet no accommodation is provided for the members of the ring, there is no stand, no shelter from the weather, in fact, as the urchins asseverate, '*no nuffin*'.*

Strong stuff! Yet these condemnations of Pellatt and the Jockey Club were as nothing compared to the extraordinary attack Caldwell launched on Prince Albert whose alleged 'crime' had been to influence Queen Victoria against attending the Derby and other important meetings. He began his lengthy epistle to 'HRH Field Marshal Prince Albert' in the mealy-mouthed way an assassin might sidle up to his victim as he wheedled:

I approach your Highness with every sentiment of loyalty and with a due sense of the delicate position I am placed in in tendering words of remonstrance to the husband of a great, a good and amiable Sovereign.

Patronisingly, he then deigned to acknowledge the Prince's attributes as a husband and father; and conceded "even in your public conduct there is much to commend," before he stuck the knife in and twisted it with a vicious glee. "I do not intend to reiterate the caustic observations which, during the height of the Crimean war, passed current in society," he wrote before he proceeded to do precisely that:

It was said that you derived military emoluments and that you were 'A fellow who never set a squadron in the field, nor the division of battle knew more than a spinster'... I certainly do wish for your own sake that you possessed some military ambition; but if you are content to be simply the paid husband of Queen Victoria, you are at liberty to remain insignificant, though eminent and unpopular, when you might command the enthusiastic admiration of the people...

All that is known of your achievements in the sporting world are either ridiculous or contemptible. You are an active 'lover of the trigger' which you may consider entitles you to the appellation of 'sportsman', but the *modus operandi* causes real sportsmen to regard you as no more one of their fraternity than a butcher or poulterer.

I remember at the period of Lord Derby's retirement from the Turf, an article appeared in *The*

---

* It was not until 1875, some time after the old private stand had been condemned as unsafe, that the Jockey Club, following considerable opposition from within its ranks, sanctioned the building of a new grandstand which included refreshment rooms and, wonder of wonders, a telegraph office for the public and press!

Times which stated that you could not 'clear a three foot hedge after a pack of harriers' and from what I have heard of your exploits with that dwarf pack which is kept at Windsor for your occasional delectation, the article was no exaggeration. It seems to be a question, when you charge a hedge, who shall be first over, the horse or the rider, and I fear that his Highness often precedes his hunter.

Character assassination completed, 'Censor' proceeded to work his way round to the main thrust of his indictment:

There is no disguising the fact that of late years our beloved Queen and family have, year by year, withheld their countenance from horseracing and only nominally patronise the sport ... The Derby was formerly witnessed by the Queen and on one occasion, in 1840, you, at the hand of Royalty, presented a handsome trophy to Macdonald, the rider of Little Wonder ... A foreigner, and unknown, it was a clever stroke of policy on your part to stimulate an interest in the darling sport of Englishmen, and in the first year of your marriage to perform an act which deluded the people into the belief that you were impregnated with British partialities.

The feigned instinct told and thrived for a time and the public talked enthusiastically of the 'handsome young Prince who was so fond of horses'. Year by year, however, the real principles which governed you gradually became manifest. The Queen deserted Epsom totally ... even the official visits to Ascot are all but relinquished and the Queen has departed from the cherished traditions of her ancestors in deserting the Heath...

The presence of Royalty at race meetings and the knowledge that the first personage in the land promoted the sports, would ultimately lead to the extinction of Turf immorality. As it is, vice, to a certain extent, is dominant; but he would be a courageous scoundrel indeed who would dare to perpetrate his villainies under the eyes of Our Sovereign Lady, the Queen.

There was more, much more, in a similar vein before the astonishingly brass-necked columnist concluded:

I have given your Highness my reasons and my remonstrations, and if you really have, as I have, the national love of Her Majesty and her family at heart, you will not despise the humble source from which these sentiments emanate, and the humbler person who addresses you in the name of 'CENSOR'.

It's safe to assume the *Sporting Life* was not as popular in the royal household in 1859 as it was later to become! But it is quite possible that Albert Edward the Prince of Wales, then a fun-loving 17-year-old yet to be initiated into the delights of the Turf, would read the paper in the not-too-distant future. He who would be king was later to echo Caldwell's argument for royal patronage of the Turf in a letter to his mother after she had rebuked him for his involvement in what she saw as a thoroughly disreputable sport. He wrote:

I utterly and entirely disapprove of what is bad about racing and I think much may be done in trying to elevate what has always been a great national sport of the country. Should we shun races entirely ... the racing would get worse and worse and these pleasant and social gatherings would cease to exist.[3]

Henry Hall Dixon, 'the Tacitus of sporting writers'.

Perhaps unsurprisingly, Caldwell's attack on Queen Vic's dearly beloved was one of the last epistles he wrote for the *Life*. His abrasive style may well have appealed to the paper's more radical readers, but there were limits!

As a replacement for the censorious Censor, Feist recruited the services (initially on an intermittent basis) of Henry Hall Dixon, one of the most gifted and popular writers of the day. A tall, shy, introspective man, Dixon had achieved national fame with his first book, *Post and Paddock* (1856) – written under his *nom de plume* 'The Druid' – which covered a broad spectrum of Turf history and his other great love, foxhunting.

The son of a major cotton manufacturer and mayor of Carlisle, he had initially chosen law as his profession and after attending Rugby and Trinity College, Cambridge, he was articled to a firm of solicitors in Doncaster where, on its historic Town Moor, he was, in his own words, "bitten by the tarantula of horseracing".

Lured away from his law books, he started writing on sporting and political matters for the *Doncaster Gazette* and was appointed managing editor of that paper at the age of 26 in 1848, but he soon outgrew the provincial weekly and two years later moved to London to join the staff of *Bell's Life*. To supplement his salary of £3 (£255) a week, he continued to write for his old paper, while he also penned political verses for *Punch* and *The Examiner*, farming articles for the *Illustrated London*

News and the agricultural journal, *Mark Lane Express*, and monthly articles for the *Sporting Magazine* under various pen names.

Within a year, the versatile north-countryman had made such an impression on the Clement brothers they offered him the editorship of *Bell's Life* but, to their astonishment and lasting chagrin, he turned it down together with the £1,000 (£85,000) salary that went with it. He preferred instead, "the freedom to carry on the work he felt impelled to do in his own way, subject only to his own will."[4]

Dixon loved to commune with nature and record the tales of the rustic characters he met on his travels among the sporting communities. It was during these rural ramblings that he gathered the material for his second bestseller, *Silk and Scarlet*, a companion work to *Post and Paddock*. The *Life* published a few extracts from the book when it appeared in the autumn of 1859, but to begin with Dixon's anonymous contributions to the paper (they never carried 'The Druid' signature) were sporadic and often sent into the office by train 'parcel' from places as far afield as Cornwall and Cumberland.

With a large family to support (he fathered 13 children, eight of which survived into adulthood) he was, by necessity, a prolific writer. His most physically taxing work and the one that gave him the greatest satisfaction was *Field and Fern* (1865); a general record of Scottish farming. In his preface to the book he revealed it had required him to...

> pluck the heart out of three summers, a winter and a spring, to travel some 8,000 miles (this includes several journeys to and from London), to sleep away from home some 250 nights, and change my bed 146 times before I wrote a line.

After his final trip north in the summer of 1863, he made the return journey from Kirkwall in Orkney on a half-broken pony he bought for £7-10s (£675). By the time he arrived back in London in the middle of a snowstorm the following February, both his wanderlust and his health were on the wane and he felt ready to accept a more permanent position writing for the *Daily News* (founded by Charles Dickens in 1846) in Bouverie Street, which was handily situated just across the road from the *Life*, where he did a double shift on Tuesdays and Fridays as a leader writer and biographer.

Working closely with Harry Feist and Edward Dorling, his mandate was wide-ranging and incorporated all aspects of sport and any political or domestic issues that might interest readers. His dry, rather cynical sense of humour, allied to his lyrical prose, made his articles an enjoyable read and he would often slip a few lighter items into his column to add colour and variety. His subjects could range from a papal sanction for horseracing in Rome to a Spanish 'bullfight' in London, just as they did in February 1870.

Coming at a time when further moves were being taken to suppress betting in England, Dixon handled the first subject with his usual aplomb:

> We read that the Pope, giving a practical instance of his infallibility, has just decreed that horseracing, which hitherto was heretical in Rome, shall now be an orthodox pastime. This little item of sporting-ecclesiastical news will take the world by surprise.
>
> 'The Pope he leads a happy life' is a proposition that nobody has hitherto cared to dispute, but the happiness has, in fitting verse, been declared to consist mainly in wifelessness together with an unlimited allowance of Rhenish wine. But his Holiness has added another ingredient to human happiness in the shape of horseracing ... it is rather singular that, at the very moment certain

influences are at work to crush horseracing out of England, the sport should receive high and direct encouragement in Rome.

Let our persecuted commission agents look to it; there is still a home for them – a place where they can issue their price lists, where betting is not exorcised and postage stamps are not objected to. In that happy land, crowns may be invested under the Crozier, while to hob and nob at the Mitre will be one of the daily amenities of speculators.

There was, however, no humour to be found in his comments on the so-called bullfight that had taken place at the Agricultural Hall in Islington. Dixon's farming affinities were evident as he ridiculed the "surpassingly absurd" event and accused the organisers of cruelty as "five or six miserable little beasts, not much bigger than calves of tender age, and about as ferocious and intelligent, were teased into something like pugnacity".

Fred Taylor, another of Feist's signings, was pugnacious enough without being teased. One of the 'noble six hundred' who had taken part in the charge of the Light Brigade, he had left the shattered remnants of his regiment, the 8th Irish Hussars, at the end of the Crimean war in 1856 to embark upon a journalistic career in Dublin from where he contributed to the English sporting press under the pseudonym of 'Ballinasloe'.

In 1863, Feist engaged Taylor to write exclusively for the *Life* by creating the role of 'Special Commissioner' for him, and the former cavalryman soon made an impression in Fleet Street, although not of the kind his editor had hoped for. Not used to taking orders from young whippersnappers, the Balaclava veteran almost threw Edward Dorling out of an upper-storey window during one heated exchange.

Despite his fiery nature, which was often fuelled by a liquid lunch at the famous Ye Olde Cheshire Cheese tavern next door to the *Life's* offices, Taylor was a great asset to the paper. The author of several books including *Recollections of a Horse Dealer* (1861) and *Life of a Nag Horse* (1862), his articles carried the authority of one who had an intimate knowledge of his subject and they helped to open doors in the racing world that would otherwise have been shut to a less-respected journalist.

In addition to signing up the best available writers, Feist was anxious to build up a network of strategically placed freelance reporters throughout the country. This team of stringers would not only provide information on horses trained in their area, but would feed the office with items of local racing news. The reoccurring notice: "Turf Correspondents are required for *The Sporting Life* at every training district in the United Kingdom. Apply, stating terms, to the Editor." rang out like a clarion call during the paper's first few months. Applicants were not slow in coming forward, but the recruitment of touts (as they would have been in all but name) on such a large scale was viewed with alarm by the Jockey Club.

Considerable pressure was put on Feist to drop the idea and, under the threat of being 'warned off' if he ignored the demands of the authorities, he reluctantly abandoned the scheme. As a result the 'Training Intelligence' column, which had contained reports from East Ilsley, Newmarket, Richmond and Middleham in the first number, was never developed and, after a few further reports from 'headquarters', it lapsed altogether.

In return for his grudging compliance, Feist gained the goodwill of many owners and trainers without whose co-operation it would have been impossible for Fred Taylor to furnish his reports on the leading stables in the run-up to each new season. Yet, there was more than a whiff of double standards in the Jockey Club's action as its members would often employ touts for their own purposes.

From racing's earliest days, a system of equine espionage had operated within the sport. Owners, anxious to find out the strength of the opposition before they put their money down, engaged grooms to spy on trial gallops and bribe stable lads for inside information.

The emergence of bookmakers at the end of the eighteenth century brought another interested party onto the scene and touting soon became a much more widespread occupation, carried on by a collection of generally disreputable and peripatetic stablemen.

The most notorious member of this unholy band was Daniel Dawson, a serial horse-poisoner who was believed to have been in the pay of the bookmakers Jim and Joe Bland when he nobbled some 20 horses over a period of years by pouring arsenic into their water troughs. This crude but effective method of 'stopping' horses not only resulted in the deaths of four of the unfortunate animals, but also cost Dawson his own life when he was hanged for his crime before a 10,000-plus crowd outside Cambridge jail in 1812.

In 1821 another tout, William Taylor, was caught watching a trial through a telescope. Like Dawson, he displayed a misplaced loyalty in refusing to name his employer and all the Jockey Club could do was to warn him off Newmarket Heath and issue a notice that it would similarly banish anyone "who should be detected in watching or divulging any trial … or who should be proved to have employed any persons to watch trials."[5]

This much-flouted law, which lacked the more effective deterrent of a rope around the neck, remained in force for almost 30 years until the miracle of the electric telegraph reached Newmarket and other racing centres to give touts the freedom to act as representatives of the press. They were employed to report on the progress of the leading classic candidates and other goings on within the racing community, but comprehensive accounts on which horses were working well, or badly, on the gallops appeared only in tipsters' circulars; John Verrall's *Racing Indicator* having set the trend in 1853.

Leaving aside the brief use of training reports in the *Life* and their equally short-lived appearance in the *Sporting Times* in 1865, this situation remained unchanged until 1866 when *The Sportsman*, a fledgling bi-weekly, made a big show of introducing them.

Initially, the *Life's* response was muted as Feist was reluctant to jeopardise the good working relationship he had built up with many of the Turf's leading players. In discussing his dilemma with the famous Kingsclere trainer John Porter, he conceded Porter was probably right to regard touting as 'obnoxious', but added: "We cannot afford to stand out. If they [*The Sportsman*] do it, we shall have to follow suit."[6]

And follow suit he eventually did when, in February 1867, he reintroduced training reports by reminding readers that "the *Sporting Life* was the first public journal which supplied such information". Why that information had then been withdrawn was passed over with the all-purpose get-out clause "for reasons unnecessary to enter upon at this distance of time". Instead, he concentrated on justifying the reports as he asserted:

> While we heartily dislike the systems of secret touting, watching trials or tampering with stable lads, we infer that a training reporter may find legitimate occupation in noting the daily doings of the horses in the various districts. Under this impression we have engaged special correspondents at the principal training quarters and they have instructions to supply their news in brief and explicit terms and confine their remarks chiefly to those horses having important and immediate engagements...
>
> For the future our readers will be kept thoroughly posted with Training Intelligence up to the hour of going to press, as the correspondents, besides the notes on morning gallops, will communicate any special matters of moment by telegram … Indeed, by the revival of Training

Intelligence in these columns, we trust we may increase our usefulness and value as accurate and faithful purveyors of all kinds of sporting news.

To begin with there were reports from Newmarket, Richmond, Middleham, Malton, Ilsley, Chilton and Fyfield and in the weeks that followed the training centres of Epsom, Findon, Hednesford, Kingsclere, Lambourn, Lewes, Stanton and Stockbridge were added.

Owners and trainers were, predictably, horrified by this turn of events and soon began to impose their own form of 'warning off' on the work-watchers who were now dignified as 'correspondents' by their Fleet Street employers. Various forms of tout-deterrents were employed to patrol the gallops ranging from prizefighters, who were "permanently retained on their establishment to strike terror into the souls of the horse-watchers and to 'drub' them as occasion might require," to vicious dogs such as the bloodhound – formerly used to track down escaped slaves in America – kept by John Scott at Malton.

The Newmarket trainer Tom Jennings, who sent out Fille de l'Air to win the Oaks in 1864 and Gladiateur to carry off the Triple Crown the following year, was involved in a high-profile court case after he had attacked a tout called John Bray in 1868. Bray, who was savagely beaten about the head with the butt-end of Jennings' hunting crop, brought an action for assault and during the case it emerged that he was employed not by a newspaper, but by Lord Stamford, a leading owner and member of the Jockey Club!

Surprisingly, the *Life* did not capitalise on this spectacular own goal by the authorities; instead Henry Dixon remarked, with some understatement, that the assault was "not calculated to enhance Jennings in the eyes of the world":

Had the trainer caught the watcher lying in ambush to see a trial; tampering with his stable lads; intruding upon private premises or placing his hands upon the horses, he might have had some justification for the outrage ... but he possessed the great advantage of being a strong man on horseback and armed with a hunting whip, while the object of his wrath was an insignificant fellow, much below even medium height, on foot and totally defenceless. Therefore, however great the provocation, the assault was at once fierce, unmanly and inconsiderate.

Bray had, in fact, been watching the horses from a public footpath and the provocation he gave was to call Jennings "a bloody fool" in an aside to a companion; a remark which Dixon considered almost as objectionable as the attack itself. To him, the expletive 'bloody' was as crude and unnecessary as most people find the use of the 'F-word' in today's society. He observed that Jennings' counsel had referred to "the hideous oaths that had been used in the altercation" and that "one of the most filthy seemed to be an ordinary expression at Newmarket". To underline this point, Dixon – who was far from being a prude – quoted the case of a parson who had…

the moral courage to preach openly against the use of a certain word, and remarked that it was so prevalent that he had heard the children of the lower orders, when out walking, speaking of 'the b——y birds a singing' … we regret to say that this loathsome expression is frightfully frequent in racing disputations … Do men who train their tongues to such vileness ever think how seriously it affects their own personal character and even defames and sullies the pursuits in which they engage?

Whether the magistrates shared Dixon's extreme Victorian values is not known, but Bray was awarded £200 (£18,000) in damages. Jennings appealed and lost, but the biggest loser was the Jockey Club whose campaign against the employment of touts by the press had been undermined by one of its most prominent members. Not that this stopped other clubmen from continuing to call for the withdrawal of training reports.

Sir Joseph Hawley, who had won vast sums from betting coups on his horses, the foundations of which had been laid in secret dawn trails, wrote a long letter to *The Times* in 1870 attacking the sporting press for "infesting" the training grounds with touts.

Feist responded by arguing that the whole system of touting had been cleaned up by the introduction of training reports in newspapers:

> In former years private touts made large sums by illicitly corresponding with individuals; frequently members of the Jockey Club or bookmakers. When regular reports were published, however, the main body found their occupation gone. Their employers no longer cared to pay them handsome sums for what had previously been valuable, privileged communications and it no longer became sufficiently remunerative to watch trials.
>
> Our reports have constantly prevented the public from being fleeced, and partially stopped the milking of 'dead 'uns' or cripples, which was formerly carried on to an enormous extent ... When The Rake broke a blood vessel just prior to the [1867] Derby, the promptitude of our Newmarket correspondent enabled us to proclaim the fact outside our office in Fleet Street within half an hour of the occurrence and not one farthing was secured, but in former times such incidents as these would have allowed the market-mongers to get thousands of pounds.
>
> In fact, touting for public newspapers has nearly killed the old pernicious system of obtaining money for 'surreptitious information'. It is only really heavy gamblers and owners who wish to make their horses instruments of gaming, who object to their teams being watched at exercise.

Having thus pointed an accusing finger at Sir Joseph Hawley, the editor continued to expand his network of 'correspondents' as the Jockey Club vainly tried its best to curb their activities, especially those who operated under its very nose in Newmarket. In 1872, the Club resolved to licence all trainers in the town and double the Heath Tax to 4gns (£380) a year for each horse that used the gallops. The *Life*, in calculating the increased charges would bring in some £3,000 (£270,000) for the Club, commented:

> The chief trainers at Newmarket can hardly grumble at this, for the resolutions have been adopted as much for their protection and their masters' as for anything else. It is notorious that under the pretext of training, individuals have, for many years, taken a horse or two to Newmarket as a mere cloak to cover touting operations. All this will be altered from the 1st of January 1873, for henceforth trainers will be compelled to obtain a licence annually and disclose the names of their employers and specify the horses under their charge.

This radical step by the authorities preceded the introduction of licences for all trainers by 32 years (jockeys were first licensed in 1880), but it did little to remove the main cause of their agitation and so, in 1876, one last effort was made at banishing 'men of observation' from the Heath when Prince Batthyany, owner of the previous year's Derby winner, Galopin, presented a petition to the Jockey Club stewards. Signed by 28 owners and trainers including such leading lights as John Porter, Mat Dawson, John and William Day and (unsurprisingly) Tom Jennings, the petition blamed "certain cheap sporting

" THREE BIG STEWARDS AND ONE LITTLE TOUT."

The stewards of the Jockey Club (l to r) Sir John Astley, Admiral Rous and Henry Chaplin, resort to extreme measures in an attempt to rid Newmarket Heath of its touts.

papers" for perpetrating a system which "if persisted in, will become intolerable". It claimed that the information contained in the reports was...

largely obtained from servants, boys and even apprentices, who are tempted to violate their masters' secrets by an organised staff of paid horse-watchers and touts, who are, as we believe, maintained at the chief training establishments in the country, at the expense of those papers.

The result of their efforts is to corrupt and demoralise, and in many cases to cause the discharge and ruin of servants and boys in training stables, and a further result is the entire destruction of confidence between the employer and the employed.

It is against this system, so dishonourable in practice, so injurious to owners and trainers, and so entirely subversive of the morality and best interests of the Turf, that we earnestly protest, and we trust that the Jockey Club will take such immediate steps as may be desirable to arrest its future progress.

The *Life*, stung by these libellous accusations, responded indignantly:

Labouring under the stigma of representing the 'cheap sporting papers', we yet fearlessly, emphatically and unconditionally deny that the training reporters employed by this journal are encouraged in any way whatever to do other than give mere records of the doings of horses in ordinary exercise work.

This rebuttal did not impress *The Times* which carried a full-column editorial on the matter. Its views were summarised in one paragraph:

It is no doubt very despicable and scandalous that the touts of the sporting papers should hang about training establishments and peep over walls at 'private trials' and give gratifications to obliging grooms, but none of these offences can be reached by the Jockey Club any more than by the law. The truth is that the modern organisation of the Turf naturally produces prophetical sporting journals and impudent spies.[7]

The *Life* deemed such remarks to be "either founded on ignorance or to be actuated by *malice prepense*," but the old 'Thunderer' was right on one thing – there was absolutely nothing the clubmen could do about it and by the end of the century the *Life* was carrying training reports from some 50 locations spread throughout the United Kingdom. They would often fill an entire page, with as many as two columns devoted solely to the action at Newmarket where the paper's resident 'tout', John Gardner, wrote a twice-weekly article under the pseudonym of 'Warren Hill'.

Unfortunately for Daniel Dawson, he was born a century too early to earn an honest crust from writing the Warren Hill column.

WELSHERS AND DEAD 'UNS

AT A TIME when the average punter was easy prey for the many welshers who infested racing, the *Life*, itself, was not immune to the fraudsters who sought to promote their schemes through its columns. Despite taking none-too-stringent steps to check the *bona fides* of its advertisers, a few 'unscrupulous tricksters' regularly slipped though the net and, much to its chagrin, the paper found itself being used as a tool to fleece the public by the very people it sought to expose.

The first of many leaders to be written on the subject appeared in November 1859 under the heading 'Advertising Commission Swindlers':

> During the present racing season we have been inundated with letters complaining of a system of public swindling which appears to have been carried out with a barefaced disregard of honesty worthy of the most desperate gangs of fraudulent practitioners.
>
> As usual in cases of public swindling, one is astonished that any individuals should exist so deficient of discrimination and ignorant of the world's ways as to fall ready dupes to fellows whose intentions are at once palpable and who only subsist by the folly of the multitude. We allude to a fraternity of swindlers who, by means of advertising in provincial and metropolitan papers, rob the public to a very large extent on the plea of undertaking to bet on commission…
>
> By well concerted plans, advertisements have obtained admission in our columns, by which some hundreds of our readers, we fear, have been unmercifully robbed … The *modus operandi* of these precious 'commissioners' is easily explained. They adopt the name of some well-known member of Tattersalls and advertise to bet on commission and not only refuse to pay when they win, but to refund money staked.

To accompany the article, two letters sent by the so-called commission agents to their victims were reproduced to illustrate the assortment of feeble excuses offered for non-payment as further attempts were made to extract even more money out of their gullible clients. Harry Feist was particularly galled by these bogus commissioners since he was in direct competition with them as his paper regularly carried such notices as:

> The Editor of *The Sporting Life* executes commissions on the usual terms. No commission attended to under £5 [£450]. Tattersalls prices guaranteed.[*]

It seemed the editor wanted it all ways and it was grossly hypocritical of him to accept advertisements from 'fellows whose intentions are at once palpable' and then launch a crusade against them after taking their money. Of course, if a suspect advert appeared in a rival paper, there was an added incentive to expose the fraud and shortly after its initial leader on the subject the *Life* was presented with a golden opportunity to discredit its arch enemy in the Strand when *Bell's Life* carried an advert announcing the setting up of a body to protect backers from welshers. It read:

> To the Racing World – Several gentlemen, having united for the purpose of suppressing the system

---

[*] Feist's days as a commission agent came to an inglorious end when he was made bankrupt in 1861.

of fraud (known as 'welshing') now so extensively carried on by certain parties both by betting and advertising, request all gentlemen willing to assist them in this undertaking to communicate with the secretary, agency office, 4 Victoria Street, Westminster. A Subscription Club has been set on foot by a number of gentlemen for their mutual protection, and proper agents being appointed to make investments for them. Subscriptions (including use of rooms with papers, periodicals &c.) one guinea [£94.50] per annum.

After remarking that the newspaper in question had given the notice "unqualified support in a variety of forms," the *Life* queried the credentials of those behind the new club:

In the first case it is essential, before the interests of the public are confided to any society, that the names of its members should be divulged ... at Tattersall's on Monday we could not find one person who knew anything whatever of those who might be the individuals identified with the project ... If the only object to be attained is the suppression of a nefarious system, we consider it a premature assumption of this nameless company of 'gentlemen' to offer to make investments unless their stability be satisfactorily shown.

Three days later, on Christmas Eve, the paper was full of festive cheer as it goaded *Bell's Life* with the news that its article had "created a deep sensation in sporting circles":

It is somewhat flattering to ourselves that, in all cases of craft and fraud, the public look to us alone for unflinching exposure ... No wonder *The Sporting Life* was not favoured with an advertisement 'To the Racing World'; the projectors of the scheme knew well enough that the transparent purpose of the 'number of gentlemen' would be seen through in Fleet Street, however well it might go down in the Strand!

In an adjacent column, a letter from 'your obedient servant, Miles' contained just the sort of information Feist had been looking for. It revealed that the promoters of the new club were a couple of ne'er-do-wells called Eicke and Barr:

The former is at present confined in the Queen's Bench for his share in the illegal sale of army commissions, and the latter was discharged about a year since when he was imprisoned under the alias of Barry. A few days since, I called upon a friend in the Queen's Bench accompanied by an officer in a cavalry regiment to whom Mr Eicke had some time ago made some proposals relative to obtaining a commission in the service. To him, Mr Eicke confided his little 'spec' adding ... they expected to make a good haul for, 'it was one of the best robberies he had been concerned in for some time'.

The *Life* also reproduced two classified ads that had recently appeared in *The Times*. Both carried the address of the suspect club and were similar in content; one read:

To retired officers and gentlemen – £200 [£18,000] per annum with a gentlemanly occupation suited to an officer may be realised by a gentleman having £300 to invest. Apply to Newton and Barry, agency offices.

Under which an editorial footnote added:

The antecedents of Messrs Newton and Barry are notorious. Newton, we are led to believe, received 12 months imprisonment for a savage assault at Beulah Spa. Barry, alias Barr, is notorious for Brown's Patient Parchment Company and was once accused of arson, his premises having been destroyed under suspicious circumstances … Barry recently offered to pay past liabilities as soon as he 'caught a secretary, a retired officer, or some subscriptions to the new Turf Purification Association dropped in'.

The gauntlet was thus thrown down in dramatic fashion and in its next number the paper reported it had been picked up and returned with interest in the form of a writ. A brief announcement stated:

The Editor and publisher of the *Sporting Life* have received preliminary notices of action and criminal prosecution for libels alleged to have been published in this journal on Messrs Eicke and Barry in reference to their connection with the new 'Subscription Club'.

And so, on 17 February 1860, ten months after 'The Great Injunction Case' the *Life* found itself back in court for 'The Great Libel Case'. Barry, who described himself as a commission agent, proved a formidable opponent. Having set his damages at £500 (£45,000) he was able to prove that no charge of arson had ever been brought against him and things seemed to be going his way until he was cross-examined by the *Life's* barrister.

Under a barrage of accusations, Barry indignantly denied he had played with marked cards at Cheltenham or had leased out a shooting ground that did not belong to him, but he did admit he had been sentenced to 18 months' imprisonment for conspiracy at cards; that he had once been made insolvent and had been remanded for 11 months for fraudulently contracting debts, and that he was also a defaulter on the Turf.

All in all, the plaintiff emerged as a man not to be trusted with either commissions or subscriptions and the jury had little hesitation in returning a verdict for the defendant, which "was received with applause". The following day the *Life* was able to announce:

Yesterday in the court of Queen's Bench at the Guildhall before Mr Justice Wightman, it was the privilege of this paper to assert a principle of vast interest, not alone to the sporting community, but to the independent public at large … We have proved the right of a public journalist to reproduce the former vices and crimes of individuals when they are seeking, by plausible devices and well-laid schemes, to outwit or, to give it its proper term, to rob, the unsuspecting…

It is not the custom of *The Sporting Life* to exalt with any vulgar exuberance of feeling over a fallen antagonist. We deny the degree of parity in this instance, and for that end think it necessary to tell Mr Barry publicly that he is a convicted scoundrel who dared to challenge the opposition of this paper to a crafty and barefaced scheme for robbery and plunder.

And as a postscript to the case, the paper paid tribute to the part played by the Jockey Club's pioneering security officer:

We consider it but fair to state that the accumulation of evidence brought forward for the defence … was in a great measure owing to the untiring energy and perseverance of Sergeant Langley of the detective force, and the accredited Turf expurgator appointed by the Jockey Club. This may serve to show how judiciously the Jockey Club acted in creating such an appointment, and in selecting so efficient an official to fill it, inasmuch as he has been an active instrument in the extinction of a scheme by which a lasting benefit has been conferred upon the Turf and the public at large.

This early instance of the press and the Jockey Club working together to stamp out skulduggery on the Turf was a triumph for Feist. Not only did it establish his paper as *the* foremost campaigning journal, but it was one in the eye for *Bell's Life* which reacted to the success of its rival with spiteful pettiness. The following week the *Life* declared:

> We had hoped to have done with Mr W Barry,[*] however, our contemporary, *Bell's Life*, after having played a part in the matter which has damaged its character and prestige beyond redemption as the 'fearless and searching' investigator of Turf immorality, arrived at its pitiable climax on Sunday last…
>
> It is positively painful to perceive that otherwise well-conducted journal converted into the ready instrument of narrow-mindedness, conceit, and ignorance when, if influenced by an enlightened policy, it should stand alone as the vigorous corrector of abuses and the beacon of sporting journalism.
>
> But it is additionally anomalous that *Bell's Life* has no one in its proprietary interests willing to step in and cleanse the Augean stable of 170 Strand of its petty jealousies, its perpetual wranglings and its rotten principles.

Wow! It transpired that the cause of all this ire was that *Bell's* had carried a report of the case which was "a disgrace to newspaper literature" in that:

> The name of the *Sporting Life* is not once mentioned, the editor's name and evidence are wilfully suppressed, and while nearly two columns are devoted to Barry's side of the question, the defendant's arguments by witnesses and by counsel are omitted.

Due credit was, however, given in the newly launched monthly *Baily's Magazine*, which declared the *Life* had:

> …gained a great and deserved reputation amongst racing men for its bold exposure of an attempted fraud. The racing world, indeed, cannot be too thankful for the courageous manner in which this paper advocated their interests, in direct contradistinction to a higher-priced and professedly higher-class sporting journal, the proprietors of which must bestir themselves or they will have some difficulty to compete with their juvenile contemporary.

---

[*] Barry's name appeared in the *Life* again in April 1870, when the paper carried the following item without comment except for the strategic insertion of an exclamation mark: "Andrew William Barr, alias Captain Barry, was charged before the magistrates at Newmarket on Wednesday with assaulting Mr Henry M Feist on the Heath on Tuesday. The assault having been proved, the bench ordered Barr to pay £2 [£180] and costs. The magistrates said if Mr Feist would swear he went in bodily fear of Barr, they would compel him [*Barr*] to find sureties to keep the peace. The complainant said he had no fear of such a person and that all he required was to get rid of the nuisance of molestation in his business. Barr protested on his honour (!) that he would not offend again and was liberated after being in custody all day from his inability to find bail."

That the 'juvenile contemporary' was not prepared to rest on its laurels became evident a few weeks later when the 1860 Flat season got underway at Lincoln. Noting the large number of welshers at the meeting, it asked:

Are these fungi of the Turf to be permitted the privilege of admission to the ring to destroy the respectability of racing, and disgust and rob individuals who would otherwise enter into the pursuit and speak well, and not ill, of betting men? … the management of such meetings ought to employ, at their own expense, a competent detective to prevent intrusion of the scum and dregs of society known as 'welshers' … or honourable betting men will lose their characters, being confounded with these ruffians who cling like barnacles to the ring.

Despite the efforts of some racecourses such as Catterick whose clerk of the course "considerably provided some stout labourers and a tar-barrel for the special benefit of the welshers,"[1] matters did not improve and racecourse robberies, assaults and general thuggery continued unabated particularly at the main meetings where the violence would often spill out into the town after racing.

One such robbery occurred during Newmarket's Houghton meeting in October 1860 when a well-known bookmaker, Billy Nicholl, was mugged. Harry Feist, who was by then standing in as 'Hotspur' for his consumptive brother Albert, first submitted his report of the incident to the *Daily Telegraph* before reproducing it in the *Life* the following day under the heading 'The Daring Garrotte Robbery at Newmarket'.

After portraying Nicholl as "a good-tempered north countryman who drives a dog cart and a very extraordinary looking horse of indescribable colour," Feist continued:

This person carries on a large, ready-money process of bookmaking chiefly among the outsiders, laying the odds to anything between a crown [£22.50] and a £100 [£9,000] or more. As a natural consequence, his receipts are great and when I state he had £1,835 [£165,150] in notes and cash at the time of the robbery, some idea of the nature of his transactions can readily be conjectured.

With great indiscretion Mr Nicholl was not only in the habit of carrying these heavy sums about with him, but, to use a vulgar phrase, 'flashed' his money in company not remarkable for withstanding strong temptations. On Friday night he had been in some such society and dearly did the poor fellow pay for his folly.

Opposite the Subscription Rooms in the middle of the High Street is a yard adjacent to one of the principal houses known as Atkins's yard. Between ten and eleven, Mr Nicholl had occasion to retire a short distance down this yard and while there he was seized from behind by two or more ruffians, throttled or garrotted and all his money together with a valuable watch and chain stolen from him. Having secured this immense booty, the robbers left their victim on the ground half dead and insensible. In this condition he was discovered, moaning piteously.

The scene of excitement which took place when the robbery was first discovered beggars all description. Betting men for once forgot 'the odds and the 'osses'; lodgings and hotels were deserted, and Fuller Andrews, that sturdy janitor, alone stuck to his post at the Subscription Rooms. Everybody else was in the streets and your obedient servant, placidly puffing his post-prandial Havana, was suddenly met by a tide of human beings tearing like madmen in all directions after the supposed robbers.

Like all indiscriminate mobs they pitched upon one unfortunate individual who was making the running for the rest and, as he happened to make the pace too good, the pursuer was himself pursued. After almost being torn to pieces, he was found to be a most respectable man and, as the police reports say, was 'dismissed without the slightest stain on his character'...

The case will doubtless act as a salutary caution to betting men against carrying much money about with them for Davies, 'the Leviathan', was similarly treated some years ago in Cromer Street from a supposed belief that he carried immense sums on his person.

The robbery may have acted as a caution to bookmakers, but the problem of 'the fungi of the Turf' remained and when the same gangs turned up at Newmarket's Craven meeting the following spring, Feist felt sure that Nicholl's muggers were among them:

An ominous fact in connection with these particular fellows rests on the circumstances that since last autumn they appear more than usually 'flash' and are clearly in full feather now, and any novice in physiognomy can tell by a glance that on one or two of the gang's countenances, rascaldom and villainy are written by the indelible hand of crime and vice.

Apart, however, from these reliable evidences of their ferocity and disposition, they are well known to have frequented racecourses for long periods as card-sharpers ... Mr Langley, the Jockey Club detective, has greatly improved matters at the ringside, but a stronger force is needed and we should have the assistance of a body of London police who are positively required to keep in check the gangs who hover about our racecourses and in the towns during the summer months...

The question is not merely one of public safety. The credit of the national pastime is also seriously at stake; and as a man is said to be known by his associates, we do not wish to be elbowed by fellows whose fondest hope is, perhaps, the possession of our money or watch by the mild means of strangulation!

But even when police were present at the most fashionable meetings, racegoers were not safe from 'the roughs' as Fred Taylor noted on Goodwood Cup day, 1864, when...

a proportionate share of the rabble were in attendance, like vultures ready to prey upon the gullibility of the well-disposed. Welshers, pickpockets and the very dregs of society were indiscriminately mixed with racing *habitués* and professionals, and the duties of the very well organised police were never more arduous and harassing.

The greatest pains were taken to keep the 'swell mob' out of the enclosure, but the scoundrels jumped the rails like stags, determined to be in and 'doing'. At one period of the afternoon I saw three of these thieves in custody at one time.

On occasions, racegoers dealt with the 'swell mob' in their own way, but matters often got out of hand as happened at Alexandra Park's inaugural meeting in the summer of 1868. Feist, who attended the north London fixture run by his former correspondent, John Verrall, reported that regular bookmakers had refused to pay the £10 (£900) fee demanded for the betting booths and as a result "a dreadful lot of professional levanters and desperadoes" moved in to take their place. When one of their number refused to pay up, the editor witnessed...

the repulsive spectacle of hundreds of people asserting by cowardly violence their supposed right to murder a man because he had welshed an individual of a sovereign or so. Welshers have never had much consideration at our hands, but the system which has sprung up recently on the Turf of permitting the mob to indulge in what Mr Gladstone terms the 'wild justice' of revenge, is most atrocious.

If the Lynch Law is not put down strongly for the future at Alexandra Park it will soon be unfit for the patronage of persons of refinement, as ladies on Wednesday were terrified and shocked at the sight of the half-naked welsher, covered with blood, led into the Grand Stand, with the mob hooting like brutes and savages… [*while*] the 'spiders' who were instrumental in the scratching of The Earl for the Derby and whereby thousands upon thousands of pounds were taken from the public, were strolling about airing themselves, totally unmolested.*

So much for the justice of the mob and its moral sensibility, which tears to pieces the poor outsider who has not 'parted' but leaves the actors of the most gigantic racing swindle of modern times to swagger about with as much ease and impunity as if they were the lords of the soil.

Feist was sailing close to the wind here but, with libel laws less stringent than they are today, both he and Henry Dixon regularly had a go at those they felt were guilty of robbing the public. As often as not, their allegations were based on circumstantial evidence, particularly when a well-fancied, and subsequently beaten, horse had 'taken a walk in the market'. Such cases provided strong grounds for suspecting skulduggery, but were notoriously difficult to prove and it was not unusual for the *Life*, under the threat of legal action, to follow up a damning accusation with a grudging retraction.

This, however, did not happen after the paper had launched a somewhat xenophobic assault on a certain Monsieur Vaillant whose top-class chaser, L'Africain, had been well backed for the 1865 Grand National.

At the time, French horses were very much in the public eye following the victory of Comte Frédéric de Lagrange's Fille de l'Air in the Oaks the previous year. Ironically, the success of the well-backed 6-4 favourite sparked off one of the ugliest riots ever seen on a British racecourse when a mob launched itself against a cordon of mounted police and prizefighters who were escorting the filly back to the winner's enclosure.

As Arthur Edwards, the winning jockey, dismounted, the enraged crowd broke forward in an attempt to snatch his saddle and so prevent him weighing in. For a moment it seemed as if sheer weight of numbers would carry the day, but then the police drew their sabres and, as the mob hesitated, Edwards, surrounded by a curious alliance of stewards and pugilists, was hustled into the comparative safety of the weighing room.

The Epsom riot had nothing to do with the fact that Fille de l'Air was the first French horse to win an English classic.† It occurred because the public, influenced by what they had read in the press,

---

* The 'spiders' were the moneylender Henry Padwick and his bookmaker friend Harry Hill who stood to lose a small fortune if The Earl won the Derby. The 'fly' who had become ensnared in their web was the dissolute and reckless gambler, the 4th Marquess of Hastings who was heavily in debt to Padwick before he scratched The Earl on the eve of the race for which his other entry, Lady Elizabeth, started a hot favourite but ran abysmally to finish tailed off behind the winner, Blue Gown. The Earl, who had beaten Blue Gown earlier in the season, was then sent to France to win the Grand Prix de Paris and, after returning to win three races in two days at Royal Ascot, was made favourite for the St Leger, but he broke down shortly before the race and never ran again. Two months later Hastings, ruined in health and wealth, died at the age of 26.

† In 1865, Fille de l'Air's stable companion, the French-bred Gladiateur, carried off the Triple Crown to earn himself the title 'The Avenger of Waterloo', an epithet bestowed on him by a *Sporting Gazette* sub-editor who headlined the report of the colt's Two Thousand Guineas victory 'Le Revanche de Waterloo'.

believed the filly had been 'stopped' in the Two Thousand Guineas for which she had also started a hot favourite only to trail in last.

Before that race the *Life* had warned readers that "certain parties, notorious for their acuteness in smelling out 'dead 'uns'," were laying heavily against the favourite, and nine months later there was a feeling of *déjà vu* when L'Africain ran in a race at Derby, a week before the Grand National. In a hard-hitting leader Henry Dixon declared:

French sportsmen have recently attained so much in honourable rivalry on the Turf they might at least learn to go 'straight'. Last summer ugly rumours reached this country in which the name of L'Africain was mixed up, and the common topic of conversation in Parisian Turf coteries was the more than suspicious running of M Vaillant's horse at Vincennes when he was first favourite and finished 'nowhere'.

With these mysterious doings we have no business at present, but simply desire to draw attention to the undoubted 'barney' perpetrated with L'Africain at Derby this week. The horse was among the runners for the Midland Steeple Chase and when the betting opened he was backed at as little as 5 to 1. Before the signal was given for the start, L'Africain had been so unmistakably operated against in certain quarters that no one would accept offers of 20 to 1 about the 'Frenchman'.

Of course, men of any racing or steeplechasing experience knew well enough what all this meant. Not to mince matters, and to give the whole thing its proper colouring, we may as well say at once that L'Africain was 'safe' or, in plain terms, was not permitted to try ... M Vaillant is, we believe, a French butcher and has probably become so used to 'carcasses' that there was nothing distasteful to him in sending 'a good dead 'un' into the market. At all events L'Africain had an ancient and fish-like smell and it would be an insult to the understanding of the public to attempt any glossing of the fact.

L'Africain took his part in the steeplechase and, when 200 yards in front of everything, the horse most conveniently went the wrong side of a post and retired from further pursuit ... Sport is noble so long as it is purely conducted, but when contaminated by thimble-rigging dodges it becomes opprobrium. M Vaillant and his advisers must be taught that in the English steeplechase field he can no more avoid detection than at Vincennes or elsewhere.

Following this debacle, L'Africain was backed down to 8-1 for the Grand National, but poetic justice intervened when he cast himself in his box *en route* to Aintree and had to be withdrawn from the race. In the meantime, Dixon's leader had created a sensation in the French press and as the ripples of shocked reaction spread back across the Channel, the *Life* took the opportunity to reassert its stand on the matter:

Our Parisian contemporaries seem completely taken aback by the line which we pursued in reference to the running of L'Africain at Derby, and they cannot understand our temerity in condemning the policy of M Vaillant, the Chantilly butcher, who, they forget, is regarded abroad with suspicion from having been 'warned off' the Imperial courses for similar flagrant practices...*

---

* This ban had been for a limited period only, but in 1866 the notorious *boucher* was finally warned off for life by the Société des Steeplechases after he was found to have run a 'ringer' at the La Marche spring meeting. At the same time, Vaillant's jockey, Reginald Riddell, received a seven-month suspension for assaulting a French Count who accused him of 'pulling' L'Africain in a race at the same Parisian racecourse. Ironically, the unfortunate L'Africain did, indeed, become a 'dead 'un' a few months later when he broke a leg in a fall at Lille.

Le Sport, which is supposed to represent the genuine sporting opinion of Frenchmen, demands that M Vaillant shall be punished, or that we shall be indicted for having circulated a calumnious libel. It so happens that an English journalist seldom commits himself to strong views on any subject without fully comprehending the obligations by which he is bound.

We see no necessity to withdraw a single sentence of what has been written on this odious subject and we even now endorse our views with fresh spirit. The 'stopping' of L'Africain at Derby, we maintain, was utterly disgraceful to all who were concerned in it, and the injuries subsequently received by the horse were regarded as a moral retribution on the entire party.

Touché, as they say!

THE TARRAGONA AFFAIR

A S THE *Sporting Life* developed in strength and depth during the 1860s, the Turf's revered but aging dictator, Admiral Rous, led the Jockey Club into a head-on clash with Fleet Street as he stretched the powers of the ruling body to what the paper condemned as "a degree scandalous and utterly insufferable".

The seeds of the conflict were sown in August 1860 when the *Life* disclosed that an unnamed official had been found to be "deeply implicated in a system of peculation". Safe in the knowledge that it held the moral high ground in what was clearly a delicate matter for the authorities, the paper took full advantage of the situation to settle a few scores with the officious officials its reporters had to deal with on a daily basis:

> The overbearing insolence of the Jockey Club officials; their ludicrous pride; their disgusting affection of contempt for the Press, prompt us to speak plainly and to ask the authorities to keep their functionaries in proper check for, as we look upon it, the default to which we have referred originated chiefly from false ideas and from the official aiming at a position above his natural sphere in society...
>
> These 'officials' are remunerated on the most extravagant scale of salaries until they absolutely believe that they are worth the high price which the Jockey Club, in their superabundance of wealth, lavish upon them, and they are backed up in treating the Press and the public with indifference and a 'bouncing' superciliousness characteristic of vulgarity and ignorance.

Two months later, the identity of the official was revealed following a Jockey Club meeting at Newmarket where it was unanimously resolved that: "Mr Edward Hibburd, late starter at Newmarket and clerk of the course at Ascot, be warned off Newmarket Heath, he having confessed to have embezzled annually large sums of money from the Ascot race-fund ever since he accepted that office, and having likewise received sums of money from the owners of racehorses."

The departure of Hibburd, who admitted to Admiral Rous "that he never made less than £1,000 [£90,000] per annum by presents from the owners of winning horses,"[1] left the Jockey Club looking for a new starter. The position was not easily filled and in the run-up to the six-day Cambridgeshire meeting, the *Life* observed the Club was "allowing several novices to try their 'prentice hands, greatly to the annoyance and risk of backers and owners of horses":

> Every race involves great pecuniary results, and backers of horses who lose their money, either by the real or imaginary incapacity on the part of the starter, are not inclined to let the excuse of 'He was only showing what his qualifications are for the post' form a plaster for their bleeding pockets.
>
> We are to have two new starters at Newmarket next week, Mr Bloss, the resident candidate, being shelved for Mr T Marshall and Mr McGeorge. Mr T Marshall has had some experience and Mr McGeorge may be a most trustworthy coursing judge, but we have yet to learn that he is capable of starting racehorses.

The niggling shadow of doubt conveyed in those final words on McGeorge, who was eventually given the job, was to develop into a dark cloud of recrimination two years later following an abortive start at Newmarket's First October meeting:

Just as the racing season is about to close, an old and ugly grievance has been opened and the patrons of the Turf are once more in antagonism ... upon the claims and qualifications of Mr McGeorge, the starter. Our readers will doubtless remember the controversy between Admiral Rous and Mr Willes upon this subject during the winter months last season, when the dispute assumed the shape of a very pretty quarrel indeed.

The Admiral was staunch and steadfast in sticking to the starter's cause while Mr Willes obstinately advanced opposite opinions and declared that the present starter was anything but the right man in the right place.

The *Life* went on to relate how Irwin Willes, a respected racing correspondent who wrote under the name of 'Argus' in the *Morning Post*, had seen his arguments borne out in that year's Derby when Ensign, who had been heavily backed by his owner, Lord Stamford, and three other horses were left at the start.

Stamford had lodged an official complaint against McGeorge who was severely reprimanded by Rous and warned that any repeat performance would result in his dismissal. It was ironic, therefore, that it was again one of Lord Stamford's horses that should be the chief sufferer in this latest instance when less than half of the 14 runners got off on level terms.

Stamford, who had a bet of £1,000 on his filly Little Lady, immediately drew up a motion calling for the starter's dismissal and, in a letter to the press, he described what had happened.

Little Lady was led back behind the starting post by Mr Dawson, my trainer, and when at least 15 lengths behind the post, Mr McGeorge lowered the flag and let about five or six horses off – the remainder having not the slightest chance. Edwards, my jockey, did not attempt to start. Admiral Rous and many other gentlemen were at the post and all agree that the start was the most disgraceful ever witnessed.

Willes, for his part, could not resist having a dig at Rous as he gave his account of the public dressing down McGeorge had received:

Lord Stamford, naturally mild, told the unhappy starter he was a perfect fool, not fit to start a parcel of donkeys, much less racehorses, and his excuse of not seeing the mare only made his conduct worse. Admiral Rous, with a spirit of honourable candour ... which forbids me for an instant in indulging in any feeling of satisfaction at seeing him a convert to my views upon the appointment of Mr McGeorge, stated he could scarcely believe his eyes when he saw such a start, which he believed to be the worst on record, and that he had got into all sorts of quarrels by standing up for him as he had done for no man before, but that it could not last any longer.

The *Life*, in summing up the situation, was remarkably impartial as it observed:

When the Jockey Club and owners of horses find a perfect starter – one who will always get horses off without a mistake – let them put the functionary in a glass case and prepare for the Millennium! Taken altogether, the scene upon Newmarket Heath as described by 'Argus' was most unseemly, and we trust the starter will not again be made to suffer from such ebullitions as those recorded. If Mr McGeorge be incompetent, let him be replaced and speedily; but to humiliate and bully the

Irwin Willes, 'Argus' of the *Morning Post*.

Admiral Rous, the dictator of the Turf.

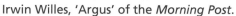

unfortunate official upon every occasion, neither pleases the public nor corrects the alleged grievance by which some owners of horses imagine they are victimised.

The Little Lady incident was but a prelude to the drama that was to follow when Rous and Willes, together with two officers of the Grenadier Guards, Lt-Col Burnaby and Capt Annesley, became embroiled in a *cause célèbre* known as the 'Tarragona Affair'.

The first sign of the brewing storm came in a report from Tattersalls that appeared in the *Life* on 8 October 1862 when it was noted: "free and outspoken comments were made on certain incidents of the First October meeting which may, or ought to, occupy the attention of the authorities. The Tarragona and Michel Grove match was put forward as one of the chief grievances."

The race in question took place over the last half of the Abingdon Mile on the final day of the meeting. Many thought it a mismatch. Michel Grove was the better horse and so he proved, winning easily by two lengths at 1-3.

Immediately after the race a series of startling accusations spread around the course. It was claimed that Burnaby, who owned Tarragona, had struck a fictitious bet with his brother officer, Annesley, for the sole purpose of misleading the bookmakers and easing the odds on Michel Grove. It was further whispered that Burnaby had instructed his jockey, John Nightingall, to 'pull' Tarragona in order to let Michel Grove win.

Hearing that these rumours had been openly discussed, if not actually fostered by Admiral Rous and another Jockey Club member, the Duke of Beaufort, Burnaby wrote to the stewards requesting a full inquiry into the matter. On the same day, Weatherbys issued a notice that was posted up in Tattersalls' subscription room; it announced that the stewards were to "call upon Lt-Col Burnaby to explain several incidents connected with the running of the match between Tarragona and Michel Grove, and the stewards recommend the Committee not to allow the settlement of the bets to take place until after the investigation."

This advice to the Tattersalls Committee, coming from a body that, since 1842, had declared that it took no cognisance of betting, was described by the *Life* to be "altogether unprecedented," while the 'investigation' was made to look decidedly questionable when it transpired that the inquiry was to be headed by Admiral Rous, a man who had not only, "expressed himself strongly on the case before hearing its merits," but who had admitted to no less a person than Annesley that he "utterly abhorred" Burnaby.

Also on the panel were Rous's brother, Lord Stradbroke, Caledon Alexander, the Earl of Coventry, Lord Glasgow and the Duke of Beaufort who had backed Tarragona. It was hardly an impartial jury and when Burnaby appeared before it he expressed the hope that "any member of the committee who might have given an opinion on the case would not be allowed to adjudicate". The request was ignored, and when Burnaby followed it up by objecting to Admiral Rous acting as chairman because: a) he was the author of the notice posted in Tattersalls; b) he had pre-judged the case, and c) he was personally hostile to himself (Burnaby), he was swiftly overruled.

Evidence was first taken from a leading bookmaker, Harry Steel, who maintained he had heard Burnaby bet Annesley an even £100 that Tarragona would beat Michel Grove. Steel had immediately offered £50 to £40, £60 to £40 and then £70 to £40 against Tarragona and when Burnaby ignored him he assumed that what he had heard was a 'flash bet' and that Tarragona was to be 'stopped'. Angry and disgusted at what he considered was "a damned ramp", Steel made no secret of his assumptions which quickly gained credence as they spread though the ring.

When Burnaby produced his betting book for inspection it was seen why he did not avail himself of Steel's odds. His bet with Annesley had not been an even £100, but one of £100 to win £200. Confronted with this evidence, which was also borne out in Annesley's book, Steel was visibly shaken and admitted he was not prepared to swear that what he had heard had been an even-money bet.[*]

With this admission the case against the two officers collapsed. Steel had made a mistake and, as a result, false accusations had been made. At this point the inquiry should have been wound up and due apologies made to Burnaby. But it was not; instead it rapidly took on the form of an inquisition as the Duke of Beaufort curtly interrupted Burnaby's cross-examination of Steel to say he had also heard the alleged bet. Being a member of the committee and not a witness, Beaufort was not only out of order, but could not be questioned as to how he might have been mistaken.

Admiral Rous, like Beaufort, was already convinced that mischief had been done and refused to accept either the written or oral word of the officers. Instead he examined their betting books with a magnifying glass "almost as big as a well-sized warming pan". Unable to detect anything suspicious, he then telegraphed the Bank of England to request the services of their handwriting expert who duly arrived the following day and promptly exonerated both men from having made any alteration to the recorded bet.

In the meantime, the charge that Tarragona had been pulled had also been dealt with. The

---

[*] Despite his defective hearing Harry Steel did alright out of the game; he became the Prince of Wales' bookmaker and when he died in 1915 he left £652,418 (£58m).

high-handed arrogance with which the committee conducted their inquiry is well illustrated by Beaufort's less than subtle approach to the issue. "Are you in the habit of running your horses straight?" he snapped at an astonished Burnaby.

The sole witness for the prosecution was the starter, Tom McGeorge – a man who owed his position to Admiral Rous, and who was now facing dismissal on the grounds of incompetence.* On top of all this, Burnaby had recently taken McGeorge before the stewards at Hungerford after the chances of one of his horses had been ruined at the start and as a result, the stewards ordered the race to be re-run when it was won by his horse. This incident, he tactfully pointed out, hardly rendered McGeorge well disposed towards him, but a prejudiced witness was of no matter to an already prejudiced jury and his objection was once again overruled.

In his evidence McGeorge claimed that Nightingall had pulled Tarragona about six lengths behind Michel Grove after they had gone about 150 yards. He said: "I thought Nightingall pulled for a waiting race and farther than was prudent." Then, being too zealous for his own good, he added he remembered the circumstances well because, "I took particular notice of the race."

When Burnaby asked him why he had taken such 'particular notice', McGeorge could only stammer: "I did not take more notice of this race than any other race, but my orders are to take particular notice of all races."

After this little gem, the unhappy starter was further discredited by the evidence of the recall flagman and the jockeys who rode in the race. The flagman, who was positioned about 150 yards down the course, said the horses were level when they passed him, but shortly afterwards Tarragona appeared to drop two or three lengths behind.

George Fordham, the reigning champion jockey who rode Michel Grove, confirmed his mount had gradually drawn clear of the filly after passing the flagman. He had heard Nightingall using his whip as they entered 'the Dip' and considered that, if anything, Tarragona had been punished more than necessary.

Nightingall stated he had been a jockey for 17 years and had never before been in front of the stewards. He said that Burnaby had put him on £25 (£2,250) to nothing if he won, but added he had told the owner he thought it was a bad (unequal) match.

The second charge was, therefore, dismissed as conclusively as the first. After four hearings spread over three days, the evidence against Burnaby amounted to nothing. Little wonder, then, that on October 18 the *Life* accused Rous and his committee of "arrogating to themselves a power to treat gentlemen as pickpockets by practically declining to hear them or believe them upon their oaths or solemn words of honour ... The power the Jockey Club possessed, they have stretched to a degree scandalous and utterly insufferable."

By this time the affair had captured the imagination of the public and was being debated in the highest society. In its next number, the *Life* attempted to put the actions of the authorities into some sort of perspective as it referred to the warning Lord Derby had delivered to the Jockey Club before he began his second term as Prime Minister in 1858:

In a letter of vigorous truth he told them of their shortcomings and reminded them of their deficiencies as the conservators of the British Turf. Still, from that period we have had no

---

* In 1863 McGeorge was replaced by his son, Tom jnr. Initially, matters hardly improved – there was a record 34 false starts for that year's Derby! But after this embarrassing hiccup, young McGeorge went on to prove himself up to the job.

improvement; there have been countless cases of suspected 'ropings' and shameful 'milkings' and, even as a late instance, there were the scandalous Old Calabar proceedings when the Jockey Club shut their eyes to the facts and never condescended to institute the slightest inquiry.*

Suddenly, and without a warning note, they have risen up like so many phoenixes from the ashes of their lethargy, burning for a victim to consume in their angry appetite and zeal for reform. Unfortunately, Colonel Burnaby and Captain Annesley happen to be in the way, and the Jockey Club, having got into their full stride, spasmodically revive their ancient tyranny. They would be Doges still.

If we could convince ourselves that this awakening were cordial and disinterested, we should have nothing to say upon the subject … [*but*] the impression upon our minds and the minds of the public, is that some of the members were irritated by having lost money upon the match and Admiral Rous, the chairman, it was shown, had spoken some time since with a personal antipathy to Colonel Burnaby…

People are asking the question 'How will it all end?' … There has been some talk of 'calling out', but neither Captain Annesley nor Colonel Burnaby would, we feel assured, be rash enough to revive what was formerly considered the final etiquette of outraged honour, but was really the fashionable ruffianism of an age less refined than our own.

Uncannily, these lines appeared on the very day the lamented H L Dillon fought his fatal duel with the Duc de Gramont-Caderousse, but if there were grounds to revive 'the final etiquette of outraged honour' – outlawed in England since 1819 – then the two Guards officers surely had them.

Before Rous's committee reconvened to return its verdict, Charles Weatherby sent Burnaby a transcription of the evidence taken at the inquiry. An attached note requested, "Should there be anything which appears to you inaccurate, if you will be so good as to mention it to me I will bring it under the notice of the members of the court."

Burnaby replied: "I cannot pretend, in the compass of a letter, to point out all the inaccuracies and omissions which I have noticed in the report, but I beg to call your attention to some of the most serious of them." He then listed some startling oversights which, when published in the *Life*, took up three-quarters of a column; the most serious of them being the report's failure to record his protest against any member of the committee who might have pre-judged the case.

Rous had certainly done so, and had also attempted to sway the committee by making great issue of a £5 bet Burnaby had made over the spelling of a word at a private house party earlier that year; the implication being that the Colonel was a trickster who was not averse to making a fast buck.

Whether Rous had a last-minute pang of conscience or whether he was too ashamed to pull the trigger after aiming the gun, he suddenly recognised the validity of Burnaby's protests. When the committee reassembled he informed its members that "owing to particular circumstances" he thought it better he should not take any further part in the proceedings, and promptly retired from the chairmanship.

This was the most damning indictment of all for, after he had "brought irrelevant evidence to bear upon the plastic minds of that already remarkably prejudiced jury" (*Life,* Oct 28), and after "all the evidence had been taken, and when all he could say against us could be said" (Burnaby, Nov 5), Rous slipped out of signing the verdict.

In summing up what it now called an inquiry into "the extraordinary expression of public feeling

---

* Old Calabar was one of the leading fancies for the 1862 Two Thousand Guineas, but a week or so before the race he was either nobbled or broke down. The *Life* claimed (without contradiction) that the brother-in-law of the trainer, Stephenson, had 'milked' £6,000 (£540,000) from the unsuspecting public by using the services of certain bookmakers to lay the horse before it was finally scratched on the eve of the race.

just before and during the match between Tarragona and Michel Grove," the committee found it was "not proved that Colonel Burnaby intended that Tarragona should be pulled ... or that he had made a fictitious bet with Captain Annesley."

The 'not proven' verdict was greeted with howls of derision from the press and public alike. The committee was variously accused of "undisguised innuendo," of "implying a stigma it dares not affix" and of having "considered insult as its highest prerogative". The *Life* denounced the verdict as "ungentlemanly, mean and shuffling" in that:

> A self-constituted body, exercising the high functions of judges of the land, sitting in Star Chamber privacy and dispensing justice with a Draconian hand ... shamble out of their own difficulty and, rather than do mere justice to Colonel Burnaby and Captain Annesley, they borrow a barbarous pedantry of Scottish law and announce that the case is 'not proven', leaving the moral stigma as black as ever.
>
> The decision amounts to this – 'We believe you guilty, but cannot legally prove you so' ... Colonel Burnaby and Captain Annesley must have apologies, full and ample, not verbal but written, that they may let their friends and the world know their honour is not healed by such an evasion of justice as that printed in the last *Calendar*.*

In its next number the *Life* was able to announce:

> Admiral Rous has written an ample and complete apology to Colonel Burnaby and, considering the inflexibility of his nature, that must be regarded as a moral phenomenon ... It is, perhaps, very painful for men of high notions to be compelled to confess that they have been guilty of an ungentlemanly course of conduct, but it seems as though the Jockey Club will not surrender until their foundations are sapped and their rottenness fully exposed.

This was not to happen for some time; in fact, the autocratic clubmen still had one underhand card left to play. In the same issue of the *Racing Calendar* which carried the infamous 'not proven' verdict, it was recorded that Lord Winchilsea had called the attention of Club members to an article written by 'Argus' in the *Morning Post* in which, he claimed, that Willes had "prejudged the Tarragona case in an offensive manner".

The 10th Earl of Winchilsea and Nottingham was George James Finch-Hatton who dabbled in journalism as a 'versifying tipster' (he gave his racing selections in rhymes) writing occasionally for the *Morning Herald* and the *Sporting Gazette* under the *nom de plume* of 'John Davis'. The fact that he now took it upon himself to attack a professional journalist from his privileged position within the Jockey Club reeked of the vindictiveness that had surrounded the whole Tarragona affair.

Winchilsea had proposed that: "Mr Willes be required to make an apology for certain offensive expressions used by him affecting the character of the Jockey Club." Admiral Rous, who had an old score to settle with his long-time critic, was quick to second the motion which was carried by 13 votes to 7. Surprisingly, one of the dissenters was Lord Stradbroke who opposed his brother by proposing that: "It is not expedient to take notice of anonymous writers in public prints."

---

* In December, a military court of inquiry set up by HRH the Duke of Cambridge, the Commander-in-Chief of the Army, exonerated both Burnaby and Annesley of any wrongdoing.

There were a few who felt it was a moot point whether this motion applied to Willes or Winchilsea, but, despite being seconded by Charles Greville, one of the Club's most senior and respected members, it was defeated by 12 votes to 10.

Inevitably, the press leapt to the defence of Willes. The *Life* could not conceal its contempt for Finch-Hatton as it declared:

Lord Winchilsea's attempted interference with the liberty of the Press has created feelings of indignation and it was well observed that things are coming to something when a dilettante peer, whose limping doggerel floods the sporting papers, takes upon himself the mission of censor of the public Press...

Lord Winchilsea knows perfectly well that pride and petulance alone instigated the measures against Willes and not a sense of insulted dignity and honour as he affects. Nor is it altogether improbable that the noble Lord was actuated by some little feeling of jealousy against so successful a writer as 'Argus' who shines in a branch of literature to which his lordship has long aspired, but without being able to struggle out of the mud of hopeless mediocrity...

Mr Willes, when he finds he is 'required' or commanded to make an apology for having exercised the privilege of free discussion and the liberty of the Press, will have little regard for the independence and dignity of the profession if he does anything of the kind. Why should he apologise, and what for?...

When the Jockey Club have performed simple justice to the two gentlemen they have persecuted; when they have recalled their shuffling verdict; when they have disavowed for the future the employment of criminal examinations and 'experts', they will be entitled to some courtesy and consideration. At present, we feel no one should extend to them the amenities they deny to gentlemen whom they have outraged and persecuted.

Willes, being the son of a major-general in the Royal Marines, was not one to be cowed by those he considered his social equals. He wrote to the Jockey Club to explain that he had written his article out of a sense of duty to the public and he would be obliged if they would specify their exact charge against him.

When the Club reconvened on November 1, only a few passages of Willes's letter were read out – those deemed most damaging to him – and Winchilsea wasted no time in proposing that the journalist should "be warned off the lands and property of the Jockey Club at Newmarket".

The folly of such an act was appreciated by only a handful of members who did their best to steer Winchilsea's clique onto a more moderate course. General Peel, a younger brother of the reforming Prime Minister, Sir Robert Peel, proposed: "That a special meeting of the Club be called for the purpose of taking Mr Willes's letter into consideration and deciding what is the best course to be adopted." Greville seconded the amendment, but it was defeated by 11 votes to 6 and the warning off motion (seconded by Lord Glasgow – ex-Tarragona committee) was carried by the same count.

As relations between the press and the Jockey Club plummeted to an all-time low, Winchilsea defended his action in a letter to *The Times* in which he claimed that Willes had brought a "scandalous charge" against the Club, to wit "they were determined to convict in the face of evidence". But this was exactly what the *Life* had stated in its leader of October 18, written *two days before* Willes's article, since when the charge had been echoed by the entire press corps. Was the whole of Fleet Street to be warned off?

Describing the warning off as "outrageous to the last degree" and "the blackest part of the whole business," the *Life* predicted:

> Lord Winchilsea will become notorious for ever as the instigator of this un-English proceeding ... When Mr Russell, the *Times*' correspondent, exposed the shortcomings of the Crimean bunglers, there were doubtless plenty of men who would have been happy to 'warn him off' that dismal peninsula, but would the English people have tolerated any slight or interference with the newspaper writer who was working and watching in the common interest of the public?
>
> Is the Turf, above all things, to be the only British institution veiled by the barbaric and despotic exercise of a Censorship? ... Lord Winchilsea should blush at the line he has pursued and we almost begin to doubt the presumed liberty of the land when the aristocracy imagine that they are privileged to put a shackle upon the voice of popular opinion.

Similar views were echoed by Charles Greville in a letter to *The Times*. As secretary to the Privy Council and a cousin of the former Turf dictator Lord George Bentinck, Greville was highly regarded as an arbitrator in personal disputes and his voice carried considerable weight with the racing community even though certain members of his own club chose to ignore it. He wrote:

> I am a very old member of the Jockey Club and a long experience has shown me that nothing is more unwise than to wage war against the Press and to endeavour to fetter the freedom of discussion upon the Turf ... Several members of experience joined with me in depreciating the course taken by the majority of the Jockey Club, but we were outvoted and the folly was committed. I am desirous that it should be known that I took no part in the condemnation of Mr Willes, but, on the contrary, that I strenuously protested against it.

With such support, Willes was not prepared to accept his banishment tamely. The following April he wrote to Admiral Rous to inform him that he intended to attend Newmarket's Craven Meeting in order to raise a case for open court. At the races 'Argus' was duly served with a notice of trespass and the case came before the Cambridgeshire Lent Assizes in March 1864.

The question the jury had to decide was whether the Jockey Club owned Newmarket Heath and, if so, whether its stewards had the right to exclude Willes from their property. Willes's counsel had no argument against the common law that was produced in evidence of the Club's right of ownership and could only plead that the jury should "save the stewards from themselves" as he asked them...

> Are these men of high position, who are honesty and integrity itself, justified in avenging what they think is a slight in a public paper by keeping a man off the land where he earns his bread? If the stewards of the Jockey Club think the defendant has degraded them, then the tribunals of the law are open to them to gain redress. But no, they look at their little piece of ground and do their little worst, endeavouring to stigmatise the defendant by classing him with defaulters and swindlers.

Unfortunately for Willes this eloquent argument was irrelevant to the question before the court and the jury found for the plaintiff although they showed where their sympathies lay when they awarded the stewards just one shilling (£4.50) damages.

Not satisfied with their hollow victory, the clubmen were to enforce their ban on Willes for a further five years; no wonder the *Life* observed:

If ever a future historian should write the decline and fall of the English Turf, one of the reasons assigned for its decay will be because it was behind the rest of the age in liberal progress and was badly governed by its chief representatives.

As for Winchilsea, he was to engineer his own 'decline and fall' with a spectacular display of arrogance. In the summer of 1865, while waiting for a train at Vauxhall Bridge in London, the 50-year-old peer met his nemesis in the unlikely form of a stationmaster named Atter who, in accordance with the regulations of the South-Western Railway Company, requested him to refrain from smoking.

Predictably, the pontificating peer refused to comply and consequently laid himself open to a court summons and the derision of his many enemies in Fleet Street. In a high-spirited leader infused with Henry Dixon's mischievous wit, the *Life* remarked:

Lord Winchilsea, who has long been so strangely ambitious of a certain kind of fame which amounts to notoriety, must, at length, be satisfied to find that he has created a mild sensation.* He has smoked to find himself famous...

The pleasant morning pipe, the equally agreeable afternoon Havana, are luxuries to which we editorially incline in common with nine-tenths of our countrymen. At the same time, we are perfectly aware of two things – that tobacco smoke is odious to some people and, moreover, that the offence is penal if persisted in after one is requested to desist on the property or premises of some of our railway companies.

Good manners, good sense and decency would induce us to extinguish the impeached pipe or cigar upon being requested to do so ... Lord Winchilsea, however, refuses to be judged by the ordinary standard under which plain mortals are estimated. His lordship stands upon the platform at Vauxhall Station, in his own estimation a 'privileged' smoker of the realm. It is, moreover, not surprising that the stationmaster, Mr Atter, should not have been aware of the 'privileges' and dignity of the smoker especially as Lord Winchilsea is described as 'an elderly man, attired in a shooting-jacket and a billycock hat'...

Mr Atter requested Lord Winchilsea to desist as coolly as if his lordship had worn his coronet instead of the plebeian billycock, showing, at all events, how conscientiously the official was discharging his duty. The blue blood of the peer was aroused; he declined to surrender the 'fragrant weed', his name and address were demanded and his lordship was compelled to undergo the indignity of being summoned to a police court...

* Winchilsea was only following the example of his father, George William Finch-Hatton, who gained notoriety by 'fighting' a duel with the Duke of Wellington in 1829. The 9th Earl had clashed with the then Prime Minister over the Catholic Relief Bill and, in a letter published in *The Standard*, accused him of seeking to "carry on his insidious designs for the infringement of our liberties and the introduction of popery into every department of the State".[2] The Duke "felt himself compelled to notice formally the petulant outrage committed upon him"[3] and demanded an apology. When none was forthcoming, he called upon Winchilsea to give him, "that satisfaction for your conduct which a gentleman has a right to require, and which a gentleman never refuses to give."[4] The two men met in a field at Battersea, but on the command 'take aim' Winchilsea kept his pistol by his side and so Wellington fired wide. Winchilsea then discharged his pistol into the air and, having stood the Duke's fire (however misdirected), felt that honour permitted him to apologise, which he duly did with an ample retraction in *The Standard*.

The immediate effect was to arouse the *cacoethes scribendi* in the proud nature of his lordship. He wrote immediately to a morning contemporary [*The Times*], showing his profundity by an assertion that if other people chose to render themselves obnoxious he should do likewise to his heart's content and become the licensed libertine of railway platforms because locomotives emitted 'grits, dust and black smoke' … but the work by which his lordship will be doubtless known to posterity is an epistle directed to the chairman of the South-Western Railway Company.

With a view to the further preservation of that extraordinary document, we reproduce it in our columns *verbatim et literatim*.

While the phrasing of the letter was muddled, the character of its writer was plain enough. Addressed and dated '32 Albemarle Street, June 28, 1865', it read:

Sir, I demand the instant dismissal of the station-master, named Atter, at your Vauxhall Station, who has had the effrontery to apply for a summons involving a breach of privilege against me at the Wandsworth bench, for what he has the impudence to term smoking contrary to your bye-laws. I beg you to observe this piece of impudence involves a breach of the privilege of the House of Lords, and that you – the chairman of the company – shall be held responsible for it. [*signed*] Winchilsea and Nottingham.

Such arrogance was food and drink to Dixon, who delighted in deflating the pompous with his incisive pen. Inspired, he continued:

To say this letter exhibits bad taste would amount very nearly to an eulogy upon it, and yet to be angry with anything so vain, weak but imperious, is impossible. It is, in reality, the condensed essence of his lordship's autobiography. Precisely in this arrogant, dictatorial tone was the instant dismissal of 'Argus' demanded from Newmarket Heath and, to the shame of the Jockey Club be it said, they listened to the demands of this self-willed, self-opinionated Earl…

Lord Winchilsea who, as a born legislator, was unaware that he was entitled to no such 'privilege' as he claimed, has found a London magistrate and a railway company less ductile than the Newmarket authorities … something of retributive justice has arrived at last and, reminding the hero of 'the billycock' of his avenger, we may be pardoned for inquiring of his lordship, in the Cockney dialect, 'Who's your 'Atter?'

After such a mauling, there was no need to rub further salt into the ignoble noble's self-inflicted wounds when he was duly convicted for the offence. The case was dealt with as a straightforward news story when it was reported that he had been fined 10s (£45) with 2s costs. It was, however, noted that "the tone of his lordship, both personally and through his counsel, Mr Metcalf, was of a most submissive description compared with the tenor of the original letter on 'privileges' which created so much surprise and amusement a few days back."

If Irwin Willes did not derive sufficient satisfaction from seeing his persecutor held up to such ridicule, then he must surely have felt he had his full pound of flesh two years later when, by a delicious irony, Winchilsea was forced to resign from the Jockey Club and withdraw from the Turf after his name had appeared – not for the first time – on the forfeit list as a defaulter. And with the death of the irascible Lord Glasgow in March 1869, the last barrier to lifting the ban on the journalist was removed.

When the Jockey Club convened for its annual meeting at Newmarket the following month, it was unanimously resolved "that the notice to Mr Willes not to come on Newmarket Heath, be now withdrawn." But by then 'Argus the exile' was also on his way out having suffered a stroke in 1868, and he died three years later at the age of 52.

A final footnote to what had started out as 'The Tarragona Affair' nine years earlier, was added in January 1871, when the *Life* published details on three recently bankrupt noblemen who had squandered their fortune on the Turf.

Lord de Mauley had claims against him of £24,402 (£2.2m); the Duke of Newcastle owed £145,000 (£13m) and lastly, but by far from least, came the 10th Earl of Winchilsea and Nottingham – family motto, *Nil conscire sibi* (To have a conscience free from guilt) – whose debts were not disclosed, but it was reported that "his lordship was not in the possession of any property whatever".

CAMPAIGNS AND CONSUMPTION

THE Tarragona Affair had shown Admiral Rous in the worst possible light, yet despite his impulsive, autocratic nature, he was widely regarded as a man of integrity and is justly recognised as the greatest of all Turf administrators. It is, perhaps, no coincidence that some of his most fruitful years in office came when Feist and Dixon were the standard bearers of a campaigning racing press.

History has never accorded credit to the literary lions of the *Life* for the reforms they helped bring about, yet the columns of the paper bear testimony to the fact that many of the improvements they called for were subsequently acted upon by the Jockey Club under the leadership of Rous who became its virtual president through a process of re-election as a steward from 1859 until his death at the age of 82 in 1877.

The second son of Sir John Rous, the 1st Earl of Stradbroke, Henry John Rous was elected to the Jockey Club in 1821 and, following a distinguished career at sea, was first appointed a steward in 1838. His initial three-year term of office was served in the shadow of another famous but tarnished Turf reformer, Lord George Bentinck who "did not scruple to do things quite as bad as the worst of the misdeeds which he so vigorously and relentlessly attacked".[1]

When Bentinck retired from the Turf in 1846 to concentrate on politics, it was Rous who assumed his mantle. In 1850, he established himself as the recognised authority on the sport with the publication of his book, *The Laws and Practice of Horse Racing*. At the same time he compiled and published the first comprehensive weight-for-age scale to be used in racing; a scale which, after 160 years and only a few minor alterations, still serves as the basis for every mixed-aged race run in the world today.

In 1855, Rous was appointed public handicapper at Newmarket and two years later, together with General Peel and Charles Greville, he was given the task of rewriting the Rules of Racing. It was while carrying out this extensive revision that the Admiral drew up a betting code from the discarded fragments of the old rules and this, when published in the *Racing Calendar,* provided a benchmark for settling all betting disputes.

He was, consequently, well qualified to arbitrate on all matters relating to the Turf but, as with all dictators, he had a low tolerance to criticism from any quarter and from the press in particular. Inevitably, the relationship between Rous and the *Life* was a stormy one, and more than one angry letter from him winged its way to Edward Dorling's father in Epsom demanding redress for a slight, real or imagined, that had appeared in the paper.

On one occasion he complained bitterly of "a most blackguard article in the *Sporting Life*" and demanded the name of the author so "I may take the necessary steps of bringing him to his senses".[2] At other times Rous and the *Life* found themselves on the same side as they fought to bring in changes that were opposed by other Jockey Club members.

One such instance concerned the naming of horses or, in the case of the obdurate Lord Glasgow, the failure to name them on the spurious basis that good names should not be wasted on bad horses. At the time there were no rules on nomenclature; some horses ran unnamed, being identified only by their pedigree, while others shared the same name and quite a few had their names changed several times during the course of their careers.

The 1859 *Racing Calendar* lists four horses of different ages called Lottery (a name made famous by the winner of the 1839 Grand National); three four-year-olds with the name of Sunbeam, and no fewer than 44 instances of two horses sharing the same name, 15 of which are of the same age. In the unnamed division, there are six horses sired by Orlando including a yearling filly that had won a two-furlong sprint at Shrewsbury in November; the last race for that age group to be run in Britain. At the other extreme, one horse had run under three different names during the course of the season.

This confusing state of affairs was addressed by Harry Feist in response to a reader's letter in November 1859. The correspondent suggested that a rule be introduced to ensure: "that all horses shall be named prior to their running in any engagement and, after being once named, to retain that name during the whole of their racing career and that there shall be no two horses of the same name." Feist was in full agreement:

> This suggestion is so simple and forcibly put and the remedy so easy, that we shall consider it an act of wilful reticence on the part of the authorities if they do not adopt a measure which would gratify the public and leave no loophole for deception. We believe that Admiral Rous did at one time suggest such a course, but Lord Glasgow's eccentricity in declining on any account to give names to his horses, caused the Admiral to falter in his purpose…
>
> At present, owners are perfectly indifferent to what names their horses receive inasmuch as they know that at any moment the cognomen can be changed as their latest fancy may direct. One individual, with more knowledge of Oriental lore than brains, this season named an animal Caifacaratadaddera, but a fresh owner, with a no less provokingly profound knowledge of Welsh, renamed the same horse Ynysymaengwyn and, on another change of ownership, these distracting polysyllables were sensibly exchanged for the intelligible disyllable of Bo-Peep.
>
> This is an instance of the present loose and absurd state of Turf nomenclature, calculated to perplex and frustrate the efforts of the compilers of future stud books and bring the practice of racing into ridicule, even if unattended by more serious consequences.

Less than six months after this article appeared, the Jockey Club took a tentative step towards clearing up a small part of the confusion by ruling that when a horse's name was changed its previous name or names would also have to be given when entering it for races.

The duplication of names, however, was allowed to continue even when, in 1866, the Jockey Club members, Lord Portsmouth and Baron Rothschild, matched their three-year-old colts, both called Robin Hood, against each other for £200 a side with the stipulation that the loser would relinquish the 'Hood' of his horse's name.

It was not until 1876 that a rule was brought in that required horses of the same name to be distinguished by the addition of Roman numerals; II, III, etc, at the time of registration, but the practice of running horses unnamed continued unchecked until 1913 when horses older than two years had to be named before they ran, and it was not until 1946 that all horses were required to be named.

Another early campaign was against the practice of owners running their horses under assumed names. These *noms de course* were registered with Weatherbys for a fee and, as the *Life* reminded readers, were initially introduced to protect the identity of "noblemen's sons, bishops' nephews, or heirs prospective to rich but pious old ladies". But, with no limit on the number of aliases an owner could adopt, the system was open to abuse and it was easy to blind the public and the bookmakers as happened in a steeplechase run at Streatham, south London, during the 1860s when…

no fewer than five of the [*six*] horses belonged to the same owner, although running in different names. Four had crack cross-country jockeys on their backs and the fifth, a comparatively unknown one named Levitt … This horse was the outsider in the betting, of course, but won easily.[3]

Such devious ploys did nothing to improve the image of racing and Feist, oblivious to the fact that he and his fellow journalists wrote under pen names or the anonymous cloak of 'Our Special Correspondent' etc, continually pressed for the abolition of the practice. In 1871, writing under his Augur alias, he stated bluntly:

The assumed name system is now adopted by the lower class of owners for none other than nefarious objects. Men of the most scandalous and even infamous antecedents, some of them existing by means too abominable to mention … are able to cheat and cozen the public by the sanction of the Jockey Club rules!

What is there that acts as a check to swindling and chicanery and as a caution to the community so much as public exposure? The rogue, therefore, who owns a horse and has it pulled, on detection does not care one iota because he is concealed under the fictitious and fantastic name perhaps of 'Mr Montague Capulet'.

The honest and candid owner who is racing in his own name has, too, a right to know against whom he is contending, or he is placed at a decidedly unfair disadvantage … The time has come for speaking out plainly against that which enables desperadoes to turn the Turf into an arena for plunder and indirect brigandage … and I trust the day is not distant when all upright and honest owners will see the desirability of abandoning their *noms de course*, or when there will be some legal prohibition of fictitious titles.

The Jockey Club, however, refused to be bullied into reform and allowed the practice to continue for a further 49 years before it was finally outlawed in 1920.

If the Club dragged its feet over this issue, it was more responsive to a leader on the derisory second-place prize money on offer in the classics. The subject received an airing in the summer of 1867 when Henry Dixon drew a parallel between selling races – in which the runner-up received a share of any surplus in the auction price of the winner – and the top races. With regard to sellers he remarked:

The interests of the owner of the second horse have been wonderfully cared for in these most paltry of races and yet, in the five great 'ribands' of the year – the Derby, St Leger, Oaks, 2,000 and 1,000 – the miserable old scale is rigidly preserved. In the two last, the owner of the second merely saves his stake; and in the three others he is only two or three 'ponies' to the good…

Year by year the amount of such stakes increases till the 'Two Thousand' has become 'five thousand' and yet the owner of the winner is still allowed to sweep almost everything into his lap. In 1866, for instance, the aggregate amount of these five races was £25,925 after deducting stakes, while all that fell to the lot of the unfortunate seconds was £175. There was, in fact, only a head, both in the Derby and St Leger, between Lord Lyon and Savernake, and yet Mr Sutton received £13,175 [£1,185,750] clear, and Lord Ailesbury £125 [£11,250].

A double injustice is also committed as not only does the owner of the second horse receive nothing, so to speak, in these races, but he incurs penalties or has to forego allowances in leading stakes all over the country by reason of his worse than barren honour. In fact, unless he has some place bets, it is a positive disadvantage to him to have his horse ridden out for fear of what it may entail.

All large stakes should be framed more liberally on this point and in the five we have named, at least a thousand should be allotted to the second horse and the third should save its stake. Such a change would, we feel assured, give general satisfaction as it would not only increase the entries and improve the place struggles, but it would effectively do away with the gross anomaly of penalising a horse for absolutely winning nothing.

Of course, the Jockey Club was always more amenable to implementing reforms that would benefit its members and within five months Dixon was able to announce:

> After 1868 the owner of the second in both the Derby and the Oaks will receive £300 and the owner of the third £150; and the terms of the Two Thousand Guineas entry for 1869 is to the effect that the owner of the second horse shall receive £200 and the owner of the third save his stake ... We are curious to know why the One Thousand conditions were not treated after the same fashion, but we trust that the Doncaster Corporation will take care that their great race is put on a level with the Derby in this respect.

The Doncaster Corporation, well used to being prodded into action by its erstwhile local reporter, grudgingly took the hint and, in 1870, doubled the prize money for the runner-up in the St Leger to £200 and introduced a third prize of £100 which, while being no great sum in a race that was worth around £5,000, was at least a step in the right direction. In the same year, the Newmarket executive brought the One Thousand Guineas into line with its counterpart.

But these successful campaigns only tinkered with the mechanics of the sport. Of much greater importance were the issues that affected the lives of those who earned a perilous, but often financially rewarding living from riding for the immensely rich noblemen and industrialists who dominated Victorian racing.

The life expectancy of a jockey was not good. Safety standards were non-existent; medical facilities lamentable and the rough riding that was the order of the day ensured serious accidents and fatalities occurred with depressing regularity. The constant catalogue of casualties prompted the *Life* to seize an opportune moment towards the end of 1865 to call for the setting up of an 'Accidents To Jockeys Fund'. The scheme, proposed 99 years before the Injured Jockeys Fund came into being, was put forward in the aftermath of a national disaster which had occurred the previous year when the reservoir that supplied Sheffield with its water burst "and carried ruin into so many families, leaving thousands destitute".*

A fund was set up for the victims and the response was so great that, in November 1865, it was closed and the extraordinary decision was taken to return half the money to the subscribers. As a result, two leading bookmakers who had collected over £1,000 from their colleagues and clients placed the following notice in the *Life*:

---

* Just before midnight on 11 March 1864, the Dale Dyke Dam of the Bradfield reservoir above Sheffield gave way and in the ensuing deluge 238 lives were lost as a wall of water swept down the valley between the Loxley and Stannington hills into Sheffield. The villages of Loxley, Malin Bridge and Hillsborough were swept away and bodies carried into the river Don were later recovered as far away as Doncaster. The relief fund raised £52,015 (£4.68m), but thousands of pounds had to be spent on litigation against the Sheffield Water Co. which, in the best traditions of all such private companies, denied responsibility before it was eventually forced to pay £13,000 (£1.17m) to the relief committee. Eighteen months after the disaster some £31,000 (£2.79m) had been paid out in compensation, but only £430 (£38,700) went to the widows and orphans of the disaster as so many families had been completely wiped out.[4]

All noblemen and gentlemen who subscribed to the Sheffield Inundation Fund through Messrs. J Stephenson and J B Morris can, on application on or before March 1, 1866 … receive back 50 per cent of the amount subscribed by them. All monies not applied for by that date will be handed over to the Committee of the Bentinck Memorial Fund for the Benefit of Decayed Jockeys and their Families.

While the *Life* naturally applauded the generosity of the racing community, it felt the excess money could be better employed elsewhere. It was left to Dixon to submit the novel proposal as he suggested, with due delicacy:

The Bentinck Benevolent Fund we all admit to be an excellent institution, but being already in a highly solvent state, we demur to its being made the recipient of the surplus in question … We would recommend the formation of a fund for the immediate relief of the families of jockeys killed or disabled on 'the flat' or across country … And we think the balance which Messrs. Stephenson and Morris will have in hand on March 1, 1866, would form a very substantial nucleus of what might be designated 'The Accidents to Jockeys Fund'.

The *Life* had given £20 (£1,800) to the Sheffield fund and, leading by example, it sent half of the returned tenner to Mrs Meany, "whose husband died from the effects of a fall while riding at Lismore Steeple Chases in October last. Poor Meany's wife and family were left quite unprovided for and we consider it a case deserving of support. The remaining £5 we shall reserve for any exigency or urgent case that may present itself."

The paper did not have long to wait. Just before Christmas 1865, a report headed, 'Tragedy in a Training Stable at Richmond, Yorkshire', announced:

A sad affair took place on Thursday evening last in the training stable of Mr James Watson, of Belleisle, near Richmond.

A trifling dispute seems to have arisen between Robert Roberts, Mr Watson's head lad, and Francis Lawrence, a jockey who, hitherto, has been a very promising youth and has ridden at many of the race meetings in the north … The former struck or, as is stated, gave the latter a slight push and Lawrence immediately ran to a rack and procured a stable fork which he threw with great force at Roberts.

The weapon entered the man's mouth and right eye and inflicted frightful injuries. Medical assistance was at once procured, but death resulted about three-quarters of an hour afterwards. Lawrence was shortly afterwards taken into custody.* He feels his position very much and there is no doubt that he committed the crime in the heat of passion.

We regret to hear that Roberts, who was a steady man, has left a widow and two children totally unprovided for. The poor fellow had lost four children who were carried off by a malignant disease within a month, and the youngest surviving child was only a week old last Monday.

The widow, as might be expected, is in a very weak and delicate state and we are glad to learn that some benevolent people are endeavouring to raise a subscription for the family and we shall be glad

---

* Lawrence was charged with manslaughter, but was acquitted after the jury heard that he had regularly received 'rough treatment' from Roberts.

to receive any contributions towards so charitable an object. This is a case which we would recommend to those subscribers who may receive back the half of their subscriptions to the Sheffield Inundation Fund.

Compared with this grim little tale, death on the racecourse was commonplace as the following, almost offhand, account of a fatality at the Epsom spring meeting of 1875 illustrates. The tragic event was not even considered important enough to be treated as a separate story, instead it was dealt with by 'Augur', but only after he had devoted the first half of his report to the inaugural meeting at Sandown Park; finally he commented:

> Remarks on the conclusion of the Epsom meeting need be but brief, though unfortunately they must be tinged with melancholy owing to the sad accident which befell the poor lad Wass, and whereby he lost his life.
>
> The circumstance was, I believe, of a purely accidental character as, in trying to come up on the inside, Wass miscalculated the opening and, his horse cannoning against a post, the lad's death was occasioned. Mr. Mannington, in whose employ the lad was, appeared much cut up by the calamity.
>
> The Epsom course is certainly a most unfortunate one in the matter of accidents, as Saccharometer and King of the Vale fell in the [1863] Derby, while last year Bugle March, Petition and Bullseye came to grief in the City and Suburban race, the last-named being killed while the rider of Petition broke a leg. The Palmyra filly also ended her days in the Maiden Plate at the summer meeting.
>
> I have no doubt that every precaution will be taken to lessen the chance of future accidents, and I strongly suggest the retention of a medical man, who would then be available at a moment's notice, with all appliances likely to be requisite, surgical and pharmaceutical; in fact, I think that a doctor ought to be specially engaged on every racecourse and every steeplechase course, although he may not be wanted once in a hundred times.

While the death toll among jockeys on the racecourse was appalling, there was an even more insidious threat to their lives than posts and fences. Flat-race jockeys, in particular, were vulnerable to serious health risks as they struggled to keep their weight down in order to ride lightly-handicapped horses in the big feature races of the day.

Mainly from poor, ill-nourished, working-class families, the aspiring jockey would begin his career in racing at the age of ten or eleven often without ever having been to school.* His chief asset was his weight. A lad, who might otherwise have been employed as a chimney sweep, was highly valued in a stable that could have a fancied horse carrying a featherweight (any weight below 4st) in a big handicap.

Little Sam Kitchener confirmed in a letter to the *Life* in 1864 that the lowest weight he ever rode at was 3st 12lb on a filly in the Wokingham Stakes at Ascot in 1840. Only ten years old at the time, he maintained that his actual body weight had been just 2st 7lb and that he had to make up the excess with "a heavy saddle and cloths"!

As the apprentice grew older and developed physically, he was compelled to resort to drastic measures in order to maintain the advantage he had over heavier and more senior riders who were necessarily limited in their choice of mounts. In major handicaps the weight range could be as much

---

* School was not made compulsory for children until the Elementary Education Act of 1876.

as 5st or more, and jockeys were literally killing themselves in their efforts to 'make the weight'. Near starvation diets, constant wasting and the use of purgatives weakened the constitution and left them open to the dreaded disease of consumption (tuberculosis) which reached near epidemic levels in the nineteenth century as it cut a fearful swathe through the ranks of the 'knights in pigskin'.

The issue was raised by the *Life* in January 1860, when the publication of the weights for the five big spring handicaps – the Tradesmen's Plate (the Chester Cup), the Great Northamptonshire Stakes, the Great Metropolitan, the City and Suburban and the Newmarket Handicap – gave John Verrall the chance to highlight what had become a dangerous and absurd situation.

Taking the Tradesmen's Plate as an example, 'Sentinel' pointed out that the weight range for the 176 entries extended from 4st 7lb to 9st 4lb and that a third of the horses were on or near the bottom rung of the handicap:

> It is simply ridiculous to find no less than 59 three-year-olds at and under 4st 12lb, although Mr Topham may produce a more flattering handicap by these means, it cannot but excite disgust amongst genuine turfites and can afford anything but satisfaction to those owners whose horses are weighted in such a manner that they must be compelled to entrust mere children to ride over such a roundabout circus course as Chester.*

Shortly after Verrall had expressed these views, Lord Redesdale, a former MFH of the Heythrope who took a paternal interest in racing, introduced a bill in the House of Lords which sought to: "Prevent the entering or running of horses carrying very light weights for any plate or money."

The sporting peer believed that the then minimum weight of 4st 7lb merely encouraged owners to keep bad horses in training and that the popularity of the big handicaps was largely responsible for an increase in heavy gambling. He was right on both counts, but the *Life* argued that he had "exceeded reasonable limits" in proposing a minimum weight of 7st:

> In the first place the minimum weight is too high and, had a more moderate course been adopted, the Bill would have received the general approval and acceptance of the sporting community. The Bill is, in effect, tantamount to a vote of censure on the Jockey Club, for had that pompous body adopted the reiterated suggestions of the Press, any legislative interference would have been unnecessary…
>
> Nothing could be more simple than for the Jockey Club to pass a rule … fixing the lowest scale of weights at 6st … while we do not pretend to depreciate entirely Lord Redesdale's measure, it is impossible not to discern some traces in it of an offensive movement against the class of racing most popular and most patronised by the less affluent sections of the sporting community.

And a week later the paper was able to announce with some satisfaction:

> Admiral Rous has poured such an irresistible broadside into Lord Redesdale's new Light Weight Bill that no one need expect it to survive his well directed attack. Not only has the chief of the Jockey Club proved the measure utterly impracticable, but the eloquence with which he defends racing men and racing practices will greatly enhance his popularity on the Turf.

---

* In 1844, the aforementioned Sam Kitchener partnered Red Deer, carrying just 4st, to an all-the-way victory over the 9st 8lb top-weight, Alice Hawthorn, in the Tradesmen's Plate.

The Admiral, whose uneasy relationship with the press did not stop him from using the columns of newspapers to further his own campaigns, had written to Redesdale on the subject and had, at the same time, leaked his correspondence to *The Times* which was well used to publishing the lucid dispatches it received from 13 Berkeley Square.

In his letter Rous echoed the *Life's* plea for "the less affluent sections of the sporting community" as he asked Redesdale:

Why should a poor man, comparatively speaking, who cannot afford to buy a good horse, not amuse himself with a bad one? It augments the revenue £3-17s per head.* Every such horse provides good wages to a man. Every breeder is lucky if he produces one good horse in ten, the proportion of a first-class horse being one in 700.

Why are you to deprive the poor man of his racehorse? the stable lad of his wages? the breeder of his profits? the country of its revenue?, and attack the liberty of the subject by not allowing persons to match their horses under seven stone?

With regard to the increased popularity of handicaps, Rous, surprisingly, confessed:

I have no mania for handicaps. No man is a greater enemy to them than myself; but knowing all the odium attached to a handicapper, I, who do not care about pleasing any man, slave at this vocation, fearing that handicaps should get into bad hands to the detriment of the Turf.

The Jockey Club subsequently presented a petition to the House of Lords which submitted that "all regulations respecting racing are better entrusted to the authority which has hitherto made rules for this great national amusement, and that the proposed Bill, should it become law, would have a prejudicial effect. Your petitioners, therefore, humbly pray that your Lordships will be pleased to refuse your assent to the second reading of the Bill." [5]

Redesdale, unwilling to force the issue, agreed to withdraw his bill after Lord Derby had assured him that the Jockey Club would raise the minimum weight to 5st 7lb for the following season. This was duly done, but the weight debate continued as the physique of jockeys gradually improved with a better diet and living standards which, in turn, required them to maintain their severe wasting regimes.

It was a vicious circle which all too often had fatal consequences and 12 years later Harry Feist was calling for the minimum weight to be raised by a further 14lb. In one short period between July 1872 and September 1873, three famous jockeys succumbed to the rigours of their profession. Two of them, one a former champion, the other the rider of two Derby winners, were in their 20s, while the third, a dual champion with three Derby victories to his credit, had reached the ripe old age of 39!

Sammy Kenyon, who won the 1866 championship with 123 winners, was the first to go at the age of 24. In recalling the career of the celebrated lightweight who weighed just 3st 5lb when he started riding in 1862, Feist listed eleven other well-known Flat-race jockeys whose lives had come to a premature end in recent years:

Two of these, H Grimshaw and little Drewe, came by their deaths through accident, the first named being thrown from his dog cart near Cambridge and Drewe while riding at Brighton races. It is to

---

* Just as there were dog licences, each racehorse had to be licensed at a fee of £3-17s (£346.50).

be feared, however, that the majority of these succumbed through the severe calls upon their constitutions, necessitated by sweating and keeping their bodies down to the minimum weight, which is another melancholy argument in favour of the wise and judicious proposition to make 6st 7lb the lowest impost in all handicaps.

On the other hand, more than one of our young jockeys that could be mentioned have been hurried to untimely and often disgraceful ends through dissipation and riotous living. No sooner has a lad made his mark as a fashionable lightweight than he is beset with all kinds of temptations, pampered with presents, deluged with drinks of the worst quality and stuffed with rank cigars or, worse still, taken 'down the Haymarket' to complete the round of the fast man's curriculum.

Few youths can withstand this vicious course of existence and the last scene of all is seldom difficult to foretell … Training and exercise are neglected and, on a sudden call to ride a certain weight, violent means are resorted to in order to get rid of the superfluity which would not have existed in the system but for irregular and pernicious habits. None of these remarks apply to poor Sammy Kenyon who fell victim to what is so dismally, but truthfully, described as a galloping consumption.

Almost a year to the day after Kenyon's untimely demise, John Wells finally lost his battle with the scales. Champion jockey in 1853 and '54, he had won three Derbys for Sir Joseph Hawley on Beadsman (1858), Musjid (1859) and Blue Gown (1868) in addition to five other classics, but his tall frame meant that he had to exist on a near starvation diet for most of his career and it eventually undermined his health.

Less than six weeks later, consumption claimed another victim when Tom French, who had won successive Derbys on Kingcraft and Favonius, in 1870 and '71, died at the age of 29. In reporting his death, the *Life* published a long letter from Dr Mead, who had taken the unusual step of providing the paper with a full account of French's medical history. The letter ended with the poignant observation:

> There is no doubt that the wasting and exposure, and the irregularity of diet from the necessities of travelling &c. shortened French's life. I consider he died a martyr to his love for his profession and a desire to do his duty to his employers.

The *Life* was quick to pick up on the fact that the doctor had attributed the rigours of wasting as one of the main causes of "hurrying poor Tom to his grave," and commented:

> It remains to be seen, after this statement, whether our racing legislators will not adopt some reform and raise the weights in all races so that our best jockeys should not be immolated … Every jockey in the kingdom should join in a petition to the Jockey Club for an alteration when they glance over the melancholy list of horsemen whose lives have been sacrificed through the unnatural process of 'wasting' which sows seeds of disease in the constitutions of the strongest of lads.

With uncanny foresight, the writer went on to observe that one popular lightweight (quite likely the 16-year-old Fred Archer who was to succeed Tom French as first jockey to Mat Dawson the following season) was…

looking fearfully ill from continual 'sweatings' to ride in handicaps and unless something be done we shall continually be shocked with the news of young men sacrificed to this pernicious and fatal system.

The number of deaths among horsemen during the past ten or twelve years has been remarkable; the mournful list comprising the names of Charlton, Bullock, Bray, Alfred Day, Plumb, Arthur Edwards, the two Carrolls, Cresswell, Drewe, Henry Grimshaw, Luke Snowden, Nat Flatman, Sam Rogers, Jem Robinson, Mr Ede, George Stevens, Wells and finally French.

More than one of these celebrities in the saddle died from accidents, such as Drewe, Henry Grimshaw, George Stevens and Mr Ede, but the majority were cut down in their youth from the dreadful strain that had been made upon their frames. It will therefore be a stigma upon the Turf if the Jockey Club do not take immediate steps to raise weights and fix a higher minimum in handicaps.

The 'mournful list' was by no means a complete or representative one. Both Rogers and Robinson had hung up their boots long before they passed on, while poor little Kenyon had, it seems, already been forgotten, as also had Jimmy Mann who won the 1866 Oaks on Tormentor and died of consumption five years later.

In addition, no account was taken of lesser lights or of English jockeys riding abroad such as George Mizen whose macabre demise had been reported just six months earlier on 1 March 1873 when a pathetic little news item announced:

The Suicide of George Mizen – This jockey, who was formerly in the service of Count Lagrange, committed suicide on Wednesday afternoon at his residence, La Morlaye, near Chantilly, by jumping down a well attached to the premises.

The deceased – who had ridden the winners of most of the principal races in France, notably Alabama for the Omnium (French Cesarewitch) 1868, and Consul for the Poule d'Essai (French Two Thousand) and Prix du Jockey Club (French Derby) 1869 – leaves a widow and two children. A small scrap of paper was found beside the well on which was written: 'This is my last day. Goodbye. G Mizen'.

Despite all this grief, the Jockey Club remained unmoved and the minimum weight was still 5st 7lb* when, on 8 November 1886, Frederick James Archer; champion jockey for the past 13 seasons, drained by years of wasting and delirious with fever, put the barrel of a revolver in his mouth and pulled the trigger. He was, like his predecessor, Tom French, just 29 years old.

---

* During the time the *Sporting Life* was published, the minimum weight in handicaps gradually climbed from 4st 7lb to 7st 10lb – this was raised to 7st 12lb in 2002 and will certainly rise again.

RULES OF THE GAME

HORSERACING was not the only sport with rules that needed updating. Cricket had evolved considerably from the game that had been played at the start of the century, but its laws had failed to keep pace with its development. By the 1860s, the need for reform was all the greater since the game was being exported to other parts of the world by emigrants and tourist teams.

In the same year as the *Sporting Life* was launched, the first overseas tour of an English XI was made, not to Australia but to the North American continent. This birth of international sport was marked by a special edition of the paper on 9 November 1859 when the front page carried a striking (for the time), three-deck headline centred across five columns:

THE LATE GREAT INTERNATIONAL CRICKET MATCHES
ENGLAND v. AMERICA, AND ENGLAND v. CANADA
ENGLAND VICTORIOUS IN ALL FIVE MATCHES

Designed to complement the reports that had appeared over the previous month, a full statistical analysis of the matches was given in the hope that the information "will be found of sufficient interest to all lovers of the noble game to cause them to possess a copy of this day's *Life* as a memento of the successful efforts of our countrymen in so brilliantly sustaining the cricketing honour of Old England." It was stated that an overseas tour had been under consideration for two years, but…

it was not until that respected English cricketer Mr W Pickering (now of Montreal) took the matter in hand on behalf of the Montreal Club that these matches were settled – the final arrangement being that the Eleven of England (and another to act as umpire), equally selected from the 'All-England' and the 'United Elevens', should play four matches against different Twenty-twos – two matches in Canada and two in America.

The twelve eventually selected were Julius Caesar, Wm Caffyn, R Carpenter, A Diver, J Grundy, T Hayward, J Jackson, John Lillywhite, Thomas Lockyer, George Parr, H H Stephenson and J Wisden. These, accompanied by Mr F Lillywhite with his well-known printing tent and paraphernalia, left Old England and the Mersey, in the *Nova Scotian*, on Wednesday, the 7th Sept., at about three p.m. for Canada; and, after a protracted passage, they reached Quebec, to their infinite delight and bodily comfort, on Wednesday the 21st Sept.

They were all heartily welcomed and most hospitably entertained throughout their tour both in Canada and America; public dinners were given to them and conveyances provided to take them to and fro to the various grounds. The people assembled in their thousands to see them play and enthusiastically applauded their exertions.

Their courteous opponents seemed honoured by contending with such players, whose skill and activity seemed equally to surprise and delight them, more particularly T Lockyer's wicket-keeping.

The popularity of cricket in America had waned since the War of Independence (1775-83) and the tourists had little trouble in seeing off the double-strength teams. In their first match against the 22 of Montreal, they won by seven wickets, and against the 22 of America, by an innings and 64 runs.

They won by six wickets in Philadelphia, and by ten wickets in Hamilton (Upper Canada), before they rounded off the series with an extra match against a combined 22, which was played in wintry conditions with England fielding in greatcoats, mufflers and gloves to secure victory by an innings and 68 runs.

Tom Lockyer of Surrey had been outstanding. During the tour he stumped 14 and caught 14 to give him an average of 5.6 wickets per match, while William Caffyn took 16 wickets for 25 runs in the match against the Americans in New York.

In a review of the various sports it had covered in its first year, the *Life* observed:

> The growing interest displayed in cricket as a healthy and manly recreation requires no fresh emphasis. In every quarter of the country, new clubs are forming and the victorious career of the cricket champions in America has not only given an impetus to the sport at home, but has excited universal emulation abroad.

Thus were sown the seeds of many a crushing defeat at the hands of the 'Colonials', although it was to be another two years before Australia received its first team from 'Old England'. That visit proved a great success especially for the promoters, the Melbourne restaurateurs Messrs Spiers and Pond, who laid out £7,000 (£630,000) to cover all expenses and cleared over £11,000 (£990,000) from their investment.

On that occasion the *Life* lifted its match reports from the Australian papers – usually *Bell's Life in Victoria* and the *Melbourne Herald* – when they arrived with the mails some seven weeks later, but for the 1864 tour the paper had the added bonus of having the great Yorkshire batsman George Anderson and Tom Lockyer as its correspondents.

Their graphic accounts of the team's adventures 'down under' were both entertaining and informative, while Lockyer was in his usual devastating form behind the wicket. In the XI's first five matches against the 22s of Victoria, Bendigo, Ballarat, Ararat and Maryborough, he stumped 27 and caught nine.*

In between their matches the team indulged in the Victorians' passion for slaughtering wildlife, potting off possums by moonlight and cockatoos and parrots by day; their cross-country treks were embarked upon with less enthusiasm. During a ten-hour overnight coach ride from Ballarat to Ararat, Lockyer related: "We were bumped about in all directions, several of us losing the rims of our hats during the journey." On arrival they just had time for a bath and an hour's rest before play.

The voyage to New Zealand in heavy seas was even worse. Most of the team were seasick and Anderson was pitched out of his bunk onto William Caffyn, who suffered a gashed forehead. Following

---

* When Lockyer died five years later at the age of 44, Harry Feist was one of many who attended his funeral at Broad Green in Croydon where the vast social divide that separated professional players from their amateur counterparts was much in evidence. It provoked Feist into firing off a blistering volley at the 'gentlemen' of Surrey: "It is well known how hard and for how long a period Lockyer had worked for Surrey. No exertion was too great for him and no effort was left untried by him when the issue of a match was trembling in the balance, and often have his batting, bowling and wicket-keeping secured success when least expected. It is the lot of many professional men to be feted and lauded when in active service and useful, but to be thrown aside when 'used up' and left to struggle on as best they may in their declining years. The Surrey County Club had not one single representative – save those of Lockyer's own class – present on Thursday. Nay, more, Mr W Burrup, the honorary secretary of that club, has never even answered a letter addressed to him by Mrs Lockyer soon after her husband's death."[1]

a match at Dunedin, the XI had to sleep on the deck of an overcrowded steamer bound for Port Lyttelton and matters did not improve when they arrived to find their hotel fully booked, so another night was spent on the floor.

At the end of the tour Caffyn signed a three-year contract with the Melbourne Cricket Club to coach their players and so helped to lay the foundations for Australia's 45-run victory over England in the first Test match to be played between the two sides in 1877.

On the debit side, the 1864 tourists also left behind an unpaid bar bill at their hotel in Melbourne which resulted in the proprietor, one John Jacob, bringing an action against the tour organiser, James Leigh, to recover the outstanding £56-10s (£5,085). The *Life* carried the story under the heading 'Liquoring-Up in Australia' as it reported that the dispute centred on what constituted 'incidental expenses'. Jacob claimed his agreement with Leigh was to board and lodge the players for 8s (£36) a head per day and to be paid extra for all drinks supplied. In evidence it was stated:

> The English cricketers, it was sworn, were very often 'treated' but seldom treated anyone in return … Nothing, therefore, was charged for but what the cricketers had themselves drunk. But some of the drinks were of an expensive character, such as soda-water and claret, or soda-water and brandy in the morning, and champagne, claret, hock etc. during the day.

When Leigh was presented with the bill at the end of the team's 26-day stay he refused to pay for the drinks. He told Jacob to get the money from the players as he had paid for their drinks on the voyage out to Australia as well as paying them a total of £2,750 (£247,500) in addition to all their reasonable expenses.

In effort to bestow some credibility on this miserly band of whinging Poms, it was claimed that rain and "the consequent detention indoors of the cricketers" was the main reason why they had quaffed so much of Mr Jacob's finest (surely the merest tipple for a 26-day stay!) – a feeble plea of mitigation the jury ignored as they found for the plaintiff.

An issue even more contentious than unpaid bar bills was that of overarm bowling. From the early 1820s, the original underarm method began to be replaced by a more forceful delivery as bowlers adopted a round-arm action to inject more pace into the ball. This technique eventually evolved into overarm bowling which came into play in 1846 even though it contravened the laws of cricket, which stated the arm should not be raised above shoulder height.

When one umpire (W H Caldecourt) boldly attempted to enforce the law at Lord's he was overruled by the MCC which continued to disregard its own rules until matters were brought to a head in the late summer of 1862 when the celebrated Sussex cricketer, John Lillywhite, 'no-balled' Edgar Willsher six times in succession in a match between Surrey and England at the Oval.

The *Life* dealt with this epoch-making event in the languid style of the day as its match report ambled its way through England's record first innings of 503. Finally, when "the clock was striking six" on the second day, the nub of the story was reached as the first Surrey batsmen went in to face V E Walker, the England captain, who opened the bowling with Willsher. After a couple of maiden overs, it was reported:

> Humphrey hit one of Mr Walker's very beautifully to square leg; but Grundy, by dint of great exertion, reached it with one hand and the first wicket fell for 4. Mr Burbidge followed and Willsher

delivered to him a 'no ball' of which he took advantage and made a fine off-hit for 4.

The next was called 'no ball' and the spectators began to wonder what was up. Lillywhite repeated his flat 'no ball' again and again, and then it began to dawn upon the imagination that at length an umpire had been found possessing sufficient moral courage to carry out Law No. 10 which runs thus: '*The ball must be bowled. If thrown or jerked, or if the bowler in the actual delivery of the ball or in action immediately preceding the delivery shall raise his hand or arm above the shoulder, the umpire shall call 'no ball'.*'

Upon this, Willsher, instead of attempting to finish the over, naturally irritated and hurt at this unexpected proceeding on the part of John Lillywhite, threw down the ball and walked towards the dressing room followed by the rest of the players. In an instant all was confusion and excitement. Cheers were raised for Willsher and counter-cheers for Lillywhite, who remained in the field until the time for drawing the stumps had arrived, surrounded by thousands of spectators.

The scene around the inside of the Pavilion beggars description. The sympathies of the public who had paid for admission were, of course, with Willsher, while those who were acquainted with the laws of the game upheld Lillywhite's decision.

At a hastily convened committee meeting, Surrey decided the match should go ahead and that "on this particular occasion" Willsher should be allowed to bowl as usual. Lillywhite, however, stuck to his guns and refused to continue to umpire unless the laws of cricket were observed. The contretemps ended with Lillywhite resigning as umpire and being replaced for the final day of the match. The resulting controversy, the *Life* observed, generated as much discussion in the press as any world issue then dominating the headlines...

This was made strikingly obvious during the past week when John Lillywhite's name suddenly became as conspicuous in the topics of the day as Garibaldi's. The civil war in America seemed to be forgotten for the moment and attention became absorbed with the uncivil war at the Oval between the partisans of the umpire and the mighty left-handed bowler, Willsher...

For years past, overhand bowling has been the subject of much criticism, and at its first introduction the old school resolutely set their faces against it as dangerous and unfair. So generally accepted, however, has overhand bowling at length become that numbers of the uninitiated were ignorant of the existence of so stringent a rule as No. 10.

In the extraordinary match which was played at the Oval during the past week the system was put upon its final trial by the determination and firmness of John Lillywhite who, though espousing the unpopular cause with the community, has emphatically enlisted on his side the sympathies of all lovers of the game. The matter is of so much importance that it may be as well to trace the origin of overhand bowling and discover how far Lillywhite was justified by precedent in 'no balling' Willsher.

In 1822, when Kent was playing against the MCC at Lord's, John Willes, one of the county eleven, introduced the system of round or straight-arm bowling and the umpire, Noah Mann, immediately 'no-balled' him. Mr Willes left the ground in high dudgeon and some other player was substituted.

The round-arm bowling eventually superseded the underhand delivery and gradually became higher and higher until about fifteen years ago when Caldecourt, who was then acting as umpire at Lord's, 'no-balled' Mr Hodson, a Sussex bowler, and about the same time, when Surrey was playing against the Marylebone Club, he 'no-balled' Sherman eleven times; the over in this instance was finished and an appeal made at the Pavilion. Instructions were issued not to call him again and the match proceeded...

Now, it is patent to the most casual observer that the batting has obtained a great ascendancy over the bowling and the effect of enforcing the present law would be to still further increase that difference as well as disqualifying a vast number of the very best bowlers, both professional and amateur, unless some counteracting plan were adopted. A remedy is most simple. Let a conference be held at the Marylebone Club with delegates from Surrey, Kent, Sussex, Nottinghamshire, Cambridgeshire, Yorkshire and other counties of cricket celebrity, and let that portion of the law which relates to the hand being above the shoulder be expunged.

As with the Jockey Club, the wheels of reform turned slowly within the MCC, but eventually this 'simple remedy' was acted on in the summer of 1864 when, by 27 votes to 20, the governing body amended Rule 10 to allow for overarm bowling. Then, just when everyone thought the bowling controversy had been finally laid to rest, Edward Mills Grace stirred things up again with an altogether different delivery.

An elder brother of the legendary 'WG', the talented 'EM' was playing in a pro-am match (Eleven Players of the South v Eighteen Gentlemen of the South) at the Oval in the autumn of 1865 when, not for the first time in his distinguished career, he found himself frustrated by the formidable Surrey batsman, Harry 'Young Stonewall' Jupp.

Built along the lines of the proverbial, Jupp was equally solid in defence and Grace finally resorted to his particular forte of lob bowling, which was uncannily accurate but was not appreciated by the cognoscenti in the crowd. When the third of his high-pitched balls sent the bails flying the spectators responded with jeers and cries of 'shame'.

While there was no rule to prohibit lob bowling, many felt Grace was taking liberties at the expense of the game. One particularly aggrieved *Life* reader wrote in to complain:

If the 'rifle practice' as I term round-arm bowling, is to be superseded by the 'shell practice' or otherwise dropping the ball vertically on the top of the wicket, much of the enjoyment of cricket will be done away with.

Jupp, he claimed, had shown his contempt for such bowling by turning his back on Grace and had "disdained even to attempt to hit the succession of balls so delivered". Quoting Rule 12, which stated that the bowler must not toss the ball "so as not to be fairly within reach of the batsman," he went on to argue that all lobs should be called 'no ball' since the batsman...

may be facing a meridian sun and, should he attempt to look upwards, he cannot see the ball with the full glare of the sun in his eyes, and, even should he attempt to keep his position at the wicket, he may receive the full force of the ball on the top of his head, dropping from a height of 20ft, as Mr Grace delivered these balls on September 30.

I am not an Englishman, and would ask Englishmen, and more especially the Surrey Club, is this fair cricket, to strike a man on the head when his eyes are shut?

While the *Life* was keen to bring about reforms to the outdated rules of cricket and racing, it initially had no such commitment to football simply because there was no standard set of rules in existence when it first appeared. Football, as played on a regular basis, was confined to the public schools and because each school played by its own rules as determined by years of tradition, they seldom met each other in competition.

There was, admittedly, a sort of communal game which had been played with no discernible rules at all in the streets of towns and villages throughout the country for centuries. This form of mob football had survived repeated attempts to suppress it; the first recorded edict being passed in 1314 when Edward II – just before he was trounced by the Scots at Bannockburn – banned football from being played in the streets of London "as there is a great noise in the city caused by hustling over large balls, from which many evils may arise."[2]

Some of those evils were addressed by Phillip Stubbes in his *Anatomie of Abuses* (1583) in which he listed football among the "develyshe pastimes" since it caused "envy, malice, rancour, cholor, hatred, displeasure, enmitie and what not else and sometimes fighting, brawling, contention, quarrel picking, murther, homicide and great effusion of blood, as experience daily teacheth."

"No change there then!" some might say, but in 1848 an attempt was made to regulate the game when representatives from the main public schools agreed on a common code which favoured the dribbling game over the handling game as played at Rugby School. Known as the Cambridge Rules since they were based on regulations adopted by that university's football club two years earlier, they outlawed the contentious practice of hacking (kicking an opponent on the shin) in order to gain possession of the ball.

But drawing up a set of rules was one thing; implementing them, quite another. It was found "that men were fast wedded to their several systems and refused to relinquish them or amalgamate with others. Eton thought the Rugby game plebeian, Rugby dubbed the Etonians cowards for not approving of hacking. One set wished to keep the ball on the ground and kick it *through* the goal sticks, whilst others wished to carry it and kick it *over*."[3]

Then on 26 October 1863, the captains and secretaries of a dozen metropolitan and suburban clubs and schools met at the Freemason's Tavern in Great Queen Street, central London, with the object of "bringing about a definite code of laws for the regulation and adoption of the various clubs which indulge in this exciting and health promoting winter pastime" – as the *Life* reported at the time.

The meeting was arguably the most important one in the history of sport since it resulted in the formation of the Football Association, the body which laid the foundations of the game that was to encompass the globe. But no sooner had the Association come into being than it began to disintegrate over the issues of carrying the ball and hacking. Under the proposed rules 9 and 10, the former would allow a player to run with the ball "if he makes a fair catch or catches the ball on the first bound," while the latter permitted a player to "charge, hold, trip or hack" any opponent running with the ball.

The 'no carrying – no hacking' brigade was headed by the Association's secretary, the Barnes captain and all-round sportsman, E C Morley, who argued: "If we have hacking, no one who has arrived at the years of discretion will play at football, and it will be entirely relinquished to schoolboys."[4] Leading the opposition was F W Campbell secretary of the Blackheath Club and treasurer of the Association, who advocated the rules which governed the game as played at Rugby School.

Matters were brought to a head at the fifth meeting of the FA on December 1 when Morley read out a letter from W Chesterman, the secretary of Sheffield FC, which had accompanied a request from that club to join the Association. In commenting on some of the rules under debate, Chesterman had observed: "Nos. 9 and 10, I think are directly opposed to football, the latter especially being more like wrestling. I cannot see any science in taking a run-kick at a player at the risk of laming him for life."

Morley and his supporters used these views to propose that the recently revised Cambridge Rules should be adopted and that hacking and carrying the ball be disallowed. What the *Life* described as "a warm discussion" then took place after which, on a vote of 13 to 4, rules 9 and 10 were expunged and replaced by two that stipulated: "No player shall carry the ball" and "Neither tripping nor hacking shall be allowed, and no player shall use his hands to hold or push an adversary."

A week later, when it was agreed that John Lillywhite should "print and publish the rules and laws of football as settled by the Association," Campbell carried out his threat to withdraw Blackheath – which was allied with Blackheath School and Percival House – as he claimed the rules savoured "far more of the feelings of those who liked their pipes and grog or schnapps more than the manly game of football."[5]

The secession of the three London clubs was a major blow to the infant Association which was now accused of lacking authority and support. No sooner had the split occurred than former public schoolboys began to voice negative 'I-told-you-so' criticisms in letters to the *Life*. One Blackheath supporter wrote:

The Association was no doubt formed with the best of motives, but I think there is now no question that it has utterly failed in its object of harmonising the rules of various clubs. No one who knew the game of football ever looked for anything but failure in such an attempt. The public schools, of course, are not to be taken into account in a matter of this kind. Each school will always play its own game; and you could sooner teach a French sailor to row like an Eton boy, than an Eton boy to play football like a Rugbeian.

In referring to the FA another jeremiad pointed out:

Even those who fondly hoped it would become a National institution find themselves compelled to recognise the stubborn fact that there are now only nine members[*] whose influence, let alone number, is quite inadequate to support its pretensions. Let anyone who knows to what extent this game is played in Great Britain think of the old association connected with every set of rules, and he will declare it puerile to believe that all the clubs (if, indeed, any) will throw away their own code and adopt that which is framed by such a fractional set of players.

The *Life*, itself, remained supportive of the 'fractional set of players' and on 2 January 1864 it gave notice that a match was to be played under the new rules between two sides drawn from the Association:

The gentlemen who set about the laudable and, it seems, partially unthankful task of establishing a set of rules for universal adoption, having so far succeeded as to be in a position to demonstrate publicly in Battersea Park this day, their practical working, deserve the congratulations and thanks of every admirer of this healthful and invigorating winter pastime.

Yet, for more than a decade the pessimistic forecasts of the letter writers appeared well founded as a rapid growth in the number of clubs throughout the country led to rival associations being formed,

---

[*] Barnes, Crystal Palace, Forest Leytonstone, Forest School, No Names (Kilburn), Royal Engineers (Chatham), Sheffield, Uppingham and the War Office.

each with its own set of rules. Yet, by the end of the 1870s, most of these bodies had adopted the laws of the London-based Association.

The magnet that drew them all together was the FA Cup competition, the brainchild of Charles William Alcock, a Sunderland-born, Harrow-educated sportsman and journalist who worked as a sub-editor on the *Sportsman* for 14 years (1869-82) before he had an all-too-brief spell writing an informative 'Football Notes' column under the signature of 'Harrovian' for the *Sporting Life* during the 1882-83 season.

Alcock had been elected honorary secretary of the FA at the age of 27 in 1870 and the following summer, after a meeting with several like-minded committee members, he invited the 50 clubs affiliated to the Association to subscribe towards the purchase of a silver cup to be competed for annually. The initial response was disappointing and in a letter to the *Life* in October 1871, he announced that the draw for the first round ties had already taken place, but "as no reservation nor restrictions are desired, any club can still be included in the first ties by signifying such intention to me at once."

The letter brought in two more clubs to boost the total entries to 15, eight of which were from London and five from the Home Counties. Only Donington School, near Spalding, Lincs., and Queen's Park, Glasgow, came from further afield, and when the former team dropped out, Queen's Park were allowed a bye to the semi-finals in which they met the Wanderers in London. The game ended in a goalless draw after which the Scots, unable to afford the cost of another trip south, withdrew from the competition leaving Wanderers to meet the Royal Engineers in the final at the Kennington Oval.

On Saturday, 16 March 1872, about 2,000 spectators paid a shilling (£4.50) admission to watch history in the making. The *Life* limited its preview of the match to a single paragraph, but found more space for its report. Fittingly it was Charles Alcock, captain of Wanderers, who won the toss and elected to take advantage of a strong following wind. The description of the game was basic to say the least, but it deserves its place in football history for all that:

> A few minutes after three, the ball was kicked off by Captain Marindin and at first was carried down towards the Wanderers' goal, but not many minutes had elapsed ere it was brought back to the centre of the ground and thence taken on into the neighbourhood of the Engineers' goal which, after a few ineffectual attacks, at length succumbed, the ball being kicked through the posts after a general bully in front of the goal.
>
> Ends were at once changed[*] and it was thought that, with the wind to aid them, the Engineers would be enabled to turn the tables; but they could not, though several times a brilliant rush on their part would bring the ball well down the ground. Towards the close, moreover, their own goals were not only most dangerously besieged, but the ball was once more driven through the posts, though the score was disallowed as Betts, who gave the final kick, was palpably 'off-side' ... When play ceased the Wanderers Club had thus become the first holders of the Challenge Cup.[†]

---

[*] In 1875 the practice of changing of ends after scoring a goal was scrapped and the half-time system was introduced together with the addition of a crossbar, instead of a tape, across the top of the goal posts.

[†] Wanderers, a team Alcock had formed out of the Forest Club in 1864, were to win the Cup again in 1873 and in 1876-78 they completed a hat trick of victories to win the Cup outright, but they returned it to the FA on the understanding it would become a perpetual trophy. Having won the competition five times in seven years, they never again reached the finals and were finally forced to disband after their best players had been siphoned off by public school old boys' clubs.

The report singled out several players for special mention, most notably the Engineers goalkeeper, Capt. Merriman, who "did his *devoir* most skilfully" and R W Sealy-Vidal of Wanderers, whose "scientific dribbling frequently elicited marked plaudits from the lookers-on". It concluded by listing the teams, but omitted to mention who had scored the vital goal (official records give the credit to the Old Harrovian and FA committee member Morton Peto Betts).

Over the next decade the FA Cup attracted more clubs to the Association and as its membership grew, so too did its authority and influence. In 1882, just ten years after the first Cup Final, the competition attracted 73 entries and for the first time a club from the north, Blackburn Rovers, reached the final. The Lancashire team, made up of players – some professional – who came from a very different background to their opponents, the Old Etonians, were beaten 1-0, but they were avenged the following year by the mill-workers of Blackburn Olympic, who gained a 2-1 win over the Old Etonians in extra time.

It was to be 18 years before the FA Cup was to return to London (when Tottenham Hotspur beat Sheffield United in a replay) and when it did it was only a replica of the £20 (£1,800), 18-inch high 'Little Tin Idol' that had done so much to draw all the different associations together. In 1895, after Aston Villa had won the Cup for the second time by beating West Bromwich 1-0 at Crystal Palace, it was stolen while on display in a football outfitter's window in Birmingham and was never recovered.

In the meantime, the ever-industrious Alcock, who also acted as secretary to the Surrey CCC from 1872 until his death in 1907, had organised a series of London-based matches between England and Scotland. The first of these 'internationals' came off at the Oval in March 1870 when the Scottish team included W H Gladstone, MP, son of the Prime Minister, but it was an Old Harrovian, R E Crawford, who gave the Anglo-Scots the lead against the run of play when he scored through "a somewhat lucky side kick," only for England to equalise in the final minutes.

A second game between to two sides was arranged the following season when, at the end of October, Alcock used the columns of the *Life* to broadcast an appeal for players:

> As it is the object of the committee of the Football Association to choose the best eleven, irrespective of clubs or distinction, they would like the names of any players who may be desirous of taking part in the match sent in before November 9.

Thus selected, the teams met at the Oval ten days later when England won by a single goal. A third 'international' the following February ended in another 1-1 draw, while a fourth meeting in November 1871 saw Alcock captain England to a 2-1 win. In its report on this match the *Life* recommended...

> that in future years the playing ground be more effectively roped and staked and that it be strongly impressed upon the spectators that this is done to prevent the players being crowded upon. On Saturday the latter were very much interfered with on this account and could scarcely see when they were close upon the goal line, the crowd rushing after the ball as it was carried first one way and then another.

It would appear that the first pitch invasion under FA rules had taken place! But these early encounters between the old adversaries were not viewed as true internationals in Scotland, where the national game had been based on the Rugby School rules ever since it had been adopted by Edinburgh Academy as a winter sport in 1855. A further objection was that some of the London-based players who

Aston Villa won and 'lost' the FA Cup in 1895; after their 1-0 victory over West Bromwich, the 'little tin idol' was stolen and was never recovered.

represented Scotland under the scorned Association rules had extremely tenuous links to 'the tartan army'. Allegedly, "one had crossed the border to shoot grouse, which was considered sufficient qualification, but it was seriously doubted if another should have been allowed to play whose sole claim was a partiality for Scotch whisky."[6]

The defeat of the Anglo-Scots in the second of Alcock's 'internationals'* was enough to spur the Scottish rugby clubs into action and a letter was sent to B H Burns, secretary of the Blackheath club in December 1870. Signed by the captains of Edinburgh Academicals, Glasgow Academicals, Merchiston (Edinburgh), West of Scotland and St Andrews University, it challenged "any team selected from the whole of England to play us a match, twenty-a-side Rugby rules."

Burns saw the challenge as an opportunity to create a governing body for the sport similar to that of the Football Association and, together with E H Ash, the Richmond (Surrey) secretary, he drafted a letter to the press. It appeared in the *Life* just before Christmas:

> Sir – An opinion has for some time prevailed among the supporters of 'Rugby Football' that some fixed code of rules should be adopted by all clubs who profess to play the Rugby game as, at present, the majority have altered, in some slight way, the game as played at Rugby School by introducing fresh rules of their own.

---

* The first officially recognised international football match between the two countries took place at the West of Scotland cricket ground at Partick in Glasgow on St Andrew's Day, 30 November 1872. The Scottish team was made up entirely of Queen's Park players and, after the game had ended in a goalless draw, the *Life* set a record for brevity with a report that stated: "The match may be described in a few words, for the Scotch had the best of the play during the first [*half*], and the Englishmen during the latter portion." The Scottish FA was formed the following year; the Welsh in 1876 and the Irish in 1880, and in 1884 a regular four nations championship was established.

Each club plays according to its own rules on its own ground so the strangers in each match, finding themselves at once at a disadvantage through not knowing the rules of the ground, confusion and disputes are generally the result. We therefore hope that all clubs playing the Rugby game will join us in framing a code of rules to be generally adopted.

As a result of this appeal, 32 representatives of 21 clubs met at the Pall Mall Restaurant off Trafalgar Square on 26 January 1871 to form the Rugby Football Union, and Leonard Maton of the Wimbledon Hornets was given the task of drafting the laws of the game – 59 in all – which were approved, without dissent, five months later. Ironically, in view of the stand Blackheath had taken on the issue eight years earlier, that club gave its full backing to Rule No 57 which stated: "No hacking or hacking over or tripping up shall be allowed under any circumstances."

Few of the rules had any relevance to today's game. Initially, only goals counted. A touchdown or 'run-in' simply allowed a free 'try at goal'. It was not until 1886 that a points system was introduced when 3 points were awarded for a goal and 1 for a try.

With the establishment of the RFU, the English wasted no time in gathering together a team of 20 players to meet Scotland.* Drawn from eight clubs ranging from Liverpool and Manchester in the north to Marlborough and West Kent in the south they were captained by Fred Stokes, an outstanding Blackheath forward who also played cricket for Kent and the Gentlemen of England.

The match took place on the grounds of Edinburgh Academy at Raeburn Place on 27 March 1871. The Scots had prepared themselves for the encounter with two trial matches, the first of which appeared to lack something in player-commitment as…

owing to the rain several of the Scottish Fifteen did not put in an appearance, but some good play was shown by those who did take part in the contest. Eleven of them were pitted against sixteen of the best of the Glasgow clubs and the result was an easy win for the Eleven by two goals and a try.

Despite going down to a 25-strong side from Merchiston in their final trial, the Scottish XX, led by Frank Moncrieff, faced the English with plenty of confidence and from the start they dominated the play. There was no score at half-time, but…

Soon after changing goals the Scotch began to make way, and Moncrieff with Cross and Richie gradually forced back the English until they secured a touch-down and try at goals, which was successfully negotiated by Cross, amidst loud cheering.

The English now kept the ball well down in the Scottish territory and at last Tobin got a touch-down, from which, however, Stokes failed to kick a goal, the wind being greatly against him. The Scotch now rallied and Cross got another touch-down (disputed for a time, but allowed by the umpires), but the place kick failed. No further advantage was gained by either side so at the call of 'time' Scotland was hailed as victorious by one goal to nothing.

And so the foundations were laid for many a bruising encounter between the old rivals during which, it may be said, the rules of the game were not always observed.

---

* The first six internationals between the two nations were 20-a-side matches before they settled down to a regular XV game from 1877 onwards.

A TRANSATLANTIC CHALLENGE

THE EARLY success of the *Sporting Life* was due in no small part to the coverage it gave to prizefighting which, by a happy coincidence, was going through one of its better phases at the time and had a worthy champion in the shape – diminutive by heavyweight standards – of the former bricklayer Tom Sayers.

While most newspapers declined to recognise 'the sweet science of bruising' which led a precarious and peripatetic existence until it was finally suppressed in 1868, the fledgling penny journal gained many thousands of readers from 'the fancy', as followers of the prize ring (PR) were called.

As the paper began to draw business away from *Bell's Life*, it started to act as an agent and stakeholder for the bare-knuckle fighters. Every edition carried a long list of challenges thrown out by boxers of varying ability together with an equal number of acceptances heralding forthcoming bouts. Typical of the often colourful notices that appeared under the general heading of 'Pugilism' are two 1865 announcements:

> Charley Turner is not surprised that Godfrey wants to fight him or Connelly, when he knows that he has had his ankle broken and Connelly his hip dislocated; but if Godfrey will send £5 to the Editor of the *Sporting Life* and articles to Charley Bray's, a match can be made for £25 or £50 a side, on the second Tuesday in January. To fight in the London district.
> Tom Cooper of Birmingham, hearing that Dan Lawrence is dissatisfied with the termination of their little brush at Warwick and that he would like to have another turn, will box him for £100 a side and, to make it worth his while, 'Ould Mas', Tom's father-in-law, will bet Dan another cool century that he gets licked. A 'pony' and articles sent to the *Sporting Life* will ensure a match.

In openly advertising, promoting and reporting on a sport that had been outlawed since the early 1750s but never entirely suppressed, the paper occupied an ambiguous position in the eyes of the law. But, as with the bookmakers' adverts it carried in defiance of the 1853 Betting Act, these anomalies were tolerated not least because the prize ring enjoyed the support of a wealthy and influential section of society.

The fight game had come a long way since it emerged as a sport in Britain towards the end of the seventeenth century when regular contests were staged at the Royal Theatre in London. Matches, or mills as they were termed, were fought without gloves or rules. Wrestling, butting, gouging, kicking, biting (*à la* Mike Tyson) and even grabbing an opponent where it hurts most (Vinnie Jones-style), were all permitted.

It was not until 1743 that some discipline was brought into the ring when the reigning champion, Jack Broughton, drew up a code of conduct under which a fighter was not allowed to hit a man when he was down or to "seize him by the ham, the breeches, or any part below the waist". A round lasted until a man went down, after which he was given 30 seconds to 'square up' to his rival by returning to his side of a 3ft square marked out in the middle of a railed platform. Failure to do so would result in a fighter being deemed a beaten man.

In 1838 Broughton's rules were replaced by those of the London Prize Ring, which were brought in partly due to a death in the ring (when the lightweight champion, Owen Swift, battered an opponent into eternity for the second time in three years), and partly to take account of the nomadic nature of the sport which now took place in remote fields or on windswept Medway islands as far removed as possible from the reaches of the law.

Contests were decided in a 24ft square, post and rope bounded ring across the centre of which a line was scratched in the turf. Instead of squaring up to each other, the fighters now 'came up to scratch' at the beginning of each round, while the rules laid down that "gouging, or tearing the flesh with the fingers or nails and biting, shall be deemed a foul" as would "the use of hard substances such as stones or stick, in the hand during the battle," while "in the event of magisterial interference it shall be the duty of the umpires and referee to name the time and place for the next meeting, if possible on the same day."[1]

For the next 30 years the fancy played a furtive game of hide and seek with the law that often ended up in running battles between the pugs and the peelers. Riots were not uncommon and when it became obvious the prizefighter's days were numbered, John Graham Chambers drew up a set of 12 regulations to govern amateur contests.

A noted Oxbridge sportsman, Chambers founded the Amateur Athletic Club (the forerunner of the AAA) in 1866 and when his rules were published the following year he got his old university chum, John Sholto Douglas the 9th Marquess of Queensberry, to lend his name and authority to them.

The 23-year-old Marquess acknowledged the honour by donating three silver cups for an annual AAC heavy, middle and lightweight championship to be decided on points of merit. So it was that, by sponsorship and social position, the name of Queensberry became synonymous with boxing and everything that is good and fair in sport, although the pugnacious patron was more renowned for bellowing "more gore, more gore" at fighters from his pitch at the ringside.

The new rules, which were eventually adapted for professional fights, differed from those of the prize ring in four main points: 1). No wrestling or hugging was allowed. 2). Rounds were to last for three minutes, interspaced with a minute's rest. 3). A fighter who went down had to be on his feet, unassisted, in ten seconds otherwise he would be counted out. 4). Fighters had to wear 'fair-sized gloves of the best quality'.

Padded gloves were still regarded with disdain by the fancy when the *Life* covered the championship fight between Tom Sayers and Bill Benjamin on 5 April 1859. Up to that time no newspaper had ever given a comprehensive account of a major fight within 24 hours of it taking place, but the new journal managed it in style, giving the contest, won by Sayers in eleven rounds and 22 minutes, four columns on the front page.

One column had been set in type beforehand. Used as a lead-in to the ringside report, it provided readers with a fascinating potted history of the heavyweight championship from the time of the first acknowledged title holder, James Figg, in 1719.

Sayers was certainly one of the great champions and was remarkable in that he was a mere middleweight who was capable of beating men 30lb or 40lb heavier than himself – he once fought and won a 109-round contest against a noted Nottingham pug, Harry Poulson, which lasted a staggering 3hr 8min.

Born in Brighton in 1826, his fighting abilities became apparent when, in an archetypal David and Goliath encounter, he floored a bullying foreman while working on the building site of Wandsworth prison in London. He had his first fight as a professional in 1849, and had been beaten only once in the eleven contests which preceded his championship victory over the 38-year-old veteran Bill Perry, 'the Tipton Slasher', in 1857.

In 1859, Sayers was at his peak, which was just as well because his toughest battle lay ahead of him. In the same issue that carried the report of his fight with Benjamin (aka Bainge), a story headed

'Extraordinary Challenge To Tom Sayers' included the transcript of a letter written on behalf of the American champion, John Carmel Heenan, by George Wilkes, proprietor and editor of the New York paper, *Wilkes' Spirit of the Times*.

Prizefights were big business for the sporting press. With the right build-up, the pre-fight publicity could quadruple the sales of a paper which would bring out special editions for championship contests. *Bell's Life* had promoted all the English title fights since its early days and this Yankee challenge not only guaranteed the paper another big pay day, but enabled it to scoop the opposition at will. Consequently, it was able to break the news of the challenge before the *Sporting Life*, which 'lifted' Wilkes' letter from its rival. It began:

> John Heenan, otherwise known as the Benicia Boy, who recently fought John Morrissey at Long Point, Canada, being unsuccessful in getting a match in this country, desires us to announce for him that he will fight Tom Sayers, the champion of England, for £200 and the champion's belt, and is ready to go to England for such a purpose, at his own expense as soon as the present engagements which Sayers is under are completed.

When Wilkes published the announcement in his own paper, he took the opportunity to introduce a bit of needle into the match by commenting provocatively:

> Should Heenan succeed in plucking the victor's belt from the body of the champion of England ... we shall look upon him as having done the country a good service by vindicating its climate from the British sneer that the human race upon this continent is suffering a constant and rapid deterioration.

Born of Irish parents in upstate New York in 1835, Heenan set off to seek his fortune in the gold fields of California in 1852, but ended up in the west coast booths of Benicia, where he made his name as a wage-packet slugger. Wiser but no richer, he returned to New York to become a minder for the corrupt Tammany politicians who ran the city and its rackets, but mixing with the mob was a high-risk business that almost cost him his life.

A few months after he had thrown down his challenge, the *Life* reprinted a report from the *Boston Herald* under the heading 'Murderous Attack on the American Champion Jack Heenan'. It related that after attending a sparring exhibition in Boston…

> Heenan was set upon by ruffians in Portland Street, who struck him from behind with a billy or a slug shot and felled him to the ground. Mr Heenan regained his feet and cleared the way before him, but he was repeatedly assaulted with clubs from behind and knocked down three times. The gang of ruffians that surrounded him were numerous enough to prevent the immediate interference of anyone who might have been disposed to save his life. Knives and pistols were flourished and one of the latter was placed at his side and snapped, but fortunately it did not explode.
>
> Heenan managed to free himself from his murderous assailants just as a hack [*Hackney cab*] was passing and got into it ... He was bleeding profusely from seven or eight wounds upon the back of his head, his right knee pan was injured and his clothing was torn and bloody ... The attack was evidently a preconcerted one ... It is supposed to have been in consequence of a grudge borne by a person who had a misunderstanding with Heenan in New York.

It took Heenan some time to recover from the assault, but by November he was back in training and the following month his representative, Fred Falkland, arrived in London to ratify the articles of agreement. This took place at the famed Horseshoe Tavern in the Haymarket run by the aforementioned dispatcher of pugilistic souls, Owen Swift, and where Sayers' principal backer, the bookmaker and theatrical agent Johnny Gideon, introduced his champion to Falkland with the words "And here's the little man himself".

The American was visibly taken aback by Sayers' lack of stature. Whereas Heenan was 6ft 1½in tall and fought at around 190lb; Sayers was a mere 5ft 8½in and tilted the scales at 154lb. Even so, when Gideon tried to up the stakes to £1,000 a side, Falkland declined, pointing out that as the betting was 2-1 against Heenan, he was not going to take evens when he could get double the odds for his money.

After a date for the fight had been fixed, the health of the fighters and their backers was proposed and "some of the choicest of the worthy host's vintage stock was heartily quaffed in responding to the same". Speeches were made followed by more toasts and, as the evening wore on, Owen Swift's 'vintage stock' was much reduced. Eventually, in the interests of legibility, it was agreed to postpone the signing of the articles until the following morning; they laid down that the fight…

shall take place on Monday, April 16, 1860, within 100 miles and above 20 miles from London. In pursuance of this agreement, £100 a side is now deposited in the hands of the editor of *Bell's Life*, who shall be the final stakeholder. The second deposit of £50 a side to be made at Nat Langham's Cambrian Stores, Castle Street on Wednesday, February 22, 1860. The last deposit of £50 a side is to be made good at Owen Swift's, Horseshoe Tavern, Tichbourne Street, Haymarket, on the 30th of March, 1860.

The deposits shall be made between the hours of eight and ten in the evening, and the party failing in any deposit shall forfeit the whole of the money then staked. The men shall be in the ring between the hours of twelve and one o'clock or the man absent shall forfeit the battle money. The expense of the ropes and stakes shall be shared equally by the combatants. The editor of *Bell's Life in London* to name the place of fighting and the referee.

All that now remained was for the fighters' colours to be designed in accordance with the custom of the time. These large handkerchief-sized silk squares represented the battle standards of the opposing camps and were worn in the waistband of the fighters and tied to their corner posts to be claimed by the victor at the end of the contest. They also provided an additional source of income for the boxers as they were reproduced in their thousands and sold as souvenirs to the fans. In Sayers' case:

The design was most beautifully executed by one of the first artists of the day and was as follows: The standard of England in the centre, with the British lion rampant in each corner, upon a cream coloured ground with a crimson border. The price of each colour was, as usual, one guinea, payable in advance on the distinct understanding that should Fortune fail to crown the gallant Sayers with the wreath of victory, the money should be returned.

Heenan chose the American eagle for his centrepiece:

The proud bird was represented on a white ground within a circle, surmounted by the popular and universal motto of the PR – 'May the best man win' – and bearing in his beak the laurel wreath of

(Left) This portrait of John Carmel Heenan resulted in a sell-out issue of the *Life* on 11 January 1860. (Right) The paper's 1859 'gratis' portrait of Tom Sayers proved so popular that even the one at the British Newspaper Library was 'half-inched' – this engraving appeared in the *Illustrated Sporting News* two years after the controversial fight.

victory. His wings were extended, and on his crest was a shield with the national stripes of America, horizontal and vertical. The right claw grasped another sprig of the immortal laurel, and the left a flight of arrows. The whole was surrounded by a red and white border, terminating in a deep blue in which shone the stars of the national flag of the Union.

As the build-up to the fight began in earnest, the *Life* inserted a half-page portrait of Heenan in its January 11th issue to complement the one of Sayers it had 'presented gratis' to readers the previous summer. The rush to obtain a copy of that particular number had resulted in the paper being sold out before midday and the demand for the handsome American's portrait was just as great.

Heenan's arrival in England five days later was in keeping with the drama that seemed to accompany him wherever he went. Having survived the attempt on his life in Boston, he had then been arrested for acting as a second at a fight in Buffalo a few weeks before he was due to sail for England. Forced to jump bail, he was smuggled aboard the ss *Asia*, in New York and when his ship docked in Liverpool, he came ashore hidden among the mail bags in order to avoid the large crowd that had gathered on the quay to greet him.

Once in London, he called in at the offices of *Bell's Life* to meet its autocratic, monocled editor, Frank Dowling, who was to referee the fight and who was most disappointed to hear that the American was not prepared to take up any of the lucrative (especially for the paper) pre-fight public sparring sessions that had been laid on for him.

Heenan explained he had come to England expressly to fight Sayers and for no other reason, speculative or otherwise. If defeated, he could not help it, and if he should be fortunate enough to win it would give him the greatest pride.

Unfortunately for the Benicia Boy his desire to keep a low profile was thwarted at every turn. Soon after setting up his training quarters at a farm outside Salisbury his cover was blown and…

> The impertinent annoyance he received from the illiterate, vulgar and obtrusive townspeople was, to him and his friends, a continual source of fretfulness and so disconcerting became this nuisance that it engendered constant fears of magisterial interference.

As with betting, there were certain areas of the country where the police turned a blind eye to the activities of the fistic fraternity, but the Americans decided not to risk arrest in Salisbury and "for the safety of the subject" moved on to Somerset. But here again "prying eyes and busy tongues" were at work and they were informed "it would be unwise to make a long stay for fear of unpleasant interruption and, as needs must … there was a flitting towards Peterborough, and then to Northampton."

Finally, Heenan's coach, Jack Macdonald, settled on Trent Lock, some ten miles from Derby. It had been a popular training camp in the past as it bordered on three counties – Derby, Leicester and Nottingham – and offered a choice of escape routes should the magistrates of one county decide to take action, but on this occasion it turned out to be a no-go area for the visitors.

The authorities were soon informed of Heenan's arrival by "a Janus-like, ninth-part of humanity" called Cook, and the hounded pugilist was arrested on Good Friday, April 6, just ten days before the fight was due to take place. In the dramatic style that the police favour to this day, a detachment from the Derby and Leicestershire constabularies carried out a dawn raid on the Navigation Inn where the Americans were staying.

That morning, the telegraph lines between Derby and London fairly pulsated with the sensational news. The report that appeared in the *Life* stated that the police descended on the inn at 5am and searched the bedrooms where they found Macdonald and his associates, but no Heenan. As the officers returned downstairs…

> a man named Henry Jackson who keeps the lock-house on the Trent bank, came into the house bringing with him a note written in pencil which he handed to the landlord. The police were in plain clothes and Superintendent Shaw said to Jackson, 'Who is it from?' and he replied, 'Heenan'.
>
> The note was as follows: 'I am waiting at the lock-house for my shoes. Macdonald must bring them directly'.
>
> The police at once proceeded to the lock-house which they besieged. The occupant, however, would not admit them upstairs and stoutly denied that Heenan was in the house. It was then agreed that Sergeant Lowndes should go to Mr Sutton, a magistrate living nearby, and get a search warrant…
>
> About ten minutes after he had been dispatched on his errand, Heenan jumped through the bedroom window and made a clear leap over the head of police-constable Hallam. He at once took to his heels and was pursued by the officers. A regular steeplechase ensued, but 'the line of the country' being new to the American and his bare feet being cut by the stones, he was compelled to stop after going over two or three fields. Both he and his friends seemed very mortified at the capture.

A trap was soon in attendance and he was at once conveyed to Derby. On the road he had a little chaff with the police. He then said he had not signed an agreement to fight Sayers and therefore his apprehension was illegal.[*] He also said, 'I have been removed twice. Why don't you take Sayers? I have been hunted about like a dog'.

Heenan, who suffered the indignity of being slung into the town hall lock-up in Derby, was later released on bail of £100 to keep the peace for six months, but with a lot more at stake than the bail money, even the mother of all parliaments was not about to stop the fight from going ahead.

The matter had been raised in the Commons at the end of February when George Hadfield, MP for Sheffield, called the attention of the Home Secretary, Sir George Lewis, to a petition which was probably not so different to the one presented to another Home Secretary (Jack Straw) 140 years later when the convicted rapist, Mike Tyson, was allowed into Britain to besmirch the name of boxing.

On this occasion, however, middle-class puritanism was the only ruling factor as is evident from the *Life's* comments on the proceedings:

Mr Hadfield has mildly permitted himself to be sent on a fool's errand to the House of Commons and has been very properly 'pooh, poohed' and laughed at by the entire legislative assembly. Had the honourable gentleman been endowed with a moderate degree of perception he might have perceived that despite the wordy clamour of certain papers, the present moment is, of all others, the most inappropriate for an attempted interference with the PR.

The forthcoming contest between Heenan and Sayers is regarded throughout England and America as a purely national affair and the particular interest centred in the fight has completely overborne the opinions of persons who profess an antipathy for pugilism. Even newspapers which formerly advertised as one of their specialities 'No reports of prize fights', are turning round and yielding to the popular craving for intelligence of the PR.

The Field, 'the country gentleman's newspaper', violates the etiquette of its pages and supplies 'Childers' graphic narrative of 'An Evening with Heenan' and *The Times*, with that shrewd sagacity which characterises its conduct, carefully collects some scraps of the Benicia Boy's trainings. These facts alone should have convinced Mr Hadfield of the increased hold pugilism is taking upon the public mind, and have reminded him that any attempt to prevent the forthcoming fight was not only uncalled for, but unwarranted by popular opinion...

The manner in which Mr Hadfield's motion was received is creditable to the good sense and discretion of our legislative assembly and, in order that our readers may fully understand the feelings which exist in the Senate relative to the fight for the championship, we re-copy the proceedings of Friday night *in extenso*.

The published transcription included the cries of derision which came from all sides of the House as Hadfield embarked on his 'fool's errand', declaring:

I rise to call attention to the petition of the inhabitants of Sudbrook Park, Petersham and Ham, complaining of a meditated breach of the peace in England by a pugilistic contest between a British subject and an American citizen for the so-called Championship of England ... The petitioners

---

[*] Heenan was telling the literal truth since Falkland had signed the agreement on his behalf.

deprecate the very vicious consequences that would arise from such an exhibition. It appears that both the time and the place of the contest are tolerably well known* (renewed laughter) and the petitioners, therefore, look to the House to take proper measures for the purpose of preventing an exhibition so contrary to the moral and religious sense of the community at large (Cries of 'Pooh, pooh').

To the delight of the chamber, Hadfield continued in this vein for some time before he asked the Home Secretary:

I therefore wish to know whether the public may rely on the right honourable gentleman doing his best to prevent an exhibition so brutal and so demoralising to the rising generation as this contest between the so-called Champion of England and the... (The conclusion of the hon. member's sentence was rendered inaudible by loud cries of 'Pooh, pooh' and laughter; one member crying out, 'Let the mill take place').

In reply, Sir George Lewis informed the not-so-learned Member for Sheffield that Sir Richard Mayne, the commissioner of police...

will probably be able to prevent that encounter taking place within the limits of the metropolitan police district. But beyond that assurance, I am afraid I cannot venture to give any positive promise to my honourable friend, because I have been informed that neither time nor place has been fixed for the proceedings and that it is probable that measures will be taken to defeat the vigilance of the police. It is, of course, impossible to say whether the police would be successful in preventing a sudden incursion into the country and the contest in question. ('Hear, hear' and laughter).

---

* Hadfield had been badly misinformed on this point. The location of all prizefights was kept a closely guarded secret in an effort to foil any attempt that might be made to stop them taking place and the articles of agreement for this fight contained several red herrings designed to mislead the authorities.

FISTICUFFS AT FARNBOROUGH

MONDAY, 16 APRIL 1860, the day fixed for the great battle, passed off without a blow being struck except, perhaps, in the sporting taverns of London which were in a ferment of excitement and confusion as legions of the fancy frantically tried to find out when and where the fight was going to take place.

In an effort to clarify the situation, Harry Feist embarked on a daunting assignment with the same heroic devotion to duty that was to become the hallmark of *Sporting Life* reporters down the ages. With due diligence, the master wordsmith sharpened his pencil, straightened his tie and, notebook in hand, went out on a pub-crawl!

He started off in the West End at the Round Table in St Martin's Close where the American party were staying, but with the exception of a few of Heenan's friends, the place was deserted. Things picked up at the Black Horse, Oxendon Street, one of several designated pubs where tickets could be bought for the fight. Here…

> we discovered the father of Tom Sayers and his brothers James, Charles and John, attended by a son of James whose mug at once indicated that he belonged to a bruising family … chaff was very plentiful and speculation, at one period, very brisk; 2 to 1 was betted freely on the Champion, one gentleman laying 200 to 80.

At the Three Tuns, Moor Street, Soho…

> we were highly pleased with the reception we met and also the company present. Amongst the latter was the well-known Champion of the hardware city, Bob Brettle, having in his possession his splendid and massive silver belt. In the company of Brettle was S Hurst, the 'Stalybridge Infant', and, assuredly, if he does not belie his cognomen no one ever did; he is one of the most powerful-looking young men that we ever encountered.

In the Horseshoe Tavern, Haymarket:

> The first person who attracted our attention on entering was Morrissey,* reclining against a partition in front of the bar puffing, in silent majesty, a 'fragrant weed' … Shortly after nine o'clock Johnny Gideon arrived, all bustle and anxiety, and at once commenced diving in his capacious pockets for Tom's colours, and passed them round with a mild inquiry of 'Won't you take one of our little man?'…
>
> A small detachment of the American party, comprising of Fred Falkland, Jack Macdonald and two or three other Heenanites made their appearance and Jack at once commenced an industrious

---

* John Morrissey, the former American champion, had beaten Heenan in Canada in October 1858. Heenan, having his first officially recognised fight, had the best of the early exchanges, but in the fifth round a left to Morrissey's body missed its target and smashed against an unpadded post. Fighting virtually one-handed from then on, he was finally stopped in the eleventh round. Morrissey declined a return bout and retired from the ring leaving Heenan to claim the title by default. The former champion went on to build up a gambling empire in Saratoga and later went into politics to become a US senator of dubious repute.

circulation of the Benicia Boy's star and stripe banners, a business which apparently throve remarkably well for Mr Falkland continually kept booking the purchasers' names as Macdonald disposed of them.

The American gentlemen who came in with Falkland … took all the 2 to 1 they were offered and at once staked their money in clean, crisp Bank of England notes in the hands of Owen Swift.[*]

From the Horseshoe, Feist moved on to Leicester Square and the Cambrian Stores owned by Nat Langham, the only man to have beaten Sayers when they fought for the middleweight championship in 1853. Then, heading east, he took a cab to the George and Dragon, Harry Brunton's popular watering-hole in the Barbican, and from there it was on to Harry Orme's hostelry where "every available place was crowded, and the good-tempered landlord seemed almost at his wit's end which call to attend to first."

Finally, the intrepid scribbler reached his eighth and final port of call as he fell in through the doors of the King's Arms in Whitechapel where the former heavyweight champion, Jem Ward, was busy denying rumours that the fight had already taken place:

After a time, as hour followed hour, the assembled crowds began to believe that the battle had yet to be fought and … betting again became brisk at 7 to 4 on Sayers. At this price our old friend Jem held a large quantity of the circulating medium and, up to the small hours of the morning, the worthy host was dispensing those good things of this life for which his hostelry has been celebrated.

By this time it was known that the fight would come off that morning; the departure point being London Bridge station. In a special edition of the *Life*, brought out on the evening of the 'Great Fight for the Championship of the World', the following graphic account was given of 'The Journey Down and Incidents of the Fight':

The hour of departure had been generally given out overnight to be not one moment later than a quarter to four, but such was the anxiety of intending excursionists to make their transit secure that as early as half-past two cabs rumbled with rapid succession over London Bridge to the terminus appointed.

The silence of Cannon Street and the Borough was disturbed by the perpetual clank of vehicles and the tramp, tramp of pedestrians wrapped to their eyes in horse-cloths as a protection against the keen morning air, and as they talked in hoarse murmurs of the great event people threw up their window sashes and stared with sleepy eyes on the mysterious beings who were traversing the streets at such an unusual hour.

The solitary policemen on their beats at once understood what was about to take place, but so far from entertaining any hostile intentions more than one 'peeler' called out to the occupants of the cabs, 'Now mind you bring good news home' or 'Good luck to Tom Sayers'.

On arriving at London Bridge station at three o'clock, we found the yard thronged with Hansoms from which young swells were alighting, while a crowd of idlers waited in a dense, dark group round the entrance, in expectation of catching a glimpse of the belligerents.

---

[*] Many sporting taverns were run by former prizefighters who made sure the local constabulary was well rewarded for turning a blind eye to the betting that was openly carried on in defiance of the law.

Tom Sayers's departure from Newmarket had to be conducted with the greatest caution, and for the purpose of disarming suspicion he was sent to London on Sunday by the half-past four o'clock train in a horse van, his friends having the precaution to disguise him in a heavy theatrical beard and mustachios … Thus protected and placed under the vigilance of two celebrated jockeys, the English Champion took up his quarters unmolested … Heenan's backers had to exercise the greatest care and he was kept in the utmost secrecy until the hour for the journey to the mill had arrived.

The tickets which were issued for the journey at £3 [£270] each, were not given out until late on the previous evening when the rush upon them was immense, but they were merely the ordinary railway tickets, with no place mentioned, and those, therefore, who were boiling over to learn the whereabouts of the encounter were left unsatisfied … Shortly after three o'clock a policeman opened the doors to the public and from that moment up to the hour of starting the first cargo of twenty six carriages drawn by two engines, soon reached completion…*

At a quarter to four, Tom Sayers, accompanied by his friends, made his appearance on the platform and all heads were immediately thrust out of the carriage windows to peep at the little man. He was dressed in a light Inverness wrapper, and proceeded to his carriage with a jaunty, good-humoured air betokening the greatest confidence.

Shortly afterwards, Heenan's majestic figure stalked along the platform, the morning duskiness giving a more stately appearance to the hero who had taken the precaution to adorn his face with dark bushy beard and whiskers to prevent any annoying identification.

Jack Macdonald introduced Tom at the carriage door to the 'Benicia Boy' and the fistic heroes shook hands for the first time in their lives, Heenan remarking with generous good feeling, 'How are you Sayers, are you well? I sure hope you are,' and after an affirmative from Tom, the contestants took their seats … The engines drew their heavy burden from the station at precisely twenty-five minutes past four o'clock. None, beyond the driver, stoker and managers knew the precise destination of the train, and many were the opinions uttered *en route* as to the probable spot…

The train took the Brighton line and nothing of note occurred until reaching the downs of Smitham Bottom, about two miles beyond Croydon, where in every field policemen were stationed along the line, and in the roads mounted patrols were seen galloping about wildly and evidently without any distinct ideas or purposes whatever. This step was probably adopted in conformity with the promise of the Home Secretary to the House of Commons that Sir Richard Mayne would prevent the fight coming off within the limits of the metropolitan districts.

For even a farther distance, however, the police showed in some force and stood on the embankments with their hands on stout cudgels or cutlasses, ready for any valorous onslaught on the followers of the PR. They had little cause for their displays, as circumstances afterwards proved, for a distance far more remote had been chosen…

On approaching Farnborough, about two miles from the camp at Aldershot, the train was stopped and it was almost immediately known that the spot for the mill had been reached and in a few moments the freight of the 'special' were clambering over fences and treading in ankle deep mud, following their leader in the shape of the possessors of the ropes and stakes…

The meadow chosen was about three hundred yards long and crossed by railway within half that

---

* Two monster trains were laid on by the South Eastern Railway even though the company had previously given assurances to the police authorities that it would stop providing transport to prizefights. It also seems strange that a policeman should facilitate the departure of spectators to an outlawed sport, but it was not until 1868, in a final clampdown on the PR, that an Act was passed which rendered railway companies liable to prosecution for running excursions to prizefights.

distance of the roped arena. The spot was very prettily situated and the various trees by which it was surrounded were at once stormed by men and boys, who were thereby enabled to obtain a perfect view of the battle ... The ring was formed of more than one thousand persons, all well-dressed and the majority comprising some of the chief members of the aristocracy and gentry, and persons famed and honoured not only in the sporting world, but in the most elevated and refined society...

Sayers was the first to show in the ring and he was received with enthusiastic cheering, and on the Benicia Boy's coming within the ropes he was also tumultuously applauded by his partisans ... The vast disparity in size and weight became apparent immediately upon the belligerents stripping to the buff. The colossal height of the American towered over the comparatively diminutive form of our English Achilles.

There was youth, size and length of reach, coupled with a gay look of determination to do or die nobly in the eyes of the British public; and when the important accessory of tremendous muscular power was taken into consideration, it was at once seen that the Englishman had a most formidable antagonist to cope with...

Harry Brunton, his old particular pal, seconded Tom Sayers in his usual, customary cool manner and was ably assisted by Jemmy Welsh, the host of the Griffin, Church Street, Borough. Heenan received all due attention from his trainer, Jack Macdonald, and Cusick, who once fought Sayers to a draw some twelve years back.

By now the *Life* had devoted 14 of its 24 columns to recording the careers of the champions and the events leading up to the fight, while its ringside report took up a further two columns and was couched in the colourful prose that had been popularised by Pierce Egan, 'the Herodotus of the London Prize Ring', half a century earlier.

Egan's style had been embellished by Henry Downes Miles, the foremost PR reporter of the day who had been especially commissioned by Feist to cover the fight for the *Life*. In his reports Miles employed an ingenious use of metaphors to prevent the constant repetition of a fighter's features. Teeth became ivories, nutcrackers and masticators; the eye was an ogle, squinter, peeper, optic, etc, while blood was turned into wine ranging from claret through to the *premier cru*.

The two fighters came up to scratch at 7.22am and the following is an abridged version of Miles' round-by-round commentary:

Round 1 – A good deal of sparring until Sayers made a lead which proved effective as he got well home with a straight hit from the shoulder on the nasal promontory and as Heenan drew the fluid up his early-troubled nostrils, 'first blood' was declared for Sayers. Heenan was evidently a little 'riled' for as Tom danced agilely around him he could invent nothing beneficial to his interests.

R2 – Heenan stopped Sayers' left prettily twice in succession. He then furnished Tom with a left-handed smack on the dial and delivered his right, almost at the same moment, to the throat. They then got to infighting and the struggle terminated in the 'illustrious foreigner' obtaining the best of the cast.

R3 – Heenan came down with good interest upon Sayers, for he struck him on the forehead, raising a neat little protuberance; the blow floored Tom like a shot from a gun.

R4 – The sun was right in Tom's daylights and considerably dazzled the clearness of his vision; he seemed unaware of it until too late for the transatlantic boy broke desperately through his guard

Tom Sayers and Jack Heenan come up to scratch to fight for the Championship of the World at Farnborough, 17 April 1860.

by one of those fearful lunges with his right and sent Sayers to mother earth again.

R5 – Heenan all alive and quite reckoning by his jaunty air that the cards were in his own hands and only wanted the due deliveries. Sayers was shifty and it was some time before his cautious manoeuvring would allow him to come at all within range; when he did, he was once more chopped down with a terrific one from Heenan's busy left hand.

R6 – Sayers began to pull himself together and, assuming a more serious air, he let go with his right mawley and slit the cheek of Benicia's child very nastily underneath the right optic causing a strong ripple of the crimson. After some ding-dong exchanges, Sayers slipped up and so the round terminated.

R7 – Heenan opened the ball readily with his left and made Tom's ivories rattle again and coloured them with Chateau Margaux. The Londoner retaliated most forcibly by dashing one in with his left on the old sore underneath the right squinter; more of the ruby. It was clear the Englishman had just begun to find out he could get his man, despite his long range and distance. Again Sayers assumed the offensive and planted his left on the snorter which sent out a full supply of the carmine as Tom jumped back and danced right away out of reach of retaliation amidst the most tremendous cheering of the strong coterie in his corner. In the close, both were down.

R8 – Sayers renewed the contest with an eager look of mischief in his eye and put in another stinger under Heenan's left peeper from which the fluid oozed again in profusion and light in that region of the States was evidently on the wane. The Boy seemed now in a very tired condition, but kept to his work undauntedly.

R9 – Tom, seeing Heenan ill-disposed to stir from his corner, pointed to the scratch. Sayers planted his left on the knowledge-box; the blow was an awful stab and it resounded all over the ring. The betting was now 4-1 on Sayers and no takers. Heenan rallied and shot out a heavy clinker on the snout which laid the tap on copiously. They countered finely, each drawing blood from the masticators.

Rather an unusual proceeding; both men stopped in their essays and were sponged without being taken to their corner. The continual effects of stopping the heavy blows of Heenan's left began to tell its own sad tale on Tom's right forearm and it was distinctly clear from the fast swelling appearance of 'the auctioneer' that he could not make any use of that invaluable 'bunch of fives'. Heenan finished this round by knocking our champion completely off his legs. They had now fought 51 minutes.

Following this gruelling 22-minute round, the next eleven were short and sweet though not for Sayers. In the 17 minutes they took to complete Heenan: "flung his man forward by dint of Herculean strength" (R11); "broke through his guard with a hot 'un right on the sniveller and floored Tom beautifully" (R14); "knocked the Englishman down again by one of his terrible left-handed plunges" (R18); "took Tom up in his arms and threw him to the ground, making it again resound, and fell heavily on him" (R20).

Sayers appeared to be taking a hammering, but he kept bouncing back and in round 26, "Tom dashed in his left and landed it slick on the canister causing a most copious flow of the claret. The Boy's head began to shake like an Aspen leaf after this disagreeable visit."

In the 27th it was noted: "Heenan's spectacle-bearer, lips and right ogle indicated that Tom had been busily at work there; the two former were greatly out of shape and the latter quite bunged up," but the American still had plenty of fight left in him.

In the 28th: "Tom, finding it very hot, ran round the ring behind the Boy, but this time he was not so fortunate as the Yankee planted on his face, ding-dong, and Tom went down." And in the 29th: "Heenan sent out his left like a flash of greased lightning and landed it on the forehead, and Tom was grassed." More of the same followed:

R32 – Tom got heavily on the proboscis and nut crackers, making the latter rattle a little. For this visit the Boy was determined to have his revenge and he lunged out his terrible left and caught Tom a stinger on the sneezer; Tom went down like shot.

R33 – Tom tried to get again on the damaged peeper, but the American neatly put the stopper on and the blow was harmless; good counters followed, Tom's left doing terrific execution with the Boy's frontispiece and cutting a deep gash under the snout. Heenan then put on the double and, drawing Tom into the meshes, at once planted his left again on the nob, and Tom was floored like a ninepin.

Two rounds later the drama increased when the Surrey police arrived on the scene, "but at once a cry was raised to block the passage and this was no sooner said than done and the 'blues' had to content themselves by being passive, if not willing, lookers-on." At this point "Heenan's face presented a hideous spectacle, his right eye quite closed and the side of the temple graced with a bump as large as a cricket ball."

The betting was now 3-1 on Sayers with no takers. Three more brief rounds followed before the fight reached its sensational climax:

R39 – When Heenan came up, the Champion caught him heavily on the snuffbox with the left and in getting away dropped his head. In an instant Heenan had got Tom's head under his left arm with one of the most fearful hugs – in fact, squeezing him like a vice. It was for some time feared that poor Tom would meet an inglorious and ignoble *coup de grâce* as he could not extricate himself, and loud and long were the groans and hisses uttered by all round the ring at the unfair treatment which many imagined Heenan was practising on the undaunted and game Sayers.

After the conclusion of this round, the referee, by some means, in the noise and uproar that ensued, was borne out of the ring and a scene of confusion ensued which we shall not attempt to describe. We will merely detail, as full as we are able, the next four rounds which were fought without referee and almost without a ring.

On coming up for the fortieth round Tom, who appeared almost without any life in him from the fearful effects of the dreadful hug, appeared anxious to make a waiting race of it, but the Boy forced the fighting and Tom was sent down by Heenan's left.

Round 41 was almost a counterpart of the 39th as Tom, in trying to avoid Heenan's left, again gave the American the opening for the hug terrific, and for a second time Tom's head was in fearful jeopardy, and had it not been for the kindly assistance of one of his friends, it might have been attended with the most painful result. As it was, when extricated, his appearance betrayed the fearful reality of what he must have suffered during the time his antagonist had him in the vice.

Ere the men came up for the next round, a great deal of angry feeling was manifested by the American party on account of the seconds of Sayers declining to go on without a referee and, on the Boy coming up, he put himself in front of Tom and let into him right and left, and not content with using his fists, raised his foot and gave Jemmy Welsh a bit of shoe-leather, and followed it by knocking Tom off his second's knee.*

After this the referee again made his appearance in the ring and at once gave directions to the backers and the seconds of both men to take them away and not think of prolonging the fight. At this juncture the police forced a passage and the ropes and the stakes were at once taken up. The fight occupied two hours, three minutes up to the time when the referee left the ring and two hours and a quarter up to the moment when the men left.

The chaos that accompanied the final rounds can only be imagined as the 22 ring-keepers – including Ned Adams who was "drunk as usual" – lashed out with their whips in an effort to repel the incensed and panicking crowd that was falling back in front of the ranks of advancing police. In the confusion, one of the partisan ring-keepers, former prizefighters themselves, took advantage of the situation to cut the ropes and lead the charge to rescue Sayers from what looked like certain strangulation.

While the *Life* deplored the ring invasion, it avoided apportioning any blame and instead described the contest as "one of the finest ever fought". It was certainly one of the most remarkable.

* Prizefighters had two men to act as their seconds; a 'bottle-man' to supply the inter-round refreshment, and a 'knee-man' who went down on one knee at the end of each round to present the thigh of his other leg, which was crocked at right angles, as a seat for the fighter.

Sayers was knocked clean off his feet at least 14 times by Heenan's stunning blows yet, until he was caught in the 'hug terrific', he appeared the likely winner despite being handicapped for much of the fight by the injury to his right arm – his famed 'auctioneer', which had to be supported in a sling for several weeks after the fight.

After such a dramatic conclusion to such an eagerly awaited contest, the arguments that followed it were both loud and prolonged. It took a month of meetings and negotiations between the two camps before a settlement was reached during which time both *Bell's Life* and the *Sporting Life* milked the controversy for all it was worth as they filled their columns with letters sent in by the rival factions and the public.

The popular view favoured a re-match, while others maintained the fight should be declared a draw and the boxers presented with a belt apiece. The appropriately named *Punch* magazine, with tongue firmly in cheek, proposed a Solomon-like solution by which the championship belt would be cut in two with each fighter taking a half!

Further fuel was added to the debate when the American papers arrived in England a month after the fight.* On May 16 the *Life* reported:

> The New York papers received yesterday are full of the fight for the Championship and, as usual, a wild spirit of boasting is indulged in, characteristic of the Yankee character. The *New York Herald* calls it, 'The settled overthrow of the British Lion' and goes on to say: 'It must be distressing to the solid islanders that the British Lion has been whipped. Worse than all, he has tried to sneak out of it in the most ignominious manner.
>
> 'The Britons, whose love of fair play is universal, stopped the fight in order to save their money. The American eagle has a right to scream like half a dozen locomotives. The poor old Lion, the bully who has been roaming up and down the earth for so many years roaring at everybody, may go away in some secluded corner and suck his bruised paws, while all Continental Europe laughs at him and is glad that the United States has done it'.

Owned and edited by the Scots-born Anglophobe James Gordon Bennett, the *Herald* could be relied upon to vilify the bullying Brits at every opportunity but, curiously, the *Life* found "among all the distortions of truth one American newspaper sanctioning a fair and impartial narrative by an American who was present at the fight."

The 'American' was actually the Epsom-born Harry Hill who had emigrated to New York in his early 20s to become a leading sports entrepreneur, and his account appeared in the same edition of the *Herald* that had poured scorn on 'the British Lion'. Hill gave his 'impartial narrative' at a press conference held at his famed Exchange saloon on the corner of Broadway and East Houston Street, Lower Manhattan, from where "it was said you could fire a shotgun in any direction without hitting an honest man."[1] After giving a detailed description of the fight, Hill took questions from the floor:

> Q. How did Heenan take his licking? – A. Like a man. I think he'd have stopped in that ring till he died. He took every blow in first-rate humour and as long as his mug could show a smile, it had a

---

* The Transatlantic telegraph cable was not successfully laid until 1866 and therefore it took 10 to 12 days for news of the fight to reach the States and then, of course, a similar time before the reactions of 'the Yankees' became known in Britain.

smile upon it. He tried to laugh two or three times after Sayers had cut him back; but 'pon my soul, his face was so out of shape you couldn't tell whether he was laughing or crying.

How was it about Sayers? – Why, the more knock downs he got the better he seemed to fight. It didn't appear to produce much effect on him, for he'd fall with the blow, and when he was down would kick his legs up in a saucy way, as if it was all sport – damnedest sort of fun I ever did see.

What kind of blows does Sayers strike? – Like a streak of lightning. You could hardly see it but you could hear a 'thud' and the first you knew blood would be streaming out of some gash he made on Heenan's mug. He spars beautifully and so does Heenan, but I think Sayers is ahead.

Did the Benicia Boy show much science? – First-rate, but I don't believe he has the judgement of Sayers; though in time I think he'll make the smartest fighter in the world.

How did they act round the ring? – Damned shamefully. Good many of the Englishmen seemed to doubt Heenan's pluck and every time that Sayers got a little the upper hand, they'd sing out 'Ere's another sure fing, ain't it, ho, ho, ho; take 'im away' and suchlike expressions, blackguarding Heenan and his friends in the worst style.

Do you suppose the referee is a prejudiced man? – No, I don't. I think he behaved fair all through and his reputation is above any suspicion of unfairness.

How do you think the fight will be decided? – As a draw, of course. You can't get around it. The referee was crowded out of the ring by those in it in the latter part, and I don't believe he will make any other decision than that it is a drawn fight.

Well, candidly Harry, who do you think is the best man? – I don't believe there's a man in the world can tell, but I believe if the fight had been kept up ten minutes longer one or other would have been whipped. They were both worse off than I ever want to be. They were game all the way through and no man can grumble for losing his money on his favourite.

Eventually, on May 18, the two fighters and their backers met in Frank Dowling's office and the following day, under the headlines 'Final Arrangement / Heenan And Sayers Agree To Fight No More', the *Life* reported it had been decided that…

two belts of equal value should be manufactured for them, and that the old belt should be left in the referee's hands to be contested for in the usual way. When this had been distinctly settled the men shook hands in the most hearty manner and, on quitting the referee's office, repaired to Jem Parish's tavern at the corner of Newcastle Street, Strand, where they consolidated their friendship over sundry bottles of wine … As our readers are aware Heenan will have to hold the trophy against all comers for a period of three years … returning to fight in this country when called upon. Tom Sayers will, however, fight no more, but retire at once from the pugilistic profession.

The new belts, made by C F Hancock of Berkeley Square, were copies of the original designed five years earlier and were of frosted silver, three inches wide and decorated with prize ring motifs and the royal coat of arms. Bearing the inscription 'Champion of England', they were presented by Frank Dowling and George Wilkes amid much pomp and ceremony at the Alhambra Palace where the long, florid presentation speeches were counterbalanced by two of the shortest votes of thanks ever made at the famous Leicester Square theatre.

Heenan, with a polite bow to the audience, declared: "My lords, ladies and gentlemen, I am not much of a speaker, but I can assure you that this is one of the proudest moments of my life and I thank you all most kindly and sincerely." The taciturn Sayers was almost curt as he mumbled a barely audible: "Ladies and gentlemen, I can say with my friend, who has just sat down, that I thank you all."

And so ended the extraordinary saga of the first recognised contest for the heavyweight championship of the world. Heenan was to spend most of the next five years in England while civil war tore his country apart. For some of the time he operated as a racecourse bookmaker, but in December 1863, with Jack Macdonald and an ailing Sayers acting as his seconds, he returned to the ring to fight Tom King for the championship.

King, a London docker, was a match for Heenan in both height (6ft 2in) and weight, 182lb (13st) and had won the championship by beating Sam Hurst, 'the Stalybridge Infant', in 1861. After losing his title to Jem Mace the following year, he regained it in a return bout ten months later and, in what was to be his final fight, he retained it by beating a ring-rusty Heenan who succumbed to a succession of body blows in the 24th round after 35 minutes of short, mauling exchanges.

In a final twist of fate, it has to be recorded that neither Heenan nor Sayers lived to see forty. Both men received some £3,000 (£270,000) in public subscriptions after their fight. Sayers invested his money in a circus and toured the country giving exhibition bouts and, quite literally on occasions, acting the clown, but as a business venture it was a failure and he turned to the bottle. He was 39 when he died from a combination of alcohol-induced diabetes and consumption at his home in Camden Town, north London on 8 November 1865. His funeral cortege stretched for three-quarters of a mile as it wound its way through a "course, brutal and blasphemous mob"[2] to the Victorian Valhalla of Highgate Cemetery where a large memorial was subsequently erected to his memory.

Following the death of his old sparring partner and the end of the American Civil War, Heenan returned to New York in December 1865. He was still nursing the injuries he had received in a train crash when returning from Ascot races in 1864, but he continued to live life to the full and it was not long before he dissipated his fortune. By 1873 consumption also had him in its icy grasp. In an attempt to stave off the disease, he journeyed west to seek out drier climes, but he had no defence against the rampant 'fell destroyer' and died at Green River, Wyoming, on October 28 that year. He was just 38.

In paying tribute to Heenan, Harry Feist, who, in his capacity as a fight referee, was well qualified to give an opinion, wrote:

> I was present at that memorable fight between him and Sayers and sat on the grass precisely where the final melee occurred. I have always entertained the opinion that from a strict point of view Heenan won. He was doing nothing illegal and Sayers was helpless and insensible. Had the referee remained at his post instead of quitting it just previously, he must have ordered Heenan to release Sayers on the score of humanity, and proclaimed the American the winner.

COMPETITION

BECAUSE the *Life* was launched two or three decades before football began to attract the sort of following that would add significantly to its readership, it relied on the prize ring to help it through the lean times when the frost was deep in the ground and an already sparse steeplechasing programme was further reduced by abandonments.

The immense boost title fights gave to its sales was illustrated by a front-page announcement headed 'Circulation of The Sporting Life' which appeared a few weeks after the Sayers-Heenan rumble:

> In speaking of the recent fight for the Championship, the *Illustrated Times* remarks, 'Not only did the subject almost entirely engross conversation, but the interest it attained added enormously to the sale of those journals which gave ample and exclusive particulars. Thus, the sale of the special edition of *Bell's Life* reached ninety thousand copies, while of *The Sporting Life*, a recently established penny paper, 360,000 copies were sold'.*

The penny paper underlined its triumph by making a small, upward adjustment to what was already a truly remarkable figure. Adding a graphic pointer for emphasis, it trumpeted in resounding block capitals:

☞ "THREE HUNDRED AND SIXTY-SEVEN THOUSAND COPIES WERE SOLD."

For its big print runs the *Life* relied heavily on the stereotyping process employed by the Dellagana printing company in nearby Shoe Lane, and three years later, sales soared to even greater heights as the imagination of the nation was again captured by the Heenan v King fight. Even the royal family became caught up in the excitement and the Electric Telegraph Company received "an express order to communicate the result immediately it was known, direct to Windsor Castle."

When it was all over, sales for the week ending 12 December 1863 topped the half-million mark and the paper was able to announce with justifiable pride:

> This unprecedented number was made up as follows: Wednesday, December 9 – 74,898; Friday, December 11 (Special) – 361,000; Saturday, December 12 – 114,980. Total – 550,878.

The massive demand for these special editions sparked a boom in sporting journals and by the end of the century approximately 130 new titles had been registered in England as all and sundry attempted to jump on the bandwagon Harry Feist had set rolling.[1] Some publications emerged into the light only to flutter and die with their first number, while many failed to survive for more than a year, but a few prospered and grew to become serious rivals to the *Life*.

The first of these was the *Sporting Gazette* which entered the arena on 1 November 1862. In contrast to many of the papers that were launched on a shoestring budget, the *Gazette* enjoyed the financial backing of "an association of noblemen and gentlemen who rank among the most

---

* The presses were kept running around the clock to meet the demand and police had to be called in to control the crowds that besieged the *Life*'s offices as they clamoured for the paper.

distinguished patrons of the Turf, the Chase and the Leash." Their number included several Jockey Club members among whom the Duke of Beaufort, Lord Coventry and Lord Winchilsea were occasional contributors to its columns.

In his introductory address, the paper's founding editor, Bill Langley, pledged that the 16-page, three-quarter sized, Saturday broadsheet would be conducted on independent principles, free from bias and with 'fair play' as its motto:

> We do not assume to be considered as the organ or champion of any class – all we ask is a 'fair start', no 'jostling' and to be judged on our merits alone; and from the many exclusive sources of information open to us but inaccessible to others, we throw ourselves upon the public with every confidence to merit their patronage and support.

The *Life*, feeling it had nothing to fear from a weekly journal that was to sell for 3d (£1.12), even carried its new rival's launch advert, but it was not so accommodating three years later when, on 12 August 1865, *The Sportsman* went on sale for just one penny. In a rare example of concord with *Bell's Life*, the team at 148 Fleet Street refused to give any publicity to the new bi-weekly which came out fighting as it declared:

> We can promise our friendly rivals as well as the two leading sporting publications which (*credite posteri*!) showed their nervous anxiety by *declining our advertisement*, that we don't intend to be 'chopped' at the start … Our creed in sport is catholic; our position independent; and our resources as large as enterprise and research can make them … A few short weeks will develop our powers and the reason we have for the faith that is in us. What we are and what we are worth will be soon known and we are content to be judged accordingly.

The proprietors of the *Sportsman* were the bookmakers, James and Sydney Smith, who were not related but had joined forces as racing confederates some ten years earlier after the former had made a killing in the betting ring.

A Manchester printer by trade, James Smith entered racing in his early 20s when he started to place bets for William Moseley, who owned the prolific winners, Bourton and Alonzo. In 1854, Smith worked the commissions for both horses when they won the Grand National and the Nottingham and Doncaster Spring Handicaps in addition to four other races all within a month, and the money he made from these carefully executed coups enabled him embark on one of the most successful Turf partnerships of the century.

As bookmakers, the Smiths were responsible for revolutionising their profession when they introduced the practice of SP (starting price) betting – as opposed to list prices – in 1864, and as racehorse owners they landed some massive gambles in major handicaps through James Smith's shrewd management of their horses.

It was little wonder the *Sporting Life* and *Bell's Life* viewed the Smiths' venture into Fleet Street with some concern and their fears were well founded because the *Sportsman* was destined to outstrip its London contemporaries in almost every department – for a time, at least. Arguably, the only paper it failed to better in its heyday was the *Sporting Chronicle* which appeared in 1871.

This northern broadsheet was edited and part-owned by Edward Hulton who, while working as a printer on the *Manchester Guardian* in the late 1860s, published a local tipping sheet, the *Sporting*

Bell, in which he wrote under the signature of 'Kettledrum' – the 1861 Derby winner. The *Bell* was similar to any number of midday racing tissues that proliferated in the big industrial towns of the midlands and the north. Printed on one side of a single sheet, it carried the latest news from the courses, the selections of the leading morning papers and up-to-date betting odds from the principal clubs.

Hulton obviously knew the time of day since "his success as a racing prophet was something phenomenal; 'Kettledrum's selections' ... attained a celebrity so widespread and genuine that he was induced to start a paper of his own."[2] This came about in February 1871 when Edward Bleackley, a local cotton merchant, gave Hulton the financial backing he needed to bring out the *Prophetic Bell*.

Initially published in a Spear Street basement in the centre of Manchester, the paper enjoyed a similar reception to that which had greeted the *Sporting Life* on its launch 12 years earlier. With Hulton's journalistic flair and inspired tipping, its sales soared as the successes of Kettledrum's selections were regularly advertised in the *Guardian*.

That autumn the *Prophetic Bell* transformed itself into the *Sporting Chronicle* after it had received an unexpected boost when the *Guardian*, together with Manchester's other two dailies, the *Courier* and the *Times*, banished all tipping adverts from its columns and restricted its racing coverage to the basic service it received from the Press Association.

This act of appeasement to the growing middle-class opposition to racing cost the *Guardian's* Turf correspondent, 'Rataplan', his job,* but proved a boon to the infant *Chronicle* which became the first sporting paper to appear on a daily basis, albeit an irregular one, as it was published from Tuesday to Friday, and "also on Monday and Saturday when racing occurs".†

Within three years it had expanded into an eight-page paper and moved to Withy Grove as Bleackley's annual share of the profits soared to £30,000 (£2.7m), while Hulton used his cut to build up the most prosperous newspaper group in the kingdom.

In addition to the *Sporting Chronicle* and the *Sportsman*, a journal of an altogether different hue made its appearance during this period in the form of the *Sporting Times* although, initially, it was not produced on the coloured newsprint which resulted in it becoming famously and affectionately known as the 'Pink 'Un'. Priced at 2d, the eight-page weekly was the brainchild of Dr Joseph Shorthouse, an outspoken and eccentric Carshalton (Surrey) practitioner who had a passion for bloodstock breeding and a violent aversion to what he called "the damnable poison of the accursed Blacklock blood".

His quarto-sized journal first appeared on Saturday, 11 February 1865. Describing itself as "A Chronicle of Racing, Literature, Art and the Drama", it was nothing if not original as was immediately apparent from its motto which proclaimed "High Toryism, High Churchism, High Farming and Old Port for ever!"

---

* The conciliatory gesture proved so costly to the papers concerned in terms of lost circulation and advertising revenue that it was not long before full racing coverage was restored in both the *Courier* and the *Times*, but the *Guardian* doggedly refused to publish racing selections for almost a century. It only resumed in 1967 when Richard Baerlein became its racing correspondent and even then it did not publish racecards or results, while the excellent Baerlein was restricted to giving just two tips a day.

† Traditionally, Saturdays were set aside for walking horses home from race meetings and Mondays were kept free for settling accounts at Tattersalls. Even after horses began to be transported by rail in the 1840s, Saturday racing was rare and remained so until the 1870s when Monday meetings also started to appear in the fixture list as the importance of betting at Tattersalls declined with the increase in SP betting.

In an inaugural address, which took up the entire front page and ran over onto page 2, Shorthouse announced that his paper would be a non-profit making concern and that most of its contributors would be unpaid or writing '*con amore*', as he put it.

For its first two numbers the *Sporting Times* carried the ambiguous line 'Published at Intervals' on its front page which, as its radical proprietor-cum-editor explained:

> …does not necessarily imply that the paper will not appear weekly for the present, but in the winter months, when there is little to chronicle, instead of filling its pages with copious quotations from trashy novels and travels, we may only publish it at intervals of a fortnight or a month. Nothing is decided yet.

In fact, the ink was hardly dry on this declaration before 'at intervals' was replaced by 'weekly', but in other respects the paper continued to be unconventional as was shown in a preface Shorthouse wrote to the short-lived training reports that were sent in from Ilsley, Malton, Middleham and Newmarket:

> We have had to condense and recast these reports. Our correspondents are so verbose and twaddling about the weather and 'horses exercising on their straw beds' that we are tired, as we should think our readers will be, of reading such rubbish.

The doctor's innovations included an entertaining 'Our Dust Bin' column that carried the appendage 'N.B. Rubbish will be shot here', and so it was as examples of "Flunkeyism, Toadyism and Turf-hunting sycophancy" in rival papers were mercilessly debunked. The *Sporting Gazette*, backed, as it was, by the Establishment, was a regular target, while the *Sporting Life* did not escape occasional, well-deserved ridicule.

Another feature, 'The Tips of the Tipsters', ruthlessly exposed the shortcomings of the opposition. Harry Feist did not fare too well in this respect since he was not only giving selections as 'Augur', but had taken over as 'Hotspur' on the *Daily Telegraph* following the death of his brother, Albert, in 1862, and had also started to write for the *Newcastle Chronicle* as 'Underhand'.

The new paper had the good fortune to get off to a flying start in this department when its chief correspondent, Gilbert Robins, a London solicitor who wrote under the signature of 'The Outsider', tipped Gladiateur (at 100-7) to win the Two Thousand Guineas. When the French colt duly obliged at 7-1, Shorthouse gleefully pointed out that Augur had dismissed the horse with the line "Gladiateur had better be left alone" in his summing up of the race.

Feist continually left himself open to the barbs of Shorthouse's journal since he was notoriously fickle in assessing the prospects of a horse in a big race and, in an attempt to cover every eventuality, he would often extol its chances one week and decry it the next as so famously happened in the run-up to the 1872 Grand National. In airing his thoughts on the race at the end of January, he had remarked:

> Casse Tête is a wonderfully fine stayer and has no more than 10st to carry. With this light burden it will not surprise me to see her carry Mr Brayley's colours into the first three as she is certain to keep going from end to end when many of her antagonists will be pumped out.

But a week later, when reporting on the latest betting moves, Feist allowed a colourful turn of phrase to betray him as he observed:

Mr Brayley took 2,000 to 100 about his couple, Silvermere and Casse Tête … but personally I would not take £1,000 to a kippered herring about any of 'Teddy's lot'. Casse Tête is sure to gallop the distance and it would not surprise me to see her in the first flight; but if she wins I publicly undertake to eat her with as little ceremony as needs be demanded.

Of course, after such a remark, the little mare, who had failed to complete the course in her two previous National attempts, jumped like a stag and outstayed her 24 rivals to romp home by six lengths at 20-1. Shorthouse revelled in his rival's discomfort and reproduced Augur's rash boast under the headline 'A Daniel Come To Judgement'. For good measure he also celebrated the *faux pas* in verse, which began:

'Bring up the horse' – the horse was brought: / In truth it was a noble dish / As ever followed soup or fish, / Not so, the hapless prophet thought … The tail looked ghastly, grim and bare / Singed of its flowing wealth of hair / The neck was roasted to a cinder / And coat was calcined into tinder / Its stuffing was a quarter sheet / The dish was garnished round with feet...

Harry Feist found it easier to eat his words. He was a good friend of Teddy Brayley, a theatrical impresario and major owner who won some £26,000 (£2.34m) on the race. In his Aintree round-up he commented: "the news of Mr Brayley's success was received in dramatic circles with the liveliest satisfaction and at the next winter banquet at which that gentleman entertains his friends at the Albion in Drury Lane, a special dish – *filet de Casse Tête* – is to be provided for your correspondent."

To help the humbled editor accomplish his task, Brayley sent Feist a huge knife and fork which he had especially manufactured for the occasion. To give Feist his due, he took the ribbing in good humour and put the implements on display in the *Life's* front window together with the three-word message that had accompanied them.

"*Bon appetite*, Augur!"

AN EXODUS OF BOOKMAKERS

WHILE Harry Feist was able to extricate himself from his Casse Tête gaffe in some style, the *Sporting Times* proved to be a thorn in his side in other ways. In particular, it was not slow to expose the *Life's* hypocritical stance over the advertisements it accepted from swindling tipsters and bogus bookmakers. Shorthouse, to his credit, adopted a refreshingly honest approach in dealing with such fraudsters:

> We allow no one to advertise in this paper unless we know them to be responsible men and therefore have no occasion to 'warn' our readers that we are 'not responsible for the shortcomings of persons advertising in our columns'. If there is a doubt about them or they are unknown to us, we equally decline to insert their announcements.[1]

The *Life*, to its shame, pursued a *caveat emptor* policy as it raked in money from patently crooked advertisers, while it claimed "the advertising sheets of our contemporaries are completely studded with 'muff-trap' announcements which we have banished from our columns," conveniently ignoring the fact that it had been willing to accept them in the first place.

In the '*Times*', Gilbert Robins responded dryly: "If this 'sensation rag', as *Bell's Life* aptly called it once in its spleen, would apply the broom a little more to its own columns and a little less to those of its contemporaries, it would do well."

During 1865, Henry Dixon wrote no fewer than four leaders on the subject and whatever his opinion was on the paper's policy of accepting 'muff-trap' adverts he had little sympathy for the greedy and the gullible who fell prey to them. In contrast to Feist, who enjoyed investing a few sovereigns on the nags and was famously liberal with his money, he had little interest in betting and was, by necessity, habitually thrifty. It was no surprise, therefore, that he did not feel compromised when it came to criticising those who lost their money to…

> the herd of reckless fellows who advertise that they are in the possession of 'certainties' and who endeavour to trap their thirteen-stamp customers by a system of wilful deception and impudent falsehood.
>
> Some of this class flourish vigorously in the advertising columns of the provincial journals and, merely to show the length to which they will proceed, we may state that one individual, who hails from Staffordshire, offers to forfeit £1,000 'if I do not send the absolute winners of the Liverpool Chase, Northamptonshire Stakes and Chester Cup'.
>
> This is a very modest offer and we think that besides the great handicaps, the advertiser might have thrown in the 'absolute winners' of the Two Thousand, Derby, Oaks and St Leger! Surely such transparent dodges must defeat their own ends, and if anyone be caught in such an ill-disguised snare, our verdict must be 'serve him right'.

These observations were remarkably cynical on a day when the *Life* carried such adverts as:

Youatt William Gray has sent the winner of the Nottingham Handicap at 15 to 1 – as certain as

Tourist, his selection last year. No change in the Northamptonshire Stakes; the one sent at 50 to 1 will win with a stone in hand. His selection for Liverpool Steeple Chase, sent at 50 to 1, has almost advanced to the front rank and another commission goes on next week. Winning, bar accident, is a certainty.

Gray's terms were not quite as extravagant as his claims as he charged the usual tipster's fee of 13 penny stamps (£4) for a week's selections.

In another leader at the end of the season, Dixon addressed the problem of bogus bookmakers who had advertised in the paper:

We have at this moment a heap of letters on our table complaining that the writers cannot get several fraudulent bookmakers to perform the highly satisfactory and necessary operation known as 'parting' … Several of these plunderers are pleading for 'time' on the ground that they have been 'hard hit' over the Cesarewitch, and if a select few of their kidney were 'hard hit' over their heads it would be mild punishment in comparison with their deserts…

It has been our constant endeavour to keep our columns as free as possible from the rotten-principled scoundrels who seek to plunder backers of horses, and we have this season refused advertisements which would have yielded us many hundreds of pounds, whenever we have been able to convict any of the pretended bookmakers of dishonesty.

Still, with all our vigilance and desire to protect the readers of this journal, it has occasionally happened that an exceptional rascal or two has succeeded in finding his way into print, thereby playing the character of a brigand on the public pocket.

But even sledgehammer denunciations of former advertisers failed to relieve the paper of its responsibility to its readers. One such warning referred to 'George Enock (alias Howes) of Devonshire Square, City':

We have again to caution the public against this notorious fellow who is at the bottom of nearly all the Turf swindles of the day. He occasionally advertises as 'The Stable Boy', 'W H Smith', 'Harry Bell', 'A Young Married Lady', 'Spencer', 'Harry Holt', 'Matthews' and 'Orlando' and was, until lately, proprietor of one or two obscure sporting publications for the sole purpose of carrying on his shameful system of depredation.

It was common practice for the more enterprising tipsters and bookmakers, both honest and dishonest, to promote their operations in their own 'sporting publications' but these tipping sheets had only a limited circulation and the principal office bookmakers still needed the megaphone of the press to advertise their ante-post prices, while the *Life* depended on their custom to maintain its level of profitability.

It therefore came as a nasty shock when, in the summer of 1869, this vital source of revenue was suddenly cut off by the arrest of several leading London layers. Among those rounded up was Billy Wright, one of the *Life's* biggest advertisers, who ran his Covent Garden business in conjunction with the racing news agency his father had made famous through 'Wright's Expresses'.

In its report on 'The Raid on the Turf Commission Agents', the *Life* noted with some concern that one of Wright's adverts had been cited as incriminating evidence and it had been shown that the

1853 Betting Act,* "applied equally to all persons concerned, including clerks and messengers, *and even to all who took part in advertising the betting offices.*"

In its next number, the paper carried a batch of 'Important Notices' issued by the commission agents informing their clients that, "in consequence of recent proceedings, business is temporarily suspended". On the same day, a few lines buried away in the news items column offered bookmakers an obvious solution to their predicament:

> The Betting Act and Scotland – It is a curious fact that Scotland is specially exempted from the operation of the Betting Act; the following being Clause 20 of the Bill: 'This Act shall not extend to Scotland'.

To drive the message home, Harry Feist made a point of calling on James Peddie, who ran a lucrative commission agency at 45 Essex Street off the Strand.† Motivated more by a desire to serve his paper than any wish to swell the coffers of his local bookie, the editor impressed upon Peddie that, since it was now obvious the authorities were not prepared to tolerate bookmakers in London, he had little to lose by a move north and the sooner he made it the better it would be for him – and the *Life*.

The discussion between the two men was intense. "The first run is everything," urged Feist. "You are surely now convinced the Betting Act does not apply to Scotland. Once you get your foot down you will be all right. Your advertisements will be a seven days' wonder, but after that only people who want to back horses will look at them."

Peddie, seeking reassurance: "Then Mr Dorling would insert the advertisements?"

Feist assured him that Edward Dorling had taken counsel's opinion on the matter and would be only too pleased to accept them. He added, candidly: "If somebody does not step in to improve matters, the *Sporting Life* will lose many thousands a year by this prosecution."

Peddie, still hanging back, argued: "The Act is bound to be extended."

"When?" challenged Feist, "Not this session at all events and in the meantime you may make your fortune."

Peddie was won over. On the Saturday following his meeting with Feist – "as steadfast and warm-hearted a man as ever breathed"[2] – he placed an advert in the *Life* and "on the evening of that day I started for Scotland, to commence the most prosperous years of my life."[3] His front-page ad announced:

> Mr James Peddie begs to intimate to his numerous clients and the public generally that he will execute commissions as heretofore to any amount on all races throughout the year (*By Letter Only*) ... Suitable offices in Edinburgh will be taken immediately, but in the meantime all remittances by Post Office orders or otherwise must be made payable to James Peddie, Post Office, Edinburgh. Scotch

---

* Commission agencies were established in order to circumvent the 1853 Betting Act. Business was conducted strictly by post. Cash bets were accepted by the 'agents' who ostensibly undertook to place them with on-course bookmakers in return for a five per cent commission on winnings, but, in reality, the money seldom left the offices unless the bets needed hedging.

† Peddie promoted his business by publishing two circulars, the *Illustrated Sporting and Theatrical News* and *The Tissue*, and was also quite an author. In addition to his autobiography, *Racing For Gold*, he produced 14 other works although most were little more than pamphlets on various subjects ranging from *The Dead Czar* (Alexander III) to *How the Bank at Monte Carlo was Broken*.

and Irish notes accepted as cash, and postage stamps may be sent for small amounts provided sixpence in the pound be forwarded for exchange. Letters containing gold, notes or stamps should always be registered.

As Feist had hoped, once the lead had been given, others soon followed. Over the next few months the classified columns of the *Life* recorded a steady migration of bookmakers to 'the land of the mountain and the flood'. In September, the drift north became an exodus when the arrested bookmakers failed to persuade the chief magistrate that they had been "acting within the spirit and the letter of the law". That month, James and Sydney Smith of the *Sportsman* together with Billy Wright placed a joint-ad in the *Life*:

Messrs Smith (late of 100 Jermyn Street, London), beg to inform their numerous patrons that owing to the recent proceedings at Bow Street against the Commission Agents and until their appeal to a superior court is disposed of, they will entirely discontinue business in England. But in consequence of very numerous applications from all classes of the racing world ... they have now much pleasure in being able to inform their patrons that they have secured premises and made arrangements by which the business will in future be effectively conducted in Glasgow and Boulogne-sur-Mer.

Subjoined to this was a letter Wright had sent to his clients. Designed to melt the hardest heart, it read:

I beg to state that the anxiety under which I have laboured since the commencement of the Government prosecutions has been such that my medical advisors have ordered me abroad for some months to come ... Until I return, I beg to recommend to your consideration the Messrs Smith who have so long and so honourably conducted a business precisely similar to that in which I have been engaged.

Within a year, what had briefly threatened to become a famine had turned instead into a pestilential plague as the exiled bookmakers, freed from the shackles of the Betting Act, filled the pages of the *Life* with their rules and ante-post prices. As a result, the paper's editorial content suffered; regular features were slashed to half their normal size, reports were squeezed out and even racecards were dropped in order to accommodate the invasive swarm of ads.

Things reached such a pass that on the eve of the 1874 Flat season more than half the paper – 13 of its 24 columns – was taken up by adverts. Disgruntled readers were left to digest what had by now become a regular "Want of space compels us to omit..." apology, which, in this instance, included the racecards for the suburban meeting at West Drayton and the West Somerset Steeplechases.

Nothing was sacrosanct, as was evident two weeks later when an aggrieved 'Special Commissioner' began his column with the resigned explanation: "Want of space having prevented my notes on the Grand National and Liverpool Cup from appearing last week, I shall now allude to those subjects only briefly..."

This unsatisfactory state of affairs was soon to be resolved in an unexpected manner. In January 1874, the Prime Minister, William Gladstone, dissolved parliament and Harry Feist, despite the articulate socialism that infused so many of his articles, immediately started beating the drum for Benjamin Disraeli, who, he noted by way of endorsement, "has frequently been seen on Newmarket Heath in company with Baron Rothschild".

In the run-up to the general election he repeatedly expressed his belief that a Tory government would be good for racing as he announced:

From all parts of the country I am glad to learn that racing men of every denomination are working hard to ensure the return of the Tories who have ever proved the true friends of the Turf while the Whigs have been the open and declared opponents or defamers of the national pastime.

And when it became clear that Disraeli had won the day, he rejoiced:

Racing interests and the national pastimes will be well and powerfully represented by Conservatives in the new and healthier Parliament. Mr T Hughes will not have another opportunity, for some time to come at least, of moving that the House 'do not adjourn' on Derby Day, or promoting abortive anti-betting Bills.

The narrow-minded and meddlesome author of *Tom Brown's School Days* has been unceremoniously kicked out of Frome and has been replaced by a Conservative, Mr H C Lopes, while Mr Hughes' antagonist on the betting question, Mr Lowther, a Conservative, has again been triumphantly re-elected for the City of York.

These facts will illustrate forcibly what I have constantly maintained, that the English people cherish their sports and will not submit to any interference with them from pettifogging Puritans or 'saintly' snobs. Society is, thank Heaven, safe from ruinous, exasperating legislation now that the 'Appeal to the Country' has been answered by so glorious an affirmative, not for the Premier and his parasites, but for Mr Disraeli and his loyal adherents.

Unfortunately for bookmakers and the sporting press in particular, one of those 'loyal adherents' happened to be a dour, black-bearded, Sabbatarian Scot by the name of George Anderson, and it was not long before Feist realised that, perhaps not for the first time, he had backed the wrong horse.

Anderson had been an MP for Glasgow since 1868 and had watched the growth of the betting business in Scotland with mounting horror. He loathed gambling and horseracing in equal measure and, like some latter-day Bruce or Wallace, he immediately took up his battle-axe to rid his country of the invading hordes of Sassenach bookies.

In March he brought in a bill that sought to extend the 1853 Betting Act to Scotland and to make it illegal for newspapers to carry any advertisement connected with betting as he claimed: "one betting house alone in Edinburgh pays a single London newspaper as much as £80 [£7,200] a week for advertising … and there are two betting houses in Scotland that are making £20,000 [£1.8m] apiece per annum." For good measure Anderson further inflamed the tender sensibilities of the sporting press by boasting: "It is only since my Bill was printed that the sporting papers have wished to appear as virtuous as possible in excluding discretionary advertisements."

The *Life* retaliated with a swingeing attack on the MP who, it disclosed, had been chairman of a failed mining company:

Mr Anderson's Betting Bill is, perhaps, more obnoxious than any that have been proposed. It aims at an interference with Press liberties as well as the freedom of the public, and it proposes an inquisitorial supervision upon personal and private communications through the post which, until now, we thought every man, woman and child in this country was entitled to expect were inviolable…

It is something like listening to 'the pot calling the kettle' when the chairman of the notorious Emma Mining Company waxes eloquent upon the ruin caused by Turf speculation. He must know that shares in the Emma Mine turned out even worse than backing a 'dead 'un' for the Chester Cup...

Mr Anderson professes a desire to 'protect the poor man who bets, from fraud', but by closing the substantial list offices in Scotland ... the new Betting Bill will simply throw the public wholesale into the hands of adventurers, welshers and professional sharpers. Statesmen have at length recognised the unalterable fact that no Parliamentary process can stamp out betting, and the time is surely approaching when it should be legalised by a system of licensing or otherwise.

Had such a regulatory system been in place at the time, there would have been no need to purge Scotland of all its bookmakers, as James Peddie pointed out in his memoirs:

For five years the turf commission business was carried on in Scotland in peace, and it might have been undisturbed to this day if a firm of swindlers had not swooped down on Glasgow. They advertised more extensively than any of the regular agents – and they could afford it, as they never, by any chance, paid a sixpence of the winnings. Some excuse was always ready to give to the unfortunate backer. It generally ended by his winnings being put on a loser. This lasted long enough to become a public scandal and the attention of Mr Anderson ... was drawn to the frauds. He drafted a Bill to suppress all betting by letter in Scotland and the Bill became law in the summer of 1874.

The outcome of the new legislation was, of course, the opposite of what Anderson had intended and exactly what Augur had forecast when he warned of a massive increase in street betting as small bookmakers would "spring up like mushrooms all over the country ... and every little town, and almost every street in great towns, will have its knights of the pencil, professional or amateur".

Meanwhile, a rash of 'Notices of Removal' in the advertisement columns signalled a mass flit to France by the Scottish-based bookies as they embarked on the first leg of what was to become a Grand Tour of Europe. But they hardly had time to settle into their new offices before the *Life* announced:

No little consternation is rife amongst betting circles in Paris owing to the government prosecution of M Oller* and other proprietors of the agencies on the pari-mutuel system. If it is discovered that the means of betting attacked are antagonistic to the French laws, it is not a wild idea to imagine that the Boulogne commission agents may find their peace of mind disturbed, and the journey to their chosen resting place but a trans-Channel leap from the frying pan into the fire.

This, indeed, seemed to be the case when Monsieur Oller and 14 other pari-mutuel operators were fined and had their machines and takings confiscated. In describing the seizure of the money as "the unkindest cut of all", Feist commented:

What a sensation of uncertainty there must have been in Rue Choiseul, or Rue 'Chisel' as it is styled

---

* Pierre Oller, a Parisian perfumer, devised the pari-mutuel betting system in 1865. Operated by machine, it works in the same way as the Totalisator, which officially came into use in Britain in 1929. All bets on each race are pooled and after deductions to cover expenses and allow for a profit, the remainder of the pool is paid out in proportions on a win and place basis.

with satirical suggestiveness by the English residents in Paris! Valentine and Wright have offices on the old cash system in the wagering quarter of the French capital admirably conducted. John Gideon exhibits a 'list' there and William Wright, the exile of Covent Garden, also set up in business after he was 'put down' in England.

The prosecutions in Paris were not against such betting offices, but against pari-mutuels and 'combination' systems alone. It had been well known for some time past that many complaints had been lodged with the Prefect of the Seine against some of the pari-mutuel operators who did not 'act on the square' and, as usual in these cases, the innocent suffer as well.

Perhaps it is not generally known that the betting each morning in Paris is most extensive on the daily racing in England and that the 'wiring away' to the French capital overnight from such places as Newmarket and Doncaster was on quite a heavy scale. Now that the pari-mutuels have been condemned, I may appropriately ask 'What is the next move on the board, gentlemen?'

As things turned out it was 'checkmate', for while the exiled bookmakers were able to enjoy a further 17 years of Gallic grace interspersed by the usual alarms and arrests before their goose was finally cooked on the pyre of a pari-mutuel monopoly, the *Life* was to be smitten by Anderson's battle-axe within the year.

The decision had been taken to ignore the amended Betting Act and carry bookmakers' and tipsters' advertisements as normal, but on 14 July 1875 the number of ads in the paper was suddenly and dramatically reduced to just three columns on the front page. The reason for this was found in a story headed 'Prosecutions of Sporting Papers', which revealed that the owners of the *Sportsman* and the *Sporting Life* had been summoned before Sir Thomas Dakin at the Guildhall and charged with "publishing certain advertisements in contravention of Mr Anderson's Betting Act of 1874".

It was a clear case of 'guilty as charged, m'lud' and, with a maximum penalty of two months imprisonment hanging over them, the recalcitrant proprietors got off lightly with a slap on the wrist and a fine of £10 (£900) with costs in each of four cases for the *Sportsman* and the same penalty times five for the *Life*.*

Having been brought reluctantly to heel, the *Life* informed bookmakers and tipsters that it could now only publish their name and address in the form of an advertisement, and so it was that 32 years after Apsley Pellatt had tried to banish all such adverts from the press, the columns of the *Life* were cleansed of what Augur facetiously chose to call:

All of those benevolent and philanthropic gentlemen, who were anxious to be perpetually doing good to their fellow beings for the trifling consideration of thirteen stamps ... Bottomley's 'special and important information' is to be consigned to limbo, Fred Osborne's 'Opinions' are to be wafted away and scattered in the desert air, George Archer, 'the King of Turf Prophets' is to be forthwith

---

* The ban on tipsters' ads lasted only until December 1883, when, as a result of a test case in the High Court, they were again admitted to newspapers. Commenting on the case, the *Life* observed: "There has for a long time been a doubt whether the publication of 'selections' or 'tips' in any form was not contrary to the law, inasmuch as they might be construed into 'inducements to bet' ... In giving judgement, Justice Mathew stated that the Act of 1853 was passed for the purpose of putting down betting houses and dealt with betting or inducing people to bet in such houses. The Act of 1874 was passed to amend the former Act and to be read with it and, in his lordship's opinion, the words (of the principal Act) referred to such betting houses and were not to be extended further. If the Court decided otherwise they would be extending the Act to cases it was never intended for and one of the results would be that any newspaper publishing a notice of any race of any kind would be committing an offence against the Acts."

dethroned and brought down to the level of an ordinary mortal! 'A secret for the Goodwood Stewards Cup' can now never be revealed, for its unfortunate possessor has no means of imparting it … Thus the world and its wicked ways will be cleansed.

Deprived of this all-important source of revenue, the paper had to fall back on the eclectic mix of adverts that had appeared in its columns from day one. These catered for the needs of an entire society; from the mundane (clay pipes, hoof ointment and trusses for ruptures) to all forms of new and wondrous inventions.

Quack doctors, in particular, rivalled tipsters with their exaggerated claims. Madame Valery's *Cosmetique Regenerateur*, "which prevents the hair from falling off and, in 90 cases out of 100, restores it when prematurely bald," competed with Cockle's Pills which were touted as the panacea for "bile, sick headache, indigestion, acidity, heartburn, flatulency, spasms of stomach and bowels, giddiness, dimness of sight, lowness of spirits, drowsiness and alarming symptoms which are frequently the forerunner of apoplexy."

There were books on all subjects ranging from *The Parrot Keepers Guide* to the indispensable *Matrimony Made Easy*, which claimed:

By following the directions you can win as many of the opposite sex as you wish. All may be married irrespective of age, appearance or position. You will also receive full particulars of how to ascertain a person's true character and disposition. These secrets, once known, can be acted upon by any person. There is no chance of discovery and failure is impossible.

Safe transport, a primary consideration of the time, ensured there was plenty of interest in George Geyelin's 'Magic Horse Taming Nose Pincher':

Although the principle of subduing a horse by pinching his nose or otherwise by taking away his breath is not now new, as applied by Mr G it is simple and infallible. The nose pinchers are fixed to the noseband and lie over the nostrils, and by pulling the reins attached to them the two prongs of the pinchers close and check the breathing. By its adoption a person can now ensure safety to life and limb without using any of those powerful bits so distressing to horses.

Dog shows were another regular source of adverts. In 1881, The Crown in Long Acre announced: "Mr Brown, of Paddington, will show his hairless wonder, imported from the interior of Africa at great cost by Cetewayo's son, the Zulu Prince." In the classified section rat-catchers were in demand to extirpate the vermin from sugar plantations in the West Indies or to capture them alive in order to supply the rat pits of the metropolis.

For those who wanted to learn this useful trade, one ad screamed: "Rats! Rats!! Rats!!! – How to destroy them or entice them and take them alive, rendering them docile and playful as kittens. The recipe, instructions and testimonials, 31 stamps. J Verity, Chemist, Bristol."

ON DOGS, RATS AND SONGBIRDS

URING the first half of the nineteenth century the public's propensity to bet on anything that moved provided a ready supply of ale was close at hand, had been temporarily curbed when the 'entertainments' of bear and bull-baiting were outlawed in 1835, while dog and cock fighting went the same way 14 years later. But the Victorian taverners were nothing if not resourceful and they soon revived an old tradition to draw in the crowds and fill their pits once more with snarling dogs and bloody gore. They did not have to look far to obtain the necessary cannon fodder.

Universally vilified, rats were the perfect candidates; not only did they provide good sport at little cost save that of paying off the rat-catcher,* but the worthy publican could claim he was performing a valuable service for his fellow citizens by dispatching as many as 200 or more 'long-tails' during the course of an evening's entertainment.

In its early years the *Life* carried numerous items under the heading of 'Ratting' or 'Canine' as challenges were issued, and contests announced and reported on. There were three main categories in which various breeds of terriers competed against each other and the clock. Most common were the handicaps in which a certain number of rats were allotted to a dog according to its weight. The general rule was that 1lb equalled one rat, but, to make matters more interesting and equitable, there were one-rat and even two-rat penalties for dogs that were especially good at the game.

One such contest took place at Charley Spalding's pit in Penkridge Street, Tottenham Court Road, in April 1859 when 'a fat sheep' was the prize. The mutton was won by:

> Mr Cooper's 18lb dog who killed a like number of rats in the quickest time, vis 1min 12sec. The next best dog proved to be Mr B Lowe's white dog Jack who, although only 8lb, was handicapped to kill nine rats in consequence of his previous performance. His time was 1min 25sec.

Dogs would also be required to kill a specified number of rats in a given time, and then there were the championship contests, the acme of ratting, in which the top dogs from different districts would be matched against each other. There were official weigh-ins for these competitions long before the practice was adopted in boxing, while the winner would be awarded an equivalent of the prize ring's championship belt.

As in the fight game, each local champion had its loyal band of followers who would back their dog with hard cash. An account of one such inter-district contest appeared in November 1859 under the heading, 'Ratting Extraordinary'. Written with as much attention to detail as would be given to any title fight, it began:

> On Monday evening the long-talked-of match between the City dog, Bob, and the Walworth dog, Joe, came off at Mr Tupper's, The Greyhound, Webber Row, Waterloo Road in the presence of one of the most respectable audiences we ever witnessed. The pit room was literally crammed to suffocation, nearly 200 persons having come to enjoy the sport.

---

* The most notorious ratoner (rat-catcher) of the time was the former boxer, Jemmy Shaw, who kept upwards of 2,000 rats in stock at his Windmill Street premises in Soho and earned a good living supplying them by the cartload to the most popular pits. Rural barn rats were the most sought after because they were clean, whereas sewer rats stank to high heaven and were likely to infect a dog's mouth causing canker.

The match was that each dog should kill 100 rats and not to be over 19lb on going to scale; the stakes to be £10 a side and the quickest dog to win. There was, besides, a silver collar of championship to be presented to the winner.

Bob is a well-known operator in the five score and odd line, having twice killed for honour at that number ... He is a fine white dog and nearly three-quarters bred, high head, tulip ears and belongs to Charley Strugnell. He has won at the fifty game, we are told, wherever he has been tried. He is now turned three years old and is in first-rate practice.

Joe is also a white dog, but long and rather flat headed. When on full crust he is eight-and-twenty pounds and on the present occasion must have been considerably stewed down to bring him within the proscribed ounces. As he is seven years old, the sweating process was not likely to be taken kindly by him and the fear was that with weight he would lose strength.

The ratting correspondent – in all probability a freelance 'penny-a-liner' – then made full use of his allotted column inches by wandering off at a tangent to rebuke some roughs he had seen at an earlier contest, for their bad language and rowdy behaviour.

"Such foolish, devil-may-care indulgence on these occasions is calculated not only to bring all sport into disrepute and put weapons into the hands of the ungodly, but to do a vast amount of injury to the very parties themselves hereafter. May we never see it repeated," he scolded before he returned to the scene of action:

At a little after seven o'clock the company began to sit down at our friend Billy's door and were received in due state and solemnity. The cellar imp received orders to turn on 'the bitter' and 'black draught' and the thirst quenching streams having begun to flow down grateful throats, the place assumed an air of business.

A brand new pit – one of the best in the village – had been constructed and at eight o'clock the young gentlemen went to scale and were both within the prescribed weight. The proceedings were opened by Tupper's trained ferret transacting a little private business on his own account. He commenced a quiet polka with a dozen of the 'varmint' then, having entered into security for their future good behaviour, he retired to his own domicile to make way for mightier folks and the first hundred long tails were boarded.

The 'starting go' was tossed for and won by Bob. The betting was all on one side – '6 to 4 Bob wins, 30 to 20 the dog in the pit' – there were, however, no takers ... Mr Saunders having been appointed referee, 'time' was called and Bob was let go to make the running in his own way. We never saw, in the whole course of our experience, a dog in such magnificent condition. His coat lay so close and so fine that it appeared for all the world like beautiful white floss silk. He had been well tutored and cared for.

He began operations rather languidly at first and many, unacquainted with the dog, thought he only meant to amuse himself with a dozen or two. About the fourth minute, however, he warmed to his work and upon being severely bitten once or twice, he made up his mind that no more of his own kisses should go by favour in that direction. He went on with a will, finally concluding the demolition of his foes in 11mins 26sec.*

---

* This was slow work compared to the record for 100 rats set three years later by Jemmy Shaw's 13lb bull terrier, Jacko, who 'demolished his foes' in 5min 28sec.

The field was immediately cleared of its slaughtered dead and the flowing cans of 'half-and-half' became masters of the situation. Strugnell ladled out the stuff in grand style, the rattle of pewters, the 'here's to you' and the clanking of the equivalent coppers were heard far above the roar of 'sweet voices' in the back rows. Everybody having liquored, 'rats' were called and 100 responded to the invitation. Mr Tupper entered the pit and announced himself as Joe's 'guide, philosopher and friend'.

Order being restored, 'time' was again called and the old dog began his prayers. His opening killing was splendid and inspired many of his admirers with confidence, but after the seventh minute it became plain the pace was too much for him. At the ninth he showed evident symptoms of distress; still, under the judicious treatment of Tupper, he worked on. At the eleventh minute he staggered slightly, but made play with great game. 'Twelve minutes' was called and he was taken out of the pit, leaving some six-and-twenty rats alive behind him.

This match is another illustration of the sporting proverb 'Youth will be served'. Joe's age beat him when matched with a younger dog of greater power. He was very much bitten and left a gory carpet on the pit floor that showed how terrifically he had contended and tried to win.

The report concluded with an earnest defence of its subject, which was obviously facing an uncertain future, as the writer observed:

There was a large muster of 'swells' at the entertainment, whilst the number of sober, broadcloth, cash-and-ledger looking people showed that ratting is not yet out of date. We never saw such an orderly, well-conducted pit; there was nothing to offend the ear or eye of the most fastidious … That's the way, Mr Tupper, to make your house attractive and respectable. Your example is well worth imitation and by continuing it you will draw the right class of customers to the sport and raise it to a much better position than it at present holds.

Unfortunately for the ratting brigade, there was always the occasional exhibitionist or deranged lunatic whose antics brought their noble pursuit into disrepute. A letter to the editor illustrated the extent of the problem:

Sir – Your pretentious contemporary, *Bell's Life in London*, which has so often been loud-mouthed about 'upholding manly diversions', inserted in its last Sunday's edition the following 'manly' announcement: 'Jack Sheppard of St Andrew's, Holborn, has made a match to destroy 30 large rats with his mouth in under 10 minutes and with his hands tied behind him, for £2 a side, to take place at J Brown's, The Sportsman, Carlisle Street, Westminster Road on Tuesday next'…

Englishmen have, from time immemorial, upheld every sport in its proper sense and I believe ever will patronise any manly game, but if killing rats in a pit as described by our leading sporting paper is considered manly, I can arrive at no other conclusion than that the sooner the human race discontinue the support of all such brutes and their patrons, the better it will be for the sporting world in general and society at large.

With the RSPCA and the police working together to suppress the 'sport', it was clear the ratter's days were numbered, although the law was ambiguous on the rights of the rat. One such case caught the eye of Henry Dixon at the beginning of 1865 when, in commenting on the extreme measures the

Kent constabulary was taking in its efforts to stamp out prizefighting, he took the opportunity to indulge in a bit of police-baiting:

> There is but one step from the sublime to the ridiculous, and in order to see how far the police desire to carry their senseless interference, it is only necessary to refer to the case reported in the daily papers of Friday wherein it will be found that their meddlesome protection has, at lengths, been extended to that interesting and inoffensive little creature – the rat!
>
> Mr Richard Cook, the keeper of a beer-house in Albany Road, Camberwell, appeared to answer a summons 'for keeping a place for baiting and fighting certain animals – to wit, the rat' … It seems that the Police Commissioner had instructed the force to keep an eye on Mr Cook's establishment and accordingly, on Boxing Night, Sergeant McClean went to the beer-shop and made the following dreadful discovery.
>
> The constable stated that he found in a shed, 'a rat-pit about 4ft high, and around it were seated seventeen men … There were also two dogs which had evidently been engaged in killing the rats as their mouths were bleeding, and on a ledge lay thirty two dead rats and close to them were fifteen live ones in a cage'…
>
> Can anything have been more contemptible than the interference with this little party of rat-killers which were engaged in watching a dog proving its eminent usefulness in the extirpation of a disgusting, a vicious and destructive species of vermin? … Fortunately, Mr Norton [*the magistrate*] showed that rats were not included in the statute … and finally dismissed the silly and preposterous summons.

If dogs and rats didn't go together in the eyes of what Harry Feist mockingly liked to call 'highly propaw society', dogs and hares certainly did, particularly on the bleak Altcar plains outside Liverpool where the Waterloo Cup was first staged in 1836. This coursing classic owed its origins and its name to one William Lynn, an astute entrepreneur who owned the Waterloo Hotel in Ranelagh Street, Liverpool. The 'Waterloo' was famed for its bear steaks which were shipped in from America, and for many years it "enjoyed a higher reputation for its cuisine and cellar than any in the United Kingdom."[1]

For Lynn, sports promotion was a natural adjunct to his hotel business which profited from the three-day race meeting held every summer on land he leased at Aintree from Lord Sefton. In 1828 he sponsored the Waterloo Gold Cup at the inaugural Aintree meeting, but of the eleven horses entered only two went to post and runners remained thin on the ground until a rival fixture at nearby Maghall was wound up in 1835.

The following year Lynn staged the first steeplechase – an optional seller – to be held at Aintree and to complement it he also promoted an eight-dog coursing sweepstake, which was run off a few miles away at Altcar. 'From little acorns' as they say! The steeplechase, a sweepstake of £10 each, with £80 added, evolved into the Grand National, while the coursing event also grew in value and prestige.

In 1837 the Waterloo Cup was increased to a 16-dog stake and the following year it again doubled in size. Finally, in 1857, it became a 64-dog stake as the fixture was extended over three days with the addition of two consolation prizes in the form of a 'Purse' for the 32 dogs beaten in the first round of the Cup, and a 'Plate' for the 16 dogs beaten in the second round.

By the time the *Sporting Life* arrived on the scene, the event had established itself as the 'Blue Riband of the Leash' with a first prize of £500 (£45,000) and it made national headlines in 1871 when Master McGrath won the Cup for the third time. The victory of Lord Lurgan's little Irish dog after his wins in 1868 and '69, made him a public hero and his followers rich men.

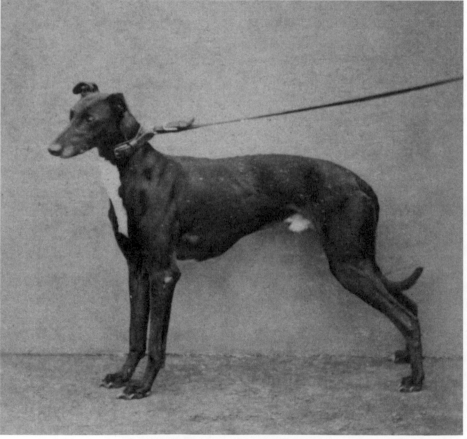

(Top) Master McGrath as painted for his owner, Lord Lurgan, after his first Waterloo Cup win in 1868
(Bottom) 'The king of the canine race' photographed by Hills & Saunders after his third win in 1871 –
reproduced by kind permission of Sir Mark Prescott, Bt.

In January, a month before the event, when Master McGrath was quoted at 100-6 in an open market, the *Life's* coursing correspondent, Charles Conquest, writing under his 'Amesbury' *nom de plume*, commented: "Every Irishman one meets insists on rejecting all the claims of fresh aspirants and sticks to Lord Lurgan and Master McGrath with a pertinacity which deserves every reward ... every man from Belfast to Cork will probably be 'on' before the eventful day arrives."

Conquest, however, refused to be influenced by all the Celtic fervour and although he went on to state that "Master McGrath is in the best of health; daily improving in condition and going in his old form," he concluded, "after what I saw of him last year I am compelled ... [*to*] repeat the opinion I have always advocated, that, as when he met Lady Lyons, he will again find his master."

So much for weak puns! When Conquest's selection, Pretender, met the Irish favourite (then a 1-2 chance) in the final, he reported:

The immense crowds upon the banks that surround Church House meadows were as quiet as Quakers when Master McGrath and Pretender were placed in the slips and, a hare coming to them directly, they were dispatched for the great trial upon which so much depended.

The pair raced together so evenly for sixty or seventy yards that it was impossible to tell which was first, but as they neared puss – a desperately weak one – the Irish champion drew a little more than clear of Mr Punchard's dog and the hare bending slightly to his side, he went with her and snapped up poor puss like a blackbird would a bread crumb – a shocking trial for a deciding course.

As may be imagined, intense excitement prevailed and as Spooner, the dog's trainer, led him back along the line of the crowd, a volley of triumphant cheers accompanied his progress ... Many traits of Irish character were brought forcibly under notice and the reckless manner in which castors were shied into the air would have gladdened the heart of the most morose hatter in the United Kingdom. I observed one excited son of Erin dancing round and upon his beaver ... shouting 'Here's a bhoy that thook a hundared to five about the darlint and niver hedged a single penny piece av it – whoop!'

In his Augur column, Feist remarked more soberly:

An immense amount of money changed hands on the result and it is quite astonishing how public interest in this contest has grown within the past few years. Formerly, the community at large were lamentably ignorant about coursing and the 'long dog', but financial speculation has caused the deepest attention to be paid to the great prize...

Master McGrath's success seems to have taken all the good judges completely off their guard as they would not listen to the possibility of a fourth-season dog becoming for a third time triumphant, more especially as 'McGrath' had been inducted into the pleasures of love and was supposed to have retired from public coursing altogether...

Probably Master McGrath is the only dog whose name was ever proclaimed in the streets of London, and the cries of the newsvendors with their 'third editions' narrating his triumph sounded like a satire upon the recent furore for war news in the same journals.*

The *Life* dubbed the black and white son of Dervock "the king of the canine race", and, shortly

---

* This was a reference to the Franco-Prussian war which had recently ended with the surrender of Paris.

after his great victory, 'the king' was summoned to meet the Queen at Windsor Castle where he received a flurry of imperial pats from the royal household.

The following day the celebrated mutt embarked on a high society whirl of London, where Lady Dawtrey and the Countess of Waldegrave both held morning receptions in his honour, and in the afternoon he was taken to Marlborough House to meet the Prince and Princess of Wales. Now acclaimed as 'The Mighty McGrath', he rounded off his day by dining at Lord Lurgan's club, Brookes in St James's, where the prospects of another Altcar foray were enthusiastically discussed. Sadly, it was not to be.

Just before Christmas 1871, the most famous dog in the world fell ill and died. At the time he was 7-1 favourite to win a fourth Waterloo and there were ugly rumours of foul play, but a post-mortem revealed he had died of double pneumonia brought on by pulmonary tuberculosis – 'the fell destroyer', consumption, had claimed another victim!

The 'Master's' lungs were so badly diseased it was estimated he'd had the condition for more than a year, which reflects even greater credit on his later performances. He was beaten only once (in the first round of the 1870 Waterloo Cup) in 41 courses and his name still inspired a sense of awe more than half a century later. In recalling coursing's halcyon days in a letter to the *Life* in 1934, a reader compared him with Fullerton, who won the Cup for the fourth successive year in 1892 having initially shared the honours with his kennelmate, Troughend, as a puppy in 1889:

> Fullerton was, no doubt, the most popular of Waterloo winners. The breed of present-day greyhounds is so lacking in fibre that we shall never see another winning the Waterloo Cup a fourth time. He then started at only 100 to 30 on the night of the draw and only 4 to 1 the following year, when he was a fifth-season dog. He was then stopped by a grueller in the opening round.
>
> I can go farther back than Fullerton, however, and venture the opinion that the late Lord Lurgan's Master McGrath was the best greyhound which contested the Waterloo Cup. I well remember that great writer, the late Lowingham Hall, telling me how, when he first saw the dog in the North of Ireland, the 'Master', his eyes all afire, seemed to mesmerise his quarry. But the crack all-rounder was Bab at the Bowster.
>
> She was not so smart a killer as Master McGrath – who, on the only occasion he was beaten, fell in the river Alt, got under the ice and was nearly drowned – and the 'Master' beat her in the final of his second Waterloo, although the luck of the course was with him. But Bab at the Bowster could run over any country, and she won 67 out of her 70 courses in public. What greyhound of these times, after having run three rounds at Waterloo, could win a 128-dog stake and another one for 64 dogs, as she did, at the end of the same season?

While the ownership of coursing greyhounds was generally restricted to the nobility and the professional middle-classes during the Victorian era, the working man had his own version of the sport which featured whippets and rabbits. Rabbit coursing may have lacked the aesthetic points of its noble cousin,* but the science behind it was as precise as any handicap Admiral Rous ever framed.

---

* Coursing was especially popular with the nobility during the Elizabethan era when the Queen instructed her Earl Marshal, Thomas Howard, the 4th Duke of Norfolk, to draw up a set of rules that would define the points of the course on which the relative merits of the dogs could be judged. Norfolk was poorly rewarded for his efforts when he was executed for treason in 1572, but his *Lawes of the Leash* survived him to become the basis for the laws compiled by the National Coursing Club in 1858.

Dogs would compete against each other over a set number of courses (usually 21) under a handicapping system which allowed the inferior or lighter dog so many 'dead rabbits'. The winner was the dog that achieved the most kills after the number of 'dead rabbits' had been taken into account. The *Life* carried regular reports of these contests and the challenges that were thrown out, such as this 1880 announcement:

> John Riley of Halliwell, near Bolton, will match his bitch Rose, 16½lb, against any other dog of the same weight at rabbits, 21 courses, 50 yards law, for £10 a side, and give a dead rabbit; or he will give ¾lb and run level; or he will take three dead rabbits from Mr Bingham's Dinah, for the same amount, Dinah not to exceed 18½lb; or will give three dead ones to any dog not exceeding 14½lb. By sending articles and a deposit of £5 to Mr James Holden, White Lion, Manchester any night this week, a match can be made.

The '50 yards law' referred to the start rabbits were given, while would-be students of rabbit coursing and ratting will note that the handicapping scale in both pursuits was remarkably similar. In the former, a bunny was equal to 12 canine ounces, while in the latter it was rat-for-pound, exclusive of penalties!

When it came to precision scoring, however, there was nothing to beat the songbird singing contests that had become popular in certain parts of London as ratting gradually died out under RSPCA prosecutions. The contrast between the two camps could not have been greater as the frenzied cacophony of squealing rats and yelping dogs was replaced by the blithesome twittering of goldfinches, linnets and larks.

The interpretation of bird song was well-understood by avian intimates who sought to relieve the drudgery of their working lives with some socially acceptable entertainment, but to the uninitiated the brief reports that appeared in the *Life* were baffling.

A typical announcement from 1871 stated that at The Mitre in Bermondsey Road: "The Whitsuntide linnet handicap proved a capital all-round success, the commodious room being well filled by the recognised members of the old and new fancy who were rewarded with faultless singing resulting in one of the highest scores of the season viz. 7.8." While at the King's Head in Broad Street, Bloomsbury: "The winning bird did 5.18; the runner up 4.19. The house is open to sing a goldfinch for the most '*sur-welts*' against anyone – Long Pat preferred – for from £1 to £6 a side."

Double treble Dutch! Enlightenment, of a kind, was provided by an extraordinary article entitled 'Amongst the Bird Fancy' in February 1872. The report, by 'Our Special Correspondent', borders on the surreal, but also gives a fascinating account of a long-forgotten hobby that was pursued with obvious dedication and pride by its followers.* Couched in a sincere, lyrical style befitting the occasion, it began:

> Deep in the classic groves of Lock's Fields, Walworth, is Rodney Road and in this same road is a snug little hostelry known as 'The Jolly Butchers' where, at certain stated times, bird-singing competitions take place.
>
> Whether the air of Walworth or Bermondsey is eminently suited to the development and training

---

* Songbird singing competitions died out in England in the 1890s following the introduction of laws to protect wild birds, but they are still popular in Belgium and parts of South-East Asia.

of singing birds is open to argument; but certain it is that, in the localities named, the twittering of the feathered tribe is gone into most learnedly and their various notes cultivated and studied with as much earnestness as ever music master bestowed on a pupil of extra promise ... Indeed, it may be asserted that no excelling performer on the pianoforte, the peerless Paganini, or even the original Orpheus himself, could ever have been listened to with greater appreciation than these London lovers of the linnet bestow on the efforts of rival songsters...

Linnets are, as other singing birds, divided into two classes called rough linnets and toy singers. The rough linnet depends on his natural note or in singing the greatest number of changes of song, but toy linnets are educated to utter particular sounds according to the fancy of the master, and when sung against each other these notes are specified, the contest, in fact, bearing a parallel to a nomination game at billiards.

The toy linnets are esteemed highest, £5 being sometimes hardly considered an equivalent for one of them, and their most valuable utterance is as follows: '*Tollick, tollick, ikky quake eeja poy chow turwheet*!' Their education consists either in taking it from a linnet already proficient, or else from being placed between such noted songsters as the woodlark or titlark, and gaining snatches of the different melodies.

The rough linnet's song consists of short bursts and the various notes are designated as an '*ikky quake*', a '*tug wizzey*', a '*chow wheet*' and '*tollick feer*'. But their best lay is a '*tollick ikky quake*', especially if there is a '*tug wizzey*' at the end of it.

Here, the writer felt it necessary to assure his doubting reader that the sound of a tug wizzey was "sweet poetry" to bird fanciers, before he proceeded to give more examples of "the rendering of bird notes by human language". Goldfinches, he claimed:

...excel all others in the variety of their musical capabilities, and amongst the technical translations of their notes are '*sippit se pet se widdy*', '*sippit ker*', '*sippit cha*', '*slam, slam se widdy*' and '*sippit se pet se widdy ker assel cha*'. Then there are the mule's notes ... '*slam slam widdle widdle se cha*'. In this case the mule inherits the '*widdling*' and the '*se*' from the yellowhammer. But now, do you know the very best '*jerk*' of a goldfinch, the acme of trained melody? ... This is it. Proprietors of goldfinches, please attend: '*Sippit slam slam widdle widdle se blink charmee charmee cha*!'

Further translations followed before the *Life*'s indomitable birdman got round to describing two competitions that had taken place between the widdling warblers during his visit to the Jolly Butchers. The first was an inter-district championship in which the Bermondsey bird "succumbed very easily, not being in his best mood. Birds are sulky, bless you, sometimes as sulky as a man with the toothache and will no more sing than they will stand on their heads."

The second contest was for a copper kettle and attracted an entry of six pairs of linnets. Setting the scene, he reported:

In a long room upstairs about fifty of the admirers of bird music were seated, one party in a corner amusing themselves with the old English game of coddam until the time arrived for the more important matter to claim their attention.

Against one side of the room was a long black plank, about as high as a man could reach, in which were driven nails for hanging the cages containing the competing linnets. Directly opposite this was the table for the two scorers, who sat with chalk in hand, ready to note down the points in favour of each bird … Between the chalk-takers sat the timekeeper with a silver watch before him, and also a bit of chalk to dot down the minutes as they passed. The time allowed for each bird to demonstrate their abilities was a quarter of an hour…

The first form to be gone through was the toss for the nails because some birds prefer to be closer to the light than others and some sing better when they can see their rival's cage. These cages, by-the-bye, are little square prisons with wood on one side and with ordinary wires on the other three sides so that the man who wins the toss for the nails can either place his bird so that he can see the other cage or not, as he pleases.

I may also here state that the practice which formerly obtained of blinding the birds by the insertion of a fine red-hot wire into the centre of their eyes is rightly scouted and that cruel operation is totally abolished.

The first pair of competitors belonged respectively to Joe and Templeton … Order being called and the game of coddam relinquished, the door was fastened and the two owners stood ready to hang up their birds. 'Time' shouted the timekeeper and instead of two brawny prizefighters coming up to the scratch as of old in answer to that magic word, two little linnets were simultaneously hung up in two little cages and 'silence reigned around'.

Then came a period of suspense, anxious faces being turned towards the cages, waiting for their inmates to sing. Minute after minute went by. Not a sound was heard. The timekeeper's chalk had already made eight strokes indicating the number of minutes which had transpired and still not a twitter came forth – not even a 'scriggle' which is the most valueless note of any.

'Take him down Joe', at last said somebody, 'he's gone to sleep'. And sure enough, as far as I could see, Joe's linnet had got his head tucked comfortably under his wing and was evidently in the land of nod. But Joe still had confidence and said, 'He'll wake up and do his score in a couple of minutes when he starts'.

Meanwhile the other bird appeared in a similarly sulky or comatose condition, the result being that the quarter of an hour expired without either of them uttering a note. This was certainly tame. Joe appeared quite downhearted and … evaporated with a quiet 'Good night, gen'l'men' and was no more seen.

It was a shame of the chalk-takers to take their fee without even scoring one little mark; but chalk-takers are inexorable and must be paid their twopence. 'Down with your deuces', was the demand after each pair of birds had competed.

The next on the list were two linnets belonging respectively to Walker and Mortimore. Walker won the toss for the nails and his bird started singing directly he was hung up. The other soon joined and for ten minutes nothing was heard but the notes of the rival songsters. A novice would have awarded the palm to Walker's bird, although Mortimore's bird was not beaten badly having scored 37 points against 44 or, to be technical, 'one score seventeen against two score four'.

Good for Walker! But there was yet a linnet mightier than his to come … the linnets of Linford and Hollaman were produced. 'Time' was again cried and Hollaman's bird immediately began pouring out his flood of melody and continued, with little cessation, during the whole quarter of an hour, doing 'three score six'.

Linford's bird only gave utterance now and then to a faint chirrup and was quite 'knocked down' although he seemed disposed to sing. But it is a fact that when one bird is much superior to another, the other one feels his inferiority and will not give utterance to a note while the better bird is singing.

Neither of the birds of Wright nor Lewis, Collins nor Lloyd, who in order succeeded, came anywhere near this performance, so Hollaman's bird was declared the winner, and if the copper kettle, of which Hollaman is now the happy owner, only sings half as sweetly as his linnet, his fireside will indeed be pleasant.

'Sweet poetry' indeed, but the feathered species was not treated with such reverence in its natural environment where everything that could fly was in danger of being blasted out of the sky. In the Scottish Highlands golden eagles were potted off with gay abandon, and prized indeed was the rare black swan that unwittingly winged its way into the display cabinet of a Victorian naturalist.

From the outset, the *Life* made a special point of promoting shooting competitions as it stated with magnificent, empire-building rhetoric: "any diversion which accustoms Englishmen to the use of arms and enables them to acquire precision of aim, must be of the first moment to a nation which is destined to influence or rule the world."[2]

Often organised by publicans in order to attract custom to their inns, the competitions usually offered livestock prizes that could range from an 840lb pig to an in-calf heifer. But in the private shooting matches set up through the paper, hard cash was always at stake. A typical (1865) notice read:

Mr. Harfield says he will accept the challenge of Mr. Banks to shoot at 50 sparrows, each 21 yards rise, for £25 [£2,250] a side. Mr. Harfield will be at our office on Tuesday, between one and two o'clock, prepared to stake, sign articles and toss for the choice of ground. The whole of the money to be staked in the hands of the editor of the *Sporting Life* three days previous to the match coming off.

In addition to sparrows; pigeons and starlings were also in the firing line and stocks of them were advertised for sale during the season, while the wildlife that was regularly obliterated on the estates of the 'upper ten' was carefully catalogued down to the last bird. On 25 December 1861, the *Life*, which, in common with other papers, published on Christmas Day up until a few years before the First World War, reported:

Lord Stamford and other great patrons of the Turf have been keeping themselves fully employed during the racing recess. In our last impression his lordship courteously forwarded us an epistle of the shooting of himself and party at Bradgate Park, and to destroy 8,476 head of game in the course of one week must be admitted to be pretty warm work even for Christmas time.

The list of game attached to the noble lord's name consisted of 4,292 rabbits, 3,609 pheasants, 482 hares, 58 woodcock, 14 wild duck, 4 snipe, 1 partridge and 16 various. The 'various' could range from crows to cats, but woe betide the 'infidel' who robbed a hunt of its sport by shooting a fox. The Victorians had a name for it – vulpicide, the killing of a fox by any means other than hunting. To the huntsman it was a crime that ranked alongside infanticide and treason.

An 1862 report of one such incident appeared under the heading 'Atrocity In The Hunting Field' as a correspondent who signed himself 'Bullfinch' related:

The Duke of Rutland's hounds met on Saturday, the 27th inst. at Croxton Park and drew Coston Cover where they found a fox starting him towards Buckminster … but a hard fate awaited him as an individual (it would be libel on the name to call him a man) shot him within two fields of the cover just as the hounds had warmed to their work.

The noble master rode up to the infidel who had hidden the murdered fox in a barn and demanded that poor Reynard should at once be given up, but the assassin, gun in hand, placed his back to the door and swore he would shoot the first man attempting to enter. However, his cowardly threat was held at its worth and the Duke, dismounting, managed to wrest the gun from him…

I was told the fellow's name is Marshall occupying a farm in the neighbourhood of Buckminster. Such an outrage cannot but obtain for him an unenviable notoriety and I would suggest that every honest man should forthwith 'send him to Coventry' … and thus, by drawing the attention of the sporting world to the outrage, banish the creature from civilised society.

To the New Labour back benches of 2004, perhaps, when Tony Blair's pettifogging acolytes condemned 'poor Reynard' to an often lingering, gangrenous death from gunshot wounds.

NO NEW THING

The thing that has been, it is that which shall be; and that which is done is that which shall be done; and there is no new thing under the sun. – Ecclesiastes (1:8)

THE OLD MAXIM that history repeats itself applies just as much to racing and sport in general as it does to any other walk of life. Controversial issues addressed by the *Life* in its early years are, today, debated just as fiercely within society. Whether the subject is 'the morality of foxhunting' or 'the brutality of boxing', the arguments have changed little over the years.

When the bookmaker, Victor Chandler, moved his business to Gibraltar in 1999 to escape the jurisdiction of the British government, he was only following the example of his Channel-hopping brethren who sought sanctuary in France in 1874. And in 2009, Hills and Ladbrokes followed suit when they moved their online operations to 'the Rock' after Gordon Brown's government slapped a 15% levy on internet bets.

Complaints about fixture clashes, small fields, and too much racing, were aired during the Feist-Dixon era when many practices, which, in recent times were acclaimed as new ideas brought in by an enlightened British Horseracing Board (now the Horseracing Regulatory Authority), were in routine operation. Such commonsense procedures as the reopening of races in the event of insufficient entries; supplementary entries; the division of major handicaps that attract a mass of entries, and the transfer of fixtures because of bad weather, were par for the course.

Similarly, ancient skills in equine management have been revived and re-introduced as exciting, new techniques. Interval training is, for instance, as old as the hills up which the horses exercise, while a celebrated American horse whisperer was doing the rounds in Britain when the *Life* first rolled off the presses in 1859.

The latter case provides a remarkable example of the parallel careers of Monty Roberts and one John S Rarey. The former, well known in America for his handling of difficult, nervous and unruly horses, came to England in 1989 to give a private exhibition of his skills before the Queen in the riding school at Windsor Castle.

The demonstration proved a great success and Roberts went on to make a major impact on the racing fraternity as he toured the UK giving performances of his remarkable rapport with horses. Flighty fillies and contrary colts all came alike to him. It would take him as many minutes to gain the confidence of an unbroken animal, saddle it and ride it around a ring, as it would take days for a traditional horse-breaker to accomplish the task.

Yet, in 1858, another American, John Rarey, using similar techniques to Roberts, gave a performance of his expertise as a 'horse-tamer' before Queen Victoria in the very same riding school at Windsor Castle. Afterwards, he also embarked on a countrywide tour giving public exhibitions in a portable lunging ring, while his fame increased among the racing community when he tamed the thoroughbred stallion, Cruiser, who had killed or seriously injured several grooms.

Like Roberts, whose *The Man Who Talks To Horses* was published in 1997, Rarey also wrote a book – *The Modern Art of Taming Wild Horses*, which was published in London in 1858 and became an instant best seller. The first edition sold 150,000 copies and revised editions were still being published in England long after Rarey had returned home to Ohio, where he died at the age of 41 in 1866.

In 1859 Rarey was engaged to instruct British cavalry officers into his ways, and that August he gave a demonstration of his skills at the Alhambra Palace, Leicester Square, where his subject was a savage Flemish stallion that belonged to the Merrett brothers of Finsbury, north London. To accompany its report of the display, the *Life* published a letter the horse's owners had sent to the American:

> Dear Sir, In reply to your note of inquiry with regard to the character of our horse, we beg to inform you that in his present condition we consider him a most dangerous animal and shall be most happy to place him in your hands to receive a lesson of obedience, and also to have your advice as to his proper management in future.
>
> The horse, having killed one of our men, is now kept securely tied up by the head with three strong ropes to prevent him from doing any further injury. He is never approached except by climbing over the partition of his stall in front of him, as no man could go into it in the ordinary way. He is a high-spirited, courageous horse, and if he could be broken of his vicious propensities, would be a most valuable one.

There were plenty of people willing to pay a guinea (£95) for a reserved seat to see Rarey work his magic that day. Described as a small, spare man with piercing blue eyes, he began by giving a talk in which he emphasised the need to treat the horse with patience and kindness; to understand its nature and capacities; to regard it as a pupil rather than a slave; the purpose, he said, was to educate the animal, not to spoil it.

The Alhambra audience murmured its approval and then gave a collective gasp as the 'killer' stallion came charging into the arena. The *Life's* correspondent was suitably impressed as he noted the beast had "sufficient mane and tail to make the fortune of any reasonable horse-hair merchant ... his eye glanced fire and, at every attempt to approach him, he plunged and neighed with astonishing shrillness."

When working with his more difficult 'pupils', Rarey would often use a certain amount of physical force by holding up their near-fore leg as he coaxed them into submission and he employed the technique in this instance, but the 'joining-up' process was identical to the way horses respond to Roberts' less coercive methods. It was observed the stallion:

> …fought with the greatest obstinacy and, even when fairly on his knees, it was upwards to half an hour before Mr Rarey could get him totally in his power. At the conclusion of his lesson, the horse, which previously screamed at the slightest touch, allowed himself to be handled all over, mounted, and finally followed the tamer in every direction as docile and gentle, to all appearances, as a gazelle.

No sooner had accounts of Rarey's performances begun to appear in the press than indignant horse-tamers began popping up all over the country. Fred Taylor, yet to be appointed 'Special Commissioner' to the *Life*, rushed to the defence of his former mentor in equine-management when he published *Telfer's System of Horse Training*. In his introduction, he claimed that Telfer had passed on his methods to a man called Robson who had emigrated to America and settled in Rarey's home state of Ohio where he practised the art. The implication was obvious as he declared:

> Our old system of Horse Taming, revived and introduced as an American discovery by Messrs Rarey and Goodenough, and professed to be taught by the former to our aristocracy, is the latest example

of American 'cuteness', 'Barnumism' and, we may add, impudence; and the object of this work is to establish the fact that the discovery is of purely British origin, and first reduced to practice by Mr James Telfer, the justly celebrated Northumberland horse-tamer.

At the same time as Taylor was advancing his claims for Telfer, *Chamber's Miscellany of Useful and Entertaining Tracts*, gave the credit to a bucolic Irishman:

> James Sulivan, a horse-breaker at Cork, and an awkward rustic of the lowest class … obtained the singular appellation of 'whisperer' from a most extraordinary art which he possessed of controlling, in a secret manner, and taming into the most submissive and tractable disposition, any horse that was notoriously vicious and obstinate.
>
> He practised his skill in private and without any apparent forcible means. In the short space of half an hour his magical influence would bring into perfect submission and good temper even a colt that had never been handled; and the effect, though instantaneously produced, was generally durable.

In truth, horse-whisperers pre-date even the 'awkward rustic' from Cork. Their secrets may have been imported into England along with the three foundation stallions of the modern thoroughbred – the Byerley Turk (c1678), the Darley Arabian (1700) and the Godolphin Arabian (1724), but it is much more likely they date back to the earliest times. To quote Xenophon (430-354BC), the famous Greek historian, military commander, philosopher and horse-whisperer – "Horses are taught not by harshness, but by kindness."

There is, after all, no new thing under the sun, as Henry Dixon illustrated in a leader he wrote for the *Life* in January 1870. In it he touched, somewhat facetiously, upon the effects of pollution on the climate (global warming) before tackling the subject which was to inflame the country 134 years later when Tony Blair's New Labour government outlawed hunting with dogs. He started off innocuously enough as he commented on the prevailing mild weather:

> People ask in vain the causes of the absolutely wondrous change in our climate. Is it the extra amount of steam puffed into the English atmosphere from thousands of locomotives? Is it the effect of paternal and perpetually 'liberal' government casting a genial glow upon the face of nature?

By this means the canny chronicler neatly manoeuvred himself into a position to attack the politicians whose repressive legislation against the popular pursuits of the working classes vexed him sorely for he was a life-long Liberal and normally an admirer of Gladstone whose ministers had recently spoken out against foxhunting. He launched into his assault with an almost tangible sense of frustration:

> Really, there is no telling where the interference of the Gladstone government is likely to end – the operations of the Executive as regards sport, having already exercised an unwholesome effect upon the public mind.
>
> A controversy, absolutely sickening, is being carried on at the present moment as to whether foxhunting ought to be pursued at all as it is inconvenient and cruel to Reynard. In the name of all that is manly, courageous and English, what are we drifting to? Seirne has been abused and satirised for weeping over a dead donkey, but the nation is making up its mind that it ought to shed tears over

every stinking fox that dies in the open.

The Puritan, we are told, 'Hung a cat on Monday for killing a mouse on Sunday'. Is it possible we are sinking into some such wretched state as that detailed above? … Humanity in sport has ever received our warmest advocacy, but when we see at last that it is gravely discussed whether it is 'moral' to hunt a fox, we begin to entertain fears, not so much for sport as for the national reputation for strong masculine sense and the Englishman's proverbial character for unaffected candour…

What matters if a million foxes perish, so long as one cavalry officer first acquires his knowledge of dashing resolution in a charge from exploits in the hunting field? Bah! We are sick of the subject and feel persuaded that it will be ill for England when her 'mimic battles' are unpopular and the chief actor's occupation is gone.

At the outset, we intended to permit the windy diatribes published on the so-called 'Morality of Sport' to pass by as unworthy of notice. Some time since we were also inclined to consider that the crusades against betting were simply steps antagonistic to gambling; but when we find outcries raised against lordly hunting and plebeian skittles, directly or indirectly stimulated by measures of the Government, it is plain that there is an unhealthy tone rising in society calculated to cast odium on our most pure and cherished pastimes.*

'Lordly hunting and plebeian skittles' were not the only sports under attack. Middle-class opposition to racing had been on the increase since the 1860s when new racecourses began to spring up in the London suburbs and meetings such as Bromley and Blackheath, Hendon and Harrow, Streatham and Southall, became synonymous with robberies, assaults and general hooliganism.

Condemnation of this 'suburban saturnalia' intensified when the steeplechaser, Voigtlander, was killed at Croydon in November 1866. The unfortunate animal met his end at what had been publicised as a 'sensation' water jump at the new Woodside course a few miles from the town centre. Sited in front of the stands, the 15ft spread of water was fronted by a fence of uncertain height (estimates varied from 4ft 6in to 6ft!), and it did indeed prove a 'sensation' though not in the way its promoters had hoped.

The publicity generated by the death of Voigtlander and the large number of fallers at the meeting due, in part, to fetlock-deep ground, led to an outcry in the national press and resulted in the RSPCA taking out a summons against the rider, Hiram 'Peter' Crawshaw. The charges brought against Crawshaw were even more sensational than the controversial obstacle, in that he did: "cruelly ill-treat, over-ride, abuse and torture a certain animal – to wit, a horse known by the name of Voigtlander – by making it leap a fence and pool of water, whereby the said horse fell and broke its back."

When the matter came before the Croydon magistrates, the RSPCA proved so inept in presenting its evidence that the case was dismissed without the defence being called, and the chairman of the bench gave costs against the Society and publicly rebuked its officers.

Henry Dixon, as a former lawyer, was well qualified to comment on the case and he castigated

---

* In 1869, a law was passed against the playing of skittles for money or beer in public houses. When, just before Christmas that year, the Police Commissioner instructed his officers to visit all London pubs to ensure the ban was enforced, Dixon was moved to write: "It almost passes belief that an ukase, at once so despotic and puerile, should have been issued by persons in office whose functions are popularly supposed to be the repression of crime rather than the interference with our national sports and pastimes … At the same moment that these experiments are being made on the morals of the people, real vice and crime are permitted and even encouraged because the energies and watchfulness of the police are misdirected."

the Society's secretary John Colam not only for displaying "the grossest legal ignorance" in the way in which he had gathered and presented the so-called evidence, but also because he had surreptitiously tried to involve Harry Feist in the prosecution:

> Never did the members of any society make a more contemptible exhibition of themselves in endeavouring to bolster up a trumpery and childish charge. Their witnesses made a strange display, more particularly the Society's officers. They had absolutely measured the water jump with a piece of string, like a couple of dressmaker's apprentices taking the width of a skirt.
>
> When Mr Simeon Sell was asked the height of the fence in front of the water jump he replied that it was 'up to his nose'… Like Voigtlander, the Society had not a leg to stand on in the prosecution and the case was summarily dismissed after such a sorry exposure as we have seldom witnessed in any court of law…*
>
> Mr Colam alienated all sympathy from his side when he read the remarks of the sporting newspapers and declared that the gentlemen who had written in these columns and in the *Daily Telegraph* were prepared to come forward and swear that the jump was of a cruel or severe description. Those writers would have done no such thing and Mr Colam was taking a liberty both with ourselves and 'Hotspur', though it is possible the *Field* may have promised the secretary its amiable assistance.

Colam, described as "one of those persons who love notoriety," was obviously unaware that 'Augur' and 'Hotspur' were one and the same. Feist, who had been critical merely of the "catchpenny style" in which the Croydon management had advertised the water jump, was wearing his Augur hat as he predicted:

> After the rebuke which has been administered, we shall hear no more of humanitarian detectives being sent into the steeplechase field to 'collect evidence' when the London streets, with their wretchedly used cab horses, present a much more wide and natural field for benevolent operations.

Little did the esteemed editor realise that he, himself, was to provide the 'evidence' for the RSPCA's next high-profile prosecution. This came about in 1870 when he was subpoenaed by the Society as their key witness in a case brought against the well-known jockey, George Holman, who was accused of "cruelly beating and ill-treating" a horse called The Doctor when finishing second in that year's Grand National.

At the time jockeys were allowed to wear spurs fitted with rowels, and Feist, in writing his 'Hotspur' report for the *Telegraph*, indicated that Holman had made free use of them as The Doctor had returned to the unsaddling enclosure with its flanks "fairly ripped up".

John Colam, still smarting from the humiliation he had suffered in the Voigtlander case, had pounced upon this expression in the belief that it provided all the proof he needed to obtain a conviction.

When the case came before the Liverpool magistrates in April, Feist was on the defensive from the start. He pointed out he had been working to a very tight deadline because the race (run on a

---

* The inefficiency with which the RSPCA tackled the Voigtlander case was not typical of the society – in the previous year (1865) it had instituted 1,085 prosecutions and was successful in all but 12 of them.

Wednesday) had started at 3.30 and his article had to be sent on the 5 o'clock train from Liverpool. When questioned by Harris, the prosecuting counsel, 'Hotspur' said he had seen two places on The Doctor's offside flank where the sweat was mixed with blood, but they had looked much worse than they really were.

Harris: "Then you mean to say that 'fairly ripped up' is a sporting phrase?"

Feist: "It would be understood by sporting men as meaning severe punishment at the end of the race. The race was only won by a neck, so it must have been a severe finish."

Harris (seeing an opening): "Severe punishment?"

Feist (back-peddling): "No; I did not mean punishment in your acceptation of the term, and the term 'ripped up' would not mean that a horse was disembowelled or that his sides were ripped through. The phrase is a figurative one. I used it simply to indicate that the finish had been severe."

Having wriggled out of that one, Feist answered several more questions before the account of the proceedings concluded: "the magistrates, after a brief consultation, dismissed the case; the decision being received with loud cheers by a crowded court."

The report of the case was accompanied by a letter that must have been written by either Feist or Holman, signed, as it was, by 'One who narrowly escaped being victimised'. It foreshadowed, with uncanny accuracy, what has already come to pass and the fears that are now being voiced by the Countryside Alliance. With regard to the RSPCA, it asked:

> What will they do next to swell their list of 'convictions obtained' and open the eyes of the rich old ladies as to the good they are doing? If things go on in this way we may soon expect to see the employees of the Society on the banks of the Thames looking out to inform against anglers, and on September 1 some ardent sportsman will discover that information has been filed against him for shooting partridges. Foxhunting and even coursing are also in danger if this Society is allowed to take such a wide range in its prosecutions.

A few months before Feist had his run-in with the RSPCA, his old sparring partner, Dr Joseph Shorthouse, found himself in much hotter water after several scurrilous articles, written by his 'con amore' correspondents, had appeared in the *Sporting Times*. Not to put too fine a point on it, the articles accused Sir Joseph Hawley of blatant fraud in that he had 'milked' two of his three entries for the 1869 Liverpool Autumn Cup before scratching them after backing his other horse to win a small fortune.

The horses concerned were the 1868 Derby winner Blue Gown, who had been kept busy since his Epsom victory having won the Ascot Gold Cup and 12 of his 17 other races; the progressive three-year-old Siderolite, a winner of his last three weakly-contested races; and Lictor, an inconsistent but fairly decent handicapper on his day.

When the weights for the race were published, Siderolite was made 11-1 favourite and was subsequently backed down to 4-1 by "cliques of speculators who constitute the members of the two principal Turf clubs" (Tattersalls and Victoria Club),* while Blue Gown and Lictor were on offer at 25-1 and 50-1.

Hawley, a firm believer in the etiquette of the ring which laid down that an owner was entitled

---

* The Victoria Club, also known as 'the Slaughter House in Wellington Street', was to become London's main betting club where bookmakers gathered to hold 'call-overs' on ante-post prices for the big races right up until the late 1960s.

Sir Joseph Hawley, 'his wretched, discontented, scowling face' had the last laugh
over his forestallers in the 1869 Liverpool Autumn Cup.

to the best of the odds about his horse, had already taken action against the forestallers in March that season when he scratched his horse, Vagabond, from the City and Suburban Handicap after it had been backed down to 3-1 favourite from 20-1, and in June he had been responsible for instigating the police raids on the London commission agencies.* So when he drew the line through Siderolite and Blue Gown five days before the race it did not come as a complete surprise.

The *Sporting Times*, however, was outraged and went for the baronet's blue-veined jugular. One particular article headed, with unsubtle eloquence, 'Representative Sportsmen – No. 1 Sir Joseph Scratchawley', carried the singularly apposite signature of 'Caustic', the pen name of Alfred Geary, a former private secretary to the Jockey Club steward, General Peel. The most infamous libel in Turf history began:

Numerous as have been the occasions on which we have pointed a moral or adorned a tale by reference to some bright example (unhappily rare) of nobility and uprightness, of honesty,

---

* In his book *Racing For Gold*, James Peddie claims that Hawley instigated the raids because the bookmaker, Billy Wright, was constantly backing his horses or installing them as favourites: "Sir Joseph was not a man to be trifled with and his friends were all powerful in Downing Street … One day there was an extra gross case of forestalling and the order went forth – the long prepared thunderbolt fell."

straightforwardness, and sportsmanlike conduct, thank God we have never been unwarily betrayed into citing the name of Sir Joseph Scratchawley.

Life on the Turf is proverbially one of ups and downs. Its losses, as a rule, far exceed its gains and if, therefore, little men or needy ones, descend occasionally to rascalities, and milk and rope, or cheat and lie, and thieve their way to winning a handicap now and then, it is to be greatly deplored, but scarcely to be wondered at.

What can then be said for the spoilt darling of the Turf ... [*who*] has had the good fortune to win four Derbys, a St Leger, the Guineas and other races too numerous to mention. He might, if he chose, get drunk every night of the year out of a different cup won by the representatives of his stable, and yet his soul craves for something more.

The noble ambition of carrying off a coveted prize or of leading back to the scales the winner of the Blue Riband amid the acclamations of thousands, begins already to pall upon his satiated palate, and he casts a longing eye on the gate-money milk-cans and the corpses of the boiled, the stiff and the dead that taint the atmosphere of the ring.

Not bad for starters! And Geary went on to insult Hawley by referring to "his wretched, discontented, scowling face" and his "exceedingly mean and crafty expression" before he turned to the race in question:

On the appearance of the weights, 'Swindlerite' [*Siderolite*] is voted the pick of the handicap and, strong in their belief in the old formula that Sir Joseph Scratchawley always goes straight and gives a run for your money, the public ... pour their money into the laps of those who have been 'put in to lay' ... The pails are full of Swindlerite and Blackleg [*Blue Gown*] milk, the market begins to be agitated; Pickpocket [*Lictor*] comes hot in the betting and Swindlerite and Blackleg are scratched.

Let us call a spade a spade – let us not, like 'Hotspur', demean ourselves by calling this 'a bold stroke' and 'firm policy'. We are sick of hearing defenders of the Turf 'diary' tell us that a man may do what he likes with his own ... A man who practices these 'market movements' as they are mildly termed, is like the man who runs wires through his hedges or sets traps for foxes. As far as any claim to the title of 'sportsman' is concerned they are in the same boat, and in that category we place Sir Joseph Scratchawley.

The bloody hand on his escutcheon is emblematic of the victims who have fallen, not in actual strife, but from the stab of the stable commissioner, and it will be many a long year before even the spurious popularity he once enjoyed will be restored to him ... We sincerely hope poetical justice will overtake the stable and that as this is the culminating point of Sir Joseph Scratchawley's frauds upon the public, so it may be the turn of the tide of the fortune which has hitherto attended him, and which his grasping policy has converted from being a blessing into a curse.

Geary's hopes that poetic justice would intervene were dashed when Lictor proceeded to land the gamble for Hawley who had staked some £500 (£45,000) on the horse at all prices down to 6-1. Not content with having rubbed salt into the wounds of his enemies, Sir Joseph immediately issued a writ for 'malicious libel' against Shorthouse and his publisher Frederick Farrah and also one against Gilbert Robins, who had recently started up his own weekly, *The Man About Town*, in which he had also libelled Hawley by accusing him of a "mean and despicable act" in that he "thought he might as well take the public money as the commission agents".

Alfred Geary escaped a summons because, although he was prepared to take full responsibility for his article, Shorthouse "had very rigid and uncompromising views as to an editor's liabilities and duties, and refused to permit his contributor to appear in the matter."[1] While this was commendable, it also exposed the doctor's failings as an editor, something he did not attempt to hide in the letter of apology he sent to Hawley as soon as he heard of the impending writ. Written two days after the offending number of the *Sporting Times* had been published, it read:

> Sir – In this journal of Saturday last there appeared an article signed 'Caustic' in which your conduct and character were commented upon in the most scurrilous and unjustifiable manner. Incredible as it may seem I was entirely ignorant of such an article having been written or that such a one would appear, or I would have prevented it.
>
> I was unable to be at the office on Friday and when I read the paper today (and I had not done so before), I was amazed, ashamed and disgusted, and I write to you to express my extreme regret and sorrow that so scurrilous a libel upon your character should have appeared in a paper with which I have any connection. I will also take care that such retraction and regret shall appear prominently in the next number of the paper.
>
> I trust this spontaneous expression of my regret will satisfy you of my sincerity in making it and cause you to forget any pain or annoyance the article may have given you; but such untruthful and gross attacks usually carry their own refutation with them and excite contempt rather than inflict pain.

Shorthouse grovelled on in splendid style, but even his sycophantic remark, "there is no gentleman connected with the Turf whose policy, as a whole, I more entirely endorse (if it not be egregious vanity in me to say so) than I do yours," failed to save him from the retribution that belonged to Sir Joseph.

Justice was delivered at the Old Bailey on 15 December 1869 when Hawley's counsel declared that that his client "would sooner have accepted an apology from a person who had met him in the street and knocked his teeth down his throat than he would accept one from a man who used expressions and terms such as appeared in *that* paper."

Shorthouse, who conducted his own defence most ineffectively, was duly found guilty of "not exercising due caution" in his journalistic duties and was sentenced to three months' imprisonment in Coldbath Fields House of Correction.

The sentence shocked even the hardened hacks of Fleet Street, particularly as both co-defendants, Robins and Farrah, escaped with a £25 (£2,250) fine, while Geary got off scot-free and eventually went to work in South Africa where his poisonous pen "frequently got him into serious trouble and, on one occasion at least, put him in danger of sudden death."[2]

Harry Feist, who had a certain admiration for Shorthouse but none for his long-time tormentor, Robins ('The Outsider'), remarked:

> Under all the circumstances, gross and scandalous as was the notorious article entitled 'Sir Joseph Scratchawley', the sentence passed can only be regarded as extremely severe, more particularly when it is contrasted with the excessive leniency displayed towards Mr Gilbert Robins ... The doctor was, however, most indiscreet in the course he took and the remarks which appeared in his paper after the libel were calculated to exasperate the prosecutor, the judge and the jury. Mr Robins, on the other hand, published abject apologies and ceased writing entirely.

This course doubtless saved him; on the contrary, Doctor Shorthouse's injudicious band of amateur writers kept the wound inflicted upon Sir Joseph perpetually open, and the Carshalton pundit might well exclaim for the future 'Save me from my friends'.

Shorthouse, it should be added, bore his confinement without undue hardship and, as a 'first-class misdemeanant', was given privileges denied to common lags.* His own paper reported that his 'loose box' was "furnished with every convenience a reasonable man can require; ink, paper, books, newspapers and letters make the place assume something of the air of home, and a cheerful fire blazes in the grate." Unwisely, it also boasted that its egregious editor had "every indulgence granted in the administration of the victualling department."

The latter fact was picked up by Irwin Willes, whose inflated ego had been pricked by the doctor's incisive pen on more than one occasion. 'Argus', ever one to bear a grudge, saw his chance to get even, and while he professed his friendship for Shorthouse in his *Morning Post* column, he sneakily added, "strange to relate the visiting magistrates do not deny him champagne with which he can drown all his cares".

The article was brought to the attention of the chief magistrate, Sir Thomas Henry, and as a result Shorthouse had his rations cut, although he was hardly on the rack when Henry Dixon visited him a few weeks later, by which time Alfred Geary had been publicly exposed as the man behind the 'Caustic' article. 'The Druid' reported:

> On the whole, our friend seemed very contented. His table was covered with writing materials and the newest sporting books and papers out, and the only bitterness in his cup was that the visiting magistrates … had reduced his champagne allowance to one bottle a day … he frankly says, in very plain Saxon, that the champagne business is hard lines, the man who told the name of the writer of the article, a miserable sneak, and that he will be devilish glad when he is out.[3]

When Shorthouse did get out in March 1870, he went to Epsom races to make his peace with Hawley. When the two men met, the doctor doffed his hat in a most unctuous manner, bowed, and blustered: "I admire you Sir Joseph. No man in England except yourself would have had the courage to prosecute me. Let us shake hands."

It was recorded: "They shook hands and were good friends ever afterwards."[4]

---

* Now the site of the Post Office's Mount Pleasant sorting office, Coldbath Fields was used for short-term prisoners although it was no soft touch for those sentenced to hard labour – convicts had to work a notorious 24-step treadmill which was known, with good reason, as 'the cockchafer'!

THE LOST LEADERS

AS A BIOGRAPHER Henry Dixon had few, if any, equals and the sporting world presented him with a broad canvas on which to portray its leading characters. All too often he found himself penning a final tribute to old friends and acquaintances, as happened in 1869 when he was profoundly affected by what the *Life* described as "A catastrophe, probably without parallel in the annals of hunting, by which Sir Charles Slingsby of Scriven Park, Knaresborough, and five others lost their lives."

The accompanying report, which appeared on Saturday, February 5, related:

The York and Ainsty foxhounds met on Thursday at Stainley House, halfway between Harrogate and Ripon. There was a good field including Sir Charles Slingsby, the popular master of the hounds ... and the weather being fine, good sport was anticipated. A fox was found, and a capital run ensued of about an hour's duration in the direction of Copegrove and Newby Hall.

On approaching the Hall, Reynard crossed the river Ure and the hounds followed. Several of the field attempted the ford some distance up-stream, but Sir Charles Slingsby and the majority of those who were close up made for the ferry, which is almost directly opposite Newby Hall, and signalled for the boat to be sent across.

The river was much swollen by the late rains and to a great extent diverted from its natural channel, being at this point some fifty or sixty yards broad. Without a moment's hesitation, however, Sir Charles sprang into the boat, followed by some fifteen or sixteen gentlemen with their horses…

The boat is flat-bottomed and large enough to carry a carriage, being 28ft in length and 10ft in width. Before it had gone a third of the distance, Sir Charles Slingsby's horse became restive and the boat swayed first to one side and then to the other and finally it fairly turned bottom upwards and all in it were thrown into the river.

Those who managed to cling onto their horses were saved, but the 10th baronet, together with the first whip, William Orveys, two hunt members, Edmund Robinson and Edward Lloyd, and the ferrymen, James Warriner and his son, were all drowned.

Dixon, as a regular visitor to Yorkshire where he stayed with his good friend Sir Tatton Sykes on the famous Sledmere estate east of Malton, knew three of the men well and had featured the hunt in an article the previous summer. Recollections of the deceased were, therefore, still fresh in his mind as he wrote:

Death is more fearful when it is directly contrasted with pleasure, and the little ferry on the Ure will be remembered from this week, so long as that river rolls its tributary waters to the Ouse, as the scene of the most frightful tragedy in hunting history.

Yorkshire can hardly believe the sad tidings. The cathedral city was in the very height of her hunting term. There were visitors a plenty, and the Club was full of the doings of Sir Charles and of news of good sport with Mr Hall and the Holderness. Now four familiar faces are lacking, and of those men, three were the very life-blood of the hunt – master, crack rider, and first whip.

Sir Charles was only 44 and ever since 1838 he had been at the head of either harriers or foxhounds … With the trigger, in the silk, or on the Stand, he was still the same quiet English gentleman, keenly observant and always speaking to the purpose. He was a master of hounds *par excellence* – not pleasant one day and moody the next – losing no friend and making no enemy. On the day of his death he was riding Saltfish, his favourite old hunter of some fourteen seasons, and the two were taken out of the river not many yards from each other.

Mr Robinson was a rollicking spirit, cast in a very different mould, loving a horse passionately and handling him across country in marvellous style … He seemed part and parcel of the York world, a very king among its horsemen with his pleasant, jaunty look, his hat a trifle on one side and invariably a horse nearby, be it in the field or at the club door, to try or to ponder over.

Orveys, too, was a ripe good servant, courteous to the field and quite a right arm to his master. The pack had gradually gone on improving under his charge till, at last, it had taken a first prize at the Yorkshire Hound Show.

When we sat on that August day beneath the Wetherby Grange chain of woodlands and hailed the first thunder drops which had rattled among those coverts for weeks, we little thought that another season, of which they were the welcome herald, would take from that well-filled master's bench one grey-haired old man who had carried the horn for forty seasons, and another in his prime of manhood. But so it was to be.

The waters closed over them, and whatever anguish may have swept through their brain as soul and body parted, their struggles were mercifully short. Those are still more to be pitied who stood on the banks waiting their turn across the treacherous tide, or who gallantly plunged in, witnesses of so hard a fate to their comrades and yet powerless to help them.

The dead are beyond the reach of regret; the living have the remembrance of a sorrow and a sight which they can never forget.[*]

At the time he wrote this, Dixon must have been acutely aware of his own mortality as his health had been failing ever since his epic trek home from Scotland in the depths of winter five years earlier. He was suffering from bronchitis and asthma and had written too many obituaries of the consumptive not to know that his own would soon appear in the same all-embracing columns. And just over a year later, on Saturday, 19 March 1870, the *Life* announced:

Readers of standard sporting literature will learn with regret the death of Mr H H Dixon (better known under his signature of 'The Druid') which occurred at his residence in Kensington on Wednesday morning at half-past ten.

The deceased gentleman had been in failing health for some years and his constitution finally broke up rapidly although he was able to attend to his literary duties up to within a few weeks … He was decidedly one of the notable men of the time and known to an immense number of masters of hounds, horse owners, breeders, trainers, jockeys, huntsmen and herdsmen, though his retiring and modest manner made him evade, as much as possible, personal identity or public notoriety…

His sporting works are distinguished by an easy fluency and a graceful diction which render them classical in contrast to other compositions; and the *Times* once said of him, as a high term of eulogy, that he was 'the Tacitus of sporting writers'.

---

[*] In his annual review of events at the end of 1869, Dixon was to add a sorry postscript to the tragedy when he related: "The first whip, who took the hounds home that sad day, also met his fate within six months, jumping over a low fence while cub-hunting."

He was a most amiable, truthful, conscientious man, and perhaps no person connected with sports and pastimes more signally preserved the dignity of his private life. Quaint and plain in dress, he was himself one of the 'characters' he could so well have depicted; and, as he strode along in his deerstalker with his stick in hand, or hovered about the secluded portions of our racecourses, few would have imagined how thoroughly refined, reflective and cultivated he was in all his tastes and predilections.

His love for anecdote was a perfect passion with him, and he sifted the traits of his subjects so completely that he could set dead worthies before the reader's eye with marvellous fidelity. When in health, his mind was bright and his spirits especially vivacious, and he delighted in quiet satire and humorous sallies with which he invariably set off his genial and chatty form of conversation with his friends.

Latterly, Mr Dixon, from his tardy and painful manner of walking and laboured breathing, attracted more than ordinary attention. Swathed round the mouth with a woollen scarf and his chest enveloped in a shepherd's plaid, he said with grim jocoseness of himself that he was 'suffering from foot and mouth disease'.

Those who were brought in close connection with him during his association with the *Sporting Life* desire to place on record the esteem and affection in which they held the deceased for his amiable disposition, his urbanity, and for many manly attributes which denoted real nobility of character.

In his Augur column, Harry Feist revealed the end had come as a merciful release:

…having been so great a sufferer for some time past, he prayed for his death and was so willing to quit the scene that he disapproved of the doctors, as he termed it, 'patching him up a little longer'. The deceased was a comparatively young man – in his forty-eighth year – one of those who look at the cheerful side of life and, being an ardent lover of nature, he strolled on his book excursions over the hills, dales and valleys of England and saw, with a finely cultivated and poetical eye, 'books in the running stream, sermons in stones and good in everything'.

Henry Hall Dixon was laid to rest in Brompton cemetery, west London without fuss or ceremony. His funeral reflected the man, since:

In accordance with his wishes, the proceedings were as quiet as possible, the followers being confined to members of his family and seven or eight intimate friends who had expressed a wish to see the last of one whose career had always been one of purity and independence and never influenced by an unworthy notice.

Inevitably, the loss of such a rare talent was keenly felt at the *Life*. Dixon was, in fact, irreplaceable and, as such, the practice of carrying regular editorials was allowed to die with him. Instead, it was decided that Feist should incorporate any comments he had on the topics of the day into his column unless exceptional circumstances demanded otherwise.

Feist was on a par with his late colleague as a writer, and because they were living at a time when there was an intellectual and literary groundswell against the inequalities of a class system that many Victorians regarded as the divine and rightful order of society, it is not surprising that their articles often reflected the need for social reforms outside racing.

It was, after all, an era when children as young as eight were sent up chimneys only to be suffocated by soot or killed by collapsing masonry, while many more suffered a lingering death from skin cancer or bronchial problems. Conditions were no better in the mines or the mills where ten-year-old girls worked on shifts that could last from 5am to 9pm; those falling asleep were strapped by overseers – accidents were a daily occurrence.

There was a strong Dickensian influence in Feist's writing as he eagerly adopted the reforming conscience of his age to attack incompetent institutions and the hypocrisy of the high and mighty. Yet his articles were often leavened with subtle humour. He had an eye for the absurd and would regularly take a leaf out of 'The Druid's' book to colour his racing 'Notes and Anticipations' with pen portraits of the towns and the people his excursions brought him into contact with.

For instance, his coverage of the Stockbridge races in the summer of '71 incorporated a moan on the late-running of the trains, a vote of appreciation for the Prince of Wales, a swipe at racing's critics, and a pen portrait of the little Hampshire village that played host to the three-day meeting. He started with the commuter's perennial complaint:

> Those who had to journey from London and back each day were compelled to endure the usual martyrdom of passengers on the South Western line. Trains crawled along, stopped at stations for twenty minutes for no ascertainable reason, and an hour behind time was considered quite good business and an approximation to punctuality.
>
> To show that such a state of things can easily be remedied on this bungled railway; when the Prince of Wales went down on Thursday, the express was at Andover to the moment. The greatest gratification was on all sides manifested at the visit of the Prince who was shown over the Danebury stables with the most profound loyalty by John Day.
>
> The Prince, in his tastes, is a thorough Englishman and to see him hastening across the paddock in his mackintosh to inspect the chief winners was significant in these days when sentimental and canting members of the Legislature are endeavouring to put down the favourite pursuits of our countrymen.
>
> When the bigoted opponents of betting and racing are fulminating indiscriminately against the followers of the Turf, they will, perhaps, be good enough to bear in recollection that it is evidently the favourite sport of the future king of England.

Here, Feist took the opportunity to attack the latest attempt by the government to bring in legislation (a forerunner to Anderson's 1874 Bill) to outlaw the bookmakers in Scotland, before he returned to Stockbridge with the remark:

> Few people, unless they have undergone the experience, can conceive the patient suffering and endurance necessary for a sojourn of a day or so in the village at race times. Miserably poor and wretchedly dirty, the natives turn their cottages to the best account and are mild, kindly people, but their domiciles are, as a rule, three hundred years behind the time.
>
> It has been well said that the only things which really live well at Stockbridge are certain carnivorous insects whose midnight excursions induce visitors to scratch themselves for all future engagements in the place! Exception must be taken to some neat, ivy-clad cottages with their pretty gardens and prim tenants and, above all, to some cosy inns. The White Hart, of which H F Haynes is the landlord, deserves honourable mention, for nothing could exceed the admirable manner in which the catering was conducted at this well-ordered establishment.

The host is well known on the Turf as a trainer, and Mr Merry's, Thomas Dawson's and other important teams are usually located for the week in the capital boxes in the rear of this clean and dainty-looking little hostelry.

The Grosvenor, which is presumed to be *the* hotel in the village, was this year turned to a most extraordinary account as it was taken *en masse* by the Bibury Club and over the principal entrance the word 'Private' was inscribed and admission refused to the public, an affair likely to be noticed on a future licensing day in the district.

Feist was happier in Brighton where, a few weeks later, his sketch of the town during race week was nothing if not varied. It included observations on the local buskers and prostitutes and – with a large dollop of journalistic licence – a drowning at sea:

All the Turf world and his wife seemed to be congregated on the spot. The aristocratic element was fully alive to the advantages of the occasion. Mornings were occupied in bracing 'dips' and pleasant strolls, or fashionable 'whips' were engaged driving friends and fair companions in dashing four-in-hands or other elegant equipages, up and down King's Road.

Evenings on the West Pier, enlivened with the admirable music of the town band, were, to use the fast expression, 'awfully jolly' … Still there may be too much of some good things. The breakfast hour, for instance, was certainly not improved by listening to the simultaneous discord of a band, the screams and too-tooing of Punch and Judy, with accompanying drum and Pandean pipes, an accordion and a pair of bagpipes played by a Highlander who looked like a dejected supernumerary from a transpontine theatre captured out of the play *Rob Roy*.

Another matter may be taken up tenderly and handled with care. It was not gratifying to notice that the cotes of Brompton and St John's Wood had let fly a concourse of soiled doves, readily recognised by their extravagant girl-of-the-period costumes, their golden chignons, powder and paint, their perennial thirst for champagne and that peculiar laugh which seems pumped up as a relief against the inward consciousness of what an anomalous place they occupy in society.

There was but one painful incident of the week, but that one appallingly tragic. Early on Wednesday morning, while hundreds of people were about the Esplanade, there came up from the beach a gurgling scream of 'Drowning, drowning – save me!' and a pair of arms and a terrified pale face were seen to rise and then sink a few feet beyond a bathing machine opposite the Old Ship.

Of the crowds of lookers-on, not one attempted a rescue. Even a couple of boatmen did no more than prod about with the end of their oars, having no other idea or means at hand, in such a place as Brighton, for saving life!

Ultimately the sunken man was trolled for with a net and hauled to the surface with a few small fish dancing about his body … That a man should lose his life in a few feet of water at so important a place as Brighton for the want of some simple implements for rescue, displays, to say the least, a disregard to awful eventualities which is unaccountable in days which boast of their humane societies.

This underlying social conscience came to the fore time and again in Feist's articles. Typical were his comments on the 1872 trial of a telegraph clerk who, in transmitting a racing telegram, had acted on the information it contained to back the horses it advised. "It is impossible not to perceive that this was a very gross prostitution of privilege and duty," wrote Feist before adding an overriding 'however', as he continued:

In defence, it was urged that Dickenson had been in the employ of the authorities for twelve years at the splendid rate of £1 weekly; that he was married, had to sustain a genteel appearance and had two children, and that the poor fellow had been tempted to pry into messages in order to eke out this magnificent emolument by occasionally 'betting a few shillings on his own behalf'.

If this be true, the real onus indirectly rests upon the Postal Telegraph authorities, for if their clerks are to be employed in such confidential duties, they should receive some salary sufficiently remunerative to place them above any petty prying temptation. Serious as the transgression is, it is cruel to think of Dickenson in a position where sobriety, industry, respectability, intelligence and integrity were all to be supported on £1 per week, and after *twelve years' service* too!

The editor was inclined to embark upon his social campaigns during the winter months when the cancellation of fixtures would result in a dearth of hard news. His sympathies for the downtrodden and his contempt for what he saw as an inefficient police force pursuing piddling prosecutions, were given a short but vigorous airing during a freeze-up in January 1874, when he used the lack of sport as a lead-in to his subject:

Anything to break this spell of monotonous apathy would be as eagerly pounced upon as has been the poor old parish clerk and sexton of Marks Tey for being found with three bits of wood – valued at one penny – the presumed property of his reverend and charitable employer, the rector of that same village.

Our police are truly wonderful in detecting such mighty crimes as this giant wood-stealing case in Essex. Yet murder stalks undiscovered, fraudulent men of high position escape with their ill-gotten gains and it is quite the exception for so mild an offence as burglary to be traced to its perpetrator; albeit, raids upon little betting men, watching licensed victuallers and 'running in' every available victim, will stand boldly out as heroic and compensating deeds to future ages.

In the case alluded to of 'the parson, the parish clerk and the penn'orth of wood', even the lawyer who defended the prisoner offered to become bail for him! This is, indeed, an example of the lion lying down with the lamb.

While Feist normally had an admirable knack of hitting the nail on the head he could also be perplexingly inconsistent in his writing which, at best, was disconcerting and, at its embarrassing worst, undermined the credibility of his campaigns. To quote just one example; in 1871 he took a definite stand against a recent Jockey Club ruling that banned two-year-old races before May 1. The edict inevitably resulted in a shortage of runners at the big spring meetings when Northampton was the hardest hit of all:

No reunion of the season was more anxiously looked forward to than this popular gathering and decidedly its most attractive features were its two-year-old contests, chief among which was the Althorp Park Stakes … The Jockey Club, however, inspired by Sir Joseph Hawley and backed by Mr Henry Chaplin, desire to 'reform' this altogether and the result has been to reduce Northampton to a mere shadow of its former self and bring it down to a level of plating. The effect of the decline was so striking that it is to be hoped the preposterous law which prohibits two-year-old racing until May 1 will soon be repealed.

Twelve months later, HMF was still bemoaning "the unwarranted and ill-judged 'interference with the liberty of the subject' in the matter of two-year-old racing" as he blamed the lack of runners at the spring meetings on 'the Hawley blight'.* But by October 1873, when he learned that the restriction was about to be lifted, instead of welcoming the news with loud hurrahs he observed:

> The present state of Turf law has worked satisfactorily and why a change should be desired is, to thoughtful persons, incomprehensible. Next season I suppose the old nuisance of spectators waiting for three-quarters of an hour in biting March winds while two-year-olds are indulging in false starts, will be revived. I am afraid that the Jockey Club are yielding to the pestering pressure continually put on them to satisfy a coterie of penurious and frail people.

And this, from one who had condemned the selfsame rule less than three years earlier! Surely, the only thing 'incomprehensible to thoughtful persons' was how he could have completed a U-turn of such remarkable dexterity in so short a space of time! Three weeks later, when it was confirmed that the ruling was to be scrapped in 1874, Feist was sitting firmly on the fence over the issue:

> That the return to the old regime will have great influence on the prosperity of the early meetings of the season is certain, and next spring we shall again see such stakes as the Brocklesby at Lincoln, the Whittlebury and Althorp Park at Northampton and the Two-Year-Old Stakes at Epsom, revived in all their glory ... I think it will be admitted that no practical benefit has been derived from the three years of restriction.

There you have it! A law originally described as 'preposterous' and then as having 'worked satisfactorily', was now declared to have been of 'no practical benefit'. Unfortunately, there are too many other examples of Feist's inconsistency for them to be brushed off with the explanation that he just had an off-day or a day off. But, whether he was running with the hare or hunting with the hounds, he campaigned tirelessly on until, on Friday, 18 December 1874, while resting at home in Croydon, he finally succumbed to the dread disease that had haunted him all his life.

Consumption had claimed the lives of two of his brothers before they were 13, while another, Edward, died from it at 21, as had his eldest brother, Albert, at the age of 32. Harry, the 'last of all the flock' in this ill-fated brotherhood, had done well to reach the age of 38. The paper he had lived for reported:

> The end was sudden and it was the close of a brilliant career which might have been finished amidst much greater glory than there was time for Harry Feist to obtain. With splendid natural abilities, with talent, nay, let us say genius, far beyond what appertains to nine-tenths of the men who have earned literary reputations within the last few years – he made less use of it to his own profit than anyone in his position we have known.
>
> He might have been a rich man – he preferred to be a generous one – and had he not befriended all save himself, and thought too much of paving the way for the successes of others who never had

---

* At a meeting of the Jockey Club in 1869, Hawley, worried about overtaxing immature horses, originally proposed that there should be no races for two-year-olds before July 1, but his motion was defeated by 25 votes to 18. The May 1 date was then put forward as a compromise and was carried by 27 votes to 8.

the grace to thank or kindly remember him for what he had done, he might have left his family better provided to face the frowns of the world than we fear is the case…

The influence of his pen was felt far beyond the range attained by other sporting writers. Nothing seemed outside his capacity. Whatever he touched upon, he adorned with an eloquence which gave his contributions to journalism a charm which was all their own, and we cannot help saying that his intense energy, his thorough acquaintance with the work to be done, his hopeful temperament, his complete knowledge of the Turf (with which he had been familiarised almost in his cradle) and his intimate acquaintance with everyone connected with the running-path, the ring and the river in their best days, helped most materially to place the *Sporting Life*, at the outset of its career, in the position it now occupies…

He was unceasing in his suggestions for advancing the interests of this paper … which he regarded as one of his own children; and we and our readers must alike feel the great loss we have sustained in being deprived of the services of one whose intellect budded so early, blossomed so brightly, but whose existence was cut off with a suddenness which startled even those who might have fancied, during the last few weeks, that the light was but flickering in its socket.

The circumstances which led to that guiding light being snuffed out were detailed in the *Daily Telegraph* as it paid tribute to its fallen 'Hotspur':

On the evening of his demise he was so much better that his friends had hope of his speedy recovery. Shortly before eight o'clock, however, he was attacked by a severe fit of illness which resulted in the bursting of a blood vessel and immediate death…

On all matters appertaining to the national pastime Henry Feist was an undeniable authority … Always ready to uphold the integrity of the sport, he was a fearless and uncompromising foe to its many abuses. As a guide he was invaluable and the rich store of information that he possessed enabled him to foreshadow coming events with singular accuracy … Personally, Henry Feist will be deeply regretted by innumerable friends. His kindly and amiable character rendered him a universal favourite, while his vivacity and ready wit made him a most genial companion.

In the *Sporting Times*, Joseph Shorthouse, now only a '*con amore*' contributor to the paper he once owned, paid homage to his old adversary even though he was, in his words, "in a very enfeebled state of body and himself almost on the verge of the grave."* His view of Feist's fatal affliction was typically unorthodox:

His death did not arise, as the papers have announced, from typhoid fever or from consumption, but like that of many others, from excitement, worry and overwork – in short, from having lived too fast, from having burnt the candle at both ends and lighted it in the middle as well.

We have been utterly amazed at the amount of work he had to do and would get through after a hard day's work at a race meeting … [*for him*] there was no rest till midnight or, as often was the case, till the small hours of the morning. He had to write reports of the day's sport for two or more newspapers, then to peruse the programme for the following day to give predictions…

It has often been remarked by his detractors that … he was not always consistent either with

---

* The good doctor was being unduly pessimistic on this score since he lived on for nine more years!

himself, with what he had written before or with the bare facts. This is not to be wondered at. Under similar circumstances, and with an amount of work to do so varied in its character and to be done under such disadvantageous circumstances, *who* would have been consistent? Very few, we are inclined to think, would have come out of the ordeal with more consistency than poor Feist.

Interestingly, Shorthouse, who could always be relied upon to come up with a controversial opinion, concluded: "We think he shone least of all as a sporting writer. As a mimic of drollery he was unrivalled by any one we ever knew … as an actor Feist must have taken high rank."

The *Illustrated Sporting and Dramatic News* also noted the late editor had obviously inherited his father's theatrical talents because, "whenever he appeared on the stage at Croydon for a charitable purpose, there was certain to be a crowded house." With regard to Feist's other attributes, it stated:

No man was better known in the sporting world and for several years he attended every important event in the kingdom. At the Ringside his face was familiar as he stood referee for many a well-fought battle, and was much esteemed for the fairness of his decisions … The deceased was a most generous man and his purse was always open to the call of the needy and distressed. Many of the Turf writers now engaged on the sporting press have to thank Mr Feist for the positions that they now enjoy, as he took great pleasure in advancing unknown men when he discovered that they exhibited sufficient promise of making successful writers.

In Manchester, Edward Hulton led off 'Kettledrum's Notes' in the *Sporting Chronicle* with a heartfelt tribute:

So poor Harry Feist is dead! One of the most genial, kindly, good-natured, well-informed and communicative of Turf writers has gone from amongst us and his accustomed haunts will know him no more. The slim figure and boyish face of 'Augur' were well known on every racecourse where his cordial manner and universal sympathies made him immensely popular…

He had long been ailing and so far back as two years ago he expressed his opinion to the present writer that the end was not far off. I regret to hear that his widow and large family are not left in very good circumstances, but I have no doubt that if an appeal is made to the sporting public, who have so often enjoyed and sometimes profited by his writings, it will meet with a prompt and hearty response.

And so it was, but not before a funeral "of rugged simplicity" had taken place at West Croydon cemetery on a cold, crisp day just before Christmas when the *Life* reported:

All that was mortal of Henry Mort Feist was laid to rest in the same grave where his younger brother Edward, who died some years ago, is buried. The severe frost of the proceeding night had covered every branch and leaf, and their outline stood out in the most beautiful relief against the snow-covered ground and the dull, leaden-coloured sky … It was a sight to be long remembered by those present. Hardened men of the world, standing round the last resting place of 'Augur' found unbidden and unwonted tears in their eyes as they gazed on the simple black coffin which bore on its lid the plain silver breastplate engraved 'Henry Mort Feist, died December 18, 1874'.

Many of those who were on hand to pay their last respects had met at Anderton's Hotel in Fleet

Street two days earlier in order to set up a fund for Feist's widow and his six children. After a working committee had been formed under the chairmanship of Charles Ashley, a former *Sporting Life* reporter who had recently become joint-proprietor of the *Sportsman*, it was announced that Admiral Rous had agreed to become its president, while four other Jockey Club members – the Earls of Coventry and Portsmouth, Sir John Astley and Sir Richard Bulkeley – were to act as patrons. Such an impressive line-up of the Turf's hierarchy was unprecedented in an era when journalists were treated with extreme suspicion, if not open hostility, by racing's governing body.

Further evidence of the respect accorded to Feist and of his all-round popularity, was provided a week later when the names of the first subscribers to his fund were published. The tabulated list took up three-quarters of a column on the front page and was headed by the proprietors of the *Daily Telegraph* who gave £200; the *Sporting Life* £103 (William McFarlane was good for £100, the odd £3 came from a whip-round among the compositors) and the *Sportsman* £60.

Henry Chaplin, owner of the Derby winner Hermit, and Sir John Astley both donated £25 as did Thomas Blenkiron of the Middle Park Stud; Leopold and Nathaniel de Rothschild £20, Lord Portsmouth £15, Lord Coventry and Admiral Rous both gave £10, Lord Falmouth £5 and Lord Courtenay £4. The Croydon Race Committee raised £34 15s; the Dorlings, through the Epsom Grand Stand Association, sent in £10; John Verrall (5gns) and Tom McGeorge jnr (3gns) also contributed.

Subscribers from the press included, from *Bell's Life*, Henry Smurthwaite (editor), R B Wormald (aquatics editor) and Charles Greenwood (destined to become famous as 'Hotspur' from 1882-1903), John Corlett, proprietor and editor of the *Sporting Times*, Bill Langley who had succeeded Irwin Willes on the *Morning Post*, Henry Harris, 'Touchstone' of *The Era*, Joe Capp (Central News Agency), William Gale (*Morning Advertiser*), Fred Taylor (*Sportsman*) and John Lovell, manager of the Press Association.

Charles Dickens jnr, whose famous father had died in 1870, was also on the list, while there were donations from the *Newcastle Chronicle*, *Liverpool Post*, *The Field*, *The Scotsman*, *Sporting Gazette*, *Sporting Opinion*, *Sporting Chronicle*, *Sporting Clipper*, *Racing Chronicle*, *Land and Water*, *Turf Guide* and the *York Herald*.

Amongst the bookmakers, Billy Wright sent in £25 from Paris, Messrs Valentine, Perkins and Burch contributed 15gns, Fred Swindell and James Peddie both gave £5, while Tom Sayers' old backer, Johnny Gideon, coughed up a guinea.

Of the jockeys, Tom Chaloner, who won the Two Thousand Guineas and Derby on Macaroni in 1863 and was to ride his fifth St Leger winner in 1875, was good for £10, while Charlie Maidment, who had the unique distinction of tying for the jockeys' championship in both 1870 and '71, put himself down for 2gns.

Among the trainers, Mat Dawson contributed £5, William Day of Woodyates and John Porter of Kingsclere, 2gns each, while Richard Marsh, who had just started training at Banstead Manor, Epsom and was to become 'A Trainer to Two Kings' (as he called his autobiography), gave a guinea.

Over the succeeding weeks, subscriptions rolled in from all sections of the sporting community. No fewer than 90 members of the Victoria and Albert Clubs contributed sums ranging from 10s to £5, while long-forgotten mortals such as W B van Haansbergen of the Woodlands Stud, Consett, and the Rev Thomas Beard of Stokesley Rectory near Norwich also chipped in, as did members of the general public who sent in postal orders or a few shillings worth of stamps.

By the end of February the fund had grown to £1,537 6s 6d (£138,350) with more to come as it was noted that "in Liverpool, Manchester, Birmingham, Dublin, Sheffield, Nottingham, Newcastle-upon-Tyne, Newmarket and other towns, gentlemen have kindly undertaken to collect subscriptions, but their lists have not yet been received."

In March, Feist's friends at the Theatre Royal, Croydon, staged a benefit evening in his memory. The company performed Craven's drama *The Post Boy* and Byron's burlesque *Aladdin*. It was a fitting tribute to a man who had taken on many roles during the course of his career and had played such an integral part in the story of the *Life*.

In his sphere, H M Feist was assuredly one of the most influential editors of all time and for the next 123 uncertain and ultimately glorious years, the *Sporting Life* was to serve as his memorial until it was desecrated by lesser men who had never even heard the name of Harry Feist.

PART TWO
THE UNCERTAIN YEARS
(1875-1918)

Taken from just below the *Life's* offices in 1897, the photo shows a typically chaotic Fleet Street with St Paul's Cathedral in the background.

A VET IN THE CHAIR

T HE LOSS of two such gifted men as Harry Feist and Henry Dixon in so short a space of time was a crippling blow to the *Sporting Life*. Feist had been the bedrock on which the fortunes of the paper had been built, while he and Dixon were responsible for raising the standard of sports journalism to a new level.

To make matters worse, Edward Dorling, who for 12 years had been Feist's right-hand man and managing editor since 1861, had left the paper soon after the death of his father in March 1873. Martin Cobbett, who worked as a sub on the *Life* and contributed a rustic 'Man on the March' column in the 1880s, described him as "one of the best working editors who ever took a paper in hand; certainly no one could be more painstaking."[1]

Firm but fair, 'EJ' was the antithesis of his elder brother, Henry Mayson Dorling, who succeeded their father in running Epsom racecourse in 1873. Whereas 'HM' was regarded as "a true martinet, a self-assured, uncompromising dictator, capable of fighting tooth and nail against anyone – be he prince or pauper – who dared to go contrary to his wishes," Edward Jonathan was fondly remembered as a "serene, kindly man, slow to anger, tactful in his dealings with others."[2]

The *Life* could ill afford to lose such a key player at this a crucial time. But so it was that within the space of five years the three men who had contributed so much to the success of the paper were all gone and with them went the dynamism that had driven the whole team forward in the face of increasing competition.

Ever since the launch of the *Sporting Chronicle* in 1871, the *Life* had been losing sales in the midlands and the north, while the *Sportsman* had, by now, replaced the ailing *Bell's Life* as its chief rival in the south. In 1866, "at the urgent solicitation of numerous subscribers," the Smiths had stepped up production of the *Sportsman* to three times a week; a fourth day was added in 1868 when they also brought out a 'double number' of eight pages on a Saturday, and finally the paper took a decided lead over the *Life* when it became a daily in 1876.

The motive force behind the move had been Charles Hitchen Ashley, a fiercely ambitious journalist who had bought out James Smith's share in the paper two years earlier. Ashley had learnt his trade in Sheffield where he started out as an apprentice printer before he graduated through the sports department of the local *Examiner* to become racing correspondent of the *Sheffield Daily Telegraph*.

In 1862, at the age of 28, he joined the staff of the *Life* and then became chief racing reporter for the *Sportsman* when it was launched in 1865. Still not content with his lot, the peripatetic pen-pusher left soon afterwards to start his own sporting news agency, which achieved a major breakthrough in 1870 when it added the recently established Press Association news agency to its list of subscribers.

Ashley was certainly better qualified to run the *Sportsman* than Sydney Smith who was now operating as a credit bookmaker from the paper's offices in Boy Court off Ludgate Hill while he continued to own horses in partnership with James Smith.

In 1875, the two men made a highly speculative investment in a three-year-old colt that had finished down the field in two outings for their Lambourn trainer, George Clement, the previous year. The unnamed bay fared no better for the Smiths in his two races that autumn, finishing last on both occasions, but this did not deter the owners from forking out £25 (£2,250) apiece a year later to enter their apparently useless hay-burner in both the Cesarewitch and the Cambridgeshire.

The fact that the horse had been kept under wraps at home since his three-year-old days meant that Admiral Rous had little to work on when it came to allotting him a weight in the two races and in his initial draft he gave him just 5st 13lb. But when the octogenarian weight-juggler sought a second opinion from the bookmaker George Hodgman, he was warned he might have seriously underrated the colt, which would be well suited by the stamina-testing two-and-a-quarter miles of the Cesarewitch.

Taking no chances, Rous accordingly raised the dark horse by 20lb to 7st 5lb, but even this massive hike did not deter the Smiths from lumping on at long odds when betting on the race began in earnest at Doncaster's St Leger meeting, where the son of Speculum was "the medium of some substantial business", being backed at all prices down to 100-6.

A week before the race, the name of 'Rosebery' was registered for the colt; a 'tip' that was not lost on those who noted that Lord Rosebery often acted as a racecourse steward with the Marquess of Hartington, and Hartington just happened to have been the name of the horse that landed some £40,000 (£3.6m) in bets for the Smiths when he won the 1862 Cesarewitch!

Final confirmation that a major coup was underway came when the news leaked out that Fred Archer had been booked for the ride. The teenage champion already had a tremendous following and now the public threw away their form books and joined in the gamble, backing Rosebery down to 100-14 behind the 9-2 favourite Woodlands, who was rated a good thing by his bookmaker-owner, the unfortunately named Fred Swindell.

It was no contest. Rosebery won easily by four lengths from Woodlands with the other 27 runners trailing in by instalments. Archer received £1,000 (£90,000) for his services, the Smiths netted another fortune and the *Sportsman's* readers celebrated as the paper had made no secret of the confidence that lay behind the horse in its final preview of the race.

But even greater things were to follow. In 1862 the Smiths had tried for an ambitious double with Hartington by going for the Cambridgeshire two weeks later but, under a 7lb penalty and (inexplicably) carrying 3lb overweight, the horse had finished fifth, narrowly beaten in a blanket finish of heads and necks.

This time Rosebery was lumbered with a 14lb penalty. Over the much shorter distance of nine furlongs he had it all to do, but with the bookmakers already committed to heavy liabilities should he become the first horse to complete the double in the 37-year history of the two races, the colt started 4-1 joint-favourite in a field of 32.

With Archer claimed to ride for his retainer, Lord Falmouth, Harry Constable came in for the mount and in a desperate finish he got Rosebery home by a neck from the Royal Hunt Cup winner, Hopbloom. And so it was that one of the best-planned coups in racing history was landed with what had started out as a four-year-old maiden.

The Smiths reportedly netted some £100,000 (£9m) over the two races. Constable had been put on at £1,000 to nothing, and young Archer was given another handsome present as compensation for having to miss the ride in a race he was destined never to win and which would ultimately play its part in his tragic death.

James Smith (forever afterwards known as 'Rosebery' Smith) invested his winnings in building the Bon Marché department store in Brixton; a business his sons ran while he continued to pit his wits against the handicapper as he shrewdly mapped out winning campaigns for a succession of progressive horses.

Such good fortune had not attended Joseph Shorthouse, who emerged from prison to find that sales of the *Sporting Times*, temporarily boosted by the notoriety of the libel case, had fallen off almost as quickly. With his journalistic enthusiasm blunted and his finances depleted, he finally cut his losses at the end of 1872 by selling out to Robert Outram Wallace, a retired Black Watch officer who was just branching out into newspaper ownership. Typically, the doctor bowed out in style with a remarkably frank farewell message that began:

> With this number my functions as proprietor, editor and manager will cease. They have been very imperfectly performed for some time past and were never done well. For the general welfare of the paper and for the edification and amusement of its supporters and readers, I have thought it best to resign all connections with it except as a simple contributor.

Not that Wallace was able to do any better. After struggling to revive the ailing journal for two years, he sold it on to John Corlett for just £50 (£4,500). The new owner had been one of the original contributors to the paper under the name of 'Don John' before he joined the *Sportsman* as 'Vigilant' in 1867. A gifted writer, he proved a great asset to that paper, but when Charles Ashley took over its management in 1874, a clash of personalities saw him return to the *Sporting Times* to clinch the deal of a lifetime.

A big man in every sense of the word, Corlett enlisted "a band of able and, for the most part, unconventional writers"[3] and "with his insatiable zest for life and sport, and the merry things of this world"[4] he gradually began to turn around the doctor's old paper.

His entertaining and informative column, signed 'Vigilant and the Wizard', helped to pull in new readers and when, for reasons of economy, the paper began to be printed on a stock of cheaply bought, pink-tinted newsprint, it was soon dubbed the 'Pink 'Un', a name that was officially incorporated into its title in 1881, when an editorial note explained that the sub-title, 'Otherwise known as the Pink 'Un', had been added because:

> *The Sporting Times* is so thoroughly known as the 'Pink 'Un' that there was a danger of some unscrupulous person starting a paper and calling it by that name, and, acting on the highest legal advice, we have ourselves registered it as part of our title.

Thus adorned, all previous inhibitions went out of the window. With Corlett's team of maverick journalists radiating their clever, subtle and sometimes ribald wit from its pages, the weekly journal flushed and blanched in varying roseate shades until it finally settled on an unabashed hue of empire pink.

This break with conformity would have been appreciated by Dr Shorthouse and it typified Corlett's outlook on life which was "the embodiment of the good-humoured, fun-loving, tolerant yet shrewd Rabelaisian ideal".[5] From a circulation of just 4,000, the 'Pink 'Un' soon reached 20,000, while the *Sportsman*, in its all-important first year as a daily, gained a host of new readers through forecasting the successes of Rosebery.

In the face of such burgeoning opposition, it was essential that the *Life* maintained its standards and its readers. It needed an editor of Corlett's calibre to fill the void left by Feist, but such men are a rare breed and Charles William Blake, who succeeded to the chair, was certainly not one of them.

Born and brought up in the ancient market town of Crewkerne in Somerset, where his father was a vet, Blake had a keen appreciation of nature and a love of country life that was far removed from the

Charles Blake, 'Augur II', a decidedly eccentric editor (1875-91).

'pen and ink' of Fleet Street.

He had set his sights on attaining high rank in his father's profession and to that end had attended the Royal Veterinary College in Camden Town, north London, where he showed himself to be a naturally talented student. His thesis on *The Comparative Anatomy, Pathology and Physiology of the Skin of all Domesticated Animals* won him the first prize medal of his year (1861) and shortly afterwards he was elected a Fellow of the Veterinary Medical Association on the strength of his essay on *The Hock of the Horse*.

It seemed as if Blake had as good a command of the pen as he had of his subject, but at the time he had no thoughts of becoming a journalist. On leaving the RVC he returned to the West Country and went into practice attending to the horses and hounds of the Cattistock and Blackmoor Vale Hunts amongst others. Being an all-round sportsman, he took advantage of his situation to have a few rides at the local hunt meetings and won a couple of races on his own horses.

But after three years in rural practice, ambition drove him back to London, where he became an assistant to Queen Victoria's veterinary surgeon, George Williams. Soon afterwards, his career took an unexpected literary turn when he began to write an occasional veterinary article for the *Life* and in February 1867, Feist dispatched him to Newmarket to report on the condition of the Derby favourite, The Rake, who had developed a hock problem.

The vet was not impressed by what he saw and roundly criticised the cauterising that had been carried out on the joint:

> …to lightly press a little bit of flat heated iron on a horse's hock, two inches above the seat of the spavin, under the impression that it will prevent disease and make him stand work, is a sheer absurdity. There is no more important joint in a racehorse, where soundness is a *sine quâ non*, than the hock … and there can be no doubt that a horse with an enlarged hock, causing a rigidity of the joint, as The Rake has, cannot possibly be so perfect or so good an animal as though such an enlargement did not exist.

The report was regarded as a scoop for the *Life* and Blake's views were borne out when The Rake was well beaten at Epsom, but whether this was because of his spavin or the fact that he had burst a blood vessel a week before the race (won by another 'bleeder', Hermit), or simply because he was just not good enough, is uncertain because he never ran again.

Blake, meanwhile, continued to contribute articles to the *Life* and in 1868, after much soul-searching, he laid down his scalpel and joined the team at 148 Fleet Street. A big, affable bear of a man, gentle in speech and with his own particular brand of humour, Charley Blake was just 26 and his knowledge of racing and style of writing were far removed from the man he was destined to succeed. He had much to learn, and still had when Augur's mantle fell on his broad shoulders at the end of 1874.

Feist had left the paper nicely set up for his successor. In the same week as he died, the *Sporting Life Companion Annual* had been launched. Pocket-sized and priced at 2d, it was marketed as "one of the most comprehensive, handy books ever published … a really valuable work of easy reference." It listed the winners of all the big races; the Waterloo Cup; University Boat Race; Thames sculling championship; Eton v Harrow and Oxford v Cambridge cricket matches; the Ring champions of England from 1719 to 1868 (when prizefighting was finally suppressed), and contained a mass of information to bolster its claim that "Such a complete sporting record at so low a price has never before been offered to the public."

The expansion of the *Life* was also reflected in a 'Terms of Subscription' notice for 1875. The cost to postal subscribers in Britain and Ireland was now 13s (£58.50) a year (newspaper postage having been halved to ½d in 1870). For France, Belgium, Prussia, Egypt, Australia, New Zealand, the West Indies, the Brazils, Cape of Good Hope, United States of America, Canada, California and most of the British Colonies, the price was 17s 4d. For the East Indies, China, British Columbia, and (perversely) for Austria, Holland, Italy, Spain and Switzerland the price rose to 26s.*

---

* This was before the Universal Postal Union (1878) laid down uniform rates for worldwide postage. Up until then, postal administrations set their own rates with an eye to obtaining the maximum possible revenue from their international services.

Whether copies of the paper were being sent to all the countries listed is uncertain, but the British Empire did extend over a quarter of the globe and even in its remotest outposts there were consuls and traders, soldiers and sailors, engineers and emigrants eager to catch up on the sporting news from home; besides which, it was felt an impressive worldwide gazetteer might reel in a few more advertisers.

Distribution was also improved in March 1875 by the earlier departure of the special newspaper trains which ran out of London; an 'Important Notice' informed readers:

> *The Sporting Life* is now delivered in the principal towns of the North of England at a much earlier hour than hitherto. Parcels are forwarded by express trains as follows: From King's Cross by the Great Northern Railway at 5.15am; from St Pancras by the Midland Railway at 5.15am, and from Euston Square by the North Western Railway at 5.25am.

A lengthy list of towns and times of arrival accompanied the notice; for instance the paper got into Peterborough at 7am, Coventry 7.48, Birmingham 8.20, Barnsley 9.55, Liverpool and York at 10 o'clock precisely, Durham 12.33pm and Newcastle 1.05.

At the same time the telegraph wires, which followed the railway lines across the country, were being extended to reach more and more racecourses. This was a natural progression from the early 1850s when the telegraph began to be adapted for commercial use by various news agencies. Stock market reports and racing results formed the bulk of the business, but the service left a lot to be desired as the companies charged "exorbitantly for late and untrustworthy information".[6] This had lasted until 1870 when, following pressure from an influential body of newspaper proprietors, the government nationalised the telegraph and it became part of the Post Office.

The new, streamlined service proved a great boon to Fleet Street in that it offered special cheap rates for the transmission of press copy and was much more reliable. The postal authorities were also quick to recognise that racing men – bookmakers, punters and journalists – were their best customers and they organised a special staff to travel around the country to handle the welter of messages dispatched to and from the big meetings.

In its first full year under State control, the Telegraph Department transmitted 164,563 racing messages of which 26,563 were press reports that "amounted to about 2,000 columns of printed matter, which, on a rough calculation, would extend to just upon three-quarters of a mile!"[7] As the telegraph expanded its network the *Life* carried weekly notices detailing the latest developments to the service. In 1872 the 'Telegraph Arrangements' for the start of the Flat season and the Grand National meeting announced:

> Lincoln Races: For the first time at any race meeting, the Wheatstone Automatic system will be worked between Lincoln and London on Monday and Tuesday next, and by this means the capacity of the wire will be increased threefold. There will also be direct communication with Manchester.

> Liverpool Races: The office at Aintree will be open from 9.30am until half an hour after the last race daily; and as the wire accommodation is greatly in excess of that of last year, the Department is in the position to do a greatly increased amount of work with the least possible delay.

Other major events required special facilities to be set up. For the University Boat Race it was announced:

Direct telegraphic communication will be established between a point close to the Ship Inn at Mortlake and London, and telegrams will be transmitted without delay to all parts of the country and abroad. The business will be conducted in the new travelling telegraph office, the position of which will be easily distinguished by a blue flag with the word 'Telegraphs' in white letters inscribed on it; a messenger in uniform will be in attendance to collect messages from such persons as may be unable to obtain access to the office.

But the great advantages offered by the e-mail of its age were of limited value to a bi-weekly paper. This was forcibly brought home during the summer of 1875 when the *Life* lagged 48 hours behind the daily press in reporting what was arguably the greatest athletic feat of the century.

CAPTAIN WEBB'S CHANNEL TRIP

CHARLES BLAKE was naturally anxious that things should run as smoothly as possible during his first year in office and, in the main, they did. Most of the major stories of 1875 – the death of Sir Joseph Hawley; the opening of an up-market racecourse at Sandown Park; the teenage Fred Archer taking his second championship with a record total of 172 winners – were reported in full, as was the England v Scotland football match which ended in a 2-2 draw after England had to play the first ten minutes with ten men because their goalkeeper, W H Carr of Sheffield, failed to arrive in time for the kick-off!

But the paper missed out in a big way when its swimming correspondent, Bob Watson, quite literally missed the boat and his chance to record history in the making when Captain Matthew Webb became the first man to swim the English Channel.

Born of Irish parents in Manchester in 1848, Robert Patrick Watson had, by a strange coincidence, passed through the hallowed halls of the Royal Veterinary College a few years after Blake, but unlike his predecessor, his heart was never in his studies and he was, by his own admission, "a kind of refractory student, careless and given to practical jokes such as muscle-throwing in the dissecting room."[1]

When he failed his qualifying exam, he pawned his veterinary books and instruments and sold the pawn tickets to ensure there was no turning back. A keen sportsman, he joined his local north London swimming club in 1870 and soon showed he was a man to be reckoned with in the handicap division of that sport, while he also proved a useful runner and for three years he competed in professional sprints on the metropolitan circuit.

At the same time the aspiring athlete entered the world of journalism when *Bell's Life* took him on as a stringer to report on the swimming competitions staged by the various London swimming clubs. However, it was not long before the tyro sports reporter found the amount of work he was required to do was hardly reflected in his pay which, at 10s (£45) a week, was often not forthcoming, so he decided to branch out on his own.

With his inherent Irish blarney, he obtained the backing he needed to publish his own paper, the *Swimming, Rowing and Athletic Record*, in 1873. The weekly journal lasted barely a year, but that was long enough to bring Watson to the notice of the *Sporting Life*, which started to carry his reports on the swimming scene.

The *Swimming Record* also caught the attention of Matthew Webb, a 26-year-old Merchant Navy captain who had recently been presented with the Stanhope gold medal of the Royal Humane Society in recognition of his brave but unavailing attempt to rescue a fellow sailor who had been swept overboard during a stormy Atlantic crossing.

Medal in hand, Webb approached Watson to ask his help in finding a backer to support him in his bid to swim the Channel. An initially sceptical Watson was eventually persuaded to introduce the persistent mariner to Fred Beckwith, who coached potential champions and children of the wealthy at the Lambeth baths, south London.*

---

* Beckwith had assumed the title 'Champion of the World' in 1851, but was well beaten in the first defence of his 'title' and was "really only a passable all-round swimmer."[2] His record as a coach was rather better and his son, Willie, became a London champion having made his public debut at the Lambeth baths a few weeks after his fifth birthday when he was billed as 'Baby Beckwith the Wonder of the World'.

In September 1874, Webb showed his prospective backer what he could do in a secret trial in the Thames. As Watson and Beckwith followed in a rowing boat, Webb swam from Westminster Bridge to Regent's Canal Dock in a steady 1hr 20mins. He would have continued for longer, but, as Watson recalled: "We grew tired of watching his slow, methodical but perfect breaststroke and magnificent sweep of his ponderous legs," besides which, Beckwith had seen enough to convince him he had found a sound betting proposition. "Get him out," he muttered impatiently to Watson. "Get him out; he'll keep us here all night."[3]

Beckwith immediately issued a challenge in the *Life* stating he was willing to back an "unknown amateur ... [*to*] swim against anyone in the river Thames, the man swimming the farthest to win," while he also sought out bookmakers and anyone else who cared to offer him decent odds against his man swimming from England to France. It was, however, too late in the season to attempt a Channel crossing that year so it was not until the following summer that Beckwith, by way of introducing Webb to the public, organised a 20-mile warm-up swim down the Thames from Brunswick pier at Blackwall to the town pier at Gravesend.

A tidy profit was anticipated from the sale of seats on a steamer that had been hired for the occasion, but a cold, showery day kept the crowds away and, while Webb had no trouble in completing what the *Life* described as "the greatest feat ever accomplished in the annals of swimming," the whole venture proved disastrous for Beckwith.

Not only did he lose money on the steamer, but he also lost his protégé as well because Webb, miffed at not getting a cut of the expected takings, promptly switched his allegiance to Arthur Payne, the sports editor of *The Standard* and proprietor of the weekly journal, *Land and Water*. A keen swimmer himself, Payne could see that Webb had the potential to achieve his ambition and, with his eye on a world exclusive, he wrote to the press to state:

> I am authorised by Captain Webb to announce his full determination to attempt the feat of swimming across the Channel ... Beyond a paltry bet of £20 to £1 he has nothing to gain by success. Surely, under the circumstances, there are some lovers of sport who would gladly, in sporting language, 'put him on so much to nothing'. Should he by chance succeed, which is extremely improbable, it would be cruel that one who would undoubtedly have performed the greatest athletic feat on record should be a loser by the event.

And nor was he. On Tuesday, 24 August 1875, while a disconsolate Watson was covering the Amateur Swimming Championships at Crystal Palace for the *Life*, Payne and three other journalists together with an artist from the *Illustrated Sporting and Dramatic News* pulled out of Dover in a lugger as Webb dived off the end of Admiralty Pier and into history.

The following day the *Life* carried a small item in its swimming column headed, rather derisively, 'Captain Webb's Channel Trip':

> The weather being very favourable yesterday, Captain Webb rather suddenly determined to commence his second attempt to swim across the Channel and plunged off Dover Pier at four minutes to one p.m. It was then supposed that he would drift westward for about two hours, eastward for six hours and a half, and then westward again for five hours and a half. Should he reach the French coast, it will be about three o'clock this morning.

Few, apart from those immediately associated with Webb, expected him to succeed in his extraordinary venture. The English champion, J B Johnson, had attempted the swim three years earlier, but it had ended ignominiously when, chilled and exhausted, he was hauled out of the sea after only an hour, but Webb was made of sterner stuff. At 5ft 8in, his solid, muscular frame tilted the scales at 14st 8lb, and in his first attempt at the crossing 12 days earlier he had battled against the tide and an increasing rough sea for over six hours before he was forced to give up.

Saturday's paper consequently carried a much more respectful front-page headline which trumpeted 'Captain Webb's Great Swimming Feat'. The main body of the story was lifted from *The Standard*, which had published Payne's graphic account of the swim, while the *Life* provided a lead-in to the report:

> A year or so ago, two or three challenges appeared in the *Sporting Life* containing offers to back an unknown amateur to swim distances which, at the time, seemed utterly beyond human endurance. They were inserted only after considerable hesitation and when they did appear, most of those who knew anything of swimming were disposed to look upon them as 'bunkum'.
>
> Subsequently, however, it became whispered about that there was a person in the habit of amusing himself of a morning by a five or six hours swim in the Thames, and then it was rumoured that Captain Matthew Webb of the Mercantile Marine … had expressed himself confident of being able to swim across the Channel from England to France.
>
> Furthermore, it was found that he was carefully preparing himself to perform the feat and when, for a reward almost nominal, he gave proof of his extraordinary capabilities by swimming from Blackwall to Gravesend, the incredulous began to open their eyes.
>
> After, in his first attempt to cross the Channel, doing a good six hours in very rough water, and showing that his zeal was tempered with discretion by retiring before becoming absolutely exhausted … the faith of those who had taken an interest in his undertaking became all the greater.

Arthur Payne's report was then reprinted in its entirety. The article is a fine example of reportage – an eyewitness account made all the more fascinating by its immediacy and the writer's intimacy with his subject. In the following slightly shortened version of the journalist's log, his description of the teeming marine life and the clearness of the sea shows just how polluted the Channel has become in the space of a few generations.

It should be added that Webb, who had insulated himself against the cold with a liberal coating of porpoise oil, used the breaststroke throughout his swim because he had yet to master the more effective and faster sidestroke, which had only just begun to find favour with British swimmers.

Payne prefaced his notes with some remarks on the floodtides and currents which had been against Webb on his first attempt, but were in his favour when he made his second plunge off the end of Admiralty Pier, which gave him a 'leg out' of almost three-quarters of a mile from the shore. He went on to relate:

> It was just on the drain of the tide and Webb swam steadily, at about twenty-two strokes per minute, as if making straight across, the tide gradually taking him westward, but it was not running fast – perhaps a mile an hour – so he was making good progress from land and but little down-channel.
>
> 1.15pm – A few jokes passed as to the utility of an empty flour barrel floating by. Toms [*Captain Toms, the pilot of the lugger*] suggested that Webb should get inside it when tired, but Webb did not see the joke.

1.35pm – The first porpoise appeared. Whether attracted by the oil or not Toms could not say, but he joined in the party for a short while and then disappeared in pursuit of a shoal of mackerel close by. The sea was beautifully calm and clear. Several small boats were convoying us; we had drifted opposite Lyddon Spout Coastguard Station.

2.40pm – Webb had some beer, and seemed refreshed and quite warm. We could hear the gunboat practising in the distance, but owing to the haze could not see her. Saw the first yellow jellyfish; these fellows sting, so he had a wide berth.

3.0pm – We saw the Calais boat and the *Castalia* come in. We are now just in the dead of the slack and leaving land fast.

4.0pm – We are now drifting back up the channel and Toms was jubilant at the good offing we had made so as to clear the suck of the tide by the Forelands.

5.0pm – Dover Castle just visible in the haze, NW by N; South Foreland N by W. Now over five miles from land; no wind whatever, sea like a millpond, I could see down three or four fathoms by shading off the light and numbers of fish, principally weavers and mackerel, could be seen while all round porpoises were rolling – in fact the whole sea appeared alive with fish. Webb now had some beef tea; still warm and confident.

5.30pm – Dover lost in the haze. The only vessel on the move was a screw steamer bound for Dunkerque, the *Ville de Malaga*. The sailors crowded to the bulwarks to see us and evidently thought we were fishing for some sunken galleon, and Webb's head was a buoy to mark the spot where the money chest was. We cheered them but they were silent, 'just like those blessed frog-eaters' as one of our sailors remarked.

6.10pm – We could hear the sound of oars and a small boat was seen vigorously pulling towards us. I recognised my colleague who had come out to fetch dispatches. It was a clever bit of steering to hit us off in the dusk and when, at 6.50, he started off again with my notes and the bearer also of news from the other 'specials' neither land nor lights were visible.

6.30pm – Webb had asked me to have a swim with him as an encouragement. The water was very cold at first but remarkably buoyant. Webb, I noticed, was swimming very high and the soles of his feet looked up skywards at each stroke.

8.35pm – Baker, the youthful diver who accompanied Webb, took him some more coffee, hot and strong. We continued rowing on through the darkness, the oars producing phosphorescence at every stroke when, at twenty-two minutes past nine, Webb called out that he had been stung on the shoulder by one of the yellow jellyfish or 'water starches' as they were called. Some brandy was quickly taken to him and shortly afterwards he said he was all right.

9.50pm – A steam tug appeared in sight and shortly afterwards joined us, but, strange to say, remained only a short time and then returned to Dover without even giving one encouraging cheer to the brave swimmer who was plodding his way through the darkness.

11.0pm – Our bearings by compass were announced. Captain Toms gave it as his opinion that we were twelve miles and a half from the South Foreland Lighthouse, eight from Cape Gris-Nez and nine from Calais. This was hopeful news for the swimmer as, allowing for the tide, he would have only five clear miles of swimming. The moon had now risen and the sound of the Calais mail-boat from Dover was distinctly heard in the distance. At 11.45 she came in sight. We burned a light which enabled those on the packet to see us and a hearty cheer went up from those on board. The night passed wearily away, but the white chalk cliffs of Cape Gris-Nez were distinctly visible in the light of the moon.

2.15am – There appeared every prospect of a successful result. Captain Webb, however, was somewhat failing in power and the lad Baker stripped and, with a life-belt around his chest to which a thin line was attached, and muffled up in a cloak, sat by my side ready for a plunge in case of accident.

4.7am – Sea calm as glass. There was sufficient daylight to see clearly what one was writing and with daylight came fresh hope. Captain Webb had taken nothing by way of refreshment but cod-liver oil, beef tea, coffee and beer. He still appeared to be swimming strongly as he was able to tread water while drinking.

5.9am – The sun had risen, but unfortunately a haze covered the land. Still Webb persevered. We had nearly reached Cape Gris-Nez when the tide turned and we drifted again eastwards in the direction of Calais.

6.50am – A slight breeze sprang up which increased by seven o'clock. It cleared the mist and caused a decided swell on the water. At this point we began to lose all hope. Webb had now been in the water no less than eighteen hours and the tide was bearing him away from the land he so longed to reach. Still there was something in his face that betokened that he would go on till he sank, and an uneasy, nervous feeling sprang up among all of us.

9.0am – We neared Calais and a boat from the Chatham and Dover Royal Mail packets put out. I believe that Webb was greatly indebted to the hearty cheers of the men on board that boat for his success. The sea was rough and Webb was exhausted, we ourselves were worn out and the sea was breaking occasionally over us. The boat belonging to the mail packet rowed to windward of Webb and acted as a kind of breakwater. Webb was now evidently fearfully exhausted, but still he laboured on as if he preferred death to defeat.

We were within a mile of shore but the tide was strong and the sea very rough. Baker now dived in and swam by Webb's side for a short time to encourage him. Webb persevered and finally touched ground on the Calais sands at forty-one minutes past ten in the morning, having been in the water for 21 hours 45 minutes.*

We sent up a ringing cheer and I am not exaggerating when I say that even among the rough seamen who accompanied us, there was not an eye on board but moistened as the brave fellow touched ground – touched and fell forward, but two men sprang from the mail boat to his assistance and, taking an arm each, he walked steadily up the sands, was placed in a carriage, driven off to the Paris Hotel and put to bed.

He was for a short time delirious after his fearful exertions, but, I am thankful to say, I left him at one p.m. in a sound and comfortable sleep. The doctor who was attending him pronounced that he was 'doing well'.

Webb became an instant hero with the British public and was feted wherever he went. Receptions, held for him at the London Stock Exchange and Mansion House, gave him entrée to the best circles of society and he was presented with many fine gifts and trophies, while £2,424 (£218,160) was raised for him by public subscription.

For a time the unsophisticated Shropshire lad enjoyed the high life, but while he was in his element

---

* It was estimated that Webb swam some 35 miles in his battle with the tides, the direct distance from Dover to Calais being about 21 miles. Despite many subsequent attempts by other swimmers, it was 36 years before Thomas Burgess emulated the feat at his 13th try, and it was not until 1934 that Webb's time was beaten when the English Olympic water polo player, Edward Temme, became only the fourth man to make the crossing. Since then children as young as 11 (a boy) and 12 (a girl) have made the crossing, while the record was reduced to an incredible 6hrs 58mins by the Bulgarian, Petar Stoychev, in 2007.

Matthew Webb's Great Channel Swim – as sketched by the artist for the
Illustrated Sporting and Dramatic News.

in water, he was unable to cope with the social whirl that surrounded him out of it and he "eventually drifted into a poor condition and sadly felt the want of money".[4]

In 1879, he embarked on a fund-raising tour of the country giving exhibitions of his powers of endurance. He would compete in six-day races, swimming 12 or 14 hours a day, and perform freakish stunts which, in 1880, included floating around a tank at the Scarborough Aquarium for 74 hours. Watching paint dry suddenly seemed attractive!

When the crowds drifted away, Webb tried his luck in America, but lost both money and credibility on his first visit and fared little better on a return trip three years later in 1882 when he beat his own flotation record by remaining in a tank for 128½ hours (five days, eight and a half hours; less 94 minutes time out) at the Horticultural Hall in Boston.

His competitive career came to an end in March 1883 when he had to retired from a 20-mile race at the Lambeth baths after which he was, quite literally, spitting blood. Already diagnosed with consumption and weighing 42lb less than when he swam the Channel, his doctor ordered him to take a complete rest from swimming, but four months later, in an effort to revive his depleted fortunes, he attempted to swim across the rapids at the foot of Niagara Falls.

It was the ultimate death or glory bid and this time the feat, which 'seemed utterly beyond human endurance' proved to be exactly that. Webb was drowned. Many believed that, knowing he was already doomed with TB, he had decided to embrace both death and glory, but Watson, who had done his best to talk his old friend out of the idea, did not subscribe to the theory as he recalled their final parting:

> As we stood face to face I compared the fine, handsome sailor, who first spoke to me about swimming
> at Falcon Court, with the broken-spirited and terribly altered appearance of the man who courted
> death in the whirlpool rapids of Niagara … let it be taken for granted that his object was not suicide,
> but money and imperishable fame.[5]

What is beyond doubt was that during his lifetime Webb had given a tremendous boost to swimming both as a recreation and as a sport. The *Life* had tapped into this new market in the summer of 1881 when it put up two 60oz silver cups for a professional and amateur championship to be held on alternate Saturdays in the reservoir adjoining the Welsh Harp Inn at Hendon, north London. The Mile Champion Challenge Cup of Great Britain, grandly declared to be "open to the world," was described as "the handsomest ever given for swimming" and a similar cup for the half-mile amateur championship commanded no less praise. In addition, there were cash prizes for the professionals and gold medals for the amateurs.

In announcing the sponsorship was designed "to assist in raising the standard of quality in the exponents of the noble and useful art of natation,"* three-quarters of a column was devoted to advocating the advantages of swimming, which had the decided plus of "rescuing life from drowning":

> Should ever the necessity arise for getting ashore from a wreck or through the capsize of a craft, or
> to help others out of such troubles, pace is the greatest desideratum … and the most expedient means
> of cultivating and developing speed is to encourage racing.

---

* There was certainly a need to learn the 'useful art of natation'. Webb's epic feat had generated a nationwide swimming craze that had resulted in an alarming number of drownings. In 1877, 2,662 people (2,140 males, 522 females) met their end in the inland waters of England and Wales. Of these 1,423 perished in rivers, 637 in canals and 602 in lakes and ponds. When these sorry statistics were released it was remarked: "No doubt many of these deaths were suicides, but by far the greater majority must have arisen from accidents – in addition to the terrible figures given, many persons were drowned off the coast."[6]

Having thus established the competition's *raison d'être*, the *Life* had the satisfaction of seeing its mile championship became part of the established swimming calendar. After Willie Beckwith had won the first championship in effortless style, the event was moved to Hollingworth Lake – 'the Weavers' Seaside' – outside Manchester where upwards of 30,000 people saw the English champion, Joey Nuttall, and the Irish-American, James McCusker, compete for the cup in August 1893.

With each man putting up £250 (£22,500), the *Life* , as stakeholder and promoter, enthusiastically built up the event after McCusker had beaten James Finney, a former champion, over a mile in the sea off Blackpool in July, while Bob Watson, who was to referee the contest, extolled the record of the host nation as he claimed:

> An international swimming match at home does not occur once in a generation. The reason is obvious. From time immemorial our best English swimmers have ruled the waves and no foreigner has yet been able to wrest from us our supremacy ... To America we sent Harry Gurr (who never returned), J B Johnson and Willie Beckwith, all of whom completely dwarfed the pretensions of their transatlantic rivals; as a matter of fact, any of the trio mentioned above could have won with the breast stroke. In Australia, undoubtedly, there are very fast swimmers, but up to the present, the relative speed of the two countries has not been practically tested in a race.

The big event came off on August 19 when the *Life* relayed the latest news from Nuttall's home town, close to the scene of the action:

> In Stalybridge there is great excitement and scarcely anything else is spoken about. The Union Jack is flying all over the town and portraits of Nuttall, McCusker and Haggerty find ready sale ... It may be taken for granted that McCusker is a great swimmer and with him in the field the prestige of England trembles in the balance. If he is to be beaten, Joey Nuttall only can bring it about, but it will be at the expense of such swimming as never previously saw the light of day.

Nuttall had won the cup for the last two years and despite being a local hero, he was an uneasy favourite. On Friday morning he was quoted at 4-5, but by the afternoon it was 'pounds to guineas' (20-21) and then even money. On Saturday he continued to drift in the betting as Jack Haggerty, a former English champion swimmer and McCusker's coach, backed his man with confidence. Watson, scenting out the source of the shekels, reported:

> It was whispered that the Irish-American had got inside 26 minutes and Haggerty declared no man born of woman had done such performances in private as McCusker. This, coupled with Haggerty's knowledge of Nuttall, made the latter's supporters cautious and consequently McCusker rose in favouritism.

By the time the two swimmers appeared on the jetty that was to serve as the dive-off platform, a flood of money had cramped the odds on the Co. Down-born challenger still further and the bookies' enticing cry of "I'll take 2 to 1" rang out across the lake. But this was one occasion when the money did not talk or, if it did, it told a lie because Joey Nuttall left his opponent wallowing in his wake as he set a new record of 26min 23sec for the four-lap mile.

And so the *Sporting Life* Mile Champion Challenge Cup became his for the keeping.

'WOBBLE' WESTON'S WALKABOUT

S PONSORSHIP, either through prize money or trophies, became part of the policy of the *Sporting Life* under the aegis of its long-time proprietor, William McFarlane, "a keen businessman of simple habits, a retiring disposition and generous instinct."[1] From its first venture into the field when it gave a challenge cup for a 50-mile cycle race at London's Lillie Bridge stadium, West Brompton, the paper went on to support athletics, swimming, boxing, motor racing, clay pigeon shooting, greyhound racing and horse racing. And for over half a century it presented a massive silver trophy for the Windsor to London marathon – a trophy that now adds lustre to the Flora London marathon.

As ever, there was a strong element of self-interest behind these promotions. As soon as a particular sport or recreation became fashionable it created a market for new readers that was always worth tapping into, and in 1877 a cycling craze was sweeping the country when the paper presented its prize silverware to H Osborne after he had won the inaugural 150-lap race in a dizzying 3hr 18m 55s, averaging 15mph.

It was less than ten years since the first bicycle race had taken place in Paris and recreation grounds throughout England were being turned into race tracks by precariously perched peddlers on their penny farthings, while a new street offence of 'furious riding' was added to the list of police prosecutions being brought before hard-pressed magistrates.

The 1870s also saw a boom in pedestrianism as the introduction of weekends and bank holidays gave the working classes greater opportunity to take part in what had become an essentially proletarian sport. The most popular events were sprint handicaps, which appealed to the public because they offered an action-packed betting medium. They were also a perfect vehicle for sponsorship, and in 1881 the *Life* entered the field by staging a series of races at the Prince of Wales's grounds, Bow, in the East End of London.

The first 'Great All-England 135 Yards Handicap' was run off in heats over two consecutive Saturdays and carried £40 (£3,600) in prize money. It seemed a particularly munificent promotion, but on closer inspection it was apparent the prize money was clawed back through entry fees and admission charges, while the lease of the ground was offset by renting out pitches to bookmakers who were an integral part of the scene.

It cost the 'peds' a shilling to enter and another 'bob' to accept after the publication of the handicap, while spectators paid 6d for admission. As the initial event attracted 235 entries (£11-15s) of which 116 accepted (£5-16s), and as 866 spectators (£21-13s) turned up for the preliminary heats and a crowd of 852 (£21-6s) watched the finals, the total receipts amounted to £60-10s; representing a profit of £20-10s (£1,845) on the initial outlay of £40 – which, all things considered, was not a bad little earner!

Each meeting was regulated by the *Life*, which stipulated:

All men must enter in their proper names and state late and present abode at time of entry, also previous performances. Any man who has won a handicap at any time and not stating it, or in any way misleading the handicapper, will be liable to be disqualified and his entrance and acceptance money will be forfeited. Any man winning a handicap after the entries are published will be put back two yards and one yard for being second; or any man running second to the winner in either of his heats will be put back half a yard. Penalties not accumulative.

Almost inevitably, with betting taking place on each heat, all manner of ruses were resorted to in order to fix races and deceive the handicapper, a role that had been allotted to Bob Watson who, as a former 'ped', was well aware of all the dodges. During the first day's 29 preliminary heats, it was noted that "more than one competitor who could have been successful, profited considerably by finishing second and sometimes last," while J Moody, who won heat 14, was disqualified "for misleading the handicapper and not correctly explaining his performances". Mr Moody, it transpired, was a member of the metropolitan police force!

At other times a subtle science lay behind legitimate coups that were planned with as much cunning as any on the Turf. Professional coaches would scour recreation grounds in search of a youngster with the potential for improvement and, having found their man, they would spirit him away to a secret training camp where he would be honed into a fully-fledged athlete.

Thus prepared, the transformed ped would return to his old stamping ground and, running off his previous handicap mark, would reward his gaffer (manager) by showing vastly improved form to land some shrewdly placed bets. One such gamble was brought off in March 1887 when a record 323 peds put their shillings down and Watson had cause to slash his handicap mark for one particular competitor after he reported:

> In the whole list of handicaps promoted by the *Sporting Life* dating as far back as December 3, 1881, the event under notice stands out prominently as the fastest ever decided ... For this unexpected revolution we are indebted to a youngster in the person of H Edwards of Walthamstow, who has been a constant entrant in handicaps organised by this paper from a boy when he was conceded 25 yards.
>
> As he advanced in years his start was curtailed but, until the event under notice, he had not exhibited form good enough to warrant his friends or the public in backing him. Last December he was taken under the wing of a party at one time identified with George Petley [*a champion sprinter of the 1870s*] and transported to Sheffield.
>
> With the reduction in weight of about 10lb and constant practice under able supervision he soon developed the necessary speed, but the secret was so well preserved that his identity was never revealed abroad and, until Saturday was well advanced, the London contingent were unaware of the youngster's formidable chance and his absence from the Metropolis.

Backed at long odds to win the final, Edwards had been given a 22-yard start in his first heat, which he won at 5-1. With his cover blown, the young Cockney easily landed the odds in the second and third rounds and burnt up the track in the final to land the gamble. Watson was left to conclude ruefully: "Thus ended a handicap fairly bristling with incontrovertible evidence as to a much needed reform in regard to the adjustment of starts and the division of class according to merit." Graded racing was on its way!

In direct contrast to the sprint handicaps, 'go-as-you-please' marathons could last for up to six days. Competitors took breaks whenever it suited them as they attempted to record the longest distance covered in the contest. The punishment they put themselves through for a prize of £30 or £40 was, quite literally, staggering. Many suffered stomach cramps from drinking too much water, while others became distinctly unsteady on their feet as a result of imbibing something stronger than *aqua pura* – a cocktail of caffeine, strychnine and brandy was a favoured pick-me-up which often resulted in a semi-conscious lay-me-down. An advert for one such contest in 1881 proclaimed:

> Great sixty-five hours go-as-you-please pedestrian tournament, promoted by the Dundee Sporting Club, will take place in Cooke's Circus, commencing Wednesday, March 12 and terminating on the following Saturday – first prize £30, with £10 added if 395 miles is done: second £12, with £8 added if 385 miles is done: third £5, with £4 added if 375 miles is done: fourth £3, with £2 added if 360 miles is done; and £2 to all competitors covering 300 miles and not getting a prize.

A lot of miles for little money! But by far the greatest endurance feat of the time was performed by the famous American pedestrian, Edward Payson Weston. In 1879, as a result of a £100 to £500 wager with Sir John Astley – a distinguished veteran of the Crimean War and no mean ped in his prime – Weston undertook to walk 2,000 miles within 1,000 hours along the turnpike roads of England.

It had been 70 years since Robert Allardice Barclay had made a name for himself by walking a mile in each of 1,000 consecutive hours over a set course on Newmarket Heath. For Weston to attempt to cover double that distance in the same time was remarkable enough but, whereas the celebrated Captain Barclay had accomplished his feat in the summer on a springy cushion of turf, the American masochistically chose to carry out his walk in the middle of winter on roads which, since the advent of the railway, had fallen into disrepair and were heavily rutted and potholed.

As had been the case with Matthew Webb, most people believed he was attempting the impossible, particularly when it became known that he had agreed not to walk on any of the six Sundays that fell within his gruelling schedule and that the actual distance of his route was 2,019 miles and 1,320 yards. Weston would, therefore, have only 856 hours (35 days and 16 hours) to complete his undertaking. He obviously relished a challenge just as much as Sir John Astley liked to have the odds in his favour when he had a bet.

The marathon walk created nationwide interest and, as the day of departure approached, it took up more and more space in the *Life* as details were given of the scheduled route which had been "laid out from the latest Ordinance survey under the direction of James Wylde, Geographer to the Queen". The long and winding road extended:

> From London to Dover, thence following the coast to Penzance returning through Cornwall and Devonshire counties to Bristol; thence to Birmingham, Shropshire, Lancashire and Cumberland to Carlisle crossing at this point to Newcastle-on-Tyne, thence to Northallerton and, after a complete circuit of Yorkshire visiting most of the prominent towns, to Retford, Lincoln, Nottingham, Derby, Leicester, Peterborough, Norwich, Yarmouth, Ipswich, Bury St Edmunds, Cambridge, Bedford, Oxford, Reading and Windsor, thus returning to London. Exclusive of London, Weston will pass through 31 counties and 190 cities and towns.

To offset the cost of his venture, 'Wobble' Weston (so called because of his exaggerated posterior movement when walking at pace) had entered into a contract with the famous impresario, Richard D'Oyly Carte, to give a series of fifty talks at £50 a time at various prearranged sites along the route. The talks were to be entitled 'What I know about Walking'!

The *Life's* Martin Cobbett was one of three journalists who had the unenviable task of accompanying Weston "to bear witness that he adheres to the conditions prescribed and that the walk is fairly and honourably carried out." Cobbett, a tall, imposing man who had made his mark as an oarsman and a swimmer, was well qualified for the job since he was a seasoned pedestrian whose "long, careless stride won him a momentous series of matches on the Leatherhead road."[2]

With newspaper deadlines normally very lax during the nineteenth century, the athletic scribe was able to file the first of what were to be a dozen long and detailed reports on the hyped hike shortly after Sir John Astley had dispatched Weston from his departure point in front of the Royal Exchange at five minutes past midnight on Saturday, 18 January 1879. From the outset it was apparent Cobbett felt the American had little chance of winning his bet as he remarked:

> The first day's work Weston has set himself is a very heavy one and we think he will not get through it in the time set forth, viz. 20 hours 25 minutes, for at the hour of writing frost has set in and for any man to get over 81 ½ miles on slippery and rough roads in the time named will be a great performance.

But Weston silenced his doubter by completing the initial leg on schedule despite the fact that "snow was falling rapidly the greater portion of the time and the wind was dead against him except from Dover to Folkestone, and between these towns the roads were in worst condition than at any other point, being ankle deep in mud."

But the state of the roads and the weather were to be the least of the walker's worries. The press, and the *Life* in particular, had done such a good job of publicising the walk that he was mobbed by huge crowds in the main towns, especially at night when the working day was done. The pattern was set on the third day when Cobbett reported:

> The scene along the road to Eastbourne will not soon be forgotten. Where all the people came from was surprising. The road was literally choked and the greatest excitement prevailed. Outside the town, Weston was met by the Volunteer band and a party of men bearing torches. Coloured fires were burnt in the streets which presented the appearance of Fleet Street on a Lord Mayor's Show day.

On the fourth day in Brighton, the intrepid ped was "mobbed to such an extent he had to take refuge in a confectioner's shop," and in Winchester at midnight on the fifth day, "but for the efforts of Chief Constable Morton and a small body of police under his direction, Weston would have been trampled underfoot." Under escort, the walker sought shelter in the George Hotel and after an hour's rest decided to press on to Stockbridge.

In an attempt to draw off the crowd surrounding the hotel, one of his party "dressed up *à la* Weston, but he did not play his part well. The natives shouted out that he had not got the 'wobble' and that it was a fraud and they vented their indignation by shying stones at the Press 'bus." By the time he left the George to complete the nine miles to Stockbridge, he was already two hours behind schedule and matters were made worse because:

> One of Weston's feet, which had been trodden upon at Winchester, troubled him much and he limped badly so his progress was slow and he had to keep continually crossing from one side of the road to the other, picking his way by the dim light of a lantern. The greater portion of the road was terribly rough, full of ruts and in other places covered with ice. This dreary march was finally terminated on Thursday morning at 4.25 when the Grosvenor Hotel was reached.

The Stockbridge Brass Band set out a little before one o'clock to meet Weston and play him into town. They acted most bravely, waiting for over three hours in the cold, and when the hero they wished to 'discourse sweet music' to did arrive, their fingers were so numbed with cold it was a matter of difficulty to raise a tune of any sort; the performer on the slide trombone being the only one who appeared to have any control over his instrument.

Weston may have escaped the crowds by his late arrival in Stockbridge, but they were waiting for him in Wimborne the following evening when the 'obdurate pedestrian' was knocked down and "in the fall cut his hand badly and received a severe shaking". Battered and bruised, he pushed on to reach the Antelope Hotel in Poole at 10.30pm. Here he downed "half a dozen new-laid eggs beat up in coffee" before setting off again to arrive at Wareham at 2am; and five and a half hours later he was back on the road again:

It is really astonishing how quickly he revives; two hours' sleep seems quite sufficient for him and his appetite is wonderfully good. Before he started he had a sumptuous breakfast consisting of poached eggs and cold roast fowl, and then he grumbled at not getting a mutton chop which he had ordered. On an average Weston swallows between twenty and thirty eggs a day, mostly taken in tea or coffee.

And so the amazing trudge through snow and sleet continued, but after a week it was reported:

The delays attendant upon attempting to walk through the large towns at night have seriously interfered with Weston's progress and unless some method is adopted of getting him safely conducted through towns, it is impossible for him to succeed and he might just as well retire from his task.

While resting in Plymouth on the second Sunday of the walk Weston wrote to Sir John Astley expressing his concerns for his own and other people's safety:

My experience while passing through Eastbourne, Brighton, Portsmouth, Southampton, Salisbury, Dorchester, Bridport and more especially Exeter, causes me to feel a terror that wears upon me more than my greatest exertions in walking, and I fear that the swaying throng, with their hearty feeling for my success, will, in their frantic efforts to see me, accidentally knock down and cripple me for life if they do not kill some child or woman...

   To prevent the possibility of accidents to anyone I propose, hereafter, to take a seat on the top of the judges' bus at the entrance to each borough and for one of the judges to learn from the town clerk the exact distance so covered and to walk an equivalent to the distance. This, I contend, will cover the conditions of our wager and gives you the benefit of the extra time consumed through my riding through the streets to gratify the courteousness of the people, who will then have no cause to crush or complain.

Sir John readily agreed to Weston's proposal, but it failed to solve the problem as the *Life's* doughty chronicler reported on February 1:

The second trial of this scheme, in riding into Penzance, showed that it entailed great loss of time and was not unattended with danger for one hour and twenty minutes was occupied in driving a distance of four miles, and in order to satisfy the curiosity of the crowd Weston had to seat himself outside the 'bus exposed to the cold night air, whereby he got a chill.

Weston had been due to give a lecture at Redruth that evening, but because of the delays he had to spend the night in Penzance and did not reach Redruth until the following morning when the town crier was sent round to announce the famed walker would give his talk in the Druid's Hall, which was "well filled" in less than quarter of an hour. On leaving the town, Cobbett, who coloured his reports with observations on the communities they passed through, noted:

> …there are several copper mines and the costumes of the women employed in breaking stones are peculiar. They mostly wear long white hoods, hob-nailed boots and short dresses; and seem quite as rough and strong as the male inhabitants.

Eventually, Weston fell so far behind schedule he had to resort to taking trains in order to meet his engagements. The distance travelled by rail had to be walked off within the 1,000 hours, but it was now obvious he had broken the conditions. Nevertheless, with the incentive of £50 a talk x 50 = £2,500 (£225,000), he plugged doggedly on and was only 22½ miles short of his target when his time ran out at 4 pm on February 28.

Despite his glorious failure, or perhaps because of it, Weston was hailed a hero, but pedestrianism, as a whole, was on the decline.[*] Cheating was so rife the public had become disenchanted and drifted away to join the growing crowds that were flocking to football matches. The event or, to be more exact, non-event that finally killed off support for the sport was the clash between the two best sprinters in England – the long-time champion Harry Hutchens and the rising northern star Harry Gent – which was scheduled to take place over 120 yards at the Lillie Bridge stadium on 19 September 1887.

The *Life*, as the appointed referee and stakeholder (£100 a side) did not stint on superlatives as it built up the match into 'the race of the century':

> The name of Harry Hutchens is well known to Londoners as the greatest wonder ever seen on the cinder path and he has held the championship of the world for the last seven years. Gent of Darlington, is a younger man and has won two Sheffield handicaps in such style that he has found supporters in Yorkshire to back him on even terms with the champion. Never before, and it may be many years again, shall we see two such splendid runners side by side as will be seen at Lillie Bridge Grounds on Monday next.

As interest in the event increased, thousands of pounds were staked on the outcome and on the day Gent was a strong favourite. Charley Blake was among an estimated crowd of 4,000 that had gathered to see the flying peds do battle and, an hour before they were due to toe the line, he witnessed an ominous turn-round in the betting after odds of 2-1 against Hutchens had gone begging:

> Little by little the aspect of the money market underwent a change not without significance to those who accept this as the surest guide to speculation, and presently Hutchens was in as good demand

---

[*] This was not the case in Scotland, particularly at the Powderhall stadium in Edinburgh which was home to the most famous professional race in the world. First run in 1870 and staged over the New Year holiday period, the Powderhall sprint was run on the same lines as the *Sporting Life* handicaps and, although its status has declined over the years it is still run off at its new home on Musselburgh racecourse.

as his opponent. Once the balance of power had been equalised, the beam quickly tilted over in favour of the Putney pedestrian and, almost as quickly as it takes to tell, the odds rose on Hutchens until 10 to 1 was offered against his rival. There could be no mistaking the nature of such a complete revolution as this, and some good judges began to hint at a sensation ending to what promised to be so interesting a race.

For once, the word 'sensation' was justified. It transpired that one or two bookmakers who had invested heavily on Gent, realised they had backed the wrong man. At first they offered Hutchens £50 to throw the race, and when he refused, they hired a gang of thugs to prevent the contest from taking place. As the runners were changing into their togs,, some 30 men, armed with sticks, knives and bottles, burst into the dressing room and, with threats of GBH and worse, forced them to leave the ground by a rear exit. It was some time before the crowd realised it had been 'sold', but eventually:

A quiet, though effectual exodus of representative sportsmen from the ground told plainly that something was wrong. Then it leaked out, and the well-kept secret spread with lightning-like rapidity amongst the crowd that there would be no race ... One by one the bookmakers took their departure; Mr Sam Mordecai, who was amongst the last to leave, closing his book with a snap and observing with an ironical smile, 'Well, gentlemen, I'll bet on the Cesarewitch!'

When the disappointed and angry spectators tried to obtain a refund they were told the gate-money (1s admission or 2s for the reserved enclosure) had been removed for safekeeping and the management was unable to issue pass-outs. This proved the final straw. Tempers flared and an enraged mob went on the rampage. Railings were ripped up, the central flag pole and telegraph board torn down, and the dressing rooms, lockers and refreshment room broken into and ransacked.

A hopelessly inadequate posse of police attempted to contain the rioters, but they were driven back by a barrage of splintered chair legs and bottles as the looted beer and whisky was passed among the crowd and consumed with enthusiasm. Bonfires were made from the debris of the pavilion and eventually the whole place was set alight.

The following day, as police raked through the smouldering ruins of the stadium, the two peds together with Dick Lewis, Hutchens' gaffer, presented themselves at the *Life's* offices to give their account of what had happened and – more importantly for them – to retrieve their stake money. Hutchens explained that 'the boys' had given him no option but to pull out: "They stood over me with open knives and bottles in their hands and swore they would murder me if I attempted to go on the path. It would have been as much as my life was worth to go out," he said before going on to name names that would never be made public as he claimed:

It was really all done by two betting men. One of them had backed Gent for a lump and when he found that he had broken down, he put up a lot of roughs to stop the race.* Why, they have been for

---

* It was rumoured that Gent had pulled a muscle in his final warm-up for the race, but years later, in an interview with Bob Watson, Dick Lewis claimed he had set up the bookmakers by staging a bogus trial a few days before the event knowing it would be watched by their touts. Hutchens played his part by running badly and the bookies took the bait and piled their money on Gent. When Lewis started to back his man just before the race, the bookmakers realised they had been duped and took their revenge. The runners finally met at the Eslington grounds, Gateshead, six weeks later when Gent, at 2-7, proved just too good for the ageing champion.

the money today that he promised them. They could not find him, but they got some and they're all drunk now.

Gent added plaintively:

I was forcibly ejected from the dressing room and hustled through a back entrance into the street, pushed into a cab and then handed over to the custody of some roughs who said they meant travelling with me in order to see that I was not injured in any way … Before leaving, they made me give them nearly all the money I had in my possession (about £6) and said that I'd got off b——y cheap as, but for them, I should have been roughly handled and that I ought to be obliged to them for looking after me.

Lewis, who was still in the stadium with some £140 (£12,600) of the gate-money when the riot broke out, was lucky to escape with his life. He had locked himself in a dressing room and was nearly roasted alive when the pavilion was set on fire. He only escaped by squeezing through a window and crawling over the roof of the stand to reach an adjoining cab yard where he hid until it was safe to make his getaway.

He claimed, unconvincingly, "if it were in my power I would return every shilling taken at the doors" and added in what was obviously a prepared statement: "This dreadful and unsightly business reflects on the heads of those too well known in the racing world, who ought to be ashamed of the paltry and unmanly part they have acted in this disgraceful and deplorable transaction."

The *Life* was equally tainted by the affair. Blake knew the identity of the guilty parties, but did little to denounce them or apportion any blame. Instead, he praised the general "forbearance and good-humour" of the crowd, which had been described in other papers as a "howling mob", and confined himself to observing:

That a few unscrupulous and unprincipled persons should have the power to permanently injure the most popular pastime of the present period and should also be allowed to debar one of the most patient, orderly and earnest crowds that has ever assembled on a running ground, from witnessing what would have undoubtedly been the race of the century, is more than a matter of regret.

It was certainly a 'matter of regret' that Blake should utter such tripe and it was no surprise that the paper came in for criticism from some of its contemporaries. While the *Sportsman* laid the blame chiefly on the Lillie Bridge management and an inadequate police presence, it could not resist having a dig at its rival as it observed:

The race had been heralded by a flourish of trumpets which gave it an undue importance and the prostitution of the healthy sport of pedestrianism is as much to be regretted as the lamentable vengeance of the mob which followed.

But to describe pedestrianism as a 'healthy sport' was as absurd as praising the crowd for its good behaviour, and it was left to *The Times* to put the matter in its true perspective as it presented an unflattering picture of the part the sporting press played in stimulating the gambling mania that had gripped all sections of society:

There is a good deal of genuine interest in athletic exercises and games of skill but, broadly speaking, the real popularity of these things – and that popularity is enormous – rests upon their adaptability to gambling purposes.

The passion for backing something or somebody permeates all ranks in this country and is nowhere stronger than among those who swell the attendance at places like Lillie Bridge. So far as can be judged, the love of gambling is spreading year by year and increasing its hold upon the sporting population.

Cheap papers, exclusively or chiefly devoted to chronicles of all kinds of sport, are now brought within easy reach of the poorest in the remote districts. They are eagerly read by thousands who never read anything else, and their information is the chief or sole mental pabulum of large numbers whose elementary education is turned to little use beyond enabling them to study the odds.

We offer no theory to account for this and no royal road to improvement. The fact is there, and ought to be recognised for what it is.

BLAKE'S DAILY BALDERDASH

B Y THE TIME Lillie Bridge pavilion was burnt to the ground by 'patient, orderly and earnest crowds,' readers had become used to, if not inured to, Charley Blake's bizarre journalese as they waded through his Augur column in an often fruitless search for constructive comments on the main issues of the day.

It was inevitable that the former vet would suffer by comparison with his predecessor, but the sad fact was that he should never have given up the profession he was so well qualified for. In his new role as editor and lead columnist, he trod a thin line between being a loveable eccentric and a guileless buffoon.

The hard, combative element that is such a necessary ingredient for a good editor was simply not in his nature. In addition, he was sadly lacking in leadership qualities and as a result his articles carried little or no authority and were often the subject of ridicule. Worst of all, however, was his evasion of the responsibility he owed to his paper and his readers.

He avoided controversy like the plague as he pursued a *laissez-faire* policy, which protected him from the confrontational wrangles that Feist had accepted as part and parcel of the job. If a tricky subject reared its head he would sweep it under the carpet in one or two dismissive sentences or simply ignore it altogether.

His blinkered approach even extended to the racecourse violence that had been on the increase since the mid-1860s when the growth of metropolitan meetings attracted the worst of the criminal element. These gate-money fixtures were run by a motley collection of bookmakers and publicans who connived with trainers and jockeys to fix races and charged the public a shilling for the privilege of viewing what had, until then, been recognised as 'a free sport for a free people'.

With prize money kept to a minimum, and rents for beer tents and betting booths to a maximum, the meetings proved a gold mine for their promoters and quickly mushroomed throughout the suburbs, as did the lawlessness that accompanied them.* Edward Spencer, alias 'Nathaniel Gubbins' of the *Sporting Times*, spoke from bitter experience when he wrote:

> We who attended the suburban meetings went racing in the full knowledge that we were extremely likely to be robbed, if worth the robbing, and assaulted as well, and grievously assaulted at that, should we dare to resist the robbers.[1]

To be fair to Blake, racecourse muggings had become such a daily occurrence they no longer qualified as news, but a riot on the scale of the one that took place at Shrewsbury (hardly a suburban course) in 1878 was hard to ignore. On November 13, a small page 3 item headed 'Latest From Shrewsbury', gave the usual information on the weather and ground conditions together with a summary of selections for the following day before it added as a postscript:

---

* In 1877, the Jockey Club, in an effort to stamp out this 'suburban saturnalia', required all courses racing under its rules to give a minimum of £300 (£27,000) in prize money (exclusive of stake money) per day. Courses unable or unwilling to meet this demand placed themselves beyond the pale and all those involved in such ('flapping') meetings faced being warned off. While this went some way towards improving the situation, the worst courses were not closed down until the following year when George Anderson MP, the scourge of the Scottish-based bookmakers, introduced a bill in parliament to prevent any race meeting being held within ten miles of Charing Cross unless licensed by local magistrates. Even then, rowdyism and robberies with violence continued to bedevil racing until the gangs were finally driven out at the end of the 1920s.

A scene approaching a riot was witnessed on the course this afternoon just before the close of sport. Welshers and thieves armed themselves with thick sticks and charged one of the gates of the enclosure, many of the ruffians forcing their way in. Many of the members of Tattersalls Ring, those who had money in their pockets, beat a retreat in a manner not the most dignified; broken hats and cracked heads were numerous before the disturbance was quelled, but to prevent a recurrence of such doings tomorrow, the Messrs Frail have obtained the services of a body of police from Birmingham.

Remarkably, apart from this passing reference to the rampant thuggery and a brief item three days later, which reported that five men had been charged with riotous conduct, there was no further mention of it in the *Life*. No editorial, no condemnation, *no nuffin*!

The *Sportsman* also dismissed the story on the day with just a fleeting reference to "the rowdy element" which was surprising because it was then running a campaign against racecourse thugs under the heading 'Scum of the Course'. However, the paper did give a full report of the committal proceedings a few days later. The extent of the violence can be gauged from the evidence that was presented before the magistrates.

A Manchester detective said he saw one of the accused, "lead a crowd of roughs, about 150 in number, towards the grandstand and there were several other mobs in other parts of the ground creating a disturbance and committing assaults." He described another of the gang leaders, William Maclean, as a well-known welsher and "one of the greatest scoundrels in the country". As the mob tried to force its way into Tattersalls, Maclean punched John Frail, the clerk of the course, while the detective was "struck on the head with a heavy stick which broke in two".

A policeman then arrested Maclean and took an iron-spiked umbrella handle from him, but the welsher was rescued by his friends and escaped into the crowd as the Tattersalls gatemen were overwhelmed by the rabble. A man was throwing coal at racegoers in the grandstand and bookmakers' stools were broken up and used as weapons. Several people were knocked down and robbed, and the stands and railings were "much damaged".

Sensational stuff! But not to C W Blake who seemed oblivious to what was going on in the world around him as he padded out his column with reams of inane waffle. He justified his ramblings by claiming it was necessary to take "a preliminary canter by way of loosening one's joints, settling one's ideas, and clearing the air passages before going into the heavy business"[2] which, to him, was anything and everything to do with racing.

All too often these 'preliminary canters' developed into marathons of unremitting doggerel on any subject that took his fancy. The vagaries of the British climate, flowers and nature were firm favourites that were given regular airings as he churned out some of the most awful garbage ever to appear in print.

In the same year (1879) that the *Life* failed to record the death of William Davies, while its rivals carried extensive obituaries on the famous 'Leviathan of the Ring', Blake provided a stunning example of his lack of news-sense and penchant for appalling prose. It appeared in the same number that reported the death of Lionel Nathan de Rothschild just six days after he had won the 100th running of the Derby with Sir Bevys, yet Blake made no mention of the deceased Baron or the fact that, as a result of his death, Sir Bevys had been scratched from the Grand Prix de Paris while *en route* to France. Instead, he launched into an extraordinary dissertation on the weather:

Poor June! Dismal, dreary, damp, bedraggled! Where are thy glories and beauties sung of by poets?

Where are thy blue skies and bright suns? Eclipsed, swamped, overwhelmed by the merciless never-ceasing rain!

Heavy lowering clouds, charged, as was the widow's cruse with a supply which never fails, have sodden with their copious weeping the depressed, helpless earth which in turn, looking pitifully but hopelessly upwards, cries faintly and more faintly still for one more glimpse of the face of the vanquished and obscured sun.

Poor June! Thy leafy glories are, it is true, left to thee in some measure, but in the absence of sunshine the dripping verdure may be compared to dancing without music. Everything seems to grow with a tortoise-like crawl, slowly and painfully, instead of leaping into life with the light-heartedness and hopefulness of youth.

Poor June! This year I am afraid thou wilt not be 'laden with the breath of roses'. Even the hawthorn has to struggle to bloom, the tightened buds having little encouragement to burst their bonds and unfold their petals. The spiked chestnut blossom is a long way behind its time, and the lilac and laburnum mourn in concert over their damp imprisonment.

The lilac and laburnum were not the only ones to mourn as Blake continued to drivel on, paragraph after interminable paragraph, before he climaxed this remarkable example of Victorian journalese with the observation:

The look-out now inclines one to sing, if there is any singing left in the world beyond the mythical notes of the dying swan, 'Oh! would I were a duck (or Captain Webb or young Beckwith) that I might swim to thee!'

It was so bad as to be almost magnificent, and each passing month and every change of weather provided the egregious editor with another excuse to impose his dementia upon his long-suffering readers. Little wonder the *Life* was losing sales to the *Sportsman*, but there were other reasons apart from the Blake-factor.

Chief among them was that the paper was still a bi-weekly and its reports inevitably suffered in comparison with its daily rival. In addition, its dogged adherence to a four-page format constantly forced it to drop items "owing to the great pressure upon our columns," while its contemporary made good use of the extra space offered by the introduction of its eight-page 'double number'.

It was not until 1880, when the *Sporting Chronicle* became a fully-fledged daily, that the *Life* took the first tentative step towards joining its rivals when 'extra numbers' on Tuesday and Thursday were published for Derby week; an experiment that was repeated for the St Leger meeting and also for the Cesarewitch and Cambridgeshire weeks. The following year 'Four Times a Week' became the norm and finally, on Tuesday, 27 March 1883, the usual *Sporting Life* title was flanked by two scrolls announcing in the word 'Daily' a belated step forward in the history of the paper.

The transition had been heralded by a month of 'Important notices to the Public' but, inexplicably, it was not backed up by an editorial on the day. It was not until 24 hours later that Blake ushered in the new era when, after his usual rambling introduction, he offered up a hymn of praise to the paper's many contributors who included W W Read, "the Surrey amateur whose batting average is the highest of the team," who had recently reported on England's first Ashes victory over Australia in Sydney.

As well as promising to cover a long list of activities including tricycling and roller skating "dear to thousands of our subscribers," and that "No 'pavement prophets' will be allowed to waste the ink and paper of this establishment," Blake asserted that 'Augur' would "contribute a letter in plain English every day" – a pledge he broke every day.

In conclusion, he declared the paper was well equipped to meet the new daily print run with three steam rotary Marinoni presses, each capable of running off 18,000 copies an hour, installed in its St Bride Street printing hall and that: "Under all changes, the *Sporting Life* colours will still be 'yellow and black', the price One Penny, and its motto 'A Fair Field and No Favour!'"

While daily publication relieved Blake of one long-standing headache, it imposed another because, instead of constantly having to drop items due to lack of space, he was now struggling to fill his pages during the lean winter months.

The traditional way for sporting journals to tide themselves over such barren periods was to commission a serial novelist to churn out a succession of chapters to run from the end of one Flat racing season through to the start of the next. During the winter of 1881-82, for instance, the *Life* 'treated' its readers to "*Beaten On The Post or Joe Morton's Mercy*, a new and original sporting novel by J P Wheeldon, author of *Miss Burton of Craigmuir, Reedyford Lock House, Tom Riley's Conquest*, etc."

There were 33 chapters of this deservedly long-forgotten tome, which was introduced with the declaration:

> We believe the work will appeal strongly to the sympathies of all lovers of sport of both sexes as, apart from the interest of a powerfully written domestic story, nearly all recognised English sports are touched upon. Racing, Foxhunting, Shooting, Trout and Pike Fishing has each its place; while a chapter or two will be found devoted to a description of 'A Night with the Fancy'. In fact, we look forward very confidently to a success for this entirely new tale from Mr Wheeldon's facile and practised pen, and, however blank may be the winter in the way of sport, subscribers to the *Sporting Life* may depend on having 'something worth reading'.

For better or worse, Blake also embraced any form of entertainment that might help to flesh out the paper on a quiet day. Among the more peculiar functions he chose to cover were the smoking concerts which had become popular towards the end of the 1870s when numerous amateur music societies were formed to allow members to enjoy the simple pleasures of a harmonious evening and a puff of tobacco without let or hindrance.

The dangers of smoking might seem a relatively modern concern, but the habit was being linked to cancer as early as the 1860s when there were campaigns to outlaw "the stinking West India plant ... [*that*] benumbs the brain, extinguishes the memory, brings on giddiness and finally engenders those terrible diseases, cancer in the mouth and softening of the spinal marrow."[3]

An account of a concert given by the South London Music Club in Brixton's Gresham Hall in 1883, implied that the smoking of 'gentle stimulants' in the streets of that unsullied suburb gave as much offence to its worthy citizens as crack users do today. The correspondent dutifully reported that "a choir of about forty well-trained voices" gave a recital of such songs as 'Nymphs of the Forest' and 'Hail to the Chief', before he embarked on the main thrust of his article which was not so much concerned with vocal harmony as it was with the disharmony caused by "interloping crazies" who sought to deny music lovers their right to smoke in concert halls.

At a time when temperance societies were flourishing, the liberal-minded scribe hardly drew breath as he applauded...

an appreciative audience in full enjoyment of the comforting weed and those gentle stimulants which local option, blue ribbons and other kindred interloping crazies, would wipe off the face of the earth if fanaticism could exert its preposterous sway; for not alone are the distillers and brewers receiving warnings from a clique of self-appointed, puritanical water bailiffs and censors whose mission is alike presumptive and impertinent, but we are now threatened with an 'Anti-Narcotic League' whose avowed object is to discountenance the use of tobacco and so forth!

Blake also capitalised on the Victorians' passion for staging grand displays such as the 1883 International Fisheries Exhibition in South Kensington, which was given extensive coverage by the aforementioned J P Wheeldon who, for two months, described every stand, boat and fish-hook on show in the mighty emporium of Exhibition Hall.

A column of the front page was given over to the opening ceremony on May 14 when, with the exception of the Queen, the entire royal family appeared to be on hand to hear the Prince of Wales voice his concern for the conservation of the oceans and express the (vain!) hope that: "without needless destruction or avoidable waste of any kind, mankind may derive the fullest possible advantage from the bounty of the waters."

On bank holiday Monday some 75,000 people paid their 1s entrance fee to see the exhibition and by the end of the month 250,855 had passed through the turnstiles, while the *Life's* piscatorial pen-pusher churned out a total of 22 columns (approximately 50,000 words) on everything from inflatable canoes (on sale at 10gns – £945) to breech-loading lance guns "for the instantaneous killing of whales after being harpooned".

While smoking concerts and exhibitions helped to fill the paper, Blake could also draw on the sporting action that took place on the other side of the world during the winter months. By the 1880s, English cricket teams had started to make regular visits to Australia following that nation's memorable victory over James Lillywhite's XI in the first Test match to be played between the two sides in Melbourne in March 1877.

The reports were usually written by one of the players who had been especially commissioned by the paper, but there was always a frustrating wait between learning the telegraphed result of a match and reading a full account of it which, for reasons of economy, was sent by sea and took about six weeks to reach London.

By contrast, news of the one-off Test at the Oval in 1882 was relayed around the country within minutes after England were defeated for the first time on home soil. Set the simple task of scoring 85 to win, they suffered a collapse of Tay Bridge proportions and lost by seven runs after Fred 'The Demon' Spofforth, proved almost unplayable by taking four wickets for two runs in his last 11 overs.

The humiliating defeat prompted Reginald Shirley Brooks, 'Blobbs' of the *Sporting Times*, to compose his celebrated mock obituary of English cricket. Suitably framed by a black mourning border, the In Memoriam notice led to 'the Ashes' becoming the Holy Grail of the game.

In addition to the cricket tours, there were regular winter events at home that helped to fill the columns. Extensive coverage was given to coursing, particularly the Waterloo Cup, and also to 'aquatics'

Within six months of its sudden death at the Oval, English cricket staged a Lazarus-like revival when the Hon. Ivo Bligh took an XI to Australia to retrieve the 'Ashes' in a three-match series. To commemorate their 2-1 victory, Bligh was presented with a miniature urn containing the ashes of a bail that had been 'cremated' after the deciding Test in Sydney. Bligh (later Lord Darnley) bequeathed the Ashes to the MCC in his will and they have remained in the Memorial Gallery at Lord's ever since, even though Australia once 'held' them for 19 consecutive years (1934–52).

encompassing sculling, yachting and rowing. In the week leading up to the university boat race, a daily column was allotted to the practice of the crews, and on the day of the race two extra editions were brought out; an 'Early Extra' with the bare result, and a 'Late Extra' with a full report.

Billiard tournaments were also a regular feature. Matches would often extend over days or even weeks as was the case in 1891 when John Roberts jnr, the 'Champion of the World at English billiards', declared he would give any player 12,000 points start in a match of 24,000 up for £500 (£45,000) a side. The challenge was aimed directly at William Peall, the spot stroke champion, and was duly taken up. Held over 12 days at the Egyptian Hall, Piccadilly, the over-confident Roberts lost his money when he failed to concede Peall half the game and was beaten by 2,590 points.

Reports on athletic meetings from around the country took up a full page two or three times a week, while there was regular coverage of the trotting meetings held throughout the year at venues such as Alexandra Park, Lillie Bridge, Abbey Hey Park (Manchester), Aintree, Blackpool, Belgrave Road (Leicester), Eslington Park (Gateshead), Blackburn, Morley (Bradford) and Shawfield (Glasgow).

The increasing popularity of rugby and football ensured both sports were given plenty of space and club secretaries were encouraged to send in match reports which the paper would, out of the goodness of its heart, insert 'free of charge'.

However, lawn tennis, which became fashionable towards the end of the '70s was given the barest coverage, possibly because the game was being promoted by a rival journal in *The Field*. More space was given to rackets and lacrosse – a game that became established in England after a touring side made up of teams of Canadian amateurs and Iroquois Indians staged a performance before Queen Victoria at Windsor Castle in 1876.

Polo, introduced from India in 1871, also had its place in the *Life*, which, in an end-of-the-year review for 1873, remarked on the matches held at Lillie Bridge:

> Hockey on horseback was one of the sensations of the past season and made the Amateur Athletic Club enclosure one of the best-frequented resorts of the 'upper ten' as might be anticipated from the frequent visits of members of the Royal family.

Golf, which only established itself in England with the foundation of the Royal North Devon Club in 1864 and the Royal Liverpool Club at Hoylake (1869), received scant coverage, but there were regular reports on the knur (or nurr) and spell matches that were played chiefly in Yorkshire and Lancashire. Known as 'poor man's golf', the game, which survives to this day, was won by the player who drove the 'knur' (a marble-sized ball) the furthest in a series of 'rises' from the 'spell', a spring trap that flicked the knur up into the air. Matches between local champions drew large crowds and were the medium of heavy betting.

Whippet racing, pigeon racing, angling, quoits, wrestling, bowls and skating (both ice and roller) were all given space in the eclectic pages, as were such obscure pursuits as clog dancing and bottle-carrying, examples of which also featured among the rich repository of challenges that appeared in the paper. Two from 1881, a year after the first world clog dancing championships had been held in Leeds, typified the period:

> Harry Collins ... is open to dance any man in the world (bar Tom Ward) twenty-one steps on the high pedestal, in clogs Lancashire style, without breaking; and match his pupil, Master Bishop, to dance any amateur in England ten steps or twenty off the toe, Lancashire style, for £10 or £50. £1 in the hands of the *Sporting Life* to bind a match. First come, first served.

> We have received articles for a match between John Howe of Westminster and George Hood of Lambeth in which the latter has agreed to concede Howe 410 yards start in an hour's go-as-you-please race, both to carry a two gallon bottle, neck downwards, on their heads; the necks of the bottles not to exceed two inches and a half across, and should either man drop his bottle he is to replace it on his head and start from where the bottle dropped. Either man to be allowed to touch his bottle, but not to hold it on his head. The match to be for £5 (open for £10) a side, and the *Sporting Life* to appoint stakeholder and referee.

'Tis a pity Charley Blake always lost his bottle when it came to addressing important issues.

THE SP WARS (1885-1925)

FOR ALL his failings, Charley Blake oversaw some crucial changes to the *Life* during his 17 years in office. Apart from the paper's transition from a bi-weekly into a daily, by far the most important of them was the employment of a reporter to compile and return starting prices from the main meetings.

Up until 1881 the paper had received its SPs from the agency run by Joe Capp, who also supplied the Central News Agency with a full racing service that included probable runners, results and race descriptions. Capp, formally associated with the racing news service run by Albert Feist, was one of the best-known characters on the racecourse. Standing 6ft 2in, he made an imposing figure with his polished top hat and bushy black beard, while his capacity for liquid intake in the watering holes of Fleet Street was legendary. It was said of him that he feared nothing on earth but closing time and "when raised to indignation his flow of language was in a class by itself".[1]

Among his rivals in a fiercely competitive market was Charles Ashley who returned SPs for the *Sportsman* and the Press Association which, in turn, passed on the information to its subscribers, while *Bell's Life* received a different set of SPs from another source. It had initially relied on William Ruff and his son before their agency was taken over by another father-son team, William and Billy Wright, but for how long it took their returns is uncertain as there was a constant shuffling of the agencies and subscribers pack.

In addition to the agencies, some of the daily papers employed their own SP men to provide a service for other Fleet Street newspapers. For a period *The Times* supplied the *Sporting Gazette*, *Morning Advertiser* and *Daily News* with its returns, while *The Standard* did the same for the *Daily Telegraph* and *The Star*. While all these reporters could generally be relied upon to relay the correct result, although instances of the wrong winner being sent out were not unknown, the SPs would often differ because each man compiled his own set of prices. There was no such thing as an official composite starting price.

The SP of a horse was, and still is, determined on the racecourse by noting the best price generally available to a decent bet in the main ring at the time of the 'off'. As the odds offered by bookmakers constantly fluctuate to reflect the latest market moves, a reporter working in one part of Tattersalls would often end up with a different set of prices to those of a rival colleague covering a different section of the ring.

In order to obtain a measure of uniformity, the reporters would confer with each other as soon as the race started. On the occasions they agreed to differ, the prices of fancied horses would usually vary by only a fraction of a point and where one reporter would return 6-4 another might go 11-8 or 13-8. The odds against a horse in the middle of the market might differ by a whole point or more, say 15-2 and 9-1, while variations could be considerable in the case of outsiders.

The prime example of this was the 1867 Derby winner Hermit, who was returned in the *Sporting Life* and most other papers at 1000-15 (66.6-1), but *The Times* and the *Sporting Gazette* maintained 100-1 was the correct SP. The *Gazette* stressed: "though Captain Machell backed Hermit at 1000-15 to win £10,000 [*£900,000*] in the last hour, 1000-10 was currently offered afterwards and such is Hermit's true starting price."

This represented a huge variation of 33 points which, when translated into cash, could mean the difference of thousands of pounds to bookmakers and backers. Yet it was only in 1864 that the SP of a horse attained any real significance in the betting world. Before then starting prices were purely of academic interest.

Bets were not taken or settled at SP. List (board) prices governed the market; the SPs published in the press merely informed the backer whether he had 'beaten the odds' or not. In such a volatile market, commission agents took every opportunity to short-change their clients and disputes were commonplace; then, in August 1864 – a year before they launched the *Sportsman* – James and Sydney Smith opened an agency office in Jermyn Street in the West End. In advertising their new venture, the bookmakers initiated a whole new era in betting when they guaranteed "the market price as laid at the start *and quoted in the papers of the following day.*" They were, they said:

> …satisfied something of the sort had long been wanted. Gentlemen who may not wish to telegraph to a race meeting or who do not want to interfere with the commission of their friends, have thus a ready and satisfactory means of transacting their business.

It was not long before others followed the lead. One of the first was Billy Wright, whose conflict of interests between being a bookmaker and running a results service that returned SPs had hardly seemed to matter before. In September an advertisement for Wright's Racing Telegram and Commission Agency announced:

> …in consequence of the uncertain state of the London market which often varies from the price the horse is at the start and at times causes great dissatisfaction … gentlemen who entrust him with their commissions … prior to eleven o'clock on the morning of a race, will be on the same price as laid at the start according to the quotations that appear in the next morning's papers.

This new system still gave bookmakers the advantage of choosing the newspapers that returned the shortest prices and on occasions they ignored their stated terms of business altogether. The 1865 Cambridgeshire provided one such example when the finish was fought out between the 33-1 outsiders Nu and Gardevisure (40-1 in some papers).

Not satisfied with pocketing the vast amount of money that had been staked on the mighty Gladiateur (the 13-2 favourite was finally vanquished under a crushing burden of 9st 12lb), many bookmakers reverted to their old practice of undercutting the few fortunates who had backed the winner. The *Life*, critical of what it described as "a very unsatisfactory settlement," commented:

> It seems that in most cases the layers, agreeing in the original instance to be bound by the quotations as returned by newspapers, have, in Gardevisure and Nu's case, so far repudiated their avowed principles as to return far shorter prices than those animals were quoted by nine-tenths of the Press, including all the sporting journals.
>
> This we consider to be highly improper, and a recurrence of such disputes will destroy the confidence already earned by several eminent commission firms which first became entitled to patronage by a steady and persistent adherence to a system they had voluntarily introduced into betting.

In general, bookmakers were reluctant to abandon the old p.p. system, which gave them a decided advantage over the off-course backer who lost his money if his horse did not run,* but eventually competition from street bookmakers, who increased dramatically as a result of the 1874 Betting Act, brought SP betting into common use.

Even so, when the *Sportsman* launched a telegram results service in 1878, starting prices were not included, but by the time the *Life* finally committed itself to publishing four times a week three years later it was evident that SPs had become a marketable commodity. Not only did they generate revenue for the papers that supplied them; they also increased the circulation of papers that published them.

The sale of evening papers, in particular, soared as every edition carried a new batch of results and SPs in the 'Stop Press' section on the back page, which was eagerly pored over by bookies and backers alike. On 10 May 1881, the *Life* staked its claim to a share of the action as it announced:

> In order to make the *Sporting Life* as complete and perfect in its racing returns as possible, we have engaged a special representative to be in the ring at all principal race meetings, and he will devote himself solely to reporting the betting which takes place on each race, and on future events ... Our representative will write as 'Man in the Ring' and commence his duties next week at Newmarket. We need hardly say how obliged we shall be for information afforded him, our sole desire being to give satisfaction to both backers and layers in this very important matter.

An accompanying house advert stated:

> We have made arrangements for the Telegraphing of Results of All Races at the principal Meetings during the year, immediately the horses pass the post. Messages will be sent to any subscriber in the United Kingdom on the receipt of 2s [£9] in stamps. In addition to the first three horses, the message will include the Starting Price Of The Winner, a feature never before introduced.

The new service faced plenty of competition not only from the *Sportsman*, which wasted no time in incorporating SPs into its telegrams, but also from the various news agencies such as MacMahon's, whose ticker-tape machines printed out the latest results in Morse Code in the offices of their subscribers.

A week before the 1881 Derby, MacMahon's placed a large advert in the *Life* which proclaimed, line by line in varying sizes of tabulated type and a fitting telegraphic style:

> They're Off! They're Off! – Time And Space Annihilated! – Epsom Downs And London – MacMahon's Telegraphic News Company (Limited) – Have Constructed – By Special License from the Government – A Direct Line Of Wire – from their – Central Offices, 8 Piccadilly – to the – Grand Stand At Epsom – During The Derby Week – Two Hundred Establishments (Of Subscribers) In The Metropolis – will be connected – Directly With The Grand Stand.
>
>   'They're Off!' – Will Be Signalled, And Will Appear Simultaneously On The Tape Of Every Instrument The Moment The Starter Drops His Flag! – Runners, Riders and Opening Quotations announced in London before the horses go to the post – Result – and – Starting Price Of Winner

---

* Play or pay, or 'all-in, run or not'; a system that originated from the early days when owners matched their horses against each other for a sum of money. If one of the parties afterwards withdrew from the agreement by scratching his horse for whatever reason, he would be required to forfeit his stake.

Published In London Before The Jockeys Weigh In – A Short Description of each Race will follow
Result – The Above Information Can Be Obtained Only Where The MacMahon Electric Indicators
Are Placed.

Meanwhile, Martin Cobbett, in his new guise as 'Man in the Ring', had made his debut at
Newmarket where Two Thousand Guineas runner-up, Iroquois, had a walkover in the first race. At
the time Iroquois was a 25-1 chance to reverse placings with his Guineas conqueror, Peregrine, in the
Derby, but a week later at Bath the *Life's* man reported that the American colt had been "backed all
over the place at 100 to 8" for the Epsom classic. Followers of market moves had further encouragement
at Harpenden a week later when "Iroquois opened at 9 to 1, but 8 to 1 was afterwards freely accepted,"
and on Derby day the plunge on Fred Archer's mount continued as the betting guru noted:

Peregrine, at intervals, was backed against the field, but owing to the strong support that was behind
Iroquois, 12 to 10 was freely on offer. Geologist, early in the market was second favourite at 11 to 2,
but left off at 6 to 1. The American Iroquois opened at 100 to 15 at which price he was heavily
backed, and the odds veered down to 6 to 1; finally 5 to 1 was freely taken, and when the flag fell he
started second favourite.

The result: 1 Iroquois (5-1); 2 Peregrine (6-5); 3 Town Moor (1000-30). And, if the *Life* is to be
believed, the jostling, boisterous crowd that had gathered outside its office that afternoon learnt of the
victory of the first American-bred Derby winner almost as soon as MacMahon's ticker-tape subscribers:

Fred Archer wins the 1881 Derby on Iroquois; the first American-bred horse to triumph in the Epsom classic.

The Derby Result At *The Sporting Life* – The start for the Derby was made at 12min past three o'clock, the race occupied 2min 50sec, and the names of the first three as they finished were posted in our window in Fleet Street at 15min past three.

Over the following seven months the paper rapidly expanded its results service and by the beginning of 1882 it was able to announce:

The Sporting Life has organised a News Department for supplying, by Special Telegrams direct from the various scenes of action, the following information to Newspapers in London and the Provinces: Results Of Races with Full List of Horses Running, Jockeys Riding, Starting Prices, Descriptions, Betting on Course, Selections each Night, and Morning Gallops of the Big Meetings, Arrivals and Scratchings. Betting In London (City), Manchester and at Tattersall's. Newmarket Training Intelligence sent at noon each day. Special Entries, Weights and Acceptances. Coursing and other Sports by Special Arrangement. Estimates for the whole or any portion of the above on application to the *Sporting Life* Office, 148 Fleet Street, London, E.C.

In the same year MacMahon's was taken over by the Exchange Telegraph Co., which had been set up in 1872 and was increasing its coverage of sport, while in 1883 the irascible Charles Ashley fell out with Edmund Robbins, the manager of the Press Association, and the *Life* stepped in to supply its service to that news agency.

Ashley then transferred his service to the *Sporting Chronicle* and so the lines of battle were drawn up for the first of what were to become known as the 'SP wars'. Initial hostilities broke out on 7 February 1885, when Charley Blake was moved to pass comment on a more distant conflict that had just taken a turn for the worse in the Sudan.

For someone who was not in the habit of expressing himself forcefully on any subject save the weather, the emotional impact of the fate that had befallen General Charles Gordon, "who has so long borne the brunt of the fray, single-handed and unassisted by his countrymen," was evident as Blake declared:

It is no exaggeration to say that indignation was never more widespread or generally expressed than when the news of the fall of Khartoum and the utter failure of all our efforts to rescue Gordon reached this unhappy country. Practically speaking, with Gordon in his hands, the Mahdi is master of the situation, having regard to the primary and expressed object of the expedition. Beyond this statement, words fail me, and I pass on to other matters more immediately within my province.

Chief among those matters were SP returns and the decision by the leading London layers "who transact business on this popular, convenient, growing and widespread system," to accept the *Sporting Life* as the ruling authority instead of the *Sportsman* whose prices had governed the betting since it became a daily in 1876

In imparting this information, Blake declared that more SP reporters would be taken on in an endeavour "to hold the scale fairly between man and man – between backer and bookmaker". From Ireland it was reported that the switch "seemed to give entire satisfaction" in Dublin and that "the papers from London by the Irish mail were all eagerly scanned for information on the point."

The papers would have been scanned in vain for any mention of this less than earth-shattering news as they were more concerned with the fate of General Gordon (whose decapitated body was already a-mouldering in the grave) and the arrest of the Irish revolutionaries, James Cunningham and Harry Burton, who had recently attempted to blow up the House of Commons and the Tower of London!

In its next issue the *Life* carried a statement from George Gibbons, chairman of the London clubs bookmakers' committee, who explained:

> The starting price bookmakers at the leading clubs have often been requested to alter the official guide from the *Sportsman* to the *Sporting Life*. This the layers have now consented to do and, as I am sure the change will meet with general approval, I have consented to the alteration.
>
> I therefore beg to give public notice that after this day (Monday, February 9) all starting price transactions, wherever entered into with me, will be governed by the prices quoted in the *Sporting Life* instead of the *Sportsman*, as hitherto. Since Saturday morning I have made a point of calling personally on a large number of my metropolitan customers and in no instance has there been a dissenting voice.

He obviously didn't call in at the offices of the *Sportsman* whose editor, Alfred Allison, dismissed the bookmakers' move with withering sarcasm:

> Let no one be irreverent enough to be mirthful; let a subdued kind of calm simmer through the compositions of all who read these words, and allow a holy feeling of awe and gratitude to pervade the mind when we announce that sundry generous starting price bookmakers have deliberately announced their intention of behaving with open handed liberality towards their clients, the noble army of backers.
>
> They announce that they are prompted to this grand display of self-denial and disregard of their own interests by the 'request of backers generally'. Then they go on to intimate that *The Sportsman* has not dealt with punters so liberally as it might have done, and therefore the journal in question is to be tabooed in the future.
>
> Under ordinary circumstances we should not have alluded to a matter of this description, but the proclamation is so uncommonly 'cool' and, withal, so unutterably impudent that it deserves some notoriety. Here is a small clique announcing that they intend to be rashly improvident and recklessly munificent during the forthcoming racing season. They care not for their own pockets – their sole desire is to benefit the division they denominate 'their clients'.
>
> This, it will be admitted, is an unparalleled outburst of magnanimity … Starting price bookmakers have never, up to the present, been especially distinguished for open-handed lavishness in the disposition of funds. That they should now evince an earnest desire to benefit their patrons may well be regarded with a certain amount of distrust.

Allison was entitled to be cynical, although many bookmakers stated in their rules which paper's prices governed their transactions or gave their clients the option of nominating the newspaper of their choice. *Bell's Life* was still preferred by some, but by now the paper was a shadow of its former self. The Clement brothers had been "reduced to abject poverty"[2] as a result of the money they had poured into their old flagship in an attempt to keep it afloat, but in 1880 they finally sold out to Henry Buck and Charles Greenwood, two journalists who were equally adept with pen or pencil.

Buck, a contributor to the *Daily Telegraph's* Hotspur column, was running a credit bookmaker's business at the time, while Greenwood, who became 'Hotspur' in 1882 and was to lend that column much distinction over the next 21 years, worked commissions for some of the country's leading owners.

The new proprietors promised to put the old journal "into a thorough state of repair ... by diminishing nothing of value, by adding everything that needs to be added and by imparting fresh vigour into every department,"[3] but, apart from incorporating training reports, it remained virtually unchanged. Its share of the market continued to decline and after two years its new owners cut their losses and sold the paper on to Hulton and Bleackley of the *Sporting Chronicle* for just £7,000 (£630,000). As one contemporary observer remarked: "There was a time when this journal must have paid its owners every year a profit considerably beyond this sum."[4]

It was a mighty fall from grace and one that even the expertise of the Manchester men failed to arrest. Inexplicably, they allowed two years to pass before taking steps to stop the lifeblood that was their readership from draining away. A tourniquet of sorts was applied in 1884 when the price of the paper was slashed from 6d to 1d and production stepped up to twice a week. But these long-overdue measures were not enough to win back the lost legion of readers and when, in a final despairing throw of the dice, Hulton turned *Bell's* into a basic four-page daily in 1885, the paper was already beyond all help. The end came a year later when a 'Special Notice' in the *Life* on Derby day announced:

> *Bell's Life* – This, the oldest established sporting newspaper in the world will, after Saturday next, retire from the field of competitive journalism. Our old friend, however, does not become extinct, but will live on in these columns, so that after the day mentioned, '*The Sporting Life* with which is incorporated *Bell's Life*' will be our title and property, together with the famous 'eye' and the motto '*Nunquam Dormio*'.

On the appointed Saturday, 29 May 1886, the editor of *Bell's Life* penned a sad and salutary epitaph as he reflected on how the paper had become "enervated and plethoric" as a result of its great success:

> Wrapped in a dignified consciousness of its own power and importance, it contemptuously disregarded the puny efforts of its imitators and waited with suicidal apathy, until they had established themselves through their own perseverance, ability and cheapness into formidable competitors ... the racing world cannot, or will not, support four daily sporting papers, all publishing a very similar class of matter on almost identical lines; and as circulation is the test of appreciation, the northern sportsman pins his faith on the opinions expressed by the Manchester *Sporting Chronicle*, whilst the southerner has equal confidence in the great ability of the *Sporting Life*.
>
> To the energetic proprietor of the latter periodical we have transferred all the copyright interests of *Bell's Life* which will henceforth be incorporated with that popular journal, and we trust that our friends and readers will extend to it the kindness they have ever shown to us. So farewell at once; for once, for all, and ever.

Meanwhile, the first SP war had lapsed into an uneasy truce as the two principal protagonists buried their differences while they cornered the market in the return of prices and busied themselves in enlisting subscribers to their service. As before, their reporters compared notes but now, when their prices differed, they agreed on a compromise in order to 'level up the lists' so just one set of SPs was issued by both papers.

This system worked to the general satisfaction of backer and bookmaker alike, although there were occasional grumbles. Such complaints usually centred on a well-backed winner; the layers would argue the price should have been shorter, while punters took the opposite view, but this was only human nature running its true course.

Then, during the winter of 1893, a protest came from an entirely unexpected quarter when Lord Shrewsbury, a steward at Wolverhampton, took it upon himself to question the SPs returned for two winners at the meeting. One concerned his own horse, Philmont, a 5-4 favourite; the other a horse called Red Pepper, a 5-1 chance. In both cases the indignant official claimed the prices should have been considerably longer.

The *Life*, understandably, took exception to this slight on the integrity of its reporter, Jim George, who was in his first year as 'Man in the Ring'.* In a leader headed 'Lord Shrewsbury and The Press' it quoted the prices that had been challenged and observed:

> For some reason or other Lord Shrewsbury was dissatisfied with these returns and on Wednesday he, along with the other stewards of the meeting, invaded the reporters' room and roundly declared that the prices were false. In proof of their accuracy the reporters procured the attendance of the solid bookmakers whose books bore testimony to the correctness of the prices. But still his lordship was not satisfied and he made the not uncommon retort of an angry man that he would write to the papers.
>
> We have been anxiously awaiting his communication, but up to the moment of going to press nothing of the nature expected has come to hand. Perhaps it will arrive tomorrow, or the next day, or about the time of the Greek Kalends.

To belittle the blustering peer even further, the paper then quoted Rule 15 of the Rules of Racing, which stated that stewards "shall not entertain any disputes relating to bets," and delivered the *coup de grâce* by remarking:

> His lordship here is plainly in a quandary for merely as Lord Shrewsbury he had no possible right to interfere with the reporters, and as a steward of the Wolverhampton meeting he had no business to approach them on the subject of betting ... Why, it may be asked, should Lord Shrewsbury assume he must be right and the reporters wrong? Certainly they had no personal interest in the return, and can he aver the same?

Apart from the occasional renegade steward running amok in the pressroom, things continued to run relatively smoothly on the SP front until a second war suddenly broke out on 26 January 1905. It was at the penultimate steeplechase meeting to be held at Newmarket that the *Sportsman*, "without

---

* Jim George, a former actor who trod the boards at Sadler's Wells, became a byword for integrity during the 32 years he was chief SP reporter for the *Life*. The story was often told of the time he was approached by a well-known owner just before a race at Derby. "I'm putting you a 'pony' on my horse at SP," whispered the owner, whereupon George snapped back: "If you do, I shall report you to the Stewards." A fastidious dresser who set a high sartorial example to other members of the racing press, George always carried a crocodile-skin bag containing a hat brush and duster "and the first thing he would do on reaching the pressroom would be to brush his hat and dust his shoes. After twirling his long, flowing moustache once or twice, he would proceed with the business of the day. Although he was so punctilious and consequential, he was withal a very likeable man ... admired and respected by men in all walks of life."[5]

any warning being given or reasons being assigned," instructed its chief SP reporter, Paul Widdison, to compile his prices independently and return them without conferring with Jim George.

At the time, the *Life* was supplying the *Sporting Chronicle* and the Press Association with its prices, while the *Sportsman* did the same for the Central News Agency and the Exchange Telegraph Co. Because the three news agencies – the PA, Central and Extel – relayed the prices on to the national and provincial press, and to bookmakers' offices, clubs and hotels throughout the country the situation quickly became chaotic as the prices returned by the two papers would sometimes vary considerably.

At first the *Sportsman's* prices tended to favour the punter. At Nottingham on January 31 there was a two-point difference in the SP of the winner, Hopeless II (10-1 with the *Sportsman*; 8-1 with the *Life*), while at Gatwick two days later there was an even greater disparity in the SPs of the unplaced horses, Marlborough Swell (33-1 against 20-1) and Mitchelstown (100-8 and 7-1).

These were huge differences and although the *Life* returned slightly longer odds on a few of the more fancied horses at the same Gatwick meeting, the cynical taunt that had been thrown out by the *Sportsman* in 1885 began to look justified. If this was a true reflection of how the two papers compiled their SPs, no wonder the bookmakers preferred to be ruled by the *Life's* returns!

A flood of telegrams and letters deluged the offices of both papers as bookmakers and punters demanded to know what was going on. The *Life* was unable to enlighten them as it commented:

> For many years the leading sporting newspapers have returned prices fair to the bookmakers and fair to the public, but a policy with which we have no sympathy is now being pursued whereby two sets of prices, where great differences are apparent, are being returned and the bookmakers and the backer greatly confused.
>
> It is common knowledge that in the great majority of cases our prices rule the settling and consequently more than ordinary care is exercised in their compilation. In this department the *Sporting Life* is particularly fortunate for Mr James George, its representative, has the reputation of being one of the soundest 'Men in the Ring' and he is happy in having the complete confidence of the bookmaker, the backer, and his employer.

On February 7 – coincidentally, the 20th anniversary of the outbreak of the first SP war – the *Life* publicly called upon the *Sportsman* to justify its action and its rival duly obliged as it explained:

> Foreseeing that something in the nature of a 'corner' in starting prices would probably result, if already it had not done so under the system of a comparison and adjustment of prices by which a rigid uniformity was ensured, we resolved to revert to an absolutely independent return.
>
> In the interests of all, the ascertainers of the odds should, we are convinced, work independently. There are no 'official prices' and it is blatant nonsense to pretend otherwise. As for the wide distribution and reputation of the *Sportsman* prices, mention of the simple facts at once disposes of all rivalry, for these odds are those prices given in the principal evening and morning papers of the United Kingdom, they are the 'tape prices' ticked out daily in hundreds of clubs, and the Jockey Club still quotes them in its *Racing Calendar*.

By now the whole of Fleet Street had joined the debate. The *Evening News* which, together with several other papers, had started to publish both sets of SPs "in order to suit the convenience of our readers," remarked:

If the *Sportsman* realised the gravity of the stake at issue, it would never have made the extraordinary announcement that 'more has been made out of our recent action in the matter of starting price returns than the situation warrants'. This is an easy and comfortable way of passing over a matter which is at present keenly engaging the attention of the whole of the racing world, but it only shows how deeply one of the chief parties concerned fails to understand the situation and its effect upon the public.

The *News* went on to speculate on how the racing authorities would deal with the matter and the following day it was able to report:

The *Racing Calendar* settled the question in the most impartial manner, for the returns for Kempton are those of the *Sportsman* whilst the *Life* prices are given for Doncaster and Leicester … This is very significant, and the one deduction to be drawn from it is that the present policy does not find favour with the stewards of the Jockey Club.

The disparity in the returns, the *News* explained, was due to the fact that it was almost impossible for any one man to determine prices on his own; an assertion that was backed up by the bookmaker, Harry Slowburn, who declared: "To do the work thoroughly and accurately at a meeting like Kempton Park, two men must work their hardest."

The *Daily Mail*, for its part, touched upon a subject that would become much more topical some 20 years later, as it remarked:

Some people advocate the establishment of the pari-mutuel, or automatic bookmaker, as a solution of the difficulty, but that would involve the legalisation of betting, which is not to be expected in England.

To the dissatisfaction of all, the situation remained unresolved for the next ten years and the two camps were as divided as ever in 1912 when the Exchange Telegraph Co. asked its regional representatives to canvass their subscribers in an effort to clarify the picture. The response showed that bookmakers in the south generally chose to be governed by the prices issued by the *Sportsman*, while those in the north, where the *Sporting Chronicle* had a large circulation, favoured the SPs supplied by the *Life*.

The reply from Extel's Brighton agent was unambiguous – "After making individual enquiry of our bookmaker subscribers I found that nobody settled on *Sporting Life* returns. This applies pretty well to the surrounding country too. I may say that the *Sportsman* is regarded down here by the majority as the last word in sporting matters."

From Glasgow – "All bookmakers in this and surrounding districts settle on *Sporting Life* prices which are the same as *Sporting Chronicle*."

Manchester – "The majority of subscribers settle on the *Life* prices."

Hull – "The bookmakers in Hull and district settle on the *Sporting Life*, but in Grimsby and district it is, as far as I can gather, equally divided, some settling on the *Sporting Life* and some on the *Sportsman*."

Leeds – "The major portion of bookmakers in the Yorkshire district pay out on the *Life*."[6]

But common sense finally prevailed and, before the year was out, the papers returned to issuing a unified set of prices. This concord lasted only until the *Life* took over the *Sportsman* in November 1924 after which the *Sporting Chronicle* started to return SPs in conjunction with the *Life*, but then began to act independently, although it did make the concession of publishing its rival's returns underneath its own – a practice that was not reciprocated by the *Life*.

At first the variations were only slight and in the spring of 1925, Joe Marshall, the indefatigable secretary of the National Sporting League, which represented bookmakers' interests, came up with some interesting figures. He remarked: "We have, with other organisations, been doing our best to bring about something like uniformity in the matter of the return of starting prices, but after all is said and done, I wonder whether it is really worth it … On a level £1 stake, I find that the total difference during January worked out at only 2s 4d; while in February the difference at the end of the month was only 10d."[7]

But as the year wore on the differences between the two sets of prices became greater and when the first three in the London Autumn Cup at Alexandra Park were all returned at different prices* the NSL decided enough was enough. Heads needed knocking together. A conference was arranged between the editors of the rival papers – W S Morley-Brown of the *Life* and W H 'Nobby' Clarke of the *Chronicle* – and other representatives of the press. The meeting took place at the Hotel Cecil in the Strand on 17 November 1925 and after a short, amicable discussion it was agreed that the SP reporters of both papers would work together to return one set of unified prices.

This arrangement survived the demise of both the *Chronicle* in 1983 (when the Press Association took over) and the *Life*, whose SP reporters were kept on by the *Racing Post*, which then returned the prices in conjunction with the PA. With the computerisation of the betting ring in 2004, however, the PA became solely responsible for checking the accuracy of the final betting show sent out by the bookmaker-backed Satellite Information Services.

In 2006, Blue Square bookmakers broke ranks when they returned their own SPs for a meeting at Ascot, since when other bookmakers have talked of returning their own prices as, with more and more money being channelled through Internet betting exchanges, they claim the on-course market bears no relation to the business they do off-course.

The wheel may yet turn full circle to the days when the Covent Garden bookmaker Billy Wright returned his own prices.

---

* The prices on the first three horses as returned by the *Life* were: 1. Congo 100-8; 2. Irish Eagle 100-6; 3. Rocketer 25-1. The *Chronicle*'s respective prices of 10-1, 100-7 and 100-7 were shorter in each instance and considerable so (by 11 points) in the case of the third horse.

TRAGEDY AND SCANDAL

T HE SHOT that rang out from Falmouth House in Newmarket early on Monday afternoon, 8 November 1886, stunned the nation. Fred Archer, a man famed throughout the British Empire, was dead by his own hand. The hero of every schoolboy, Archer was idolised by the poor and courted by the rich. He had dedicated his life to riding winners – far more than anyone else ever had – and now he had paid the ultimate price.

It was as if he had made some Faustian pact, which required him to forfeit the lives of those dearest to him – his wife, his brother, his infant son – together with his own before he was 30. In return he gained immortality as the greatest jockey that ever lived.

Born in Cheltenham on 11 January 1857, Frederick James Archer was the son of William Archer who, while still in his teens, spent two years in Russia riding for the Tsar. When he became too heavy for the Flat, Archer senior switched to jumps and climaxed a successful career by riding Little Charley to victory in the 1858 Grand National.

Fred, together with his two brothers, Billy and Charlie who also became jockeys, was taught to ride from an early age and spent most of his days in the saddle much to the detriment of his elementary education. Like many other children who went into racing, he was almost illiterate when he was apprenticed to the Newmarket trainer, Mathew Dawson, a few weeks after his eleventh birthday.

Dawson, a much-respected, forthright Scot, came from a large racing family whose "judgement of a yearling is held in as high repute as their irreproachable taste for whisky."[1] His judgement did not stop at horses and *usquabae*, however, for he saw in his nervous, sensitive pupil a depth of character that was not immediately apparent in a child who was desperately homesick and afraid of the dark.

When John Corlett visited the Heath House trainer in the spring of 1868 to write a 'stable visit' article for the *Sporting Times*, Dawson pointed out young Archer to him and remarked: "There's a little fellow I shall be able to make a jockey of. He wants hands at present, but he's the pluckiest lad I ever had."[2]

Archer had his first ride the following year and finished last, but in 1870 he rode the first of his 2,748 winners on Athol Daisy at Chesterfield. At the time he had no trouble in making the minimum weight of 5st 7lb and was confined to riding the stable's lesser lights in handicaps, but before he was much older his battle with the scales began.

In 1874, when he won his first classic – the Two Thousand Guineas on Atlantic when carrying 3st of dead weight – and his first championship with 147 winners, he could just about get down to 6st with severe wasting, but by the end of the following season when he rode a record 172 winners, his absolute minimum was 7st 2lb.

In 1876 he broke through the 200 barrier for the first time (a feat he was to achieve seven more times in the ten years that were left to him) when his total of 207 winners placed him 132 in front of his nearest rival – a truly amazing margin of superiority.

By now he was spending most of his spare time in the Turkish bathhouse Mat Dawson had built for sweating his horses as was the fashion of the day. He was tall for a jockey at 5ft 9in, and by his early twenties, when his weight used to approach 11st during the winter, he had resorted to taking an explosive purgative which became famed as 'Archer's Mixture'. Once, in a mischievous moment, he persuaded an acquaintance to take a small dose of his 'medicine' to settle an upset stomach – the unwitting victim spent the next 24 hours commuting at high speed between bedroom and bathroom!

Charming, modest and courteous out of the saddle, Archer was the very opposite in a race. He would scream obscenities at anyone who got in his way and on one memorable occasion so terrified an apprentice blocking his path to his favourite pitch on the rails, that the lad, who was under orders not to expose his horse, shot to the front and won in a canter – much to the disgust of both Archer and the winner's connections!

In an era when rough riding was the norm, he would resort to any tactic he thought he could get away with in order to win. Once, when his younger brother, Charlie (to whom he was devoted), tried to sneak up on his inside he put him over the rails, and, when riding the 1878 Oaks and St Leger winner, Jannette, in the following season's Doncaster Cup, he dug his spur into the shoulder of the challenging favourite, Isonomy, who, nevertheless, got up to win by a head.

Nor did Archer spare his own mounts. One particular unruly animal, Muley Edris, had felt the sting of his whip too often for comfort and took his revenge by savaging the jockey just 25 days before he was due to ride the favourite, Bend Or, in the 1880 Derby.

The muscles in Archer's upper right arm were badly torn and his doctors told him there was no way he would be fit in time to ride at Epsom. They were right, but it didn't stop the obsessively driven champion. He returned to action at Manchester 17 days later and, from nine carefully chosen rides spread over the four-day meeting, he broke through the pain barrier to win on four of them.

On the Sunday before the Derby, he was in France to ride the hot favourite, Beauminet, in the Prix du Jockey Club. Again it was evident he was under-strength, but his determination to win was unaffected and, with his long legs and crouching style, he virtually lifted the colt to victory in the dying strides. Even then there was still some doubt as to whether he would ride Bend Or, but four winners from five rides on the opening day of the Epsom meeting were enough to satisfy the colt's owner, the Duke of Westminster, that a one-armed Archer was preferable to a fully fit substitute.

On the day, Archer had his injured arm heavily strapped up and supported by a metal brace, while Bend Or was having his first race of the season as he had been laid up with sore shins during the spring. The sceptics declared that a crippled jockey on a crippled horse could never win the Derby, but the public's faith in the champion was such that his mount was sent off 2-1 favourite.

No one rode Epsom's tricky, switchback course better than Archer. His iron nerve and a total disregard for his own (or anyone else's) safety, was to see him win on five of his ten Derby mounts and five City and Suburban Handicaps in six years. It was well said that "at times he rode with sheer desperation and achieved the seemingly impossible,"[3] and this was one of those times.

In a race that quickly found its place in the annuals of Turf history, Robert the Devil, a marginally better horse than Bend Or, appeared to have opened up an unassailable lead in the straight, but Archer was inspired and seemed to infuse his mount with his special brand of steely determination. Gradually they began to reel in the leader.

Inside the final furlong they were at his quarters. Rossiter, on Robert the Devil, snatched a look over his shoulder, panicked and unbalanced his horse. Archer instinctively went for his whip, but dropped it in agony. Yet, inch by inch, the gap closed. Two strides from the line the two horses were inseparable and in one last desperate lunge the champion forced the chestnut's head in front.

The crowd went wild. Many swore it was the greatest race he had ever ridden. Under the circumstances it probably was, and the magnitude of the performance became even more apparent when, at the end of the week, he announced he was going to have further treatment on his arm and would not return until it was properly healed – two months were to pass before the cry of 'Archer's up' was heard on the racecourse again!

In 1881 Mat Dawson made Archer a partner in his Heath House stables and two years later the jockey married the trainer's niece, Helen Rose Dawson. Success, wealth, health and happiness; Fred Archer had it all, but it was not to last. Within a year of their marriage Nellie Rose lost a son at birth, but a year later a daughter was born and as Archer hurried home from Aintree where he had won the Liverpool Autumn Cup on Thebais to take his score for the season to an unprecedented 241 winners, he reflected on how fortunate he was.

"I thought at the time," he told a friend later, "I wonder why I should be so blessed? There really does not seem to be anything in this world that I can or ought to want."

Poor Fred. Two days later his beloved Nellie was seized with convulsions and died in his arms without recognising him. Archer was inconsolable. A few years earlier his elder brother, Billy, had been killed in a fall in a piddling three-runner selling hurdle at Cheltenham, then he lost his infant son and now his wife; he felt as if the very soul of his being had been ripped from him.

Persuaded to take a few months' holiday in America, Archer was back in time for the opening of the 1885 season at Lincoln where he was cheered to the echo as he rode past the stands on his way to the start. Back in the old routine, he did not spare himself as he buried his grief in an unremitting schedule pursued with demonic dedication.

He took more mounts than ever before (667) and rode 246 winners (a massive 37 per cent strike rate), a record that was to stand until Gordon Richards surpassed it 48 years later. He won all the classics bar the One Thousand Guineas and turned in another superhuman effort to win the Derby on Melton. It was said the two cracks of the whip he gave the colt in the last few strides could be heard above the roar of the crowd.

The following year the mental and physical strain was beginning to take its toll. He was betting heavily and losing, and for the first time in 12 years he was headed in the jockeys' table. More self-critical than ever, he convinced himself that he was riding below form, but victories on the outstanding Ormonde (Derby and St Leger) and Minting (Grand Prix de Paris) helped to restore his confidence.

Then, in October, he made what was, in effect, a suicidal decision when he passed over his Derby and St Leger winner, Melton (9st 7lb) in favour of St Mirin (8st 6lb) in the Cambridgeshire – one of the few major races he had yet to win. A week before the race he travelled to Ireland to ride at the Curragh. He spent a day reducing his weight from 9st 4lb to 8st 12lb and then, to the delight of the crowd, won on two of his three mounts.

He returned to England looking ill and drawn, and for three days before the Cambridgeshire he barely ate at all. He had backed St Mirin at long odds to win £30,000 (£2.7m) and was confident of collecting although on the eve of the race he confided to a reporter: "I have never won the Cambridgeshire and if I don't succeed tomorrow, I'll never try again."[4]

He never did. Putting up 1lb overweight to ride at 8st 7lb, he brought his mount to master the favourite, Carlton, inside the final furlong and after beating off the challenge of Melton he appeared to have his race won until The Sailor Prince, racing on the opposite side of the course, got up in the final strides to win by a head.

Drained to the core, depressed beyond measure, Archer was now riding on willpower alone, but that was still enough to see him win on five of his eight mounts on the final day of the meeting. Already unwell, he caught a chill at Brighton the following Wednesday, but stayed on to ride at Lewes the next day. Badly beaten on the first two favourites, he finally realised he could not go on. He returned home and took to his bed. In his bedside cabinet was a revolver he had been given a few years earlier following a spate of burglaries in Newmarket. The rest, as they say, is history.

At the inquest his widowed sister, Emily Coleman, who had been looking after him, stated: "A little after two o'clock he asked to speak to me alone ... when the nurse left the room, I walked to the window to look out and he said, 'Are they coming?'. I heard a noise and looked round. He was out of his bed by the side next the door.

"I saw something in his hand and ran to him. I saw it was a revolver and tried to push it to one side, but he put one arm round my neck and thrust me against the door. The revolver was in his left hand. He shot himself in the mouth and seemed to fall flat on his back. I screamed while we were struggling, but he never spoke."

Archer's doctor, John Wright, stated that on the Friday morning the jockey had a high fever and the next day he called in Dr Latham for a second opinion when they had diagnosed typhoid fever. On Monday, Archer seemed better, but was very depressed. "He had the idea that he must die," the doctor said.

Wright left his patient at 9.30am and did not see him alive again. On examining the body, he found that death had been caused by a bullet passing through the two upper cervical vertebrae, severing the spinal cord. He considered that Archer was so unhinged as not to be accountable for his actions, and a verdict of 'suicide while in a state of temporary insanity' was returned.

As the news and manner of Archer's death was telegraphed around the world the shock of its impact can only be imagined. In Fleet Street even the most talented wordsmiths struggled to convey the depth of public feeling and the *Sporting Life* simply admitted:

> Words fail us in giving point to the deep regret we would express at the death of this world-famous jockey, and we are certain that this feeling will find an echo in the hearts of myriads, not only in this country, but in other countries where his name had indeed become a household word.
>
> Even the children, as they played hobby-horse in the streets, may often have been heard chattering of Fred Archer and, in their mimic way, emulating his deeds.
>
> Emperors, Kings, Princes, Dukes, Duchesses, Lords and Ladies, merchants and tradesmen, and all, from the highest to the lowest, whether they took an interest in racing or merely made it the subject of conversation, knew the name of Fred Archer and knew that they were talking of one who by his probity and perseverance; by his great talent and unswerving devotion to his 'masters', as well as by his geniality and kindness in private life, had raised himself to a pinnacle in his profession and in public estimation never before achieved by one in his calling.
>
> His was indeed a name to conjure by in a thousand ways, and wherever the English tongue is spoken 'Fred Archer' has long been familiar by sound to those who had never seen him, but had simply heard of his marvellous prowess and proud position. Now, alas, all that is left of poor Fred Archer is clay. A more tragic end to a triumphant career, a more awful check to a future full of promise, would be hard to conceive.

In his column, Charley Blake expressed his feelings in his own ingenuous way:

> Alas, poor Fred! Your usually cool brain must indeed have been on fire or you would never have lost hope of life and given up all the grand future that was before you for the 'suicide's poor shift'. Horrible word! To have been killed on the racecourse; to have died after fighting with the 'pale horseman' to the last stride and the last gasp, would have been to end a life of triumph in a grave of glory. No! my poor Fred. You must have been mad, mad, mad! But Heaven will shelter you, I doubt not, for your heart was ever right and your temper good and kind.

This portrait of the 13-times champion Jockey by Rosa Corder, RA, was given as a wedding present to Fred and Nellie Archer in January 1883; 90 years later it turned up in a north London antique shop where it was bought by racing buff, Michael Amey, for £12. NB. The diamond tiepin was given to Archer by the Prince of Wales (later Edward VII).

'Good and kind' Archer may have been, but he was not beyond reproach. During the champion's last few years it was widely rumoured that he and another leading jockey, Charlie Wood, were operating a jockeys' ring. The matter was raised at a meeting of the Jockey Club in April 1884, when Sir George Chetwynd asked the stewards whether they were aware: "that it is openly stated that a conspiracy exists between certain jockeys and so-called professional backers of horses to arrange the result of races for their own benefit, and, if they have heard of such statements and believe it possible such a plot exists, what steps they propose taking to deal with the matter?"[5]

Lord March, the senior steward, confirmed he and his fellow stewards knew of the rumours but, as no formal accusations had been made to them, they had not taken any action although they would do if any direct evidence was placed before them – a favoured excuse for inaction that is wheeled out by weak governing bodies to this day.

Archer, with his innate will to win, was unlikely ever to have thrown a race himself; in fact, he rode some of his best races against his own money, as happened at Windsor in 1884 when he got a headstrong colt called Westwood up on the line to beat the even money favourite who was carrying his £500 (£45,000) bet. But, at the same time, he was giving the nod to a betting syndicate and his association with Wood, whose reputation for pulling horses was notorious, put him in a position to know which horses were 'off' and which jockeys could be squared.

He was, therefore, at least an accessory both before and after the fact. It could even be argued that his involvement in race-fixing contributed to his death. Always highly-strung and an innate worrier, was it a conscience racked with guilt that made him cry out "Are they coming [*to get me*]?" in those last demented seconds?

While he was alive, however, the Jockey Club was unwilling to act on the matter. One or two members were undoubtedly anxious to cleanse the Augean stables that flourished under their very nose in Newmarket, but iconoclasts they were not – the scandal simply would have been too great.

It was Archer's death that paved the way to one of the most sensational purges ever carried out by racing's rulers. The removal of 'undesirables' extended to the highest echelons of society and the first to be rooted out was George William Thomas Brudenell-Bruce, who had succeeded to the title of Lord Ailesbury just a few weeks before the champion jockey's untimely demise.

At the age of 23, the 4th Marquess was eager to pursue a racing career that would equal that of his great uncle, the 2nd Marquess. His noble ancestor had not only been Master of the Horse to Queen Victoria and a distinguished member of the Jockey Club, but had owned many top-class performers including the 1860 St Leger winner, St Albans, and his luckless full-brother, Savernake, beaten a head in both the Derby and St Leger of 1866. But young Ailesbury was more of a chip off the old block, his dissolute father having drunk himself to death before he was 30. Offensive and foul-mouthed, boorish and obese, he was known to the racing world as Billy Stomachache (a play upon his ample girth and his family seat at Savernake in Wiltshire).

Matters were not improved by the unsavoury company he kept or by the fact that his horses were with John Tyler, a clever but crooked trainer. It was not long before the inconsistent running of the Ailesbury horses began to be commented on, and in August 1887 there were angry scenes at York's Ebor meeting after young Teddy Martin had clearly not done his best to win on the wayward owner's Everitt.

The gelding had started 4-1 joint-favourite for the Harewood Plate on the strength of a runaway win in the Wokingham Stakes at Ascot two months earlier and, despite Martin's efforts to throw the race, he dead-heated for first place. As was the custom of the time, there was a run-off between the two horses and this time Everitt, at 1-6, beat his rival as decisively as he should have done in the first place.

Unfortunately for Ailesbury, one of the officiating stewards was his fellow peer, John George Lambton, the 3rd Earl of Durham, a fearless and energetic member of the Jockey Club who was determined to stamp out the scandal of non-triers, no matter what the cost.

At Durham's insistence, an inquiry was held into the race and, after hearing evidence from Ailesbury, Martin and Tyler, the stewards concluded: "either an attempt was made to win by an unjustifiably and dangerously short distance, or that Everitt was wilfully stopped." The matter was referred to the stewards of the Jockey Club and five weeks later, following two further inquiries, their findings were published in the *Racing Calendar* – they were dynamite:

> It was proved to the satisfaction of the Stewards that Lord Ailesbury, in the presence of J B Tyler, his trainer, gave orders to Martin not to win the race, but that Martin, finding himself in a prominent position towards the finish, hesitated to carry out his orders, the result being a dead heat. The Stewards further satisfied themselves that similar orders had been given by Lord Ailesbury on previous occasions. Notices were served upon Lord Ailesbury and Tyler warning them to keep off Newmarket Heath and the Stewards severely reprimanded Martin, and cautioned him as to his future conduct.

To warn a peer of the realm off the Turf, while giving his jockey a second chance was a remarkably egalitarian act. The clubmen had atoned for the scandal of the Tarragona affair in one fell swoop and, in an ironic reversal of roles, it was the editor of the *Sporting Life* who had cause to hang his head in shame as he tried to pretend the whole disgraceful business had never happened.

The warning-off notice was carried without comment alongside Blake's 'Current Events and Anticipations' column which ran to some 3,500 words. Readers who ploughed through it in the hope that 'Augur' might give an opinion on what was, up till then, the biggest story of the year, were to be disappointed, but not surprised.

Prompted by "a nippiness in the air and the advisability of changing the summer or autumnal garb for winter clothing," Blake led off with the observation that "the world at large owes a lot to its tailor". His barely credible dissertation included such statements as: "bad boots are an abomination in the eyes of civilisation … a good hat imparts a marvellous charm to the manly countenance that it adorns … the ceremony of putting on gloves before going to church is part and parcel of the Christian religion."

When he eventually got onto the subject of racing, the purblind editor began by referring directly to the journal that had published the warning-off notice: "One of the most interesting items of information in this week's *Racing Calendar* is..." – "surely the Ailesbury case," his readers must have thought – but no, it was "...that relating to the St Leger of 1889." It was only after he had rambled on about the entries for a race that was not due to take place for another two years, that C W Blake stiffened the sinews, summoned up the blood and – dismissed the Ailesbury story in two of the shortest sentences he ever penned:

> With regret I read the decision of the stewards of the Jockey Club in the Everitt case today. The full text appears elsewhere and it would serve no purpose to further dilate on such an unsavoury matter just now.

That was it! The slogan, 'The paper the professionals read', which was proudly carried under the title of the *Sporting Life* in later years, certainly did not apply in 1887 especially when matched against its contemporaries.

Henry Smurthwaite, who wrote the lead column in the *Sportsman* under the signature of 'Vigilant', was of the same mind as Blake, but his journalistic conscience forced him to address the subject as he commented:

> It stands to reason that in a matter so momentous the most careful consideration has been given to the case. The decision, therefore, must be accepted as one meeting justice. Before banishing Lord Ailesbury from the Turf – this means far more than mere deprivation of a particular amusement – those who sat in judgement must have weighed anxiously all that was laid before them.
>
> The scandal is a great one and all who have the interest of horse racing at heart regret it deeply. Yet these are the people who will heartily admit that, in fulfilling to the utmost extent what they believed to be their duty, the Stewards of the Jockey Club have done well. Lord Ailesbury is a young man, and what young men do in hasty temper or in the folly of a moment, can often be wiped out in course of time.* I shall write no more on a matter which it is painful to touch at all.

---

* In this case, time was not on the young man's side. The opprobrium Ailesbury brought upon himself was total; it not only meant banishment from the Turf, but from society. Crushed and ostracised, he increased his pace along his father's well-trodden path of dissipation and self-destruction and, eight years later, he achieved his goal when he died of a heart attack at the age of 31.

In his office at Withy Grove in Manchester, Edward Hulton had no such qualms. Whereas Blake had made his fleeting reference to the affair at the end of his column and Smurthwaite had buried his observations in the middle of his, Hulton tackled the subject head-on as he made it his lead. Having given the background to the case, he stressed:

> It is impossible to extend much sympathy to the chief actors in this discreditable business, and if the Stewards have inflicted the heaviest sentence in their power, it must not be overlooked that their decision did not rest entirely upon the Everitt case.
>
> Matters of this kind do not, as a rule, improve when subjected to close investigation and the Stewards seem to have been made aware of other delinquencies which, no doubt, influenced them in the sentence they have passed upon Lord Ailesbury and his trainer.
>
> The present season has witnessed so many glaring instances of in-and-out running – inconsistencies that could not be reconciled by the ordinary canons of reasoning – that official notice was urgently called for and, having put the hand to the wheel, it is to be hoped that the Jockey Club will not stop until they have purged the Turf of the evils that surround it. There must be no hesitancy or attempt to shield persons of high degree and so long as they act firmly and without fear or favour, they can depend upon the full sympathy of the public.

Bravo Edward Hulton – a journalist to the last! And nor was there any hesitancy on the part of at least one Jockey Club member, the then 32-year-old Lord Durham, in his determination to 'purge the Turf of its evils' by exposing similar scandals even though the greatest of them involved a former senior steward in Sir George Chetwynd.

It was ironic, and possibly significant, that it had been Sir George who first brought the festering rumours of a jockeys' ring into the open in 1884. In the light of subsequent events, his motives for doing so are debatable. He was, after all, directly implicated in the allegations as he retained Charlie Wood to ride the horses he had in training with Richard 'Buck' Sherrard at Chetwynd House stables in Newmarket.

Was the canny Baronet trying to lay a smoke screen for himself and his jockey by taking a gamble that the Jockey Club stewards wouldn't act on the matter? He must have had a fair idea of how they felt about tackling Archer on the subject, but he could not have anticipated the champion's dramatic exit from the scene; an exit that left both himself and Wood exposed to the full rigour of Jack Durham's reforming zeal.

As with Admiral Rous, Durham was inclined to be impulsive once he got an idea into his head and there is no doubt he believed the worst of the rumours that surrounded Wood and Chetwynd. It was said the jockey owned many of the horses that ran in Sir George's name, and that Chetwynd connived at the frauds and profited by them.

Proving this was a different matter. Under Feist, the *Life* would have been a useful ally, but with Blake in the chair 'Determined Jack', as he was appropriately known, had to look elsewhere for someone brave enough to bait the trap he had set for Wood. He found his man in W H Bingham Cox, the proprietor and editor of a little tuppenny weekly, the *Licensed Victuallers Gazette*. Prompted by Durham, Cox waded into the fray in November 1887 when his 'Sporting Gossip' column delivered the blatant accusation:

> There was a great deal said concerning the Everitt scandal, but how about the running of Success at Lewes and Alexandra Park when Charley Wood nearly pulled its head off on each occasion?

And just in case this wasn't enough to spur Wood into seeking legal redress, he gave the jockey another prod the following week after George Barrett had rounded off the season by winning the Manchester November Handicap on the 9st 12lb top-weight, Carlton, who had finished unplaced under Wood at Derby ten days earlier. With a passing dig at his fellow scribes, Cox taunted:

> The sporting reporters were all loud in praise of Barrett's horsemanship on Carlton. Master George managed to win this time so, of course, it was all right. Anyhow it was better than what we saw of Charley Wood's performance on the same horse at Derby.

Wood was furious. Six times runner-up to Archer in the jockeys' championship, he had finally won his first title with 151 winners and must have been looking forward to more glory days to complement his saintly Epsom Derby double on St Blaise in 1883 and St Gatien who dead-heated with Harvester the following year. To be denounced by a pipsqueak rag that was aimed at publicans and the catering trade was too mortifying for words, but, after consulting his solicitor, the not-so-saintly jockey decided to ignore the insult rather than face exposure in open court as he would have to do if he sued for libel.

This was not what Lord Durham planned, but he still had one card left to play and it was an ace. Determined to compromise the jockey and his employer in public, he chose the annual end-of-season Gimcrack Club dinner to deliver the most sensational speech ever made at that prestigious gathering.

Many of the high and mighty who congregated at York's famed Harker's Hotel that December evening had expected some sort of attack from the crusading Earl, but none was prepared for the onslaught that assailed their burning ears. Durham began by referring to a recent *Racing Calendar* notice, which warned that the stewards would withdraw the licence of any jockey found to have an interest in any racehorse or to have been engaged in any betting transaction.

Similar warnings had been issued ever since jockeys were first licensed in 1880, but they were never enforced chiefly because it was well known that Fred Archer betted heavily and also owned horses – in fact, he had his colours (cerise and French grey hoops) registered with Weatherbys up to the time of his death.

Durham now expressed his fears that the latest edict would "not be worth much more than waste paper" if the Jockey Club failed to act upon it. "On the other hand," he said: "If we enforce this rule we shall see a very different list of names of principal winning jockeys at the end of next season.

"Surely the Stewards do not ignore what every racing man knows, namely, that one or two jockeys bet in large sums and are the virtual owners of horses which run in other people's names. It is notorious that one well-known jockey does this ... If I add to this that it is a generally accepted fact that this jockey pulls horses in order that he may make money out of them, I think you will agree that this is a very serious evil to the Turf."

There was more than one spillage of port as these damning accusations reverberated around the oak-panelled banqueting room, and Durham had barely started.

"No owners of horses ought to put up any jockey suspected or known to be guilty of pulling horses. Unfortunately, I know very many honest and straightforward owners of horses who employ the services of a notorious jockey because he rides well, and because they adopt the selfish principle that it is better to have him on their side than against them.

"I go further than this. Some owners employ him because they think that he can square some other jockeys in the race and thus ensure the victory of his mount – if he has backed it. I consider such

a policy on the part of owners to be a direct encouragement to malpractices on the part of jockeys ...
But the darkest part of the matter is this – that the owners, or nominal owners of the horses to which
I am alluding, win large sums when their horses are successful, but do not lose much when they are
beaten.

"If you wish to purify the Turf you must go to the fountainhead ... The higher a man's position
on the Turf, the more needful is it that he should be above reproach. If we find that such a man or such
men continue with impunity to break the rules of racing law and the code of honour amongst
gentlemen, let us treat them as they deserve to be treated – as unfit to mix with us and associate with
us in the sport we love."

Short of actually naming names, Durham could not have been more explicit. Everyone knew
whom he meant and Chetwynd immediately demanded that his accuser either withdraw his allegations
or fight a duel. Durham did neither; instead he reasserted his charges in a letter to the senior steward,
Lord Hastings. He maintained that the matters addressed:

> ...have been commented upon both in the Press and upon every racecourse in England for a
> considerable time; that this state of things is dishonourable to the sport whose interests you have
> specially in charge; that nothing but a public inquiry ... can possibly satisfy the requirements of the
> case; and that from such an inquiry, if Sir George Chetwynd has the courage to initiate it, I do not
> shrink.[6]

Sir George did have the courage. He brought an action for slander in which he sought £20,000
(£1.8m) damages. Wood, meanwhile, had changed his mind about suing Cox. He had been left with no
option when the Jockey Club stewards refused to renew his licence as a result of an inquiry they held
into the running of Success; the horse he allegedly pulled at Lewes and Alexandra Park.

The case of Wood v Cox was heard at the High Court in June 1888 and served as a preliminary
to the main bout between Chetwynd and Durham which, after many delays, finally took place in the
same court a year later. In both cases the only real winners were the lawyers who represented the cream
of their profession both in ability and in fees.

Durham, who had promised to back Cox in any legal action that might arise from his articles,
instructed the country's foremost barrister, Sir Charles Russell QC (later Lord Russell of Killowen), to
act for the defence. Wood secured the services of Sir Henry James QC who, nine years earlier, had
acted for the tout, John Bray, in his successful prosecution for assault against Tom Jennings.

As Wood had feared, he was subjected to a merciless grilling by Sir Charles, who maintained that
after Success had been beaten at Lewes (where he drifted significantly in the betting) the gelding's
trainer, Robert Peck, accused the jockey of riding a weak finish saying, "if I had thrown my umbrella
at you, the horse must have won." But the arguments surrounding the inappropriately named Success
– a selling plater that only ever managed to win one race – were tame compared to the information the
QC winkled out of Wood with regard to his finances.

Under cross-examination, the jockey freely admitted that a large proportion of his income was
derived from betting. Over the last four seasons his riding fees had averaged £1,900 (£171,000) a year,
and when presents from owners and the proceeds of his betting were taken into account, he calculated
his income would be about £4,000 a year.

Russell, having established that Wood had several times received £1,000 for winning a race, put
it to the jockey that a more realistic figure would be £10,000 a year.

Wood, to the accompaniment of laughter from the packed court, exclaimed: "Oh, dear no! It would be about £5,000 or £6,000. I have a wife and five children. I have a house at Newmarket and rent a house at Brighton."

"And carriages and grooms?" queried Sir Charles.

"I've no carriages or grooms," the jockey replied jauntily. "But I have a boy to black my boots." (Laughter).

"You have ponies for the children? – Yes, I have one pony at Brighton. My hunters I turn out."

"How many do you keep? – I keep about two." (More laughter).

At this point Wood, needled by the response his answers were drawing from the public gallery, decided there was no point in sparring with the great barrister any longer and he staggered his inquisitor with his reply to the next question.

"You own your own house at Newmarket," asserted Russell.

"Yes," replied Wood quietly and deliberately. "It's in the High Street. I also own Lowther House, also in the High Street. I own the Greyhound Hotel, the Black Horse Hotel, Chetwynd House in Station Road and the new training stables in the same neighbourhood. There is accommodation there for 48 horses. They are rented at £500 a year, so I'm the landlord and jockey of them.

"I also own two little cottages of £20 or £30 each, as well as some small buildings – hardly cottages – letting at about 1s 6d a week. I also have a share in a large coopering business at Argyle Walk, Limehouse. I have a little over £4,000 in these works. I also own a breeding establishment at Cheveley and about 35 acres of land."

Wood, his eyes twinkling with mischievous delight, smiled faintly at his adversary as he relished the impact these disclosures had upon the court. As he savoured his moment, he garnished it with what appeared to be an afterthought by adding that he also had about £12,000 (£1.08m) invested in consols (government securities).

Sir Charles, for once taken aback, struggled to compose himself as he asked: "Is that all you have got; just think again?"

Pausing momentarily for dramatic effect, the second largest property owner in Newmarket coolly replied: "Yes; I think that's all."

Having established the extent of Wood's fortune, Russell then proceeded to expose his notoriety. It was not a difficult task as witness after witness implied that the jockey had not acquired his wealth by an adherence to the straight and narrow.

Major Egerton, the Jockey Club's chief handicapper, stated that Wood's reputation "amongst a very large majority of men who made racing a study was as bad as could be as regard pulling horses and general malpractices on the Turf."

John Corlett, who had a string of horses in training at Newmarket so well was the *Sporting Times* doing, was eloquent in his indictment as he declared: "The very atmosphere of the Turf is redolent with suspicion with regard to him."

"He has a reputation for pulling horses?" pressed Sir Charles, unnecessarily.

On receiving the affirmation he wanted, Russell felt confident enough to play devil's advocate as he posed the rhetorical question: "It's been suggested that the same thing has been said of every jockey?"

At this point Baron Coleridge, the Lord Chief Justice, eager to display his limited knowledge of racing, chipped in: "Except one." To which Sir Charles provided a precise, but polite correction: "Except two, I believe m'lud – Tom Cannon and John Osborne."

Despite the weight of hearsay evidence against Wood, it could not be proved that he had pulled Success, and after sitting for eight days the jury took two hours to return a majority verdict in his favour, although the derisory award of a farthing (6p) damages told its own story. It was a story that was to be repeated 12 months later when the entire cast of barristers and witnesses reassembled for the Chetwynd v Durham case.

The main difference this time was that the case was tried by arbitrators rather than by a common jury. In the light of Wood's award, Sir George was all for arbitration; Lord Durham was not. In a letter to Lord March written a fortnight before the hearing, he explained:

> One of my objections [*to arbitration*] was the difficulty which I foresaw in obtaining a tribunal of sufficient weight and authority to deal with the intricacies of legal form. This difficulty was more than realised, for it subsequently transpired that although the Club as a body seemed to wish that the action should be tried by arbitrators selected from its members, one refusal after another amounting to some forty in all, came from individual members who were asked to act in that capacity.

Eventually it was agreed the acting stewards – James Lowther, Lord March and Prince Soltykoff – should shoulder the unwanted responsibility.

For his part, the editor of the *Life* for once accepted his duty to his readers and devoted unlimited space to the dispute that had split the racing world in two. The rift had even divided the Prince of Wales (who supported Chetwynd) and his racing manager, Lord Marcus Beresford, who gave telling evidence on Durham's behalf.

The hearing got underway on 10 June 1889 and, with a four-day break for Royal Ascot, continued until 28 June. The charges were detailed in two clauses. Basically, the first was that Sir George employed Wood to stop his horses when they weren't wanted and to square other jockeys in a race when the money was down. The second was that he knew what was going on and connived with Wood in breaking the rules.

The case attracted nationwide interest and on ten of the 12 days the court was in session Charles Blake, as 'Court Observer', wrote a full column commentary on the proceedings which, when added to the verbatim evidence carried by the paper, amounted to 34 columns or some 80,000 words – the equivalent of a lightweight book!

Descriptive writing was something Blake was comfortable with and his pen portraits of the principal witnesses were particularly illuminating. With regard to Sherrard he suggested the trainer "might sit as an artist's model for a Friar Tuck. There is a stubborn, quarterstaff wielding appearance about him that is corporally impressive. He is a sturdy witness." But it was Beresford, "with his straightforward, manly method," who outshone them all in giving evidence:

> There is no mistake about Lord Marcus. He may even be said to better the typical individual who calls a spade a spade. His style, always clear and keen and unwasteful of words, occasionally borders on epigram. Take, for example, his description of Wood in two aspects – according to his view, Wood when he was trying ... would get the best place and was jealous about inches. When he was not trying he would take the worst place and was careless about lengths. Throughout, Lord Marcus's descriptions were graphic, uncompromising and militant.

On the eighth day, the jockeys' ring was discussed. There was a lively exchange between the leading counsels after Russell had accused Chetwynd of adopting the proverbial posture of an ostrich over the matter – a most unfair charge since it was Sir George who first brought the matter to the attention of the Jockey Club. Blake did not pick up on this point, but remarked:

> Sir Charles Russell's application of the figure of the hunted ostrich to Sir George Chetwynd was not permitted to pass unchallenged by Sir Henry James.
>
> With regard to it – 'How came he to hide his head in the sand?' asked Sir Charles – it might be said that honours were even after Sir Henry had finished with the bird. 'There were six or seven in the jockeys' ring. Wood alone was finally removed. Four were still riding. Down to the moment Wood's licence was refused, men as honourable as any on the Turf had employed him.'
>
> With these answers, elicited in rapid succession, Sir Henry James handled the ostrich with splendid scorn – and wrung its neck.

On the ninth day, Lord Durham gave his evidence:

> He faced Sir George Chetwynd with a table between them, and made his statement with cool clearness. He sat, one leg over the other, with a glass of water handy and varied his study of the documents on his knee with a tug at the O.P. [*left*] end of his moustache. In whatever else they differ, Sir George Chetwynd and Lord Durham have this habit in common.

Cross-examined by James, Durham stuck to his guns and declared he believed Chetwynd was, at the very least, an accomplice after the fact. When asked to name the other owners he felt were guilty of the practices he attributed to Sherrard's stable, Durham refused to name them in open court, but agreed to write them down.

> The names were written and submitted. 'Fold it up,' said Sir Charles Russell, as the paper was passed over. This was done. The names were duly read by each of the leading counsel and then the paper reduced to smithereens by Sir Charles. The proceedings went on at a lively rate from this point, Lord Durham ... believed that Wood was alternately robbing and standing in with Sir George Chetwynd.

Sir George, for his part, "gave his evidence with full and gentlemanly frankness". He admitted he relied on betting to maintain his lifestyle and that he only paid Wood a retainer when he could afford to and had, in fact, not paid him for several years. But most importantly he was able to show, through his betting books and evidence provided by Sam Lewis, a well-known moneylender, that he had lost money by backing his horse Fullerton – a horse Durham had implied was run for Chetwynd's benefit, only winning when he had backed it and being pulled by Wood when he hadn't.

This was the crux of the dispute and the fact that Sir George had been able to refute it seemed to augur well for him even though it was shown he was in league with Wood over the ownership of some of the horses that ran in his name. It therefore came as a surprise when the arbitrators followed the example of the jury in the Wood v Cox case. They found for the plaintiff, but awarded him just a farthing damages. Having set his sights on £20,000, it was, as Sir George is reputed to have remarked, "Damned short odds!"

In commenting on the findings under the sub-heading 'The Mountain In Labour Which Brought Forth A Mouse', Blake wrote:

The chief figures in the Chetwynd v Durham case – the stewards of the Jockey Club presided as judges with
Prince Soltykoff flanked by James Lowther (on his right) and Lord March.

The great case of Chetwynd and Durham has turned out a veritable *mus in monte* except to those
who pay the costs and, as honours are equally divided in this very important respect, most people
are left as much in the dark as ever, and few people are quite certain which side has won...

According to many grave opinions the verdict is against Sir George Chetwynd inasmuch that by
awarding him a farthing amount of damages, his honour is assessed at the worth of the smallest
coin in Her Majesty's United Kingdom. On the other hand, there are people who assert that Lord
Durham's accusations can also be worth but a farthing, seeing that the powerful words 'not true in
substance or fact' are used as applying to the first paragraph [*detailing the main charge*].

It might not have been obvious to Blake, but there was no doubt who had lost. Guilty or not,
Chetwynd was a beaten man and, in the light of the farthing indictment from the stewards, he had no
option but to resign from the Jockey Club and retire from the Turf. He thus attained a similar notoriety
to that of the profligate Marquess of Hastings whose widow he had married in 1870, and his brother-

in-law, the defaulting Lord Winchilsea. It was a remarkable hat trick for aristocratic arrogance and folly, though Chetwynd at least departed from the scene with dignity and there are grounds for believing he was more sinned against than sinning.

The *Life's* 'Court Observer' certainly thought he had been hard done by, and in commenting on the resignation Blake lamented:

> Sir George Chetwynd dies like a hero. There is no wail of the martyr about him. He simply accepts the situation as becomes a man judged by his fellows and without acknowledging the correctness of the verdict, bows to the tribunal before whom he elected to be judged ... In the course of time Sir George Chetwynd's bitterest enemies – if he has any – may think and acknowledge that a mistake has been made. No man could have exposed his dealings more openly, fairly and squarely, and perhaps there are few who would have come so well out of the ordeal.

In 1891 Chetwynd published his memoirs chiefly "to preserve a record of the facts connected with an action which I felt it my duty to bring against a nobleman who had traduced my character."[7] Even his 'bitterest enemies' must have had some doubts as to the extent of his guilt and may also have felt some sympathy for him as he admitted:

> ...the feeling of indignation which I experienced when first so unjustifiably and inexcusably assailed has not worn away, nor ever can do ... what Lord Durham did was to bring as foul a set of charges against an innocent man as was ever drawn up on the sheet charges at the Old Bailey, and this was surely not an excusable proceeding![8]

Sir George spent the rest of his life in racing exile and died in Monte Carlo at the age of 67 in 1917.

Lord Durham continued to campaign for what he believed to be best for racing. He was undoubtedly one of the foremost Jockey Club reformers of his or any other time, but his disconcerting habit of dropping the stewards in the proverbial did not make him particularly popular with his fellow clubmen.

As an owner-breeder his successes were limited, although he won Newcastle's prestigious Northumberland Plate on three occasions and gained his only classic victory when Beam won the Oaks the year before he died in 1928.

Buck Sherrard, merely a pawn in the affair, was allowed to continue training after he had moved to a new yard in Royston. Capable horseman though he was, he was never able to achieve the success that had come his way when Wood was riding his horses and mapping out their campaigns. He retired in 1910 and died two years later.

Charlie Wood did not get his licence back until 1897 when he showed he had lost none of his flair by partnering Galtee More to victory in the Triple Crown of that year. He gave up riding in 1900 and trained for a few seasons before he retired to live in Eastbourne, where he died with a healthy bank balance and an untroubled conscience at the grand old age of 90 in 1945.

THE IRISH CONNECTION

FOR MORE THAN three decades Bob Watson proved a mainstay to the *Life*, acting as its representative at many events either as a reporter or referee and very often both. It was said he never ducked the issue in either capacity even though his referee's fee of five per cent of the purse at boxing matches was barely adequate danger money if his decision upset a volatile crowd.

While he may have missed out on the scoop of a lifetime when Matthew Webb did the dirty on him – "I taunted Webb with this ingratitude and for a very long while we were bad friends"[1] – other assignments provided him with plenty of good copy, and a trip to France to cover an illegal prizefight in the spring of 1888 proved particularly eventful.

Since the suppression of the old fight game in 1868 the law had been rigorously enforced against those who chose to do battle with the 'raw 'uns' and as a result all the big fights were staged on the Continent where, rightly or wrongly, it was felt that the police shared the views of the French boxing writer 'Mermeix', who declared:

> We haven't the slightest objection to these English ruffians (*goujats*) coming over here to batter each other about for money on French soil. Let them understand that they can make us other visits of the same nature and we shall be very glad to see them on one condition – one of them must kill the other. There would be then one Englishman less in the world.[2]

Not that a true-blooded Englishman took part in the rain-sodden slog between Charlie Mitchell and John L Sullivan, when they met behind a rubbing house on the gallops of Baron Gustave de Rothschild's Chantilly estate on 10 March 1888. Both men were born of Irish emigrants – Sullivan near Boston, USA (1858) and Mitchell in Birmingham, UK (1861) – and had first met in New York in 1883 when the contest had to be stopped in the third round to save Mitchell from further punishment.

The re-match was to prove a more even-sided affair since Sullivan had led a splendidly dissipated life during the interim and was not the formidable force he had once been.

Mitchell, who was not far behind the 'Boston Strong Boy' in the boozing stakes being a boon companion of the talented but dissolute amateur rider George 'Abington' Baird, had asked Watson to go to France to set up a venue for the fight, but when the *Life's* man arrived in Paris he was told the nobleman on whose estate he had hoped to stage the fight had just died. It was not a good start and things were to get much worse.

When the Chantilly site was finally settled on, a band of shady-looking *étrangers* in the unlikely guise of a wedding party descended on the little racing town. In an effort to avoid drawing attention to themselves the two camps had agreed to limit their number to just 32 although, as the fight got underway, they were joined by several liveried gamekeepers and a few of the local jockeys and trainers.

Exclusive as the encounter was, it proved a poor exhibition of the noble art as both men injured their hands – Sullivan his right, Mitchell his left – in the early stages of the fight which quickly deteriorated into an ungainly maul. Finally, after 3hrs 11min interspersed with numerous stoppages as both men took long rests on the ropes, the exhausted and bloodied pugs agreed on a draw in the 39th round.

It was only then that the real action started. As a soaked and dispirited Watson was making his way back to Chantilly he was arrested by a mounted gendarme, but made his escape when '*le flic*' galloped off to assist in rounding up the main body of spectators.

When the fugitive journalist, muddied and dishevelled after a cross-country detour over hedges and ditches, was finally able to dispatch his copy to the *Life* the following day he reported that 24 of the party had been arrested including both fighters, who had been released on bail after spending the night in jail. He added that the men had no option but to surrender to the police since:

> To refuse to obey would have been foolish and dangerous in the extreme for these gentlemen are not over-particular in their usage of people they take into custody, particularly Englishmen, whom they mortally detest. To have been violent, as is sometimes the case in England, would have ended in swords being drawn and as some of the men in custody were armed with six and eight-chambered revolvers, the result would have been serious.

Serious indeed! A master of understatement was our Bob.[*]

Sixteen months later the *Life* recorded the end of an era when it devoted a full page to what was to be the last of the great bareknuckle fights. This time the contest came off in the United States where Sullivan faced a fellow Irish-American in Jake Kilrain, who had Charlie Mitchell as one of his seconds.

On 8 July 1889 the two men met outside the town of Richburg, Mississippi, to fight for $2,000 and the diamond-studded belt put up by Richard Kyle Fox, a former printer on the *Belfast News Letter* who had emigrated to America in 1874 and made his fortune when he took over and transformed the ailing *National Police Gazette* into a salacious, under-the-counter weekly tabloid that reported on sport, sexual scandals and crimes of the worst kind.

Apart from the *Police Gazette's* championship belt, the law's ambiguous relationship with the prize ring was reflected by the fact that Sullivan's coach, Bill Muldoon, was a former New York cop, one of the timekeepers was the ex-deputy marshal of Dodge City, Bat Masterson, who was reporting on the contest for the *New York Morning Telegraph*, and the referee, John Fitzpatrick, was soon to become mayor of New Orleans.

It was all very Irish, but no State authority wanted the fight to take place in its back yard. The *Life*, which received its report by cablegram from New Orleans, carried the dramatic headline 'State Troops and Gatling Guns Ordered Out', as it described how the militia patrolled stations along the St Louis to Nashville railway line as trains ferried fans to the fight. At Richburg it was reported:

> The Sheriff eventually put in an appearance with the intention of preventing the fight taking place in Mississippi. However, after a little coaxing, he was prevailed upon to leave the ringside and he ultimately found a comfortable seat on the Grand Stand.

What the man with the star saw was a war of attrition fought out under a blazing midday sun as Kilrain adopted hit-and-run tactics and continually prevented Sullivan from mounting a sustained attack by going down on one knee to the first probing blows. In the 44th round, after 'Jawn L' had refreshed himself with a drink of cold tea liberally laced with whisky, it was reported:

---

[*] Watson at least got home safely unlike Archie McNeill who went to Rouen the previous December to cover the Jake Kilrain v Jem Smith fight for the *Sportsman*. McNeill went missing on the return journey and was later found washed up on the beach at Boulogne – foul play was suspected, but never proved.

SEVERAL SPORTS GATHERED IN FLEET-ST ABOUT 2 O'CLOCK

Big-fight weigh-ins at the *Life* attracted big crowds right up until they came to an end in 1929. In 1950 the *Life* published a letter from an old-time messenger boy, J G Jones, who recalled some of the bareknuckle fighters who stood on the office scales; they included the heavyweight champions Jake Kilrain, Jem Smith, Jem Mace, Charlie Mitchell and Frank Slavin. Jones particularly remembered the West Indies-born Peter 'Black Prince' Jackson playing a visit in 1889: "He was over six feet tall and magnificently proportioned. His unscarred face shone like ebony as he smiled at me with glistening white teeth. On his head he wore a silk hat. A morning coat, fashionable trousers, patent shoes, spats, white kid gloves and a gold-knobbed stick completed his outfit. 'Say boy,' he drawled. 'Is the editor around?' "

Sullivan was attacked by a fit of vomiting which lasted several minutes. Kilrain manfully stood in the middle of the ring until he had recovered himself. They went at it again. Kilrain smashing his antagonist in the stomach in the hopes of disabling him. Sullivan put in two good counter hits on the jaw, Kilrain going down. This so exasperated Sullivan that he lost his temper and at the end of the forty-fifth round when Kilrain fell down, Sullivan jumped on him and looked round at the referee. No notice was taken of the claims of a foul.

Eventually, after 75 gruelling rounds lasting 2hrs 16mins, Mike Donovan, one of Kilrain's seconds, threw in the sponge "much to Mitchell's disgust". Sullivan was still the undisputed world champion but, not for the first time, his victory celebrations were soured by the legal repercussions that had become part and parcel of any prizefight.

With warrants out for their arrest, the two fighters fled north and a week later Sullivan was in Chicago where a reporter from the *New York Herald* found him:

> …well-loaded with stimulants to maintain his drooping courage … The prospect of real labour under the supervision of a chain gang driver in the Mississippi pine forests has entirely destroyed his appetite for all save drink.

Both boxers were finally arrested and once again Kilrain came off worst as, in a perverse twist of justice, he was found guilty of 'assault and battery' and was sentenced to two months' imprisonment, while Sullivan pleaded guilty to prizefighting and got off with a $500 fine. The arrests and the resultant lawyer's fees proved to be the last straw for both Sullivan and the prize ring. When the champion next stepped into the ring to defend his title against James Corbett at the Olympic Athletic Club in New Orleans on 7 September 1892, he was wearing gloves.

"In all the fights I have been in under the London Prize Ring rules I have not only lost money, but have also had the care and worriment incidental to arrests, trials and penalties,"[3] he explained as he famously stipulated "The Marquis of Queensberry Rules must govern the contest. I want fighting, not foot racing."

Sullivan got his fighting all right. A few weeks short of his 34th birthday with his constitution weakened by too many late nights and too much booze, he was out-boxed by 'Gentleman Jim', and after 1hr 19mins of torrid punishment he failed to beat the count in the 21st round.

The *Life* published a special 7am fight-edition for its report, which came from Dalziel's Agency in America, and two days later it carried a salutary postscript in a short item from the same source:

> John L Sullivan is the most miserable man in America. Ever since his defeat by Corbett his jaw has been too stiff to permit of any eating, but it has not interfered with drinking and the ex-champion has been drinking heavily. When he drinks he becomes maudlin and he wept in a public house last evening, making the historical remark, 'Yesterday I had a million friends. Today I have not one'.

The fight marked a watershed in boxing, and the role the *Life* played in promoting the sport at this time helped the paper through a distinctly rocky period. Not only did it stage gloved-bouts under its own rules at the Ormonde Club in Walworth Road, south London, but it held weigh-ins for important contests at its office.*

The paper also had some gifted writers to kept Augur's despairing readers from switching their allegiance to the *Sportsman*. As with many of the foremost fighters of the day, there was a strong strain of Celtic blood flowing through their veins. Chief among them were Ned Healy and Elliot Hutchins who had worked together on the *Irish Sportsman* (forerunner of the *Irish Field*) in Dublin during the early 1870s.

Hutchins, a graduate of Trinity College, Dublin, came to England to join the *Life* in 1875. A popular little man, he wrote under the signature of 'Solon' until he took over the role of Special Commissioner from George Lowe in 1891. The Solon pseudonym – taken from a leading Irish stallion named after the famous Athenian magistrate – did him justice since he was described as "the greatest judge of a horse that I can recall"[4] by Meyrick Good, who had an extremely long recall as he wrote for the *Life* for a record 60 years – 1897-1957.

Hutchins had an extensive knowledge of the *Stud Book* and although breeders frequently sought his advice on mating arrangements, he failed to profit from his own modest endeavours in that sphere. He always kept a broodmare or two at home and, whenever he could, he would send them to the sons of his great idol, the outstanding Irish racehorse and sire Barcaldine, who was, himself, a son of Solon.

---

* The tradition of holding weigh-ins at the *Life* started with the last of the great bare-knuckle bruisers and continued until 1929 when the Italian giant, Primo Carnera, posed a problem. After it was found there were not enough weights in the office to balance the scales, a 12st 4lb promoter had to stand in with two 56lb weights to level the beam at 20st 4lb (284lb). That night the 6ft 7in Carnera decked his Deptford opponent, Jack Stanley, twice in the first round before the referee stopped the fight after 1m 48s. Half an hour later the 'Ambling Alp' was back in the Albert Hall ring to take out Pat Tarling, another British horizontal, in similar fashion. Carnera went on to become world champion by knocking out Jack Sharkey in 1933, but he lost his title a year later when he was floored ten times in 11 rounds by Max Baer. Other world champions to have weighed-in at the *Life* included Jimmy Wilde (flyweight 1916-23), Georges Carpentier (light-heavyweight 1920-22) and Maxie Rosenbloom (light-heavyweight 1930-34), while many British and Empire champions also stood on the *Life*'s scales and signed articles of agreement at the editor's desk.

Elliot Hutchins and George Lowe, who was to succeed Charles Blake as editor of the *Life*, as sketched by the famous *Punch* cartoonist, Phil May, in 1891.

But his much-vaunted judgement let him down badly when he sold the best horse he ever owned after it had shown only modest ability as a two-year-old. As fate would have it, the horse, Chaleureux, a grandson of Barcaldine, did not stop improving after joining the shrewd Newmarket trainer George Blackwell who placed him to win ten races in two seasons when his 1898 victories included the Chesterfield Cup, the Cesarewitch and the Manchester November Handicap.

The task of having to report on these races was particularly galling for Hutchins whose remorse often seeped through between the lines. When he saw his transformed plater display "immeasurable superiority" over his galloping companions in a pre-Cesarewitch workout, he lamented "one cannot but regret, for the colt's own sake, that all his training days were not spent under his present trainer's charge."

And again, when tipping Chaleureux for that race, he remarked that the improvement made by the horse "should serve as a warning not to hastily discard shapely, sound-limbed thoroughbreds solely because of unsuitability in youth to two-year-old scampers." Sadly for Hutchins, it was 'a lesson too late for the learning'. He never really got over the disappointment, and perhaps it was just as well he did not live to see his old horse become the sire of Signorinetta, the winner of the Derby (at 100-1) and Oaks in 1908.

As the *Life* had remarked at the time of his death three years earlier: "Poor Elliot, though one of the kindest hearted of men, was never one of Fortune's favourites."

While Hutchins came to England to further his career, Ned Healy chose to remain in Ireland from where he dispatched his beautifully crafted articles on an intermittent basis for over 30 years (there were long and lamentable periods of enforced economy at the *Life* when his column was dropped along with those of the American, French and Australian correspondents).

Born in Pollardstown on the borders of the Curragh in 1847, Edward Behan Healy learnt his trade under one of Ireland's foremost racing men, Joseph Osborne, who was an author and journalist of considerable merit in addition to having owned and trained Abd-el-Kader, the first horse to win successive Grand Nationals (1850-51).

Osborne compiled and published an annual *Steeplechase Calendar*, wrote the standard work, *The Horsebreeders' Handbook*, and was, for many years, chief correspondent for *Bell's Life*. Writing under the signature of 'Beacon', his articles carried significant weight both at home and abroad and his young disciple achieved a similar standing after he had graduated from the *Leinster Express* and the *Irish Sportsman* to become sports editor of the *Irish Times*.

Healy was best known in the Irish press as 'Vates', a *nom de plume* he adopted some years after the original 'Vates' (John Harrison of the *Morning Advertiser*) had died, but it was as 'Rory O'More' that he penned his first full-length article for the *Life* in 1878. Up until that time the paper had made do without a regular Irish correspondent as the country's racing simply did not merit one.

The sport had sunk to a pitifully low ebb as a result of a number of factors that had come together in the wake of the great potato famine (1845-49), which left its mark on all aspects of Irish life. Not only did tens of thousands die of starvation and disease as mass migration tore the heart out of the nation, but, within a decade or so, many of the Turf's staunchest patrons died off and their studs were dispersed with the best horses being sold abroad to England and the Continent. Things reached such a state that in 1863 – when nine of the 17 Royal Plates were won by the English-trained Tourist – the Royal Agricultural Society set up a committee to inquire into the deterioration of the Irish horse.

Matters had improved considerably by the time Healy was commissioned to write a short series of articles for the *Life*, but just when it looked as if they might develop into a regular column, the country and its sport was hit by political unrest after a bad harvest in 1879 sparked fears of another famine.

In October that year the republican-backed Land League was founded with the object of achieving land reform for the hard-pressed tenant farmers. With its president, Charles Stewart Parnell MP, the leader of the Home Rule Party, championing its cause in the British parliament, the League instituted an anti-hunting campaign, which was directed against Anglo-Irish landowners rather than the principles of the hunt.

When Parnell was imprisoned for 'treasonable practices' two years later, the situation deteriorated as the League called on tenants to withhold their rents, which, in turn, resulted in the movement being outlawed by Gladstone's government. This small but important chapter in Ireland's turbulent history was reflected in the columns of the *Life* as Healy was asked to chart the course of events that not only disrupted hunting, but racing as well.

Although an ardent nationalist, Healy was, nevertheless, fiercely opposed to the radical policies pursued by the League and was not afraid to say so. In November 1881, he described the movement as "the most pernicious organisation which was ever permitted to disturb a country" and declared:

> From the moment the Land League expressed its determination to manifest opposition to hunting it was easy to foresee that such a policy was merely the thin end of the wedge which, in time, would be driven home against racing and other pastimes.
>
> All this was devised solely to annoy and banish the moneyed classes or at least those amongst them who closed their pockets to the beggarly importunity of the League. But by degrees society is regaining confidence, the action of the Government is tranquillising the disaffected, hunting in many districts goes on unmolested and ere the old year departs I have hopes that the old land will have settled into its usual quiet grove.

Some hopes! On 6 May 1882, the newly appointed Chief Secretary for Ireland, Lord Frederick Cavendish (Gladstone's nephew), and the permanent Under-Secretary, Thomas Burke, were stabbed to death in Phoenix Park by members of the nationalist sect, the Invincibles. Revolution was once again in the air.

In England the seriousness of the situation was reflected in the fact that, for the first time since Lord George Bentinck introduced the custom in 1847, there was no Derby-day adjournment of parliament, which was too busy rushing through an emergency Prevention of Crime Bill for Ireland.

In Ireland, race meetings that were seen as potential rallying grounds for insurgents were cancelled, while those that did go ahead were heavily policed by armed troops. Yet, despite all the unrest, Healy remained optimistic that the situation would soon improve. He expressed his hopes in a pre-season article in March 1883, when his Rory O'More signature was replaced by a 'From Our Irish Correspondent' byline as he was finally taken on as a regular weekly columnist.

Making good use of the latest word to enter the English vocabulary after Capt Charles Boycott, a Co. Mayo land agent, had been ostracised by his neighbours for opposing the Land League, he reported:

> That the Irish have a strong inherent love of racing and the kindred pastimes cannot be denied and though, beyond question, hounds have been poisoned and masters boycotted, it is also equally true that the great bulk of the Irish people were loud in their denunciations of acts so vile.
>
> The boycotter's reprehensible programme was never in full swing in Ireland as levied against any of the field pastimes, for Ulster escaped completely, whilst Leinster too turned a deaf ear to the wicked cry of 'Stop the hunt!'. However, in the principal province the contagion spread somewhat and the 'Killing Kildares' were, for a time, mute as tombs.
>
> Now all is right once more and the first immediate result of the patching-up between landlord and farmer was the fixing of the premier race meeting in the country for April 3 and 4. In 1882 it was a case of 'no hunting, no Punchestown'; in 1883 it is a case of plenty of hunting and glorious Punchestown in a more attractive garb than ever.
>
> Right has happily triumphed most notably in Kildare – the premier sporting county of the thirty-two on the Irish map – and men who once cheered the No Rent Manifesto, and shouted 'Down with the Kildares!' are now back to a state of normal reason and doubtless feel all the better for the change … Many of the men themselves were passionately fond of a day on the trail of a fox or a stag, and it may be noted here that Parnell (Ireland's 'uncrowned king') is as good a man to hounds as one would see with the Quorn or Pytchley.

When the new season got underway with the traditional Easter Monday meeting of the Ward Union Hunt at Fairyhouse, Healy reported that, despite the improved situation, the Lord Lieutenant of Ireland, "the hard-riding, sport-loving and well-liked Spencer" who gave a £100 cup for one of the races, had decided that discretion was the better part of valour and had remained "in the midst of his mounted escort in Dublin":

> It were shaming modesty if I did not admit the reason of his absence. In Ireland, alas! there are too many who will die with a feeling of hatred of any Viceroy, simply because he is the Queen's representative in the country, and with these malcontents it matters not a straw whether the ruler guides the people with a silken thread or puts them on the wrong side of iron bars. He will be hated all the same.

A month later, 'Our Irish Correspondent' had cause to mention Spencer again as he gave a graphic account of a country still on the rack; riven by mass migration and the aftermath of political assassinations:

> We live in the midst of curious contradictions in this green and bloodstained island, and whilst on one hand it is easy to count many signs of improving times and near at hand prosperity, there is no lack of scenes of destitution and its wonted results.
>
> This week the excellent Earl Spencer rode forty miles with one change (Ballina to Balmullet) to see – what think you? The Viceroy went forth on this dreary trip in order that he himself might behold the arrangements for the emigration of our poor people to the great Western Continent, and these same poor folk are leaving the land of their birth in hundreds, flying from barren wastes and seaweed food to such new homes in America as Fate may provide...
>
> Surely there are no signs of prosperity about scenes such as these, and yet in other parts of the Irish picture there is much that is bright and hopeful. And better by far than anything upon which the eye can rest, is the feeling now abroad that we are really at last on the mend – that we are, in fact, emerging from the long and dreary night of darkness and of crime in which Ireland has been enwrapped for too long a period.

Healy went on to expand upon the 'darkness and crime' as he referred to the fact that five of the men found guilty of the Phoenix Park murders were shortly to he hanged at Dublin's Kilmainham jail by Marwood, the Lincolnshire executioner. Several of those involved in the plot had been on the peripheries of racing including Ned McCaffrey, a small-time bookmaker, and Michael Kavanagh a cabman who "has been for years an attendant at all the race meetings near Dublin and possessing that speedy mare used on the memorable 6th of May, he could always get his own price for tooling it down to, say Baldoyle or Fairyhouse."

Returning to more mundane matters, the Irish chronicler remarked on the number of rural race meetings that were springing up all over the country and which provided local breeders with the incentive to aim for the ultimate – a Grand National winner:

> They breed from a better horse this year than last year and so, in improving their young stock, they make a market for themselves, for it is only in excessive bad times that the Irish hunter fails to command his full value. Some wonderfully good animals are found at these small affairs and, if my

memory serves me aright, I think it was at a small countryside race meeting, running for a 'tenner', that The Lamb was first seen.*

It was a mighty leap from this article, both in time and progress, to the day when Healy was able to record the first success of an Irish-trained horse in the Epsom Derby. This came about in 1907 when Orby, bred and owned by Richard 'Boss' Croker and trained on his Glencairn estate outside Dublin by Colonel Frederick McCabe, landed a major patriotic gamble after he had been backed down to 100-9 from 66-1.

It was a glorious affirmation of the journalist's unbounded faith in Irish racing, and just as a dog (Master McGrath) had united the 'green and bloodstained island' in nationwide celebrations in 1871, so too did a horse achieve a feat that generations of politicians and terrorists have failed to accomplish.

Overnight, Orby became the peoples' horse even though some tried to claim him for their own – when the victorious nag was paraded through the streets of Dublin, one ecstatic old biddy greeted McCabe with the immortal line: "Thank God and you, Sir, that we have lived to see a Catholic horse win the Derby!"[5]

This great day for Ireland came in the twilight of Healy's distinguished career. His final article for the *Life* appeared on the day he died – 16 August 1910. It had been written over the weekend just before he was taken ill at the Grand Hotel in Tramore where he was staying for one of his favourite race meetings.

To the end he remained true to the high standards he set for himself both in his work and in his private life. Tributes to him were many, and they varied little in their assessment of a man who was described as "a landmark in the history of Irish sporting journalism" (*Irish Field*), and as "one of the best and most loveable characters whom it could ever be one's privilege to meet or be associated with" (*Freeman's Journal*).

The *Life* declared "a more upright, charitable and cultured gentleman has not been known to the racing community," while similar sentiments were echoed in a whole range of publications including *Sport*, the popular Dublin weekly which Healy had edited and written for since the early 1890s.

At a time when racing in his country was going through one of its most difficult periods, Healy had written: "Despite all the sullen gloom which just at present clouds the Irish outlook, some rays of hope appear upon the horizon like summer sunbeams in the ever doubtful yet certain future."[6]

Ned Healy, himself, was surely one of those 'rays of hope'.

---

* Bred by a Co. Limerick farmer named Henchy, The Lamb was eventually leased to Lord William Henry Poulett for whom he won the Grand National in 1868 and again in 1871, but his triumphs were clouded by tragedy. Both George Ede, who partnered the little (15.2hh) iron-grey gelding to his 1868 win, and Ben Land, the successful trainer that year, met untimely ends. Ede, a leading amateur who rode under the name of 'Mr Edwards', was killed in a fall on The Lamb's stable companion, Chippenham, at Aintree in 1870. Land, a great friend of Ede who had ridden for his stable for 14 years, blamed himself for the death and, haunted by guilt, he gave up training jumpers and finally, his misery compounded by gambling losses, he committed suicide in 1872. His end was all the more terrible since he failed to make a clean job of cutting his throat and lingered on for four days before he died. To complete the sorry saga, just one month later The Lamb broke a leg while running in the Grand Steeplechase at Baden-Baden and had to be destroyed.

THE TRODMORE COUP

TOWARDS the end of June 1891, the following notice appeared in the *Life*:

> Several friends of Mr Charles W Blake, 'Augur', have expressed a desire to present him with a testimonial on the occasion of his reaching his fiftieth year … It is, however, clearly to be understood that no pecuniary object is aimed at but that the matter is simply put forward as affording evidence of good fellowship and appreciation. For that reason subscriptions are limited to one guinea downwards. The full list of subscribers will be announced soon after July 10 (Mr Blake's birthday) when the whole matter will be closed.

Sadly, the matter was closed before Blake reached his 50th year. The pressures of work had been chipping away at his health for some time although this was not reflected in his last article, which appeared on July 4. Written in his own inimitable style, it portrayed a man who was content with his lot. True to form, he led off with the weather, taking as his text a quotation from Longfellow: "How beautiful is the rain! / After the dust and heat / In the broad and fiery street / In the narrow lane / How beautiful is the rain!"

Expanding on his theme, he went on to deliver what amounted to a valediction as he imparted one final piece of Blakeish wisdom to his readers:

> We hear nowadays of many messages from many prophets, but the best message that any age can receive from any prophet, be he sporting or otherwise, is 'Be content!' This, maybe, is a hard saying when anything is provocative of the reverse of contentment; when the skies are weeping and the sun is sulking and the streets are strewn with slosh. But lately there has been every inducement to contentment, as for the most of a month the sky by day has been glorified with the sun and beautified by night with the stars – those 'holy lamps of heaven'. It has indeed been a luxury to live, surrounded as we have been by flowers and amply supplied by fruits.

'It has indeed been a luxury to live!' It was almost as if he knew his time had come. Shortly after he had written these lines, Blake was taken ill and left the office early to return home where he was felled by a stroke the following day. He never recovered consciousness and died three days later. Poor old Charley would have appreciated the 'In Memoriam' penned by his anonymous colleague, 'Old Port':

> The daily task, the common round proceed, / We live our life, the great world swings along; / But gone from out our heart is light and song, / Though in the face our sorrow none may read.
>
> Our chief is dead! – dead! Nothing now but clay, / That form pulsating so with joy of life; / That mind that never stooped to petty strife / Is quieted, and he has passed away.
>
> So strange, so swift, so silently he went; / Our loss we learn, but scarce can realise; / He, tender-hearted, true to all, and wise, / Was called away ere his loved form was bent!
>
> No common sorrow mourn we; O our grief! / Vacant that chair – no more that hand we grasped! / O could not Death some less-loved form have clasped / With icy touch, and left us our great Chief!

Apart from this awful dirge and the reproduction of a profile on Blake, which had appeared in *Man of the World* two years earlier, the *Life* carried no other tribute to its editor. It was left to John Corlett in the *Sporting Times* to testify to Blake's all-round popularity after he had attended the funeral at New Southgate cemetery in London:

> Amongst his personal friends – and their name is legion – he was beloved as a genial and generous comrade … and the flowers we placed on his grave today and the tears that are shed will be but outward tokens of a heartfelt grief.

The question of a successor was soon decided. At the time, the editorship of the *Life* was regarded as "one of the prizes of the newspaper world and is reputed to be worth £1,500 [£135,000] per annum"[1] and once again it went to an insider who lacked the necessary qualities to lift the paper out of the rut it had fallen into.

George Shortland Lowe was but a conservative version of his predecessor. A towering (6ft 3in), well-built, kindly fellow with a bushy moustache and a slouching walk, he was, like Blake, a West-countryman born near Brent, Somerset, in 1840. Thanks to a helping hand from the famous Devonshire sporting parson, the Rev. Jack Russell of terrier fame, he had started to contribute articles on hunting to *Bell's Life* when still in his teens and in 1861 he moved to Paris to become that paper's French correspondent. Writing as 'Anglo Saxon', he held that post until the outbreak of the Franco-Prussian war in 1870 drove him back to England where he became a recognised authority on foxhounds.

He played a major role in establishing the Kennel Club in 1873 and, as its secretary, did much to develop the society, while he also founded and edited the *Kennel Gazette* as he continued to write for *Bell's Life*. When that paper was taken over by the *Life* in 1886, Lowe was appointed Special Commissioner to replace William Morris, a former Newmarket trainer who was in failing health and ready to accept the less demanding task of writing a weekly 'Round and About Newmarket' column under the signature of 'Martingale'.

Lowe fulfilled his new role with a solid diligence until he took over the chair in 1891 when he gave a much-needed new slant to the Augur column as items on foxhounds replaced Blake's weeping skies and dying swans. The new editor's doggy dissertations often appeared at the beginning of July when his annual stint as a judge at the prestigious Peterborough hound show gave him the perfect excuse to delve into his favourite subject.

In 1899, one such article headed 'Hounds and High Breeding' asserted: "Foxhunting has had much to do in making England what she is," before it went on to draw an interesting parallel between horse and hound:

> It may be a questionable point as to whether thoroughbred horses or hounds were first bred on scientific lines, but at any rate hounds came the quicker to perfection. They were the objects of much thought and study by the year 1750 and the matches that took place between the years 1780 and 1795 showed that the greatest amount of excellence had been obtained.
>
> They were run for £500 a side over the Beacon Course at Newmarket and a challenge was issued to match a bitch called Merkin for £10,000 a side against any other. Very fortunately this species of gambling over foxhounds died out, but all the ideas about breeding them were retained, and how remarkable it is now to see a race of hounds after a 120 years' breeding … keeping up a standard for bone, symmetry and working qualities down to the present time.

When Lowe was not extolling the glories of the ducal packs of England, he liked to hark back to 'the good old days' by dipping into the files of *Bell's Life*, but one thing in the lead column remained constant but variable and that was the weather, although, to his credit, GSL always kept his observations on this subject short and to the point.

On August bank holiday Monday 1898 there was only one word to describe the weather and that was 'hot'. In London it was 78°F (26°C) in the shade and bookies' runners were finding it warm work as they did the rounds on what was one of their busiest days of the year. The *Life* carried the cards for four home meetings that day – Hurst Park, Ripon, Birmingham and Newton Abbot – in addition to Baldoyle in Ireland and Vincennes in France, while the *Sportsman* had the bonus of a hunt meeting at Trodmore.

The card for Trodmore was typical of its kind. There were the usual races for hunt subscribers; a farmers' plate, a hunters' flat race, a hurdle and a chase as well as a handicap hurdle of £40. The first of the six races was due off at 1.30, and appended underneath the last race was a list of 'Arrivals'. The names of 24 of the 46 horses entered were given together with the postscript, 'Others expected'. The Trodmore programme had also been sent to the *Life* by the clerk of the course, G Martin, who politely requested that his annual holiday fixture be included in the paper as usual, but because of lack of space the card ended up on the spike.

By midday that Monday the huge nationwide industry of illegal betting was in overdrive as bookmakers' agents in barbers' shops and tobacconists, grocers and newsagents, pubs and clubs, gathered in cash bets from their customers. 'Runners' would then collect the bets before noon, while others stationed themselves at regular sites on street corners where they could rendezvous with their clients as 'watchers' kept a look out for prowling policeman.

Most street bookmakers had an arrangement with the local plod whereby their men were allowed to go about their business unmolested provided a weekly contribution was made to police 'funds'. Those not prepared to make such 'donations' found their agents were constantly harassed and arrested.

There were quite a few harassed bookies in London that memorable bank holiday afternoon as their runners brought in a surprising number of bets on horses engaged at the Trodmore meeting. In particular, there was a lot of money for Reaper in the handicap hurdle. The five-year-old was also included in doubles and trebles with other horses at the meeting as well as likely favourites at the principal fixtures.

As the evening papers published only the results from the main meetings, the layers had an anxious wait until the sporting papers appeared the following morning. Those who took the *Sportsman* were dismayed to find that Reaper had won "very easily" at 5-1 and many of the doubles and trebles which included Reaper had also come up. Most bookmakers paid out grudgingly, but others refused immediate payment on the grounds that they settled only on the prices returned by the *Life*, which had not published the Trodmore results.

It was not long before telegrams and letters (a same-day delivery service operated then) from bookmakers asking when the Trodmore return would appear in the paper began to pile up on George Lowe's desk. At the time, Lowe had no reason to suspect there was anything amiss so he simply had the results cut out of the *Sportsman* and sent to the printers to be reset in *Sporting Life* type.

The results duly appeared in Wednesday's paper, but by a freak coincidence a printer's error had converted Reaper's price from 5-1 to 5-2, and the literal brought in a whole new spate of inquiries from aggrieved bookmakers who had already paid out on the *Sportsman's* prices.

The *Sportsman's* editor, Sam Downing, was similarly deluged with queries and, perhaps for the first time, he asked his staff "where the hell is Trodmore, anyway?" When no one was able to enlighten him, he sent off a telegram to the obliging Mr Martin who had wired in the programme and results from a post office in St Ives, Cornwall.

When the telegram was returned 'addressee not known', Downing contacted Lowe to find out what was going on. An embarrassed Lowe had to admit to his 'scissors and paste' job, and as the two men compared notes the awful truth dawned on them that they had been duped into helping execute the most celebrated fraud in racing history.*

Never has a front-page story been sat on so tightly. Both papers maintained a strict silence as the matter was handed over to the police. There were strong suspicions that it had been an inside job, but despite interviewing the staff of the *Sportsman* and the telegraph clerks in St Ives, the police drew a blank. Finally, three weeks after the coup, the following statement appeared in the *Sportsman*:

> 'Trodmore' Race Meeting – On August 1 we published the program of a race meeting purporting to be held at Trodmore, Cornwall, and on August 2 a report of the alleged meeting. Both the program and the report were sent to us by a correspondent who signed himself 'G Martin, St Ives, Cornwall'.
>
> Investigation has shown there is no such place as Trodmore and that no race meeting was held on August 1 in the neighbourhood of St Ives, Cornwall. It is obvious, therefore, that 'Martin' by himself or in league with others, invented the program and report in question for the purpose of defrauding bookmakers, several of whom have communicated with us.
>
> We are endeavouring to trace the fraud to its source, and meanwhile would recommend agents who received commissions in connection with the meeting to withhold payment and to forward to this office the names and addresses of any persons who sent commissions to them.
>
> It appears that our contemporary, the *Sporting Life*, was the victim of the same fraud, a return of the fictitious meeting appearing in its columns on August 3.

The *Life*, meanwhile, uttered not a word, but in the offices of the *Sporting Chronicle*, Edward Hulton allowed himself a wry smile. A year earlier, under a contract drawn up on the sale of *Bell's Life*, William McFarlane, the *Life's* reclusive proprietor, had obtained a High Court injunction to prevent his Manchester rival from publishing the *Sporting Chronicle* and its weekly sister paper, the *Handicap Book*, in London. The *Chronicle*, therefore, had little sympathy for the *Life* as it commented smugly:

> In days of old, bogus programmes and returns of race meetings were occasionally foisted upon London newspapers by designing persons for nefarious purposes. The object of the device was to swindle the bookmakers, but we thought that in these days of telegraphy, explicit maps and comprehensive gazetteers it was impossible to carry out so old a scheme of robbery as ancient as thimblerigging and the three-card trick.
>
> We feel sorry for our London contemporaries who, with all the parade of exclusive news in big type, set forth the programme of an alleged meeting at an alleged place called Trodmore followed by an 'adequate' return of the sport wherein runners and prices were given with much 'accuracy'. It now transpires that Trodmore, as a racing centre, existed only in the imagination of the inventive genius who supplied our contemporaries so promptly and so fully.

---

* Downing never got over the ignominy of being hoaxed, it played upon his mind so much that it eventually drove him insane and five years later he was confined to an asylum where he died, aged 48, in 1906.

The same 'gentleman' favoured this paper with his 'information', but for us 'Trodmore' was not on the map. The delinquent should be brought to justice and surely our London contemporaries who have been 'spoofed' will spare no expense to discover his individuality.

As the Manchester men chortled, the coup became the talk of Fleet Street. Speculation was rife as to who the 'inventive genius' was and how much had been made out of the bookmakers. The *Daily Telegraph* devoted a whole column to the fraud and observed:

All the animals ran at pretty prices and the 'accumulator' principle could have been followed to a profitable tune by the person or persons, who promoted, ran, judged, reported, and 'returned' this phantom meeting.

For the layers of odds we can feel little sympathy – for the takers, if the allegations made be true, they may find that a sense of humour, adulterated with fraudulent intent, is apt to beget unpleasantness with magistrates and recorders and judges and their retinue. There are already sufficient facilities for betting upon our over-abundant flat and steeplechase fixtures advertised in the official broadsheet [*the Racing Calendar*], and everything else, real or bogus, should be left severely alone.

Under the heading 'How To Dupe Bookmakers', the *Daily Mail* remarked:

It is not every professional who will take bets in the case of countryside leather flapping meetings of the character of this bogus Trodmore one, but the most appears to have been got out of those who would. Some of the Fleet Street division were tapped for considerable sums bearing in mind the character of the 'fixture'. The prices of the successful horses were beautifully graduated, the first winner being returned at 5 to 4 against. Two 5 to 1 chances won, and oddly enough these figured in nearly all the double events and accumulative bets.

The Star's headlines proclaimed 'A Daring Turf Fraud / Little Bookmakers Spoofed By An Entirely Bogus Meeting' as it pointed out:

It is the provincial man and the street corner man and the amateur bookmaker who will suffer because they usually take bets on any event and are quite likely to have taken bets on a program that appeared in the *Sportsman* and to have paid on the published results. What else can they do?

What else indeed! They could hardly go to the police and complain since they themselves would have been arrested for breaking the law. It was, as the *News of the World* declared, "Perhaps the most extraordinary swindle ever perpetrated" – all the more so because those responsible got clean away with their ill-gotten gains, although their identity was known to more than a few journalists and bookmakers.

Years later, the *Life's* Meyrick Good admitted he had "a pretty shrew idea" of those who were behind the sting. Without naming names he stated:

One was a billiards reporter, the other a sub-editor and the third a racing journalist. The last-named, whom I knew well, was conveniently 'laid up' for a couple of months from the moment the police offered a £100 reward for information which would throw light upon the ramp.[2]

At the time there was a general closing of ranks in 'the Street'. Many scribes shared a sneaking admiration for the inventive geniuses who had so cleverly stitched up the bookies, and reporters who, ten years earlier, had left no stone unturned in their efforts to track down 'the Ripper', were notably reluctant to follow up any lead that might reveal the identity of 'the Reaper'.

Even the outspoken Theodore Andrea Cook, whose column, 'Men and Matters in the World of Sport', added a much-needed sparkle to the *Life* every Wednesday, was not about to rock the boat. A week before the *Sportsman* admitted its part in the fraud, he had pointed out how powerless a journalist was to prevent chicanery in racing; a subject he might well have brought up to excuse his failure to mention the coup:

> I have no doubt there are many evils attached to the Turf which (in its best interests) ought to be abolished. But – as the result of a pretty lengthy experience – I have found it useless for any writer to moralise upon what may be called the *histoire inedite* of the Turf. Much may be done by the vigilance of daily and weekly sporting papers to scotch malpractices, but no man who knows the Turf can pretend to believe that any writer – whatever his authority – can be potential in killing them.
>
> Some of our readers may doubt this. Well! let any writer who is ambitious of lashing evildoers upon a racecourse take the pains to read *Essays on the Turf* published years ago by 'Nimrod' and thus learn vicariously his own impotence. It can't be done.

Not that this uncharacteristically negative view deterred Cook from having his say on other matters which George Lowe, in true Blakeish tradition, failed to address. He had, in fact, become the voice of authority in a publication that had long since lost its way as a *news*paper, and the subjects he tackled were many and varied.

COOK'S CAMPAIGNS

FROM THE TIME Theodore Cook first started to write for the *Life* on a freelance basis in 1894, he promoted sport in all its forms and fiercely defended it against the puritanical spoilsports who were then so prominent in middle-class society. The ranks of the ungodly could range from the Matlock and Bath district councillors who, in 1899, banned boating and the playing of cards on a Sunday, to the country's farmers whose use of barbed wire was causing havoc in the hunting field.

Once Cook took up a cause he did not let it drop. Terrier-like, he would worry away at his prey week after week even though, in the case of barbed wire (an American invention of 1874 which carved up a lot more than the prairies), it took years rather than months before an uneasy compromise was reached between farmers and huntsmen.

'Old Blue', as he signed himself, launched his anti-wire campaign in November 1894 by quoting R S Surtees' celebrated hero:

> It was the boast of Mr Jorrocks years agone that 'hunting possessed all the glories of war, with but 25 per cent of its dangers' – but *autres temps, autres moeurs*! Hardly a week passes but some awful accident is reported from the prevalence of that devilish invention, barbed wire; hence the hour is at hand ... when combined action must be taken in the matter.

Cook's solution was to outlaw the 'devilish invention', but that was never going to happen even though an increasing catalogue of lacerations, broken limbs and fatalities to both man and beast led to the resignation of a number of MFHs. There was even talk that some hunts might be forced to disband when, during the winter of 1898-9, Cook led his column with a brief news item from the Yorkshire Post: 'Lord Middleton has decided that his hounds will cease to hunt, on account of the barbed wire about.'

Bewildered by this "sudden change of front in what has always been a very sporting neighbourhood," 'Old Blue' commented:

> That English farmers, especially *Yorkshire* farmers, should wittingly cut their own throats in this absurd fashion is emphatically one of those things no fellow can understand! I presume they have counted the cost! Lord Middleton is not an MFH to do things by halves and when he comes to any decision of this nature depend upon his 'going right away through with it', as the Yankees say. Egad! The above resolve is enough to make old Sir Tatton Sykes fairly rise from his grave.

Eventually, most farmers agreed to take down their wire during the hunting season and Cook was able to mark up another success on his impressive CV. Born in Exmouth, Devon, in 1867, he was head of school at Radley and captain of football and boats. At Wadham College he rowed in the trial eights in 1887 and '88, winning in both years to earn himself a place in the defeated Oxford crew of 1889. He captained the English fencing team in Paris (1903) and Athens (1906) and represented the Amateur Fencing Association on the British Olympic Council. He also served on the International Olympic Committee for ten years and drafted the rules for the 1908 Olympic Games in London.

His versatility as a journalist was no less impressive. In between filling his column with such controversial and diverse subjects as 'should women hunt', 'the degeneration of the Englishman' and 'the cycle tax', he went to Stockholm at the behest of Joseph Pulitzer to interview King Oscar II on the Samoan arbitration treaty which was being thrashed out by Germany, Britain and America.

At the time, Cook had just taken over as editor of the influential London evening paper, the *St James's Gazette*, but after a year in the chair he fell out with its German proprietor and, following a couple of short stints as a leader writer on *The Standard* and the *Daily Express*, he joined the staff of the *Daily Telegraph* in 1901. Throughout this time he continued to furnish the *Life* with his weekly column, which, for ten years, brought in a bulging postbag to the paper's office.

In spite of his upper-class background, Cook did not toe the Establishment line; instead he championed some unfashionable causes that marked him out as a man ahead of his time. In 1903, for instance, he rattled quite a few gilded cages when he denounced, with italicised emphasis, the accepted way of shooting game as he posed the question:

> In what way can the battue even savour of sport or how can the performers therein be dubbed sportsmen? *No pursuit deserves the title of sport which taxes nothing beyond the organ of destruction in those who follow it*. In the battue we find hundreds of pheasants, reared by hand almost of the keeper, and scores of hares enclosed within nets, driven in the very face of sportsmen posted in advantageous positions, to be slaughtered wholesale. Does anybody call this sport? What sense or sport is it to kill huge quantities of game artificially reared and semi-domesticated?

Since Edward VII's annual bag of game birds (of the feathered variety) rivalled that of the most ardent 'lover of the trigger', Cook's scornful censure was courageous at a time when the press's obsequious pandering to royalty bordered on the obscene – and he went further as he extended the scope of his article to include birds of prey:

> All our large and rare birds are fast disappearing under the current rage of making what is termed 'collections in Natural History'. This object is, perhaps, legitimate enough in itself but, carried to excess, these would-be collectors will very soon destroy the balance of nature and leave us to contend with more subtle and mysterious enemies.
>
> We are therefore in danger of becoming vulgar game killers without sport, and mere bird stuffers without even the pretence of a necessity for the acquisition of knowledge by a murderous onslaught on all by which that knowledge could be obtained. In the best interests of sport and humanity, I ask our great landowners to pause ere following such a suicidal system. Only let some of those in high places set their faces against it, and Fashion will do the rest.

This barely disguised appeal to the King brought in a flood of angry letters from shooters and landowners, as well as a plea for the protection of the wildlife that was being wiped out along the banks of the Thames. The latter came from F R Wilkinson of the British Museum who, Cook reported:

> …laments that a system of barbarous Philistinism is banishing, if it has not already banished, the otter, the grebe, the kingfisher, the moorhen, etc. from the river. They are shot, ruthlessly trapped and otherwise destroyed simply because the angling societies grudge them their tribute out of the multitude of coarse fish with which the river still abounds. Oftener than not, however, they are 'butchered to make a Cockney's holiday'.

He thanks the *Sporting Life* for having the courage to decry the *battue*, the senseless massacre of English birds, etc. and asks that we will also lift up our voices against this equally destructive form of Vandalism, so to speak. I gladly do so, for it is a national question. The sooner some Act is passed giving absolute protection to what may still be left of the Thames fauna, the better.

On this subject it has to be said that Cook was writing as a convert, and for a paper that carried regular reports on the packs of otter hounds that operated throughout Britain. Four years earlier, 'Old Blue' had cheerfully scorned a reader who had written in to complain about the hunting of otters in the very same river:

A lot of adverse criticism has been recently vouchsafed at the wanton destruction (*sic*) of otters in the Thames. 'The more so', says a kind correspondent from Maidenhead, 'because rewards have been offered by the Thames Angling Society for each animal killed'. This is another contention I, for one, cannot readily understand.

Naturally the disciples of rare old Izaak* are wishful to preserve the finny tribe, and where a deadlier enemy to such than the otter? But, as I am advised, the TAS do not wish to exterminate the otter, far from it. They simply desire to keep them down so that fishing may not receive undue injury. Where does the 'wanton destruction' come in?

Moreover, compare with the present, the old-time form of otter hunting as depicted in Somerville's famous *Chace*: 'Pierced thro' and thro' / On pointed spears they lift him high in air; / Wriggling he hangs, and grins, and bites in vain. / Bid the loud horns, in gaily warbling strains, / Proclaim the felon's fate; he dies, he dies.'

In the modern revival of otter hunting the spear has no part or place. Where, then, does the alleged 'cruelty' come in? Is not this yet another case of strained Humanitarianism?

The light on Cook's road to Damascus must have been dazzling to bring about such a *volte-face*, the more so since he was normally stubbornly consistent in his opinions. He had, for example, particularly strong views on the 'shamateurism' that was so rife in cricket during the extended reign of W G Grace, and he condemned the practice in no uncertain terms when the matter was brought out into the open in 1896.

At the time there was a lot of resentment among professional players over payments made in the form of expenses to the top amateurs; a situation not improved by the fact that the professionals were regarded as socially inferior to their counterparts. While they played together as a team, the two camps were segregated off the pitch on what was very much a first and third-class basis. They used separate ground entrances, changing rooms and dining rooms, while salaried players were also expected to act as general dogsbodies to their social superiors, but what really rankled them was that they were not so well paid as the so-called amateurs.

Undisputed king of the shamateurs was the nation's hero, Dr William Gilbert Grace, who received £1,500 (£135,000) *plus* expenses from the Melbourne Cricket Club when he took a side to Australia for the 1873-4 season, while the seven professionals in the team had to settle for £170 (£15,300) a man. The disparity was even greater on the 1891-2 tour when Grace doubled his fee to £3,000, and received full expenses for taking his wife and two children with him. Lord Sheffield, the president of Sussex CCC

---

* Izaak Walton – author of the classic work, *The Compleat Angler* (1653).

who funded the tour, was poorly rewarded by the boorish antics of his star player who led his team to a 2-1 defeat in the Test series.

When playing at home it was no secret that the doctor asked for and got more than 'reasonable expenses', but such was his dominance of the game and the fact that he could put thousands on the gate, the Marylebone Cricket Club turned a blind eye to this blatant abuse of its rules in much the same way as the Jockey Club had allowed Fred Archer a free rein in the betting stakes. Then, during the summer of 1896, the issue was blown wide open when five of the leading professionals asked for double the normal £10 match fee for playing in the third and deciding Test against Australia at the Oval.

It was a sensational move and its timing rocked a complacent Establishment to its core. On Saturday, August 8, the *Life* announced with typical understatement:

> In connection with the England and Australia match at Kennington Oval on Monday, we are officially informed that a serious difficulty has arisen as regards the constitution of the England Eleven. Early in the week a communication was sent to the Surrey committee signed by Lohmann, Gunn, Abel, Hayward and Richardson, demanding £20 each for their services in the match.
>
> The Surrey committee, without in any way discussing the question of whether or not £20 is an excessive sum, resented the position taken up by the players and made them an offer of the same terms on which the professionals played in the England match at Manchester last month of £10 and expenses. These terms Lohmann, Abel, Hayward and Richardson have declined to accept and, according to the latest advices, neither they nor Gunn will take part in Monday's match.

As England had won the first Test at Lord's (where Lohmann and Richardson dismissed the tourists for 53 in their first innings) and Australia had levelled the series at Old Trafford (where Lohmann did not play), everything rested on the Oval match, but the Surrey committee refused to be held to ransom on their own ground, more especially since four of the rebels (all except Nottingham's Billy Gunn) were their own players.

The *Life* backed the Club in its stand, but mindful of the fact that it was preparing to build a new pavilion at a cost of £38,000 (£3.42m), it reasoned:

> Considering what an enormous attraction cricket is at the present day and the large amount of money that is made out of the biggest matches, we do not think £20 an excessive fee on such occasions as Monday's contest for players of Abel's and Richardson's standing, but at the same time we cannot approve of the action now taken by the Surrey professionals...
>
> If the leading professionals of all counties had, at the beginning of the season, made a requisition to the MCC and the Lancashire and Surrey committees that the fee in the three test matches should be £20 per man we should have been glad to back them up, but to raise the question of terms in the third match after taking the ordinary fee in the first two seems to us an ill-judged and illogical proceeding.

The 'strike' was the main story in all the London papers over the weekend when the reasons for the revolt were discussed in depth. The consensus from a wide range of interested parties was that the payments made to Grace (who, it was said, was to receive £50 for the match) and other top amateurs were the source of the problem.

By Monday the situation had been partially resolved as Bobby Abel, Tom Richardson and Tom Hayward had buckled under the pressure and, having "placed themselves without reserve in the hands of the Surrey committee," were reinstated in the team. But then another crisis arose from an unexpected quarter.

The great 'WG' had taken umbrage that the Surrey committee had not issued a denial regarding statements made in the press, and he made it clear that he would not play in the match until they did. The crucial Test was rapidly developing into a farce before a ball had been bowled. There was only one thing to be done. Charles Alcock, the long-time secretary of Surrey and an old friend of Grace, put his conscience to one side and issued a statement that would be the envy of any Downing Street spin-doctor:

> The Committee of the Surrey County Cricket Club have observed paragraphs in the Press respecting amounts alleged to be paid or promised to Dr W G Grace for playing in the match England v. Australia. The Committee desire to give the statement contained in those paragraphs the most unqualified contradiction.
>
> During many years on the occasion of Dr W G Grace playing at the Oval at the request of the Committee of the Surrey County Cricket Club in the matches of Gentlemen v. Players and England v. Australia, Dr Grace has received the sum of £10 per match to cover his expenses of coming to and remaining in London during the three days. Beyond this amount Dr Grace has not received, directly or indirectly, one farthing for playing in any match at the Oval.

With Grace mollified and an improvement in the wet and windy weather, play finally got underway at 4.55pm and the day ended with England on 69 for 1 – the fallen wicket belonged to Dr Grace who was out for 24. Nor was the beefy 48-year-old able to do any better in a disastrous second innings when he managed just nine runs before he was clean bowled and England were all out for 84. All appeared to be lost before two professionals, Bobby Peel (6 for 23) and Jack Hearne (4 for 19), saved the match and won the series by bowling out the Aussies for just 44 on the rain-ruined wicket.

On the same day, Cook had his first chance to air his views on the dispute. Predicting it was "but the thin end of the wedge" in the payments question, he claimed the spirit of the game was being destroyed by the mercenary attitude of certain amateurs and clubs:

> One of England's leading patrons of cricket lately said that the game is rapidly becoming 'unreasonable in its expenditure, immoral and selfish in its tendencies, and, worst of all, dishonest and unclean in its traffic'. A formidable indictment indeed, but who can gainsay the statement?
>
> The grandest of games, which has given pleasure to generation after generation, has now become, to all intents and purposes, a mere moneymaking affair. Gate money is now the prevailing factor where once the love of sport held sway, and it is a fact long known that many of our leading amateurs make a pretty penny out of it year after year...
>
> Nobody desires or expects your average amateur to play in representative or county matches without reasonable expenses, for, in that case, those not too well endowed with this world's goods would, perforce, go to the wall. But are our amateur cracks content with reasonable expenses? Is it not notorious that very many of them receive an amount per match out of all proportion to the term 'reasonable expenses' – enough, in fact, to satisfy the claims of two or three professionals?...

George Lohmann. – © [Popperfoto]/Getty Images

If cricket is to resolve itself into a matter of £. s. d., let all share equally alike say I. All very well for one gentleman to talk of 'the arrogance and extravagance of the professional', but he knows very well that he himself could not afford to devote most of every succeeding week to cricket, etc. as he now does 'on bare expenses alone'. The knife cuts both ways.

By quoting Grace and pointing an accusing finger at him, Cook was charged with personalising the matter, a charge he refuted the following week when he insisted:

…as the question has attained national proportions it must be thoroughly thrashed out. It is not one of individuals altogether, but of principle, yet, if the cap fits, well and good even though it be Dr Grace or anybody else. It would please me immensely if some dozen of our leading amateurs including 'WG' could honestly say that they had never received one penny beyond actual expenses during their career. But can they? … it certainly behoves the MCC to look into the matter as soon as may be – following suit to the Football Association and the AAA – for the future of cricket is at stake.

In his next column Cook had the backing of some grey-bearded wisdom as he related:

For many weeks past I have been endeavouring to emphasise the opinions of *modern* cricketers as regards the urgent necessity of divers reforms ere another season. As luck would have it, I got an idea of what our *veterans* think the other day, for at a recent cricket match of note I found myself seated cheek by jowl with a whole posse of ancient warriors, including Jackson of All-England and Kent fame … it was interesting and pleasing to learn that these old-time worthies, men who bore the brunt of cricket from years agone, are quite in unison with those who fain would see many and speedy reforms in cricket government nowadays.

I am afraid the ears of our gentlemen amateurs (?) must have tingled, for they were spoken of with scant respect by more than one. Indeed, they all seemed to think, with most other people, that in the all-absorbing question of payment – 'expenses' if you like – the MCC has practised disingenuousness and encouraged injustice.

The charges levelled against cricket's ruling body from both inside and outside the game finally began to have their effect, and a month later Cook remarked:

I note with great satisfaction that the MCC authorities are at length awakening from their long spell of inaction as regards the best interests of cricket. They sadly wanted waking up, that's certain, and the only question now is whether they are beginning to arouse to their responsibilities a trifle too late. For others, besides myself, now openly accuse them of lamentable apathy and join in one's condemnation of the lack of system in cricket legislation.

'We revere the MCC but take no notice of its dictums'; 'the present cricketers are like a flock of sheep without a shepherd, each goes his own way, in some cases irrationally, but unchecked'; 'The MCC has seldom done anything to earn either respect or allegiance'.

Such are a few of the very latest opinions of prominent patrons of the game, not mudslingers, mark you, and who can gainsay any one of them? … A proposal has emanated from high quarters that a constituted governing body, representative of all the counties, shall be instituted at once; for only then, it is urged, shall we get anything like management.*

Most of us have a sort of reverence for the MCC and would ten times rather let its council manage affairs than anybody else, but it must be one thing or the other. Either the MCC must stand up and assert itself as a ruling body once and for all upon the lines of other kindred organisations, or it must give place to some sort of elective council in the manner proposed. At present our greatest of national games is under no form of systematic government whatever. It rests with themselves.

---

* A similar proposal had been made by the *Sporting Life* as early as 1863 when it called for the setting up of a 'cricket parliament' to replace the MCC as it urged: "Some more comprehensible and responsible form of government than that which has hitherto existed for the regulation of the national game of cricket has become absolutely necessary." Yet it was not until 1904 that an Advisory County Cricket Committee was formed along the lines it had advocated. The new body ran the county game separately from, although still strongly influenced by, the MCC. In 1969, when the game in Britain was given a formal constitution to enable it to attract public money, a Cricket Council was established, comprising two main bodies, the Test and County Cricket Board and the National Cricket Association. The MCC's place on the Council derived from its traditional role as lawmaker and owner of Lord's; the game's chief source of revenue. A further change in 1997 saw the replacement of the Cricket Council by the England and Wales Cricket Board, which has overall responsibility for the game 'from the playground to the Test arena'. The MCC still has a seat on the management board.

In conclusion, 'Old Blue' added a postscript to the original dispute as he bade farewell to the 'amateur' colonials with the provocative observation:

So, the Australian cricketers who left our shores last week are to receive £700 [*£63,000*] per man as his share of the proceeds of the recent tour. This – upon the highest authority – affords food for serious reflection.

Under the threat of being replaced by the proposed governing body, the MCC did reassert some of its authority on the game, but did little to address the thorny problem of shamateurism and it was not until 1963 that the distinction between amateurs and professionals was finally abolished. Nevertheless, the bold protest made by Lohmann and Gunn did result in professional Test-match players having their fee increased to £20 in 1898 after their cause had been taken up by the outstanding Yorkshire and England captain, Lord Hawke, but by then it was too late for George Lohmann.

Blue-eyed and fair-haired, with shoulders hewn from Royal Oak, he had been England's outstanding bowler for almost a decade. His high, deceptive deliveries had taken over 200 wickets in each of three consecutive seasons (1888-90), while his record of 112 Test wickets for an average 10.75 runs in 18 matches speaks for itself.

A dashing batsman and a fine slip-fielder, whose career was checked only by the onset of tuberculosis in 1892, he spent over two years in South Africa in an attempt to regain his health and returned to play for Surrey and England in 1895, but 1896 was to be his final home season and at the time of the Oval Test he probably realised he was sacrificing his last chance to play for his country.

His stand was, therefore, all the more heroic and he was much mourned when he finally succumbed to the dread disease five years later at the age of 36. In paying tribute to a man he knew well, Cook wrote:

Personally 'Our George' was immensely popular both in England and abroad, while professionally, it is not hyperbole to say he was the very finest all-round cricketer Surrey ever had. He was 'thorough' to the backbone, and to see him gradually luring some of the best batsmen to their own destruction in the field was a revelation to most.

Finally, he was one of Nature's own gentlemen, although a professional, and did much to raise the tone and standard of his colleagues generally. He inveighed against the 'shamateur' in and out of season as the *Sporting Life* correspondence files can testify, and was forever protesting against the tactics of sundry of this order.

Meanwhile, the amazing Grace continued to bat on in his own indomitable way until a year before his death at the age of 67 in 1915. The following year Theodore Cook, by then editor-in-chief of *The Field* and still a regular contributor to the *Life*, received a knighthood for his services to sport and the community.

Howzat!

THE AMERICAN INVASION

THE FINAL YEARS of the nineteenth century witnessed some revolutionary changes in journalism and in racing. In Fleet Street, newspapers were transformed by the introduction of the Linotype machine, which, as its name implies, was able to set a line of type automatically as opposed to the age-old process of making up each line by hand.

Keyboard operators could set type eight times faster than the old compositors and the ease of the procedure resulted in papers taking on a new look as page layouts assumed a much greater importance. The popular press led the way with T P O'Connor's *The Star* (1888) and Alfred Harmsworth's *Daily Mail* (1896) carrying an attractive mix of short, easy-to-read news items under eye-catching, multi-deck headlines.

An American invention, the Linotype machine changed the face of the British press forever in much the same way as another 'import' from the States transformed racing – it, or rather he, was a diminutive young jockey by the name of Tod Sloan.

James Forman Sloan – unkindly called 'Toad' as a child (a nickname he converted to 'Tod' asap) – first saw light of day in Indiana in 1874, but was a long way from being a natural-born horseman. Initially afraid of horses, he finally followed his brother Cassius ('Cash') into racing but his early career was far from auspicious.

When he was not falling off, he was being run away with and, at the age of 20, he was on the verge of quitting the game when, more by accident than design, he found that horses ran better for him when he crouched forward over their withers instead of sitting upright in the saddle as the conventional style demanded.

Sloan was not the first to adopt this 'forward seat' in America, but it suited him so well that within a year he had gone from being a jockey whose reputation was so bad it was said that trainers only put him up to get their horses handicapped (i.e. beaten), to one who was in demand for exactly the opposite reason.

As his strike rate soared to an impressive 30 per cent in 1897, the formidable US stock market speculator, James R Keene, asked him to go to England to ride his St Cloud II in the Cesarewitch and Cambridgeshire, a double the owner had landed with Foxhall in 1881. Sloan jumped at the chance, but when he made his debut at Newmarket on the eve of the Cesarewitch, the 'experts' in the stands were not impressed.

He was inevitably compared to the black American, Willie Simms, who had introduced the crouch style to Britain two years earlier when he created a minor sensation at Newmarket's Craven meeting by winning on his first ride, Eau Gallie – one of 20 horses shipped over from the States at the beginning of the year by Richard Croker and Mike Dwyer; two of the biggest owner-gamblers on the American circuit.

When the shock of Simms' initial victory had worn off and he started to get beaten on horses made favourite by the weight of their owners' money, his style began to be ridiculed by the press and public alike. He was dubbed 'the Christy Minstrel' after the Newmarket trainer, Joe Cannon, first saw him on a horse and observed dryly: "He looks a bit lonely up there without a banjo!"[1]

The *Life* was not as scathing as some, but when Simms was beaten on a hot favourite at the Guineas meeting, its reporter remarked:

It was both instructive and amusing to see, when pitted in a finish against such a master of the art as 'Morny' Cannon, how bunched up and helpless to assist his mount the darkie was except by needless punishment of the whip, and those who have gone into raptures on the donkey-boy style must admit the superiority of the time-honoured mode.

Despite partnering three more winners, Simms was unable to get any outside rides and later that summer he returned to America from where he gave his critics a two-digit salute by riding two of the next three Kentucky Derby winners. It was, however, still a biased jury that judged Sloan when he failed to make the frame on his first ride in England. The *Life's* reporter at Newmarket noted that Sloan rode in a "more bunchy style than Simms":

…as his mount comes head-on to you, the jockey's cap is hardly discernible above the horse's ears. And with our insular prejudice to overcome he failed to create a favourable impression on Libra, who steered an erratic course.

The 'insular' scribe had no reason to revise his opinion when St Cloud II was well beaten the following day, but two weeks later Sloan made his critics sit up and take note when he opened his account in decisive fashion at the Houghton meeting. The occasion was doubly memorable since it saw all four races on the first day started by 'the Australian machine' (a two-strand, barrier gate) which, after a series of trials, was gradually introduced over the next few years to replace the flag start.

Well-used to a similar starting mechanism in America, Sloan got a flyer on his mount, Quibble II, and made all to win by six lengths, while he was beaten just a neck on his only other ride that day, when he "didn't strike one as getting so much out of him as he might have done with a more backward seat." When the jockey was beaten a head on St Cloud II in a blanket finish to the Cambridgeshire two days later he was again damned with faint praise by the *Life's* man, who insinuated the American had dropped his hands in the dying strides, allowing his mount to be pipped on the post by Kempton Cannon on Comfrey:

…if the American method may possibly have its advantage in driving runners quickly away from the post, very few who saw the last few strides of the finish would declare against the English system of sitting down in the saddle for the final tussle. At the same time … all unprejudiced observers must allow Tod Sloan to be an artiste in his own line. Furthermore, this jockey made many friends by his cheery, plucky way of accepting defeat and it is much to be regretted if he really did ease St Cloud II just the wrong side of the post under the impression that he had the race in hand.

Whether Sloan was guilty of such a crucial error is a moot point, but he certainly wasn't 'cheery' when the result went against him. He was spitting feathers! Many years later the judge's decision still rankled as he declared, in a ghosted autobiography littered with factual errors: "I shall always believe – in fact I *know* – that Comfrey, who was given the race, was only third; Sandia being second, three-quarters of a length from me."[2]

But neither a dubious decision nor the carping criticism deterred Sloan. The pasting he had received from the American press in his early years had made him immune to such attacks and he was determined to see out the rest of the season in England.

At first rides were hard to come by, but he made good use of those that came his way and it soon became clear he had something special to offer. Punters were quick to latch onto him and on the final day of the season at Manchester he rewarded them in spades when he won on four of his five mounts. Like the ranks of Tuscany, even the *Life* could scarce forbear to cheer as it remarked:

> The hero of the day was the clever little American who promises to become as popular an idol with the British public as the late, lamented Fred Archer ... the Lancashire folk 'Sloaned' themselves on each of his mounts, careless of what the animal might be.

The 188-1 accumulator took Sloan's strike rate in England to 34 per cent with 20 winners from 58 mounts and, even more importantly, it boosted his bankroll by no small amount. The fact that it was against the rules for jockeys to bet did not worry him. He had always been a gambler and, for a while at least, he was a successful one.

At the time, racing in the States was under attack from a strong anti-gambling lobby and there were fears it would be wiped out altogether. From a peak of 314 racetracks listed in *Goodwin's Official Turf Guide* for 1897, the number was drastically reduced by State legislation until only 25 tracks remained in 1908.

The sport's big players could see which way the wind was blowing and when Sloan – who had stopped off in Monte Carlo to play up his luck on the roulette tables – arrived back home in January 1898 the tales of his triumphs gave many in racing an urge for transatlantic travel. Breeders, owners and trainers saw England as a safe haven where valuable bloodstock could be unloaded and rich pickings reaped.

The American thoroughbred had already proved itself more than capable of holding its own in the land of its forefathers. Richard Ten Broeck, who had owned the mighty Lexington for most of his racing career before selling him on to become the most influential North American stallion of the nineteenth century, brought a few horses to England in 1857 and soon made his mark when Pryoress featured in a historic triple dead-heat for the Cesarewitch which she won in the run-off.

Ten Broeck, a former Mississippi riverboat gambler and owner of the famous Metairie racetrack in New Orleans, also landed the Goodwood Stakes (1859) and Cup (1861) with Starke, while in 1881 the American-bred, owned and trained Iroquois was sent out by Jacob Pincus to win the Derby and St Leger for the tobacco millionaire, Pierre Lorillard.

In the same year, Foxhall, also bred in the States but not entered in the classics, proved an even better horse than Iroquois when he gained victories in the Grand Prix de Paris, the Cesarewitch and Cambridgeshire before going on to win the Ascot Gold Cup in 1882.

During this period, a number of American jockeys came and went without making any impact, but from the day J F Sloan first unfurled the Star-spangled Banner on Newmarket Heath the manual of English jockeyship, which had been sacrosanct for two centuries and more, was destined to be torn up and rewritten before the old queen died.

Not that the ingrained convictions of generations of horsemen were swept away in one season. At first the cocky little American was viewed as a flash in the pan; just another colourful thread in the rich tapestry of racing, but even traditional diehards were forced to question their beliefs when he returned to England in the autumn of 1898 to ride for Lord William Beresford and Pierre Lorillard, whose horses were trained by the Newmarket-based American, Jack Huggins.

Bill Beresford VC (he won his gong for saving the life of a fellow soldier during the Zulu wars in 1879) was the third son of the Marquis of Waterford and, like his brothers Marcus and Charles, was a fast-living, fun-loving socialite. He had taken Sloan under his wing in 1897 and despite their vastly different backgrounds the two men were kindred spirits united by their love of gambling, and gambling was what the American invasion was all about.

When Sloan set sail for England on the ss *Deutschland* in September 1898, he was accompanied by a motley collection of gamblers, touts and hangers-on who felt they could fleece the British bookies by following their little man. They were right, and for the next few years the Ring was hammered by fair means and foul.

The plunder was immense as Sloan led the charge at Newmarket's first October meeting where he pulled everything out of his bag of tricks as he coaxed and cajoled, rousted and romped his way to victory on 12 of his 16 mounts. Five of his winners came on the final day of the meeting. He had been due to ride at Alexandra Park the following day, but "owing to indisposition" was unable to fulfil his engagements! The *Life's* 'insular' reporter must have been similarly indisposed due to the large portion of humble pie he had to eat since it was Theodore Cook who filed the report that afternoon:

> 'Twas indeed a marvellous record on the little man's part, showing, as it did, that he can ride a finish as well as wait in front, and those who had hitherto seen him only sitting still on a winner were compelled to admit that he can finish with the best ... and irony gave way to admiration of the exponent of the new style.

Sloan's onslaught came in the same week as a draft of 42 yearling fillies, sent over from California by James B Haggin, came under the hammer at Newmarket. The prices they fetched were described as "simply extraordinary" although an aggregate of 7,250gns (£685,125) was no more than loose change to Haggin who, having made his fortune as a lawyer during the Californian gold rush, had built up the largest stud in the world – the 44,000-acre Rancho del Paso, which, at its peak, boasted some 2,000 thoroughbreds.

The American invasion was by now well and truly underway and Elliot Hutchins, the *Life's* Special Commissioner, was just one of many who paid tribute to its leader:

> Sloan's judgement in race-riding is marvellous. He keeps his opponents on the stretch – a horseman thorough from beginning to end. Whether his system will revolutionise jockeyship is another matter. But certain it is that our professors have much to learn as regards judgement of pace, which is at the little American's fingertips.

Cook, writing in his column the following week, was more cautious in his appraisal. In his uninhibited style, as distinctive as that of his subject, he observed:

> So Tod Sloan is the man of the hour. He has certainly 'arrived' with a vengeance and (according to some folk) his position of Triton among the minnows is assured so far as English jockeys go. Others go in for hero-worship on a scale that would even have made Carlyle sit up – and he was pretty smart that way. In a paper now before me I see him described as 'an Archer, Fordham, Wood and 'Morny' Cannon all rolled into one'.
>
> My yes! Against this view of the position in general I take no objection. He is emphatically a fine horseman and a grand judge of pace and conditions withal; moreover *he is right in luck just now*. Whether he is going to out-ride, out-manoeuvre and generally play skittles with our best English jockeys, however, is quite a different story. Frankly, I don't believe it; unless, as alleged, his style is altogether superior to our English ditto.

One gentleman seems to think Sloan's style so (mathematically) superior that it makes a difference in his favour of a stone or two. We shall see. If so, the solution of the problem is easy enough. Our young jockeys must adopt the American style of riding, and that speedily.

And that, more or less, is what happened. A few of the old school either couldn't or wouldn't adapt, but there were plenty who did for it is in the nature of jockeys to be followers of fashion. It was not just a matter of redistributing their weight over the horse's centre of gravity by pulling up the stirrup leathers, shortening the reins and leaning forward over the withers (which also reduced wind resistance); it involved a complete change of riding tactics.

The traditional way of race-riding had evolved out of the races Charles II staged at Newmarket during his reign (1660-85) when his King's Plates were run as four-mile heats, the winner being the first horse to win two heats. Because it would often take four or five heats (16 or 20 miles) to decide a contest, horses did not cover the full distance at racing pace; rather a sedate hack-canter would dictate affairs until the closing stages when the jockeys would unleash their mounts in a mad dash for the winning post.

A less extreme version of these tactics was still employed in the 1890s and Sloan took full advantage of it since he, like all American jockeys, had been taught to ride against the clock which governed the pace races were run at on the uniform, level, Stateside tracks. Taking distance and ground conditions into account, he was able to regulate a horse's pace instinctively in order to give it the best chance of getting from A to B in the fastest possible time.

Many of his races were won from the front. He would let his horse bowl along at its natural cruising speed as he counted off the furlongs, while his rivals restrained their mounts as they waited to pounce at the finish. But when they did make their move they often found that Sloan, in the best traditions of the poker player, had kept a little bit extra up his sleeve and was able to hold them at bay.

His dominance over the home division was so evident that, in the run-up to the 1898 Cesarewitch meeting, an advertising tipster in the *Life* stated his service provided "a boon and a blessing to would-be Sloan supporters". The 'boon' was simply that he was offering his clients a daily list of the horses the midget money-making machine would be riding at Newmarket – all for the price of 15s (£67.50)!*

This, in itself, was a mighty compliment to Sloan's ability, but the ultimate accolade came from one of his English rivals, Fred Rickaby, who, when asked for his opinion of the American replied: "If I were an owner I should not run a horse unless Sloan rode it."[3]

By the end of the season Sloan had notched up 43 winners from 98 mounts – a truly awesome strike rate of 43.9% – and at the Gimcrack Club dinner that December no less a figure than Lord Durham applauded the positive influence the American was having on race-riding.

In praising his judgement of pace, the straight-talking Earl could not resist having a dig at the outmoded tactics of the English jockeys. He declared that very few of them had any idea of what pace meant as they seemed to ignore the basic fact that the horse which could cover the allotted distance in the fastest time would win the race. Sloan, he said, had shown them how a horse should be ridden in a race.

Such views were all too much for the editor of the *Life*. George Lowe was aghast. "I very much question whether some of his Lordship's opinions will be endorsed by the majority of Englishmen,"

---

* The *Life* and its contemporaries did not start to publish riding arrangements until the early 1920s and it was not until 1992 that the Jockey Club brought in the overnight declaration of jockeys.

he wrote indignantly as he gave voice to an ancient insularity that had long pervaded the Turf:

> It has been a somewhat strong belief during, perhaps, two centuries that England is quite unsurpassed in the matter of every kind of horsemanship. To get along over a country, to ride difficult horses, and more particularly to ride a race, has been thought to be the veritable birthright of the Englishman; and so to be told by such an authority as Lord Durham that we must learn this and that from America, sounds something like what the little boys used to say in the street about teaching your grandmother to suck eggs.
>
> I had hitherto thought that the Sloan furore was a bit overdone, but to hear a very distinguished member of the Jockey Club declare that the presence of Sloan was a good thing for this country is something more than I quite like on purely patriotic lines.
>
> I am old enough to have seen Alfred Day ride, both in the hunting field on a favourite hunter he had called Stonehenge, and also in landing Mincepie for the [1856] Oaks, when the second, Melissa, with a cross-country sort of jock on her, should have won by two or three lengths.
>
> Alfred Day was absolute perfection in seat and hands, and the way he dropped on an opponent in the last fifty yards could never be forgotten.[*] I have also thought that Wells was the most elegant horseman imaginable. He was long in the leg, but very perfectly made and his combination with even a little horse like Rosicrucian was the very poetry of grace. Then there was another beautiful rider called Quinton I used to admire, and the freedom of Fordham, the easy manner of Tom Cannon and the vigour of Jem Goater did much to make me fairly love racing.
>
> It may be said, 'Yes, but these were jockeys of a past generation and they are gone'. I admit it, but I have often thought that Morny Cannon resembles both his great uncle, Alfred Day, and his father Tom Cannon and that in judgement of pace, style and grace he is very little inferior to either.

Lowe went on to praise Jack Watts for his 1896 Derby win on the Prince of Wales's Persimmon before he concluded defiantly:

> I can admit that Sloan is a very good jockey to win races ... He has particularly good hands and does not pull horses about, but to even think of him as a race-rider with the names I have mentioned is altogether out of place. We admire our great jockeys for their elegance and grace; are we to exchange their style and everything for a pattern that resembles very much a monkey on a rail?

The short answer to that was 'yes'. The new style was initially adopted and then adapted to suit the wide variety of British courses, not that Sloan was one to travel the country in pursuit of winners. While he had a natural affinity with horses and was especially effective on a highly-strung animal or one that had been soured by too many hard races, he lacked the hunger that had driven past champions such as Archer.

Sometimes he would not ride from one week to the next as he preferred to spend his days hobnobbing with the rich and famous. A good shot and a decent bridge player, he was on everyone's guest list, and to ease his entry into high society he changed his middle name from Forman to Todhunter

---

[*] George Lowe might have been conservative in his views, but he was obviously a fair judge of genealogy whether he was writing about foxhounds or jockeys for, in citing Alfred Day as a perfect exponent of his art, he was, after all, talking about Lester Piggott's great, great, granduncle!

Tod Sloan, the dandy Yankee.

in order to avoid the embarrassment of explaining away his nickname.

His personality was reflected in his dress-sense which proclaimed him to be a swell of the first order. Fastidious to a degree, he had his own valet and would take two or three trunks of clothes with him whenever he went on a journey of any length. Included in his luggage were at least a dozen pairs of shoes (size 1½), a case containing about £5,000 (£450,000) worth of diamond-studded tiepins, and a ready supply of large Havana cigars.

When in England he based himself not in Newmarket, but at London's fashionable Hotel Cecil in the Strand, which also became the haunt of major American plungers such as the bookmaker Riley Grannan, John 'Bet-a-Million' Gates and young Charlie Dwyer whose father, Mike, had fallen on hard times since his trip to England in 1895.

Sloan claimed he had little to do with these high-rollers, but he made no attempt to hide his dealings with bookmakers at the races – a blatant breach of the rules that was highlighted by the radical weekly journal, *Truth*, in the same month as Lord Durham had praised Sloan at the Gimcrack dinner. Its racing correspondent asked:

Is the rule against jockeys betting to be suspended or ignored in the case of Sloan? Any English rider about whose betting transactions there was such open gossip would quickly find himself off the Turf altogether and I really do not understand why there should be one law for our own jockeys and another for Sloan or any other foreigner.

When Sloan's application for a riding licence is sent in to the authorities next spring it may be hoped that the stewards will make him understand exactly upon what conditions it is granted to him, and that if those conditions are in any way infringed it will, *ipso facto*, be withdrawn.

That the Jockey Club did not act on the matter for another two years was mystifying, particularly as the *Racing Calendar* published its usual annual warning notice to jockeys a few weeks after the *Truth* article had appeared:

The Stewards, having on previous occasions observed that many jockeys have been in the habit of betting on horse racing and/or receiving presents in connection with races from persons other than the owner of the horse they ride in such races, give notice that such practices will not be tolerated and any jockey who may be proved to their satisfaction to have any interest in any racehorse or to have been engaged in any betting transactions, or otherwise to have disregarded this notice, will have his license at once withdrawn.

Typically, Sloan ignored this warning when he returned to England for the start of the 1899 season since, in this one respect at least, he felt he was no different to any other jockey – they all liked to bet – besides which, his immense popularity with the public had added an air of arrogance to his natural cockiness. Just like Fred Archer, he felt he was untouchable and could do as he liked.

This was a dangerous stance to take at a time when a significant section of society still expected a jockey to know his place which was no more than that of a well-paid servant. This, in essence, was the message Theodore Cook put across in his column as he replied to a reader who had written to him on the subject in March 1899. Referring to the way the dandy Yankee had been fêted in the popular press the previous year, he wrote in his usual forthright style:

To read the gush about Sloan, vouchsafed almost daily – the type of trousers he wore, the number of visitors he had, and even what cigars he smoked – was almost nauseating ... Sloan is a very genial fellow and a fine horseman, but that is no reason why he should be set up as a god for the admiring crowd to worship.

My correspondent thinks that this sort of thing lowers the Turf and he is not far out ... Quoth he, 'that our jockeys should be encouraged to smoke cigars, play billiards and volunteer opinions without restraint in the presence of their betters of either sex, is one of the saddest anomalies of our modern civilisation. The day is at hand when the people of England will pay little respect to men and women with handles to their names who do not respect themselves'.

This was not far off indicting the Prince of Wales who had an easy-going racecourse relationship with the jockey and acted on his advice when it came to betting. That advice proved well worth following in 1899 when Sloan enjoyed his best British season despite picking up a three-week suspension (which he turned into a six-week holiday in America) for disobedience at the start of a race at Sandown.

His 108 winners from 345 rides placed him fifth in the championship table behind Sam Loates (160 winners from 727 rides), but he was now having to face increasing competition from his own compatriots. Not only was he up against the Reiff brothers, Lester and Johnny, who had arrived in England with the American trainer Enoch Wishard that summer, but in 1900 he had to contend with two former US champions in 'Skeets' Martin and Danny Maher, as well as others of lesser rank including the whip-happy Ben Rigby, Alex Covington, Eddie Jones, Clem Jenkins and Peter Maguire.

One for all and all for one, this happy band of brothers saw out the old century in style as they dominated the finish of race after race. At Royal Ascot, Sloan, Martin and the Reiff brothers won 16 of the 28 races. Tod topped the table with six victories headed by his 100-7 Gold Cup winner, Merman, who only ran in the race after he had worked his charms on the horse's owner, the actress Lily Langtry.

Sloan skipped Goodwood, preferring to return to America for his favourite Saratoga meeting, but his absence only emphasised the Yankee dominance as the Reiff brothers won 12 of the 25 races, and Lester went on to end the season as champion jockey. The first American to win the title, his 143 winners from 553 mounts placed him six in front of Sam Loates (809 mounts), while brother Johnny was third with 124 winners. Sloan had 82 winners from 310 rides to tie for sixth place with Morny Cannon.

But amid all this star-spangled success, there was the ever-present evidence of high-stakes betting and much talk of doping and race-fixing together with an increasing number of stewards' inquiries into rough riding and inconsistent running. Some of the erratic riding stemmed from the Americans' inability to balance their horses on the undulating courses or to correct them when they started to roll about under pressure. But on other occasions the tactics were deliberate and downright dangerous, as when Sloan carved up Morny Cannon in the Portland Plate at Doncaster that September.

Riding Lucknow for the Prince of Wales, Sloan repeatedly hampered Cannon on the champion sprinter, Eager, who was just beaten in a desperate finish. Eager's trainer complained to the stewards about Sloan's riding, but in deference to the winning owner, he stopped short of lodging an official objection.

To pacify Eager's connections the stewards suspended Sloan for one day, but allowed Lucknow to keep the race as they did not want to spoil the meeting for 'Good old Teddy', whose ill-tempered Diamond Jubilee had just landed the Triple Crown by winning the St Leger to complete an outstanding year for his owner, who had also won the Grand National with Ambush II.

Shamefully, the officials' pandering to royalty was matched by the supine way both Elliot Hutchins and George Lowe reported on the race. Not only did they fail to comment on Sloan's reckless riding, but they also omitted to mention that he had been suspended. Hutchins even praised the tiny prima donna who "shone out quite at his best when on Lucknow".

The *Yorkshire Post* saw things very differently. Referring to the rule governing the draw position, its reporter observed that Sloan…

has taken upon himself to disregard Rule 138 … he generally makes for the inside just as Archer used to do at a time when there was no rule against such a proceeding. Immediately the flag fell he took Lucknow across to Eager and not once but three times, did M Cannon have to pull Eager up. Eventually Sloan found himself where he wanted to be, on the rails … [*and when Eager made his challenge*] Sloan pulled Lucknow out from the rails and bumped Eager who had been separated from him by a couple of yards, knocking him out of his stride. This gave Lucknow the race.

A month later at Newmarket's second October meeting, there was even greater cause to question the tactics of the Americans when several supposed good things were turned over. Lester Reiff, in particular, was 'hooted' by the crowd after he had been beaten on two consecutive odds-on shots, Escurial and Americus. The running of Americus in his match against Sonatura in the Challenge Stakes was inexplicable. It should have been a virtual walkover for the Richard Croker-owned favourite, who was meeting his rival on 27lb better terms than in the Portland Plate, but he was beaten four lengths after Sonatura had been significantly backed.

Even Hutchins felt obliged to remark that the afternoon's racing "never will conjure up pleasant recollections". Alfred Watson put it more bluntly in the *Badminton Magazine* as he reported: "criticisms, freely passed on trainers and jockeys, were extended to the Stewards of the Jockey Club who were derisively christened 'the Three Blind Mice'."

The stewards did, in fact, inquire into both races, but took no action against Reiff although, in the case of Escurial, they did issue him with what amounted to a public warning in the *Racing Calendar* which stated: "though the stewards were not altogether satisfied, they did not consider that the evidence was such as to convince them that the horse had been pulled, or to cause them to withdraw L Reiff's licence."

Two weeks later 'the three blind mice' were presented with their evidence in Braille when Sloan rode the French horse, Codoman, in the Cambridgeshire. It was no secret that the jockey had backed his mount at long odds to win an enormous sum (£66,000 = £6m, according to his autobiography) and that some of his compatriots were in on the gamble. While Danny Maher appeared to make too much use of the 3-1 favourite, The Raft, Lester Reiff gave the third favourite, Good Luck, too much to do – "there seemed to be an error of judgement somewhere" (*Sporting Chronicle*) – but Codoman was still beaten fair and square by the Irish raider, Berrill.

Trained by Phillie Behan whose brother, Jack, had sent out Irish Ivy to win the race the previous year, Berrill was ridden by the up-and-coming John Thompson who, Hutchins noted, was "a jockey of remarkable latter-day improvement since adopting the forward American seat."

Sloan had thus been beaten at his own game and, as with Archer, the Cambridgeshire proved to be his downfall. On the following day he was interviewed by the stewards with regard to the bets he had on the race and the fact that an American gambler, who had no connection with Codoman, had promised him a large 'present' if the horse won. Sloan admitted to both charges and considered himself reprimanded. No further action was taken at the time and he rode out the remainder of the meeting, winning the final race on the 13-8 favourite, Encombe. It was to be his last ride in England.

He had already decided to finish the season early so he could enjoy a few weeks on the town before returning to America, but by this time a controversy had broken out in the press over some disparaging remarks Lord Durham had made on the inability of the stewards to curb the wayward ways of the American jockeys.

This criticism was decidedly rich coming from a man who had publicly praised Sloan just two years earlier and had completed his three-year term as a Jockey Club steward only that April. Sam Pitman, the racing correspondent of *The Times*, was quick to take Durham to task for "casting a slur upon his late colleagues," a charge 'Determined Jack' answered in a letter to the paper. In it he asserted:

> If the remarks I have recently made are 'a slur upon my late colleagues' they are none the less a true description of the present state of the English Turf, and no practical racing man will accuse me of want of courage or of timorous discretion if I decline to make myself responsible for the inaction of our Turf authorities.

Durham went on to quote a number of instances of "unscrupulous riding" by the Americans and named Sloan, Martin and Rigby as the chief offenders, although he did concede that Danny Maher "rides very well and seems a most respectable boy". He also referred to several cases of inconsistent running, which he felt should have been looked into, and in particular, he cited the suspect riding of Lester Reiff

In the *Life*, Theodore Cook sided with the slighted for whom he had an affinity since he had spent several years in the States as a postgraduate tutor to Ralph Pulitzer, the son of Joseph, the proprietor and editor of the popular *New York World*. Cook, who learnt as much from Pulitzer senior about journalism as he taught junior of the ancient classics, described Durham's attack on the Americans as a bolt from the blue and observed:

> Most people will agree with the late President Lincoln that the value of an opinion altogether depends upon the sort of person holding it. Had any faddist ventured upon such a scathing indictment of Turf procedure, for instance, what sportsman would have cared one two-penny cuss? As it is, Lord Durham's words have to be considered and weighed most carefully...
>
> Read the context of his remarks. Frankly vouchsafed, he dubs American jockeys a very blackguardly lot and American trainers, etc very little better. Now this is a serious charge and (I say emphatically) *not justified by fact*. It would be most unjust to call a flock of sheep wolves because there happens to be one or two of the vulpine family amongst them masquerading as vegetarians.
>
> So in the case of American jockeys. Some of them may be 'outsiders', but are our own English jockeys all satisfactory? ... Throwing stones is a dangerous pastime. *They are apt to rebound.*

A few weeks later, as the controversy escalated and doping was being discussed openly in the press, 'Old Blue' drew upon his second-class degree in Classical Greats:

> I am aware that Dame Rumour nowadays beats the rolling stone of Sisyphus in a canter. Give a dog a bad name and we all know the consequences, but petty slander is a cruel adjunct of sport. I can authoritatively say that such slander sticks to sundry American jockeys like the shirt of Nessus – lacerating their very spirit. Others (more hardened) bear it even more philosophically than Socrates did the ducking from Xanthippe; yet, I repeat, it is cruel work ... why this sudden distrust – to put it mildly – of Yankee procedure? It isn't English, it isn't sportsmanship, it certainly isn't just.

Cook, who enjoyed swimming against the tide more than most, returned to the subject the following week when he implied that envy and malice lay behind the accusations:

> Philosophers and psychologists when they reason on human nature do not realise the enormous place which *pure spite* occupies in its motives and actions. It will be remembered that when Telemachus visited Gorenia he was generously entertained and afterwards politely asked *if he happened to be a pirate*. I cannot help thinking the American contingent has been similarly treated by many.

Pirates or not, the days of Tod Sloan, Lester Reiff and company were numbered. A week after the Cambridgeshire, Leopold de Rothschild indicated the way the wind was blowing in a letter to *The Times*:

I feel convinced that energetic measures should at once be taken to remedy the present state of the Turf, which, everyone agrees, is in anything but a satisfactory condition ... there ought to be no difficulty in dealing with jockeys who disregard the rules of racing ... if one or two of the chief offenders were severely dealt with the others would be amenable to reason.

And so Sloan's fate was finally sealed. In December a notice in the *Racing Calendar* stated that as a result of the inquiry the stewards held into the jockey's Cambridgeshire dealings they had "informed him that he need not apply for a licence to ride". They could have added 'ever again', but that was not the way things worked in 1900. The refusal to grant a licence was like a warning off; it was open-ended. There was no prescribed period of banishment; it all depended on the prevailing circumstances and how the stewards felt about it.

For Sloan the ban was to last a lifetime. He returned to England in March 1901 to ride work at Newmarket, but his most influential supporter, Bill Beresford, had died a few months earlier and with him went any hope of an early reinstatement. He reapplied for his licence in subsequent seasons, but did not help his cause by involving himself in a series of betting coups on the Continent.

In 1903 he was behind the success of Rose-de-Mai, who landed a "purely American coup" in the Prix de Diane (French Oaks) as a result of which the French authorities rather churlishly warned him off for a minor misdemeanour. The following year he rode for a short time in New Orleans, but his heart was not in it and he never made any serious attempt to resume his career in his home country.

Instead he dabbled on the peripheries of French and Belgian racing, managing horses for wealthy owners who kept him in the style to which he was accustomed. Throughout it all he courted controversy like the actresses he was so fond of and finally, in 1915, he suffered the indignity of being deported from Britain as an undesirable alien after being convicted of running an illegal gambling club in London.

His remarkable talent dissipated forever, Tod Sloan's fortunes went into inexorable decline and he died in the charity ward of Los Angeles City Hospital in 1933.* In his four seasons in England he had ridden in 811 races and won 253 of them. His UK strike rate of 31% was less than Fred Archer's (34%), but considerably better than both Lester Piggott's (24%) and Gordon Richards' (22%). Unlike them he was never a champion, but his followers always regarded him as one.

Lester Reiff, on the other hand, did win the championship, but his reign was a short one. Having survived several high-profile inquiries into his riding, he was finally warned off for stopping De Lacy, who was beaten a head by Richard Croker's Minnie Dee, ridden by brother Johnny, at Manchester in September 1901.

Remarkably, the *Life* carried the warning off notice without comment. George Lowe felt that any publicity given to the affair would simply aid the rampant Anti-Gambling League in its efforts to get betting banned, but this didn't stop 'Vigilant' from sketching in the background to the case in the *Sportsman*:

> The warning off of Lester Reiff was only what was anticipated by those who have carefully watched his riding for the last few months ... if it were worth while to do so I could give half a dozen recent instances in which his performances have been more than suspicious, the worst feature of the case being that they were foreshadowed by the state of the market. It cannot be said that he has not been

---

* A year before his death Sloan suffered a final indignity when he was arrested for violating California's anti-gambling laws by acting, for a stunt, as a starter in a turtle race! In a rare moment of humility he admitted: "My downfall was due to a swollen head and high living. I had £100,000 once and lords and ladies sought my company. I lost my money through bad friends and unfortunate speculations."[4]

given every chance; indeed, it is the opinion of most people that no English jockey would have been allowed so much rope. But there is a limit to everything and that limit has been fairly reached at last.

And the authorities were not finished, not by a long chalk. Six months later, just before the start of the Flat season, Theodore Cook's warning that the stones thrown at the Americans were liable to rebound came to pass. In a sensational double-barrelled blast, Lord Derby's jockey, Fred Rickaby, was warned off, and Otto Madden, who had succeeded Lester Reiff as champion, had his licence withdrawn.

It says much for the stewards that they were prepared to go to such lengths to clean up racing, but drastic measures had to be taken as the campaign for the suppression of betting was growing by the day. The *Calendar* notice that rocked the racing world read:

> The Stewards of the Jockey Club, when considering applications for licences to ride during the coming season, made enquiry into several cases in which jockeys were stated to have associated with persons of bad character on the Turf, and to have been guilty of offences under the Rules of Racing. At the close of the enquiry, the stewards refused F Rickaby a licence and warned him off Newmarket Heath. O Madden was refused a licence to ride, and some others were severely cautioned for association with persons of bad character.[*]

The scandal was great. Otto Madden was the second reigning champion to fall foul of the authorities in two years and he rode for Dick Marsh who trained for Edward VII – the Prince of Wales having succeeded to the throne on the death of Queen Victoria in 1901.

Fred Rickaby, from a long-established racing family, had ridden as first jockey for George Lambton's stable for the past nine years. He had won the 1896 Oaks for Lord Derby on Canterbury Pilgrim and had finished the 1901 season among the top ten jockeys with 72 winners.

Today, the story would have wiped everything else off the front page, but in 1902 it did not even merit a headline in the *Life*; instead Lowe buried the news at the bottom of his column which, as ever, led off with remarks on the weather. When he finally got around to addressing the subject his comments were risible. In an effort to play down the impact of the bombshell, he declared: "It has been expected for some time that the Jockey Club would not grant licences to Rickaby and Madden, through the fact that these jockeys had ridden for men convicted of grave frauds."

Indeed? Were, then, Lord Derby and the King's trainer complicit in employing jockeys who rode for these criminals?

Poor Lowe, who doubtlessly had the *unconvicted* Richard Croker[†] in mind when he spoke of 'grave frauds', waffled on naively:

---

[*] Madden had his licence restored in 1903 when he quickly re-established himself as a champion, a title he retained in 1904. Rickaby had obviously associated with even worse characters than his colleagues since his ban lasted for three years. He resumed riding in 1905, but unlike Madden or Charlie Wood, he was never able to regain the patronage he once enjoyed and after managing only 26 winners in four seasons he retired to live in Hove, near Brighton, where he died at the age of 72 in 1941.

[†] Born in Co. Cork in 1841, Richard 'Boss' Croker migrated to America with his parents as a child. As a young man he ran rackets for the corrupt Democratic Party organisation that controlled city politics in New York from its Tammany Hall headquarters on East 14th Street. In 1874, he was tried for the murder of a rival gangster, but was released when the jury failed to reach a verdict. Rising in the ranks under the notorious William M Tweed who, as 'boss' of Tammany, siphoned off millions of dollars from the city treasury, Croker eventually took over as 'boss' in 1885, and in 1891, when he just happened to be chairman of Tammany's finance committee, he launched himself into racing by buying a stud farm and a string of

All right-minded people will applaud the action of the Jockey Club, and it should be a lesson to jockeys not to associate in any way with persons of doubtful character. It is no use to say that such persons are not known, as they are known particularly well, and here should come in the real assistance of the police in keeping bad characters out of the betting rings and other enclosures.

As I have frequently written, the Jockey Club is one of the greatest powers in the Kingdom to prevent malpractice, and its punishments are most severe and far-reaching. There is, consequently, no necessity for legislation on Turf matters.

Not from the government, perhaps, but the Jockey Club still had much to do as it hauled itself into the new century. By 1902 the American invasion had all but run its course, but its more insidious effects were just beginning to surface as the doping menace that was to haunt racing for the rest of the century, began to sweep the country.

---

racehorses. When Theodore Roosevelt appointed a Senate commission to inquire into Tammany's activities in 1894, Croker slipped off to England where he stayed for three years before he returned to New York in the hope that the storm of reform had blown itself out. It hadn't, and in 1901 he lost control of Tammany and returned to pursue his racing interests in England. In 1905, following the refusal of the Jockey Club to grant his trainer a licence, he sold his Wantage mansion and Berkshire stud and retired to his native Ireland, where he bought and built up the Glencairn estate adjoining Leopardstown racecourse outside Dublin. Two years later, his home-bred colt, Orby, ridden by Johnny Reiff, won the Derby to realise the dreams of a nation and a fiercely determined, but infamous owner.

A LETHAL LEGACY

WHEN the American trainer Enoch Wishard and his assistant, William Duke, disembarked from the ss *Manitou* on its arrival at London's Royal Albert Dock in the summer of 1899, they brought with them a medicine chest of equine 'tonics' that was to prove a veritable Pandora's Box for British racing.

Wishard was paying his second visit to England having initially tested the water in 1896 when he had been encouraged by the modest success he achieved with even more modest horses that were transformed into half-crazed winners by his magic potions.

Doping was not illegal at the time and drugs had been used in racing in one form or another since at least the middle of the eighteenth century when coca leaves were first imported from Peru. It was not long before the cocaine obtained from the plant found its way into racing, although the preferred stimulant of the time was alcohol.

Early training manuals recommended that racehorses should be given a pint of sack (sherry) a day, while spirits were openly administered on racecourses during the nineteenth century when it was a common sight to see "the use of stimulants being resorted to in many instances in the hope of 'priming' the faint-hearted ones to 'screw their courage to the sticking place'."[1]

The John Scott-trained Taraban was a celebrated example of the beneficial effects of port – "which is supposed to have an extraordinary effect in improving the speed and temper of animals of every description"[2] – when he returned to form with the help of his favourite tipple to win the Goodwood Stakes and Northumberland Plate in 1871.

On the debit side, there was always the risk that a jockey would empty the bottle before the horse got its share. Scott's brother, Bill, often rode 'under the influence' but that did not stop him from winning the St Leger a record nine times before his career and his life was brought to a premature end by alcoholism and cirrhosis of the liver.

Even Jockey Club members thought nothing of giving their horses a slug of the hard stuff if they thought it might do them some good. Sir John Astley, a senior steward in his time, wrote of a favourite quad:

> Good old Drumhead! he was the very kindest and quietest of horses. I once gave him some whisky before he ran at Shrewsbury as I thought he didn't quite struggle as gamely as he ought, and the old boy liked the cordial so well that he followed me round the paddock in hopes of another suck at the bottle.[3]*

Of course, horses also could have too many sucks at the bottle. When the Derby winners St Gatien and Melton clashed in the Jockey Club Cup at Newmarket in 1886 it was said that Melton had "so much whisky given to him before the race that Tom Cannon, who rode him, declared the horse was quite drunk."[4]

Drunken jockeys were one thing – drunken horses quite another, but the American trainers who

---

* Drumhead made all the running to win at Shrewsbury in November 1878. He was doubtlessly fortified with more 'cordial' the following year when he carried his 16st 6lb owner to victory in a £500 match with fellow steward, Caledon Alexander (16st), riding Briglia over one and a half miles at Newmarket.

arrived in England at the turn of the century had no need to rely on the uncertain effects of alcohol. They had refined doping to a fine art and were able to give a horse just enough of a stimulant to give it an edge without burning it out.

Enoch Wishard was a skilled trainer who was perfectly capable of improving a horse without the help of drugs, but a quicker road to riches lay in their use. He specialised in buying jaded horses of proven ability for modest sums and rejuvenating them with his equine elixir to land some major gambles before selling them on at a tidy profit.

His greatest success in this department was achieved with Royal Flush, his only purchase (for 400gns = £37,800) at the Newmarket December sales in 1899. The fully exposed six-year-old had won four consecutive handicaps, including the prestigious Cumberland Plate at Carlisle, in the first half of that season, but had then lost his form and was considered to be past his best.

This was far from the case. He reappeared the following year in the colours of the American gambler, James Drake, and, ridden by Johnny Reiff, landed close on £100,000 (£9m) in bets for his connections when he won the Royal Hunt Cup at Ascot by a head and then went on to romp home by six lengths in the Stewards Cup at Goodwood.

Royal Flush inevitably shot up in the weights as a result of these victories, but that didn't stop him winning two more races before the end of the season, much to the chagrin of his former owner, Fred Lee, who had only sold the horse so he could become a Jockey Club handicapper!

Wishard ended the 1900 season with more winners (54) than anyone else, while his former assistant, Duke, who had set up on his own, won 29 races – a modest foretaste of what he later achieved when he and his medicine cabinet moved to France, where he won the Prix du Jockey Club three times in four years.

It has to be said that Jack Huggins, who sent out the Lester Reiff-ridden Volodyovski to win the 1901 Derby, was one American trainer who detested the use of dope, but he was in the minority as his countrymen took full advantage of the Jockey Club's reluctance to introduce any rule banning the use of drugs.

George Lowe reflected the general ignorance that surrounded the subject when he added his voice to the growing debate in November 1900:

> That the so-called 'doping' can make horses faster than their natural abilities can allow is not considered possible by anyone endowed with a mode of reasoning, but horses, like humans, might be rendered unconscious or semi-conscious and in that condition do something superhuman or super-equine bordering on temporary insanity.

Quite so! In the same month a number of eminent vets and other interested parties gathered at St James's Hall in Regent Street to discuss the issue. Chaired by A Cope, president of the RCVS, the meeting lacked the vital ingredient of expert knowledge and after a lot of time and hot air had been expended on discussing the comparative merits of English and American training methods, an exasperated Cope exclaimed: "What we do want are some gentlemen to make some remarks about doping. If there are any gentlemen who know anything, kindly put up their hands."

There was an awkward silence and a lot of searching looks before a Dr Dongal eventually came forward and stated that doping was only harmful when drugs were used to stop a horse. If a trainer used them to improve a horse's performance in order to make it win then "no reasonable man could blame him".

This observation was greeted by a chorus of approval, which was hardly in keeping with the spirit of the conference. Finally, the *Life's* industrious reporter, who managed to churn out nearly 2,000 words on the abortive proceedings, concluded:

The chairman, having again called for anyone 'who knew anything about doping' without response, declared the meeting closed, and the company dispersed after forty minutes sitting without any advancement in the art of doping.

It's a pity the Bishop Auckland vet, Jimmy Deans, was not on hand to enlighten his colleagues. For some years he had been supplying trainers with cocaine-based 'speedy balls' to gee-up their jaded nags, while he considered himself to be a pioneer in the field of needlework. In a letter to the *Yorkshire Post* in 1900, he stated with pride:

As the first veterinary surgeon in England to attempt the hypodermic injection of a stimulant into a racehorse before running in public, I confidently assert that it is possible to treat a horse by this method, not only once but many times, without having any detrimental effect, either immediately or in the future. I have a horse under my care at present which has always run a stone better, or even more, after being injected, and has never suffered in any way through the injection.

Details also started to appear in print on how doping was being carried out in the United States. One particularly well-informed American correspondent reported:

Whatever may be the case in England, there is no doubt that drugs are largely used in this country for the purpose of stimulating racehorses. This practice is far more common in the West than on the Atlantic coast, for the horses in the former locality are of a much lower class. Indeed, many of them are cripples who have outlived their usefulness as racers and are only retained by their owners in the vain hope that a strong injection of dope may some day cause them to forget their infirmities and run one of their old-time races...

The most popular way to do this is still with a syringe, but many now prefer a capsule administered via the mouth or rectum, especially if much time may elapse before the start takes place. The prescription generally used for injections is: Cocaine, 8 to 10gr; carbolic acid, 1 to 2 drops diluted with 30 drops of distilled water, to this some trainers add 10 drops of a one per cent solution of nitro-glycerine. The recipe has frequently been used to advantage, but any increase in either of the ingredients named has always caused disaster.[5]

Especially, one assumes, when ladling in the nitro-glycerine. The American journalist's cliché of horses exploding out of the gate (stalls) takes on a whole new meaning!

Despite the accumulating evidence, the Jockey Club remained reluctant to legislate against doping for the simple reason that there was no sure way of detecting the presence of drugs in a horse. Wishard, who returned to the States a rich man at the end of 1900, knew this well enough and was on safe ground when he declared he was willing to have his horses examined "even to the extent of using X-rays on them".[6]

Nevertheless, some early moves were taken to outlaw the practice on the Continent and towards the end of 1900 an item in the *Life* stated:

The Jockey Clubs of Austria and Hungary have decided that, in all cases of doping, the offenders are to be excluded from the racecourses under the supervision of the two clubs, but that the administration of whisky, sherry and champagne as stimulants to horses shall not be regarded as prohibited.

This happy compromise did nothing to check the wave of doping that swept across Europe as American trainers sought out fresh fields to conquer. By 1903 it had become such a problem at the imperial hippodromes in St Petersburg and Moscow that the authorities took drastic steps to combat the menace. That August the *Life* reported:

A correspondent informs us that stringent rules have been made against the use of any drug on the racecourse, and the long period during which horses engaged in the races of the day have to remain out in the open under the eye of the stewards would appear to have minimised the field of action of the 'doper'.

A professor at the Veterinary College of Riga has studied the question and has discovered that the saliva of 'doped' horses is fatal to frogs when injected. A veterinary surgeon at the Zarakossel meeting has tried the effect of injecting the saliva of different horses having taken part in racing. It appears that more than one frog has died and the remainder of the saliva, with the remains of science's victims, have been sent to Riga for further investigation.

So it was, with a mounting mortality rate among Russian frogs, that the frontiers of science were extended; nor did they croak in vain. The following month it was reported that Jack Keene, who trained for the immensely rich Michael de Lazareff, had been warned off the Turf in Russia.*

Meanwhile, the Jockey Club finally started to take steps to bring in its own legislation as doping had become such a scandal that "one constantly saw horses who were notorious rogues running and winning as if they were possessed of the devil, with eyes starting out of their heads and the sweat pouring off them."[8]

History has always credited George Lambton for convincing the authorities that action needed to be taken since he claimed, in *Men and Horses I Have Known*, that he doped five of his horses – "some of the biggest rogues in training" – with the full knowledge of the Jockey Club stewards so they "could see for themselves what the result was". The result was that four of the horses won and the other finished second, but, curiously, of the three horses named by Lambton in his book, two of them ran and won a month *after* the Jockey Club had already taken action on the matter.

It was on 30 September 1903 that the stewards proposed an additional clause be incorporated into Rule 176 which dealt with corrupt practices, and the new rule was confirmed in the *Racing Calendar* on 22 October:

If any person shall administer, or cause to be administered, for the purpose of affecting the speed of a horse, drugs or stimulants internally, by hypodermic or other methods, every person so offending shall be warned off Newmarket Heath and other places where these rules are in force.

---

* John Oliver Keene allegedly turned out a remarkable 116 winners in three and a half months during this period.[7] Following his banishment he trained in Japan for a time, but eventually returned to America where he laid out Keeneland racecourse on his Lexington estate in Kentucky.

The rule became operative in 1904, but it was to be another six years before it was introduced for jump racing and it was not until 1914 that the first official saliva test (which proved negative) was taken on a horse. It is inconceivable that doping with stimulants was not going on during this time and that it continued for many years after, yet it was not until 1930 that the first trainers were warned off for the practice.

But that's another story, and a grim one at that!

THE SCOTTISH REFORMATION

O N 5 NOVEMBER 1900, in the best of British traditions, bonfires were lit across the land and effigies burnt, but they were not all of Guy Fawkes. On many a village green 'President Kruger' blazed merrily away as the end of the Boer War was celebrated. True, a peace treaty had yet to be signed, but that very day the *Life*, in common with other newspapers, had published a letter from Field Marshal Lord Roberts of Kandahar which indicated the messy conflict was all over bar the shouting – the 'boys' were coming home.

Dated September 30, the communiqué from British Army Headquarters, Pretoria, was given the imposing headline 'Letter from Lord Roberts to the Editor of the Sporting Life':

> Sir – Will you kindly allow me through the medium of your paper to make an appeal to my countrymen and women on a subject I have very much at heart and which has been occupying my thoughts for some time past.

In a word, the little teetotaller's thoughts were centred on booze as he anticipated the reception his conquering heroes would receive on their return home. 'Bobs', as he was known to one and all, expanded:

> My sincere hope is that the welcome may not take the form of 'treating' the men to stimulants in public houses or in the streets and thus lead them into excesses which must tend to degrade those whom the nation delights to honour, and to lower the 'Soldier of the Queen' in the eyes of the world – that world which has watched with undisguised admiration the grand work they have performed for their Sovereign and their country...
>
> I am induced to make this appeal from having read, with great regret, that when our troops were leaving England and passing through the streets of London, their injudicious friends pressed liquor upon them and shoved bottles of spirits into their hands and pockets – a mode of 'speeding the parting friend' which resulted in some very distressing and discreditable scenes.

Tut-tut! The Boers, of course, had their own way of 'speeding the parting friend'. On the very day this letter was published, they launched a new offensive with raids on British outposts in the Orange Free State and the Transvaal. The war, which had started a year earlier, was far from over; it still had 19 more bloody months to run during which time the world watched with undisguised horror (not admiration) as some 26,000 women and children died of hunger and disease in British concentration camps.

Throughout the whole mismanaged campaign the *Life* kept readers up to date with events by publishing the official dispatches issued by the War Office, while George Lowe dissected and analysed its effects in a series of jingoistic essays on 'The Lessons of the War'. As the conflict escalated amid mounting press and public criticism, the editor remained Blairishly contemptuous of both domestic and world opinion. In forecasting the end of hostilities in his New Year's Day message for 1902, he declared:

> The foe has become debased as well as largely demoralised, and it is daily more evident that it is to

an aggregation of the scum of Europe, a horde of desperadoes no more deserving of the treatment accorded to a fair-fighting foe than so many banditti, we chiefly owe the dragging on of the struggle … We need not trouble ourselves about the opinion of the Continental Press, respectable and 'reptile', for we know from past experience that outside Great Britain any stick is considered good enough to belabour the country which the intelligent (?) foreigner hates, envies, and vainly makes believe to despise.

Strong stuff! More's the pity he did not tackle racing's problems with the same vigour. Had he done so he could have given his paper the lift it so badly needed at a time when its very existence was under threat from falling sales and proposed anti-gambling legislation, but he appears to have become wholly indifferent to its fate. The *Life* looked like a paper on its last legs; its page-layouts lacked thought and design; news stories were lumped together as single-paragraph items in one column or used as fillers regardless of their importance.

In common with the rest of Fleet Street, Lowe was obsessed with the doings of the Edwardian set. In 1903, he started a daily 'In the World of Sport' column, sub-headed 'News about notable people', which served as a virtual court circular with its opening items centred on the royal family's agenda. For the big race meetings such as Epsom, Ascot and Goodwood, upwards of half a column would be devoted to listing 'The Company' present, while news of high-society weddings and grand balls would often be given priority over important racing and general sports items.

Inexplicably, the obituaries of magistrates who had no connection with the sporting world were also meticulously recorded, while mundane fillers such as: "At a special meeting of the Dalkeith Town Council yesterday afternoon, the chain was placed around the chief magistrate's neck amid applause." must have caused much grinding of teeth amongst the paper's disenchanted and dwindling band of readers.

Almost without exception, these 'briefs' and any news story of note emanated from the news agencies. The car crash in which Danny Maher was seriously injured during the summer of 1903 provides a perfect illustration of the lamentable depths to which the *Life* had sunk. On Saturday July 11 it was reported:

> The Press Association's Newmarket correspondent telegraphs: 'Mr George Blackwell, the Beverley House trainer, has just received a telegram stating that Danny Maher, the well-known American jockey, met with an accident whilst riding in his motor car in the neighbourhood of Caterham, Surrey, this afternoon, and that the base of his skull was fractured, whilst he had also sustained other injuries of such a nature that a London specialist had been telegraphed for'. Danny Maher, it may be mentioned, was riding at Lingfield yesterday.

Underneath this announcement was a 'Latest' bulletin, which was a re-write of the PA report with a dangerous piece of hearsay tagged onto the end – "Late last night a rumour was current that a telephone message had been received in Newmarket stating that Maher had since expired."

The *Sportsman* actually worked the rumour into its headlines – 'Shocking Accident to D Maher / Reported Fatal Termination' – but in every other respect its report was vastly superior to that of its rival:

> We greatly regret to learn that an accident of a very serious character happened yesterday evening to D Maher, the American jockey, near Godstone.

Maher, after riding at Lingfield races during the afternoon, started to return to London on a Panhard automobile belonging to Lord Carnarvon which had been lent to him by his lordship. Maher himself was driving with the chauffeur seated by his side.

About half-past five when nearing Godstone at a rapid rate, something apparently went wrong with the steering gear of Maher's car and he collided with terrific force with another car in which were a lady and a gentleman. Maher and the chauffeur were hurled violently out of the machine which was completely wrecked. Both men were found in an insensible condition suffering apparently from fracture of the skull. They were removed to Caterham Cottage Hospital where at a late hour last night they remained in an unconscious condition. Grave fears are entertained about their recovery.

All the essential ingredients of a news story were there; the who, what, when, where and why. The paper went on to state the passengers in the other car had escaped serious injury, and only at the end of its report did it incorporate the rumour of Maher's death.

Given the story broke relatively late on Friday night, the *Life* could be forgiven for its sketchy account, but with 48 hours in which to gather further information, there was no excuse for the apology of a follow-up that appeared in Monday's eight-page number. The only mention made of the 'expired' jockey (who was riding again seven weeks later) was a two-paragraph item headed 'The Accident to Danny Maher / Message from the King'. Once again the news, such as it was, was supplied by the PA:

The Press Association, telegraphing on Sunday night, says: 'Danny Maher, the American jockey who met with a serious motorcar accident on Friday, has passed a good day and the doctors are now very hopeful of his ultimate recovery. Trottman, the chauffeur, is a little better, but his condition is still serious'.

Following telegram was received at Caterham Cottage Hospital yesterday from Eastbourne: 'The King enquires after Maher. His Majesty wishes to know how he is. – Equerry-in-Waiting, Compton Place, Eastbourne'. Miss Smith, matron, replied: 'Maher had a good night and was progressing favourably'. Mrs Langtry wired: 'She was grieved to hear of the accident; glad he was so much better'.

That was it! Not another word was given to the jockey on a day when space was found for nine column inches of PA copy on 'The Memorial Bust of Sir Arthur Sullivan'!

The *Sportsman*, in contrast, sent a reporter to the hospital and gave half a column to the story. The account was no masterpiece, but it was intimate and up-to-the-minute:

I have just left D Maher and he could not be going on better. His brain is as clear as possible and the headache is not so bad. He keeps quiet and dozes nicely, which is what the doctors want him to do.

He is an excellent patient with the pluck of ten men and so unselfish that he has no thought of himself, the one drift of his conversation being 'Tell me, now tell me, is the other boy bad?' this being in reference to Trottman, the chauffeur who was with him in the motor. They were the first words he said when I found him on Friday in a semi-pool of blood in a cottage at the scene of the accident and it has been the same ever since.

The anonymous reporter, whose account was no doubt corrupted in transmission from 'semi-conscious in a pool of blood', went on to praise the hospital staff and added:

The hall of the hospital reminds one just now more of an editor's room in a newspaper office than anything else, every available table being smothered inches deep in telegrams which have arrived not in twos or threes or tens and twenties, but literally in hundreds. One was from the King, delivered by special messenger this morning. A smile lit up the jockey's face, defying the bandages and the scars and the gashes, and making him look like his old self.

…and so on. This was the new, on-the-spot, human-interest style of reporting that had been pioneered by *The Star* and the *Daily Mail*. Faced with such competition, which was no more than the basic coverage any newspaper would give to a major story, it was obvious drastic steps had to be taken to save the *Life* from oblivion. Lowe had to go.

The huge task of reviving the moribund journal fell to William Will, who, at the age of 36, possessed all the drive and strength of purpose that had been so noticeably lacking in those who had controlled the paper for far too long.

Born in the heart of Aberdeenshire, Will gained his early journalistic experience on his local paper, the *Huntly Express*, before he progressed to the Aberdeen *Press & Journal* and then on to the popular illustrated Scottish weekly, the *Bon-Accord*, climbing the usual promotional rungs of sub-editor, chief-sub, assistant editor and editor, as he went.

It took the Herriot-Watt educated Scot little more than a decade to reach the top of that particular ladder and he was soon hankering for further advancement after the lure of Fleet Street had brought him to London in 1898. He quickly made his mark working alongside Theodore Cook on the *St James's Gazette* and became its news editor when Cook moved on in 1900. Three years later the challenge of resurrecting the *Sporting Life* beckoned and, with the backing of 'Old Blue', he was appointed managing editor towards the end of 1903.

As Will set about hauling the paper back from the brink one of his first moves was to bring in a former colleague to act as his deputy. This was W S (William Smith) Morley-Brown who had worked for the *Aberdeen Journal* group for 20 years, the last eight of which had been spent as editor of the town's *Evening Express* for which he compiled a daily sporting notes column.

Loaded down with farewell gifts, which included a purse of sovereigns from his colleagues and a marble clock from his local cricket club in recognition of "his past services to the 'Aberdeenshire' and cricket generally in the north of Scotland," Morley-Brown arrived in London at the end of February 1904 and from that day on the *Life* started to breathe again.

The transformation the two Scots brought about in a relatively short space of time was dramatic. They revitalised the paper by opening it up to highlight stories and make the whole layout more attractive. Articles, reports and racecards were given more space and were consequently easier to identify and read. The design of the football pages (two on a Monday) was greatly improved, and the slab of solid type that had been the Augur column for so many years was broken up by relevantly placed three-quarter inch square indents (later replaced by crossheads) containing a few words to indicate the subject or race under discussion.

The daily grind of writing the lead column was now taken on by Arthur Graham, an able journalist who was also to have spells as 'Solon' and 'Special Commissioner' over the next 18 years, but Will reserved the right to don the 'Augur' mantle whenever he felt the need to air his views on a subject. And this he did both vociferously and often as he campaigned against the anti-betting brigade that was posing an increasing threat to the paper, and to racing.

In 1905, a further improvement was made with the belated installation of a bank of Linotype machines, 15 years after the *Scottish Leader* in Edinburgh had become the first paper in Britain to take on the trade unions by using the labour-saving device that was advertised as 'A one-man machine – A type foundry in itself'.

The 'out with the old, in with the new' policy also applied to editorial content as the fawning coverage given to royalty and the aristocracy was phased out in favour of more relevant features. Of all the changes made, the most valuable in terms of reference was the inclusion of an annual list of obituaries and a chronological summary of the year's main sporting highlights.

First published to cover 1905, the tabulated obits extended to five columns by 1909 when they were categorised under the headings: 'The Turf', 'Cricket', 'Golf', 'Football' and 'Miscellaneous'; while the deaths of notable horses and greyhounds were also recorded. Among the departed souls that year was: "G S Lowe sports journalist and one-time special correspondent for *Bell's Life* in France. Oct 9."

No obituary had appeared in the *Life* at the time of Lowe's death and the deliberate omission of the fact that he had been editor of the paper was a mean and shoddy way to record the passing of a man who, for all his failings, had served the paper for 16 years.

In 1910 the obituary columns were further swollen as the competitive spirit of 'those magnificent young men in their flying machines' began to take its toll. The Hon. Charles Rolls became the first British casualty and the tenth in all when he was killed at Bournemouth on July 12, just a few weeks after he had made the first non-stop return flight across the Channel.

Rolls would have been better sticking to the roads. In 1904 he had joined forces with Henry Royce to design and produce a superior motorcar, and three years later the 6-cylinder Rolls-Royce Silver Ghost was proclaimed 'the world's finest car' after he had driven it in an endurance test for 14,371 miles back and forth between London, Edinburgh and Glasgow.

It was, however, as "the most enterprising as well as most daring of British aviators" that Rolls was remembered by the *Life*, which noted that "death has laid an especially heavy hand upon those adventurous spirits who have set out to solve the baffling and dangerous problem of the conquest of the air."

The adjoining list of departed 'adventurous spirits' was not quite an A to Z of fatalities, but it came pretty close to one. Chávez had died after crash-landing following his flight across the Alps on Sept 13; Delagrange was killed in a crash at Pau, Jan 4; Erbsloeh, the winner of the Gordon Bennett balloon race in 1907, died in an airship accident in Rhenish Prussia, July 12; A Hoxsey, who set a new altitude record at Los Angeles on Boxing Day when reaching a height of 11,474ft, went 6ft under five days later.

D Kinet met his end at Ghent on July 10; Le Blon at St Sebastian, April 2; M Michelin at Lyons, May 13; J R Moisant, the first to accomplish a Paris to London flight, at New Orleans on Dec 31; Robl, a former champion cyclist, at Stettin, June 18; Wachter at Reims, July 3, and M Zosily at Budapest on June 2.

On the roads the death rate was even higher as the quest for speed took its toll of both drivers and pedestrians. The dramatic impact of meeting one's end behind the wheel (or under the wheels) of a speeding 'mechanical monstrosity' had resulted in a lot of negative press for the car. Back in 1903, when the Paris-Madrid race was abandoned after a series of crashes had claimed the lives of a number of drivers (Marcel Renault included), their mechanics and spectators, Theodore Cook had felt compelled to defend the 'Juggernauts of death' by putting the contrasting forms of horse-power related fatalities into perspective. The statistics showed that over the previous 12 months 411 people had been killed and 2,991 injured in accidents involving horse-drawn vehicles.

By 1905 the *Life* was running a weekly motoring column that was to develop into a two-page spread during the golden days of the Bentley Boys, Le Mans, Malcolm Campbell *et al*, and that winter William Will came up with another winner when he arranged with the veteran boxer, Jem Mace, to publish his autobiography in serial form.

Mace was a living legend whose long and varied career spanned three continents and offered a fascinating insight into the final decades of the prize ring. He had won the middleweight championship of England in 1860 and the heavyweight championship a year later. In 1870 he became the first undisputed world champion when beating the American champion and ex-Brit, Tom Allen, in New Orleans and he pioneered the transition from bareknuckle fighting to gloved boxing in Australia and New Zealand, where he tutored the Cornish-born Bob Fitzsimmons who later won the world heavyweight title by beating 'Gentleman Jim' Corbett in 1897.

The old bruiser was still fighting exhibition bouts at the aged of 74 in 1905 and Will milked his story for all it was worth which, in terms of attracting new readers and winning back old ones, was quite a lot. His inspired scoop, more than anything else, helped to restore the *Life's* long-lost dignity as it boasted:

> The publication by the *Sporting Life* of the history of the famous pugilist is creating an immense amount of public interest, and the demand for copies of the paper containing instalments of Jem Mace's boxing career is unprecedented. Readers should therefore make a point of possessing a copy of the *Sporting Life* every Monday on which day the instalments appear.

The first part of Chapter 1 was published on 4 December 1905 and ran to three columns, but as the tale progressed the space allotted to it was gradually whittled down to a single column in order to keep it running for as long as possible. In the case of 'Jem Mace and his Battles', this lasted until 25 June 1906 when chapter eleven ended with a '*To be continued*' tag which, disappointingly, it never was, although what had already appeared formed the basis for an extended autobiography that was published in book form under the title *Fifty Years a Fighter* in 1908.

Photographs – mainly mug shots – were also introduced by Will to replace the old single-column woodcut illustrations, while bylines began to be used on a regular basis. The name of G Wagstaffe Simmons, which was to lend distinction to the paper for 50 years, appeared above the main football stories, and R P Watson emerged from behind the cloak of his 'Paul Pry' pseudonym as the chief boxing reporter.

Captain E G (Teddy) Wynyard, an excellent but cantankerous all-round sportsman, and J N (Jack) Crawford, the bespectacled teenage prodigy who was "probably the greatest school cricketer in the history of the game"[1] were playing in and reporting on the MCC tour of South Africa; the Hon. Southwell Fitzgerald wrote authoritatively on rugby, and there were occasional articles by other top players including J A Lambie, the top-scoring Queen's Park forward and Scottish international footballer (1886-88).

Less distinguished contributors remained anonymous; some acknowledged simply by bracketing their sport with an 'Our' prefix and an 'Expert' suffix, while others wrote under a series of bland pseudonyms. Cricket notes were by 'Long Leg'; motoring by 'The Wheeler'; golf by 'Stymie'; hockey by 'Full Back', etc.

More space was also given to articles on bloodstock breeding at a time when the paper had two budding authorities on the subject in Ernest Coussell and Edward Moorhouse. Coussell, who wrote under the signature of 'Ithuriel', had joined the *Life* from the *Sportsman* in 1902, while Moorhouse traded in his position as racing editor of the famous London evening, the *Pall Mall Gazette*, to become 'Special Commissioner' following the death of Elliot Hutchins in 1905.

Together, the two men did much to counteract the advantage previously enjoyed by the *Sportsman,* whose William Allison was regarded as the leading expert on thoroughbred breeding until the eminent vet, James Bell Robertson, made a belated entry into journalism at the age of 50 when he started to write for the *Sporting Chronicle* as 'Mankato' in 1910.

Coussell and Moorhouse were destined to make a far greater impact on the thoroughbred world than either of their contemporaries when they founded the British Bloodstock Agency in 1911.* The following year they also made a huge contribution to racing literature by launching the universally acclaimed *Bloodstock Breeders Review* as a quarterly magazine.

Meanwhile, at a more mundane level, Will decided that if advertising tipsters could make easy money by supplying gullible clients with 'special late information' gleaned from the *Life* for the price of a penny and sold on for half-a-crown or more, there was no reason why the paper itself shouldn't get in on the act. In the run-up to the 1906 Flat season, a craftily drafted notice headed, 'Special Selections By Augur', announced:

> For a long time 'Augur' has withstood numerous requests to give his readers the benefit of the information which he may have received subsequent to the publication of his letter and previous to racing, but so pressing have the demands become of late that at last he has given way.
>
> He has made arrangements whereby during the flat-racing season he will wire two special selections daily for a fixed weekly fee of £1- 1s. In order to meet the wishes of the other class of his readers, who like only an occasional wire, 'Augur' proposes sending special selections when he has particularly good information. The charge for these occasional wires is £1 for five. One wire will be sent for 5s [£22.50].

This pricey midday service was soon extended to include the jumping season, but readers almost certainly got better value for money later that year when the first *Sporting Life* racegoers' trip to France for the Grand Prix de Paris was organised. The three-day excursion was run in conjunction with the Thomas Cook travel firm and cost just 5gns (£472) all in. This included first-class travel from Victoria (2.20pm) on Saturday to the Gare du Nord (11.25pm); the drive to Longchamp on Sunday; admission to the 5fr enclosure (the 20fr enclosure cost an extra 12s 6d), and a tour of Paris on Monday before departure for London at 9pm arriving back at 5.29am – 'tired but happy,' as they say.

As the first-class return fare to Paris was £4-7s-10d, the trip offered outstanding value to the 60 enthusiasts who set out under the guidance of Edward Moorhouse to see that year's Derby winner, Spearmint, attempt to become the first English horse to win the Grand Prix since his maternal grandsire, Minting, carried off the prize 20 years earlier.

Expectations of a successful outcome were high. The *Life* advised: "English visitors may easily

---

* Moorhouse, who was also instrumental in setting up the Thoroughbred Breeders Association in 1917, resigned from the *Life* in 1913 after the paper's owners, Eleanor and Walter Broomfield, had tried to muscle in on the BBA. The Broomfields then set up the Anglo-Foreign Horse Agency, under the management of Friedrich Becker who also took over the role of Special Commissioner. Unfortunately, Becker, being German, was interned during World War I when the paper's attempts to rival the BBA came to an ignominious end. In 1921 Moorhouse rejoined the *Life* as Special Commissioner, a post he held until he retired in 1924 to concentrate on editing the *Bloodstock Breeders Review*. Coussell continued to contribute breeding articles to the *Life* on a freelance basis until his death in 1947.

clear their expenses by backing the son of Carbine," and many did when Major Eustace Loder's 300gns bargain-buy made all the running under Bernard Dillon to win by a hard-fought half-length, but the odds about the broad-blazed bay were cramped.

The pari-mutuel in the *pelouse* (public enclosure) paid just 21fr to a 10fr stake, while in the *pesage* (paddock enclosure) backers got a miserly 19fr for their *dix francs*; a difference which was "the result of the heavy investment in Spearmint by English visitors". It was noted that "A movement is on foot in France to have the investments 'outside and in' put together so that one uniform price can be returned."

On his return, Moorhouse filled a column on the party's adventures and concluded:

The experiment was, I think I may say, unanimously voted a success. So much so that it seemed to be taken for granted that we shall repeat the venture next year and in successive years. 'This will develop into a big thing,' said one gentleman. 'It is a splendid idea and why nobody thought of it before I can't imagine.'

The trip did, indeed, 'develop into a big thing' catching on to such an extent that it eventually evolved into what is now the annual October invasion of Paris for the Prix de l'Arc de Triomphe.

A MARATHON TROPHY

TOGETHER with the improvements brought in during the Scottish reformation period, some peculiar items also crept into the paper. One of the most bizarre appeared in June 1904 when readers were confronted with the block-capital headline 'IS THERE A CURE FOR DRUNKENNESS?'

The column-length tract that accompanied this arresting query was "An interview with Canon Fleming by Fred A McKenzie (*Daily Mail* Special War Correspondent In Japan)," which the strictly teetotal William Will had lifted from the *Windsor Magazine*.

In claiming that alcoholism was rife among the working classes, the article touched upon a new insidious threat, "which attacks the most finely strung of the intellectual classes. The drug habit is not yet so prevalent here as in some of the great cities of America, or as in Paris, but it is growing and growing rapidly."

But there was salvation for the afflicted. Fleming, "the well-known vicar of St Michael's, Chester Square, London," advocated a six-week course of injections and tonics: "I have seen men go in perfect wrecks and come out at the end with their bleared eyes bright, their willpower restored, their manhood brought back. The cures I have seen seem almost miraculous," he averred.

This unexpected vote for temperance was actually topped on 16 July 1908, when the campaigning editor felt a need to boost the 1904 Entente Cordiale by leading the paper with an article by 'Our French Correspondent' written in – what else? – French!

The occasion for this bold, if not altogether universally acclaimed venture into bi-lingual journalism was the Olympic Games which were being staged in London in conjunction with the Franco-British Exhibition. Originally scheduled to be held in Rome, the games had been switched to London in November 1906 when the Italian government decided it did not have the resources to fund them as well as deal with the national disaster caused by the eruption of Mount Vesuvius earlier that year.

Thanks to Theodore Cook, who was on the council of the recently formed British Olympic Association, the *Life* was able to break the news of the switch five days before it was officially announced in the rest of the press. The scoop did not go down too well with Lord Desborough, chairman of the BOA, but he had other things to worry about as he had less than two years in which to find the money to finance the games and to design and build a stadium capable of staging them.

It was a mammoth undertaking, but providentially, Imre Kiralfy, a man of great vision and energy who specialised in putting on spectacular shows, was in the process of laying out an enormous building complex on a 140-acre site at Shepherd's Bush, west London, to house the Franco-British Exhibition. Over the previous three decades the Hungarian-born Kiralfy had designed and organised a series of extravaganzas in America and at Earl's Court and Olympia in London, but, even by his standards, the 130,000-capacity stadium required by the BOA presented him with a mighty task.

It was not until 31 July 1907 that the construction firm of Messrs Alexander Findlay drove the first stanchion into the ground, but in ten miraculous months a 6,000-strong workforce labouring around the clock completed the colossal steel and concrete coliseum. With ten miles of seating for 68,000 spectators and ranks of terracing for almost as many more, the *Life* acclaimed the stadium as "the largest, most costly and best appointed the world has yet known". It incorporated a 660-yard banked concrete cycle track laid outside a 586-yard cinder running track with an infield the size of two football pitches and a massive 109yds x 16yds open-air swimming pool in the centre of the arena.

Adjacent to the stadium, the exhibition compound contained twenty domed palaces, eight huge halls (400ft x 70ft), four show villages (Indian, Ceylonese – with elephants – Senegalese and Irish) and lots of smaller buildings all linked by 30 miles of paths and 12 miles of canals along which a flotilla of pedaloes ferried the marvelling public. The whole white-plastered creation resembled a great White City, and so it became known.

But, for all the good work Kiralfy and the BOA put into the fourth modern Olympiad, the games were marred by political controversy, bad weather, poor attendances and charges of biased judging and professionalism, but in the end the Olympic spirit won through thanks to a gutsy little Italian by the name of Dorando Pietri.

From the outset, the games had been portrayed as a battle between Britain and the USA, and by the end of the first week the *Life* was able to proclaim:

July 18, 1908, will be historical in the annals of sport. Foregathered at the Stadium were the chosen athletes of the world in such widely differing sports as archery and cycling, tug-of-war and swimming, steeplechasing and fancy diving. And Great Britain, though not invincible, won eight of the ten finals, while two were shared between the other countries; United States taking the discus (as at Athens) with a record throw, and Germany the fancy diving. To put matters shortly, that means we have now won 15 events of the 27 decided at the Stadium, the United States being second with five, Sweden third with three, Germany has two and France and Italy one each.

But the disputes had already started. In the tug-of-war the Americans were easily pulled over by a team of Liverpool policemen (one of three teams representing Britain) and walked off in a huff complaining that the heels of the Scousers' boots had been fitted with special steel rims. Inspector Harry Duke, coach of ultimately victorious City of London team, maintained the boots were regular police issue, but offered the Americans a rematch "in which both teams shall pull in stockinged feet". The challenge was not taken up.

Then, in the 400 metres final, the American, John Carpenter, was disqualified for deliberately hampering the British champion, Wyndham Halswelle. The race was declared void and a re-run ordered, but the other two American finalists withdrew in protest and so provided Halswelle with the first and only walkover in Olympic history.

But it was in the marathon that the greatest drama occurred. In the previous three revivals of the games, at Athens, Paris and St Louis, Missouri, the race had been run over 25 miles, the distance which, as legend has it, Pheidippides ran in 490 BC when he carried the news to Athens of the Greeks' victory over the Persians on the plains at Marathon.

The 1908 renewal was originally due to be run over 25½ miles from the Long Walk in Windsor Park to the White City, but it was then decided to tailor the event to give the royal family a grandstand view of the start by moving it to the East Terrace of Windsor Castle. This added half a mile to the race which, when tagged on to the two-thirds of the stadium circuit the runners had to cover in order to finish in front of the royal box, made a grand total of 26 miles and 385 yards (42.195km), which later became the standard marathon distance so memorable did the 1908 contest prove.

Blessed with a fine, sunny day in contrast to the opening week, the race brought out massive crowds. The serried ranks lined the route which ran north-east through Eton and Slough, past the

Dorando Pietri provides the iconic image of the 1908 London Olympics.

Langley Marshes to Uxbridge, through the rustic villages of Ickenham and Ruislip, and on to Pinner, before it turned south-east to skirt the bottom of Harrow Hill on the lower Sudbury road, then on past Wembley, Craven Park and Wormwood Scrubs, and so, finally, to the packed White City stadium.

The *Life*, in common with the rest of the country, expected the British runners to dominate, and when the early leader was broadcast in the stadium it reported:

> What a shout went up when, in stentorian tones, the message was delivered through the megaphone: 'One mile, Clarke of Great Britain, leading, with A Burn of Canada, second!' It was cheerful to know that the Old Country was prominent at the start.

The 'Old Country' was still at the head of affairs when the next announcement was made at the four-mile stage, and again at nine miles and 12 miles, but at 18 miles a groan went through the crowd when it was relayed that C Hefferon of South Africa was in the lead chased by the Italian, P Dorando (as his name appeared in the programme). The final, dramatic stages of the race were related by the *Life* in a confusing mix of tenses, which gave the report a curious vitality:

> It was known that the Italian was leading and that, except for a sudden collapse, he must win. And now he enters. Not with a swinging gait and alert step, not as a conqueror in a great athletic event. It was painfully apparent that Dorando had run himself to an absolute standstill.
>
> He staggered down the cement track onto the cinder path, but he could not run. He was done. He walked, then tried to run, but the powers of his body were not responsive to the workings of his half-delirious mind. He stumbled; he fell!
>
> Officials crowd around him; they minister to his requirements; they encourage him with words of cheer. They tell him the race is almost won. Will he not finish his glorious work by making one more effort?

The poor, tired body is once more called upon. He is on his legs; he starts, staggers, and a second time he falls prone. It seemed that exhausted Nature could do no more, and that even in sight of the tape he would lose the deathless prize which he had so gallantly struggled to win.

It was a painful, pitiful, heart-breaking scene. The cheers which rolled round the ground to encourage him reached his tired, dazed brain. Yet one more effort.

Her Majesty the Queen watched with tender, womanly sympathy the Italian's brave attempts to conquer his physical weakness, and tears, which she did not seek to hide, were in her eyes.

How earnestly the thousands upon thousands of people who watched the grim tragedy wished that Dorando would yet reach the goal of his ambition. He is again making his way round the track, and not much more distance remains to be covered. Will he succeed in breaking the tape? Less than twenty yards from the finish he falls down in a convulsive heap.

Has he done so much to be beaten by cruel Fate in the last few yards? It seems so, for Hayes, the American, has now entered the Stadium and is running steadily round the track. Dorando has apparently lost. But no; the frantic appeals to the Southerner to complete the race produce the desired effect. He is once more assisted to rise and he wearily finishes the last few yards.

He has broken the tape; he falls into the arms outstretched to receive him, and is immediately placed on an ambulance and removed to his dressing room.

Inevitably, the Americans protested and Pietri was disqualified for receiving assistance, but, although denied victory, his spirit and determination had captured the heart of the nation and its Queen. At the medals presentation ceremony the following day the 22-year-old former messenger boy from Carpi, northern Italy, received a personal consolation prize from Queen Alexandra. The *Life* described Pietri as "a proud and happy man" as he walked around the track fully recovered from his almost certainly drug-induced collapse:*

Then came the great, the triumphal moment for him. He marched up the steps and faced the dais where the Queen was smilingly awaiting him, and in that sweet and gracious manner so characteristic of Her Majesty, she handed him the handsome gold cup amid a tornado of cheers that must have been heard miles away.

The French correspondent, whose reports had grown smaller by the day, was less unctuous as he commented:

Le geste de Sa Majesté a réparé une injustice flagrante, et Hayes peut emporter aux Etats Unis la médaille d'or le challenge de Marathon; il ne sera jamais consideré ici comme le vainqueur des Marathon 1908. Ce dernier est, et sera toujours Dorando, l'Italien. [The gesture of Her Majesty has repaired a flagrant injustice, and while Hayes may carry off the marathon gold medal to the United States, he will never be considered here the winner of the 1908 Marathon. This is, and always will be Dorando, the Italian].

More importantly from a domestic point of view, was the fact that Great Britain had emerged well

---

* Cocaine tablets or grains of strychnine washed down with champagne were widely used by long-distance runners to give them a final boost and were even recommended in some training manuals of the time.

on top in the medals table with 38 golds against the 22 won by the United States. Sweden came next with 7 victories, France 4, Hungary 3, Norway, Germany, Canada and Italy 2 apiece and one each for Belgium, South Africa and Finland. The nation's resounding triumph in the stadium events, thanks to its numerically superior 736-strong team, was acclaimed under the defiant crosshead 'Britons Not Degenerates':

> After the general chorus as to British degeneracy in athletic sports ... we are surely entitled to claim in no proud spirit of boasting, but with a degree of proper pride, that we are still in the front rank of athletic nations.

The only major disappointment had been the eclipse of the marathon men. Their failure prompted Jack Andrew, the secretary of the London Polytechnic Harriers who had organised the event, to institute an annual international race "to encourage long-distance running in the hope of retrieving the lost laurels of Britons in this connection." To this end he approached William Will to ask if the *Sporting Life* would put up a trophy for a race run over a similar route to that taken by the Olympic athletes.

Will was all for the idea. He realised it would be a great publicity coup for the paper as the sensation of the Pietri drama had created a worldwide craze for marathon running. William McFarlane, the long-time proprietor of the *Life*, had died the previous year and the paper was now owned by his widow, Eleanor, who readily agreed to give £500 (£45,000) for a perpetual trophy that was to become the envy of the athletics world. Designed and manufactured by the Goldsmiths and Silversmiths Company of London the huge, ornate sculpture was not the sort of silverware that could be raised aloft in a victory salute. The 4ft 6in tall monolith was described by the *Life* as...

> classical in design, the principal feature consisting of a solid silver model representing Pheidippides, the Greek athlete, in the attitude of running. The statuette stands upon a square oak pedestal having at the angles solid silver Corinthian columns. Each of the sides bears a richly decorated silver panel surrounded by laurel, one panel portraying a classic scene depicting Pheidippides' death after conveying to Athens the news of the battle of Marathon; another contains a medallion portrait of Miltiades, the Greek general at Marathon, and a third a medallion portrait of King Edward VII.
>
> All the decorations in these panels are executed in relief, while the front panel bears the title of the trophy in a ribbon, also in relief, and behind this appears a caduceus of Mercury. Upon each of two of the four sides of the base are projections supporting finely modelled silver figures of Victory and Fame respectively, and the plinth carries a number of silver scrolls for engraving the names of winners, divided by festoons of laurel. The presentation inscription is engraved on a silver plate and the trophy is fitted in a specially constructed oak case.

The race was to be strictly for amateurs, which put paid to any hopes that it would bring about a Pietri–Hayes rematch since both men turned professional soon after the games in order to compete in richly endowed marathons in America, where the Italian comfortably beat his Irish-American rival in each of their three head-to-head encounters.

The first running of the Polytechnic–*Sporting Life* marathon took place on Saturday, 8 May 1909, when the paper devoted three columns to the event that had brought together a representative field of 68 runners selected from the four home nations as well as from France, Germany, Italy, South Africa and Switzerland.

(Left) *The Sporting Life's* £500 (£45,000) marathon trophy was first run for in 1909 and is now associated with the Flora London marathon – © Museum of London picture library.
(Right) Harry Barrett the first winner of the trophy at Stamford Bridge stadium with the *Life's* editor, William Will, on his left. – © University of Westminster Archive Services.

In a section headed 'Hints to Competitors and Rules', it was stated that drugs were forbidden; that each runner would be allowed two attendants on bicycles; that the official caterers, Oxo, would provide their requirements en route and that "A special car will follow with the competitors' clothing, and a similar car will be in readiness to pick up all who abandon the race." The 'crocks car' must have become somewhat cramped by the end of the day since 28 runners including F H Reay, who was "discovered dead-beat in a hostelry near Sheen," failed to complete the course!

Victory went to Harry Barrett, a Hounslow electrician, who won in a time of 2hr 42m 31s. Much was made of the fact that he had beaten Johnny Hayes' Olympic time by almost 13 minutes, but since the race had started in Windsor Park and finished at Stamford Bridge stadium rather than the White City, the times could hardly be compared.

The *Life* had tipped Barrett to win and took added satisfaction from the fact that only two of the eight foreign runners had managed to finish "so that one result of the race has been to show that for pluck, speed and stamina, Britishers have not deteriorated but are still able to hold their own against the best that the world can produce to oppose them."

It also noted with approval that the 27-year-old Barrett "abstains from alcohol and tobacco," but added, somewhat tetchily, that the third man home, Harry Green, was not such a paragon of virtue since he "does not altogether eschew alcohol".

To capitalise on its publicity coup, the paper brought out a 16-page penny booklet on marathon running and two years later, when the tippling Herne Hill harrier, Harry Green, beat the Canadian, Mike Ryan and 47 others, it was quick to claim a share of the glory:

> A few years ago Green discovered he could run well over a long distance and he went systematically to work to improve himself. He obtained a copy of the *Sporting Life* publication *How to Become a Marathon Winner* read it, assimilated it, moulded his running upon it, and soon met with success.

Despite the abandonment of the 1910 race due to the death of Edward VII and a four-year hiatus during the First World War, the race for the *Sporting Life* Trophy quickly achieved worldwide status and from 1912 until 1968 it was the official British trial for the Olympic marathon. Not that the home brigade had a monopoly on the event. In the three years preceding the WWI, it was won by a Canadian, a Swede and a Tunisian.

In 1919, when run as the Victory Marathon and confined to members of the British and Allied forces, the race was started by George V and won by Ed Woolston of the Machine Gun Corps. It was a remarkable performance from a man who, six months earlier, was still in hospital recovering from the effects of being gassed at Ypres in May 1918.

The Lincolnshire farmer, Bobby Mills, produced another upset when he beat the Italian champion, Valeria Arri, in 1920 and he showed that win was no fluke by going on to complete a 'Poly' hat trick before being beaten by Axel Jensen of Denmark in 1923.

In 1924 victory went to Duncan McLeod Wright who beat his Shettleston Harriers club-mate, Sam Ferris, by 45sec, but two months later, Ferris left wee Dunkie Wright toiling in his wake when he finished fifth in the Olympic marathon in Paris.

That performance marked the beginning of an extraordinary reign for the RAF (Uxbridge) harrier, who had his name engraved on the *Life's* trophy no fewer than eight times from 1925 to 1933, only missing out in 1930 due to illness. And it could well have been more had he not been posted out to Iraq for five years just before the 1934 race.

Despite Ferris's dominance at home, the popular Ulsterman was never able to win an Olympic gold. He finished eighth in Amsterdam in 1928 and was second in Los Angeles in 1932 when he left his run just too late to catch the exhausted Argentinean, Juan Carlos Zabala, who held on to win by 17sec in a record time of 2hr 31m 36s.

Bert Norris of the promoting club was the next multiple-winner, running up a hat trick in 1935-37, but he failed to make the Olympic rostrum in 1936, although the wiry little Sheffield bricklayer, Ernie Harper, who had finished fourth to Norris that year, ran the race of his life to be second to the Korean, Kitei Son, in Berlin.

In 1940, war conditions forced the race to be run over private roads in Windsor Park and from 1941-45 it was held over a four-lap course adjacent to the Polytechnic Harriers stadium in Chiswick, west London. The race reverted to a Windsor-Chiswick route in 1946 when George VI sent a record field of 99 on its way, but Olympic laurels again eluded the trophy's winners when the games returned to London in 1948.

This time the marathon was run over an out-and-back northern route from Wembley stadium to Radlett, Herts., but the jinx that had denied Sam Ferris Olympic gold struck again when the Welshman,

Tommy Richards, winner of the trophy in 1944-45 and runner up in 1947, was beaten 16sec by another Argentinean, Delfo Cabrera.

In 1951, Jim Peters emerged as a live Olympic prospect when he had his name engraved on the trophy's silver scrolls for the first time. The Dagenham optician underlined his claims the following year when he set a new record of 2hr 20m 42s in the race, but in Helsinki he could not live with the amazing Emil Zatopek – no one could. In the space of eight unforgettable days, the red-vested Czech army lieutenant tore the heart out of his opponents as he ran away with the 10,000 metres, the 5,000 metres and then the marathon at his first attempt over that distance.

Peters came back from that humbling experience stronger and more determined than ever, and in 1953 he clipped two minutes off his Poly record. Remarkably, he set another world best of 2hr 17m 39.4s in the event the following year,* but by now the strain of his punishing 20-miles-a-day training schedule was beginning to show.

In reporting Peters' victory, the *Life's* athletics correspondent, chief sports sub and night editor, Arthur Robins, writing under his 'Clubman' pseudonym, predicted:

> I will hazard a guess that this will be his last season over the gruelling marathon journey. At the finish he looked almost all in and it would not surprise me if he confines his actions to the track after the Empire Games race in August.

The Empire (Commonwealth) Games were held in Vancouver that year and the prescient Robins, a marathon runner himself in his younger days, went on to quote Peters as saying that he understood the course was "apparently a bit of a killer". It almost was. On a sweltering summer's day not made for long-distance running, Roger Bannister won his 'Mile-of-the-Century' duel with Australia's John Landy – the only other man to have broken the four-minute mile – just as Peters was approaching the stadium, an incredible 17 minutes (some three miles) ahead of his nearest rival. The report echoed the agony of Pietri's collapse 46 years earlier:

> Hardly had the cheering died away after the Bannister-Landy mile, when a frail looking figure in white shorts and vest, tottered into the stadium. The crowd of 35,000 rose to cheer the Marathon winner home from his gruelling run. But Jim Peters was not home yet. His head rolling from side to side as he gasped for breath, he fell to the track with a lap still to go. For a full two minutes he lay motionless.
>
> A hush fell on the horrified crowd. Police and doctors gathered round, knowing that to help him meant his disqualification. Other events came to a halt, and the athletes saw the gallant Peters climb unsteadily to his feet. He tried to run on, but almost immediately he was down again. The courage which had driven him more than the distance round the Equator since he took up marathon running eight years ago again brought him to his feet.
>
> From side to side of the track he reeled in agony. Down again and then up. A few anguished paces and down again. Fifteen minutes after he had entered the stadium he had covered only 150 yards. He must have fallen 20 times.
>
> At last he crossed what he thought was the finishing line. Mick Mays, the English masseur,

---

* The time taken to cover the 26m 385yds has been whittled down over the years until the record now stands at 2hr 3m 59s, recorded by Haile Gebrselassie of Ethiopia over the flat Berlin course in 2008.

wrapped his arms around the exhausted runner and carried him from the track. Mays, too, had mistaken the finishing-line. There were still 220 yards to go. The line Peters crossed was that which had been used for the finish of the mile.

Nothing could have been crueller and it was little wonder that the 35-year-old Peters announced his retirement from athletics a couple of months later.

In 1962, the *Life* also retired from the field when it withdrew its trophy from the marathon. The Polytechnic had been struggling for some years to finance the race and, having failed to coax the paper's new *Daily Mirror*-dominated management into providing the necessary funds, they found a new sponsor in Callard & Bowser, the famous makers of butterscotch – 'a most valuable energy food'.

In the race programme, Arthur Winter, the organising secretary, recorded with deep regret that "the *Sporting Life* could not accept the division of the credit that would have been necessary had their trophy been retained as the premier award of the race." And for the next seven years one of the most famous trophies in the world languished out of sight and out of mind under a dust sheet in a strong-room at 93 Long Acre, the headquarters of Odhams Press, owners of the *Life* from 1920 until 1961 when the firm became a subsidiary of the International Publishing Corporation (IPC) and the paper joined the *Mirror* group.

Then, in 1969 as the Poly marathon celebrated its diamond jubilee, Winter wrote to Odhams to suggest the trophy be linked to the Olympics. Almost in desperation, he added that he felt the directors of the *Life* "never realised the great part their trophy had played in developing the athletic manhood of this country". His proposal that it should be held by the club whose runner was the first Briton to finish in the Olympic marathon found little favour with the company's publicity manager, Eric Sykes.

In referring to the splendid hulk of Edwardian silverware, Sykes unwittingly rivalled his comic namesake as he replied:

It is my opinion that in conception and execution it belongs to the period when it was first presented … For that reason, I discussed with my colleagues the possibility of modernising it by removing the sculptured Marathon runner which forms the apex of the trophy and mounting it on a simple plinth to make it more acceptable to present-day standards. This, of course, would involve additional expenditure which, to be frank, we have no wish to incur.

Fortunately, a horrified Winter vetoed the proposed decapitation and, following further correspondence, it was agreed that the trophy should be given by a deed of gift to the Polytechnic on the understanding that it would be presented as a national award for long-distance running and "taken out of the partisanship of club athletics altogether". But by now the race was in decline. While it was attracting bigger fields, a corresponding increase in traffic made the problems of policing the route safely insurmountable and in 1973 the Windsor to Chiswick course was abandoned and a new route brought in, starting in front of Windsor Castle and finishing at the local athletic grounds.

In 1976, the egg-marketing organisation, Goldenlay, took over as race-sponsors and by the time the former Olympians Chris Brasher and John Disley inaugurated the London marathon in 1981, the *Life's* mighty trophy had become just one of many awards ranging from pewter tankards to egg-cups that were presented to runners and inter-area teams.

When the Poly marathon lapsed in 1988, the trophy was put on display at the Victoria and Albert museum, but six years later, following talks between Chris Brasher and Charlie Wilson, editor-in-chief of the *Life*, it was returned to its proper place on the world's athletic stage as it became officially linked to the London marathon.

Today, its ever extending scrolls record all the winners of the Flora-sponsored event, so Paula Radcliffe's name has joined those of Harry Barrett, machine-gunner Ed Woolston, 'Smiling Sam' Ferris, Jim Peters and a host of other long-forgotten heroes who pounded out the miles on the long and winding road from Windsor to London.

In 2003 the name of Chris Brasher was added to the trophy's title as a fitting tribute to the 1956 Olympic 3,000 metres steeplechase champion who had died that February. And so the Chris Brasher-Sporting Life Trophy now serves as a permanent memorial to two outstanding front-runners.

THE FIGHT AGAINST THE FADDISTS

T HE ARRIVAL of William Will at 148 Fleet Street in 1903 was a timely one in many ways. Not only did he put the *Life* back on its feet, but he was also responsible for organising an effective opposition to the 'faddists' as the paper scornfully dubbed the alliance of clergy and middle-class moralists who made up the Anti-Gambling League.

Formed in 1890 with the express purpose of wiping the whole ungodly caboodle of bookmakers, tipsters and the racing press off the face of the earth, the League was led with crusading zeal by its honorary secretary, John Hawke, who had the support of some influential politicians and churchmen. Foremost among them were the League's president, the Earl of Aberdeen, Lord Davey and the Bishop of Hereford, while its 23 vice-presidents included an archdeacon, a couple of deans and a smattering of reverends.

In 1901 the movement was presented with a heaven-sent opportunity to achieve its ends when Aberdeen, Davey and the Bishop of Hereford were appointed to a House of Lords select committee set up to inquire into "the increase of public betting amongst all classes and whether any legislative measures are possible for checking the abuses occasioned thereby".

Following a lengthy investigation, the nine-man committee concluded that "the increased prevalence of betting throughout the country is largely due to the great facilities afforded by the Press and to the inducements to bet offered by means of bookmakers' circulars and tipsters' advertisements." Consequently, it recommended that all such inducements should be made illegal.

It was what the sporting press had feared and yet it seemed only reasonable to expect that if the newspapers could not regulate themselves with regard to the advertisements they accepted, then the law would have to do it for them.

The *Life* may not have been too particular about the *bona fide* of its advertisers during its early days, but now both it and the *Sporting Chronicle* demanded 'proof wires' from tipsters confirming their selections before the start of racing. In this, however, the two papers were in the minority. The *Sportsman* imposed no such conditions, while other papers, particularly the provincial press, blatantly connived with their swindling clients.

It was standard practice for newspapers to charge tipsters three or more times the normal rate for adverts, in return for which the more disreputable journals left spaces in the draft notices which proclaimed the names of the 'winners' purportedly given by the tipster and, "No matter what won, someone in the newspaper office would fill the name in where blanks had been left for the purpose."[1]

Bookmakers' circulars, which evolved from the old tipping sheets, came into being as a result of Anderson's 1874 Betting Act. Barred from advertising their ante-post prices in the press, the layers simply published their own 'newspapers' containing "the latest market movements on all future events," and advertised them quite legally in the press where they were offered to the public "Free on receipt of address".

During their 17-year sojourn in France, bookmakers ran off these circulars on their own presses. In Calais, James Webster published the *French and English Turf Chronicle*, while William Wilson brought out the *Calais Record*. In Boulogne, Valentine, Hardaway and Topping had the *French and English Sportsman*; Morey and Janey, the *Bow Record* and George Waller the *Continental Turf Gazette*.

When the French government brought in a pari-mutuel monopoly in 1891, the banished bookies simply packed up their presses and moved on to Holland where they continued business as normal. Ten years later the Lords select committee appeared to recognise the absurdity of the situation when it noted: "The plan of giving licences to bookmakers has been adopted in some of the Australian Colonies, and if it were introduced into this country it might possibly diminish street betting and also do much to check fraud and dishonesty, both on the part of the bookmaker and of the backer."

But then it ducked the issue by claiming, "the establishment of such a system in this country is open to serious objections ... it would mean the legal recognition of the bookmaker and necessitate the making of betting debts recoverable by law."

Oh dear! Oh dear! To think that such a dreadful eventuality should ever come to pass! What happened instead was that three members of the committee, Lord Davey, the Bishop of Hereford and Lord Newton, spent the rest of their political careers vainly attempting to curb the swindling activities of bookmakers, tipsters and a compliant press.

Unfortunately, most of their well-intentioned bills were drafted in such a way as to be seen either as an attack upon the liberty of the subject or on the freedom of the press and, while they would often pass through the House of Lords unopposed, they were invariably strangled in the Commons.

The campaign against betting had been on the increase ever since the *Life's* earliest days when the paper's success resulted in an avalanche of sporting publications and an accompanying surge in betting.

In 1874 an attempt was made to outlaw all betting when private prosecutions, taken out under the 1853 Act, were brought against the lessees of several metropolitan racecourses and the stewards of the Jockey Club. The latter case created a sensation when Henry Chaplin, the owner of the Derby winner Hermit and MP for Mid-Lincolnshire, was served with a summons which charged him and his fellow stewards, Lord Falmouth and Admiral Rous, with having "knowingly and willingly" permitted betting to take place on Newmarket racecourse during the July meeting of that year.

But the prosecution, like so many others, floundered in a sea of legal ambiguity as the judiciary, comprising the finest legal brains in the land, could not agree on what constituted a 'place' for betting within the meaning of the Act.

In 1891 the Anti-Gambling League brought a new wave of prosecutions against on-course bookmakers, the Jockey Club and the lessees of Kempton Park and Northampton racecourses. The case was won in the High Court, but was overturned on appeal to the House of Lords. Despite this reverse, the League made a major impact in fostering and promoting the movement against racing and betting. Amongst a flood of evangelistic pamphlets it issued was the 1893 publication *A Blot on the Queen's Reign* in which John Hawke quoted from an editorial in *The Times*:

> Betting is no longer the exclusive appanage of aristocratic dissipation; it is the delight of shop men and servants; it roars daily along Fleet Street with its unsavoury following of touts and roughs; it forms the favourite reading, morning and evening, of the clerks on their way to and from the banks and counting houses of London and other great cities; it lies in wait for the schoolboy almost as soon as he begins to feel an interest in athletic competitions; it entraps, we are assured, even women and children; it is a main element in the miserable story of an immense number of embezzlements and frauds.

Hawke went on to cite other outlets for gambling that included lotteries, newspaper competitions and the stock market together with its plebeian equivalent, the bucket shops where bets were made on the rise and fall of individual share prices.

He maintained that these "prolific sources of misery and ruin, of destruction of life and degradation of soul" were alien to a Christian society, and he aimed to exorcise "their volume and power of evil" by making all betting illegal "for rich and poor, on credit or for ready money". Failing this, he called for the publication of starting prices to be banned, "as betting is increased and facilitated by the Press acting as an intermediary by quoting the betting odds." More specifically he claimed:

High class sporting papers like the *Field* would have nothing to fear; their columns filled with the varied interests of country life and manly sports, while those which depend but to a moderate extent on betting will soon accommodate themselves to circumstances and provide healthier food for their readers.

As to the ones which exist entirely on the vicious habit of betting, pandering wholesale to the evil and battening on the unwholesome excitement, they are pests of society which would perish in deserved contempt; their proprietors are nothing but gambling touts and their offices should be dealt with as Common Gaming Houses.

Predictably, George Lowe had chosen to ignore these Hawkish rants as he argued:

Such people have always existed and my principle has been to refuse them the publicity they are always craving for in the newspapers. Without some sort of ventilation to air their wretched and gloomy views, they can cause very little annoyance and no harm; consequently it is the better plan to treat them with silent contempt.[2]

The *Sportsman*'s Special Commissioner, William Allison, saw things in a very different light and in 1894 he was instrumental in setting up a body to fight Hawke and his disciples. On November 3 that year, his paper issued a four-page supplement to announce it had formed the Sporting League to, "resist the encroachments of the various bodies who occupy themselves in interfering with the sports and recreations of the people."

It stated that more than 400 leading sporting representatives, including such Jockey Club luminaries as the Earls of Durham, Lonsdale and March, had been appointed to the League's council, while an accompanying editorial warned of what could happen if the country reverted to Cromwellian times:

Again and again it must be impressed on the public that all the many varieties of sports, recreations and pastimes are as one in the view of the Puritan 'faddists' and must be defended as one. Therefore, the poor man's skittle-alley or his whippet will be protected as jealously as the richer man's hunting or his racehorse…

We know that on the only occasion in our history when the Puritans got the upper hand, they repressed and punished all human pleasure, whether it were theatre-going, horseracing or the humble sports on the village greens. History repeats itself whenever the chance is afforded and we know from this past experience how we should all be ground down and trampled underfoot if we should ever be foolish enough to let the shrieking sisterhood of women and reputed men attain really to power.

This call to arms ended with a special message for the team at 148 Fleet Street…

We do in all sincerity wish it to be understood that our efforts have in no sense whatever been in the comparative narrow interests of *The Sportsman*, but for the great cause in the interests of which all sporting papers exist ... We are sure they and the British public will alike feel that the Sporting League is far removed beyond the little journalistic rivalries which are healthy enough in their way, but are altogether out of place when touching a subject of national importance.

But 'little journalistic rivalries' tend to be magnified out of all proportion when a paper is in trouble, and the *Sporting Life* gave the League a very cool reception indeed. In fact, Lowe refused to acknowledge its existence until he was forced to when its president, the Jockey Club's James Lowther, devoted most of his Gimcrack Club dinner speech to promoting its aims.

Theodore Cook, at least, gave the new body a guarded welcome:

I fancy it savours of the 'much ado about nothing' order, moreover giving undue colour to the idea that sport can be damaged by the quips and cranks of a few mad enthusiasts on the ramp. But now that it is *un fait accompli* it behoves every sportsman to join the ranks and do all that lies in his power to strengthen its operations everywhere, in which case 'twill become a power in the land indeed. For (as has truly been said) the great charm of sport is that it knows neither rank nor station nor politics, peer mixes with peasant, merit is its only passport to favour, and its universal motto '*Vive le Sport!* – may the best man win'.

However, a few weeks later as the League campaigned on behalf of the dual Grand National winning rider, John Maunsell Richardson, who was a Tory candidate in the Brigg by-election, 'Old Blue' hardened his views as he observed:

I regret to note inclination is being evinced by the newly formed Sporting League to take an active part in politics as a representative body which, mark my words, will be fatal to the best interests of sport if persevered in. All may be of roseate hue now, but, sooner or later, the rift in the lute will be discernible and, as sure as fate, party feeling, which has been known to sever long-standing ties of friendship, aye, even put father and son at loggerheads, will show its cloven hoof.

Dozens of influential sportsmen decried this departure from what they had deemed the non-political objects of the League the other night, and for myself I quite thought it was founded for defence, not offence. As I said at the onset, by all means combine for mutual advice and protection if you like, but as for politics in any shape or form 'We'll have none of it' is the cry of the vast majority of sportsmen where'er located.

This was a remarkably naive stance for Cook to take since the main purpose of the League was to support those who were in a position to oust the faddists from power and it was churlish of the *Life* to ignore the part the organisation played in the Lincolnshire by-election when Richardson was returned thanks to the strength of the sporting vote.

As the battle between the opposing Leagues escalated, it drew in other sections of society. Town councils found themselves divided over whether public libraries should censor the newspapers in their reading rooms by blacking-out the racing columns with an inked roller – a practice that started soon after the Anti-Gambling League was founded, and which was to continue in some libraries until the legalisation of all betting in 1961.

In 1894 a row broke out between the Sheffield council and the Free Library committee after the council had given its backing to 245 petitions from various religious societies demanding blacking-out. Following a heated debate, the council was outvoted and had to back down over the issue, but other libraries were only too willing to apply the censor's ink be it black or white. When referring to the action of the Aston (Birmingham) Free Library committee that autumn, 'Old Blue' noted cynically:

…as regards racing intelligence and the current odds, they have cut the Gordian knot by erasing all such from the London and provincial newspapers *in toto*. The first idea was to 'blacken' out the latter in highly suggestive style, but after sitting in solemn council awhile, an amendment in favour of 'whitening' was unanimously carried, emblematic of the purity of their motives I presume!

The extent to which the gambling paranoia had grown was illustrated in a letter the *Life* published during the summer of 1896 under the heading 'The Liberty of the Subject':

Sir – Are we descending into a position of white slavedom, and is the liberty of the subject to be entirely ignored? We, the drivers and conductors of the Atlas and Waterloo Association of Omnibus Proprietors, have just received notice that 'If any driver or conductor be known to back horses he will be instantly dismissed'.

Surely after working day after day, fifteen hours and a half with scarcely time for meals, men should be allowed to have their shillings on 'Augur's' big-lettered selections without running the risk of losing their situations.

When the masters journey to Liverpool to see the National run, or to Ascot on the Hunt Cup day, perhaps they only go to see the racing and do not have a bet!

I withhold my name and address from publication, or I should be instantly dismissed, you bet. – Yours etc. A White Slave.

Meanwhile, the hypocrisy of the faddists was constantly being exposed by Cook in his 'Men and Matters in the World of Sport' column. Never short of material to draw on, he noted in June 1895 that the Rev Hugh Price-Hughes, a vice-president of the Anti-Gambling League, had "put his foot in it somewhat severely" in that…

the reverend gentleman, whilst preaching against horseracing, betting etc … thought it not amiss to insert advertisements relating thereto in the Non-conformist paper which he conducts. *The New Age* promptly sits upon him for this and takes him to task in great style. Let these ultra-purists wash their dirty linen among themselves, I have no patience with any of them. Yet the latter contemporary is consistent at any rate. I agree that, as a vice-president and great high priest of the faddist party, Mr Hughes 'ought to know better than to advertise horseracing in a Methodist journal'.

It is really too comical for anything. But by the same token other contemporaries I wot of pursue exactly the same tactics, raving against betting etc, in one column whilst giving detailed up-to-date odds in the next. Comment is needless.

Cook made a habit of dining out on pontificating parsons and the following year, while reflecting on the hugely popular victory of the Prince of Wales's Persimmon in the Derby, he took a Scottish minister to task for having had the temerity to criticise the heir to the throne for his association with the sport.

From Her Majesty the Queen – God bless her! – downwards, congratulations galore poured in upon the Heir Apparent and one would have thought that even the extra goody-goody section of society would have (at least) ceased their fuming in such a case. But no! the Rev. Dr Fergus Ferguson must needs give vent to what Carlyle would have dubbed 'more d——d impertinences' the other night in Glasgow.

He thought that if some colporteurs were sent to Epsom, perhaps the Prince might be induced to try for a higher race than the Derby, and peradventure Lord Rosebery's soul might be saved also. This fairly takes the biscuit and knocks all the rant of Chadband and Pecksniff into a cocked hat! He who has the amazing presumption to discuss the morals of his future King, let alone the morality of the Turf, should himself be as holy as severe, and cannot be aware that '*Incedit per ignes suppositos cineri doloso*'.* [Roughly, 'He who walks through fire must expect to get burnt'].

The campaign against betting even found favour in Fleet Street where, in 1903, the *Daily News*, owned by the Cadbury brothers of chocolate fame, dropped its coverage of racing and inserted in its contents bill the words 'No Betting or Turf News'. The move was welcomed by the trade journal, the *Newspaper Owner*, which commented:

We wish it well and hope the time will speedily come when other newspapers will follow the example of *The Daily News* and at any rate eliminate betting quotations from their pages. If this were done, it would contribute more than anything else to stop the growth of this great national vice.

What the *Newspaper Owner* omitted to mention was that *The Star*, the popular London evening also owned by the Cadburys, devoted most of its early editions to racing and made a special point of advertising Captain Coe's selections in its contents bill!

Despite all this hypocrisy, the faddists continued to make ground as they encouraged town and county councils to bring in bye-laws for the suppression of betting. In 1903, prosecutions soared in many parts of the country as inoffensive newspaper sellers were pounced upon in the street and hauled before the beak under a law that stated: "No person shall frequent any public place for the purpose of selling any paper devoted wholly or mainly to giving information as to the probable results of races."

Those who sold the *Life* only escaped prosecution because of the extensive coverage it gave to other sports, but by now the faddist threat was being taken seriously at its offices. William Will, unlike Lowe, believed in taking the fight to the enemy and as soon as he joined the paper he began to promote the aims of the National Sporting League, which had been formed in 1902 by an alliance of northern bookmakers who had been snubbed by the original body.

Will not only let the new organisation set up its headquarters in an office at 148 Fleet Street, he also agreed to act as its treasurer. Years later the League's secretary, Joe Marshall, acknowledged the

* Racing's debt to the Prince of Wales (Edward VII) during this testing time cannot be overstated and it was underlined by the *Life* when he died in May 1910. The paper went over-the-top with its tribute headline, 'Greatest Monarch Of All Time', but William Will was not far out when he observed: "Without doubt King Edward's influence was largely responsible for the successful resistance to the attacks of the faddists. When a monarch of his character and dignity deigns not only to patronise a sport, but to intimately associate himself with it, the fulminations of *soi-disant* Puritans against that particular pastime might be regarded as ludicrous were they not an insult to the Throne ... Within living memory the term 'a racing man' was practically synonymous with that of 'vagabond' in the minds of the middle classes, and it is largely due to the late King Edward that the idea that the racecourse is nothing more nor less than a sink of iniquity has been removed from the minds of all but a few irreconcilables."

contribution the non-betting, teetotal, church-going Scot had made to the NSL when he wrote: "I frankly admit that had it not been for the wise counsel and splendid assistance which we received from the then editor of the *Sporting Life*, Mr W Will, our Society would have gone under."[3]

The NSL certainly needed all the help it could get in rallying its troops because it was to be badly outmanoeuvred in 1906 when Lord Davey's Street Betting Bill, which had been brought forward every year since 1894, was finally adopted by Henry Campbell-Bannerman's Liberal government and passed into law.

Under the old bye-laws the maximum penalty that could be imposed on a street bookmaker was £5, but the new Act allowed for fines of £10 for a first offence, £20 for a second and £60 (£5,400) or six months' imprisonment with hard labour for a third offence. It also closed all the loopholes the illegal layers had exploited in their efforts to circumvent the confused betting laws by stating that the word 'street' included…

> any public bridge, road, lane, footway, square, court, alley or passage whether a thoroughfare or not, and the words 'public place' shall include any public park, garden or sea-beach and any unenclosed ground to which the public for the time being have unrestricted access, and shall also include every enclosed place … to which the public have a restricted right of access, whether by payment or otherwise … Nothing contained in this Act shall apply to any ground used for the purpose of a racecourse for racing with horses or adjacent thereto on the days on which races take place.

Because the Act was aimed specifically at the working classes, it was as inequitable as its predecessors, and was condemned as such by Will in an editorial that December:

> We agree with the arguments that this is class legislation and that what is law for the working man should be law for the rich man, but we argue from the point of view that the House of Lords and the House of Commons have no moral right to dictate to either the rich man or the poor man what he shall do with the money that he has honestly worked for. The liberty of the individual which is the bedrock of the greatness of the English-speaking race is too sacred a thing to be surrendered to an unholy alliance of bishops, stockbroker MPs and Non-conformist parsons.
>
> Let it be conceded that the street is not a proper place for betting and we are at once face to face with the only real solution of the betting question; the licensing of bookmakers to carry on their perfectly legitimate business in registered premises.

In another column, a tabulated list of the number of street betting convictions obtained in major English towns and cities over the past three years provided an interesting league table of how vigorously the various district authorities had pursued their quarry.

London, predictably, headed the list with its conviction rate rising from 3,276 in 1903 to 4,997 in 1905; Newcastle came next with 864 convictions in 1905 followed by Birmingham (680), Liverpool (139) and Manchester (109). At the other end of the scale just five worthy citizens of Blackpool breached the bye-laws in 1905 and in the sporting county borough of York nary a soul, although there was one sorry transgressor in 1904.

Two weeks later the contents of a letter which the Anti-Gambling League had sent to Lord Davey was leaked to Will, who took the opportunity to admonish those in racing who had displayed such an apathetic attitude towards the threat posed by the clique of "self-righteous and meddlesome cranks" that made up the faddist lobby.

Under the three-deck headline 'The Enemies Of Racing / A Call For Action / Organise! Organise!' he quoted from the letter in which the League boasted of the part it had played in urging councils to suppress betting, and also cited a cumbersome sentence from its journal, which, for added emphasis, he highlighted in bold type:

> **'England will never be the England that she should be until horse racing, and all that appertains to it, is swept away with the bosom of destruction.'**

Having got his reader's attention, 'Augur' continued:

> In the letter of thanks to Lord Davey which, curiously enough, bears the same date as the new Street Betting Act – 21st December, 1906 – the executive of the Anti-Gambling League are good enough to inform us what will be the next step when they say: 'at the same time we consider that the omission of racecourses from a Betting Act leaves the scope of any such measure incomplete'.
>
> That last word, 'incomplete', explains a lot. Now, how long are racing folk going to stand this meddling with their affairs? ... The time has gone by for a policy of *laissez-faire*. Racing men must organise and when they do organise it must be an efficient organisation that shall speak in no uncertain manner to every member of Parliament.
>
> Why should the fads of a minority override the wishes of the majority? The sporting vote, properly organised, should be sufficiently strong to make it plain that racing men will tolerate no further curtailment of their liberties.

It was a call to arms which Will and the *Life* were to repeat *ad nauseam*, but all too often it went unheeded or was undermined by the actions of rogue bookmakers and unprincipled newspaper proprietors who, in their greed to line their own pockets at the expense of the gullible public, played into the hands of Mr Hawke and his followers.

FOOTBALL BANDITS

PIECEMEAL legislation, proposed and passed by pontificating politicians, seldom achieves its desired objective and, as with the Betting Acts of 1853 and 1874, so it was with the Street Betting Act of 1906. It accomplished nothing and only aggravated the supposed evils it was designed to suppress. No sooner had the Act come into effect than many of the country's street bookmakers took themselves off to Holland to set themselves up as 'football accountants'.

This latest scheme to relieve punters of their 'hard-earned' had its origins in the competitions run by most sections of the British press. Some papers required contestants to fill in the missing words in a given section of text, while the sporting press offered prizes to any clairvoyant who was able to select the winners of six nominated races on a given day – an early 'Scoop6' in fact. The competitions were free to enter, but each entry had to be made on a coupon printed in the paper. The more coupons sent in, the better the chance of winning; and so the sales of numerous minor rags were boosted far beyond their merit.

In 1883 the *Sporting Life Racing Guide** introduced a 'Name the Winners' competition which started off with a prize of 5gns and, with an extra 5gns added to the pool each time it was not won, built up to a maximum of 50gns. The competition was soon bringing in 9,000 entries a week and such was its success that by 1898 the pot had been increased to 250gns (£23,625), an amount that was doubled for Cambridgeshire week when, if six winners were not found, 200gns could be won for five winners and 50gns for four.

By this time the national press had latched onto the increasing popularity of football to run similar competitions in which readers were required to forecast the results of specified matches. Newspaper football coupons quickly became a craze that swept the country and it was from this lucrative pool that the football accountants emerged, dripping with the anticipation of easy money. They were not to be disappointed.

From rented offices in the Dutch towns of Middelburg and Flushing they cast their net far and wide as they posted off their pseudo newspapers such as the *Football Chat, Football Record* and *Football Sport*, and the haul was mighty indeed as the circulars brought in coupons and postal orders by the sack full. Any punter lucky enough to submit a winning coupon was told his entry had not been received and even if he took legal action and was successful in court, the bookmaker would simply plead the Gaming Act (of 1844) under which gambling debts were not recoverable in law. Thus was daylight robbery conducted with impunity under the sanction of the State.

The football bandits flourished unopposed for more than four years before the Dutch authorities showed them the red card when, on 6 March 1911, a multi-deck headline in the *Life* announced: 'Betting in Holland / English Bookmakers in Peril / Result of Football Betting':

> For several years English bookmakers in Holland have been subjected to 'alarums and excursions' in consequence of threatened legislation which was to destroy the whole system. The faddist party, a very small one, had made futile efforts to create trouble, but little progress was made for years, indeed until betting on football and cricket results became part and parcel of the Anglo-Dutch system.

---

* Initially, a pocket-sized penny publication, the weekly *Racing Guide* (1880) had no editorial content and was essentially a form book that also carried programmes for the following week's racing.

Then many moderate members came to the assistance of the faddists and their agitation culminated in the passage through the second chamber of the Dutch Parliament on Friday of a stringent measure, which calls for the suppression of bookmakers and totalisators at all race meetings. English bookmakers will not, after the passing of the Bill, be allowed to conduct their business in Holland, and in his speech in the debate, the Minister of Justice declared that bookmakers dealing with clients by post would have to leave Holland under pain of imprisonment.

The following day a leading article by 'Augur', which lacked William Will's authoritative imprint, gave a remarkable example of the sort of double standards usually employed by the faddists as it explained why the *Life* had set its sights against football betting. With all the fervour of a campaigning bishop, 'Augur' cried:

We of the *Sporting Life* have always opposed this form of speculation as bitterly as we know how. Right at the start we recognised the fearful evils that might result from the propagation of 'skill' competitions and 'totalisators' on football matches and decided that so far as advertisements re football were concerned, there was 'nothing doing'...

Why? Well, just because this wretched business of betting on football has been the means of bringing all forms of speculation into disrepute. Betting on horseracing and betting on football are as different as chalk and cheese. They are as the poles asunder. Betting and horseracing are necessary concomitants. Betting and football is an incongruous and demoralising combination.

All the boys in the street have a nodding acquaintance with football and the men who play the game. For one penny they can take a chance in a £50 lottery. You and I know just how much chance they have; but they, poor, innocent youngsters, really believe that there are benevolent gentlemen resident in Holland who are itching – yes, positively itching – to give away something for nothing.

What is the result? We find mere children dabbling in speculation. We find office boys stealing their masters' stamps in order to back, say, Tottenham Hotspur or Chelsea, and we get the blame! 'Ruined by Betting!' is a poster which catches the eye at every turn ... To put it mildly, betting on football is just about the lowest rung on the ladder of speculation. It is a dirty business which we have always condemned.

For sheer, unadulterated hypocrisy this took some beating, but the paper was right on one thing – it was 'a dirty business'. Later that month the *Life* published a long article on the subject by Walter Randall, secretary of the bookmakers' regulatory body, the Turf Guardian Society, that exposed the unabashed greed with which bookmakers and their accomplices in the newspaper world fed off the gullible public:

The scenes outside the Flushing Post Office on Saturday evenings, after the English mail has come in, have often been commented upon. Envelopes have been hurriedly opened in the streets and in the cafes, and not infrequently the only enclosure of any interest to the addressee has been the postal order ... in some cases where a postal order for 1s. accompanied a coupon which should have resulted in a win of £20 or £30, the envelope, coupon and postal order have all been destroyed together...

The Turf Guardian Society for some time has had a rule that no member shall be professionally engaged in betting on football and it placed itself in communication with several of the newspapers in which football accountants' advertisements appeared, in an endeavour to get the proprietors to see eye to eye with it. The second attempt to bring the Press into line was as abortive as the first...

A few months ago the advertisements of a certain provincial bookmaker were occupying, week by week, a whole page of a sporting paper. It was known that this business was being engineered by a man who, at the best, was recognised as a notorious defaulter with a long list of undischarged betting liabilities.

Not only did his advertisements appear, but the paper went out of its way to recommend its readers to place their commissions with this advertiser who was, it assured them, a thoroughly reliable and honest man. The editorial notice to this effect and the full-page advertisement appeared in the paper in question on the very day on which the defaulter and his fellow conspirator ... were arrested for fraud.

While Randall stopped short of naming the guilty parties, his article was a much-needed wake-up call to his own industry and the press, and he concluded by warning:

...unless some practical measures are taken by sound advertising commission agents and the Press and possibly by the recognised racing and betting tribunals, to give a greater measure of protection to the public, we may all, at no very distant date, be discussing the clauses of a Bill introduced in our own Parliament with the view to imposing further restrictions upon Turf transactions.

In this he was not wrong, not that the bookmakers in Holland, both honest and dishonest, were unduly concerned. When the Dutch Betting Bill became law in May 1911, these unsung forefathers of the EU simply upped roots and once again moved on to pastures new on what had become their Grand Tour of Europe.

The flamboyant Martin Benson, the self-proclaimed 'Prince of Turf Accounts' who traded under the name of 'Douglas Stuart', led the way as he placed a large front-page advert in the *Life* to announce he had relocated from Flushing to Basle in Switzerland, and by the end of the month the remaining bookmakers had followed. Topping & Spindler, a firm that had evolved out of the old Valentine & Wright partnership, chose Lucerne, but most of the others plumped for Basle.

And the bookmakers were not the only ones on the move. A few weeks before their flit from Holland, William Will, who had joined the *Life* in its hour of need and had played such a vital role in reviving its fortunes, resigned his post to move on to bigger, if not better, things.* In paying tribute to his boundless energy and editorial command, the paper he had served so well for just over seven years stated:

---

* Will went into the management side of journalism, initially with the *Graphic* newspaper group before becoming a director and London manager of Allied Newspapers Ltd when the Berry brothers, Lord Camrose and Lord Kemsley, formed that company in 1924 – principal titles in the group included the *Sunday Times, Daily Dispatch, Sporting Chronicle* and *Empire News* as well as various provincial papers. In 1926, Will was appointed a director of the Press Association (he was chairman in 1931-32), while he was also deputy chairman of Reuters and served on the council of the Newspaper Proprietors Association. Outside Fleet Street he was a leading light of the Scottish community in London, serving on the boards of various societies including a spell as president of the London Burns Club (his book, *Robert Burns as a Volunteer*, almost manages to portray the immortal Rabbie as a teetotaller!) and was also an elder of the Church of Scotland. On the outbreak of WWII he became chairman of the Newspaper and Periodical Emergency Council which liaised between the industry and the government. Under his direction newspapers accepted a voluntary system of censorship, while he won many battles with officialdom over unnecessary restrictions on the freedom of the press. In recognition of his service Will was appointed a CBE in 1945. He retired to Scotland and died in Dundee at the age of 91 in February 1958.

He has left behind him a record of services and success in this comparatively short period of which any man might be proud. It is not too much to say he has stamped his personality on every branch of sport ... His strict integrity, charm of manner and keen sense of humour have won and kept for him a host of friends, not only in England, but in the Colonies, in America and on the Continent.

Such a man was going to be hard to replace. His loyal lieutenant, W S Morley-Brown, seemed the obvious choice, but he was surprisingly passed over in favour of yet another Aberdonian, William Lints Smith, who had followed Will onto the *Aberdeen Journal* and then worked alongside him on the *St James's Gazette* before taking over from him as news editor when Will moved to the *Life*.

Morley-Brown, understandably miffed at not getting the job, left to become sports editor of the *Daily Chronicle* and its weekly sister paper *Lloyds News*, while his position of assistant editor was filled by Ben Bennison, a talented writer and former sports editor of *The Standard* and *The Tribune*.

Along with Bennison, Lints Smith brought in a number of fresh features to enhance the paper; in particular, he made good use of the caricature sketches of Chas Grave and, soon after he took over in April 1911, he began to use photos of race finishes and other events for the first time. Action photos, as opposed to posed portraits, had featured for some years in quality weeklies such as the *Illustrated London News* and *Sporting Sketches* in which their reproduction was perfect, but on the newsprint used by the *Life* they tended to lose definition and on occasions the inky images were all but indistinguishable.

Despite this, the increased pictorial aspect of the paper made it more attractive, while its outlook was broadened by the introduction of a 'World's News in Brief' column and articles by the famous playwright W Buchanan-Taylor ('Bayard'). That summer a review of Diaghilev's Ballets Russes Company at Covent Garden noted: "Nijinsky was a revelation. He seemed more often above ground than on it; he seemed to float through the air like a swallow on the wing" – just like the 1970 Triple Crown winner, in fact!

The new editor was also a great believer in the appeal of a well-conducted interview* and led by example when he featured Henry Chaplin, by then the Turf's senior statesman, in the 1911 Derby-day issue. It was quite a scoop for the paper and a fortnight later it scored again when it gave a front-page spread to a Bennison 'Special Interview' with Jack Johnson, the first black heavyweight champion of the world, who had just arrived in England "willing to fight anyone for £6,000 [£540,000] win or lose".

Bennison was bowled over by the charismatic 33-year-old American – "A more entertaining man or one who has shaped his notions more clearly it would be impossible to meet ... A great, imposing, remarkable man is Johnson" – but the racial prejudice that had dogged the boxer in the States resurfaced when he arranged to fight the popular British champion, 'Bombardier' Billy Wells, at Earl's Court in London.

The Free Church Council led the way in calling for the fight to be banned and in a letter to *The Times* headed 'A Menace To Public Life', the Rev J H Shakespeare, secretary of the British Baptist Union, claimed that whatever the outcome of the fight, "white and black will be pitted against each other in anger, revenge and murder ... there can be no greater disservice to the negro race than to

---

* Newspaper interviews became popular in America during the Civil War in the early 1860s, but they were regarded as an invasion of privacy in England and did not gain acceptance in Fleet Street until the late '80s when they were used to great effect by William Stead, the famous editor of the *Pall Mall Gazette*.

encourage it to seek glory in physical force and in beating the white man ... every voice which exalts animal passion in them is that of an enemy."[1]

The Archbishop of Canterbury wrote to Winston Churchill, then Home Secretary, urging him to stop the fight, and following similar calls from a bevy of bishops, Sir Robert Baden-Powell and the Lord Mayor of London, Churchill caved in and, without giving any grounds for his decision, declared the proposed contest would be illegal – a decree that put the future of British boxing in jeopardy.

On the strength of this ruling the DPP took out a summons against the boxers who appeared at Bow Street magistrates' court on September 28 to answer the charge that they planned a breach of the peace. Johnson took it upon himself to cross-question the Crown's chief witness and ran rings around him, but it did him no good as a High Court injunction was taken out to prevent the fight taking place.

The *Life* described the whole charade as "one of the greatest controversies that has ever been waged round the ring; a controversy of much bitterness, gross and wicked misrepresentation and distorted perspectives."

The following year saw more of the same when the Bishop of Hereford introduced a Gambling Advertisement Bill that would have made it impossible for any newspaper to publish starting prices. The Bishop's bill – one of many he introduced during a long political career – was eventually withdrawn only to be replaced by Lord Newton's Betting Inducements Bill which sought to prevent "the writing, printing, publishing or circulating in the United Kingdom of advertisements of any betting or tipsters' business."

The bill, which passed through the Lords but was blocked in the Commons, resulted in the sporting press making a belated attempt to put its house in order, and on 19 February 1913, the PA sent out the following statement over its wires:

The Press Association is authorised to announce that a conditional agreement has been arrived at by the *Sporting Life*, the *Sportsman* and the *Sporting Chronicle* and the majority of the weekly sporting papers, to cease publishing tipsters' advertisements. It has also been arranged that the insertion of bookmakers' advertisements will be regulated by a Press control committee to which official and unofficial information will be confidentially submitted.

Lints Smith had been instrumental in setting up the new body, the Newspaper Association for the Control of Sporting Advertisements, and in a PA interview which accompanied the announcement, he stated, with a degree of hyperbole:

Lord Newton's Bill has reopened the floodgates of calumny and misrepresentation, and given the enemies of racing a fresh opportunity for their destructive campaign.

It was an unwise measure in my opinion and I believe the sporting Press in general holds that view, but we all recognise that Lord Durham, Lord Derby and Lord Newton have the best interests of racing at heart and while we cannot agree with them in the step which was taken by Lord Newton, we are showing by the financial sacrifice – amounting each year to many thousands of pounds – we are making that we are anxious to meet the wishes of the ruling authorities to the utmost possible extent ... we expect, in that case, to hear no more of Lord Newton's Bill or any other measure for the curtailment of the betting facilities of the nation or the restriction of racing.

In this matter Lints Smith had his supporters in parliament and the Jockey Club. At a meeting of the NSL in January 1914, John Denison-Pender, MP for Newmarket, stressed that the leading sporting papers were the only guide the working man had as to who were the honest bookmakers and if their adverts were banned the punter would suffer.

Lord Lonsdale viewed the proposed legislation as a direct threat to the press and wrote to the editor to say: "I think it would be a terrible blow to the country if the daily sporting papers ceased to exist as such papers are a guide to the public as to what goes on in the sporting world and help so much to keep all sport pure and clean."[2]

Of course, neither the Betting Inducements Bill nor the Anti-Gambling League or all the years of parliamentary debate and legislation that had preceded and was to follow the 1906 Street Betting Act had the slightest effect in curbing man's instinctive desire to speculate in order to accumulate. Theodore Cook had summed up the situation perfectly in the autumn of 1894 when he mused on the activities of the faddists:

> I wonder if any person outside Bedlam really imagines that betting can be suppressed by Act of Parliament or that British folk will submit to such a breach of the liberty of the subject ... Betting is inherent in human nature, has flourished since the good old days of Adam, is carried on in every country under the sun, civilised or uncivilised, and all the Leagues in Christendom will have about as much effect in stopping it as Canute's little farce down by the sea. Moral suasion may prompt people to abstain if they wish it, but force never!

And so the battle rumbled on until it was drowned out by the thunder of guns from an altogether different sort of conflict in which a generation of young sportsmen were sent to a place called 'The Front' from which they never returned.

'PREPARE FOR THE HORRORS'

Sportsmen of every kind,
God! We have paid the score
Who left green English fields behind
For the sweat and stink of war![1]

DURING the golden summer of 1914, just before the world plunged patriotically and enthusiastically into an abyss of unmitigated horror, William Lints Smith was surprised and not a little flattered to be offered a managerial position on *The Times* by its proprietor, Lord Northcliffe (né Alfred Harmsworth).*

In his short time with the *Sporting Life* WLS had done much to extend the scope and appeal of the paper, but now he felt it was time to move on. At his farewell dinner at Simpson's in the Strand, he was praised for his "determination not to spare himself" and for his "never flagging regard for the comfort and happiness of the staff". He had been, it was generally agreed, an excellent editor.

For his replacement it was a case of welcome back W S Morley-Brown. Initially passed over for the job, the sagacious Scot had the good grace not to hold that fact against the joint-proprietor and managing editor, Walter Broomfield, who had acquired his share in the paper along with his marriage certificate to the widowed Mrs Eleanor McFarlane in 1909.

It was not the best of times to take up the editorship of a sports paper. Barely a month had passed since the Archduke Franz Ferdinand, heir to the Austro-Hungarian throne, had been gunned down in the streets of Sarajevo, and already most of Europe was in arms.

Just before his departure, Lints Smith had started a 'War News' column compiled from reports issued by the Central News Agency. It first appeared on July 30 when the headlines 'British Precautionary Measures / Austria's War Plans' reflected the doom-laden messages that had been posted on the billboards in Fleet Street that week.

The countdown to what David Lloyd George was to describe as 'organised insanity' had been relentless: Monday, 27th *The Times*: 'European Peace in the Balance'; 28th *Daily Telegraph*: 'War Cloud – England's Plan for Mediation'; 29th *Daily Mail*: 'Austria Declares War – Official'; 30th *Daily Chronicle*: 'Austrians Shell Belgrade'; 31st *Daily Herald*: 'Stop the War!'; Aug 1, *Daily Sketch*: 'Germany's 24 Hour Ultimatum to Russia'; 2nd *News of the World*: 'Germany Declares War'. And on August bank holiday Monday the *Herald's* board displayed just one word – 'Armageddon'.

The front page of the *Sporting Life* that day carried a list of 62 athletic meetings that were scheduled to take place throughout the country, while its athletics editor, Charles Otway, set out his reasons for the continuance of sport. It was a case that was to be argued many times during the next four years as the paper fought for its survival while other journals, hit by rising costs and starved of advertisers, faded away and died. A cross-country runner of some note, Otway began:

---

* As associate manager, Lints Smith had the task of tailoring the paper's finances to wartime requirements. In 1922 he became general manager and held that position until he retired in 1937, during which period *The Times* "rose to a degree of prosperity it had not known for over half a century".[2]

The shadow of war hangs heavy over England today and it may be held that graver matters than sport should concern the people. But sport, and especially athletic sport, has been a powerful factor in the making of the British character and when the time comes athletic sport will give of its best to the nation as it did in the dark hours of the South African War.

And the time had come; on page 5 the latest war news announced:

Germany has declared war on Russia and her ally, France, and the first shots of the tremendous European conflict have been fired. The fateful news was conveyed in the following message: 'St Petersburg, Saturday. The German ambassador, in the name of his government, handed to the Foreign Ministry a declaration of war at 7.38 this evening – Reuter'.

Reuter is informed that at 3.30 yesterday afternoon an official telegram was received announcing the fact that the Germans had invaded France and crossed the frontier of Cirey. Cirey-les-Forges is a town in the Department of Meurth-et-Moselle on the Vezouse. A Liege paper says the Germans numbered 20,000 and were repulsed with heavy losses.

The following day three columns were taken up with news of the conflict as War Office telegrams summoned Britain's sportsmen from the field of play, while many events had to be cancelled due to the general mobilisation.

On August 5, the front page of the *Life* looked much the same as it did on any other day.* Half the page was taken up with training reports; there were two columns of adverts, a column on the forthcoming Doncaster sales, the results from Newton Abbot and the usual 'Replies to Queries' correspondence.

The inside pages carried reports from Tuesday's three meetings; the card and form for the second day at Brighton; the results from a trotting meeting at Blackpool; snippets of news on rabbit coursing and croquet, and regular features on golf, tennis, boxing, swimming, athletics, etc. It was not until page 4 of the six-page number that readers learnt the nation had entered the abattoir of war. Under an advert for Scrubb's Ammonia – 'Marvellous Preparation; Invaluable for Toilet Purposes' – just over a column was devoted to this not altogether uninteresting item.

In an age when 'England' was interchangeable with 'Britain', the initial block-capital paragraph delivered the news in short, sharp, staccato sentences:

England is at war. The fateful news was flashed to the ends of the earth late last night. Earlier in the day the English government had called on Germany to respect the neutrality of Belgium. Germany's reply was to declare war on England.

The following official notification of the German declaration of war was made from the British Foreign Office at a quarter to twelve last night: 'His Majesty's Government has been informed that Germany declared war on this country at seven p.m. this day, and that His Majesty's Ambassador was handed his passports. A state of war therefore exists between Germany and this country as from seven p.m. on August 4'.

---

* Tradition died hard in Fleet Street; the *Life* did not start to carry the main story of the day on its front page until the 1920s and it was not until 1966 that the front page of *The Times* carried news instead of adverts.

On the same day, remount officers began to scour the country for suitable horses. It was to prove a rude awakening for many a well-groomed thoroughbred whose ability was not of sufficient merit to save it from being given a one-way ticket to the Front, for Britain, unlike the major continental powers, did not have a national stud to draw on.

While France, Russia, Germany, Austria and Hungary had laid out vast sums to buy English and Irish horses for their state studs, years of under-funding had left the nation's light-horse breeding industry quite unable to meet the demands of a full-scale war despite the costly and humiliating lessons of the Boer War. Then Britain's reserves were quickly exhausted and some 24,000 horses had to be bought from Hungary after which it was found that, through the combined incompetence of the Remount Department and the sharpness of the dealers, the animals were quite unsuitable for the task in hand.

The French, at least, had learnt from the Franco-Prussian war and had established a National Stud to ensure a ready supply of quality cavalry horses – a source from which the French Saddlebred (*selle francais*) emerged to make such an impression on British jump racing in the closing decades of the twentieth century through the exploits of the King George VI Chase winners, Nupsala, The Fellow and Algan, and many others.

Had such worthies been around in August 1914 they would have been as swiftly pounced upon as was that year's Grand Steeplechase de Paris winner, Lord Loris, who, together with his jockey Alec Carter, joined up at the outbreak of war when the *Life's* French correspondent, Victor Breyer, editor of *L'Echo des Sports*, commented:

> The announcement that Lord Loris, Mr James Hennessy's crack chaser and winner of the big Auteuil steeplechase, has been requisitioned for service in the French Army need not cause astonishment. In the present crisis France is determined to have the 'best of the best' in every department and Lord Loris ought to be the finest charger in the field for he is a strong, sound and sturdy horse.[*]
>
> This year he has won in prize money close upon £10,000 and had he been an entire horse the Government would have gladly given more than that sum to have had him for one of their National stallion depots.
>
> As I have frequently explained in the columns of the *Sporting Life*, the heads of the French War Office have long been convinced that the best cavalry horse is the one bred by a thoroughbred stallion from a good Normandy or half-bred mare. That is why they have acquired over 200 English thoroughbreds that have won great races on the Turf whose services can be obtained for a nominal fee by breeders and farmers who keep brood mares … I think it will be proved in the war now convulsing Europe that the French cavalry is far superior to what it was in the Franco-Prussian conflict of 1870.

Unfortunately for the cavalry, the mechanics of war had moved on since 1870. Two inventions in particular – barbed wire and the machinegun – had made the old-fashioned cavalry charge obsolete, a fact that should have been made obvious to the generals by the carnage at Omdurman in 1898 when an Anglo-Egyptian army under Sir Horatio Herbert (later Lord) Kitchener returned a score sheet of 'Maxim gun 11,000 – Dervish forces 48'.

---

[*] Strong and sturdy Lord Loris may have been, but he wasn't bomb proof. The following month he was fatally wounded by shrapnel and a few days later Alec Carter suffered the same fate. A week earlier Carter had tempted fate too far when he wrote to a friend: "I seem to have a charmed life. Although four horses have been killed under me, I am without a scratch."[3]

Nevertheless, the noble quad still had a major role to play in the Great War and at their peak during the summer of 1917 there were some 460,000 horses and mules pulling guns and ambulances or carrying supplies for the British army. In one of many letters the *Life* received from Lieut J Fairfax-Blakeborough during this period, the young cavalry officer (whose name that was to become very familiar to readers over the next 60 years) sketched a brief portrait of 'The Thoroughbred in War':

Some of these old horses – once the pampered inmates of racing stable loose-boxes, fed with carefully sieved oats and dampened and shaken hay – now stand fastened to a line in the open, herded with all manner of common foreigners, eating corn and chop out of a nosebag, and hay you daren't shake. *Sic transit gloria mundi*!

And yet their glory has not departed. They are looked upon with respectful awe and something akin to sentimental interest as horses which were bred for the great national sport and once took part in it ... Over and over again have I found this out here in France – the marvellous fascination and wondrous affection and sympathy there is between man and horse.

But the wastage was horrendous. Horses died like flies from exhaustion, exposure, disease and enemy action, or drowned in the sea of mud that was Flanders. A constant supply of remounts was needed and only blue-blooded aristocrats such as the 1914 Derby winner, Durbar II, were excused duty. In the case of the American-owned, French-trained Durbar, it was reported in September 1914:

Mr Duryea's horse was at Marle when the war began, but was removed in a great hurry to Senlis when the former place was threatened by the Teutonic hosts. The Negro groom wrapped the Epsom hero in an American flag and covered his horse-cloth with a placard which read as follows: 'This is Durbar II, the Derby winner. He is neutral'. The Germans respected the horse's 'neutrality' and he and his stable companion, Shannon, were allowed through and are now in a place of comparative safety.

Meanwhile, thousands of less celebrated horses had been requisitioned or voluntary given up at home. In the first two months of the war the *Life* revealed:

Sixty-seven leading British hunts have contributed 8,684 hunters to the War Office and from the stables of eighty notable masters have gone forth exactly 1,000 remounts. The editor of *Baily's Magazine* estimates from the replies kindly made by masters of foxhounds, that fully 10,000 regular hunting men are with the Colours, the majority having elected to take on 'foreign service' duties, whatever they may be.

Others rallied to the flag from all corners of the Empire. On the same day as the paper carried the news on Durbar, it reported that the famous Indian cricketer, K S Ranjitsinhji, who had played for Cambridge University, Sussex and England in a distinguished first-class career that dated from 1893, was doing his bit for the war effort:

The magnificent action of the Indian ruling Princes in regard to the war has caused a thrill to pass through England and unbounded satisfaction will be felt in sporting circles that the old-time idol of the cricket field, 'Ranji' now the Maharajah Jam Sahib of Nawanagar, has played his part in the time of crisis as well as ever he did when he represented England on the playing fields.

We are able to state officially that he has called his subjects together at Jamnagar, and there delivered a remarkable speech to them, explaining the cause of the war. He told them quite plainly that he was not asking them to help at a crisis in which he too was not willing to join heart and soul, and at every, and any cost.

'You will be glad to know,' said His Highness 'that I have placed the humble and limited resources of my State at the disposal of the Empire by my letter to the agent of the Government. I have promised to raise and maintain a force of one thousand able-bodied men to fight for the Empire, to give 200 horses and fifteen motors, over and above two squadrons of Imperial Service Lancers.'*

Before long, however, Britain had to turn to America and the Argentine in order to replenish her stocks and by the end of 1915 Lord Kitchener, the Secretary of State for War, estimated the government had spent some £12m (£1bn) on acquiring remounts from those countries. That vast sum was to increase dramatically over the next few years and not all of the expensively bought horses (in terms of seamen's lives and shipping) were to reach their destination.

The story that emerged after the *Georgic* had been sunk by the German cruiser *Möwe* while transporting 1,200 remounts from America to France in 1916 is surely one of the most harrowing accounts of its kind. It was told by one of the veterinary surgeons who had been picked up by the *Möwe* and watched from its deck as his own ship went down. The vet, O E McKim, related that as the crippled *Georgic* settled lower in the water some 25 to 30 horses were swept overboard by the heavy seas:

> They swam round and round in the icy water, some of them for hours. A splendid chestnut struck out straight for the raider. I recognised him as one of my pets. So close did he get that I could hear his breath coming in rasping sobs ... It was exactly like a swimmer reaching for safety just before he is spent.
>
> I could not stand it. Rushing to the German commander, I begged him to shoot the animal rather than leave him to struggle his life away trying vainly to claw up the side of the raider, as he was. The commander took careful aim with his Mauser pistol, which had an adjustable stock that made it capable of being used like a rifle, and fired. It took four shots to end the poor creature's misery ... Another grey horse which I recognised swam for probably an hour and a half round and round the *Georgic* before the water closed over his head ... It was terrible.[4]

It was what the *Life's* prescient football correspondent, George Wagstaffe Simmons, had forecast at the start of the war. In a front-page article that must have had a sobering effect on those who were predicting the whole unfortunate business would be over by Christmas, he wrote under the crosshead 'Must Prepare For The Horrors':

> We all hope, and hope most fervently, that hostilities will not be prolonged, but proud nations are in conflict, and it would be contrary to the teachings of history for any to sue for peace until the

---

* By 1915 a third of the British forces on the Western Front were made up of Indian sepoys, ironically fighting for a country that occupied their own against a country with which they had no quarrel.

country's resources have been exhausted. It is necessary, therefore, to hold ourselves in readiness for a campaign that may spread over a long period.

Whether, however, it be long or short there must be much misery and much destitution. Now that the first flush of war is upon us and our minds are exalted by the fervour of our patriotism we can see with our mental eyes only the glory of war. Its horrors will be upon us all too soon and the country that is best prepared for them will be best able to recover from the shattering blows it will receive.

Five days later, on August 20, the *Life* published the first casualty list to be issued by the British Expeditionary Force. It contained just six names; three dead and three injured. Apart from General Sir James Grierson who had died of a heart attack, the others had been involved in motoring or flying accidents; among them was Major Arthur Hughes-Onslow who had died of his injuries.

'Junks' as he was known to his friends, thus became the first notable British sportsman to perish in the war. As well as being an accomplished cricketer and polo player, he was regarded as 'the best of the soldier riders' and had won the Grand Military Gold Cup at Sandown three times from just four rides in the race – Bertha in 1888, County Council (1898) and Marpessa (1903); his only other mount had finished second in 1899.

The prestigious steeplechase (which was not run from 1900-2 owing to the Boer War) quickly became a jinx on those who had won it. In a matter of weeks both Capt Charles Banbury, who rode Sprinkle Me to back-to-back victories in 1909-10, and Lt-Col David Campbell, who won successive runnings on Nelly Grey and Parapluie in 1896-7, were wounded, the former fatally so.

Campbell, who had also won the Grand National on The Soarer in 1896, was hit as he led the 9th Lancers in one of the first cavalry charges of the war when, like so many others, his company was cut to pieces by a combination of barbed wire and machinegun fire. He recovered to fight on in the trenches and survived the war, but Capt Leon Denny, who rode Royal Blaze to win the Sandown race in 1906, was killed in action in May 1915, while Admiral Christopher Cradock, who finished third in the 1906 race, had gone down with his ship, HMS *Good Hope*, which was sunk with all hands in the battle of Coronel off the coast of Chile in November 1914.

It was not long before the casualty lists began to appear on a daily basis. Even restricted, as they were, to officers who had achieved distinction in the field of sport, they sometimes had to be printed in minuscule 8pt type to fit in all the names.

In August alone the French were estimated to have lost 200,000 men, and by the time the first battle of the Marne was over there were another 250,000 casualties on both sides. These mind-numbing, but nicely rounded statistics only took on any real meaning when familiar names were added to them; men whose sporting exploits had made them nationally famous or at least hometown heroes.

To those more personally acquainted with them, the endless columns of 'our glorious dead' were soul-destroying. Capt. Frank Starr, an army PT and bayonet instructor based at Aldershot, had more than a nodding acquaintance with most of the men on the front line.

Starr wrote for the *Life* under the pseudonym of 'Navarm' and also supplied the brief biographical sketches of the sportsmen in the casualty lists. It was a task he found almost unbearable and his pain and outrage were evident in his articles. On September 18, seven weeks into the war and a day after the Kaiser first asked the American President, Woodrow Wilson, to seek peace terms from the Allies, Starr spoke for the vast majority of his countrymen as he gave his answer to such a proposal:

To one who has known every officer and almost every man in the Army for the past quarter of a century, the task of reading, day after day, the list of casualties is a duty that almost paralyses one's pen, and leaves only an overwhelming desire for vengeance upon that misguided monarch who is robbing our Army of the flower of its manhood.

Yesterday's list from the Headquarters of the Expeditionary Force contains names of officers whose successes in the world of athletics would fill a whole issue of the *Sporting Life* were I to chronicle all they had done on the field and track and all the assistance they have rendered by influence and example to the followers of athletic pastimes.

Starr, whose invaluable contributions were curtailed when he was posted to France at the end of 1916, went on to pay tribute to some of those he had known best before he concluded:

> …but one might go on indefinitely multiplying instances of officers whose fine sporting qualities have helped our little British Army to beat back the Kaiser's hordes and whose deaths will be avenged by their fellow sportsmen a hundred-fold during the progress to Berlin which is down in the Army fixture list for 1914-15.

That particular fixture was to be postponed for 30 years; meanwhile, the repetitive headline 'Latest War Casualties' would, when space allowed, carry a sub-heading detailing which particular field of sport had been hit. One day it might be 'Famous Rugby and Polo Players killed', the next 'Well-known Cricketers and Footballers in the List', but always the catalogue of carnage was there to testify to the terrible sacrifice that was being made in 'the war to end all wars'.

Some deaths had bizarre repercussions on mundane events at home. Two weeks after Lieut W Macneill of the 16th Lancers had been killed in action in October 1914, his horse, Maxim IV, landed the odds of 4-7 in the Plodders' Steeplechase at Nottingham. It was only after the horse had won that the stewards were made aware of Macneill's fate and under Rule 82, which stated that all entries became void upon the death of the owner, they had no option but to disqualify the horse.

Macneill, an intrepid amateur rider who won a sizable side-bet by remounting to complete the course on Fool-hardy in the 1911 Grand National, had quite possibly been mown down by the murderous, ten-rounds-a-second, fire of a Maxim machinegun, but that irony was lost on those who had backed his horse and had to forfeit their winnings.

The rule under which Maxim IV was disqualified had been making a mockery of racing for ages by denying some of the best horses of their generation the chance of competing in the top races, but the Jockey Club had consistently refused to act on the matter. Now, surely, urged 'Augur', it was time it did:

> On many occasions, and during many years past, readers of the *Sporting Life* have had placed before them reasons, which appear to be good and sufficient, for the abolition of the rule of racing which renders null and void all entries made by an owner or breeder who subsequently dies … A few days ago I pointed out that instances of this sort must inevitably occur very frequently during the continuance of this greatest of all wars and I had hoped the stewards of the Jockey Club and National Hunt Committee would have passed some measure, even if it were only to operate temporarily, to do away with the injustice which must necessarily be

inflicted upon the relatives of officers who have sacrificed their lives in the service of their country.*

Morley-Brown, who was to turn the lead column into an editorial platform to campaign for the continuation of racing during the war, went on to point out that the Irish Turf Club had scrapped the rule soon after the start of the war, and added: "It is to be hoped that this excellent lead will soon be followed by our own Turf legislators. The present appears to be the ideal time for similar action."

But it was a vain hope. As was so often the case, the Jockey Club lagged sadly behind the Irish on such issues and, perversely, it was the ardent reformer Lord Durham who continually thwarted the efforts of other clubmen to have the archaic rule removed. Fatefully, two days after his 'void entries' article Morley-Brown reported:

> For the second time since the commencement of the war the Lambton family, of which the Earl of Durham is the head, has suffered a grievous bereavement, the news having just been received that the Hon Francis Lambton, the Earl's youngest brother, was killed in action on Saturday last.

In a short tribute to the fallen officer, who had trained a string of 40 horses at Park Lodge stables in Newmarket before the war, the editor revealed that Lord Durham's nephew, Geoffrey Lambton, had also lost his life in the fighting a few weeks earlier.

Many other old and influential racing families were to be bereaved during the conflict. Among those cut down were the brother officers and cousins, the Hon Neil Primrose (son of the former Prime Minister, Lord Rosebery) and Major Evelyn de Rothschild, whose deaths in Palestine were announced on successive days in November 1917.

Such 'related' deaths were a common occurrence amongst the pals' battalions that were formed to bolster the regular army at the outbreak of war. Men from the same trade, town or district, joined up together and, on a private's pay of a shilling (£4.50) a day, fought and died together. It was not unknown for an entire family of brothers, or a village team (be it rugby, football or cricket), to be wiped out in a single action.

Among the most famous of these companies was the 23rd (First Sportsman's) Battalion of the Royal Fusiliers, which was formed by Edward Cunliffe-Owen after his wife had launched a recruitment campaign for men of up to 45 used to "hunting, shooting and outdoor sport". Known as the 'hard as nails corps', it was saluted by the *Life* in November 1914 as the men set off for their training camp at Hornchurch in Essex:†

> How the organisation of such a battalion had appealed to the public was shown by the huge crowd which had gathered to meet them on their arrival on the parade ground opposite Knightsbridge

---

* It was not until 1929 that the void nominations rule was finally scrapped. Legal action was taken to remove the anomaly after the 1927 Derby winner, Call Boy, was prevented from running in the St Leger by the death of his owner, Frank Curzon. The benefits of its repeal were almost immediate as Cameronian – whose owner-breeder, Lord Dewar, had died in 1930 – was able to run in and win the following year's Two Thousand Guineas and Derby in the colours of his late owner's nephew, John A Dewar.

† The battalion entrained for France a year later. From the 219 officers and 4,768 other ranks who served with the First Sportsman's, the number of those killed, missing or wounded in action totalled 128 officers and 3,102 other ranks.[5]

Barracks. Rousing cheers greeted them as, accompanied by the sound of bugles, they lined up nearly a thousand strong...

Their plain khaki carried no badge or ornament to mark them out from a hundred other regiments, yet as they swung by, four by four, through the raw, foggy streets, it must have been apparent even to the most casual observer who cast a curious glance at them, that this was no ordinary battalion. They were, in a sense, a very mixed lot – mixed in size and especially mixed in age. There were huge men – one towered above all others, a giant in height and breadth, a twenty-stone man – and there were wiry, little fellows and stocky, medium-sized men.

It was the same in every field of sport; the working classes, fired up by a spirit of adventure and the chance to escape the drudgery of their poverty-ridden lives, enlisted in their ten of thousands together with the upper-classes who, inspired by the public school traditions of duty and honour, were to learn too late Horace's 'old lie', *Dulce et decorum est pro patria mori* – It is sweet and glorious to die for one's country.

Rugby gave of its best. Of the four London-Scottish teams that turned out on the last Saturday of the 1913-14 season, 45 of the 60 players never returned from the trenches. Their commitment was illustrated in an article which appeared in October 1914 under the heading 'Rugby Men and the War / Rush of Famous Scots to the Colours':

At the S.R.U. meeting last week it was mentioned that in clubs which had furnished details nearly 650 out of 800 playing members had joined the Colours, and of the remainder of the clubs it was impossible to ascertain the exact number because practically all the playing members are in the Army. Of the Scottish Rugby Union Committee, four are actually at the Front – Dr J R Greenlees, the president, R F Neilson, W L Church and J M B Scott – while all the internationals are serving in one capacity or another. Rugby matches are now confined to the schools and to occasional contests between regimental teams. Some of the latter can put a fairly warm lot into the field!

But it was not long before those regimental teams were sadly depleted. Scotland had already lost two of its internationals in Ronnie Simson and Jim Huggan who were killed at Aisne in September; the latter, a RAMC officer, while tending to a wounded German soldier. And by the end of the year two more Scottish and three English internationals had been added to the list. Then, on 16 January 1915, the *Life's* rugby correspondent, 'Phoenician', reported:

The melancholy list of famous Rugby players who have laid down their lives in the Great War continues to grow. The present week has brought news of the death of one of the most consistent Scottish forwards of recent years in F H Turner who was playing so recently as October last when he turned out for the Liverpool Scots against the 9th Royal Scots in a match at Edinburgh.

Turner was not only a fine player but a fine captain, and he led the Scottish team last season* in matches with Ireland and England, against each of whom he secured four caps for his country; while he had three against Wales, one against South Africa and played three times against France.

---

* Turner had, in fact, captained Scotland in all four internationals in 1913, but he was replaced by Dave Bain and then by Eric Milroy in 1914. None of them survived the war. Bain was killed that summer and Milroy on the Somme the following year.

He was a member, as were also the late Lewis Robertson and C M Usher, who is missing, of the side which gained Scotland's most memorable victory of recent years when the greatly esteemed English team were beaten at Inverleith in 1912.

Fred Turner was just one of 111 British rugby internationals whose lives were to be snuffed out in the slaughter. In the same month as his death was reported, the former English captain, Percy Kendall, also serving with the Liverpool-Scottish, paid the ultimate price and four months later a sniper's bullet claimed the life of the game's golden boy, Ronnie Poulton Palmer, who had led England to their second successive Grand Slam victory in 1914.

The dashingly elusive centre had played alongside Turner when they won their rugby blues at Oxford and also when they turned out for the formidable Liverpool side of 1913-14, but they were in opposition in March 1914 when they both scored in a thriller that saw England retain the Calcutta Cup by one point (16-15) at Inverleith. Nine of the other players who took the field that day were also to have their names added to rugby's roll of honour.

Reports of Poulton Palmer's death in the national press on May 8 were overshadowed by news of the torpedoing of the Cunard liner *Lusitania* with the loss of 1,200 lives, but the *Life* paid him a fitting tribute as it declared:

Among the many splendid sportsmen whose loss in the European War we have to mourn, none stood higher in general esteem, none was more distinguished in his particular branch of sport, and none had established a more lasting fame as a player than the late R W Poulton Palmer, whose death was announced yesterday. Thus both England and Scotland have lost their Rugby captains, and of the men who played under them in the season 1913-14, J H D Watson and F E Oakeley on the one side, and J L Huggan on the other, are gone.

After listing other internationals and Varsity blues who had played their last game for their country, the paper concluded:

It is appalling to think of the many splendid careers which have thus been cut short – and many of them held out the highest promise in other fields than that of sport – but events such as the Germans latest outrage on the *Lusitania* convinces us of the stern necessity of the sacrifice. It is unhappily only too probable that we shall have many more such reminders of the great part that sportsmen are playing in this war, and we must console ourselves with the reflection that after it has been fought out to the bitter end, the credit of sport will stand the higher for the gallantry of those who have fallen.

And the reminders came thick and fast. The day after this article appeared, England lost another fine player in Harry Berry (4 caps) and before the month was out the lives of Scotland's Jim Pearson (12 caps) and Ireland's Basil Maclear (11 caps) had also been wiped out. Their names have faded with time, but Edgar Mobbs, a flying winger who was capped seven times for England between 1908 and 1910 and who captained his home team, Northampton, for six seasons, is still commemorated by the annual Mobbs Memorial match, played between the Barbarians and an East Midlands XV.

Described as "one of the most popular players of the last decade" in the report on his death in August 1917, Mobbs had formed his own company at the outbreak of war when he recruited some

250 men for the Northamptonshire Regiment. Rising in the ranks from sergeant to Lt-Colonel, he went out in style when, with a blend of bravado and madness that befitted the occasion, he led a charge on a machinegun post at Passchendaele by punting a rugby ball ahead of him. His body was never recovered.

The Dominions, too, paid a high price. New Zealand lost one of her greatest adopted sons when Dave Gallaher perished in the charnel-mud of Flanders after the war had claimed the lives of two of his brothers. Born in Co. Galway, Gallaher was revered as the founding father of the All Blacks and had captained the 'Originals' on their epic 1905-06 tour of the UK when they ran up 830 points and conceded just 39 in 32 matches; a controversial 3-0 defeat by Wales being their only reverse.

But the grim chronicle could go on for ever as, indeed, it seemed to do on New Year's Day, 1915 when a 'Toll of the War Among Sportsmen' list took up six columns spread over two days. The fallen officers ranged from: "Abell, W H, Major Middlesex Regt. Polo player and well known in the hunting field," through to "Yate, C A L, Major Yorkshire Light Infantry. Fine polo player and rider to hounds and organiser of regimental sport. Awarded Victoria Cross for gallantry at Le Cateau, where, when all other officers were killed or wounded and ammunition exhausted, he led his 19 survivors in a charge in which he was severely wounded and died in a German hospital."

The *Life's* mournful roll-call was hardly calculated to help Lord Kitchener recruit men for his New Army. The initial lemming-like rush to join up had resulted in 1.2 million men in uniform by the end of 1914, but as the casualty lists grew, even the most ardent patriot began to have second thoughts about laying down his life at the behest of a bunch of largely incompetent generals, inept politicians and squabbling imperialist monarchs, three of whom – Kaiser Wilhelm II, King George V and Tsar Nicholas II – were cousins; the first two being grandsons of Queen Victoria, the 'Grandmamma of Europe'.

When Kitchener's famous 'Your Country Needs YOU!' poster made its appearance to point an accusing finger at the 'shirkers' who had yet to enlist, it did much to boost the number of recruits to 2.25 million by September 1915, but when this was still not enough to feed the guns, conscription was introduced for the first time ever in 1916.

Until then, the pressure on men to join up had been unrelenting and the press played a major part in the campaign. As the death toll mounted day-by-day, it seemed perverse that the same columns that recorded the slaughter could be devoted to recruiting more cannon fodder for what was to be the 'final' big push, but so it was.

The *Life*, itself, trod a narrow line as it encouraged sportsmen to take the king's shilling at the same time as it campaigned for the continuance of sport in the face of increasing calls from the lay press for a halt to racing and football. In November 1914, on the same day as it was announced that Douglas Arthur Kinnaird, the eldest son of Lord Kinnaird, the president of the Football Association, had been killed in action, Wagstaffe Simmons felt impelled to defend Charles Clegg, the chairman (1889-1923) of the FA Council:

> I call attention to a recent utterance by Mr Clegg with a view to putting an end to the assaults that have been made on the FA and – I quote from a London contemporary – 'its Kaiser-like chairman, who is largely responsible for the disgracefully miserable response of Association footballers who are content to go on playing their games while other and better sportsmen shoulder their rifle in the service of their king'...

> I quote the words used only so recently as last Sunday by Mr Clegg when addressing a huge

gathering at Sheffield, on the occasion of the annual Football Sunday in that city: 'There is no doubt that more men are wanted, but every man will have to settle for himself what his duty is. I will say this for myself – I do not want to commit anybody else to it – that every capable man who, without good cause, refuses to help, is a coward and a traitor to his country'.

It would not be possible for more direct and straightforward language to be used.

In his desire to "restore the proper perspective as to football and recruiting," Simmons failed to mention that he, himself, was a member of the FA Council, but he was able to show there was no lack of volunteers among rank and file players:

Amateur football and minor professional football has made a magnificent response to the urgent call for recruits … The estimate that, to-date, well over 100,000 Association players and officials have enrolled themselves in the forces is extremely modest. Not merely hundreds, but thousands of amateur clubs have suspended operations this season because they have not enough playing members to continue. There are numerous instances in which every member has put on his country's uniform; the man with the slightest spark of patriotism who is able to enlist does so as a matter of course.

The next day Frank Starr endorsed those claims as he wrote:

If space would permit, the publication of a list of footballers now serving in Kitchener's New Army would furnish a very effective knock-out blow to those who, while remaining at home themselves, are shrieking wild denunciations of the professionals who are doing the same.

I knew, of course, that nine-tenths of Kitchener's men were athletes, but I did not guess how many were athletes of standing until I accepted a position this week upon an Aldershot military football committee … And Aldershot represents but one-seventh of the new Force! If similar enquiries were addressed to all the training centres the probability is that a list might be published that would stagger the killjoys who, by libelling sportsmen in general and footballers in particular, fancy they have done their duty to the country and are now immune from military service.

There was, nevertheless, a lack of recruits from the big London clubs and in January 1915 this was reflected in a 'name and shame' report on the Footballers' Battalion, the 17th Middlesex,* then in training at London's White City, which had been turned into a military camp. It was left to an anonymous army officer to hand out the white feathers as a 'Special Correspondent' commented curtly:

The professional footballers are over a hundred in number and they are in a separate platoon. There ought to be many more and I place on record the statement of one of the officers on this point:

'We have, I think, a good cause for complaint against some of the clubs. Brighton and Hove with its 13 or 14 players, Clapton Orient, Millwall, Plymouth Argyle, Watford, Luton Town, Croydon Common, Nottingham Forest and some other clubs have done well, but others have been most disappointing.

'We have Coquet from Fulham, but where are the other players? Where are the first class players from Chelsea, from Tottenham Hotspur, from Arsenal? We want those players to understand that

---

* Altogether, three footballers' battalions were formed; the 17th, 23rd and 27th Middlesex Regiment.

they have a duty to their country as well as the Millwall, Crystal Palace and players of other clubs I have mentioned, and that it will be a disgrace for those who should enlist if they fail to do so...

'The players who are the darlings of the football public have a unique opportunity to show that they are not only alive to their responsibilities, but are prepared to discharge them and in discharging them they will set an example that will be followed by thousands of others. It is up to them to enrol themselves without delay'.

The phrase, 'alive to their responsibilities', was somewhat unfortunate since so many of those who did enlist were soon relieved of all their responsibilities, Donald Bell among them. A full-back for Bradford Park Avenue and one of the first professional footballers to enlist, Bell won a Victoria Cross (awarded posthumously) for taking out a machinegun post five days before he was killed on the Somme in 1916.

On the first day (July 1) of that insanely orchestrated bloodbath when the PBI (Poor Bloody Infantry) were told to *walk* in ranks towards the enemy lines, the 8th Battalion of the East Surrey Regt. went into action by dribbling footballs ahead of them. Capt W P Nevill, who led his men over the top that day, never returned, but three weeks later one of the footballs arrived back at the battalion's Kingston barracks.

The *Life* reported that the depot's commandant, Col H P Treeby, DSO, showed the ball to his men and declared: "With splendid gallantry this and other footballs were dribbled under a withering shellfire right up to the German trenches. The football fields have become the battlefield of the world's war, and today we are reminded by this football of how splendidly that game is being played…"

It was a splendid example of how the top brass glossed over the blackest day in the history of the British Army when its casualties totalled 57,470. Heart of Midlothian lost three of its players in the first few hours of what was to be a five-month long battle which also claimed the lives of five West Ham players and three from Clapton Orient (as Leyton Orient was then known).

Many other top league players were k.i.a. including two Scots who had scored the winning goal in FA Cup Finals – Sandy Turnbull for Manchester United in 1909 and Jimmy Speirs for Bradford City in 1911 – as well as Eddie Latheron of Blackburn Rovers and England, and Walter Tull of Northampton Town, who overcame racial prejudice to become the first coloured commissioned officer in the British Army. Recommended for a Military Cross (never awarded) in January 1918, he was killed two months later. His body was never recovered.

Cricket lost some 80 first-class players including the England caps William Booth of Yorkshire, Kenneth Hutchings of Kent, and Leonard Moon of Middlesex, who all fell at the Somme in 1916. But perhaps the best of them was Colin 'Charlie' Blythe, who was killed at Passchendaele in November 1917. Despite the usual pressure on space, the *Life* devoted three columns to Blythe whose tally of 100 wickets in 19 Tests placed him among the best. Tributes came from the outstanding all-round sportsman C B Fry and Kent's former captain, Lord Harris, who declared, "Of the galaxy of brilliant left-hand bowlers whom Kent has given to the cricket field, Charlie Blythe was surpassed by none."

In other sports the cost was no less great. In 1915 the headline 'Heavy Loss To Lawn Tennis' paid tribute to the four-times Wimbledon singles champion, Tony Wilding, who won the first of his titles in 1910 when he beat the defending champion, Arthur Gore. Born and brought up in Christchurch, New Zealand, Wilding was to add four Wimbledon doubles titles and as many Davis Cup successes for Australasia to his laurels before his unique talents were wiped out when his Auber's Ridge dugout took a direct hit from a shell on May 9. The same battle also claimed the life of Wyndham Halswelle, the 1908 Olympic gold medallist.

Sometimes the brief casualty notices contained more than just bare biographical details. When the Australian 110 yards swimming champion and 1912 Olympic gold medallist, Cecil Healy, was killed in 1918 his commanding officer, Major Middleton, wrote: "By Healy's death the world loses one of its greatest champions, one of its best men. Today, in the four years I have been at the Front, I wept for the first time."

There were tears enough to form an ocean. Among the jockeys who made 'the supreme sacrifice' was Fred Archer's nephew, Charles Archer jnr, who died in hospital during the botched Dardanelles campaign of 1915, while F L Rickaby was fatally wounded in France just a few weeks before the armistice.

A son of the classic-winning jockey, Fred Rickaby, Frederick Lester followed in the steps of his father when be became first jockey to George Lambton at Stanley House, Newmarket, in 1912. The following season he won the One Thousand Guineas and Oaks on Jest, and he went on to win the former classic three more times in the next four years; on Vaucluse (1915), Canyon (1916) and Diadem (1917), only being let down for the nap hand by his 1914 mount, Glorvina, who finished a close second.

Described by the reigning champion jockey, Steve Donoghue, as "one of the best," Freddie had a short but varied war, having joined the Veterinary Corps in 1916 before transferring to the Flying Corps and finally moving on to the Tank Corps. Rickaby's name was to live on through his infant sons, Fred and Bill, who were to continue the family's long association with racing (the former as a leading trainer in South Africa, the latter as a top class jockey) while his sister, Iris, became the mother of another jockey best known by his late uncle's middle name.

But the list is as endless as the regimented rows of gravestones that bear silent witness to the futility of it all in war cemeteries across Europe. Lambs to the slaughter, motivated by a sense of duty, and a blend of peer-pressure and jingoistic propaganda dished out by politicians and the press on a daily basis.

In November 1915 a perfect example of this psychological blackmail appeared in the *Life* underneath an item which recorded that 155 men were missing following a collision between the minesweeper, *HMS Hythe*, and another ship off the Gallipoli peninsula. Carrying the initials 'W.V.K.', it took the form of a poem entitled 'Be a Man!'

Be a man today, sonny! / Join before you must: / You've a debt to pay, sonny, / Be the sort we trust. / Shall conscription tarnish / England's sacred name? / Go and join the Army / Out of very shame.

Married, did you say, sonny? / Never mind the wife: / She will get her pay, sonny, / You can bet your life / Children? There's a trifle / Set aside – Now then, / Sonny, where's your rifle? / Kitchener wants men.

Can't you hear them singing / 'Somewhere' out in France? / Cheer on cheer is ringing, / At the word 'advance'. / Go and help the boys, sonny / Force the foe to run; / England first of all, sonny, / Till we've licked the Hun!

Leaving aside the breakdown in rhyme in the middle verse, anything more patronising would be hard to imagine. It's a fair bet that this particular page was used for something other than reading by the boys (some as young as 14) in the trenches who received the paper post free thanks to a scheme designed to boost its sales.

From the start of 1915, notices began to appear under multi-deck headlines such as, 'Sporting Life In The Trenches / The News The Soldier Likes Best / Our Free Postal Offer To Readers', followed by wordy declarations on the importance of 'the favourite service paper' to the morale of the troops, and the pledge that:

> For the sum of 6d a week, paid in advance, we will undertake to send a copy of the *Sporting Life* daily, post free, direct from our publishing office, to any soldier or sailor, friend or relative whose heart our subscriber may wish to gladden by a daily budget of sport ... Letters containing subscriptions should include the full name, rank, number and other particulars of the chum to whom it is intended the *Sporting Life* shall be sent.

At the same time, the paper began to ask for sports equipment, playing cards and other games for the troops and binoculars for the officers, while there were constant appeals on behalf of various war charities. The response was magnificent and at the end of 1916 a humble Morley-Brown announced:

> It has been the supreme privilege of this journal, through the generosity of its readers, to render as agreeable as possible the lot of many thousands of soldiers and sailors, both on active and home service, since the early days of hostilities.
>
> I need hardly explain that this happy result has been achieved by the provision of altogether extraordinary numbers of boxing gloves, footballs, packs of playing cards, and chess, draughts and domino sets, while the donors of some hundreds of pairs of race-glasses must not be forgotten in the general scheme of thanks I am now expressing.
>
> It is not unreasonable to assume that the daily distribution of the *Sporting Life* in the trenches has helped to while away many hours which would otherwise have been wearisome – at any rate, I have amongst my most treasured possessions several letters to that effect.

In one such letter an officer in the King's Royal Rifles expressed thanks on behalf of his men for a few packs of playing cards, before he concluded:

> May I add that it is common knowledge among the troops what wonderful work your great sporting journal is doing, not merely for the fellows out here, in the way of healthy, clean amusement, but also for our future comrades-in-arms in training at home, and for the great Sportsmen's Ambulance Fund.
>
> Those of us who come through after we have licked Germany (I don't like the cold expression 'after the war') will not forget the *Sporting Life*. I predict a very large increase in your circulation, for undoubtedly you have made hosts of new friends. My own copy passes through many hands daily. Once I caught my batman about to light a brazier with one copy a week old. For days after he appeared to be suffering from shellshock. – Yours sincerely, R O Edwards, Capt. K.R.R.

The Sportsmen's Ambulance Fund mentioned in the letter was particularly close to the editor's heart. He served on its committee under Lord Lonsdale and seldom missed an opportunity to plug the fund which had set itself a target of £40,000 (£2m) to pay for 100 ambulances that would be used on the Allied fronts.

In February 1917 the paper carried a photo of one of the ambulances with 'Presented By *Sporting Life*' emblazoned on its side, together with the inevitable appeal for more money. In acknowledging some of the many contributors to the fund, Morley-Brown pleaded:

The Sporting Life

"BELL'S LIFE IN LONDON."

POST Your CHEQUE TO-DAY.

POST Your CHEQUE TO-DAY.

No. 13,144. [REGISTERED AT THE G.P.O. AS A NEWSPAPER.] LONDON, FRIDAY, JULY 7, 1916. [DAILY.] PRICE ONE PENNY.

BRITISH SPORTSMEN! ATTENTION!

READ THIS PAGE!

This is Not an Advertisement, but a Special and Urgent Appeal by a British Sporting Newspaper to the Sportsmen of GREAT BRITAIN.

What is this Fund?

IT IS AN EFFORT TO RAISE

£40,000

TO PROVIDE MEANS TO CONVEY WOUNDED SOLDIERS FROM THE FIRING LINE.

Motor Ambulance Transport IS Urgently Needed ON THE Fighting Fronts.

WHAT HAVE YOU Done For THE FUND?

EACH CAR COSTS

£400

And the Minimum Number the Committee of the Fund wish to Present is

100 Cars.

THE SUBSCRIPTIONS RECEIVED TO DATE ARE ABOUT

£6,000

AND THE PROMOTERS FEEL SO CERTAIN BRITISH SPORTSMEN WILL PROVIDE THE MONEY THAT

50 Cars

HAVE BEEN ALREADY ORDERED.

What is this Fund?

IT IS A FREE-WILL OFFERING BY

SPORTSMEN

AT HOME, TO THE SPORTSMEN FIGHTING IN THE GREAT ADVANCE.

Every Individual Sportsman Fails in his Duty Unless he Helps.

WHAT ARE YOU Doing To Do For THE FUND?

If You Have Worked Before,

WORK HARDER NOW;

And if You Have Subscribed Already,

SUBSCRIBE AGAIN.

ALREADY 20 Cars

HAVE BEEN HANDED OVER TO THE SIR ARTHUR DU CROS CONVOY AND OUR FIGHTING ALLIES BY H.M. QUEEN ALEXANDRA, ON BEHALF OF THE FUND COMMITTEE, & ANOTHER

30 Cars

ARE NEARLY COMPLETED.

QUEEN ALEXANDRA AND LORD LONSDALE INSPECT A CAR.

HER MAJESTY QUEEN ALEXANDRA, who is evincing much interest in the Fund, inspecting one of the British Sportsmen's Motor Ambulance Cars at Marlborough House. Standing by the Car is Lord LONSDALE, the President of the Fund.

British Sportsmen's Motor Ambulance Fund.

PRESIDENT:
The Right Hon. The EARL of LONSDALE.
Hon. Secretary: Mr. A. F. BETTINSON, National Sporting Club, London.

WHAT LEADING SPORTSMEN ARE DOING.

(1) Racing Men are generously supporting this Scheme. Collections are regularly made at Race Meetings, over £184 being contributed at Lingfield.

(2) Boxing Men and Boxers have done, and are doing, a lot to help the Fund. A Collection at the National Sporting Club realised over £1,000. Boxing Tournaments are being organised in London and important Provincial Centres.

(3) The Football League has contributed £400.

(4) Billiards: A big Tournament will be held at the National Sporting Club NEXT WEEK, when all the Leading Professionals will be playing. Tournaments and Special Matches are being played in various centres.

(5) Help has been given by followers of all kinds of Sport, and every Sportsman in Great Britain must DO HIS BIT and make the Fund a Success.

SEND YOUR CONTRIBUTION TO-DAY TO
The TREASURER, British Sportsmen's Ambulance Fund, National Sporting Club, Covent Garden, London, W.C.

W S Morley-Brown took every opportunity to promote the British Sportsmen's Motor Ambulance Fund, in this case devoting the whole front-page to it on 7 July 1916 when the bloodiest and most insanely orchestrated battle in history (the Somme) was in its seventh day.

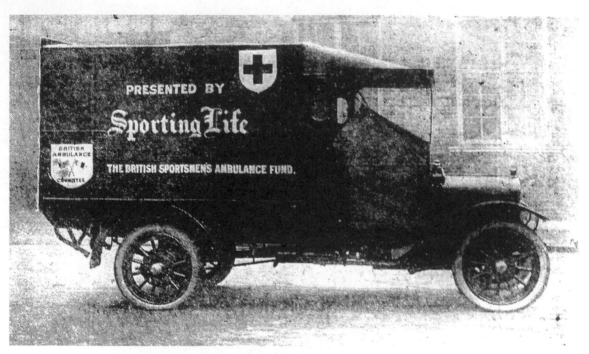

A *Sporting Life* ambulance destined for the Allied fronts in 1917.

There are profoundly urgent reasons why this appeal should be promptly and unselfishly responded to. It is an open secret that early in the coming spring there will be a mammoth simultaneous offensive by the Entente Powers, and every possible motor ambulance that can be obtained will be needed for the purpose of saving life and ameliorating the suffering of those who are daily and hourly fighting our battles.

It has been estimated by high authorities that every car sent out saves the lives of at least from 400 to 500 Tommies, and the value of the work done by those cars on the British, French, Russian, Italian, Serbian and Rumanian fronts is incalculable.

British sportsmen and those who have co-operated with them in this effort find more than sufficient reward in the fact that they have rendered valuable service to those branches of the Armies that are engaged in saving life instead of destroying it.

Meanwhile, the holocaust raged on.
Unabated.

RACING AND THE WAR

THROUGHOUT the war the *Sporting Life* was to wage its own battle against the usual faddist sections of the press, the public and parliament that sought to bring a halt to racing for as long as the conflict lasted – or even longer. And, for once, the opposition did not come entirely from outside the sport as there were some within its own ranks who felt it was morally wrong to continue racing while the flower of the nation were laying down their lives for King and Country.

On practical grounds alone, racing was opposed because it was reliant on the railways for ferrying horses to meetings, and trains were essential to the war effort.* For the first three weeks of the war all racing was cancelled as the State took control of the railways to rush troops and munitions to France.

At the same time many racecourses were taken over by the military to be used as training camps or as internment camps for alien residents who were rounded up in their thousands as spy-phobia swept the country. Other courses became POW camps, motor transit depots and munition dumps, while several grandstands – most notably Epsom's – were turned into makeshift hospitals.

When racing was resumed on August 28 it was roundly condemned in newspapers that had already called for the cancellation of all sport, prompting Morley-Brown to hit back under the heading 'Hypocrisy And Cant At Work / Senseless Outcry Against Sport':

> At a time when there is, or ought to be, absolute freedom from internal dissension, I regret to note in the columns of many of our lay contemporaries a tendency towards the belittlement of sport of every description. Indeed, if one were to believe everything one reads on the subject, it would appear that participation in racing, cricket, football, rowing and other sports of the nation almost amounts at the present time to an act of disloyalty of the most reprehensible character.
>
> This, too, in the face of the announcement that His Majesty the King has expressed the wish that racing shall go on as usual and that the royal horses will be entered and run out for their engagements during the remainder of the season. With King George's noble example before them, surely it is sheer impertinence on the part of those who suggest that there should be a total cessation of all sport during the period over which this lamentable war is to last.

A few weeks later, as a result of mounting unease among its own members, the Jockey Club held a meeting to discuss the situation. In a circular issued beforehand the stewards forestalled any serious objections they might have faced by explaining that they believed racing should continue where possible because "its cessation would have the immediate effect of throwing out of work a very large number of people entirely dependant upon it for their livelihood".

They added that many of the stable lads employed by the 290 licensed trainers had already enlisted, while the majority of those remaining were married men, boys and those unfit for service. There were also 54 racecourse companies employing full and part-time staff who, if made redundant, "might be compelled in the near future to apply for relief to funds which will be urgently needed for cases of unavoidable distress". These reasons were sufficient to sway the doubters and it was

---

* Motorised horse transport was virtually unknown in 1914 and by the time moves were made in that direction petrol rationing had been introduced and a ban placed on using motors to attend race meetings.

unanimously decided that racing should continue "where the local conditions permitted, and the feeling of the locality was not averse to the meeting being held".

Despite this conciliatory approach, those who were opposed to racing in peacetime redoubled their efforts to have it banned in wartime. Always quick to exploit any situation that might aid their cause, they were presented with an open goal in February 1915 when it was reported that wounded soldiers lodged in the hospital that had been set up in the luncheon-room annex of Epsom's grandstand were to be turned out so that racegoers attending the spring meeting could dine in comfort.

Not surprisingly, the report sparked a general outcry against racing. Questions were asked in parliament as editorials in the national press, accompanied by columns of letters from an outraged public, inflamed the situation. Matters were not helped by the autocratic nature of Henry Mayson Dorling, the general manager of Epsom racecourse, or by the fact that the Duke of Portland had written to *The Times* to say that it would be an affront to the Allies if the high-profile meetings at Epsom and Ascot were allowed to go ahead.

As a member of the Jockey Club, the Duke's opinion commanded respect particularly when he backed it up by scratching his horses from their engagements.

Morley-Brown responded as best he could to what was an indefensible situation by accusing the faddists of promoting the controversy. He wrote of the "wave of madness" that had invaded newspaper offices and declared it was beyond his comprehension how:

> Several ordinarily staid and sound journals have … allowed themselves to be inveigled into a discussion inaugurated in and out of Parliament by people who are no more interested in racing – except from a desire to do the sport harm – than the Germans were in the maintenance of peace in the critical days preceding the outbreak of war.

At the height of the uproar the *Life* published a column-length letter headed 'What Our Soldiers Think Of The Agitators', prefaced by the italicised paragraph:

> *I enclose you a short article dealing with racing in wartime from the point of view of the private soldier at the Front who has returned to England wounded. It is not merely a personal opinion; nine out of every ten men in our regiment, at any rate, hold the same views. If the spoilsports could only hear a few remarks made about them in the trenches they might perhaps abandon their attitude – E L Thompson. (A private in the 2ⁿᵈ Batt. Coldstream Guards, who is now in the Royal Surrey County Hospital, Guildford).*

In what was a timely defence of sport, Thompson referred to a wounded colleague who had set his heart on going to the Cup Final,[*] as he commented scathingly:

And yet there are pseudo-patriots in this country, who, if they had their own way, would deprive him

---

[*] The 1915 'Khaki' Cup Final in which Sheffield United beat Chelsea 3-0 at Old Trafford was the last to be played during the war. In its review of the match the *Life* inserted a separate item headed 'The Sterner Game'. It reported that Lord Derby, who was in charge of recruitment and was on hand to present the Cup, had addressed the 50,000 crowd: "He said the clubs and their supporters had seen the Cup played for and it was now the duty of everyone to join with each other and play a sterner game for England. He felt sure he would not appeal in vain; we had a duty before us, and every man must face it and do his best."

of the one pleasure to which he is looking forward particularly. They would have stopped Association football and thus put an end to the favourite topic of conversation in the trenches and the billets in ruined French villages...

We went out to France to fight for our King and country, and to preserve the national institutions so dear to the heart of Englishmen. We return to find that one of our greatest national institutions – the Derby – is threatened for the first time in history. Has a single one of the men responsible for this attack fired a shot in defence of his country against Germany? At the Front we regard these spoilsports with the utmost contempt.

The Epsom controversy finally died down when assurances were given that the wounded would not be moved out of the hospital but, like the heads of the Hydra, no sooner had one anti-racing campaign been dealt with than others took its place.

At the beginning of May 1915, *The Times* published a letter which described how an officer on his way to France missed his train because racegoers at Waterloo were "struggling in hundreds" for the Hurst Park race specials "while a great many officers and men and their sorrowing relations had literally to force their way through this throng to reach the train which was to take the soldiers to Southampton *en route* for the Front."

The issue of race-trains quickly escalated. In parliament, Lord Claud Hamilton, chairman of the Great Eastern Railway Company which served Newmarket, asked whether, "having regard to the very invidious position now occupied by railway companies in this matter, will the Government take the bold and patriotic course of stopping all race meetings during the continuance of the war?"

The inquiry was endorsed by ringing cries of 'hear, hear', and when the Home Secretary, Reginald McKenna, replied that a ban on racing would be too contentious an issue to be proposed at that time, he drew enraged howls of 'No' from all sides of the chamber. Taken aback by such a vociferous response, McKenna then got the biggest cheer of the day as he hastily added: "If I may judge from that expression of opinion on the part of the House that answer may reasonably be altered."

The mood of parliament was due to a series of recent events that had hardened the hearts of all politicians and the nation in general. That spring, Winston Churchill's Dardanelles campaign had lurched from one disaster to another as the loss of six battleships to mines in March was followed by the horrendous casualties that accompanied the Allied landings at Gallipoli in April.

At home, the bombardment of coastal towns by the German fleet; an increase in Zeppelin raids; the torpedoing of the Lusitania, and the use of chlorine gas against the Allies on the Western Front had led to anti-German riots throughout the country.

On top of all this, there was widespread criticism of the government's handling of the war; in particular it was being blamed for the shortage of shells that had resulted in the failure of the first major British offensive that spring. It all built up into an intolerance of anything that might be seen to interfere with the war effort and politicians from all parties were quick to pounce on racing and use it as their whipping boy.

The inevitable blow fell on May 19 when Walter Runciman, president of the Board of Trade, wrote to Capt Harry Greer, the senior steward, to inform him that parliament was strongly against the continuance of racing as it threatened "the rapid and unimpeded transit of troops and munitions" and consequently:

...we think it necessary to ask the Stewards of the Jockey Club to suspend all race meetings in Great

Britain after this week for the duration of the war. The only exception to this general suspension should be at Newmarket, the peculiar circumstances and industries of which, dependent as they are entirely on racing, combine to make this exception expedient.

The Jockey Club, having already pledged itself to be bound by any decision that might be taken by the government, had no option but to agree to the demand, but many in racing shared Morley-Brown's view that "the interests of the vast army of racing employees and their dependants have been sacrificed in an altogether unnecessary way". The editor felt the stewards had been cowed by "the clamour set up by the Harmsworth newspapers consisting of *The Times*, *Daily Mail* and *Evening News*," and he accused Herbert Asquith's Liberal government of subterfuge:

> The Government, as everyone knows who has carefully followed the trend of recent events, is in difficulties and by way of distracting attention from its own shortcomings has been only too glad to find any side issue which would serve the purpose of diverting criticism into other channels.
>
> Thus, however unwittingly, the Stewards of the Jockey Club have played into their hands, and on the eve of the Whitsuntide recess, the Government have contrived very cleverly to drop a bombshell which, in their view, was quite likely to give people something else to talk about. In this they have undoubtedly succeeded, as the only subject discussed in town yesterday was the stoppage of racing, and so, for the moment, even the Government's internal quarrels were forgotten.

The reaction of other papers to the ban was given the following day when the majority reflected the sentiments expressed by an editorial in *The Times* which, under Lord Northcliffe's wartime direction, was a committed enemy of racing:

> We need hardly say that for ourselves we heartily welcome this wise, if somewhat tardy, decision conveyed to the Jockey Club as a request by the Government, and we fully believe that it will commend itself to every man of decent feeling ... This is no time for the transportation of undesirable mobs in racing specials; the railways must be given over unreservedly to the exigencies of the war. It has long been evident that racing had ceased to exist as a social pleasure. It will now cease to exist as a hindrance and an obstruction.

On the same day, the Jockey Club went some way towards placating the racing community by announcing that extra meetings would be held at Newmarket and that substitute races for the classics would also be run there, but this didn't appease an unnamed French journal, which was quoted in the *Life* as having declared on June 2:

> Today the Derby should have been run, but Mr Runciman killed it with a stroke of the pen. Something of England has disappeared. Something so traditional, so national, so inherent to the life of the country one would have thought that even revolution could not have touched it. The Government in five seconds changed the legendary Blue Ribbon into a band of crape. Fifty years ago, day for day, Gladiateur won the Derby for Count de Lagrange. Last year, Durbar's success was the second French victory in the English Derby. Austria won in 1876 with Kisber. The Germans have won the Derby of 1915!

And just to drive the message home Morley-Brown reported that racing had resumed at Hoppegarten in Berlin. Under the heading 'Germany's Example To England', he quoted *Deutscher Sport*, which justified the resumption by explaining: "The needs of the many racing establishments and the employees had to be considered as had also the demands of the public for racing, the severe conditions notwithstanding."

Supplied with this ammunition he challenged: "Apparently the sport is in a highly flourishing condition in the land of our great enemy, and if it can go on there without let or hindrance, why not in its natural home?"

As British racing ground to a halt, the *Life* switched its attention to Ireland, where the sport had been unaffected by the war. With a warning to readers: "Irish time is considerably behind ours – 24 minutes 48 seconds, to be precise – and bookmakers must therefore revise their rules so as to make allowance for this," the paper dispatched Jim George to return the SPs, while Tom Healy, who had taken over as Irish correspondent on the death of his father, Ned, in 1910, extended his reports.

A number of jockeys and horses also caught the ferry to Dublin, before they returned for the resumption of racing at Newmarket on June 15 when the first of five extra meetings sanctioned by the government attracted massive fields and huge crowds. On sun-baked ground that would normally have reduced fields to single figures, a total of 520 runners (214 on the first day) contested the 21 races held over the three days.

No other racecourse could have coped with such numbers, but the town was quite unable to accommodate the influx of racegoers. Beds were already at a premium as the area had become a vast army training camp for 4,000 troops and many visitors had to sleep out on the heath on Tuesday and Wednesday night, while the race-day crowds were swelled by the walking wounded from Cheveley Park which Mrs Harry McCalmont had turned over to the War Office for use as a hospital.

Punters got off to a good start when the 11-10 chance, Pommern, coasted home in the hands of Steve Donoghue to win the 'New' Derby, while the June Stakes, a substitute for the Coronation Cup, also went to the hot favourite, Black Jester. But the 'New' Oaks fell to a 20-1 shot, Snow Marten, owned by Ludwig Neumann, a German-born, London businessman who had escaped internment thanks to his friendship with the royal family.

The *Life's* Special Commissioner, Friedrich Becker, was not so fortunate and had been interned on the Isle of Man the previous month. Morley-Brown was hardly sympathetic to the plight of his former colleague, if an article he wrote at the time is anything to go by:

> Alien enemies are, or ought to be interned, which is only another way of saying that they are kept in comfort and ease at the country's expense, but apparently there is no fund upon which the respectable racing stable employee can rely for support during the period he is compulsory turned out of work. We are, however, always solicitous for the welfare of our enemies, and devil may care what becomes of our own people.

Of course, internment worked both ways and in Germany a number of English jockeys who had been riding in that country at the outbreak of war suffered the same fate as Becker. Among them was Fred Winter, who won the Oaks as an apprentice on Cherimoya in 1911 and had been appointed first jockey to the Kaiser in 1914 when he was installed in grand style at the imperial stables at Graditz only to be marched off to the internment camp at Ruhleben outside Berlin a few months later.

As 1915 progressed, a national paper shortage gradually reduced the size of the *Life* which appeared as a four-page issue on the first day of the Newmarket December sales when the main topic of news was the dispersal of Colonel Hall Walker's bloodstock.

Walker, a member of a Warrington brewing family whose father had been mayor of Liverpool, achieved his great ambition when The Soarer carried his colours to victory in the 1896 Grand National, while his home-bred Minoru – when leased to Edward VII – provided him with further glory by winning the 1909 Derby. The owner of three other classics winners, he had, in October 1915, offered his entire bloodstock interests to the country as the basis for a national stud.

The thoroughbred stock, which comprised of 2 stallions, 30 broodmares, 8 horses in training and 30 yearlings and foals, together with 600 head of cattle, were to be a gift to the nation, while the government was to buy his Tully stud in Co. Kildare and his Russley Park training establishment in Wiltshire. As the bloodstock had been valued at £75,000, and a similar sum was being asked for the two properties, it seemed an unbeatable bargain but, amazingly, the offer was turned down. Since the government had already spent £12m on buying remounts from overseas, its decision could only be put down to a prudish refusal to connect itself with racing.

The rebuffed Walker (later Lord Wavertree) then went ahead with his plans to sell off his horses at Newmarket. The dispersal of such a valuable consignment created an immense amount of interest and bloodstock agents were looking forward to some fat commissions when, late on the eve of the sale, Walker received a telegram from Lord Selborne, president of the Board of Agriculture, which read: "Gladly accept your generous gift of your horses and livestock. Buy your properties at Russley and Tully."

The eleventh hour turn-round reflected the inept way the government – now a coalition under Herbert Asquith and the Tory leader, Andrew Bonar Law – had been conducting the war. The expense of shipping most of the horses from (and back to) Ireland was the least of the inconvenience caused.

When the purchase of the stud was discussed in the Commons the following March it emerged that Walker had been paid just £65,625 (£3.28m) for his two properties totalling 1,100 acres, and that Harry Greer, who was due to end his term as senior steward that April, had agreed to act as an unpaid director of what had now become the National Stud; but even then some MPs weren't happy.

Sir Frederick Cawley, a bloodstock breeder himself, asked how any ministry could go about preaching economy after buying the stud. It would be a questionable experiment in peacetime, he said, and could be of no use in wartime, while F D Acland, secretary to the Board of Agriculture, made no secret of his opposition to the deal when he declared he regarded racing as "a very low form of sport".

Despite this petty prejudice there had been an unexpected breakthrough for racing that winter when the government gave permission for a limited number of National Hunt meetings to be held in 1916. The concession was granted subject to strict and deliberately class-biased conditions. No race-specials would be run and racegoers were even forbidden to use normal train services, instead they had to travel by road; admission to the course would be by a voucher system and only the club and reserved enclosures were to be used. The minimum entrance charge was set at 15s (£37) as opposed to the normal cheap enclosure rates of a shilling (£2.50) or half-a-crown (£6.25).

Fixtures were granted to five courses: Gatwick, Lingfield, Windsor, Hawthorn Hill (Maidenhead) and Colwall Park (Malvern). The first of these Friday-Saturday meetings was held at Gatwick in January when a select crowd of about 1,000 motored to the course. The following weekend the *Life* carried a front-page advert for 'All Motors Ltd' which was running a taxi service from 36 Great Portland Street to Lingfield. Fares included admission to the reserved enclosure and ranged from 25s (£62) by charabanc to 35s (£97) by car.

In the same month, another concession was squeezed from the government when it agreed to four southern courses staging an extra 24 days of Flat racing in addition to the 39 days that had been scheduled for Newmarket. This led to an outcry from northern courses that had been left out because the Board of Trade was determined not to give munition workers in the industrial towns an excuse for a day off at the races.

Liverpool, in particular, felt the loss of Aintree which had been turned into a munitions area, and for the next three years the Grand National suffered a similar fate to the Derby in that it survived only as a shallow substitute staged at Gatwick, where it was first run as the Racecourse Association Steeplechase in 1916.

Racing over specially constructed fences that proved a lot less formidable than the famous Aintree obstacles, it was won by Vermouth, whose owner donated the £1,000 prize money to a fund for disabled servicemen, while films of the race were sent out to France to be shown to troops at cinemas that had been set up behind the front line.

On the day, racegoers had, in keeping with the conditions laid down by the government, travelled to the course by road even though the Board of Trade had spent much valuable time and money in issuing posters that urged the nation to save petrol and avoid 'motoring for pleasure'. Inevitably, the faddists made the most of this bureaucratic bunkum and their indignation was further inflamed when the Great Eastern Railway, contrary to restrictions and the professed views of its chairman, ran race-specials from London to Newmarket for the three-day Craven meeting in April.

More letters poured into *The Times* and more questions were asked in the Commons, where common sense seemed to be singularly lacking, but by then the harassed government had other things to worry about. On Tuesday 25 April 1916, the lead to the war news column in the *Life* announced:

> At noon yesterday serious disturbances broke out in Dublin. A large body of men identified with the Sinn Feiners, mostly armed, occupied Stephen's Green and took possession forcibly of the Post Office where they cut the telegraphic and telephonic wires. Houses were also occupied in Stephen's Green, Sackville-st., Abbey-st., and along the quays.
>
> In the course of the day soldiers arrived from Curragh and the situation is now well in hand. So far as is known here, three military officers, four or five soldiers, two Loyal Volunteers and two policemen have been killed and four or five military officers, seven or eight soldiers and six Loyal Volunteers wounded. No exact information has been received of casualties on the side of the Sinn Feiners.

Despite the situation being 'well in hand' the rebels held out for another three days, and by the time they surrendered the death toll on both sides had risen to 450 with more than 2,600 wounded. The Easter Uprising, which resulted in martial law being imposed throughout Ireland, brought the country's racing to a halt for six weeks and occupied the minds of politicians for a time, but it was not long before the question of motor transport to race meetings was again being debated and in August petrol rationing was introduced with private motorists limited to 8 gallons (36 litres) a month.

By the end of the year the Coalition government had collapsed, Asquith had resigned and David Lloyd George had become Prime Minister. The year also saw the loss of Lord Kitchener when *HMS Hampshire* was sunk off the Orkneys, while on the racing front the "universally beloved and admired" Danny Maher lost his battle against tuberculosis at the age of 35 and the *Life's* long-time correspondent, Bob Watson, died at 67.

In bidding farewell to "a keen worker, a faithful servant and a staunch friend," the *Life* remarked:

"There was not a branch of sport upon which he was not regarded as an authority and in which his services in an official capacity were not frequently sought." The respect accorded to Watson was demonstrated when a benefit was staged for his family at the Blackfriars Ring that summer. The five-hour programme included boxing bouts and performances by famous variety artists. Among those present were Watson's old pal Charlie Mitchell, the reigning British heavyweight champion, Bombardier Billy Wells, and the former lightweight champ, Dick Burge, while some 200 wounded 'Tommies' were invited along as guests.

The music hall star, Marie Lloyd, who was married to the Derby (Lemberg, 1910) winning jockey Bernard Dillon, donated a rope of Teresa pearls to the auction, while her sister, Alice, sent a gold watch from America, and Watson's own collection of sporting memorabilia was sold off — included were the fight colours sported by Tom Sayers in his mill with Jack Heenan at Farnborough in 1860. It was, truly, the end of an era.

By 1917 the transport of horses to race meetings by train had been banned and for the New Year meeting at Gatwick the clock was turned back almost 80 years when all 75 runners were walked to the course. Blind Hookey, the winner of the first race, took five hours to complete the journey from Robert Gore's Findon stables, while other horses made similar hikes from Epsom and Lewes.

Racing had proved it could exist without the use of railways, but no sooner had it done so than another obstacle was thrown in its path. At the end of January, following the rejection of its latest peace proposal, Germany resumed unrestricted submarine warfare and the heavy toll its U-boats were taking on shipping — 134 merchant ships were sunk in the first three weeks of February — threatened Britain's food supplies.

With the predictability of ducks flying south in the winter, letters began to appear in *The Times* complaining that the consumption of oats by racehorses was unacceptable at a time when the price of bread was soaring and there was the possibility of food rationing. As ever, politicians were quick to build on these fears and on April 19 Charles Bathurst, secretary to the Ministry of Food, claimed that the full oats ration for a horse over a year could support 20 or 30 people. He added threateningly: "The question might arise before long whether it is in the highest national interest to continue racing."

A few days later, the director of Food Economy, the former *Daily Mail* journalist Kennedy Jones, stated in a letter to *The Times* that the bloodstock industry could survive during the war by limiting racing to the five classics and a few events for two-year-olds. This, he maintained, was sufficient to determine the best horses of their generation: "Thus the 4,000 horses now in training would be cut down at once to about 80 or 100 horses."

The fact that Jones — a racehorse owner himself — was quoting the number of horses registered on 1 March 1914 as opposed to just under 2,000 on 1 March 1917, showed the sort of spin the anti-racing lobby was employing to achieve its ends, ends that were duly attained on April 29 when the following notice was issued to the press:

> The Stewards of the Jockey Club, having received intimation that the War Cabinet considers it undesirable that further racing should take place after the conclusion of the First Spring Meeting, have cancelled all 1917 fixtures after that date [*May 4*].

The announcement outraged the racing community. Less than three months earlier the government had given the go-ahead for 13 meetings, amounting to 44 days, to be held at Newmarket on the basis of which many provincial trainers had taken leases on stables in the town and surrounding area. That they now felt betrayed was no surprise.

Under the headline 'Methods of the Faddists Triumph at Last', Morley-Brown viewed the decision with a mixture of cynicism and anger – the latter sentiment being reserved for the aforementioned Northcliffe acolyte, Kennedy Jones, an abrasive Glaswegian and once proud holder of the hotly contested 'most hated man in Fleet Street' title:

> So the blow has fallen at last! The faddists have won the last trench in their State-aided onslaught on a great and vitally important British industry ... Those who must inevitably suffer in consequence of the decision now arrived at will be able, however, to enjoy the supreme satisfaction of knowing that their discomfiture removes what has been apparently the main obstacle to the successful propagation of the war.
>
> At all events, the opponents of racing will henceforth be free to devote their whole energies to the prosecution of the stupendous task in hand ... but woe betide them when our soldiers come back from their well-earned conquest and demand pastimes of a more exhilarating kind than dominoes and draughts.
>
> In this sense we may take it for granted that Mr Kennedy Jones will never again be re-elected as Member for the Hornsey Division or, for that matter, any other constituency in which the true sporting spirit prevails. One regrets very much to have to write in this strain of a gentleman whom we had come to regard as a good sportsman, but since he has worn the mantle of officialdom he has gone the way of so many others in the same boat.
>
> It is not given to every man to keep his head and maintain a true perspective under the influence of newly acquired importance. The assistance afforded them by Mr Kennedy Jones, one does not hesitate to state, has been the deciding factor in the faddists' triumph and he will always be remembered as one who deserted his friends of the racing world in their hour of direst need.

Amid a forest of doomsday headlines that reflected the industry's reactions to the ban, John Gardner in Newmarket focused on the provincial trainers who had leased stables in the area and were thus "doubly burdened with rent, rates and taxation, in addition to huge expense". For dramatic effect he added:

> At midday two dead horse carts were busily employed and the town had the appearance of a deserted French village on the approach of the Germans. Tradesmen and the hundreds of families dependant on racing are much alarmed. Most of the houses had been let for the season and now nothing but extreme poverty stares us in the face.

At the time the government dropped its bombshell, its Food Controller, Lord Devonport, who, the *Life* reminded readers, "was a retail grocer before political devotion to party secured for him a handle to his name," was busy drawing up an oats allowance for thoroughbreds. When the scale of rations was issued the following week it was seen that stallions and broodmares had been exempted, but colts and fillies were to be limited to 7lb a day and geldings were to get no oats at all, something, one would have thought, that had already been denied to them!

While George V called for a restraint on bread consumption without, it has to be said, telling his subjects to eat cake, the *Life* shot the oats kite out of the sky with a front-page letter from a mathematical genius known to history only as F Charly of 24 Oakley St, London NW. Headed 'Feeding The Racehorse / A Pertinent Fact For The Food Controller', it read:

> Sir – While three million Britons are fighting for liberty abroad, three hundred faddists are filching away their liberties at home and paving the way for a Puritanical tyranny infinitely worse than anything our avowed enemies could have inflicted upon us.
>
> No man who has given ten minutes thought to the subject is deluded by the statement that the rationing of racehorses has been prompted solely by a desire to benefit the populace. Not a word has been said about rationing the hundreds of thousands of hacks and carriage horses kept solely for pleasure, but 2,000 thoroughbreds are selected because they are associated with sport.
>
> Allowing a thoroughbred a hundredweight of oats a week, he consumes, approximately, 2 ½ tons a year, which means – on a basis of 2,000 horses in training, and that is well over the mark – 5,000 tons a year.
>
> If this were milled and prepared for human food, it would yield about 2,500 tons or the equivalent of 2 ounces per annum to every inhabitant of the United Kingdom! And for the sake of these two ounces an industry in which millions of pounds have been invested and which has taken hundreds of years to build up, is to be completely crushed.

As the esteemed Mr Charly implied, the oats issue was merely a pretext for the ban, a fact confirmed when the *Racing Calendar* published a report of the meetings that had taken place between the Jockey Club stewards, Lord Devonport and Lord Derby, the new Secretary of State for War. It emerged that Derby had tried to dissuade the War Cabinet from imposing the ban, but the government claimed "that public opinion, which was shared by members of the Cabinet, was opposed to racing at the present moment, and it was therefore advisable … there should be no more racing as long as the war lasted".

The revelation that 'public opinion' had prompted the ban raised a whole new storm of protest in the sporting press which was inundated with letters from a very different section of the public to that which wrote to Geoffrey Dawson, editor of *The Times*. The *Life's* headline on May 7 'The Truth Revealed at Last: Not Oats, but Prudery' said it all:

> Public opinion, we are told, demands that racing should be put an end to, but where is the overwhelming volume of antagonistic public opinion to which the War Cabinet have succumbed? … Most of the supporters of racing in Parliament, including the two members for Newmarket, are at the Front and under such circumstances, therefore, it would be hopeless to look for a vote favourable to racing in the event of a division being forced on the matter in the House of Commons.
>
> Yet, with a Chamber composed mainly of people who no longer faithfully represent the views of their constituents, we find ourselves compelled to submit to the sort of 'public opinion' thuswise expressed. Public opinion forsooth! Pacifism, conscientious objectors, Little Englandism, fads and faddism of every description – these are the elements of which the present-day Parliamentary forces are largely composed, and will continue to be until a much-needed General Election takes place.

The *Life's* battling and embattled editor was inevitably accused of self-interest by his enemies as, day after day, he kept up his relentless and none-too-subtle barrage against:

> …the congregation of humbugs and hypocrites who nowadays earn their four hundred a year by

impeding the conduct of the war by … asking stupid questions regarding other people's business. [May 8].

…a handful of fanatics who dislike everything that brings joy to the hearts of their fellow beings … with characteristic cunning these miserable beings wait until reliable 'public opinion' is to be found only in the trenches, and then press home the advantage secured at the cost of the life and limb of the brave fellows but for whom their own unworthy skins would be in dire jeopardy. [May 10].

At the same time he pointed out that racing was continuing "in full swing" in Germany as he observed:

One cannot help feeling that the Germans must derive great comfort and encouragement from the belief that their submarine campaign has brought about the cessation of racing in England … It is an amazing fact that while racing is prohibited in England and Ireland it is going on, if not exactly as usual, to a greater or lesser extent everywhere else. Even in France, where the enemy is still mustered in great force, it has been found possible in the vital interests of horse-breeding to make a resumption at Chantilly, which famous training centre itself was not so very long ago threatened with occupation by the invading German hordes.

And if Morley-Brown was up in arms, it was as nothing compared to the fury felt in Ireland, where a deputation of breeders and owners informed the Chief Secretary that the ban would throw 20,000 men and boys out of work and do irreparable damage to an industry that had already supplied 300,000 horses for the war. They might also have added that while the War Cabinet's crutch of 'public opinion' might apply to a clique of letter writers to *The Times*, in no way could it be attributed to Ireland. On the contrary, the decision to stop racing was an affront to public opinion.

There were certainly no faddists among the Irish MPs. They were, to a man, behind their constituents, and the fact that the ban was being imposed at a time when Lloyd George was making major efforts to bring about a satisfactory conclusion to the vexed question of Home Rule beggared belief. It was a blunder of staggering proportions.

In an interview with 'a *Sporting Life* representative', an exasperated John Dillon, the Nationalist MP for East Mayo, exclaimed: "Heaven knows there is sufficient bitterness in Ireland as it is, and anything more calculated to aggravate that bitterness than the stoppage of racing could hardly be conceived."

The Irish outcry and the threat of another uprising soon had the weak and vacillating government back-pedalling. Its first concession was to allow the Curragh meeting of May 8-10 to go ahead provided it was recognised there could be no more racing afterwards.

Admiral Sir Hedworth Meux, MP, a member of the Jockey Club and the Lambton family, soon saw which way the wind was blowing and on May 11 he pinned down Bonar Law with a series of questions which culminated with the query: "Does that mean that if any concession is granted to Ireland, a similar act of justice will be granted to England?"

To which the Leader of the House coolly replied: "It is the intention to act in the same way in all parts of the United Kingdom." The very next day the Irish Turf Club received the go-ahead to hold meetings at Dundalk and Phoenix Park for the week ending May 19 – Bonar Law had, it seemed, brought forward Irish Home Rule by five years!

More concessions followed and eventually a fairly normal programme was restored in Ireland on the understanding that no racing would be held during harvest time when all labour would be turned to the fields. Meanwhile, appeals for a limited resumption of racing in England were rebuffed with a stubborn effrontery.

The transparent dishonesty of the government's actions generated a nationwide protest not only from those within the industry, but from outside it as well. The councils of the Royal Agricultural Society, the Hunters' Improvement Society and the Shire Horse Society all condemned the ban, while the National Workmen's Council organised a massive petition among its members calling for racing to be resumed.

A Racing Emergency Council was set up under the chairmanship of Horatio Bottomley, MP, a vociferous supporter of the sport, but also an unabashed self-publicist and silvery-tongued fraudster whose activities in the latter sphere paid for his string of racehorses, mistresses and champagne lifestyle before they eventually earned him a seven-year jail sentence for embezzlement.

But the most influential movement to emerge from the crisis was the Thoroughbred Breeders Association (TBA), which was formed at a conference held at Tattersalls subscription room in Knightsbridge on 14 May 1917. Lord D'Abernon, who had just won the One Thousand Guineas with Diadem, was nominated president, while Edward Moorhouse, the motive force behind the new body, became its secretary.

A month later, following a meeting between Moorhouse and several pro-racing MPs, a cross-party committee was set up under the chairmanship of Sir Hedworth Meux to protect the interests of the horse-breeding industry in parliament. The War Cabinet, meanwhile, was learning all about the strength of true public opinion as mass meetings in Sheffield, Manchester, Newcastle and London demanded the resumption of racing.

Finally, the voice of the people began to be heard and, on June 20 'Augur' informed his readers that the government: "fully appreciating the grave political changes that were likely to result from the next General Election ...if the efforts of the cranks in Parliament were not speedily stopped ... will almost immediately make an announcement that will ... be gratifying, if not quite satisfying, to the sporting public."

The announcement duly came two weeks later, when Sir Albert Stanley, the new president of the Board of Trade, wrote to Sir John Thursby, the new senior steward, to inform him: "the War Cabinet have now decided that, in view of the national importance of horse breeding, a limited amount of racing may be allowed in England from the middle of this month to the close of the season."

It was, in its way, one of the most remarkable about-turns in parliamentary history. The twelve days lost to racing as a result of the ten-week ban were made good by the allocation of the first fixtures in the north since 1915 when three days were allotted to both Manchester and Stockton, while Windsor and Brighton were also allowed three days each. Newmarket had all its fixtures restored with three extra days added for good measure.

At the same time, the oats allowance for horses in training (which were to be limited to 1,200) was set at 15lb a day, while the added bonus of a two-day meeting at the end of September was later granted to Ayr.

For Morley-Brown it was a personal victory that was acknowledged by readers who wrote in to express their thanks for the campaign he had waged:

I must say I have enjoyed reading the outspoken articles and letters appearing in your valuable paper and the bold fighting front the *Sporting Life* has shown during the racing ban, and I shall always stick to the old paper after this. *J Stock, Sawston, Cambridge.*

> Several people have asked me to express their entire appreciation of the indispensable part borne by the *Sporting Life* in the recent struggle for racing; indispensable because of the indifference or even hostile attitude of the lay papers generally. *J H Smith, Brighton.*

The editor was entitled to take a bow. He also felt justified in warning readers off the Harmsworth press and what he called "the Bouverie Street cocoa organs" – the *Daily News* and *The Star* – owned by the Cadbury family, whose Quaker beliefs set them against all forms of gambling unless it helped to sell their papers:

> I sincerely hope that all good sportsmen will remember, now that racing is about to be resumed, the names of those newspapers under faddist control, and steadfastly decline to subscribe to them ... Let them remember that certain journals, which have played an active part towards the abolition of racing have, in ordinary times, made a special feature of the publication of racing news and will, now that the sport is re-established on a firmer basis than ever, endeavour to enlarge their wartime circulation by resorting to all the old tricks.

The resumption of racing at Newmarket on July 17 was a truly festive occasion. With a ban now placed on motors being used to attend race meetings, every conceivable form of horse-drawn transport was pressed into service, and as the editor clip-clopped his way out of town to the July Course he noted:

> The only people to be benefited by the new arrangements are the cab and fly proprietors who will, of course, reap a rich a harvest until the day of the motor returns. Their voracity in the matter of charges was less pronounced than might have been expected under the circumstances, but in any event I am not sure that we are strictly entitled to criticise anything in the shape of 'profiteering' so long as the Government set the example by charging a fifty per cent increase on railway fares.

In another column, under the eye-catching headline 'The Gas-Bag and Racing', it was reported that a party of racegoers had chartered a bus which "caused no little consternation and amusement on the way to the course. The 'motor' had previously been propelled by petrol, but yesterday it carried on top a huge gas-bag, not unlike a balloon, and by this means it conveyed its passengers to headquarters!"

Manchester's first meeting coincided with the August bank holiday and offered soldiers home on leave a blessed relief from the horrors of war. The Corporation laid on 60 trams to ferry the crowds to the course on Saturday and Monday when the *Life* commented:

> Never was the need of some relaxation for the hard-worked munitioneers better demonstrated than by the big crowds that came from the surrounding districts which have been working day and night ... There was a wonderful array of khaki and the blue of the wounded, the Executive entertaining a thousand gallant men who had been maimed and broken in the recent big offensive.

But racing's reprieve was short-lived. At the end of October the president of the Board of Trade informed the NH Committee that "it has been found impossible during the coming winter to give any facilities for meetings under National Hunt Rules. He fears, therefore, he cannot agree to such meetings being held." Once again Morley-Brown railed against the decision as he called on the NH authorities to fight the ban:

> Surely it is not the intention of the Stewards to accept tamely and without protest of any sort so vague a refusal as has been conveyed to them. They will, and must, demand reasons from Sir Albert Stanley and see that these are forthcoming. They have been told that facilities for meetings cannot be granted. What facilities?
>
> There are no facilities available just now, and there have been none since the ban on flat racing was removed in July. The only condition imposed was that road travel, which alone was permissible the preceding winter, must be abandoned and progress to meetings only be allowed by rail – no special trains being provided. It is misleading, therefore, to talk of facilities that do not exist.

And once again the decision was reversed within two months when a limited weekday programme of fixtures was allowed. As a Whitehall farce this one was set to run for as long as the war lasted, and the way things were going that looked as if it might be forever.

After three months' fighting with the usual appalling casualties at Passchendaele in what was the third battle of Ypres, a major breakthrough had been achieved in November when, in a surprise attack at Cambrai, some 370 British tanks, grinding along at 3mph, smashed their way through the Hindenburg line. It was a rare success for Field Marshal Haig, command-in-chief of the British Army, but ten days later the Germans launched their own 'surprise' counter-attack and recaptured all the lost ground.

And 1918 did not dawn any brighter; on New Year's Day the *Life* carried a list of almost 200 gentlemen riders (those who were members of select clubs such as Boodle's, Carlton, Turf, etc. as opposed to rank and file amateurs) who had 'fallen in action' since the start of the war.

On the domestic front there were an increasing number of strikes among the exhausted workforce and in the Commons the same coterie of MPs seemed more intent on bringing about a halt to racing than winning the war. Foremost among them was George Lambert (Lab. South Molton, Devon), who, in January, resurrected the old chestnut of oats rations for racehorses. In his reply, Bonar Law said that the War Cabinet now felt that the effect of a complete stoppage of racing on "the habits of the people" would be out of proportion to the savings made in cereals. This, of course, was more political poppycock as Morley-Brown, by now an expert in exposing such humbug, pointed out:

> If the habits of the people are really the object of so much solicitude on the part of the Government, how does it come about that the Railway Executive Committee is forbidden to provide special train accommodation, and that the working classes are debarred from participation in racing owing to the sport being taboo on Saturdays? This hardly looks as though the habits of the people have been very seriously studied, unless by 'the people' he means those who have sufficient leisure to be able to attend midweek meetings.

The 1918 Flat season started with fixtures being granted to ten courses from Lewes in the south to Haydock and Stockton in the north, but as a result of a new German offensive launched in March, racing was once again restricted to Newmarket after May 31 because of "the increasing strain on the railways".

In June, when the Germans were once again threatening Paris and victory for the Allies seemed as far away as ever, it was announced that there would be no jump racing that winter; a declaration Morley-Brown greeted with undisguised scorn:

This latest edict of the War Cabinet denotes a really amazing advance on the part of our rulers in the direction of foresight. The usual complaint is 'too late, too late, always too late', but where racing is concerned apparently it is deemed necessary to formulate plans six months ahead.

He went on to point out that horses had been walked to meetings for the past 16 months and at populous centres where racecourses were not occupied by the military, people could get to the races by bike or tram with no call on railway facilities. "What was the conclusion to be drawn from all this?" he asked as he answered: "The faddist element is the master of the situation."

In September, the indefatigable editor exposed more double standards when he revealed that flapping meetings were being held throughout the country and one such fixture had recently taken place at Brighton:

> We have no great objection to the holding of such meetings, although it is obvious that their value from the point of view of the breeding industry is practically nil. They, however, doubtless provide recreation and enjoyment for some sections of the community; and it is to be assumed that they do not interfere with the prosecution of the war. But what the plain man cannot understand is that, if it is possible and permissible to hold meetings under unrecognised rules at Brighton and other places, why on earth it should not be also possible to hold meetings under Jockey Club Rules.

This legitimate query did not make Morley-Brown very popular with flapping fans since, four days later, the *Life* reported that the War Cabinet, in its drive to achieve victory on the Western Front, had acted with unusual alacrity and that "a Defence of the Realm Regulation has accordingly been made prohibiting any meeting at which racing with horses, Galloways, or ponies takes place".

It was, of course, the key to winning the war. The fortunes of the Allies had already begun to turn thanks largely to America's belated arrival on the scene, and in the succeeding weeks the war-news headlines told their own story.

On Sept 19: 'Fine British Push / Complete Success On 16 Miles Front'; Sept 25: 'Bulgarian Rout / Further Big Advance On Salonika Front'; Oct 7: 'Germany Asks For Armistice / Chancellor's Message To US President'; Oct 16: 'Surrender First: Talk After / America's Plain Words To War Lords'; Nov 1: 'Exit Turkey: Rout Of Austrians / New Allied Attacks In Belgium'; Nov 7: 'The White-Flag From Berlin / Official Delegation Wait On Foch'; Nov 9: 'Yes' Or 'No' By Monday / Foch Refuses Hun Request To Stop Fighting Now'.

And suddenly it was all over. On Tuesday 12 November 1918 the block-capital headlines in an emaciated, single-sheet edition announced: 'Germany Rendered Impotent / Sweeping Nature Of The Armistice Terms / Ex-Kaiser And Kaiserin In Holland':

> The great world war ended at 11 o'clock yesterday morning. The Allies' Armistice terms were signed by the German delegates at Marshal Foch's headquarters at 5 a.m. and became operative six hours later. By these terms … it has been made impossible for Germany to continue the war. Her acceptance of the terms is, in fact, Unconditional Surrender.

The *Life's* response to the end of hostilities was almost muted; there was no wild rejoicing or triumphal hallelujahs in its shrunken columns. The cost had been far too great. Instead Morley-Brown focused his thoughts on the coming general election as he prepared to settle some old scores.

On the same day as it was announced that jump racing would be resumed at Manchester on New Year's Day, he produced four questions which "all sportsmen should ask parliamentary candidates canvassing for their votes," and pointedly remarked:

> The approach of a General Election has a wonderful effect upon the slumbering consciences of members whose desire it is to return to Westminster, and while I hope that all our friends still entitled to affix M.P. to their names will retain the honour, I sincerely trust that in the critical times to come they will endeavour to put up a more determined fight against faddist intrigue than in the past.

On polling day, December 14, as women (those aged 30 and over) prepared to exercise their hard-earned right to vote for the first time, the paper published a 'List of Candidates Who Have Declared Themselves on the Side of Sport' and urged readers to vote for Lloyd George and his Coalition government. And two weeks later when all the votes had been counted, a three-deck headline proclaimed: 'Sportsmen In New Parliament / Gratifying Success Of 'Sound' Candidates / Faddists Badly Beaten Everywhere'.

As Morley-Brown had so often forecast in his strident editorials, the election had been a true reflection of public opinion and it resulted in the Coalition being returned with a massive majority of 234. The one blot on an otherwise glorious landscape for the doughty editor was that the Hornsey electorate of north London had been unsporting enough to return Mr Kennedy Jones as their MP, but that was something he could live with. He had, after all, carried his paper through a most crucial period and while it is impossible to say how much his vigorous campaign to keep racing going had influenced the powers that be, it certainly earned the *Life* the loyalty and respect of all associated with the sport.

And for the next 80 glorious years that loyalty was to be repaid through its pages as a collection of gifted, unconventional and occasionally ill-disciplined journalists educated, enlightened and entertained generations of discerning readers.

PART THREE

THE GOLDEN YEARS
(1919-98)

This advert for the Primo Carnera v Larry Gains fight helped to draw a record crowd of 70,000 to the White City stadium in May 1932. 'The Ambling Alp' was hot favourite to beat the Canadian champion, but lost on points over ten rounds. Stanley Longstaff ('Straight Left'), the *Life*'s boxing correspondent before he became the urbane PRO for Ladbrokes, reported Gains as saying: "Carnera is strong, but he does not know how to land a good punch." Carnera claimed: "Five I won, three were even. How do I lose then?" Carnera went on to become world champion the following year by knocking out Jack Sharkey at Madison Square Gardens.

A LAND FIT FOR HEROES?

T HEY WERE promised 'a land fit for heroes', the lucky ones who returned from the trenches, the maimed and the blind, the shell-shocked and the insane. Instead they found a nation racked by industrial unrest, war debts and fears of revolution, elements that were to congeal and fester into mass unemployment, riots and hunger marches.

Racing, having endured the dithering diktats of a succession of wartime governments, was now hit by a series of strikes in the railway and mining industries. In the first three years of peace, a total of 68 meetings amounting to two months' racing were lost to industrial action. A miners' strike in October 1920 brought the sport to a halt for three weeks and put paid to the Cambridgeshire, which had been run without interruption since its inception in 1839. The following year another mining dispute resulted in no racing for most of April and the Newmarket Guineas meeting being crammed into one day.

But the first strike to stop the sport came at the end of September 1919 when 400,000 rail workers, faced with imminent pay cuts, downed tools. With the railways still under State control, the government placed full-page adverts in the press to argue its case. Its concluding question 'Is The Strike Justified?' was answered with an emphatic 'No' by the *Sporting Life*, which also condemned the decision of the stewards to go ahead with racing on the opening day of Newmarket's first October meeting.

Because racehorse transport was still heavily reliant on the railways, many intended runners were unable to reach the course and local trainers were left to mop up the races. For once the *Life* found itself in agreement with *The Times*, which actually boycotted the meeting by refusing to publish either the programme or the results. Describing the day's sport as "farcical" (the remaining three days were abandoned at the 'request' of the government), Morley-Brown declared: "racing in present circumstances is absolutely contrary to public interest and the policy advocated in the Government's daily communiqué to the nation."

In his Warren Hill column, John Gardner, the paper's long-time Newmarket correspondent, was scathing in his denunciation of the strikers:

> Whilst racing has been struggling for its very existence for the last five years it is sad indeed to see many of those who have had a nice quiet time at home hauling in big wages now attempting to undo all that our soldiers have done by strikes of the most disgraceful kind.
>
> Railwaymen here say that they did not want to come out, but were told to. That, however, is no excuse, and the way they left their duties with packages strewn everywhere and corn left to spoil in the sheds, shows a vindictive malice aforethought. The intention of the strikers is to starve the country into submission, and this should compel the Government to do far more to the culprits than merely defeating them.
>
> There is talk of trouble even in racing stables, but let those concerned take warning in time, for there is no shadow of doubt that many owners of horses, including some of our wealthiest, will give up racing altogether. They say that as things are now there is very little pleasure in it and they do not care much if they continue or not. They had a tremendous struggle to keep going through the war and any extra worry will snap the last thread.

Gardner's cry of 'wolf' had been heard before in Newmarket, most notably in 1901 when more than 600 stable lads went on strike after their demand for a 25 per cent increase on their standard rate of £1 (£90) a week had been rejected, and if things were bad then they were even worse in 1919. That January the *Life* carried a letter headed 'A Living Wage / Plea for Better Treatment of Stablemen', which read:

> Now that our leading Ministers have expressed convictions that horse breeding and racing is one of our greatest national industries, it is quite time that something should be done to secure a fair living wage for the attendants who spend their whole lives in a breeding or racing establishment...
>
> I will quote the wages paid by one, if not *the* most fashionable of jumping stables in England where horses worth thousands of pounds are trained and under the care of these men who are expected to do three or more horses each for the beggarly wage of from 30s to 35s [*£60 to £70*] per week. Out of this their board and lodgings cost from 25s to 30s per week. How are they to get clothes and boots at their present price to keep themselves respectable, as required, out of this altogether insufficient wage?
>
> It is to be hoped that someone in authority will take this up at once for us, and see that this cruel injustice is put right. (Signed) 'Stableman'

But justice in the form of 'a living wage' was in short supply in post-war Britain and what little there was had to be fought for. Workers who had the backing of a powerful union were better off than most, but for those unable to bargain from a position of strength the cause was hopeless. When the police tried to set up their own union in the summer of 1919, some 6,000 were sacked for going on strike; as a result the crime rate soared and the army had to be called out to deal with riots and looting. It was little wonder the papers were full of talk of revolution and Bolshevism.

It did not take long for the discontent to spread to racing and in October 1919 the stable lads in Epsom came out on strike after their demand for a £2-10s (£100) minimum wage had been rejected by the trainers. While the racing establishment predictably condemned the strikers, Augur was sympathetic to their cause:

> Truth to tell, the lads appear to have reason on their side, though the facts concerning the contending parties have never been set forth in full detail. If it is the owners who are at fault, surely they will see their way to follow the example of their contemporaries in France who have agreed to an increase of training charges ... as sportsmen, let us be fair to the lads and see that they are not the only ill-paid section of the community. *

The Epsom branch of the Discharged Soldiers Federation did what it could to help. It paid the weekend butchers' bills of the married ex-servicemen on strike and provided mid-day meals for their schoolchildren and milk for those under school age, but with no support from stable staff in other racing centres, the strike collapsed after a month and the lads returned to work no better off than they were before.

But for some the milk and honey flowed – for a short time at least. In the general euphoria that followed four years of heartbreak and horror, sport flourished as never before. Crowds flocked to

---

* Stable lads were to remain 'ill-paid' for many years to come. In May 1938 the Lambourn lads began a ten-month strike when they also demanded a minimum weekly wage of £2-10s (by which time the £ was worth 30 per cent more than it had been in 1919), but this time the dispute was due as much to the argument over union recognition as money.

racecourses and football grounds in record numbers and in every arena new stars emerged in an international firmament.

Tennis fans were captivated by the flamboyant flair and balletic agility of the French champion Suzanne Lenglen, who won the first of her 15 Wimbledon titles in 1919 by beating the seven times English champion, Dorothea Lambert Chambers, in an epic 10-8, 4-6, 9-7 encounter. The 8,000-plus crowd that crammed into the Worple Road centre court that day finally convinced the Wimbledon authorities that a larger site was needed and in 1922 they moved to their present home in Church Road.

In that same year, the extrovert American golf pro, Walter Hagen, won the first of his four British Opens and England's finest batsman, Jack Hobbs, celebrated his 40th birthday before going on to amass a record number of runs (61,237) and centuries (197) in a first-class career that spanned four decades (1905-34).

Racing still had its wartime darling in Steve Donoghue who began the decade with an unprecedented hat trick of Derby victories before a shy young miner's son took over his mantle as the people's champion. Gordon Richards won the first of his 26 titles in 1925 and retired in 1954 with a knighthood and a record 4,870 winners from 21,828 mounts.

Horsepower of a different kind made the headlines in the '20s as an elite band of well-heeled enthusiasts known as 'the 'Bentley Boys' got their kicks on the world's first banked racing circuit at Brooklands in Surrey, and at Le Mans where the dark green, two-ton monster machines ruled supreme in the 24-hour race for four brief but glorious years.

Others, hooked on adrenalin and glory, set their sights on the land and water-speed records. Foremost among them were the former fighter pilots, Malcolm Campbell and Henry Segrave who, together with the Welshman, John Parry Thomas, drove ever more powerful cars as they pushed the record up from 136mph in 1923 to 301mph in 1935. But all too often the 'speed kings' addiction proved fatal and they perished in a mass of flames and twisted metal.

It all made for sensational news, and Fleet Street rode high on the boom that swept the nation as the space allotted to sport in the national press was extended from a few columns to two or three pages. For the *Sporting Life* it was the dawn of a new era. The paper had emerged from the war battered and emaciated, but otherwise intact. However, after almost 60 years of holding its price at a penny, it had been forced up to 2d in 1918 and at the end of May 1920 another penny was added. In explanation it stated:

> We have been compelled to take this step owing to the tremendously heavy and ever-increasing cost of producing a daily newspaper. The price of paper is almost six times higher than it was in 1914, and will assuredly go higher still; salaries and wages have risen enormously during the past few months; and the working hours of all classes of newspaper men have been greatly reduced, necessitating increased staffs at very high rates of pay compared with even a short time ago … It may be stated that over 350 newspapers and periodicals have been increased in price during the present year, and the list is being added to daily.*

The year had started with the *Life* moving out of 148 Fleet Street, which had been its home since 1859. Its publishing office transferred to nearby Shoe Lane and advertising joined the editorial department that had been based at 27 St Bride Street, just off Shoe Lane, since 1904. The move had been

---

* The increase lasted barely a year before it was cut back to 2d. It was not until 1946 that the price returned to 3d, but from then on regular increases forced the price up until it reached £1 in the paper's final year.

brought about by the death of the paper's joint proprietor, Eleanor Broomfield, and the subsequent sale of the old offices.

For the widowed Walter Broomfield it marked the end of his involvement with the *Life*. In July 1920 he sold the paper to the printing and publishing company, Odhams Press Ltd, and retired to lead the life of a country squire, training a few of his own National Hunt horses at Longdon Chase, Hindhead, in Surrey.

The *Life*, meanwhile, continued much as before under its new owners. Founded in 1847 by William Odhams, the Long Acre-based firm had just started to expand into mainstream publishing under the direction of its chairman, Julius Salter Elias. It had recently acquired the popular weekly journal, *John Bull*, which was, according to its former proprietor, Horatio Bottomley, "devoted to the fearless exposure of frauds and defrauders" thus proving the old maxim 'it takes one to know one'.

Elias, a shy, eccentric but inspired businessman, placed both *John Bull* and the *Life* under the direction of his trusted editor-in-chief, John Dunbar. The son of a Scottish farmer, Dunbar was a keen horseman and a staunch trade unionist and, initially at least, he was happy to leave W S Morley-Brown to his own devices.

This was not altogether to the *Life's* advantage since its editor had become too set in his ways to fit comfortably into the new style of journalism that had been brought in by wartime exigencies. The reduction in the size of newspapers had resulted in tighter editing and more effective presentation of stories. A report that might formally have taken up a full column would be cut back to half that size by judicious pruning without losing any of its news value. The main facts were contained in the first paragraph or at least they should have been, but this was not always the case with the *Life* as was evident from a racecourse report filed by Augur in 1920.

Whether Morley-Brown wrote the column for Saturday, January 17, is uncertain, but whoever it was, one thing is certain, it needed rewriting. Headed 'Excellent Sport at Hurst Park Meeting', it began in time-honoured fashion:

> The continuance of extraordinary mild weather for this time of year, coupled with the prospect of excellent sport, ensured a big attendance for the opening of the Hurst Park meeting yesterday.
>
> So far as the racing promise was concerned, it was amply fulfilled, fields being good except in one instance. Unfortunately there were one or two somewhat serious mishaps to riders, but that is a circumstance over which no management has control and it is hardly necessary to add that on no racecourse in the country are arrangements more perfect than those prevailing at Hurst Park.

It was only after this mincing introduction that readers were told that Frank Cullen had been "badly hurt about the back and neck" in a 'somewhat serious mishap' that resulted in the unfortunate jockey's death 24 hours later.

In contrast to Saturday's rambling intro, Monday's paper gave just two column inches to the jockey who had been held in high regard by his employer, the Epsom trainer William Nightingall. The sparse details revealed he was 27, married with one son, and a nephew of the well-known Irish trainer, W P Cullen.

Cullen's death was just the first in a spate of fatalities that finally brought about reforms in racecourse safety and the provision of financial help for the dependents of jockeys killed or injured while riding under 'Rules'. The *Life* was to lead the way in demanding these reforms, but in a world still numbed by the carnage of war, it was some time before even it raised its crusading banner.

DEATH ON THE RACECOURSE

TWO MONTHS after the death of Frank Cullen, the headlines 'Fatal Accident At Hawthorn Hill / Promising Young Rider Loses His Life' announced the fate of Len Ward who met his end at the Maidenhead course when his mount fell at the final hurdle and landed on top of him. There were few details on Ward who had only recently ridden his first winner, but at the inquest it was stated he had died within half an hour from shock and internal injuries. Pathetically, his last words were "I think I'm dying".

When another jump jockey, Alf Parnham, died without recovering consciousness following a fall at Hurst Park in February 1921, Augur at least refrained from leaping to defence of the racecourse management. This time an agency report supplied the details. Parnham had ridden on the Continent before the war when his successes included the 1907 Romanian Derby, and, "Though he was not in the front rank of his profession, he was a particularly painstaking and a reliable jockey."

A week later, Harry Ward, no relation to Len Ward but another jockey 'not in the front rank of his profession', was killed at Gatwick. One might expect that two deaths in seven days would merit some sort of editorial comment, but there was none; the annihilation of the nation's youth in the war had diminished the impact of individual tragedies at home and just one small item recorded the barest details – unmarried, from Durham, attached to Alec Law's Findon stable.

Six weeks later, a French Lieutenant, Joseph Cosse, died from injuries received in a fall at Sandown's Grand Military meeting. The mounting toll of fatalities was becoming alarming, and because jockeys were not covered by State insurance, the families of those killed or badly injured on the racecourse were reliant on handouts from the Rendlesham Benevolent Fund, set up by the National Hunt Committee in 1902.

There was, however, such a heavy and constant demand on its resources that it was able to offer only limited help and it was left to the racing press to step into the breach. Over the years the *Life* must have raised tens, if not hundreds of thousands of pounds through its appeals to the public.

Frank Pearse, who began his career as an office boy on the *Life* in 1879 and graduated through the ranks to become the Press Association's chief racing reporter in 1903, was renowned for his fund raising activities and in 1921 his efforts were applauded by Edgar Wallace in a letter to the *Life*. In paying tribute to Pearse, who had recently helped to raise some £2,000 (£70,000) for Joe Plant, a former Flat jockey who had fallen on hard times, the famous novelist, playwright, journalist and racing enthusiast, wrote:

> I should be glad if you would allow me a little space to express the gratitude which a very large number of racegoers feel towards Frank Pearse who, through your hospitable columns, succeeded in raising the money to put Plant beyond the fear of want. It has not only been the Plant Fund that has benefited by the indefatigable Mr Pearse. He is the most assiduous worker on behalf of racing charities I have ever known and personally I never see him coming towards me on a racecourse without wondering who is the new unfortunate who is going to benefit by his industry.

Wallace learnt of the latest 'new unfortunate' on the day (12 December 1921) his letter was published, as the same edition carried the news that Fred Cheshire had been killed at Sandown.

Cheshire, who had gained his most important success when winning the 1913 City and Suburban Handicap on Drinmore, therefore became the sixth jockey to lose his life on a Home Counties course in less than two years. This time there was a wife and three children in need of support; something, surely, had to be done.

The impetus for action came in a letter to the *Life*, which pointed out that the French Steeplechase Society had recently taken steps to ensure that the children of any jockey who lost his life on the racecourse would be provided for until they reached the age of 17. The correspondent went on to suggest that the NH Committee should establish an insurance scheme to cover all jockeys in the event of accident or death:

> It should be an easy matter to provide or raise say £1,000 to form the nucleus of such a fund, which could be kept going if every owner running a horse would insure his jockey against accident. If each owner paid a premium of about 5s per race the fund would guarantee the dependants at least £500 in the event of a fatal accident and a competence to cover the period of being laid up in such cases as a broken leg, collar bone, etc.

The *Life* backed these suggestions to the hilt, but didn't wait for the authorities to act. The next day it published its first subscription list to the Cheshire fund after Jim Killalee, who trained the horse that gave the jockey his fatal fall, had called at the office to kick-start proceedings with a donation of £70.

With Christmas fast approaching, contributions flooded in along with a swingeing denunciation of the safety procedures in operation on NH courses. The criticism came in a letter from a Harley Street physician, George de Vine, who slated the "primitive and inadequate arrangements" which, he claimed, "would not pass muster at a Pampa pony meeting in Central America". In particular, he cited the carts that served as ambulances:

> First of all the antiquated horse-drawn vehicle is too slow and, as speed is often a very vital factor in these accidents, on this one point alone it stands condemned. Secondly, it is open and thus even if a rider has escaped serious injury he runs the risk of contracting pneumonia – no remote contingency in a person perspiring heavily, exposed to our winter blasts. Thirdly, a rider falling on the far side of the course cannot be reached by a vehicle, or at least so I am informed. If this is really so it is nothing short of scandalous.

The doctor went on to urge the use of motor ambulances;[*] that slip rails be inserted to give access to any part of the course and that all racecourses should have a warm ambulance room with plenty of hot water bottles to relieve the shock of a heavy fall. Sadly, hot water bottles were of no help to Willie Smith who met his end at Gatwick less than a month after Cheshire had been killed.

One of the most popular jump jockeys of the time and a brother-in-law of two fine Flat jockeys in Fred Winter and Morny Wing (who was to win the Irish championship nine times before he retired in 1949), Smith had headed the table in the curtailed 1917 season and had numbered the Grand Sefton

---

[*] Sometimes horse-power was best. In a report on the 1926 Cheltenham Gold Cup it was stated that the long delay in bringing an injured jockey back to the medical room was caused by "the unsuitability of the ambulance in use, which, owing to its weight, could not be taken onto the course".

(Aintree), the Victory (Manchester) and the Grand Annual (Cheltenham) among his recent big steeplechase successes.

This time a widow and four children were bereaved and, as yet another fund was launched, Augur renewed his calls for a compulsory insurance scheme funded, in part, from jockeys' licence fees. By now the whole of racing's formidable press corps was calling for action to be taken, while letters from the public put further pressure on the authorities to act. One reader wrote:

> The Stewards of the Jockey Club and owners cannot expect *The Sporting Life* to run around with the hat every time a jockey is killed or injured … Last year £704,500 [*£26m*] was paid to various owners in stakes. Let the Stewards of the Jockey Club stop 5 per cent from the value of each race won and form a fund.

By the time of Smith's funeral, his fund had reached £1,500 which, the *Life* noted, was a remarkable achievement "especially as the present appeal follows so closely upon those on behalf of Plant and Cheshire".

Two weeks later it was announced that the NH Committee was considering the question of insurance, news that prompted Augur to remark that the matter should also concern the Jockey Club since Flat jockeys were "not immune" from serious accidents – a warning that was soon to be fatally fulfilled.

That summer it was confirmed that jump jockeys would be covered by a policy of £1,000 (£42,000) against death while riding in a race. Both jockeys and owners would contribute to the scheme. The jockey's licence fee of £1-10s (£63) would be divided between the Rendlesham Fund and the insurance fund, while owners would contribute 2s 6d (£5.25) to the latter account each time they used a professional jockey.

By the end of the year the Jockey Club had followed suit, with owners and jockeys each contributing 1s (£2.10) per ride to a fund. That jumping was the poor relation of the Flat was plainly borne out by a scale of distributions that valued the life of a Flat jockey at £2,000, while they were to receive £12 a week for temporary disablement compared to the £3 awarded to NH jockeys.

But payments, however inequitable, did not stop accidents and, in retrospect, the page of the *Life* that carried the news of Willie Smith's death was chillingly uncanny. Alongside the main report were two other stories, one headed 'More Winners For Mr Adam Scott'; the other 'Parfrement Resumes Riding' – within four years both men would also be killed on the racecourse.

Georges Parfrement was the most famous international jump jockey of his time. He had won the Grand National at his first attempt when he partnered the French-bred five-year-old, Lutteur III, to victory in 1909, the same year as he gained the first of his three pre-war wins in the Grand Steeplechase de Paris, while he also won the Scottish Grand National in 1915.

The Chantilly-born jockey's other major successes included two Grand International Chases at Sandown and in March 1923 he rode North Waltham to victory in the Imperial Cup on the same course. Later that month, his mount finished first in the Liverpool Hurdle, but was subsequently disqualified for bumping and boring. Upset at what he felt was an injustice, Parfrement declared he would never ride in England again, and he never did. Three weeks later, he was killed in a fall at Enghien outside Paris.

The veteran amateur rider, Adam Scott, who bred and trained his own horses at Alnham, Northumberland, with considerable success, met his end when he broke his neck at Kelso in March 1925. He, too, had ridden a Scottish National winner and in 1921 his horses won eight of the 12 races at the two-day Perth Hunt meeting, while in 1924 he achieved a long-held ambition when his Jazz Band, ridden by Charlie Smirke, gained a hugely popular victory in the Northumberland Plate at Newcastle.

Two other high-profile deaths occurred during this period when Charles Hawkins and Clyde Aylin, were killed within two weeks of one another at the end of 1922.

Hawkins was well known in Britain, France and Ireland where he numbered the Irish Grand National, the Leopardstown Chase and the Galway Plate among his successes. In 1915 he achieved the rare feat of riding winners over fences, hurdles and on the Flat in one afternoon at Cork, and the following year he headed the NH jockeys' table in Britain as he ferried back and forth across the Irish Sea during a much curtailed wartime season.

At the beginning of 1919, a badly broken leg kept Hawkins out of the saddle for 16 months during which time almost £2,000 was raised for him through the columns of the *Life*. On his return, he resumed his career in France riding for James Hennessy, but in December 1922, just a few days after the paper had reported a revival in his fortunes, he was killed at Auteuil on the final day of the season.

Aylin, like Hawkins, was English, but had ridden in Ireland since 1904. Equally adept under both codes he was at his peak in 1922 and had just won the championship with 70 winners when he suffered fatal head injuries at Leopardstown's Christmas meeting.

In announcing the opening of a fund for Aylin's widow and six children, the *Life's* Irish correspondent, Tom Healy ('Harkaway'), wrote: "The fund will be a bumper success for Clyde Aylin knew everyone and everyone knew Clyde. He won for himself a unique place in Irishmen's hearts because he was straight." It was a fine epitaph.

The dismal toll of fatalities continued in 1923 when Peter Jones took a tumble in a Flat race at Bogside in October. At first the Beverley-based jockey did not appear to be seriously injured and he went out to win on his next ride, but he collapsed on his return to the weighing room and died in hospital that night.

Two months later, the year ended on a sombre note when the leading amateur rider, Capt. Geoffrey Bennet, received serious head injuries at Wolverhampton. As with Aylin, 'Tuppy' Bennet was at the height of his powers having won that year's Grand National on the 13-year-old Sergeant Murphy, a horse he had partnered to victory in the previous year's Scottish National at Bogside.

At the time of his accident on December 27 he was involved in a thrilling battle for the jockeys' championship with Fred 'Dick' Rees and Jimmy Hogan, all three having ridden 62 winners apiece with just three days of the season remaining. When he died without regaining consciousness 17 days later the *Life* described him as "one of the most brilliant and dashing riders of his own or any other time".

Poor Arnold Higgs, the 19-year-old son of dual champion Flat jockey (1906-07) Billy Higgs, was just beginning to show his brilliance when he suffered fatal injuries in a fall from his father's horse at Chester's May meeting in 1924. And the year ended as it had begun when Andrew Thomson died of injuries received at Sedgefield on Boxing Day.

Of all the deaths (12 on British racecourses) over this appalling five-year period, Bennet's resonated the most. A great favourite with the crowd, he had earned the plaudits of almost everyone except the owner when he finished a distant fourth (and last) on Turkey Buzzard after the horse had fallen three times in the 1921 Grand National. On his return to the unsaddling area the gallant captain was met by a furious Mrs Hannah Hollins who proceeded to chase him around the paddock wielding an umbrella and uttering the most unladylike oaths.

With Bennet's death a bizarre thread emerged linking him with Willie Smith and Charlie Hawkins as all three had ridden Sergeant Murphy in the Grand National. Smith had finished fourth

Sergeant Murphy (Geoffrey 'Tuppy' Bennet up), winner of the 1923 Grand National with his trainer George Blackwell. 'The Sergeant' had finished fourth in the 1920 and 1922 Nationals when ridden by Willie Smith and Charlie Hawkins respectively – in the space of two years Bennet, Hawkins and Smith were all to lose their life as a result of racecourse falls, while Sergeant Murphy met his end in 1926.

on the horse in 1920, while Hawkins occupied the same position on him in 1922 having remounted on the first circuit after 'the Sergeant' had slipped into the ditch that was then in front of the fence at the Canal Turn.

Three jockeys – two of them wartime champions the other the reigning amateur champion – who had ridden the same horse in the National, all killed in the space of two years. It was unbelievable; it was deplorable, and the grim cycle was completed in 1926 when the 16-year-old Sergeant Murphy broke a leg at Bogside and had to be destroyed. The following day the same unforgiving Irvine fences claimed the life of Billy Watkinson who had won the Grand National on Jack Horner just three weeks earlier. Never was there such a disastrous chapter of fatalities among the top echelon of jockeys.

In view of the earlier tragedies, the article that appeared in the *Life* in February 1924, a month after Bennet's death, was long overdue. Written by the paper's chief racing reporter, Meyrick Good, it was headed, 'Hurdle & Steeplechase Accidents / How They Happen And How To Avert Them: Suggestions To N.H. Committee'.

A grandson of the famous Woodyates trainer, William Day, Good had joined the *Life* in 1897 after a four-year apprenticeship on the *Wiltshire County Mirror* and was destined to serve a record 60 years on the paper before he retired at the age of 80 in 1957. During his long career he added his voice to numerous campaigns for racing reforms. He argued the case for an overnight draw in important handicaps, for stricter regulations on the use of the whip, for better racecourse veterinary facilities and (more controversially) for the Cesarewitch to be run on a round course at

Newmarket,* but none was more important than his call for crash helmets to be made compulsory.

In attributing the increase in accidents to bigger fields and the faster pace at which races were being run, Good cited the metal helmet that was compulsory for jockeys (both Flat and jump) in Australia and New Zealand, but which most British riders objected to wearing. The answer, he reasoned, lay with the authorities:

> I am perfectly aware that English jockeys scorn the steel cap on the ground that it has a rather unmanly appearance; but if it were made compulsory for the head guard to be worn, as is the case in Australia, no exception would be taken to it and many a nasty knock would be saved.
>
> My friend, the late Capt Bennet, who was the most fearless amateur rider of modern times, would in all probability have been alive today had he been in the habit of wearing a protection to the head. An aluminium or even a cork skullcap might have been sufficient to change what unhappily proved a fatal accident at Wolverhampton, into just an ordinary mishap.
>
> The leading steeplechase jockey 'down under' – the Fred Rees of Australia – is Tom Moon who recently had his skull protector photographed and the picture revealed no fewer than nineteen deep dents in it, any one of which would have been enough to cause severe concussion and possibly death.

It seemed a scandal that the authorities should need their attention drawn to such a pressing issue, but at least something was done about it – under NH rules at least. That October, skullcaps became compulsory for jump jockeys, but they were a far remove from the efficient Australian helmets.

The design approved by the NH Committee was merely an unfastened resin cork cap that usually came flying off as soon as the rider hit the ground, if not beforehand. They were first worn at a Cardiff meeting where the *Life's* man noted: "the need for chinstraps was shown by the fact that a couple of riders lost their helmets on the way round".

Yet, despite this glaring deficiency, it was not until 1962 – *38 years* after they had been introduced – that skullcaps were fitted with chinstraps. Worse still, helmets were not made compulsory on the Flat until 1956 when the deaths of four jockeys (all attributable to head injuries) in the space of two months finally persuaded the Jockey Club to act.

During the intervening years scores of other jockeys had been killed or suffered severe brain damage that could have been prevented had the Australian helmet been adopted. It was a damning indictment of those who governed racing at the time – nor did it say much for the 'power' of the press.

---

* In 1958 a round course, known as the Sefton course, was laid out at Newmarket joining the Rowley Mile course three furlongs out and six races from a mile to a mile and three-quarters were run over it during that season. However, the jockeys were never entirely happy with its bends and cambers and it was not used after 1969.

THE RACE GANG WARS

WHEN Flat racing resumed with a full fixture list in 1919, a much reduced thoroughbred population left runners thin on the ground and almost 100 races resulted either in a walkover or a match, while three and four-horse fields were the norm. Hard ground also contributed to the dearth. Only 16 horses turned out to contest the six races on the opening day of York's big May meeting when the Zetland Stakes for two-year-olds was one of several events to be declared void during the season after all 45 entries were withdrawn.

Even the turnout at Royal Ascot was sparse. Over the four days, six races were three-horse affairs, the Hardwicke and St James's Palace Stakes were both reduced to a match and there was a walkover for the £1,000 added Churchill Stakes. But despite the lack of horses, racecourse executives throughout the country reported record attendances as three million demobbed servicemen with money to burn swelled the crowds.

With such rich pickings to be had, there was fierce competition for the unregulated bookmakers' racecourse pitches and it was not long before gang warfare broke out as racketeers fought for control of the best sites.

For years racecourse violence had been on the increase. Ever since racing became a spectator sport the big meetings had attracted fraudsters, muggers and pickpockets. Each faction had their era of notoriety. In the early part of the nineteenth century thimble-riggers plagued the courses before they were finally routed in a pitched battle with police and a mounted force of stewards and their followers on the Town Moor at Doncaster during the 1830 St Leger meeting – 150 pea-and-thimble merchants were arrested and sentenced to varying terms of hard labour at Wakefield prison.

The extension of the railways in the 1840s and '50s and the increase in metropolitan meetings during the 1860s and '70s saw welshers and card-sharpers flourish as never before, while bookmakers began to employ ex-prizefighters for their own protection as the gangs became more violent, organized and numerous.

The public, however, were left unprotected and with each passing decade the *Life's* letters column testified to the rising rate of crime, which was particularly bad in the cheap enclosures. During the summer of 1898 one battered racegoer who had paid 3s 6d (£15.75) for entry to Windsor's silver ring, related:

> After backing the winner of the first race, I went for my money and was instantly set upon by four or five ruffians who snatched part of my ticket and I was hurled to the ground. Later I found scores of backers in the same plight as myself and out of sixty or seventy bookmakers only about a dozen were paying out, with the result that free fights were occurring every few minutes. Surely it is time bookmakers should be registered and not allowed to rob people with impunity. I would also advise those who manage the meeting to visit any respectable Northern or Midland enclosure where much better protection is secured. – Yours, &c. 'A Victim'. King's Norton, August 14.

The letter echoed the grievances of hundreds of others who were then writing to the *Daily Telegraph* in response to a campaign the paper had launched under the heading 'Roughs and the Turf – A Crying Scandal'. Complaints concerning "the outrageous increase of criminality, blackguardism and brutality" filled its columns for more than two weeks during which time many writers were critical of the racing press: "The sporting Press keep their mouths shut. It does not pay them to complain and, again, their reporters would be marked men and sure to be maltreated if they wrote on the subject."

The racecourse executives and the police were equally culpable. It was claimed that the violence was the result of "the scandalous inaction and mismanagement shown by the executive of the companies owning the racecourses," and that "if you complain to the police on a racecourse of any assault, abuse, robbery, violence or welshing, in nearly every case the intelligent officer assures you that he is powerless to do anything and he would advise you to go away and let the matter drop."

Constables were accused of drinking at the bars with men who, minutes earlier, had "committed acts of brutality under the very noses of the police," while qualifications for admittance to the main ring had become a farce: "A few years ago one had to be introduced, but now the greatest scum get into Tattersalls." At any meeting "the merest tyro at racing could walk round the rings and point out to anyone scores of undoubtedly familiar thieves and blackguards, members of well-known, regular, organised gangs who attend race meetings, men who should never have been allowed to enter or remain on licensed premises."

Lord Greville, who was not a member of the club he censured, wrote: "The Jockey Club should cease being afraid of its own shadow and issue a notice to clerks of the courses – who are the real offenders – that in future, if they allow this state of barbarism to exist, no further licence will be granted."

All this correspondence, the *Telegraph* concluded, was proof of:

> …the unquestionable license enjoyed by gangs of roughs and desperados; of the failure of executives to suppress these offences; of the unsuitableness and corruptibility of many of the officials employed; and of the impotence or unwillingness of the police to act decisively and smartly – or, as a matter of fact, to act at all.[1]

It was no surprise, therefore, when violence erupted on racecourses that were awash with money in 1919. Everyone wanted a piece of the action and in a bloody feeding frenzy the gangs fought amongst themselves over territorial rights, while corrupt racecourse employees exploited the situation to the full:

> Gatemen, ring officials and others were making big money by selling pitches to bookies, admitting known thieves to the Ring and trafficking in pass-out checks and complimentary tickets with racecourse undesirables on a vast scale.[2]

Gangsters would establish their own men on the best pitches splitting profits on a 50/50 basis, while others provided 'services' to bookmakers that ranged from 'protection' to the tools of the trade which, at 2s 6d (£5) an item, provided a rich source of income. The 'tools' included betting tickets, lists of runners, small wooden pallets for the bookmakers to stand on, and chalk and water for marking up and wiping off prices on the boards.

Other gangs employed less subtle means to extract their levy. Bets would be shouted out to bookmakers without advancing the necessary cash. If the horse lost – so what? But if it won payment was demanded and if the 'winnings' were not immediately forthcoming, bottles, hammers and razors were used as 'persuaders'.

Most cities and major towns had their racecourse gangs, but the most formidable of them operated out of Birmingham. They ruled the roost, working courses throughout the country until their London rivals took exception to their raids on the southern tracks. Initially there were numerous London mobs – principally Jews and Italians based in the East End and operating independently of one another – but after the war most of them joined forces with the six Sabini brothers from Saffron Hill, close by the old haunt of the Victorian street bookmakers at 'the ruins' off Farringdon Road.

The turf wars then became a north v south battle fought chiefly on southern courses. Some courses attracted trouble more than others and following outbreaks of violence and "virtually unchecked robbery by pickpockets" at Salisbury's Bibury Club meeting in July 1920, Augur commented:

> Ruffianism, I regret to hear, has again been greatly in evidence and although meetings at Salisbury have always had an evil reputation in this respect matters have never been so unsatisfactory as during the post-war gatherings. This is so serious a reflection upon the police arrangements that surely something will be done to remedy matters ere another meeting comes round.

At the same time, *The Times* demanded that the Jockey Club set up a permanent police force, funded by the racecourses, to deal with the thugs. This was precisely what the *Life* had called for as far back as 1861, but its appeal went unheeded then and this latest timely advice also fell on deaf ears – at least until things had become much worse.

By the spring of 1921 the clashes between the gangs had escalated into a shooting war. Within weeks of a revolver being brandished during a fracas at the Greenford trotting track near Ealing, a member of the Birmingham mob was charged with the attempted murder of a rival gangster following a shooting in the silver ring at Alexandra Park. In referring to the incident Augur remarked:

> It is deplorable that the pleasure of numerous visitors to the north London meeting was marred in consequence of the presence of a gang of undesirables who have lately been in evidence not only on the racecourse, but at trotting meetings. There were a few ugly incidents, but fortunately Messrs Pratt had reason to anticipate some trouble and the force of police and detectives was considerably strengthened, and the trouble was confined to comparatively narrow limits ... Every step should be taken by racecourse executives, the railway authorities and the police to make it impossible for pests of all descriptions to make themselves, if not a positive danger, certainly a nuisance.

This was understating the situation to some extent – bullets flying around crowded enclosures were more than 'a nuisance' – and when a bloody fight took place on the road out of Epsom on the final day of the Derby meeting two months later the *Life*, in common with the *Sportsman* and *Sporting Chronicle*, ignored the incident which made front-page news in the national press.

Presumably, Morley-Brown took the view that as the violence took place away from the racecourse there was no need to further blacken racing's name, but for whatever reason, it resulted in a good story ending up on the spike. It transpired that the Birmingham gang had formed an alliance with a group of Leeds bookmakers to sort out the Italian-Jewish mob who had taken over their pitches on the Downs. Rather than risk a battle in the open, about 40 Brummies ambushed the coach in which they believed their London rivals were travelling, and it was only after faces had been slashed, skulls cracked and arms broken that they discovered they had actually attacked their northern allies.

Considering the Leeds men were hopelessly outnumbered it was remarkable that no one was killed although five were seriously injured. The police later caught up with the gang at the George and Dragon pub in Kingston and made 28 arrests; most were well-known thugs (one had 18 previous convictions, another had been sentenced to seven years penal servitude for manslaughter) and subsequently 17 of them received jail sentences ranging from nine months to three years with hard labour.

But prison was no deterrent to gangsters when easy money was to be made, and week after week there were reports in the general press of the mob rule sweeping the racecourses. In July 1921, at the same Salisbury fixture that had been condemned by Augur a year earlier, the police came under attack after they had made several arrests at the railway station. A rabble of about 50 East Enders attempted to free their partners in crime and five of them were later jailed for assault and obstruction.

A week later three brothers were accused of attacking a Hurst Park bookmaker and his clerk with bottles after he had refused their demand for £2-10s protection money but, as in many similar cases, the bookmaker was too frightened to give evidence against his assailants who walked free.

In August, the Birmingham 'boys' were in action at Bath where they attacked several bookmakers and their clerks with hammers and sandbags in the town, while motorists and pedestrians on their way to the races were stopped and robbed. The assaults continued on the racecourse where a bookmaker had to draw a revolver to defend himself. On this occasion, at least, Morley-Brown was moved to comment on spiralling wave of violence in his 'Occasional Notes' column, which he had started shortly after the war:

> Yesterday's disturbances are attributed to a long-standing feud between certain London and Birmingham 'bookmakers'. [*] All the men likely to give trouble in this respect are known to the police, and it would be a comparatively easy matter to see to it that they had no opportunities of attending race meetings unless they intended to behave as responsible citizens. Racecourse executives too should take every precaution to keep undesirables off the course – not a difficult problem if attacked in whole-hearted fashion. A little determination now will save a whole heap of trouble in the future.

But determination was lacking in all but the legitimate bookmakers who took matters into their own hands the following week when they formed the Racecourse Bookmakers and Backers Protection Association to guard themselves against "victimisation at the hands of blackmailers, defaulters and other undesirables who frequent racecourses".

Headed by the respected Walter Beresford and comprised chiefly of southern layers, the 137-strong body was given a cautious welcome by the editor:

> The formation of a Racecourse Protection Association for the purpose of protecting racegoers from hooligans and other undesirables is, no doubt, a necessity under prevailing conditions, but it is a thousand pities that it should be left to the public to protect themselves against lawbreakers.
>
> That, surely, is the duty of the police aided by the executives of race meetings and unless that protection and aid are freely and fully given it will, we fear, be difficult, if not dangerous, to root out the evil. Recent happenings have shown to what length those racecourse pests will go and unless the most drastic means are taken by the authorities to repress completely the activities of those roughs

---

[*] Most gangsters described themselves as bookmakers when they were arrested because it accounted for any large sum of money they might be carrying. As a result of this and the failure of government to license and regulate bookmakers, the profession got an even worse name than it already had.

and blackmailers not only will attendances at race meetings greatly diminish, but the sport itself will assuredly suffer in popularity and material support.

While the Jockey Club gave the Association its blessing, it stopped short of providing any form of practical help and consequently the bookmakers had to resort to the desperate measure of buying over members of the gangs that had been terrorising them. Thugs were taken on as minders; Darby Sabini, the godfather of the Italian mob, was hired as a steward of the new body and Edward Emmanuel, head of the Jewish mafia, was appointed vice-president. It came as no surprise, therefore, when these unlikely defenders of the ring started to demand 'royalties' for the printed lists of runners they sold to bookmakers at 2s 6d a copy.

The RBBPA (later re-launched as the Southern BPA) refused to bow to this latest form of blackmail and courageously sacked its 'protectors' which left its members exposed to renewed violence. By 1923 things had become so bad there was talk of government intervention and of banning racing at 'open' courses where most of the trouble occurred – at places such as Bath, Brighton, Epsom, Goodwood and Lewes where bookmakers set up pitches on common land outside the racecourse enclosures.

Eventually, a series of meetings between Home Office officials, the stewards of the Jockey Club and senior police officers, resulted in the setting up of a force of some 60 salaried ring inspectors – mostly retired CID officers – operating under the supervision of two former army majors, George Wymer and William Bebbington.

This Jockey Club appointed force was empowered to keep troublemakers off the course; patrol the betting ring and keep order by liaising with police, bookmakers and the racecourse management. A working relationship was also struck up with the chief gang leaders who gained a measure of respectability by co-operating with the new body.

By this time regional Bookmakers Protection Associations (BPAs) had sprung up all over the country and as they began to weed out the welshers from their midst, the National Association of Bookmakers was formed in 1932. The NAB set up a pitch committee to confer with the Racecourse Association (RCA) which had been given the right, under the 1928 Racecourse Betting Act, to compel on-course bookmakers to bet in specified places. Pitches were allocated to established bookmakers on the basis of seniority.* A newcomer would be considered only when a vacancy occurred and only if he had two BPA members to vouch for him, and so the grip of the gangsters was broken as the legitimate layers regained their positions in a well-regulated ring without having to fight for them.

It was an object lesson in what could be achieved by presenting a united front, and while there were isolated outbreaks of racecourse violence both before and after the Second World War they had little to do with the old pitch battles, but were rather an unwelcome overspill from the urban protection rackets the gangs had moved on to.

Meanwhile, the bookmakers had another fight on their hands. This time they faced a foe far more formidable than the Birmingham mob or the Sabini gang. He was known as the Chancellor of the Exchequer, one Winston Leonard Spencer Churchill by name.

---

* This system worked well enough for many years although it operated against the more adventurous layers. A senior bookmaker in the favoured front row might only be prepared to accept bets of up to £1,000, while a newcomer in the back row would willingly take ten times that amount. Eventually, a growing movement for reform of the ring in the 1980s and 90s led by on-course layers such as Dougie Goldstein and Barry Dennis, resulted in an injection of new blood in 1998 when bookmakers were able to sell their seniority by auction and pitch positions found their own value.

CHURCHILL'S INIQUITOUS LEVY

HISTORY highlights 1926 as the year of the General Strike, but the nine-day stoppage was a mere fleabite for racing compared with the events that surrounded another strike later that year. True, the sport suffered in May when the country was held to ransom as two million workers came out in support of a million miners who had been locked out by pit owners after refusing to accept wage cuts of up to 50 per cent.

The *Sporting Life*, in common with other newspapers, did not appear for two weeks, and racing once again ground to a halt along with most of the trains as an assortment of vehicles were pressed into action by volunteer drivers to ferry essential supplies around the country. When the paper reappeared on May 18 after the TUC had left the miners in the lurch,* its motoring correspondent cum strike-breaker, the racing driver Alan Hess ('White Line') who had been in charge of a lorry depot in London, reported:

> Among the potent factors which went most entirely to break the strike and which completely upset the plans of the strikers' leaders, none played a greater part than road transport. A railway strike, while it may occasion the fear of some inconvenience, will never again be regarded as a serious menace to industry or to the travelling public...
>
> As to the drivers, no praise is too high for them. Private limousines, sports cars, omnibuses, 5-ton lorries, all were handled with the same skill and the same zest. High speed journeys with despatches from one end of the country to the other, or 10mph treks with 6 tons of eggs aboard from Plymouth to London – it was all in the game.
>
> Many well-known racing drivers were doing valuable work. Attached to Scotland Yard or the Ministry of Transport were such men as Major Segrave, Capt Woolf Barnato, R N N Spring and Capt Frazer Nash; while buses were being driven by Parry Thomas, Kaye Don and J Cobb. Capt Malcolm Campbell, Gillette and R B Howey, I understand, were driving railway engines.

Morley-Brown acclaimed the return to work as a triumph for common sense, a faculty that was noticeably lacking in another dispute that grabbed the headlines in the *Life* six months later when the unimaginable happened – the bookmakers went on strike! Their protest was against a betting tax that had been brought in by the Chancellor of the Exchequer, Winston Churchill.

The 'iniquitous levy' had been prompted by the findings of a parliamentary select committee that had been set up in 1923 to investigate the feasibility of a tax on betting. After holding 15 meetings and interviewing 40 witnesses the committee was hopelessly divided and finally, on a vote of 11 to 7, decided a tax was practicable, but not desirable.

The committee's findings were contained in a Blue Book of 672 pages, the gist of which could be summed up in its three-line assertion that "an *ad valorem* duty of 2½ per cent on the amount staked in each bet will produce an annual sum of £5,000,000 and its realisation can be safely relied upon."

This assurance was based on the unrealistic assumption that illegal betting would be suppressed and that street bookmakers would be licensed and also pay the tax, something that would require a

---

* The miners held out until November when they were eventually forced to accept longer hours for less pay.

complete revision of the class-biased betting laws, which, for the past 70 years, successive governments had refused to touch.

Street betting in the 1920s was a highly organised and flourishing business despite all attempts to suppress it. In London alone an average of 62 policemen were daily engaged in the prevention of illegal betting at an annual cost to the Police Fund of £26,000 (£1m). Under the Street Betting Act of 1906 any person found guilty of taking or making bets was liable to a fine of £10 for a first offence, £20 for a second and £60 or six months imprisonment on a third conviction.

To safeguard himself the street bookmaker had his bets collected by 'runners' whose services were dispensed with after two convictions. He also paid commission to agents who allowed their premises to be used as betting offices, and often ran his own quasi-social betting clubs. Because of the inequitable laws, he not only had the support of the public but, in many cases, the sympathy of magistrates and the police, especially in the latter case, if he contributed a little something towards his local constabulary's funds.

Police corruption was widespread. In Liverpool the going rate in the 1920s was £1 (approx £45) a week per constable during the Flat racing season and £1 a fortnight during the jumping season.[1] For this the bookmaker obtained protection from arrest for his men and information on any impending 'show raid' from his police informants.

Prosecutions, therefore, were difficult, sporadic and sometimes waived altogether. Walter Womersley, the Mayor of Grimsby, was one magistrate who refused to take street betting cases because, he reasoned: "I do not think it right that the rich man can have his bet by phone, not incurring any penalty, whilst the working man who puts a shilling on may be run-in and fined."

It was against this background that the Conservative Prime Minister, Stanley Baldwin, stated in the Commons at the beginning of 1926 that the practical objections to a betting tax were "almost insurmountable" – a view shared by most of his Cabinet who were anxious to avoid ruffling any faddist feathers in a controversy over the morality of the State deriving a revenue from 'the evil of betting'.

Typically, however, Churchill was undaunted by 'practical objections'. He was seeking new sources of revenue for the Treasury's war-ravaged coffers and in betting's untapped millions he saw his crock of gold. With his usual bulldog tenacity he brushed aside an initial rebuff from the Cabinet and won them round in time for his Budget speech on 26 April 1926.

Addressing a sceptical House he announced: "I have caused an examination to be made of various methods of optional or luxury taxation … betting is certainly a luxury and it is certainly optional … I propose, therefore, to put a tax of 5 per cent on every stake made upon a racecourse or through a credit bookmaker." Bookmakers would also be required to take out an annual certificate for themselves and their offices, at a cost of £10 each.

This was one step away from legalising cash betting shops, but the government was not prepared to go the whole hog and reform the betting laws although Churchill freely admitted they were unsatisfactory and brought the law into disrepute: "I am not looking for trouble," he said, " I am looking for revenue … I propose to leave the anomalies, the inequalities, and the prohibitions where they are. My object is to tax legal betting only, and to leave illegal betting in the same position as it is at present."

While the Establishment press welcomed the tax, the *Life* was dead-set against it. It pointed out that it would be the only tax on turnover in the nation's fiscal system; its estimated yield of £6m was unrealistic, and it would lead to widespread evasion and an increase in illegal betting. Only street bookmakers stood to gain as punters transferred their custom from the credit bookmakers in order to avoid the tax.

As when it predicted a major increase in street betting as a result of the 1874 Betting Act, the paper was to be proved right on all counts, but Churchill was not about to throw any of his vanities on a bonfire at the behest of his critics who were many and varied.

Together, if not exactly hand-in-hand, deputations from the clergy, the bookmakers and the Jockey Club converged on Downing Street with an assortment of manifestos and arguments against the tax. The Free Church Council claimed the tax "would strengthen the appeal of betting by giving it State sanction," while the Scottish Christian Social Union declared it would be "unworthy of a Christian nation to raise revenue out of the people's degradation".

The Jockey Club maintained the tax would "have a very disastrous effect on racing and consequently upon the breeding of the thoroughbred in this country," but the Thoroughbred Breeders Association viewed it as a chance for racing to claim a share of the revenue. It urged that "a reasonable proportion of the proceeds, on lines similar to the practice of other countries, should be devoted to the endowment of the race prize-fund or to the direct support of the horse-breeding industry in this country."

The bookmakers, conveniently ignoring the fact that it was once common practice for them to charge a 5 per cent commission on winning bets, claimed that they faced ruin as all the money available for betting would be taxed away.

Jim Sutters, a leading layer, forecast: "The attendance at race meetings will be substantially diminished and consequently the revenue from the entertainments tax will be seriously depleted and income tax at present derived from bookmakers will be reduced to a minimum.* Many race meetings in the United Kingdom will be forced to close down and important industries dependant on racing will be ruined. The proposed tax puts a premium on street betting and will add enormously to the duties of the police."

Variations on these themes filled the letters' column of the *Life* throughout the summer and autumn of 1926 as the countdown to the imposition of the levy gathered momentum. It was not long before their doom-laden predictions kindled a sort of mass hysteria that infected even the most level-headed and responsible of men.

F W Wilmot, clerk of the course at Lingfield, wrote: "I have no hesitation in saying the betting tax will cripple every racecourse in England within two or three years. It will be the death knell of racing. What will become of the 300 stallions, 6,000 broodmares and the 4,690 horses that ran in 1925? They will be of little value."

The Hon. George Lambton, the much-respected doyen of his profession, pointed out that the majority of his fellow trainers depended upon betting for their livelihood, and that, when the cost of transport, forage and labour was added to the effects of the tax, he knew many of them would be forced to give up.

Others asked whether the Chancellor had considered how many men would be thrown out of work because of bookmakers closing down, or how the fall in attendances would reduce racecourse dividends to shareholders. Had he, they wondered, taken into account, the loss to the railways due to fewer people travelling to race meetings; the loss to the Post Office due to fewer people sending telegrams to their bookmakers, etc. etc.

Above all this wailing and gnashing of teeth, the *Life* continued to hammer out its own message to the Chancellor; it was little different to the one that Harry Feist had advanced 67 years earlier:

---

* It was estimated that £250,000 (£10m) was derived in income tax from bookmakers, while there was a 10 per cent entertainments tax on admission to places of amusement, football matches, race meetings, etc.

If the Government is determined to extract revenue from betting, the sanest, fairest and most economically sound way would be a system of licensing and registration of bookmakers and betting premises. As it stands the proposed betting duty is morally wrong because it taxes those people who keep within the law and leaves untouched those outside the law. Tax without legalisation is wrong in principle.

But the Chancellor was not for turning. He answered his critics in typical Churchillian style: "There are four predictable lines of argument against the tax," he growled. "The tax will bring about a horrible increase in betting; there will be a horrible decrease in betting; the Government ought not to touch an evil thing; the Government should go the whole hog and face the entire problem of lotteries and gambling."

As the *Life* finally accepted that the Rt Hon Member for Epping had his Dardanelle blinkers on, it could not resist the pun as it observed:

It looks as if Mr Churchill will add one more to his lengthy list of political gambles and go down in history as the man who put the Chance in Chancellor!

In July, Churchill lived up to this billing when he announced that he had decided to reduce the proposed tax from 5 per cent to 2 per cent on-course and 3½ per cent off-course. The reason for the cut was, he claimed, the result of an examination of a leading bookmaker's accounts. His initial calculations had been based on a legal betting turnover of £170m, but it was now apparent a more accurate figure was £275m (£112bn). It was not the government's policy to break the betting business, he said, when he could reap the required revenue with a lower rate of tax.

Morley-Brown, who had revived his editorial column to give more weight to the paper's anti-tax campaign, viewed the reduction with well-founded cynicism as he accused the Chancellor of window dressing:

Mr Churchill is rather like the shopkeeper whose sale tickets look exceedingly alluring, but really represent a big percentage profit on the cost price, though they speak of enormous sacrifices. It is very easy to gain public favour in Parliament or in business by taking a definite stand – followed by considerable 'concessions'.

When the tax came into effect on 1 November 1926 at Birmingham and Wye, the on-course bookmakers settled on a 2½ per cent (6d in the £) deduction from winning bets. The ordinary punter accepted the situation philosophically, but professional backers demanded that the layers meet them half way in paying the tax. Most bookmakers agreed, but they were not happy. Turnover, they claimed, was down by 50 to 60 per cent. Something would have to be done.

Something was done two days later at Windsor. As the horses made their way to the start for the first race the bookies' boards in Tattersalls remained blank. Confused racegoers tried in vain to get a price, but the layers remained shtoom. The race was run without a bet being struck and the pattern was repeated for the second race in which Steve Donoghue's mount, Bohemia, was expected to start a hot favourite.

Then, just before the 'off', the ring's silence was broken when a leading bookmaker shouted "I'll bet on this race – 6 to 4 the field". The odds were never laid. The blackleg was quickly surrounded by a crowd of angry colleagues who soon persuaded him it would be in his best interests to remain within

Bookmaker Jack Hale with his 2% tax vouchers at Birmingham races on the day the betting tax came into force on 1 November 1926 – © [Kirby]/[Hulton Archive]Getty Images

their ranks. More skirmishes followed after Bohemia got home by a short head. A frustrated punter, having seen two of his good things go in unbacked, cried out "We want the Tote." They were very nearly the last words he uttered as a gang of bookmakers' henchmen pounced on him and GBH was only averted by the speedy intervention of the police.

After the fourth race, the bookmakers held a meeting in the stands. One by one they denounced the tax and agreed to boycott the meeting the following day. Pickets were appointed and their efforts, combined with the publicity the strike received, resulted in only 30 people paying admission to Tattersalls. Once again no prices were returned and betting throughout the country was effectively frozen as all bets were declared void.

As a demonstration of the power of the pencillers the strike had been an unqualified success, but as an exercise to bring about the repeal of the tax, it was a total disaster. In an editorial headed 'Wrong

Tactics At Windsor', Morley-Brown pointed out the strike had merely provided advocates of the Tote with another reason for its introduction. The bookmakers' action, he declared, had been "futile and fatuous":

> It is all very well to claim that it was a means of focussing public attention on the imposition by the State of an unjust burden on a section of the community. Both bookmaker and backer are articulate and their protest could have been heard with more force and reason before the Finance Bill became an Act of Parliament…
>
> Laws on the Statute Book of Great Britain are repealed or amended only by strenuous, unremitting and honest endeavour on strictly constitutional lines. It is on these lines that the newly formed but influential Betting Duty Reform Association will work and if they have the wholehearted support of the sportsmen of this country, their efforts must be crowned with success.

By the end of the year the bookmakers' BDRA had a campaign fund of £20,000 and was learning to fight with political weapons. By using 'damned lies and statistics', figures were produced to show that betting turnover had fallen by 65 per cent since the imposition of the tax. "Street betting is flourishing at the expense of the credit bookmaker," they moaned. "Evasion is rife," they howled. "The honest layer is having to sack his clerks and pay the tax himself in order to remain competitive," they sobbed.

But the lament of the layers was undermined by those who advertised the thriving state of their business in the *Life*. The day after Call Boy won the 1927 Derby, Jim Sutters gleefully announced: "All records broken. On Derby day we had our biggest turnover since we started business 37 years ago." Such exultant claims were hardly calculated to gain the sympathy of the Chancellor, particularly as the same Mr Sutters had given evidence before the 1923 select committee and assured them that any tax on betting would ruin his business.

The *Life*, meanwhile, had conducted an in-depth inquiry into the effects of the tax. In February 1927 the paper announced:

> We are satisfied from the information of a confidential character that has come into our possession that the evasion of the Tax is on a more comprehensive scale than was imagined even by those behind the scenes.
>
> There is a general opinion among the bookmakers who are honestly endeavouring to meet the exacting demands of the State that the Bets Tax in its present form cannot be generally enforced. It could not be if officials were multiplied a thousand-fold and the entire receipts of the Tax were used up in the cost of collecting it.
>
> The unanimous verdict of bookmakers who desire to carry on their business in conformity with the law of the land … is that the *ad valorem* principle must go and that a system of licensing must take its place. There is another vital point on which there is agreement. It is that the 1853 Act should be so altered as to permit of cash betting, at least by post. Every person carrying on a betting business would then be licensed and street betting badly hit.

Political opponents of the tax took up the call as they demanded a complete revision of the betting laws. In March, Arthur Dixey (C. Penrith and Cockermouth) asked the House for leave to introduce a bill that would legalise betting. He had made the same request in 1926 when he was refused by 126 votes to 99; this time the vote against him was 143 to 44. The herd instinct in parliament was obviously gaining momentum.

In May, Lord Newton, whose Betting Inducements Bill of 1912 had sought to outlaw bookmakers' advertisements, moved the second reading of a bill designed to legalise cash betting. This, he claimed, would end street betting and boost the betting duty revenue by no small amount. His about-turn had been prompted by a visit to a betting shop in Dublin where a similar tax operated after the law had been amended to legalised off-course cash betting with licensed bookmakers.

In a backhanded compliment to the Dáil Éireann, Newton declared: "I confess that it never occurred to me that we should learn from the Free State, but that only shows how mistaken one can be … If the result of ready-money betting offices in Ireland has been a success, why on earth should it not be a success here?"

The converted peer won a second reading for his bill by 44 votes to 23, but it was then referred to a committee of the whole House and was heard of no more.

Meanwhile, the *carte blanche* way in which the excise authorities issued bookmakers' permits was making a mockery of the law. Welshers, who had been driven off the racecourse by the BPAs and the Jockey Club's policing body, applied for and received them without question. With their newly acquired State authority, they then brazenly advertised they would bet 'tax-free' which, of course, they could afford to do if they had no intention of honouring winning bets.

The honest bookmaker consequently had his business undermined and also lost out to a legion of defaulting punters. In 1927 the National Sporting League had the names of some 30,000 defaulters on record and by the end of the year the Douglas Stuart firm had paid £25,000 (£1m) in duty on bad debts – money it had no chance of recouping since, under the 1844 Gaming Act, gambling debts were not recoverable in law. The situation was intolerable.

To expose the absurdity of the law, Martin Benson (aka Douglas Stuart) sued a defaulting client for the recovery of the tax (£2-12s-6d) on a £75 losing bet. The punter, who had won £223-15s from the firm the week before, admitted the £75 debt, but refused to pay it or even the tax on it by pleading the Gaming Act.

On the same day in the same court, another bookmaker sued the same punter over an unpaid £65 bet, which the punter again refused to pay. The judge, who declared he would not pass comment on the defendant's moral character, gave judgement with costs for the defaulter in both cases. The *Life* was not so reticent in passing comment:

> The legal decision has been given in a Court of Justice, that a person who has a bet with a bookmaker may plead the Gaming Acts if he is sued for the amount of tax on his bets. This is so preposterous a position of affairs that the Government, whatever else it may or may not do in connection with the Acts that govern betting, should abolish this State-fostered dishonesty.
>
> In effect the State says to a punter: 'Betting is legal and we compel the bookmaker to pay a percentage of the stakes to us, but we have so arranged matters that you need not pay the bookmaker anything. If the bookmaker sues you even for our share of the plunder we will non-suit him and make him pay all the costs'… How much longer can this farce continue?

The farce even extended to street bookmakers who were being fined for pursuing an illegal calling without a certificate. A spate of such prosecutions in the summer of 1927 elicited a flurry of furious editorials. One scathing denunciation was delivered after two Manchester bookmakers had been fined £10 each for failing to take out permits:

> These men were doing something in taking bets in the street, which the law declares is a crime, but

the State steps in and says, 'If you commit this crime you must take out a State certificate. When you have done so you must pay us 3½ per cent of the stakes, and you must pay income tax on your profits. After we have made you take out a certificate and we have had our share of the money that passes through your hands, we shall prosecute you for breaking the law'.

It is a scandal of the first magnitude that the State should insist on sharing the proceeds of an illegal calling, and should then prosecute those who are their partners in crime. For hypocritical humbug this cannot be equalled in any civilised country in the world.

At the height of this State-sponsored bedlam, the racing authorities approached the Chancellor to ask for a share of his ill-gotten gains. The TBA, in particular, impressed upon Churchill the advantages of establishing a new and reliable source of revenue through the installation of totalisators on racecourses. In his reply, Churchill told them that if the Tote was ever legalised that would be the time for racing to press its claims for any funds that might be left over after the Exchequer had taken its cut.

Encouraged by this gratuitous hint, the Jockey Club set up a committee to inquire into how betting could be made to contribute to the maintenance of racing. It came as no surprise when the committee, under the chairmanship of the senior steward, Lord Hamilton of Dalzell, a staunch advocate of the Tote, concluded that the industry would best be served by alterations in the law that would enable the totalisator to operate on racecourses and allow for the collection of fees from on-course bookmakers.

That November, Churchill announced that the Cabinet had considered the committee's report and had decided that if a private member's bill seeking the establishment of the Tote was introduced and obtained a second reading in the Commons, the government would provide facilities for its passage into law.

The Tote was on its way, unwittingly promoted by its natural enemies. At the time the Chancellor gave his blessing to the machine, he had just received the returns for the first full year of the tax. The figures underlined the *Life's* claims that evasion was taking place on a massive scale since the duty had yielded just £2,766,000 (£110m) – less than half the expected revenue.

Churchill had always demanded proof of evasion;* now that he had it, he listened more attentively to the bookmakers as they enlightened him on the dodges employed by the big punters in association with compliant layers. In many cases only 1/20th of the tax was paid as pounds were being treated as shillings; bets were recorded as shillings and the official settlement took place in shillings by cheque, while the remainder was paid secretly in cash. Many bookmakers, they said, had turned to evasion in a desperate effort to retain clients who objected to paying tax on losing bets.

There was, in addition, an ugly undercurrent attached to the business. In June 1928, Churchill told the House: "I'm continually being informed of evasion, but when I press for information that would enable a prosecution, there is a singular and rather sinister reluctance to furnish details. People who might give information to the Government go about in physical fear."

The following month the *Life* had the satisfaction of welcoming the Chancellor as a reluctant convert to its cause when he announced he would consider substituting a system of graded licences in place of the tax in his 1929 Budget and, as an interim measure, he would reduce the tax to 1 per cent

---

* Further proof, if it was needed, was supplied by Sir Francis Floud, the chairman of the Customs and Excise Board, when he gave evidence before a select committee on estimates in January 1929. He told them it cost £150,000 a year to collect the tax and that duty had been paid on only £95m out of the estimated £200m turnover (a figure the *Life* described as "immeasurably below the true amount"). From the total tax paid it appeared that 15,194 registered bookmakers earned an average of £144 a year!

'Tex' on the tax as he brilliantly derides Winston Churchill's iniquitous levy.

on-course and 2 per cent off-course. It was, to borrow a Churchillian phrase, the beginning of the end. The paper noted:

> In all the 28 years that have passed since Mr Churchill first came into the House of Commons, he has never been so subdued and humbled as he was when he withdrew the existing taxes and asked the House to substitute lower rates.

The bookmakers now scented victory and were not slow to follow up their advantage. Up until 1926 they had been, as a class, predominantly Conservative, but the tax had transferred their allegiance to the Labour Party, which made it quite clear it would abolish the 'iniquitous levy' if and when it was returned to power. Mustering their forces as never before, the bookmakers threw their whole weight into the political arena as their various associations provided organised and financial support for Labour candidates in every marginal constituency by-election.

The *Life* had long since forecast the tax would spell disaster for the Tories and in January 1928, when a popular Unionist candidate was defeated in a Northampton by-election, it reasserted its claims under the heading 'Red Light For The Government' as it predicted: "A changeover of a few hundred votes in a large number of constituencies would be sufficient to sweep away the present Government majority."

During the winter of 1928-29 this warning was hammered out week after week as the paper ran a four-month long series of open letters to the Chancellor. Written by a Tory backbencher who signed himself 'A British Sportsman', the full-page, large-print epistles spelt out the folly of the tax and its consequences. And on March 23 'A Valedictory Summing Up' appealed to Churchill that...

> because the Tax has failed to benefit the revenue, because it is monstrously unjust, because it outrages the accepted canons of political economy, and further because it is a menace to the future of the Conservative party, you will be courageous enough to admit your mistake and take the earliest opportunity of rectifying it in the only satisfactory way in which it can be rectified – ABOLISH THE TAX.

On the same day, it was reported that the 24-year-old Labour candidate, Jenny Lee, had overturned a Conservative majority by the stunning margin of 8,606 votes in the North Lanark by-election. In acknowledging the work of the bookmakers' agents who had canvassed the constituency under the slogan 'Fair Play For Sport', the *Life* asserted:

> There is abundant evidence that prior to the recent series of by-elections the Government did not regard the sporting vote as a factor seriously to be reckoned with in the constituencies. The view was taken that the sporting vote could not be organised. It has been. And the result is a series of disasters for the Government culminating in the sledgehammer blow delivered by North Lanark.* In every election in which there has been direct effort by sportsmen there has been a highly satisfactory effect on the poll. The Bets Tax is now doomed. It must go.

---

* This was a bit of an exaggeration. The defeat of the Tory/Unionist candidates in the mining communities of North Lanark and Northampton was more a result of the government's unpopular support of the colliery owners than anything to do with the betting tax.

And go it did. In his Budget speech on 15 April 1929, Churchill admitted the tax had been a fiasco and more trouble than it was worth. He blamed its failure on "the volatile and elusive character of the betting population" for placing the honest bookmaker "at an invidious disadvantage compared with his more slippery and unsubstantial rivals".

In an effort to salvage some dignity out of what was a humiliating and personal defeat, he then excused himself by quoting Burke: "If I cannot have reform without injustice, I will not have reform," he declared defiantly.

The *Life* was understandably jubilant as it claimed: "Throughout the racing world the death of the tax is recognised as a triumph for the policy constantly advocated by *The Sporting Life*." And to drive the point home, the paper published a letter from J T W Huckin, chairman of the NSL and the BDRA:

> As one with intimate knowledge of every phrase of the movement and efforts that have been made for the abolition of the *ad valorem* Tax … may I be the first to congratulate *The Sporting Life* and its Editor on the result.
>
> The Betting Duty Reform Association and kindred bodies have every reason to appreciate the immense service you have rendered. The consolidation of all factions into one united body, the formation of the Joint Committee, the preparation of an alternative scheme from which the Chancellor's new proposals are founded, are all efforts in which you took a leading part, giving hours and days of time, columns of space and much careful thought to every section of the work…
>
> You may well be proud of the service you have rendered to the racing world. And now, with the cancer cut from racing, and the dawn of brighter days, I sincerely hope that the interests you represent will share in the healthier and happier times that are before us.

LONG LIVE THE NANNY GOAT

'THE TAX is dead, long live the Tote,' chorused the racing's establishment in unison and even Churchill was moved to raise a cheer in his 1929 budget speech when he declared: "We have as a monument to the betting tax, the healthy machinery of the totalisator." Not that he was prepared to let bookmakers off the hook entirely. He proposed to replace the tax with a duty of £40 on every telephone in a bookmaker's office, which, he estimated, would bring in £500,000 a year, but his scheme never got off the ground.

In May the country went to the polls and although the Conservatives won the popular share of the vote, they lost a massive 152 seats and a hung parliament resulted with Ramsay MacDonald heading a minority Labour government. It would be too simplistic to say that Churchill's blind obstinacy over the betting tax brought down Baldwin's administration, but it was certainly a contributory factor.

The new Chancellor, Philip Snowden, who had repeatedly expressed his detestation of "the very close association between the State and the evil of betting," promptly scrapped the proposed telephone duty on bookmakers, but stopped short on carrying out his threat to repeal the Act that had paved the way for the Tote the previous summer.

Because the 1853 Betting Act made it illegal to monopolise any part of a racecourse for betting purposes, the Jockey Club had drawn up a Racecourse Betting Bill to replace it and so enable a central racing authority to erect and operate totalisators and charge bookmakers five times the normal admission fee for the right to bet on-course. The Jockey Club and NH Committee were to have direct control of the operating body and would use the funds it raised for the benefit of horse-breeding and racing in general.

The sponsorship of the Tote Bill, as it became known, was undertaken by Major Ralph Glyn, the backbench Tory MP for Abington, but it was long odds against it obtaining the second reading it needed for government support. For a start, Glyn was just one of 300 MPs who had balloted for the privilege of using one of the ten days that had been set aside for debates on private members' bills.

But this was one 30-1 shot that came up. Glyn's name was the fifth to be drawn and the debate on his bill was fixed for 16 March 1928. In the meantime, arguments both for and against the Tote filled the columns of the *Life*. Many hailed the machine as the panacea for racing's ills, but others maintained it could never be effectively employed on Britain's widely spaced and little-raced courses.* The *Life* fell into the latter category and also opposed the bill because it reeked of class legislation in that it would give the racing authorities control of on-course betting to benefit owners and breeders at the expense of the poor punters.

The bookmakers, predictably, were against the machine for more insular motives. The BDRA actually affected a sense of stricken horror as it wailed: "If the Tote is permitted, it is then but a short step to State lotteries, premium bonds, casinos and the whole gamut of gambling media." This was breathtaking hypocrisy coming from a body that represented the very bookmakers who were advertising their own totes in the *Life* under such names as the National Pari-Mutuel or simply,

---

* In 1928 there were 105 racecourses staging an average of six day's racing a year. Of these, 26 courses were restricted to Flat racing and 57 to NH racing, while 22 held meetings under both codes.

The Totalisator.* In fact, after the war, the big four bookmakers, Douglas Stuart, Jim Sutters, Bert Fry and Joe Lee, got together to run a tote from Liestal in Switzerland, an advert for which trumpeted: "SP Guaranteed as Minimum. The average returns of the Pari-Mutuel are 50 per cent above SP."

Come March, the parliamentary debate on the Tote Bill was both fiery and prolonged and the *Life* gave full coverage to the historic and histrionic exchanges, which began with ironic cheers from the Labour benches as an embarrassed Glyn stated that the bill would have to be amended because it had been discovered that, under the Vagrancy Act, anyone using the Tote could be run in for being a rogue and a vagabond!

After the bill had been seconded and the motion put to the House, a Labour MP (William Kelly, Rochdale) moved its rejection on the grounds that it would confer a monopoly on the Jockey Club and NH Committee. Major Crawfurd (Lab. Walthamstow) then voiced the popular view that the real object of the bill was to "correct a miscalculation made by the Chancellor of the Exchequer and to save Mr Churchill from having to admit for the first time in his life that he is wrong," while Snowden wryly suggested a more fitting title for the measure would be 'The Chancellor's Relief Bill'.

Opposition to the bill was not confined to the Labour benches. Tom Oakley, a staunch Tory supporter of the BDRA, contended that it would give a subsidy to the already rich owners and breeders in the form of increased prize money and bloodstock prices.

Lord Stanley countered this by maintaining its object was to set up a co-operative service to end the bookmakers' monopoly. Besides, he argued, people who derived a profit from the betting industry should pay a small contribution to owners and breeders who kept the show on the road.

The Home Secretary, Sir William Joynson-Hicks, though opposed to gambling, neatly dismissed opposition claims that the Tote would add to 'the evil of betting' by remarking: "I believe that betting is inherent in human nature as well as in the Labour Party!"

Those who opposed the measure because it would give the Turf authorities the power to enrich themselves and their ilk at the expense of poor punters, had their fears partially allayed when Churchill indicated that the government was not prepared to accept the bill as it stood. The question of the Jockey Club's relationship with bookmakers and the Exchequer would have to be gone into, he said.

However, the Chancellor did repeat the TBA's plea that more money was needed in racing if England was to maintain her position as 'the fountainhead of the thoroughbred'. He also claimed the Tote would do much to rid the Turf of its race gangs. The contrast between British and French racecourses (where the pari-mutuel had enjoyed a monopoly since 1891), was, he declared, a contrast between 18th century barbarism and the new civilisation of the 20th century.

Finally, the debate was wound up, a division taken and the votes counted. It was close, but the 'ayes' had it by 149 votes to 134. Ralph Glyn and his supporters were jubilant, but, in their celebrations, they allowed the opposition one last throw of the dice. The normal procedure after a private member's bill has received a second reading is to send it to a standing committee for its final drafting. Many of the Tote's advocates assumed that this would be the case in this instance and left the House happy in

---

* Ironically, bookmakers were responsible for bringing the pari-mutuel to England. Two years before Pierre Oller's machine (invented in 1865) was first installed on French racecourses, a news item in the *Life*, dated 13 August 1870, reported: "At the Wolverhampton Police Court on Thursday John Lyshon and Charles Tollett of Birmingham, were charged with having used an instrument of gaming called a 'pari-mutuel' on Wolverhampton Racecourse. The defence was that the instrument of gaming mentioned did not come within the [1853] Act inasmuch as it had nothing to do with the issue of the bet, but merely recorded the transactions on the race. The magistrates, however, decided upon convicting and sentenced the defendants to seven days imprisonment with hard labour."

the belief the day had been won, but the opposition, realising the government's weakened position, moved that the measure be further dealt with by a committee of the whole House.

If carried, this would have killed the bill stone dead. The government would have been unable to find the time for it as well as the measure's other stages. There was panic among the Glynites; messengers were sent out to recall the departing MPs and the round-up was just enough to defeat the motion by 128 votes to 126.

The Tote Bill had survived by a whisker, but during the next few days civil servants from the Home Office and the Treasury completely redrafted it according to the designs of the government. The Jockey Club had intended to nominate its own seven-man Tote Board, but the Home Secretary insisted on a statutory body of 12 members, five of whom were to be government appointees including the chairman.

This major change spawned a whole series of new clauses that transformed the bill from its terse, simple format, into a complicated chronicle of legislative verbiage. When it reached the report stage, Ramsay MacDonald asked how the House could proceed with a bill so drastically altered; the original operative clause had consisted of seven lines, he said, now there were 141 lines!

In fact, of the original draft only one and a quarter lines had survived: "Nothing contained in the Betting Act, 1853, shall apply to any..." But the Speaker ruled that as the initial bill was in the nature of a skeleton and the amended bill was the same skeleton clothed with flesh and blood, he could not advise its withdrawal.

Because of all the complexities, the government was obliged to fulfil its promise to back the measure and, in announcing it was being given two extra days, Stanley Baldwin added that government whips would be put on it for its third reading. Its success was now assured. On July 19 it was carried by 218 votes to 122, passed swiftly through the Lords and entered the statute books as the Racecourse Betting Act of 1928.

The hallelujahs from the Tote's supporters were loud and prolonged and in their euphoria some wild predictions were made to a wondering world. The TBA's president, Lord D'Abernon, who was made a member of the Tote's governing body, the Racecourse Betting Control Board (RBCB), when it was formed that August, forecast that the machine would have a £66m turnover within a few years, while the Board, itself, announced that "a substantial surplus" would be available to racing after the first year of operation.*

This heady optimism was a world away from reality, but the Board had been blinded by glowing reports from countries that had a Tote monopoly and/or centralised racing. The *Life's* reservations on the practicality of operating a totalisator under the very different conditions that prevailed in Britain had been dismissed as bookmakers' propaganda, but now the truth was to be borne out as the Board spent vast sums of borrowed money in its effort to find suitable machinery.

There was no lack of choice. Long before the Tote Bill became law, owners of 'fraud-proof and infallible' totalisators were advertising their machines in the *Life*. Some were primitive mobile units installed in converted double-decker buses, while others were already operating in private gaming clubs in London and other cities. But even before it had been formed, the RBCB was denied the best equipment available when the Jockey Club failed to secure the British rights to the Premier Electric

---

* It was five years before the Tote was in a position to contribute anything to racing and even then it was the merest trickle (less than £10,000) from the promised river of riches that was to flow into the sport. By 1961, when the RBCB was reconstituted as the Horserace Totalisator Board, the Tote's turnover had crept up to £33m, half of what Lord D'Abernon had expected 'within a few years'.

Totalisator, which operated throughout Australasia and India and had been installed at Longchamp in 1927.

This missed opportunity was compounded when the Board opted for the inaptly named Lightning Totalisator for Newmarket's Rowley Mile course with its 22 day's racing a year and also for Newbury (16 days), but the machine's suppliers failed to meet their delivery deadline and when it was finally installed it lasted only a few years before it was scrapped in favour of a more basic model that had been developed by the RBCB.

In the meantime, the Board decided to create regional pools of portable equipment to service the country's remaining courses, but this scheme proved so costly and impractical that the idea of providing the majority of courses with a fully automatic Tote was abandoned. Instead a manually operated system was adopted, which was both slow and inefficient. Somewhere along the line of discarded machinery, the thought must have occurred to the Board that the money would have been better spent in paying off the £2.25m (£90m) loan that was needed to put the Tote on its feet.*

It was on decidedly unsteady feet that the Tote made its eagerly awaited debut at Newmarket and Carlisle on 2 July 1929 when the *Life's* on-course representatives sent back reports of basic errors and deficiencies. The decision to have a different codeword printed on the tickets each day to prevent forgeries was understandable, but to choose the word 'Bogus' for the first issue showed why the Tote soon became derisively known in rhyming slang as 'the Nanny Goat'.

Because the machines were not yet fully automated it took about 15 minutes to calculate the dividends after each race, while some cashiers appeared to lack elementary maths. At Carlisle, the paper's scrupulously honest reporter received £5 for his five 2s tickets on an even-money winner, £4 of which he returned to "the astonished clerk". A few lucky punters also benefited from an over-generous payout at Newmarket before the mistake was spotted, while many more were unable to get their bets on:

> Five minutes before the 'off' a bell rang within the precincts of the purchasing office in the paddock and all booths were immediately closed despite the fact that people were still queuing up to bet. Recovering from their surprise, the disappointed ones stampeded for the bookmakers who were only too ready to do business.

On the second day of the Newmarket meeting the benefits of a competitive market were dramatically illustrated when the bookmakers, keen to show that they could match any dividend the Tote might throw up, offered 100-1 bar three in a five-horse race. The result was a gift to bold headline writers when The Bastard, one of the 100-1 shots that would normally have started around 100-6, beat the even-money favourite.

The Tote paid odds of just 19-1; the bookmakers had made their point, but at a price. Their off-course colleagues were not amused and within days the National Sporting League announced that its

---

* In all some £93,000 (£4m) worth of machinery was written off. In January 1934, the *Life* reported: "Hundreds of tons of totalisator equipment were sold at the Baltic Exchange yesterday by order of the Racecourse Betting Control Board. Intricate machinery from Hurst Park, Newbury, Ayr and Hamilton Park, installed at tremendous expense, was sold at scrap prices since, for reasons of economy, the totes there will in future be operated by hand. The goods offered included 68,000 electric lamps, nearly 30,000 yards of cable, ten motor lorries, 25 automatic cashiers and twelve and a half tons of papers and ticket strip." It was not until 1945 that the RBCB was able to pay off its bank debt, and it took another five years before it redeemed all its debenture stock.

members would impose limits of 33-1 in ordinary races and 100-1 in ante-post races, no matter what SPs were returned from the course.

Two weeks later, the Jockey Club, anxious to capitalise on the generally favourable press the Tote had received, announced the first of the benefits it had declared the machine would bring to racegoers – admission to the Newmarket grandstand for the October meeting was to be reduced from £1 to 15s. Somewhat reluctantly, a few other courses followed suit and even the railway companies joined in on the short-lived altruistic spree. In August, combined rail and admission tickets from London to Kempton Park were offered at the bargain price of 4s (£8), which resulted in huge crowds and record takings of £35,000 (£1.4m) on the Tote over the two-day meeting.

It was evident the machine was a big hit with the public largely due to the fact that it accepted place bets and 2s stakes; a field in which most bookmakers were unwilling to compete.* Indeed, one of the first effects the Tote had on the betting ring was to drive small layers (most of whom were habitual welshers) out of business, but its popularity soon had the *Life* calling on the Turf authorities to take action against a common habit that was penalising punters. Under the banner 'Fair Play For Totalisator Place Backers', it demanded:

> Having taken cognisance of betting and sponsored the introduction of the Totalisator, it behoves the Stewards of the Jockey Club to protect the interests of those who bet with the machine in the place pools by making a definite ruling regarding the riding out of horses for the minor places. There have been instances recently of horses being eased out of the first three when their winning prospects were hopeless, a practice which will not be appreciated by the new public which has been attracted to racecourses since the Tote's appearance.

The jockeys' habit of dropping their hands when beaten was not quite as bad as the Tote operator who dropped a nought from the win dividend on a horse called L'Habit Vert at Gatwick that August. Those who had backed the 25-1 chance were predictably upset when a win dividend of just 18s 6d was declared, particularly as the place dividend paid 49s 6d. But racegoers had become so used to the eccentricities of the 'Nanny Goat' by this time they resignedly collected their winnings without question – or at least 31 of them did before it was discovered that the dividend should have been 180s 6d.

Great was the embarrassment. When the punters who had already cashed in their tickets were told to apply to the RBCB for the balance of their money, the *Life* pondered: "How the Board will decide the claims, goodness only knows. It is quite probable that they will receive more claims than they had tickets." Tut-tut, such cynicism!

A few days later a Tote official happily reported that there had been no bombardment from fraudulent claimants, which was, he said, a tribute to "the extreme honesty of the sporting fraternity".

That did it! The floodgates opened and claims poured in by the score until there were demands for the settlement of 213 units. The Board ruefully met 30 of them.

---

* In its first full year the Tote derived 25 per cent of its custom from the 2s punter, while only 1.5 per cent of its sales were to those who placed bets of £10 or more.

A NEW LIFE

URING the spring of 1927, when the battle against Churchill's 'iniquitous levy' was at its height, W S Morley-Brown suddenly took his leave of the *Life*. Apart from his three-year spell (1911-14) as sports editor of the *Daily Chronicle*, the doughty but pedantic Scot had served the paper well for almost quarter of a century.

He had done much to revive its fortunes under the inspired leadership of William Will, and during his own period in office he had carried it through the traumatic years of the Great War and had been a motive force in co-ordinating the fight against the betting tax. Yet his departure went unannounced in his own paper.

There was no farewell dinner; no tributes or presentations, as there had been for his immediate predecessors, Wm Will (1903-11) and Wm Lints Smith (1911-14), and even his colleagues were caught unawares. Adair Dighton, who had taken over as Special Commissioner on the death of William Allison in 1925, was no great penman, but in a dozen words – "he was conservative to the core and hated any idea of acceleration"[1] – he provided the key to the editor's silent exit. Major changes were afoot that were not for him.

In 1925 Odhams had acquired *The People* as a bad debt after having taken over as its printers the previous year. Under the skilled management of J S Elias and his right-hand man John Dunbar, the circulation of the Sunday paper soon rose from 300,000 to touch a million and more machines had to be brought in to handle the increased print run.

In order to avoid the new machinery standing idle on the days when *John Bull* (published on Saturdays) and *The People* were not printed it obviously made sense to transfer the *Life* to the headquarters of Odhams Press at 93 Long Acre and this duly took place in May 1927 just two months after Morley-Brown had vacated the chair.

The move to the West End had been on the cards for some time and with Dunbar overseeing operations and planning a complete revamp of the paper it was, perhaps, understandable that the old man should choose to move on. He was, after all, the wrong side of 60 and had additional interests to occupy him in his role as vice-president of the British Olympic Association. It was not the time to embrace a new style of brash, in-your-face journalism that was completely alien to him.

That style, which he viewed as a general lowering of journalistic standards, had been reflected in a week of tantalising 'Look out for the BIG SURPRISE' editorial notices that preceded the flit to Long Acre and which culminated with one that proclaimed:

> Here is the big surprise – A NEW *Sporting Life* Out Next Monday May 16. A new *Sporting Life*! Something better and far more comprehensive than ever attempted before in sporting journalism! New blood! New methods! Even new paper and new types! There are surprises, indeed, for the sporting man when he opens the NEW *Sporting Life* on Monday morning next!

The punter was promised: "more experts to advise him – more red hot information flashed from the course – more news about form and the paddock. He will find, too, the news served up in a more convenient, more accessible manner – news on which he may put his finger the moment he opens his paper." Readers were further advised: "The prowess of women in sport will have the attention that it so richly deserves. Motor Racing, the new sport Greyhound Racing, Golf, Athletics, Polo – all legitimate sport will be discussed at length, as never before, in the new *Sporting Life*."

Monday's paper was, indeed, a revelation. For a start, the 12-page issue was much more pictorial with 28 pictures compared to the seven that had appeared in Saturday's eight-page number. As varied as they were numerous, they included shots of a shapely Mlle. Simone de la Chaume teeing off in the British Women's Open Golf Championship at Newcastle; the 20-mile National Road Walking Championship at St Albans, and the *Life's* work-watchers, featuring the famous 'Yorky' Edwards, on Newmarket Heath.

Art and effort had been lavished on page displays. Light, airy and easy on the eye, the front page was completely redesigned. A banner headline gave added impact to the layout as news stories were spread across the whole page instead of being sandwiched into three columns flanked by two columns of adverts on either side.

Not that ads had been banished entirely from the front page. In the bottom right-hand corner a two-column block announced: "Jack Hobbs' Bats Free – 500 Bats, specially selected by Jack Hobbs, each one bearing his personal signature written in ink in his own hand, free and post-free to you in exchange for 250 coupons from packets of 20 B.D.V. Cigarettes, or 500 coupons from packets of 10 B.D.V. Cigarettes." – The 'King of Cigarettes' was priced at 6d for 10 or 11½d (£2) for 20.

All in all, the new *Life* represented a vast leap forward to the forefront of modern journalism and it had the best of all starts when 'Augur' (Willie Standring) went through the card on what was the opening day of York's big May meeting; not that the winners took much finding with five short-priced favourites going in along with an 11-4 chance.

Nevertheless, it gave the paper another platform from which to proclaim its rebirth and for the next three days the front page carried scores of 'Greetings From The Great' that had been elicited from famous sportsmen and prominent figures such as Earl Jellicoe, the controversial commander of the British Fleet at Jutland: "I send best wishes for the future success of *The Sporting Life* in supporting clean sport in every branch."

Malcolm Campbell, who was to break the land-speed record nine times between 1924 and 1935 raising it from 146mph to 301mph, wired: "Your long success is due to the high journalistic standard which you have always maintained, and I wish you all prosperity for the future." And the thriller writer, Edgar Wallace, extolled: "I think today's number is a splendid improvement on anything attempted in daily sporting journalism."

In acknowledging the paeans of praise, an editorial on Tuesday declared:

If the good wishes of its friends can make for success, then the new *Sporting Life* will have a triumphant career. Shoals of congratulatory telegrams and messages reached us yesterday. We are grateful to the senders and will do our best to justify their hopes.

Obviously, an enterprise such as this – a venture unique in the history of sporting journalism – can reach perfection only by degrees. We are glad that the first issue pleased so many of our friends; we hope – we mean – to do better and better. Many of the messages that reached us spoke of the 'starvation' of certain classes of sport by the newspaper Press. We shall endeavour to remedy a defect we have long realised...

Basking in the reflected glory of what were chiefly John Dunbar's labours was the paper's new editor, Chris Towler, a fast-living, fun-loving scribe who delighted in entertaining the chorus girls from the Windmill Theatre both in and out of his office. It would be hard to imagine a more different character to the austere Morley-Brown.

Born near Middleham, North Yorkshire, in 1880, Towler had learnt his trade on papers in Blackburn and Manchester before he became editor of the *Weekly Mercury* in Birmingham in 1908. At the outbreak of war he joined the Army Service Corps and saw action in Palestine and Mesopotamia, rising from the ranks to staff captain. On his return to civvies he became a sub on *The People* working under the great Hannen Swaffer, and when Odhams took over that paper, his way was paved towards the editorship of the *Life*.

Pitched in at the deep end, he took up Morley-Brown's fight against the betting tax with a passion and his efforts to bring about its abolition earned him the respect and appreciation of the bookmaking fraternity and many influential racing men. And while he came in on the crest of a wave, it was not all plain sailing. Barely a month after the re-launch, his paper reported:

> Residents in the vicinity of Long Acre were roused from their sleep at about four o'clock yesterday morning by a roar that must have seemed to them like an earthquake. It was an earthquake in miniature. Behind the premises of Odhams Press in Wilson Street practically half of the street away from the main building collapsed ... building operations had been in progress for some months to house machinery to cope with the ever increasing circulation of *The People* and *The Sporting Life*.
>
> A new brick wall 3ft thick had been built, several iron girders, each weighing seven or eight tons had been placed in position ... For some reason, at present unknown, the ground beneath the roadway subsided, and the brick wall collapsed carrying with it some of the iron girders, as well as a huge crane which had been in use during the building operations. Fortunately no one was engaged on the job at the time.

It was, truly, a groundbreaking year for the *Life*, which celebrated its renaissance by running a series of reminiscences from celebrated sportsmen. First up was the billiards champion, Tom Reece, whose entertaining articles ran on a daily basis for a month. When these finished, Frank Mitchell, the South African and Yorkshire cricketer and rugby international, stepped in to tell his stirring tale and he, in turn, was followed by Reece's great rival, Melbourne Inman, the professional billiards champion from 1912 to 1920.

There were sensational stories too. In the summer of 1927, the former Rochdale bricklayer, self-made multi-millionaire and racehorse owner, Jimmy White, committed suicide at his King Edward's Place Stud near Swindon, and the *Life* scooped the whole of Fleet Street by publishing his remarkable life story as told by 'an intimate friend'.

The revelations ran for eight days and their blend of adventure, romance and tragedy touched the emotions of every reader. White had ventured everything in a bid to raise the money he needed to gain a controlling interest in an oil company he part-owned, but it proved one gamble too many and when it failed, rather than face financial ruin, he chose to top himself with a ghastly cocktail of prussic acid and chloroform.

As with all such exclusives, the sales of the *Life* soared in an *annus mirabilis* that saw its reporters in the news for a variety of reasons. In January Charles Packford, who wrote on rugby under the pseudonym of 'Touch Judge', achieved the rare distinction of getting himself banned from the Murrayfield press box by the Scottish Rugby Union.

As versatile a reporter as he had been a sportsman during his days at Oxford at the turn of the century, Packford's impressive track and field CV boasted more than 200 prizes for 12 different sports including rowing, golf, tennis and swimming, as well as county caps for football, cricket and hockey. An international athlete, he won eight championships from 100 yards to one mile in addition to hurdle races and the long and high jump, while his speed and agility made him an outstanding rugby wing three-quarter.

It can safely be said that he knew what he was writing about, and it was because his opinion was widely respected that he incurred the wrath of the SRU when he launched an attack on the notoriously elitist stance that body took against the merest whiff of professionalism. Taking as his cue an extravagant remark made at a function held in honour of the Union's autocratic president, James Aikman Smith, he wrote:

> We read that in the opinion of Sir George Adam Smith, principal of Aberdeen University, Aikman Smith is 'the Napoleon of Rugby football' and that 'it is impossible to be too grateful to him for all he has done for Rugby, not only in Scotland, but also in England'.
>
> It would be interesting to know what the president of the Scottish Union has done for us in this country ... the Union over which he presides has attempted time and again – possibly unwittingly – to wreck friendly relations between the home Unions and those of the Dominions ... If it were not for the English, Irish and Welsh Unions we should not have welcomed the All Blacks here in 1924; we should not have had the pleasure of meeting the Maoris this season, nor should we be anticipating, as we are, the visit of New South Wales in the first half of the 1927-28 campaign. Yet all these teams have assisted in the promotion of greater interests in the game.
>
> The Scottish Union is alone, apparently, of the opinion that the Rugby Unions of the Dominions, if not actually hot-beds of professionalism, are yet flirting with the idea and our overseas players do not like the insinuation ... There are, of course, certain uncharitable people in the Rugby world who still believe that the financial disaster connected with the game between Scotland and the All Blacks in 1905 is really responsible for the present attitude of the Scottish authorities.[*]
>
> Since then Scotland, by the creation at the time of some imaginary grievance, have not met a Dominion side, and by this act of isolation alone they have rendered a disservice to the game. If England, Ireland and Wales welcome overseas teams, this should be sufficient guarantee to Scotland that there is no question or doubt as to their amateur status.
>
> It must not be imagined for a moment that the Scottish Union has had the solid support of its members in their many peculiar activities to 'purify' the game. They have on innumerable occasions annoyed those fine sportsmen over the Border by adopting an attitude of glorified isolation, and they will not be forgiven for a long time by their own people for refusing to play the 1924 All Blacks.

As can be imagined, all this did not go down well too well with Aikman Smith and when Packford

---

[*] When the first All Blacks team to tour Britain arrived in September 1905, Scotland dismissed them as serious rivals and refused to give them a £200 match fee. Instead it was agreed the New Zealanders could have the gate receipts after the deduction of expenses, but under the captaincy of Dave Gallaher, the 'Originals' proved a sensation. They began their gruelling 32-match tour by thrashing the highly-rated Devon XV 55-4 and by the time they arrived at Inverleith everyone wanted to see them. The game was a sell-out and the tourists not only scored twice in the last five minutes to beat Scotland 12-7, they made £1,700 from the match. They went on to beat Ireland 15-0 at Lansdowne Road and England by the same score at Crystal Palace. When they met the Triple Crown winners, Wales, just before Christmas they were unbeaten in 27 games with a tally of 801 points to 22, but they lost 3-0 in Cardiff after the Scottish referee controversially disallowed what would have been an equalising try in the last ten minutes.

The *Life*'s John Melhuish, ('Mel'), sees the All Blacks performing the haka on their 1924 tour of England.

went to pick up his press pass for the Scotland v France game at Murrayfield that weekend, H M Simpson, the secretary of the SRU, informed him that he was *persona non grata*. In commenting on the 'ban' the *Life* remarked:

> The amusing part of the interview lies in the fact that 'Touch Judge' then asked Mr Simpson if he would be allowed to buy a ticket. 'Oh yes' was the reply, 'You can have a stand ticket on payment of ten shillings', and so seated in Block D Row V No. 13, our representative had a far better view of the game than he would have had from the back of the stand where the Press are seated. The ticket for this particular seat, by the way, was originally stamped 'Complimentary', but this Mr Simpson carefully erased!

The wounds Packford inflicted with his incisive pen had obviously not healed two months later when the annual clash for the Calcutta Cup took place at Murrayfield:

We applied again in the usual way for a Press pass for next Saturday's Scotland v. England match, but this has been refused by Mr H M Simpson, the Scottish secretary, 'with regret'. This regret may have been because ten shillings was not enclosed with the application; we do not know. But whether Mr Simpson's tears are genuine or of the genus crocodile, we are not concerned. Quite clearly his Union declines to grant us the right to witness and report upon an international match. It is all very childish – and so completely futile that next Monday's *Sporting Life* will contain a full description and criticism of the match by 'Touch Judge'.[*]

Matters could hardly have been improved by this waspish response, but it is worth noting that Packford's criticism might well have nudged the SRU into reassessing its policy, because when the New South Wales Waratahs toured Britain that winter the Scots took them on at Murrayfield and beat them 10-8.

Meyrick Good was another *Life* man to make the news in 1927 when he gave the first horserace commentary ever broadcast on air in what was a landmark year for the BBC. In January, the Corporation had staked its claim to a share of the sports media market with a commentary on the England v Wales rugby match at Twickenham and over the following months it expanded its coverage to include the University Boat Race, the FA Cup Final, Wimbledon, the Derby and St Leger.

Newspaper proprietors viewed this move to outside broadcasting as a threat to their interests and were reluctant to allow their top men to sign up as commentators, but Good was uniquely qualified for the job. On two previous occasions he had been summoned to Lord Derby's box at Aintree to 'read' the Grand National for George V; a command performance he later described as "the greatest honour and compliment I have ever been paid in my journalistic career,"[2] and it certainly helped to clear the way for his lead role in what his paper called the 'BBC's Important Aintree Experiment'.

On the day of the historic broadcast, which went out through the Daventry transmitter to all parts of the UK, Ireland and many European countries, the *Life* carried a small front-page item headed 'The King to Hear the Race Described':

> The King will view today's contest for the Grand National Steeplechase from Lord Derby's stand and will be immediately on the right of *The Sporting Life* representative Mr Meyrick Good, who is broadcasting the race for the B.B.C. ... His Majesty will hear all the incidents of the parade, the line-up for the start, and the race as it is described. The commentator will give the first three horses past the post and the remaining candidates to finish and continue until the first three are back in the unsaddling enclosure.

Good had his work cut out with a then record field of 37 facing the starter, but the race could not have worked out better for him. Not only was his commentary voted a great success, but he had backed and tipped the winner, Sprig, who was trained by his good friend Tom Leader with whom he had horses for more than 20 years.

As Sprig started to forge ahead up the long run-in under young Ted Leader, Good, momentarily forgetting he was on air, roared out 'Come on Ted, you'll win' – a cry that was echoed from the stands and by millions of his listeners as the well-backed 8-1 favourite, battled on gamely to hold on by a

---

[*] With some nostalgia for 'the good old days' it can be recorded that the Scots were triumphant in both these games. They thumped the French 23-6 to extend their dominance over their Gallic rivals to 8 wins, lost 3, drawn 1 since they first met in 1910, while the game against England was won 21-13 to level the Calcutta Cup score at 20 wins apiece with 9 games drawn.

'Tex' sketches some of the owners, trainers and jockeys associated with the main contenders for the 1927 Grand National

Sprig and Ted Leader are led in by 74-year-old Mrs Partridge after their victory in the first race ever to be broadcast on radio; the *Life*'s Meyrick Good was the commentator.
© [Central Press]/[Hulton Archive]Getty Images

diminishing length from the one-eyed, 100-1 chance, Bovril III. And, as with so many Grand National heroes, there was a 'story' behind the homebred nine-year-old who was winning the race at his third attempt:

> Sprig used to belong to Mrs Partridge's son Richard, an officer in the Shropshire Yeomanry, who was killed a few weeks before the Armistice. He left the horse to his mother who, not being a 'racing woman', kept him as a pet and only consented to have him put into serious training because she thought it was 'what Richard would have wanted' ... Mrs Partridge is now both the happiest and saddest woman in England. She is seventy-four years of age and had her two other sons killed in the Boer War.

The BBC's entry into sports broadcasting resulted in the *Life* starting a weekly 'Radio Notes' column to cater for interest in the new medium, while its pledge to give more space to minority sports extended to running regular columns on darts (by J A Peel, secretary of the National Darts Association) and pigeon racing (by 'Quartermaster').

News on the 'doos' led the paper in June when the headlines 'Great Pigeon Disaster / 3,000 Birds Lost In Channel Storm' announced the fate that had overtaken the birds from the Worcestershire Federation on their flight from Rennes in France. The estimated loss to the lofts was said to be in the region of £10,000 (£400,000). The following month a happier story – 'Welsh Miner Wins Great Pigeon Race Prize / San Sebastian Results: Silver Trophy From The King' – told of the success of an Ogmore Vale Club fancier whose bird had made the flight from Spain in just under 28½ hours.

It had taken Charles Lindbergh five hours longer to make the first solo crossing of the Atlantic in the *Spirit of St Louis* two months earlier, while there was also front-page coverage of a British aviation triumph that September when Sidney Webster piloted a Supermarine-Napier S5 seaplane to victory in the Schneider Trophy in Venice.

'Britain's Greatest Air Triumph / Schneider Cup Won At Terrifying Speed Of 281 Miles An Hour / Flight-Lieut. Webster Gambles With Death And Wins' roared the block-capital headlines as the lead story reported that a quarter of a million people had watched the event in which only two of the six competing planes managed to complete the 350km (217-mile), seven-lap course with its 20 'Corners of Death'.

It was the first of three successive victories for the Supermarine in the international race, which not only won the cup outright for the Royal Aero Club in 1931, but also led to its young designer, R J Mitchell, going on to the develop the Spitfire, which was to play a leading role in winning a greater battle for air supremacy nine years later.

Other highlights in the *Life's* 1927 calendar were Cardiff City's 1-0 win in the FA Cup Final after Arsenal's goalkeeper had fumbled the ball into his own net; France's first rugby victory over England (3-0) since their first meeting in 1906; Joe Davis's win in the first world snooker championship (a title he was to hold until he retired 20 years later) and Major Henry Segrave setting a new land-speed record of 203mph in his monster 1,000hp Sunbeam ('The Slug') on Daytona Beach, Florida.

In July the *Life* staged its own day's motor racing at Brooklands with a programme of seven races devised by its motoring correspondent Alan Hess. The day attracted the cream of British drivers and with the famous handicapper, A V Ebblewhite, staggering the starts from 21mins 48secs down to scratch, the paper was able to claim "Never before have such exciting finishes been witnessed at Brooklands."

Malcolm Campbell won the opening 15-mile drivers' race in an 8-cylinder Bugatti beating Hess's 3-litre Austro-Daimler by 1.6sec; George Duller, the outstanding hurdles jockey who was equally at home behind the wheel of his Bugatti, won the fourth race, while the feature event, a 102-mile, 37-lap, 19-car handicap, was won by John Cobb driving a Vauxhall at an average speed of just over 111mph.

Cobb's race might well have ended in disaster as his car returned with a three-inch screw embedded in a rear tyre. As Hess remarked: "When it is realised that a moment before, the car had been hurtling down the Railway Straight at nearly two miles a minute, it will be appreciated that Providence was kind to Cobb – and to the spectators."[*]

Sport on wheels also took on more unorthodox forms and coverage was given to the Auto-Cycle Union football cup final that was staged before a large crowd at Crystal Palace in March. Coventry, captained by J Montgomery riding one of his own 350cc manufactured bikes, duly maintained their unbeaten record (held since the team was formed in 1924) by hammering Douglas, their Isle of Man rivals, 12-1.

On a more general front, betting forecasts, which had been carried by evening papers for some years, but had been opposed by Morley-Brown on the grounds that they could mislead the punter, were introduced for the day's principal meeting. Similarly, jockeys' riding arrangements, which had made a tentative appearance in 1919 became much more detailed thanks to the 'probable runners and riders' service the Press Association's racing editor, Fred Harrison and his reporter, Harry Humphries, started in 1926.

But the most significant change to the *Life* in 1927 took place four months after its re-launch when the back page was given over to one particular sport or, to be more precise, entertainment. The paper, like everyone else that autumn, was going to the dogs.

---

[*] Cobb went on to set three land-speed records taking it from 350.2mph in 1938 to 394.2mph in 1947, but his luck finally ran out in 1952 when he was killed in an attempt on the water-speed record of 178.5mph. The 54-year-old former RAF pilot was clocked at 206.8mph on his first run over a measured mile on Loch Ness when his 3 ton, 6,000hp jet-powered boat, *Crusader*, hit the wake of one of his support vessels and disintegrated in much the same way as Donald Campbell's *Bluebird* did when attempting to break the 300mph barrier on Coniston Water 15 years later.

GOING TO THE DOGS

He and his dogs went growling on their journey to that very notorious place called Belle Vue, near Manchester. I stood for a moment looking after him, and said to myself, that if there was a man in England beyond the reach of sovereign grace that man was Niff.

SO WROTE the celebrated Rochdale chronicler and saver of souls, John Ashworth, in his collection of short stories *Strange Tales From Humble Life* published in 1865. The irredeemable Niff was typical of the working-class man who sought to supplement his meagre wage by running his dogs at Belle Vue and other such 'notorious places' – usually public recreation grounds – throughout the country.

The races were well-organised affairs run as handicaps over a straight course that varied from 100yds to 220yds. The dogs, mainly whippets but sometimes terriers or small lurchers, were graded according to weight and ability. Those that could cover 200 yards in 12secs ran from scratch, while a yard-per-pound start was allowed for the lighter dogs. Prize money ranged from 50s up to £25.

To the uninitiated, the races presented a surreal spectacle. Each dog had a handler at the start who, after taking up his allotted handicap position, would crouch down on one knee beside his charge, holding it by the ears or scruff of the neck with one hand and by the root of the tail with the other. On the command 'Pick up dogs', the mutts were lifted by the tail so they were angled at 45 degrees to the ground and, at the crack of the starting pistol, they were launched forward in what was literally a flying start to land running, while their owners stood at the finishing line calling their dogs and frantically waving a rag lure.

These 'rag races' had long been a passion among the mining communities of the midlands and the north and were just starting to become popular in London in the mid-1870s when, instead of using a rag, a mechanical lure was devised in the form of a stuffed hare skin mounted on a trolley. The trolley was slotted into a grooved rail set in the ground and pulled along by a manually operated windlass.

The contraption had its first public trial at the famous sporting hostelry, the Welsh Harp at Hendon, on 9 September 1876 when, in a bid to raise the status of the sport, the races were confined to greyhounds and run on the same knockout basis as coursing with the dogs paired against each other.

The trials proved a success particularly for the *Life's* coursing correspondent, Charles Conquest ('Amesbury'), whose dogs "cleaned out the lot," and an inaugural meeting at the 'Harp' was arranged for October 7 when a 16-dog stake of 2gns each and an eight-dog stake of 1gns each were to be run off.

Conquest's son* acted as secretary and stakeholder, but despite a fair turnout, the day was marred by torrential rain and mechanical failure. The 1hp engine brought in to operate the windlass proved too powerful and resulted in either the wire breaking or the hare-trolley jumping out of its rail.

When a return was made to hand-cranking "everything went as well as possible" except for Conquest whose entry was beaten in the first round of the 16-dog stake. The eight-dog Kingsbury Stakes did, however, attain a place in greyhound history since it was won by Charming Nell who became

---

* Charles Conquest jnr eventually succeeded his father as the *Life*'s coursing correspondent writing under the pseudonym of 'Lambourne', but he "was fitted for anything but a journalist. Even if he did know more about greyhounds than racehorses, he was illiterate and I should say never had more than a year or two's schooling. His copy had to be more than soled and heeled; it had to be practically rewritten."[1]

A whippet is given a flying start by his handler at Canning Town, east London, 1927.
© [Popperfoto]/Getty Images

the great grand dam of Fullerton, the only dog to win the Waterloo Cup four times. But enthusiasm for the mechanical hare soon died out because the races, which were run over a straight 400 yards, failed as a betting medium since they were almost always won by the fastest dog.

What was needed were a few bends to blend speed with agility and so bring out the natural skill of the coursing greyhound, but it was to be another 50 years before such a track was built in Britain. In the meantime, the popularity of whippet racing increased. By the turn of the century dog racing took place on a daily basis (Sundays included) in the London area. Meetings were held at such venues as the Royal Standard football grounds at Walthamstow, the White Hart grounds at Tottenham Hale and Pacey's athletic grounds at Clapton.

But it was in America that the foundations of modern greyhound racing were laid after an Irish emigrant, Owen P Smith, staged as a tourist attraction the coursing of jackrabbits in an enclosed field. The venture backfired badly when there was an outcry against the slaughter of the bunnies, so in 1907 he built a small track outside Salt Lake City and had a stuffed rabbit skin towed around the circuit by a motorbike. The dogs gave chase, but the public stayed away.

Years passed before Smith tried again with a motorised trolley at a track in California, but because betting was illegal in that State the project flopped. Undaunted, he moved on to Tulsa in 1920 and this time, with bookmakers in attendance, and using an electric lure, he was on a winner. Two years later he took his apparatus to Miami where he staged the Greyhound Derby at Hialeah and from there dog racing took off – big time.

In 1925 Charles Munn, a Philadelphia businessman, acquired Smith's patent for the hare on the (unfulfilled) promise of a share in any profits that might accrue from the establishment of the sport in England. That was the last Smith saw of Munn. The dogged pioneer died in 1927, a year after Munn had teamed up with Brig-Gen Alfred Critchley and one or two other like-minded entrepreneurs to lease 12 acres of land opposite the Bellevue Gardens recreation grounds in Manchester.

Stands were built and a track laid down in record time as some £22,000 (£1m) was sunk into the venture. The Greyhound Racing Association was formed and the respected coursing judge and vet, Major Leslie Lyne Dixson, was recruited to bring in owners and buy up cast-offs from the top coursing kennels. On Saturday July 24 1926, Belle Vue stadium opened for business when 2,555 curious punters turned up to chance their luck on the six races. The honour of winning the first race – a £15 (£690), seven-dog, 440-yard event – went to the 6-1 shot Mistley, a Waterloo Cup semi-finalist with half a tail, who bolted home by eight lengths.

When the gate receipts were totalled up that night the GRA found itself £50 out of pocket, but the novelty of what Winston Churchill was to deride as 'animated roulette' soon began to draw in the crowds. By the end of its extended three-month season 333,375 people had passed through the Kirkmanshulme Lane turnstiles and 154 dogs, which cost their owners £1 a week to keep on site, had run at the track. Almost overnight (37 nights to be precise), the GRA was able to pay off its bank loan and make plans for more tracks, this time in London.

Critchley, a First World War hero who was to win the amateur golf championships of France, Belgium and Holland in the 1930s, was a man of great energy and vision who tackled all his projects with an unbridled enthusiasm that infected everyone around him. Unorthodox, forthright and impetuous, it was said of him that he never lost a friend – or an enemy.

At the end of 1926, 'Critch' and his fellow directors took a lease out on the White City stadium, Shepherds Bush, which had fallen into disrepair since its use as an army training centre during the war. In a frenetic burst of reconstruction, the concrete cycle circuit was ripped out, the terraces roofed in, and a turf track was laid down on the old running track.

By June trials had started with the electric hare. These were seldom dull and provided visiting journalists with plenty of colourful copy. The eccentric antics of the 'barmy bunny' soon earned it celebrity status. 'Rupert', as it was dubbed, initially refused to exert itself and trundled around the track as if it was on a Zimmer frame rather than a high-voltage electric trolley, but later on it went to the other extreme as a surge of current sent it rocketing around the 525-yard circuit in a blur of fur.

In an attempt to achieve a happy medium, further complications arose and, without warning, Rupert would suddenly go hurtling backwards. Headlines such as 'Hair-Raising Hare Racing' lit up the front page of the *Life* and on June 14, just four days before the scheduled opening night, the one-line header 'Hare Goes On Strike' told its own story:

> Everybody and everything at the White City is active, except the hare. Gangs of engineers have been busy throughout the weekend and yesterday were still engaged in trying to speed-up this obstinate hare, but he steadfastly refuses to be hurried ... He did nothing but stand in an outstretched position staring with glassy eye at the reproachful crowds that gathered around him.

Two days later the problems appeared to have been ironed out as readers were informed 'Rupert Wakes Up – Everything Ready at White City', but the out-of-season mad March hare still had one last trick to perform. The following day it was reported:

> At 5.30 the hare made several rounds of the course, but then suddenly switched off onto the brake siding and ran through the brake onto the sandbag shutters with a terrific crash. The trials were naturally postponed until after 8 o'clock when, retaining nothing of its original shape, the hare worked perfectly and ten trials were run off satisfactorily. It is hoped the hare trouble is now finished.

As a result of 'the hare trouble' the opening meeting had to be postponed until Monday June 20 when Rupert was on his best behaviour throughout the eight-race card. Admission to the cheap enclosure was just 1s 2d (2d entertainment tax) and a crowd of some 25,000 raised a mighty roar as the traps sprang open for the first race at 7.30pm.

The thrill of seeing six sleekly sculptured canine aristocrats racing full pelt around the track at 38mph captivated the Londoners, and even the *Life's* dyed-in-the-wool coursing correspondent, D H (Douglas Harold) Watson-Wood, could scarce forebear to cheer. Reflecting on what many of his colleagues condemned as 'the prostitution of coursing', 'King Cob' wrote:

> 'If you had never seen a coursing meeting you would call this marvellous,' said a friend to me on Monday and in a nutshell he explained the popularity of the new sport as probably not one in every hundred of the thousands that were present had ever witnessed the coursing of a hare.
>
> To them the turns and the wrenches and the work were unknown quantities. They saw, and gloried in, greyhounds brought to a state of physical perfection by their trainers, and watched them race round a track under conditions of comfort that are only found on a racecourse.
>
> Honestly, you cannot wonder. Forget that wrench that won Pentonville his 'Waterloo' or the pluck that earned Running Rein his Centenary Cup. Put aside the oiled boots, the innumerable mackintoshes and the inevitable Altcar umbrella. The White City is different. The dogs are the same, but there is no chance of your being reduced to a sponge-like mess with rain or snow, and the spectacle is wonderful.

Others were less enamoured. Lord Sefton, on whose land the Waterloo Cup was held, had left members of the National Coursing Club in no doubt as to his views on the new sport when he presided over a meeting of the Club that February. In response to Lyne Dixson's plea that the NCC should hold talks with the GRA in order to protect its traditional winter season from the encroachment of track racing, Sefton scotched any prospect of diplomacy as he snapped: "I hope we will fight to the bitter end against the recognition of the Greyhound Racing Association."

The overlapping of the respective seasons was, however, inevitable. Even though the GRA initially restricted its season to seven months from April to October, the managers of other tracks, which were springing up all over the country, saw no need to be bound by any obligation to coursing and were keen to race throughout the year.

The Irish, as ever, had been quick on the uptake. Tracks in Belfast (Celtic Park) and Dublin (Shelbourne Park) opened in the spring of 1927, and by the time the GRA established its second London track at Harringay that autumn, the *Life* was devoting the whole of its back page to the dogs.

With White City and Harringay racing on alternate nights from Monday to Saturday, space was at a premium because the paper was also carrying selections and form for Birmingham's two tracks, Hall Green and King's Heath, as well as for Blackpool, Bristol, Edinburgh (Powderhall), Hull, Leeds, Liverpool (also doubly represented by Stanley and Breck Park), Manchester, Sheffield (Darnall Wellington) and Southend.

The Kursaal track at Southend even attempted to race on Sundays that summer, but this was fiercely opposed by the *Life* in a lead article headed 'Kill Sunday Greyhound Racing' which reflected an editorial view and a society very different to that of the 1980s and early 90s when the paper campaigned vigorously for Sunday racing:[*]

> The policy of *The Sporting Life* on the question is what we feel our readers will expect of us. We have constantly raised our voice against any extension of the incursion of organised sport on the first day of the week. We do not believe the sporting public wants Sunday racing and while we are not killjoys, we are entirely opposed to it.

This stance, combined with condemnations from the unlikely alliance of the GRA and the Lord's Day Observance Society, forced Southend to abandon its plans, but in all other respects dog racing continued to expand at a phenomenal rate. The reason for its success is not difficult to see. First and foremost 'the dogs' offered inexpensive entertainment for the working classes at a time that was convenient to them – the evenings. The floodlit tracks were also built within the catchment area of the city suburbs and for a few pence fare on the bus or tram and a shilling (£2.35) entrance fee, they could have all the excitement of the racecourse at a fraction of its cost.

Crowds of 40,000 or 50,000 were soon regarded as normal at White City which played host to the Prince of Wales (later Edward VIII) within a month of its opening. Stars of stage and screen, and owners such as the Queen of Greece, the Duchess of Sutherland, the Marchioness of Blandford and the Countess of Ranfurly also brought respectability and a touch of Royal Ascot sophistication to the tracks.

In the first nine months of 1927, no fewer than 68 greyhound-racing companies were registered in the nationwide rush to get in on the action; even the British Borzoi Club held trials for its breed at Blackpool "to ascertain whether they are adapted for racing with the electric hare". The answer was an emphatic 'no' as only three of the 20 trial dogs completed the course.

After the electric hare came the electric rat, and for a short time fox terrier racing was all the rage in London. Betting was fierce at the Stadium Club in Holborn where a 150-yard circuit was laid out, while at the Coliseum, Charing Cross, six races a night, including three over hurdles, were staged over a 75-yard course.

The over-excitable terriers provided wonderful entertainment but chaotic racing though nothing compared to the tentative trial that was held for cheetahs at the White City one night after the crowds had gone home although some bookmakers stayed behind to watch the fun. What followed is best described by Alfred Critchley:

> We put a big bit of steak on the electric hare, and the bookmakers arrayed themselves on the barrier overlooking the track, just past the starting trap. The raw beef came hurtling round, the starting trap was opened and out came the cheetahs (four of them). One got away to a good start, while the

---

[*] Official Sunday racing (both dog and horse) with betting finally took place in Britain in 1995.

others ran a few yards and then stopped. They then had a look at the bookmakers and walked slowly towards them. The bookmakers scattered like pigeons, and rushed up the steps to the back of the stadium ... By this time the one on the track, getting bored, stopped, turned, and came back to his pals ... So ended cheetah racing in England.[2]

By the time the silly season had run its course, the *Life* calculated the Exchequer was raking in at least £10,000 (£470,000) a week in entertainment and betting tax from the dogs, while the paper also profited from the bonanza through an increase in circulation and advertising. Unlike the Chancellor, however, it gave something back to the tracks that autumn when it put up £500 (£23,500) for a hurdle race at White City and a stylish silver challenge cup for a Yorkshire Championship at Leeds.

Eliminating heats for the *Sporting Life* Greyhound Grand National were run off at Edinburgh, Liverpool, Birmingham, Manchester and the two London tracks before the four-dog final took place at 'the City' on Monday, October 10. The evening was a resounding success. "There has been nothing quite like it since greyhound racing was introduced as a national sport," the paper boasted after a record crowd of 80,000 had packed into the stadium to see the champion jockey, Gordon Richards, present the trophy to the owner of the Manchester dog, Bonzo, the 13-8 favourite, who beat the locally-trained Jasserand by half a length.

Seven weeks after the GRA wound up its season on October 22, another London track opened its doors when nearly 70,000 'greycing' fans packed into a refurbished and revitalised Wembley stadium that had seen little action since Cardiff City beat Arsenal in the FA Cup Final back in April. December also saw the Greenford track introduce mixed afternoon meetings with five dog races interspersed by two trotting races.

On the stock market shares in greyhound companies soared. Within days of their issue in September, the 1s deferred shares in Wembley Greyhound Racecourse Ltd were changing hands for ten times that amount. And in December shares in the GRA Trust were so heavily oversubscribed that those who applied for 1,000 received only 50. On their first day of trading, the 1s shares closed at 5s 9d.

Dog prices were also rocketing. On the Saturday before the 1928 Waterloo Cup, the *Life* carried a special four-page greyhound supplement that included adverts for forthcoming sales. Of the two big greyhound repositories in London (Stollery's at the Barbican and Aldridge's in Upper St Martin's Lane), Aldridge's were selling 110 dogs that day and their sales on February 25 and March 10 were already full.

Campbell, Parker & Co of Moor Street, Birmingham were selling 100 greyhounds on February 23; the monthly sales at Sewell's in Lower Mount Street, Dublin, were due to take place the following day, and 24 hours later, Henry Manley & Sons in Crewe were offering a catalogue of registered dogs that included entries from Lord Lonsdale's kennels. In an article headed 'World Market for Greyhounds' it was stated:

The ever-increasing popularity of greyhound racing, not only in this country but abroad, is evidenced by the almost feverish demand for dogs of undoubted breed regardless altogether of the cost. For instance at Aldridge's Repository, London, Messrs W and S Freeman have sold a considerable number of dogs to go to France, while several Americans over here at the present time are buying freely for shipment to the United States. At one of Messrs Campbell Parker's Birmingham sales the other day a great number of the dogs were bought for export to China.

Whether the mutts destined for China were for the track or the table was not specified, but amid all the frenetic wheeling and dealing, there was an obvious need for a control body to regulate the burgeoning industry. To this end the National Greyhound Racing Club was established in January 1928; independent of the promoters, its main aim was to protect the punters, 5,656,686 of whom had attended GRA tracks in 1927.

The Club's jurisdiction was accepted by the leading tracks whose managers formed the National Greyhound Racing Society to administer the sport. Those tracks that declined to accept the authority of the NGRC placed themselves beyond the pale and continued to operate independently on a similar basis to the flapping meetings that took place outside Jockey Club control.

There was certainly a need for strict regulation if the industry was to protect itself against the skulduggery that exists in any sport where large sums of money can be won by cheating. Unsavoury elements had already begun to emerge the previous summer when the Belle Vue trainer, H A Wilson, became the first person to be warned off all tracks under the control of the GRA after he admitted to the charge of "grossly improper conduct in connection with the running of greyhounds".

An even bigger sensation had occurred in September 1927 when six Belle Vue dogs were poisoned as a result of being given a strychnine-based tonic by an inexperienced trainer's assistant. Because the bottle had not been shaken the strychnine was concentrated in the last few doses and it resulted in the death of Tall Oak who held the track record of 27.8sec for 500yds. It obviously had been a genuine mistake, but the GRA was so keen that the new sport should be seen to be 'clean' it suspended the trainer, Tom Fear, from holding a licence at any of its tracks.

At the same time as the GRA was setting its house in order, there was a mounting campaign against dog racing from the usual quarters. In October, the Anti-Gambling League took out a summons against the Association for "openly keeping and using the stadium at the White City for the purpose of betting with persons resorting there and unlawfully, knowingly and wilfully permitting betting to take place."

The League claimed that bookmakers had been allotted "at least a thousand" places with concrete posts set in the ground for them to hang their boards on. Because the posts created 'a place' under the 1853 Betting Act it was ruled that an offence had been committed and the GRA was accordingly fined £50 with 100gns costs.

The year ended with an even bigger bombshell being delivered by the Home Secretary, Sir William Joynson-Hicks, after a deputation of MPs had approached him on the subject of dog racing and betting. Just before Christmas, the *Life* published a statement from the Tory Minister that sent shivers through the greyhound world:

> For some time past I have been very much influenced by reports that have been given to me in regard to the very doubtful effects on the wellbeing of the community of this enormous expansion of greyhound racing … I think it would be well that those who are investing in this form of sport should realise that the development has been so sudden and so extensive that any Government must devote very serious attention to it and I accordingly feel it my duty to give at least this warning hint to those who may be investing their money in the undertaking.

In addition to this 'warning hint', religious groups and social welfare organisations were urging politicians to bring in legislation to curb the growth of the tracks. In February 1928, Chris Towler addressed the subject in an editorial headed 'Strange Mentality':

The human mind is a curious thing. That of the anti-sport section of the community is a fearsome creation. The outlook of the average opponent of sport is of the narrowest possible description and he betrays his lack of breadth in every step he takes in his attempt to interfere with the liberty of action of others. Just now the 'antis' are concentrating largely upon manufacturing opposition to greyhound racing. It is just what we should have expected that one of their main arguments against its continuance is its popularity.

Macaulay accurately summed up the 'antis' when he wrote that the Puritans opposed bull and bear baiting not because it was cruel to the animals, but because it gave pleasure to the spectators. Much of the opposition to greyhound racing today has its origin in a similar unworthy motive. If the fanatics were allowed to have their own way England would indeed be a dismal land. The sports and pleasures of the people would be abolished by Act of Parliament, or be permitted only in such emasculated form as to rob them of their chief attraction.

But 'Cometh the hour, cometh the dog' as into this cauldron of puritanical politics and sanctimonious sanctions blazed a hound that captured the imagination of the nation and transformed Churchill's scorned 'animated roulette' into a sport of canine heroes.

Bred in 1926 by Father Martin Brophy, a Co. Offaly parish priest, Mick the Miller was the runt

Mick the Miller, the epitome of a well-muscled greyhound in his prime; the photo is signed by Mick's part-owner, Arundel Kempton.
Reproduced by kind permission of Sir Mark Prescott, Bt.

of the litter and almost died of distemper when a puppy, but against all the odds he survived to become as famous as his legendary ancestor, the three-time Waterloo Cup winner, Master McGrath.

Father Brophy was a firm believer in the parable of the talents and like the 'good and faithful servant' he reaped a rich harvest from the bookmakers as his dog farmed some of the top races in Ireland during his first two years on the track.

Seeking fresh fields to conquer, the sporting padre entered 'Mick' for the Greyhound Derby at White City in 1929 and took as much of the 25-1 ante-post price on offer as his meagre stipend would allow. In July those odds vanished in the record time of 29.82sec that it took the Irish flyer to win his Derby qualifying heat by eight astounding lengths, and a week later he was a 4-7 shot to win the 525-yard final.

But there is no such thing as a racing certainty and on the first bend the favourite collided with two of the other three finalists and was knocked out of the race. Fortunately for those who had backed him, a 'no-race' was declared and in the re-run Mick proceeded to win with some ease "amid a scene of great enthusiasm".

Bought for £800 before the race by London bookmaker Albert Williams, Mick the Miller was afterwards sold on for a record £2,000 (£95,200) to Arundel Kempton, vice-chairman of Wimbledon greyhound stadium, where he spent the rest of his career with the legendary trainer, Sidney Orton.

In 1930 he ran up a sequence of 19 wins over a five-month period during which time he won a second Derby, but he was denied an unprecedented hat trick in that classic when a re-run was ordered in 1931 after another dog had been involved in fighting. Mick had initially prevailed by a head in a desperately close finish, but that hard race and his five years took their toll in the re-run and he finished last, although he gained his revenge over the winner, Seldom Led, in the 700-yard St Leger at Wembley that October.

This turned out to be his last race and the *Life* hailed it as the greatest triumph of his career in which he won 61 of his 81 races and over £9,000 in prize money, setting six world-record times in the process.

An enthusiastic tail-wagger, he endeared himself to the crowds with his evident *joie de vivre* and style of running, which was not designed to prolong the life of his backers. Habitually a slow starter, he was often hampered on the first bend, but he had the class and track craft to get himself out of trouble and turn the tables on his rivals. It was said Mick was as good a judge of pace as the jockey Harry Wragg, whose swooping late challenges had earned him the moniker of 'The Head Waiter', and he certainly timed his arrival on the greyhound scene to perfection.

It was his celebrity status more than anything else that helped silence those who denounced dog racing. And during the dark days of the depression when strikes and unemployment, hunger marches and naval mutinies (at Invergordon), threatened to plunge the nation into anarchy, even Winston Churchill just might have secretly agreed with Brig-Gen A C Critchley CMG, DSO (and later CBE) that greyhound racing had proved "a great antidote to Bolshevism".

THE IRISH SWEEPS

THE PHENOMENON of the Irish Hospitals Sweepstakes took Britain by storm at a time when the economic depression was at its worst. By 1931 three million people (25 per cent of the workforce) were unemployed, whole towns were on the dole, and subsistence funds were almost exhausted. Many of the dispossessed saw the purchase of a 10s (£24) Sweeps ticket as a chance to escape their grinding poverty. But the government viewed it as a national scandal that the public was contributing millions of pounds to benefit the Irish Free State (and, it was whispered, the IRA) when the money was badly needed at home.

The fault, of course, lay not with the governed but with those who governed. In 1930 the legislature had been left at the post when the Dáil Éireann took the initiative and authorised the holding of a sweepstake on three races each year for the benefit of Irish hospitals.

It was not as if the fine, upstanding members of the British parliament had been taken unawares. For years they had been urged to bring in a State-run lottery to ease the burden of the nation's crippling war debts, yet the Home Office had continually spurned the chance, cowed by a small clique of humbugs and hypocrites who would denounce any such lottery as 'the evil of gambling'.

Yet many of these same politicians would happily buy a ticket in the Calcutta Turf Club Derby draw that had become a worldwide institution since Lord William Beresford started it as a private sweepstake in 1887. And if it was not the Calcutta, it would be any one of the countless other sweepstakes that were run on the Derby by political clubs and associations in order to boost their party's fighting funds. While the clubs may have been private, the sweeps certainly weren't and were therefore illegal under the 1823 Lotteries Act. Yet, despite their proliferation, prosecutions were rare and spasmodic.

Because of this and the fact that many other sweepstakes were run simply to line the pockets of their promoters, the *Sporting Life* had long campaigned for the introduction of Premium Bonds, which, the paper argued, would furnish the Exchequer with valuable funds and provide the public with a safe and potentially rewarding means of investment.

After the First World War, many nations went some way towards replenishing their exhausted treasuries through State lotteries, while sweepstakes on major English races were also run by private organisation from the Continent. In 1919, on the same day as the *Life* reported that a soldier from Stoke Newington had won £11,178 (£470,000) on the Army 'Victory' Cambridgeshire sweep run from Lille in France, the question of Premium Bonds again cropped up in the Commons.

As on previous occasions, the Chancellor of the Exchequer refused to be drawn on the subject and his evasion prompted Morley-Brown to renew his plea for some form of State lottery:

> There are big Government lotteries in France and Germany ... and it is a known fact that in the case, at least of the French lottery, a lot of British money is being sent across the Channel, the flow of which could be instantly stopped if our benighted and namby-pamby legislators could rid themselves of the silly notion that while it is right and proper to dabble in stocks and shares and in other 'doubtful' transactions, it is intensely wicked to put a bit into a lottery.
>
> What a hypocritical lot we are; at any rate those who are set over us in high places! I am convinced – and I am far from being alone in my conviction – that if the 'sense' of the nation were taken on

the lottery question, the answer would be an emphatic 'Yes'. That it will come one day is certain, and the day is not very far distant either.[*]

In the meantime the usual disreputable tribe of fraudsters cum bookmakers began to re-establish themselves in Switzerland and advertise sweeps on the 1920 Grand National and Lincolnshire Handicap. To its credit, the *Life* stamped on them from the start:

Since the success of the Army sweepstakes organised in France last year a number of other people have been sending out circulars broadcast asking for subscriptions to this or that sweepstake on forthcoming races in England and the majority of these cases are, on the face of them, just a means of obtaining money without any intention to meet obligations. So far as this paper is concerned it will not, in future lend itself to giving any publicity to any 'sweepstakes' whatsoever. We have had numerous instances lately of the use of the name of the *Sporting Life* on circulars of this description. It is unauthorised and actionable at law.

This self-imposed ban fortunately saved the paper from publicising the 1920 Victory Club Derby sweep run by Horatio Bottomley MP, the Independent member for South Hackney, who ended up behind bars two years later when he was found guilty of embezzling £218,415 (£8m) – a fraction of what his fraudulent schemes had netted him over the years – from his wartime Victory Bonds ruse.

However, no sooner had Bottomley started sewing mailbags in Wormwood Scrubs, than the *Life* was compelled to reassess its policy on sweepstakes when an enterprising Irish bookmaker by the name of Richard Duggan took the first step towards benefiting himself and his nation, and transforming the lives of thousands of ordinary folk around the world. In October 1922, Tom Healy announced in his weekly 'Harkaway' column:

The £10,000 Manchester November Handicap sweep organised in aid of the Mater Misericordiae Hospital in Dublin is certain to prove a very big success for it has been taken up most enthusiastically and I may add that there are no grandmotherly people here who think that the national character is about to be ruined because one invests 10s in a ticket for a sweep … Everybody who is anybody in sport in Ireland has a ticket and a very considerable amount of support has been received outside Ireland. The point to bear in mind is that a most deserving charity is being helped.

Healy went on to report that Duggan had deposited £10,000 (£420,000) with the Lord Mayor of Dublin before a ticket had been sold, and ended with the blatant plug "Mr Duggan has his offices in Ireland at 38 Dame Street, Dublin, and he has a large staff dealing with applications at that address."

With the *bona fide* of his undertaking established and another £10,000 pledged to the cash-strapped Mater Misericordiae hospital for lending its name to the project, Duggan was taking a tremendous gamble that he would be able to recoup his £20,000 outlay plus expenses, but he needn't have worried.

What he made out of this initial venture is uncertain, but the word was it was no small amount and four months later he ran another £10,000 sweep, this time on the Grand National, in aid of Dublin's

---

[*] Morley-Brown was somewhat premature in his prediction. Premium Bonds were not introduced until 1957, and it was not until 1994 that the National Lottery came into being.

Holles Street cancer hospital. And once again the sweep was publicised in the *Life*, which announced at the beginning of January:

> Mr Duggan has again received the sanction of the Free State Government to organise and carry out the sweep on similar lines to those connected with the Manchester November Handicap … It might be interesting to recall that for the last sweep, tickets were purchased by people living within the gates and walls of Buckingham Palace and 10 Downing Street, but they had no luck … the winning ticket – Torelore – was drawn by a motherless girl in Londonderry; the second prize by a poor person in Glasgow and the third by a professional footballer in Preston.

And the money came rolling in. Even before Sergeant Murphy won £5,000 for his Plumstead (London) ticket holder it was reported that Duggan was putting up £20,000 for a sweep on the Derby in aid of the Meath Hospital in Dublin.

By this time herds of bookmakers were pounding the streets of Dublin in search of needy hospitals on which to shower their largesse, but they were brought up short when the Dáil banned all future sweepstakes. Duggan somehow managed to circumvent the law by having his Derby sweep drawn in Switzerland even though that country had recently driven out the British bookmakers by outlawing all forms of gambling.

Meanwhile, in England the sweepstakes craze continued in defiance of the law. In 1923, a Conservative MP won £25,000 on the Stock Exchange Derby draw, while the winner of the London Meat Traders Derby sweep in aid of St Bartholomew's Hospital received £13,000. In Yorkshire, the Otley Unionist Club paid out a thumping £31,517 (£1.4m) to a Skipton girl who had drawn the Steve Donoghue-ridden winner Papyrus; almost as much again went to those who held tickets on the placed horses and the 16 other runners in the race, while the Red Cross also benefited from a sizable donation.

Predictably, cross-party jealousy gave rise to questions in parliament. The Tory Home Secretary was asked why the police had prohibited a sweep organised by the Ilford Independent Labour Party while other lotteries such as the Otley sweep, promoted by the Conservative Association, were allowed.*

In the spring of 1924, Dick Duggan showed he was not to be thwarted when he formed an alliance with Sidney Freeman, a partner with Martin Benson in the Douglas Stuart bookmaking firm, and approached Morley-Brown with a 'skill' competition that required contestants to place in order of merit ten Derby winners from a selected list.

The first advertisement for this so-called 'Derby Scheme' run in aid of the Meath Hospital appeared (significantly?) on April 1. Details were sparse, but the fact that £25,000 in prize money was "in the hands of the editor of the *Sporting Life*" was good enough for most people. Perhaps because Morley-Brown knew he was sailing close to the wind, the 'Scheme' received no editorial endorsement and only a few more adverts appeared in the paper on the run-up to the Derby.

Behind the scenes, however, the promotional effort was massive. A million circulars and half a million pamphlets were sent out to Douglas Stuart clients and members of sporting organisations, while £250,000 worth of 10s tickets were printed.

---

* As a result of this publicity the police prosecuted the promoters of the Otley sweep, but because they were unable to prove the actual sale of the tickets the case was dismissed. In 1924, a pre-emptive raid was made on the Otley operation and 9,000 books containing 180,000 tickets were seized along with thousands of counterfoils. The secretary of the club was fined £50 and the money was returned to subscribers.

The draw was made on the Friday of Derby week when the £10,000 first prize went to an Egham (Surrey) housewife; second prize of £5,000 to a London civil servant, while five contestants shared the third prize of £2,500. The remaining £7,500 was distributed among 598 ticket holders – 66 receiving £73 each and 532, £5 each.

For the record, the winning order was: 1 Flying Fox (1899), 2 Papyrus (1923), 3 Galtee More (1897), 4 Captain Cuttle (1922), 5 Sunstar (1912), 6 Diamond Jubilee (1900), 7 Spearmint (1906), 8 Humorist (1921), 9 Minoru (1909) and 10 Orby (1907).

The whole operation was decidedly iffy and it was no surprise when legal proceedings were taken against its organisers, although it was only on the technicality that the tickets and accompanying literature had not carried the printer's name and address. With a maximum penalty of £5 for each illegally printed document – two million in all – hanging over them things did not look too good for the printer, Ernest Cutts, or Sidney Freeman, the publisher.

Cutts, however, pleaded ignorance and got off with a £3 fine, which was a whole lot better than ten million quid, while the summons against Freeman was dismissed after he claimed the competition was identical to a 'Golden Ballot' run by the Labour Party and which had been held to be perfectly legal. Because of this decidedly grey area the *Life* escaped prosecution, but the usual hot air was expended on the subject in the Commons where Ramsay MacDonald's Labour government was enjoying its first taste of power.

The day after the Derby, Lord Curzon, entered the chamber brandishing a copy of the *Daily Herald*, the official organ of the Labour Party, and asked the Home Secretary, Arthur Henderson, if he was aware that the paper had carried a large batch of socialist-sponsored sweeps results in its classified columns. The Tory peer then began to reel off the 'offending' organisations in alphabetical order starting with the Amalgamated Society of Brassworkers' Benevolent Fund and reaching the Hammersmith Labour Party before he ran out of steam and concluded "and some 30 other sweeps of a similar character".

Ignoring Labour cries of 'Stock Exchange!' and to the accompaniment of Conservative cheers, Curzon went on to ask Henderson if action had been taken against the organisers of these sweeps as had been the case with the Otley sweep and whether he proposed to take proceedings against the paper that had carried the results.

George Lansbury (Lab. Bow and Bromley), the founding editor of the *Herald*, then got to his feet to point out that similar information had appeared in newspapers for the last 25 to 30 years without any action being taken. While another MP chipped in mischievously: "Has the Home Secretary's attention been drawn to the fact that a member of this House has won a very considerable sum?" (the Liberal MP, Harcourt Johnstone, had a share in a £36,000 winning ticket in the Calcutta Sweep).

Amid the usual bear garden uproar that followed, Henderson replied that he had been unaware of the sweeps Curzon had mentioned and did not know if the police had taken any action against them, but he would consider the suggestion. With regard to the press, he admitted it was difficult to know where to draw the line. "There is not a single newspaper in the country that does not today report the result of one of these draws in which a member of the House was concerned," he conceded. "Am I to be asked to proceed against all of those newspapers for announcing that?"

While the politicians huffed and puffed, Duggan decided not to push his luck any further and put his schemes on hold until another attempt was made in the Dáil to legalise his sweep. This came about through a private member's bill introduced in 1929 thanks to the support of Joe McGrath who, as Minister of Labour in the first Free State government, had backed Duggan's venture from the start.

The following year the Public Charitable Hospitals Act sanctioned the setting up of a private trust to run sweepstakes for the benefit of Irish hospitals. Duggan, with his experience and contacts in the field, was an automatic choice to promote the operation together with his political ally, McGrath, a former IRA gunman who had spent time at His Majesty's pleasure for his part in the Easter Uprising of 1916.

A third and no less important figure in the enterprise was Capt Spencer Freeman, a brother of Sidney who helped Duggan set up the 'Derby Scheme' in England. An engineer by profession, Freeman was also a born organiser and entrepreneur who was to play a vital role in running and publicising the sweepstakes which, as before, were held on prestigious English races.

Once again the Manchester November Handicap was chosen for the launch, since it always attracted a large field and plenty of public interest as a major ante-post betting event that traditionally brought down the curtain on the Flat season.

Six selected hospitals were allotted 20 per cent of the pool, while a hefty 30 per cent was set aside for expenses and promoters' fees, leaving 50 per cent to be distributed in prizes. The total pool of £658,618 (£32m) far exceeded expectations which had been lowered when the British Home Office made a belated attempt to stop the flood of money flowing across the Irish Sea by instructing the Postmaster General to intercept letters addressed to the Hospitals' Trust.

This desperate 'finger in the dyke' tactic only prevented a trickle of sterling from reaching Dublin. From the 9,031 letters opened just £6,960 was returned to the would-be subscribers who quickly found other ways to dispatch their cash.

With a surplus of funds to play with, Freeman invited the editors of all the principal British papers and news agencies to attend the draw in Dublin on an all-expenses-paid trip. Feeding and watering the elite of the Street soaked up a considerable portion of the money, but the publicity it generated was worth it. Overnight, the Irish Sweep became world-famous and Chris Towler, as one of the invited guests, ensured the *Life* gave maximum coverage to the draw, which took place when the final acceptors became known five days before the race.

Delighted to be among the bevy of young nurses who had been chosen from the hospitals that were to benefit from the Sweep, the editor reported on the carefully orchestrated build-up on the eve of the draw:

> Guarded by mounted policemen, the ten boxes – exactly like ballot boxes – were removed today from bank safe deposits and taken with due impressiveness to Mansion House, where the ceremony of mixing the counterfoils began.
>
> The counterfoils, over a million of them, were emptied from the containers and spread on a number of immense tables. The mixing staff consisted of over 200 women. They stood shoulder-to-shoulder round the table shuffling heaped up papers with their fingers. Then they formed a living chain moving round the tables continually shuffling the papers. Some of them even removed their shoes and crawled among the papers…
>
> All this elaborate mixing was but a preliminary for today when the counterfoils will again be shuffled for an hour before they are placed in an immense revolving drum from which they will be drawn.

With 33 of the 78 race entries standing their ground at the final forfeit stage on the Tuesday, the draw took almost four hours to complete. It was only then that the wheeling and dealing began in earnest as those who had drawn fancied horses, and whose names and addresses were published in the press, were inundated with offers for their tickets from the big credit bookmakers and syndicates of professional punters.

The chief speculator was Arthur Bendir, the head of Ladbrokes, who formed a syndicate with Martin Benson, Sidney Freeman and others to buy shares in as many tickets as possible since the odds were greatly in their favour as they were guaranteed at least a portion of the £49,143 that was to be split equally among the 'also rans'.

The first major beneficiary of the Sweep was a night porter in a Cork hotel, who drew the 7-1 ante-post favourite, Saracen, and accepted £10,000 (£490,000) for a half share in his ticket. No sooner had he done so than the rains came down turning the ground against Saracen who drifted out to 20-1 on the day and finished 13th. Result: one very happy ex-night porter.

The other side of the coin was represented by those who had drawn outsiders and were anxious to see their horses in the line-up. As the race's prize money (1st £1,276, 2nd £125, 3rd £75) was paltry in comparison to what ticket holders stood to win, owners of the 'no hopers' were offered shares in tickets to run their nags. How much these incentives boosted the field is uncertain, but only five of the final acceptors dropped out leaving 28 horses to take their chance on ground that was barely fit for racing.

All this excitement was played out against the background of a nail-biting finish to the jockeys' championship with Freddie Fox going into the final day with a 127 to 126 lead over Gordon Richards. Walter Meeds, who had become the *Life's* chief SP reporter in 1927, summed up what was at stake as he wrote:

> Never in the history of the Manchester meeting ... has a day's sport been fraught with such vital importance as that of today. Even those with only a smattering of racing knowledge are interested in the November Handicap ... which has achieved worldwide notoriety as a result of its connection with the Irish Hospitals Sweepstake.
>
> By 2pm, weather permitting, the destination of undreamed of wealth will have been decided and a fortunate few will benefit from the sporting instincts of the many. Naturally such a colossal undertaking has created a deal of adverse criticism in some directions, while in other places nothing but praise has been heard about those far-seeing enough to blaze the golden trail.
>
> Whether the sequel will be the sanctioning of State lotteries or sweepstakes similar to the one under discussion only the future can disclose. After all, what harm has been done? None to my way of thinking.

And certainly none to the Dublin hospitals that benefited to the tune of £131,798 (£6.5m), nor to the three Belfast men who clubbed together to buy the ticket that drew the 25-1 chance, Glorious Devon, who, with Gordon Richards putting up 2lb overweight at 7st 5lb, ploughed through the mud to win by three lengths.*

It was also a bookmakers' benefit as Arthur Bendir's syndicate had bought a half share in the winning ticket for £3,300 so when the first prize of £204,764 was split up, the Belfast men received £34,127 each, while Bendir and his associates pocketed £102,382.

---

* Having also won the first race, Richards was now one up on Fox, but his rival fought back to draw level in the fourth race, before he took the fifth and the championship on the odds-on Isthmus. The crowd went wild and Freddie responded not with a flying dismount, but by "removing his cap and waving it".

The £81,905 second prize went to a Canadian in Vancouver who, under the laws of his country, faced the prospect of his winnings being forfeited to any informer who cared to take the case to court, while the £40,953 third prize was won by a Worksop widow. The success of the Sweep resulted in more questions being asked in parliament, and when the Home Office again failed to give any encouragement for a British sweep angry letters started to appear in the *Life*. One exasperated reader wrote:

> Here we have some of the finest institutions in the world for attending to the sick and injured, and nearly all of them handicapped through lack of funds, while at the same time the means are at hand that would produce sufficient money to put them all on a sound financial basis. People are already talking about the Grand National Steeplechase, which is fixed for March 27 next, and but for our antediluvian law that prohibits the holding of sweeps, the vast sum that might be kept at home for the benefit of our hospitals will go to another country.*

And that sum was vast indeed as the Grand National sweep dwarfed the inaugural one by more than £1m. With their cut increased to 25 per cent of the pool, the Irish hospitals benefited by £438,990 (£21.5m), while 25 per cent of the first prize of £354,544 went to an Italian café owner in Battersea, but, once again, it was the Bendir syndicate that cleaned up. Their shares in 28 of the 43 runners included three-quarters of the winning ticket on Grakle, and realised an overall profit of £250,000. The second and third prizes went abroad with £177,272 going to Buffalo, USA, and £118,181 to Cape Town.

Bendir apart, the shrewdest move was made by a 60-year-old Durham miner who sold 14/15th of his ticket on the 5-1 favourite Easter Hero for £17,000 (£850,000) and saw the dual Cheltenham Gold Cup hero brought down at Becher's on the second circuit.

In order to give more people a winning chance, the distribution of prizes was radically altered for the 1931 Derby. With 33 final acceptors, the prize fund of £1,900,544 was split up into 19 units of £100,000. Each unit gave £30,000, £15,000 and £10,000 to the first three horses, while there were 570 prizes (19 x 30) of £833 for those who had drawn the remaining 30 acceptors, plus 3,800 cash prizes of £100.

This time the draw for the horses took six hours, and another two days for the cash prizes. The winning ticket numbers listed under the respective horses filled a whole page of the *Life* and the one-line ticket details for the £100 prizes took up 18 columns (three pages) of closely packed type.

There had never been anything like it, and with each succeeding year the pool grew bigger despite the concerted efforts of the British postal authorities and customs officials to stem the flood of incoming tickets and outgoing cash and counterfoils.

A huge, clandestine network sprang up around the distribution and sale of the tickets as they were smuggled across the border into Ulster in coffins and milk churns and by all manner of ingenious dodges. From Belfast they enjoyed a clear run to the mainland and from Dublin they came in by the suitcase load on fishing boats and ferries.

There was also the tri-annual 'Dash to Dublin' to return the counterfoils before the closing date. Sweepstakes agents, drawn from the large Irish communities in Britain, were on a 20 per cent

---

* In the autumn of 1932 Spencer Freeman left the Hospitals' Trust to set up a sweep on the Continent to aid British hospitals, but shortly afterwards he rejoined the Irish organisation. He explained in the *Life*: "I was prepared to go into the question of raising money in this way for British charities. Now I find that such is the opposition, not only on the part of the government, but also on the part of many influential people interested in English charities who are opposed to accepting money except through traditional sources, that I have decided not to proceed."

commission for every book of tickets they sold and they descended on the Irish capital in their thousands, forming huge queues outside the Plaza ballroom, the main receiving centre in the city.

In February 1933 it was estimated as many as 5,000 made the 'dash' with their Grand National counterfoils. Spencer Freeman was forced to increase his clerical staff to 3,000 and extend the closing deadline by two days to cope with the rush, but by this time the Free State hospitals were among the best equipped in the world thanks largely to the speculative instincts of the Brits.

After the 1932 Derby Sweep had brought in a record £4,128,486, it was stated in the Commons that British subscribers had contributed £13,285,000 (£650m), or roughly 75 per cent of the total, to the first six Irish Sweeps. It was primarily to deal with this embarrassing situation that the government set up a Royal Commission on Lotteries and Betting in the summer of 1932, and in March 1934 Lord Hailsham introduced a Betting and Lotteries Bill that embodied many of the Commission's recommendations.

Driven through parliament by a government that was locked in a bitter dispute with the Irish Free State over a £100m debt,* the Act legalised the small lotteries that had always been run by social clubs, churches and offices, provided they did not offer cash prizes and their profits went to a good cause, but outlawed large-scale lotteries such as the Irish Sweep and provided for severe penalties to be imposed on anyone selling tickets in them or giving publicity to them.

Its immediate effect was to impose a news blackout on the Sweep in the British press. Stories on the lucky winners were taboo as they might be "calculated to act as an inducement to persons to participate," while Irish papers for sale in the UK were censored with all reference to the ▉▉▉ blotted out. Even the Irish radio was jammed when it tried to transmit news on Dick Duggan's brainchild. But the tickets still got through, although eventually, with the oxygen of publicity denied to him, Freeman switched the main focus for ticket sales to the United States, despite the fact that the Sweep was also illegal there.

Ironically, Duggan, who had done so much to help Irish hospitals, died of cancer in 1935 at the age of 57, but his legacy lived on in the benefits the Sweep brought to his country and also to Irish racing through the driving force of its most influential and ardent advocate, Joe McGrath, who was to win the Epsom Derby in 1951 with Arctic Prince.

In 1962, McGrath transferred the Sweep on the Derby to its Irish counterpart and with an initial sponsorship injection of £30,000 (£480,000) from the Hospitals' Trust coupled with Freeman's promotional genius, the Curragh classic was transformed into an international event that placed Irish racing on a footing with the best in the world.

But while the Irish Sweeps Derby flourished, the glamour and excitement of the Sweep itself gradually faded and in 1987 it was replaced by a State lottery. Meanwhile, as the British National Health Service continued to struggle against ever rising costs, the politicians in Westminster's House of Humbug continued to dither and dally over the question of a national lottery.

---

* On coming to power in Ireland in 1932, Eamon de Valera had suspended the payment of annuities due to the British Exchequer under the Land Purchase Acts of 1926. Ramsay MacDonald's National Government retaliated by slapping a 20 per cent tax (soon increased to 40%) on all livestock imported from the Free State. Irish bloodstock breeders were faced with ruin and de Valera was forced to subsidise them at a rate of 20 per cent until he finally negotiated a settlement with Britain in 1938.

BATTLING AGAINST THE OLD GUARD

T URF REFORM was as high on the agenda of the *Sporting Life* during the inter-war years as it had been when the paper was first launched in 1859, and the task of achieving much needed improvements was certainly no easier. Autocratic and conservative to the core, the Jockey Club opposed each and every call for change that emanated from a campaigning press.

The louder the calls, the more obdurate the authorities became. At times it seemed to be a battle of wills as Fleet Street's finest chiselled away at the sport's deficiencies and abuses, but gradually the persistent drip, drip, drip of printer's ink began to wear away the Club's resistance and one by one the old bastions began to crumble.

In 1920, more than half a century after the *Life* had first condemned the practice, owners were no longer permitted to race under an assumed name.

In 1927, the rule that allowed a jockey to 'stop' a horse in favour of another in the same ownership was scrapped when all horses were required to run on their merits.

In 1929, the absurd 'void nominations' rule was done away with, and in 1936 a long and hard-fought press campaign finally led to the appointment of stipendiary stewards.

The use of professionals to advise honorary racecourse stewards was long overdue. The latter's ignorance and wilful neglect of their duties constantly brought racing into disrepute as when, in 1915, an objection at Gatwick had to be carried over to the Jockey Club's London offices the following day because one of the stewards had left the course early. The weariness of Morley-Brown's comments on the matter spoke volumes:

> It occurs to me that it is time once more to protest against the practice so common amongst stewards of departing before the last race is run and so leaving the contest to take care of itself. In this latest instance Sir Claude de Crespigny, one of the two stewards officiating for the day, remained at his post to the end, but he, of course, could not adjudicate upon the objection alone and as, apparently, there was no substitute available to take the place of his fellow steward the matter had necessarily to stand over.
>
> The amount of inconvenience this sort of thing causes all round is very great and although it is gratifying that on this occasion the matter was settled within 24 hours, even that brief delay ought not to have been necessary.

The Jockey Club finally addressed the matter in 1922 when even the senior steward, Sir Samuel Scott, acknowledged there were "too many dummy stewards who either knew very little about racing or never attended a meeting,"[1] a remark that gave Augur the opportunity to renew his call for 'stipes':

> It is for this reason that the appointment of paid stewards has been so frequently advocated. The agitation has not yet born fruit, but it is gratifying to find the subject is arresting the attention of the Turf rulers … The question of inconsistent and suspicious running was also dealt with, and the difficulties of the local stewards emphasised. These difficulties are really the strongest argument in favour of paid stewards.

Local stewards are unable, under their powers, to effectively investigate cases in which the vastly improved form of a horse is involved. In other words what happens at one meeting is no concern of those officiating at another. With stipendiary stewards it would be entirely different. These would go the round of the meetings, like other officials who are paid for work performed.

There was, of course, the question of funding. When, in 1931, the Jockey Club limply proposed that a scheme for the employment of paid stewards' secretaries should be drawn up "at some future date" it was anticipated the money would come from the Tote. But as the machine proved to be more of a lame duck than a golden goose, the idea was put on hold until the legalisation of off-course credit betting through Tote Investors Ltd in 1936 provided the Racecourse Betting Control Board with the necessary funds.

It was not only in the stewards' room that there was need for a drastic shake-up. In 1920 the paper renewed its pre-war campaign for the appointment of an official supervisor of entries owing to an alarming increase in the number of well-backed horses running in, and often winning, races for which they were not qualified.

Both bookmakers and backers suffered on these occasions. On-course layers had usually paid out on the result before the objection (which could be made up to two weeks after the race) was lodged, while punters who bet with credit bookmakers would have their accounts debited when the objection was sustained.

Following the disqualification of three short-priced winners (4-7, 5-4 and 2-1) in the first two months of 1920, Augur returned to the old complaint with renewed vigour:

> Probably in the long history of the Turf there have never been so many disqualifications on the grounds of wrongful entry as during the present jumping season. No wonder that backers and layers alike are in a state of ferment and have largely lost confidence in official management of the business side of racing … surely it ought to be the duty of someone at the Registry Office to point out the error and refuse the entry.

The fact was that no official was required to check the entries. It was left to the racing press to monitor each meeting and while the majority of 'not qualified' horses were spotted in time, there were always a few that slipped through the net. By the autumn of 1921 the *Life* was weeding out ineligible entries on a weekly basis, but it missed Fiddle Bridge who won a handicap chase at Nottingham in October only to be disqualified a few days later because the race had been for horses that had not won a chase of £80 and Fiddle Bridge had won three such races in the space of a week in 1920.

Six weeks later the headline 'Wrong Nominations At Haydock Park' alerted readers to the fact that two horses were not qualified to run in the Wigan Steeplechase which was for horses that had not won a race over three miles or upwards and both Shannon Vale and Young Brian had won over three miles in 1920. Yet, despite this advanced warning, Young Brian was allowed to run in the race although he got no further than the second fence where he refused. It was only then that the stewards acted on the matter and took the unusual step of issuing a notice to the press.

In view of the number of similar cases that had occurred recently, the statement could only be explained by the amount of port the officials must have downed over lunch. It read: 'In view of the fact that this is the first case of its kind that has been dealt with under National Hunt rules the stewards only imposed a fine of £5 on the trainer, Bickley, for carelessness in addition to a caution.' The *Life's* response was direct and withering:

Torpidity – studied, we think – seems to pervade all departments of officialdom in horse racing – not a sporadic infectious complaint like influenza … but a permanent supineness which stops action no matter whether dictated by the interests of sport, the interests of justice or by the crudest common sense…

The question will naturally be asked 'Why was Young Brian allowed to run when the authorities were apprised of his ineligibility?' And I put a further query. Whether it is to be understood that in future under National Hunt Rules a horse that is unqualified can run in a race with no worse punishment than the infliction of a fine of £5 [£170]? If so, there is surely an El Dorado for those who dare, now and then, to enter an unqualified horse for a race with the chance of allowing layers to wager on a 'cert'.

This was dynamite. It implied that trainers, deliberately running an ineligible horse, could tip off a compliant bookmaker who could then lay the horse until the cows came home safe in the knowledge that it was certain to be disqualified if it won. The fact that officials and stewards might be complicit in such a plot was barely conceivable. But three weeks later, on New Year's Day 1922, the *Life's* form expert who hid his identity behind the initials 'GH', pointed out that since the Fiddle Bridge case the paper had highlighted 12 instances of horses not qualified to run and there were two more at Manchester that afternoon.

The New Year Chase was for horses that had not won a steeplechase of £90 or more, and Hectic had picked up £97 for winning a chase at Hexham in October, while Padraig, the winner of a handicap hurdle at Limerick Junction during the summer, was in a race confined to horses that had not won a handicap hurdle!

Because the respective owner-trainers of the horses involved, Adam Scott and J P Hogan, made entries on an extensive scale, the *Life's* man felt they could be forgiven the occasional mistake, but there was no excuse for the handicapper who had presumably assessed Padraig on the very race that made him ineligible for the Manchester event. In renewing his call for stricter scrutiny of entries, he declared:

Before their last meeting the National Hunt Committee were apprised of the scandal, but for reasons of their own … they remained slumbering at their posts. Insufficient proof of the evil could be pleaded earlier on, perhaps, but the plea is no longer a good one. Case after case has been given in our columns and writer after writer in reputable journals has supported our appeal, appreciating the damage done to horseracing by the looseness of the methods of those who control its destinies.

The following day it became clear that 'GH' had been casting pearls before swine as the headlines 'Hectic Disqualified / Sporting Life's Warning Ignored' revealed an astonishing story of official incompetence – or was it connivance?

The New Year had not cut its teeth … when the 'object lessons' about which I was writing yesterday were crowned with one of the most glaring cases of a wrong entry leading to disaster which it has ever been my painful duty to chronicle.

Hectic ran in the first race decided anywhere in this country in the year 1922. It was tipped by many sporting prophets as the likely winner, but it fell to the lot of the *Sporting Life* to point out that however well the horse performed it could not win the New Year Steeplechase … The voice of the *Sporting Life* is heard as clearly in Manchester as in London and many of the officials on the course must have known what it would mean to backers and bookmakers if Hectic was allowed to run…

We do not forget that the Manchester executive had special reason to be on the alert in regard to entry surprises … My readers will remember that in 1919 Powerful came in first for the Rothschild Maiden Plate at Castle Irwell, but was disqualified as the horse was not a maiden at closing.

It seemed inconceivable that the stewards had allowed Hectic to take part in the race and that Adam Scott had insisted on running the mare even after the paper's on-course representative had again warned him that she was not qualified.

Bookmakers were as surprised as any when Hectic was declared a runner and at first offered 5-1 about her. Under ordinary circumstances this would have been a generous price for a horse that had won eight of her last ten races, but the weight of (uninformed) punters' money soon forced her down to 5-2. When Hectic duly obliged, the trainer of the runner up, Dunstanburgh, promptly objected on the grounds that the mare was not qualified, finally forcing the stewards to act and disqualify her. A serious breakdown in communications then added to the fiasco as it was reported:

It was known by many that the objection lodged by Threlfell, as trainer of Dunstanburgh, had been sustained, but some considerable time elapsed before it was signalled on the number boards. In the meantime scores of bookmakers had paid out considerable sums over Hectic, which … they will never see back. It is believed the notice did appear subsequently, but the high wind dislodged it from the frame and many backers of Dunstanburgh must have remained in ignorance that he had been awarded the race until learning of the fact from the evening papers.

Scott was fined £25 for carelessness and afterwards apologised through the paper to those who had lost money on Hectic, adding, cryptically: "Having so many animals, I am a very busy man, to say nothing of the trouble the income-tax people give me."

As the repercussions of the debacle rolled on into a second day, Augur pointed a surprisingly feeble finger at those who had fined Scott by remarking: "it is not altogether clear that the stewards themselves were not guilty of negligence in failing to inquire into the circumstances before instead of after the race."

On the same day, GH returned to the fray with yet another instance of a wrong entry (this time at Bogside) and, in referring to "the chorus of support for our demand," he quoted comments from almost every noted racing journalist in the country. He then followed up his earlier insinuation that the unscrupulous might be mining gold from an El Dorado of ineligible entries with an even more pointed accusation:

There is, as we know, an authority that, like Caesar's wife, is 'above suspicion', but if that authority is persistently obdurate, wilfully deaf to reason, when the public see this authority's apathy imitated, reflected and – what shall I say? – *probably* taken advantage of, am not I justified in hinting that people who may have been regarded hitherto as honourable men may fall under the suspicion of being actuated by ulterior motives?

Two weeks after this damning indictment, the NH Committee found the clerk of the course at Manchester, Cecil Frail (who also officiated at Haydock where Young Brian had been allowed to run), "culpably negligent, in that he took no steps in the matter" after he had been told there was "some doubt" as to whether Hectic was qualified to run. He was fined £25 and severely cautioned as to his future conduct as a licensed official.

The stewards, who had overall control of the meeting, were never called to account and a supervisor of entries was never officially appointed, although there is no doubt that entries began to be checked more thoroughly because there was a sudden and dramatic drop in the number of unqualified horses being sifted out by the *Life*.

Nevertheless, there were still a few that escaped detection at the Registry Office and at Newmarket's July meeting in 1922 the paper spotted that Most Beautiful, who had won the Nassau Stakes worth £807 two years earlier, was in the Milton Handicap for horses that had not won a race of £500. But the case that created the greatest stir was unearthed 12 months after the Hectic affair. By a strange coincidence it was also at Manchester, it was also in the New Year Chase and was also trained by Adam Scott, but this time the *Life's* warning was heeded and Scott was fined another 'pony' for his 'carelessness'.

While the paper could claim success in its demand for stipendiary stewards and at least a moral victory in its campaign for the stricter supervision of entries, it found the old guard firmly entrenched in other areas as it continued to press for reforms that could only benefit the sport. Following a spate of abandonments because of snow and ice at the beginning of 1928, it suggested that the NH Committee should grant new dates for the fixtures that had been lost to compensate the racecourses and "the thousands of folk who are directly or indirectly dependent upon racing for their means of livelihood," but the response it received to its proposal was in keeping with the wintry weather:

> Discussing the matter with several racing officials at Plumpton, however, one of our representatives was informed that applications for additional fixtures were pretty certain to be turned down. But why? … During the next two months, racing on the first two days of the week is practically confined to the Midlands, while the Fridays and Saturdays are devoted to the South…
>
> What logical argument, then, can be advanced against a few additional dates being granted to the South, say, at the beginning of the week and to the North at the end? … The idea strikes us as being both practical and practicable and we commend it to the powers that be. Racing just now requires all the encouragement it can get.

Indeed it did. Attendances had been badly hit by the betting tax and the counter attraction of greyhound racing, but in a follow-up story the next day it was stated that while most clerks of the courses were in favour of the proposal they accepted that "the ruling body of the sport would not be likely to entertain applications for new fixtures which might lead to over-crowding of programmes."

During the *Life's* early years such concerns would not have arisen as it was common practice to allot new dates for meetings lost to the weather, but such flexibility had long since ceased to operate. So it was that official intransigence denied Easter Hero the chance of winning his third Cheltenham Gold Cup when the NH Meeting was frozen off in 1931 and six years later robbed Golden Miller of a likely sixth successive Gold Cup victory when the second and third days were wiped out by snow and rain, although, perversely, the NH Chase was saved by transferring it to the April meeting.

The paper met with a similar negative response later in 1928 when it proposed the introduction of evening racing during the summer to stem the flood of racegoers going to the dogs. This time there was opposition to the idea from racing's professionals and it was not until 1947 that the Jockey Club gave Hamilton Park the go-ahead to hold the first evening meeting in Britain. As anticipated, it proved popular with the public and it was not long before racecourses throughout the country were applying for evening fixtures.

The list of similar innovations suggested by the *Life* is a long one and the initial impact they had on the ruling bodies were invariably the same; they bounced off them like paper pellets off a dinosaur, but no attempt was ever made to put the proposals directly to the authorities. At the time such a move would have been unthinkable.

"There was no liaison between the Jockey Club and the racecourse Press. The one did not want it; the other did not expect it,"[2] instead, journalists merely floated their suggestions for reform in their paper and hoped that they would be taken up – eventually.

On the eve of the 1934 Flat season, Meyrick Good excitedly led the paper with what he obviously felt would be a godsend to racing and punters alike:

> The Lincoln executive have a great opportunity to make the first important handicap of the season more popular with backers by creating a precedent and arranging for the draw for places to take place overnight. Positions at the starting gate could then be shown on the day's racecard. There is nothing in the rules to prevent this innovation. It is done in other countries and is generally regarded as a boon.
>
> It may be argued that some horses may drop out between the time the draw takes place and the decision of the race, but it would be an easy matter for horses to move up a peg or two. An owner friend of mine races every winter in South Africa and he tells me that the draw for the Durban Handicap is always published on the card and is known to owners with horses engaged in the race on the night before the race. Why should England always lag behind in such matters?

Why indeed! But Good should have known better, his suggestion was far too revolutionary for the Jockey Club and the following day his anticipated scoop proved a damp squib doused by the short announcement:

> Mr Stanley Ford, the Lincoln Clerk of the Course, declined to create a precedent by making the draw for the Lincolnshire Handicap yesterday. Although there is nothing in the Rules of Racing to prevent the draw being made the day before the race, it was thought inadvisable to vary the existing procedure until such time as overnight declaration of runners is made compulsory.

But overnight declarations were still a long way off as many owners and trainers objected to having to commit themselves to running their horses 24 hours before a race. In order to stave off the growing demands from press and public for accurate racecards, trainers had agreed to supply details of their intended runners and riders to the Press Association, which relayed the information on to their subscribers, but the system was always open to abuse by those who would inform the PA that their horse would not run when, in fact, they were planning to land a mighty coup with it.

When a 'surprise' runner that was not among the 'probables' listed in the newspapers bolted home there was an inevitable 'we wuz robbed' outcry from off-course punters. But although the Jockey Club could see that a 24-hour declaration system would bring more money into racing through Tote Investors Ltd, they refused to align themselves with the rest of the racing world as they, once again, put their own interests (those of the owner) before that of the sport they professed to serve. It was a classic case of cutting off their nose to spite their face.

A STAFF OF EXPERTS

BETWEEN the wars the *Life* was particularly well served by a solid body of scribes who pooled their talents to cover every aspect of sport. As with any team of players they all had their strengths and weaknesses. Some were slow but precise, others fast but slipshod. There were young reporters who were slaves to their art, and hardened hacks who churned out their copy in a never-ending race to beat their deadline and get back to their local before closing time.

In 1934, when the paper underwent a minor facelift, it was able to boast:

Regularly employed in the task of reporting and commentating upon events of the day will be upwards of 100 *Sporting Life* writers and critics. No other journal in the world has such a staff of purely sporting experts to supply up-to-the-minute reports on all that is happening in the world of sport.

Most of these 'experts' were short on literary flair, but they wrote with an authority that could only be gained from an in-depth knowledge of their subject. Many had participated in their own particular field of sport as amateurs, some were involved in an administrative capacity and one or two were still competing at the top level.

Meyrick George Bruton Good could hardly have been more intimately connected with racing. Following the death of his father, he had been adopted as a child by his famous grandfather, the Woodyates trainer William Day, and his association with the great horses of the past dated back to 1882 when, at the age of five, he had been lifted onto the back of Foxhall, who had been ridden to victory the previous season by no less an immortal than Fred Archer.

Despite this early initiation in the saddle, he failed to pose a threat to his cousin, the six times champion jockey Morny Cannon, although he did have a few rides on the Flat as an amateur before WWI. More successful as an owner, he had a number of decent horses that won him some 50 races over as many years, and in 1941 he became secretary of the re-launched Racehorse Owners Association (ROA), while he was also a director and later chairman of Fontwell Park, laid out in 1924 by his uncle, the Arundel trainer Alfred Day.

Immensely proud of his family connections – hence the title of his first book of memoirs, *Good Days* – he may not have been able to match the stylish fluency of Sidney Galtrey, 'Hotspur' of the *Daily Telegraph*, or the concise phrasing of Jimmy Park, 'Ajax' of the *Evening Standard*, but he had some of the best connections in the business. At a time when many hacks went in awe of the ruling authorities, Good was on friendly terms with most Jockey Club members, while he had the respect and trust of the leading owners, trainers and jockeys, and they were the contacts that mattered.

A firm believer in keeping himself in the best company and running his horses in the worst, he had an air of aloofness, which did not make him the most popular man in the pressroom particularly as he considered himself to be a cut above many of his fellow scribes. One story that offers an insight into his character tells of the time he was seen in deep conversation with a leading trainer of a Cesarewitch fancy. A rival newshound, eager to pick up a few titbits of information, hovered around until the discussion was over and then sidled up to the great man to query: "What did he tell you Meyrick?" "Tell me?" snorted Good indignantly, "Tell me! He was *asking* me."

 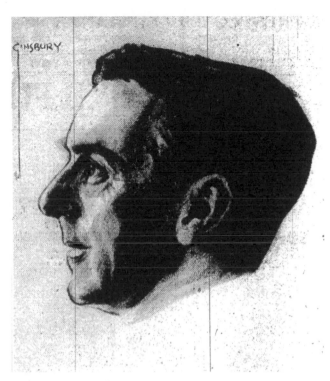

Two crusty individuals: (Left) Meyrick Good ('Man on the Spot') wrote for the *Life* for a record 60 years before retiring in 1957. (Right) Walter Meeds, the paper's chief SP reporter from 1927-61 – the portraits are by Joseph Ginsbury whose charcoal drawings of notable personalities appeared in the *Life* on a regular basis from 1929 to 1934.

For many years Good compiled, with the help of trainers, a table that gave the vital statistics – height, girth measurement, depth of bone and distance from hip to hock – of the leading Derby contenders. Published on the day of the race under such headings as 'Form to the Inch', the figures were of purely academic interest, but they could also bring in a valuable tip from the trainers as they did in 1954 when Joe Lawson added: "If my charge runs as well as he measures, he will win."

Those who took the hint were rewarded with a 33-1 winner as his charge – who measured 15.3½hh, girth 71in, bone 8in, hip to hock 39in – was Never Say Die who gave the 18-year-old Lester Piggott the first of his 30 classic successes.

When Meyrick Good died at the age of 85 in May 1962, Ben Clements, the last of the six editors he had served under, described him as "A great character; a wonderful colleague." It was not a sentiment shared by Walter Meeds who loathed the man with a passion; a feeling that was reciprocated in spades.

For more than 30 years these two crusty individuals conducted a cold war against each other that lowered the temperature of the pressroom by several degrees – no mean feat in a hothouse environment that not only promotes healthy rivalries, but can also incubate petty jealousies of a particularly virulent strain.

In the case of Good v Meeds, their mutual antipathy was fuelled by a head-on clash of personalities. Meeds was a dour, gritty northerner who had spent some 20 years on the *Sheffield Daily Telegraph* and the *Yorkshire Telegraph and Star* before he joined the *Life* as chief sub-editor in 1922.

Five years later he took over as chief SP reporter and occasionally ventured outside the betting ring to report on other sports. He had been an accomplished athlete in his youth winning medals for boxing, swimming, running and football, and his great love was the world-famous Powderhall sprint in Edinburgh which he never missed covering.

A secretive operator who kept himself to himself, Meeds was best described as "a professional of professionals. He did not wear his heart on his sleeve, nor in any other visible position either, but though he could be remorseless as an enemy, he could be a good friend to those who succeeded in winning his confidence."[1]

Two other stalwarts of the racing staff were Willie Standring and Sam Long whose careers were interlinked through the papers they served and the positions they filled.

Born in Oldham in 1869, Standring started out as a teenage chronicler for Accrington Football Club before he joined Edward Hulton's *Athletic News* working under its editor Jack Bentley, the long-time president of the Football League. In 1902 he moved on to the *Sporting Chronicle* and for the next 20 years wrote the Kettledrum column, while he doubled up as the paper's coursing correspondent, 'Donald', during the winter months.

In 1922, Standring switched camps and joined the *Life* as 'Augur', filling that position for ten years before he took over from Sam Long as 'Warren Hill', a column he was still writing up until a few weeks before his death in May 1945.

Strongly independent and forthright in his dealings with others, Standring remained to the last a chubby, ruddy-faced, jolly little man who "never made the mistake of being unduly influenced by what he heard, preferring to be guided by what he had seen on the racecourse and on the training grounds."[2]

Robert Carwardine Long, (known to one and all as 'Sam'), was a tall, erect son of a Wiltshire farming family who entered journalism after serving as an army instructor at Sandhurst during WWI. He started off on the *Sportsman* writing the 'Vigilant' column before he replaced Standring as 'Kettledrum' on the *Chronicle* and in 1929 he joined the *Life* as 'Warren Hill' with a formidable reputation for picking out winners.

Unfailingly kind and helpful, he formed some valuable and long-lasting friendships during his four years at 'Headquarters' where he was respected as a shrewd judge of form. At a time when the Jockey Club employed a dozen handicappers each with their own opinion of a horse's ability, trainers would often ask Long for advice on where to run their horses, and when the nursery season came around they were guided by his two-year-old handicap which was later published at regular intervals in the *Life*.

With his knowledge of the form book, it was only natural that Capt. R C Long, as his byline appeared (he was promoted to Major when he rejoined the army in 1941), should eventually take over the Augur column and he quickly gained a faithful following that included the bookmaker, William Hill, who never failed to read the pundit's summing up of a big race.

Hill would even consider hedging any outstanding bets he held on Augur's selections as Long had an impressive record in handicaps such as the Cambridgeshire in which he tipped three winners in four years from 1936-39 – Dan Bulger (7-1), Artist's Prince (13-1) and Gyroscope (100-6). During the same period, he twice won the naps competition against 17 other national and provincial tipsters, and was runner-up to his stable companion Jimmy Cox ('Solon') in 1937 and third to Meyrick Good ('Man on the Spot') in 1938, realising an impressive level-stake profit of almost 100 points over the four seasons.

Long also had the distinction of having given the first racecourse commentaries in Britain. This took place at Doncaster in May 1933 when Councillor Wilburn, the go-ahead chairman of the race committee, introduced the facility chiefly for the benefit of racegoers in the cheap enclosures who could see very little of the racing.

The commentaries were much appreciated by the vast majority, but when repeated at the St Leger meeting 'influential patrons' in the members' enclosure complained they distracted them from 'reading' the races. To placate them a compromise was reached whereby the sound was cut off from the grandstand but broadcast at full strength to the massed crowd on the inside of the course. But the innovation was a step too far for the Jockey Club which actively opposed commentaries until they were once again tried on an experimental basis at Goodwood in 1952.

With furlong markers erected over the final half mile to help the commentator (in this case *Raceform's* Bob Haynes), the broadcasts were a success and one more little step out of the dark ages was made the following year when they were brought into general use.

In addition to its racing staff, the *Life* employed some of the most respected sports writers in the country. Its chief football correspondent for half a century was George Wagstaffe Simmons, one of the foremost authorities on the game in Britain.

Player, official, administrator and legislator, Wagstaffe Simmons had represented Hertfordshire on the FA Council from 1901-27 and was a member of the International Selection Committee and Rules Revisions Committee for a similar number of years. He had refereed at every level of the game from junior cup-ties to internationals and was manager of the British team that won the 1912 Olympic tournament in Stockholm.

A fine amateur player himself when he turned out as centre-half for St Albans and Hertford in the final decades of the nineteenth century, he was chairman of Hertfordshire FA for over 40 years and was also vice-chairman of Tottenham Hotspur from 1944 until his death in 1954 when he was still writing leading articles for the *Life* at the age of 87.

GWS was no less talented as a cricketer and for many years he was an automatic choice for the Gentlemen of Hertfordshire and other local county teams. He wrote on the game under the pseudonym of 'Cover Point' and also liked to diversify as the paper's drama critic when the opportunity arose.

From the time he joined the *Life* in 1905, he fought many battles in an effort to protect the integrity of football, his *bête noir* being transfer fees. At the beginning of the century he was responsible for introducing measures to limit them to £350 (£31,500), and although the clubs got around the rules in various ways, he never gave up his attempts to control them. His last article, written a week before he died, offered the FA an eight-point solution to what he saw as an insidious problem but, as he anticipated at the time, his proposals were never taken up.

While his involvement with the administrative side of football may have compromised his writing on occasions, from the time he left the FA Council in 1927, Simmons was never afraid to criticise his former colleagues if the need arose. Indeed, two issues over which he held widely differing views to those of his fellow Council members hastened his departure from that body.

During the summer of 1927 he gave his backing to the *Life's* campaign to have football players numbered as they were in rugby, but in the face of such die-hard opposition from the likes of the FA secretary, Fredrick Wall – "Very undesirable and quite unnecessary" – and Spurs manager, Billy Minter – "Those who attend our matches at White Hart Lane are familiar with the game and they know in which position a man is playing. As his name is on the card that is all that is required."[3] – it was not until 1939 that the Football League finally voted by 24-20 to make the wearing of numbered strips compulsory.

Simmons was also strongly critical of the FA's demand that clubs should not lease out their grounds for dog racing, an edict that backfired in spectacular fashion when Wembley was bought by a greyhound consortium in September 1927, forcing the FA Council to withdraw its order. Five years later, however, its Emergency Committee inexplicably proposed: "That clubs in membership of the Football Association must not sub-let their grounds for the purpose of being used for greyhound or speedway racing."

At a time when many clubs were facing bankruptcy due to the depression, it seemed perverse to deny them this valuable lifeline and the *Life's* man predictably poured scorn on the proposal:

> The resolution is to be considered by the Council that have arranged a meeting for themselves in London on Friday so that they may attend the England v. Scotland match at Wembley the following day! Do the Emergency Committee of the FA Council know that Wembley is one of the chief centres in England for greyhound and speedway racing?...
>
> I do know that some Association clubs have been assisted to a very liberal extent by owners of tracks used for the two sports they are asked to ban. The FA with its six figures of surplus assets, does not assist any club to the extent of the smallest coin of the realm. Suppose others are willing, for the sake of football, to come to the rescue, where is the ground for the proposed embargo?
>
> During the past ten years the FA have made a profit out of the matches played at Wembley of between £60,000 and £70,000. To be consistent they should not have permitted themselves to make a penny profit from them.
>
> What a farce it all is! I believe in calling a spade a spade, and my opinion is that to pass the resolution asked for by the Emergency Committee next Friday would be a humbugging, pettifogging and unjustifiable attempt to besmirch sports that are just as honestly and just as well conducted as Association football.

Faced with this public rebuke from such a respected authority, the Emergency Committee was left with no option – it withdrew its resolution.

While Simmons was able to draw on his years of experience to add gravitas and sound judgement to his articles, Thomas H Wisdom had all the vitality and exuberance of youth on his side when he became motoring editor of the *Life* at the age of 23 in 1930.

Attached to the *Daily Herald*, which had been acquired by Odhams in 1929, Wisdom was not only a talented writer, but he had the invaluable asset of being able to compete with success in the sport he wrote about. During a racing career that spanned 40 years he competed in all the great events winning his classes in many of them. His record included 25 Monte Carlo rallies, doing best overall when second with his co-driver, Donald Healey, in 1952; a dozen assaults on the Le Mans 24-hour marathon in which he set the 1,500cc record in 1950, and nine Mille Miglias, Italy's lethal 1,000-mile road race in which he won the Grand Turismo class on three occasions.

He drove every sort of car from the MG Midget and the Austin A40, to the Aston Martin DB II and the famous Jaguar XK120 in which he led for most of the way in the 1953 Portuguese Grand Prix before his brakes started to fail and he faded into third place behind Felice Bonetto in an Alfa Romeo.

It did not take Tommy Wisdom long to make his mark as a scribe behind the wheel. Less than a year after he started to write for the *Life* he was brought in as a last-minute replacement driver for Dudley Froy, who broke an arm when he crashed during practice for the RAC Tourist Trophy on the Ards circuit outside Belfast. It was Wisdom's first road race and he had just 24 hours to get used to handling Froy's powerful Invicta which combined Rolls Royce quality with Bentley performance, although, on this particular occasion, it fell short on reliability. He reported:

> Just before 11 o'clock the 45 cars which are to battle for Britain, Italy and Germany over the 410 miles of twisting roads which make up the Ards circuit are lined up before the pits. Sharp on the hour the limit cars are sent away – the supercharged MG Midgets will need a lot of catching with their big start; just over 60 miles.
>
> After what seems an interminable wait the flag falls and our group goes off. Close on the heels of the others in our class we skid round Mill Corner and shoot up Bradshaw's Brae at 70mph. A lightning glimpse gives us an impression of an overturned car in the first mile. Hard on the brakes and we are safely round the corner where Ruben came to grief in his Bentley two years ago.
>
> Down the hill to Newtownards, then a 100mph shoot under the railway bridge, the car 'crabbing' as we take the slight left-hand bend. A sharp right-hand turn into the village square and we gain another three miles an hour by cutting across the pavement. Round a series of 70mph curves, over a blind level crossing and so into Comber village with its two sandbagged right-hand bends. 'O.K.' shouts Hatcher, my mechanic, who sits with his eyes glued to the gauges.
>
> Six miles of winding roads – 65mph is the limit for safety here – a couple of railway bridges that can be taken at 75 if you put your front wheel within an inch or so of the wall; then a straight mile with the slight left-hand bend where Dudley Froy crashed in practice.
>
> Skidding madly on the stones on Dundonald hairpin and then we pass the stands. From the pits we get the 'O.K.', and the first lap is finished and another twenty-nine to do. Casualties mark the route on the third lap. After skidding over a furlong down Bradshaw's Brae, we see Earl Howe in his Alfa Romeo shoot off the road backwards at 80mph – he was not so lucky as we were. Another lap and Tim Birkin, in the green Alfa Romeo comes to grief in a butcher's shop – his brakes failed.
>
> Re-fuelling at halfway – a gulp of beer and we are off again. The engine is faster if anything, but the brakes have gone and third gear has to be held in.
>
> I drive one-handed for a few laps then we get the 'flat-out' signal. After a conference at 100mph, Hatcher holds the gear in when required and we do our best to carry out orders. So it goes on until we see the yellow flag – it would have been chequered had we been among the leaders – and we draw into the pits.
>
> We have won our class and have averaged only five miles an hour less than the record speed at which the race was won in 1929. And – satisfying thought – we are among the nineteen who finished the course out of the 45 starters.

The report was typical of Wisdom's crisp, unpretentious style, which gave his readers a vicarious thrill and placed him laps ahead of his more sedentary pressroom colleagues. There were, however, more sobering occasions when he had to record the deaths of his fellow drivers as was the case in 1933 when he was competing in the world's fastest race, the annual 500-mile event at Brooklands:

> I have just taken over the MG Magna from my colleague at the pits, and the little car is getting into its stride again. Suddenly a streamer of flame licks out from behind a car ahead. It is too far away to see who it is, but a moment later there is a great column of flame and smoke shooting up.
>
> Half a dozen of us approach the Fork, that difficult, high-speed bend just opposite the pits and the grandstand. Brakes are applied, and the whole bunch slithers and slides from well over 100 miles an hour to 70 – there is no time to reduce speed further.

A car is upside down in the centre of the track, already burned out of recognition. Officials, police and firemen are endeavouring to get onto the track. Flags are being waved. A few yards from the blazing car a still figure lies face downwards on the track. A fireman is rushing forward with a fire extinguisher, for the figure is ablaze.

But the race goes on. That is one of the traditions of motor racing – whatever happens the race must go on – but there is not a single driver who does not wish it were over. On the next lap we see the ambulance at the side of the track and a still figure is being carried to it. The blazing car is still in the centre of the track surrounded by firemen. It is a dangerous business for the smoke obscured the track ahead, and officials are rushing to and fro … Never has a race seemed so long.

THW went on to report that the ill-fated driver was the experienced 28-year-old amateur, M B Watson, who died of his injuries in Weybridge hospital a few hours later.

James Armour Milne, the *Life's* athletics correspondent during the 1930s and 40s, might not have been able to match the words of Wisdom when it came to writing, but he did prove himself to be a top-notch competitor on at least one important occasion when he landed quite a coup for the paper.

The Dunfermline-born Milne had covered the Berlin Olympics for the *Life* in 1936 and the sight of Jesse Owens burning up the track to the smouldering fury of Herr Hitler inspired him to redouble his own efforts to win Scotland's celebrated Powderhall sprint. He had competed at the Edinburgh stadium in the 1920s, but was very much a dark horse when he returned under his track name of 'Jimmy Saxon' in January 1938.

Walter Meeds was one of the select few who knew his colleague had been turning in some impressive times under the supervision of two top coaches in London, but he was in an awkward position when it came to previewing the event since he had been entrusted with placing some sizable bets on Milne and obviously could not give the game away by declaring his man was a certainty. In the end he compromised by including Milne in a short list of four; observing that he was "temptingly handicapped" and a likely winner despite a four-year absence from the track.

Just before the first of the 28 preliminary heats was run off, there was a sudden market move for 'Saxon' who was quickly established as overall 3-1 favourite "and those who supported him had several fair bets at 100 to 8".[4] It looked as if Meeds had done his job, and Milne certainly did his by burning off his rivals to win his heat by three yards.

To Meeds the final was now all over bar the shouting. Seldom has a more confident forecast – be it for man or beast – ever appeared in any newspaper than the one he wired through from Edinburgh that night:

> Granted that he 'doesn't fall down', it appears inestimable odds on Jimmy Saxon bringing Powderhall honours to London for the first time since 1870, the inaugural year of the world-famous New Year professional sprint … [he] seems to have over half a second in hand of his most formidable rivals … Seldom does such a certainty as Saxon represents slip past the lynx-eyed handicapper Chris Lynch … No final summing up appears necessary. Barring accidents, Saxon's victory can be confidently predicted.

'Fill yer boots' in other words; and the confidence was fully justified. The following day's headlines trumpeted 'Sporting Life Athletics Expert Wins Powderhall Handicap / Five Yards To Spare In Final Dash' as Meeds reported:

Powderhall, the biggest meeting of the year for professional track runners, wound up yesterday with one of the most dramatic victories ever recorded in the world-famous sprint. Jimmy Saxon … landed odds of 3 to 1 on when he broke the tape in the final, five yards ahead of Willie Scott, last year's winner, who, on the four yards mark, was set to give his rival eleven yards…

From the moment the starts were published I realised that Saxon, despite his 35 years, must win if he could find anything like his old form. Monday's heat revealed he was almost as good as ever and the manner in which he went through his task in the final is the most eloquent tribute to the training of his mentor, Cecil Bailey, and the beneficial air of Battersea Park.

The next day the man himself told his story. Dismissing talk that a huge betting coup had been landed or that he had not been 'off' for the past 12 years so as to get a favourable handicap mark, he declared:

I had been working towards my goal for only three years and, but for breakdowns in training, I would have tried in 1936 or 1937. My last preparation seemed doomed to have the same unsatisfactory ending. Two weeks before Christmas I spent two days in bed with influenza, and I pulled a thigh muscle a week ago today.

Scott Dryburgh, my masseur, nursed me through to the day of the heats and I was able to give the leg enough hard work to return the fastest time for the first round. Cecil Bailey, who was responsible for the regulation of my work on the track, has always held the opinion that my best days were not over when I forsook the Highland Games…

Credit too, should be given to Bill Thomas, trainer of Jack Lovelock and many other famous athletes, for the patience which he has shown in working for the perfection of my new style of running. Although it is likely that I have run my last race I shall adhere to the traditions of pedestrianism in not revealing exactly what I showed to Cecil Bailey and Bill Thomas in my trials, but I ran much faster than the Powderhall time suggests.

In short, he was what every punter dreams of — a racing certainty! For Milne and his backers the only galling aspect of his triumph was that Meeds (if he is to be believed) had failed to get their money on "owing to the sensitive market and their commissioner being forestalled".

Celebrations at the *Life* were also muted. On the eve of the race the staff had been stunned by the sudden death of Chris Towler who had been taken ill just a few days earlier. Despite his habit of borrowing money from staff to fund his betting habits and then 'forgetting' to pay it back, Towler had proved a capable editor since taking over from Morley-Brown in 1927 and in its tribute, his paper stated:

During his association with *The Sporting Life* he worked untiringly for the good of sport in general and for horse racing, greyhound racing and boxing in particular. His efforts during the difficult days of the betting tax — efforts which culminated in the abolition of that harsh imposition — will be gratefully remembered by all connected with the Turf.

An authority on boxing, his broadcast talks on old-time 'mills' delighted thousands in this country and America. President of the British Bullmastiff League, he was one of the best judges of this breed. Many famous sportsmen have bullmastiffs bred by Captain Towler from his favourite bitch, Nita.

Always genial, ever ready with a helping hand, *The Sporting Life* staff mourn a chief and loyal friend, and extend sincere sympathy to Mrs Towler in her great bereavement.

In addition to the points mentioned, Towler had boosted the standing of the *Life* through the introduction of a bi-weekly breeding page written by Adair Dighton, which brought in increased advertising from the principal studs, while he had also proved an important fund-raiser for the Royal Veterinary College in its hour of need.

In 1932 the college launched an appeal for £25,000 to enable it to reach a target of £100,000 (£5m) that was required to restore the crumbling Camden Town buildings in which Charley Blake had excelled as a student some 70 years earlier. Towler took up the challenge with a will and for five months hardly a day went by when the front page did not carry an update on the latest subscribers. Headlines such as 'His Majesty The King Supports Our Fund', helped to promote the cause which was duly achieved and earned the editor a personal vote of thanks from the dean of the college, Sir Frederick Hobday, better known today for the equine respiratory operation that bears his name.

Following Towler's death, the baton was passed on to Arthur Bernard Clements who had joined the paper as chief sub-editor in 1929 after honing his skills on the *Evening Despatch* in Birmingham. In 1932 'Ben' (he was never known by his real name) had become assistant editor, and he regarded his elevation to the chair at the age of 40 as the fulfilment of his ambitions.

He had always wanted to be editor of *The Sporting Life* or *The Times* and in his later years he became fond of garnishing his accomplished after-dinner speeches with the quip that the *Life* had got to him first!

A WARTIME WEEKLY

T HE Four Horsemen of the Apocalypse were already saddling up for another global rampage when Ben Clements eased himself into the editor's chair at the beginning of 1938. This time, however, the role of wartime editor was to be very different to the one taken on by Morley-Brown 24 years earlier.

From the outset, the paper distanced itself as far as possible from the conflict. There was no daily 'War News' column nor did it publish the endless lists of 'fallen sportsmen' that had been such a harrowing feature of the 1914-18 slaughter; in fact, for most of the war it existed only as a weekly paper put together by a skeleton staff of no more than half a dozen journalists, and it very nearly never came out at all.

When racing was suspended at the start of the war, most directors of Odhams wanted to close down the *Life* for the duration, but because their chairman, Julius Elias, or Baron Southwood as he became in 1937, harboured a protective instinct for the paper, he told Clements he could incur losses of up to £500 (£25,000) a week in order to keep it going.[1]

This noble gesture was not appreciated by those who wrote to *The Times* protesting about the amount of newsprint that was being 'wasted' on sporting publications. In parliament, too, there were the usual demands for a complete stoppage of racing, and there *were* times when it did grind to a halt, but in the main the government was pro-sport and every effort was made to keep a limited programme going throughout the war.

The first intimation the paper gave that the world was on the brink of its second conflagration in 25 years came on the eve of the new football season when, on 25 August 1939, the front page carried a bland, single-sentence announcement from the Football League – "Saturday's matches will take place unless there is war, in which case it is unlikely that the Government will allow big gatherings of people." The following day the inevitable crept a little closer as readers were informed:

> The Foreign Office has warned persons intending to spend their holidays abroad not to leave the country, in their own interests. In consequence all organised visits to the Continent have been cancelled. These include *The Sporting Life* trip to Ostend for the Grand International (to be run tomorrow), which was to have left Victoria station at 10.45 tonight.

Six days later, the crisis resulted in Folkestone becoming the first race meeting to be abandoned because of the crisis due to "the curtailment of railway facilities owing to the evacuation of children from London". In the same issue, the motoring column had some tips for those thinking of driving in a blackout, the most useful being – "they would be strongly advised not to".

On Saturday, September 2, the front page was littered with abandonment notices. The Doncaster yearling sales; the London to Brighton walk; the RAC Tourist Trophy at Donington, and county cricket matches from Old Trafford to Lord's, were all called off along with many speedway and greyhound meetings; football, however, went ahead as normal. There was also an important announcement on the international situation:

> In the House of Commons last night the Prime Minister, Mr Neville Chamberlain, stated that the

British Ambassador had been instructed to present an ultimatum to the German Government stating that by invading Poland, Germany had committed an aggressive act, which called for the immediate implementation by the Government of the United Kingdom, and of France, of the promise to come to Poland's assistance. Unless we received an assurance that Germany would suspend all aggressive acts, and were prepared to withdraw their forces from Polish territory, H.M. Government would, without hesitation, fulfil their obligation to Poland.

On Monday, the headlines 'Government Ban Sports Gatherings / Hopes Of An Early Resumption Of Racing' set the pattern for the way in which the paper was to deal with the war for the next six years:

After the Prime Minister's broadcast yesterday announcing that this country is at war with Germany, the Government issued the following statement: 'Sports gatherings and all gatherings for the purposes of entertainment and amusement whether outdoors or indoors which involve large numbers congregating together are prohibited until further notice.' Everyone will endorse the Government's determination to pursue the grim business in hand with wholehearted endeavour, but the period of all work and no sport cannot be indefinitely prolonged if the nation's morale is to be kept at its present peak. The tonic effects of racing, greyhound racing, and football are incalculable, and we hope and believe that a modified fixture list will be permitted.

The ban on racing lasted for six weeks and put paid to the eagerly awaited St Leger clash between the outstanding French and English Derby winners, Pharis and Blue Peter, while the rugby internationals involving the New Zealand (league) and Australian (union) teams were also cancelled. The Kiwis managed just two games before their tour was called off, while the Wallabies arrived in Southampton the day before war was declared and spent their brief stay toiling on Torquay beach filling ARP sandbags.

In towns where sand was not so readily to hand, speedway dirt tracks were scooped up to fill the bags, but during the deceptive months of the phoney war the public were more in danger from IRA bombs (Piccadilly Circus and Euston station were early targets) than from any that might be dropped by the Luftwaffe.

When the expected onslaught failed to materialise and restrictions on sport were relaxed, the *Life*, which had initially announced it would be published only on Saturdays until racing resumed, returned to its daily format after just three weeks, but with no racing to cover it was hard pressed to fill its columns and Meyrick Good and Willie Standring had to come to the rescue by drawing on their lengthy reminiscences. Good's memoirs ran on into 1941 and formed the basis for his first book, *Good Days*.

Meanwhile, most of the country's 92 racecourses were requisitioned by the military along with some training stables. Newbury, which staged racing up until September 1941, disappeared under 35 miles of concrete roads and railway sidings in 1942 when it became a vast supply depot for the American Army, while much of Newmarket Heath was used as a satellite aerodrome for RAF Mildenhall. Its flat, open spaces offered a perfect base for Bomber Command, and badly damaged planes returning from raids over Europe were often diverted there to make emergency landings on the hallowed turf.

In 1943 one aircraft failed to clear the formidable rampart of the Devil's Dyke[*] and ploughed up part of the July course which staged all the fixtures at Headquarters during the war as well as hosting substitute races for the Derby and the Oaks. The St Leger, having been lost to history in 1939, led a peripatetic existence as it flitted from Thirsk to Manchester to Newmarket (1942-44) and finally on to York in 1945.

It was on the July Course that racing resumed on a relatively normal basis in 1939 when, on October 18, 169 horses contested seven races, with a 12-noon start to allow racegoers to get home before blackout. In other areas of sport, however, things were far from normal. Football was being played on a regional basis with ten leagues operating across England and Wales and two in Scotland.

Teams bore little resemblance to those that had turned out on the first day of the season. Many footballers were in the forces and those who took the field were paid just 30s (£70) a match, which resulted in a mass movement of players from one club to another as they either returned to their home towns or moved away to find work.

In 1940, a less fragmented north-south league with 34 teams in each was introduced along with competitions for servicemen and charity internationals, which ran throughout the war and drew capacity crowds to Wembley (90,000) and Hampden (133,000). Some star players such as Everton's Tommy Lawton, who earned 18 wartime caps for England, occasionally 'guested' for other teams and on Christmas Day, 1940, he helped his own club gain a 3-1 victory over Liverpool in the morning and then scored both of Tranmere's goals in their 2-2 draw at Crewe in the afternoon.

Most clubs struggled to muster a full team and there were times when spectators found themselves filling in the gaps as when Northampton Town met Arsenal in November 1940. A typically brief report stated:

> Five home players failed to reach the ground. After a wait of 40 minutes Northampton started with eight men – and lost seven goals. Reinforced by three volunteers in the second half, the team held their own and the score was 8-1.

Two years later Wolves were reduced to cradle-snatching when they fielded 14-year-old (and 57 days) Cameron Campbell Buchanan in their match against West Brom. Their forward line averaged just 17½ years, but despite their inexperience they won 2-0, with Buchanan contributing to both goals.

Greyhound racing was restricted mainly to Saturday afternoons, while cricket survived chiefly as a series of one-day matches. Teams representing the London Counties and the British Empire toured the country raising money for war charities, and there were also matches between combined county sides as well as different branches of the services. These seldom merited a mentioned in the *Life* because, following the suspension of the *Sporting Chronicle* in November 1939,[†] it was felt that the maximum amount of space should be given to racing as the paper started to run a series of promotional notices that had a hint of desperation about them:

---

[*] The Devil's Dyke, also known as 'The Ditch', runs across Newmarket Heath in a northerly direction dividing the July and Rowley Mile courses. Believed to have been built by Boudicca's Iceni in 61AD as a defence against the Romans, the eight-mile earthwork rises 90ft from the bottom of the ditch to the top of the rampart at its highest point. After the 1943 accident, which caused the postponement of the Guineas meeting for a week, the rampart was levelled for 100 yards to give a clear approach to the main runway. By a happy coincidence the landscaping also gave post-war racegoers a view of the Cesarewitch start for the first time.

[†] The paper was amalgamated with the Manchester *Mid-Day Chronicle* and was published only on race days. It did not reappear in its usual format until 1946.

No sport can flourish without the help of publicity of the right kind. This applies to racing with special force. The publication of programmes and results, form of horses, probable runners and jockeys, and authoritative betting returns is essential to the well-being of a great industry. With the advent of war and the shortage of newsprint, *The Sporting Life* remains the only national daily newspaper which continues to give these features the same prominence as in peacetime. To maintain this expensive service we need your help. It is a small thing we ask. Buy *The Sporting Life* every day.

Newsprint became even scarcer in April 1940 when Germany invaded Norway and cut off a vital source of wood pulp to British mills. As the price of paper soared, the press barons, Lord Kemsley and Lord Beaverbrook, got together to set up a Newspaper Supply Company to distribute newsprint on an equitable basis. In a rare act of Fleet Street solidarity, papers that had plentiful supplies agreed to pool their stocks for the benefit of those that had little or none, and there was co-operate buying of newsprint from Canada and Newfoundland to supplement domestic supplies.

The war took another turn for the worse in May when the Nazis marched into Holland and Belgium to, as Hitler put it, "protect their neutrality". As refugees began to flood into Britain, the *Life* started to give more prominence to the situation as it published the adventures of some of the returning ex-pat sportsmen.

One lucky escapee was the former Sunderland, Sheffield Wednesday and England international, Bill Marsden, whose playing career came to an end when he broke a bone in his neck during the 1930 Germany v England match in Berlin – the first to be played between the two sides since the 1914-18 war – which ended in a 3-3 draw.

Under a Roy of the Rovers-type heading, 'Soccer Coach Under Fire / Thrilling Experiences Of Bill Marsden', a report described how the Holland-based coach had been woken up by German transport planes circling overhead as they prepared to land on a nearby beach. The footballer, carrying a small suitcase containing his international caps and medals, had been shot at as he made his way to the British consulate in The Hague, after which he and his wife made their escape on a train packed with refugees and captured German airmen: "The Nazi pilots appeared to be a fine set of men, but the parachutists seemed to be of sub-normal intelligence," Marsden observed.

Herbert Ellis, one of several English trainers who had been based in Belgium where his son, Stan, was a leading jockey, returned to report that many racehorses had been slaughtered to prevent them from falling into German hands. "There was such a glut of horsemeat, I wasn't even able to give my horses away," he told an agency reporter.

Those fleeing the Low Countries were soon joined by their French-based compatriots who included the jockeys Tommy Dunn, rider of the last winner at Auteuil before the Germans entered Paris on June 14, and George Bridgland who, after joining the RAF, took time off to win the 1941 St Leger on Sun Castle and the 1944 Oaks on Hycilla, (post-war he also won the 1947 Derby on the French-trained Pearl Diver and as a trainer sent Cambremer over from France to land the 1956 St Leger).

The returning trainers included Claude Halsey, who also served with the RAF for the remainder of the war before setting himself up at Somerville Lodge, Newmarket, where Pearl Diver completed his Derby preparation, and Dick Warden, the man who was to introduce Sheikh Mohammed al Maktoum to British racing in 1977 after he had bought him his first racehorse, the subsequent four-time winner Hatta, for 6,200gns.

By the end of May, when the British Expeditionary Force was being evacuated from Dunkirk, Liverpool's full-back, Jimmy Harley, made seven cross-Channel trips with the Royal Navy and might well have picked up the Duke of Norfolk who was among the 340,000 Allied troops rescued from the beaches. Harley, who, at the age of 18 in 1936, became the youngest winner of the famous Powderhall sprint, recounted:

> We were bombed by planes, bombarded from the shore, machine gunned from the air and attacked by torpedo boats … From our decks the soldiers blazed away with every available weapon. Three enemy planes and possibly a fourth were brought down. It was the toughest spot I've ever been in.[*]

The *Life's* French correspondent, Colonel E E 'Teddy' Wilford, a WWI veteran, got away two weeks later on the last boat out of Bordeaux, but there were many who did not make it home. Among those killed in the fighting was the popular amateur rider and trainer Kim Muir, who, two months earlier, had partnered his own horse, Another, to finish ninth to Bogskar in the Grand National.

Amid all the chaos and carnage, the *Life* suddenly expanded its general sports coverage by bringing out a 12-page number on Mondays. Designed to boost the battered morale of the nation as well as the sales of the paper, the enlarged editions contained columns by the incomparable Henry Longhurst (golf) and the 1936 Olympic 1,500 metres gold medallist, the tousle-haired New Zealander, Jack Lovelock (athletics).

There were also regular features on swimming and cycling by two of the foremost writers in their field, W J Howcroft and B W Best, as well as occasional articles by Phil Bull, writing under his 'Wm K Temple' *nom de plume*, and lighter contributions from such heroes as England's former Test cricketer P G H 'Percy' Fender. An introduction to one of the latter's articles proclaimed:

> When PGH was captain, every game in which Surrey played was 'alive' from start to finish. The finest match-winning skipper since the days of the 'Old Man' here tells the story of one of his earliest and most spectacular of successes as captain – against Leicestershire in June 1922. Set to get 153 in 80 minutes, the runs were knocked off in 63 minutes, Fender's contribution being 91. He scored 28 of the last 29 runs in eight minutes, finishing the game with a drive into the dressing room that nearly killed Strudwick.

But however much the paper tried to present an air of normality there was no disguising the threat to the nation and there were increasing calls for a halt to racing. In the Commons the Home Secretary, Sir John Anderson, was in the minority as he argued: "Experience has proved that if workers are to maintain their efficiency for more than a limited period some measure of relaxation is essential. For that reason the Government has been anxious not to interfere unduly with facilities for sport and recreation."

Lord Reith, the puritanical director-general of the BBC, saw things differently and his decision to substitute a programme on 'A visit to an arms factory' in place of the 1940 Derby broadcast was roundly condemned by the racing fraternity. Lady Wentworth, who contributed an occasional article on the Arabian horse to the *Life*, wrote in to declare: "the suppression of the broadcast is simply childish and penalises those who stay at home to save petrol and assist in easing the work of the police."

An estimated 10,000 did attend the Derby, which was won by Pont l'Évêque, owned and trained

---

[*] Harley was to be in a few more tough spots before he was through (he was mentioned in dispatches for conspicuous gallantry during the disastrous Dieppe raid in 1942), but he survived them all and returned to play for Liverpool until 1947.

by Fred Darling who had only entered the colt when the race was re-opened that February. Once again, however, the special trains and streams of race-bound traffic caused eruptions in the Commons and on June 19, to no one's surprise, racing was suspended until further notice.

In the same number of the *Life* that imparted this news, the threat of an imminent invasion was graphically illustrated by three War Office-issued ID silhouettes of German transport planes – the Junkers JU 90, the Focke-Wulf 200 'Condor' and the Junkers JU 52, "the most important troop carrier and the one normally used for parachute dropping," with its unmistakable, snout-like, central engine mounting.

Readers were asked to "Take a piece of cardboard and paste the photographs side by side and hang them in a prominent place" – a request that was no doubt carried out with enthusiasm by stable lads in Berkshire from where it was reported:

> It has been suggested that lads employed in the racing stables in the Lambourn district should be mounted on bicycles to help round up German parachute troops. Dozens of lads – many of them not much bigger than the rifle they will have to carry – have joined the 'Parashots'. The area of the Downs they will have to patrol is considerable, and one bright notion was that racehorses should be enrolled too, the division to be called the South West Mounted. The idea of valuable bloodstock careering about while the lads took pot shots at descending German troops did not appeal to their employers. Hence the bicycle as an alternative.

The 'Lad's Army' scheme would have appealed to Henry Longhurst who dispensed some much-needed light relief in his 'Golf Mixture' column even when England's green and bunkered courses were being desecrated in order to prevent the Luftwaffe from trundling down their fairways:

> It seems that the Home Office survey of golf courses on which it might be possible for enemy aircraft to land has shown, at any rate in the southern area, that in all but a few isolated cases such landings would be extremely unhappy. Over the weekend I talked to the secretaries of nearly a dozen clubs and only at three was there any possibility of their having to take special precautions.
>
> The most drastic case was one in Kent, where, so I gathered, they are to dig a trench 18 feet wide, right across the course. I fancy it may make an excellent hazard and I can see it being preserved permanently as a souvenir of the Second World War. They might christen it 'Goering's Folly' or some such name.

With the suspension of racing, the *Life* reverted to an eight-page weekly published on Mondays. A statement read:

> It has been with the utmost regret that the decision to cease daily publication has been taken, but in present circumstances it is the only course that we can pursue. At great cost to the proprietors, *The Sporting Life* has kept faith with the racing public during the difficult days of the past nine months. Every meeting under Jockey Club and National Hunt Rules has been reported and the Starting Prices, upon which depend the whole fabric of the sport, have been faithfully returned by our representatives. This important service we hope to render again when a resumption of racing is possible.

This time the stoppage lasted for three months and when it was announced that the ban was to

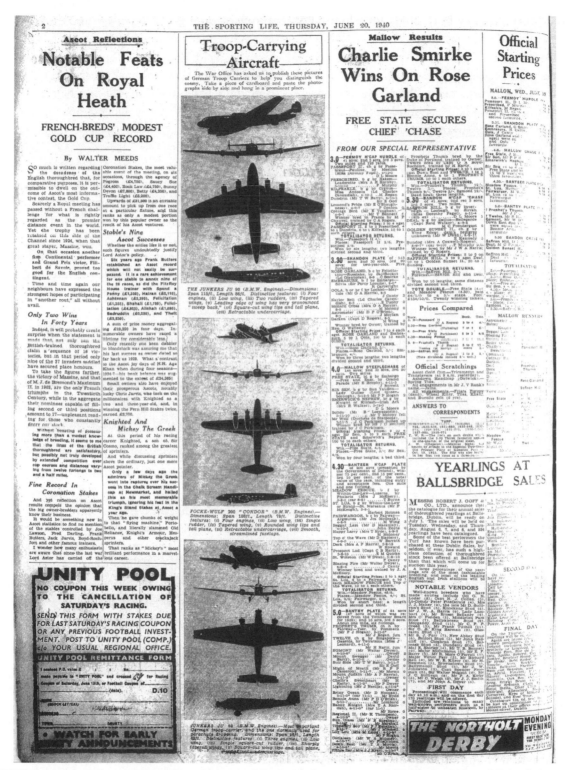

With the threat of an invasion hanging over Britain in the summer of 1940, the *Life* published these ID silhouettes of three German troop-carrying aircraft.

be lifted on September 14 to allow for a limited programme of racing, the paper greeted the news with a 'not before time' observation:

> Horseracing is, in all respects, the greatest and most important of our national sports and it has seemed unreasonable to the racing and breeding communities that there should be a ban on its promotion, while greyhound racing, football, cricket – to say nothing of cinema and theatre entertainments – were permitted.

Plans to resume daily publication were, however, thwarted by government restrictions and the *Life* was to remain a weekly for the next four years. Meanwhile, the blitz on London had begun in earnest and, although the paper carried no direct reports of the bombing even when Fleet Street was badly hit, a reader from a safer time was given a glimpse of the lottery of whistling death in Longhurst's lucid prose.

The Bedford-born journalist, radio and (post-war) TV commentator who also wrote for the *Sunday Times*, *Evening Standard* and *Tatler*, always had one eye on the clock as, like many fine exponents of his art, he could not begin to write until an approaching deadline forced him to it – even if it was in the middle of an air-raid as was the case one weekend that September:

> Difficult to write at times like this. As I sit in my basement, the table shakes and I bounce in my chair as the grocer's goes up in smoke and small stones at the end of the road. Is it wrong to think, and write, of golf in times like this? I think not. We can only live from hour to hour, and it will help us to dwell mentally – there goes a whistler; a quarter of a mile away, I judge – on times that are past. Times that we hope may come again.

But for too many those times were never to return, and in another number during that fateful, fearsome summer, Longhurst devoted his entire column (half a page) to the all-round sportsman and fighter pilot, Bill Fiske:

> Last week they buried a good friend of mine and a fine fellow. His name was W M L Fiske. We first met when we used to play golf together at Cambridge. Fiske was an American who, by long acquaintance, had come to love England. He died fighting for us in one of the air battles over the Channel. He was short of stature, good humoured and immensely tough. He was afraid of nothing in this world, and into little more than thirty years he had crammed enough experience to last most men a lifetime.

Longhurst, too, was not short on experience. He had won his first golf trophy at 14 along with a scholarship to Charterhouse and Clare College, Cambridge. He captained the Cambridge University golf team and, in pre-war tournaments, had won the German amateur championship and was runner-up in the Swiss and French equivalents.

He was, therefore, well qualified to recall some of the great rounds he had seen played, as when the beefy, broad-shouldered Lawson Little made Prestwick look like a pitch and putt course in the 1934 British amateur championship or when Henry Cotton achieved the 'impossible' in the last round of the 1937 Open at a rain-sodden Carnoustie. But golf was not entirely sacrosanct to him, and in one of his last articles before he went off to war he touched upon the 'Dig For Victory' campaign that had seen many racecourses ploughed up and parts of Newmarket Heath turned over to arable land.*

Underneath the three-deck headline 'If They Can Grow Carrots On Carnoustie / The Game Matters Not At All / Food Before Fairways', he wrote:

> Mr Tom Johnstone, Secretary of State for Scotland and the man who shook the industrial world to its foundations the other day by renouncing a £100-a-week [*£4,200*] salary on the grounds that he 'did not want to make money out of the war' has ordained a survey of golf courses. Those that are suitable he hopes to see doing their bit by handing over anything up to 18 acres for food production. Bunkers and greens are to be spared.
>
> I suppose I shall be expected to rise in arms against such heresy. In fact, I am afraid I do not. Mr Johnstone is unduly charitable with his demand of 18 acres. I can tell him the names of a good many courses, not one acre of which ought ever to have had any function but the growing of cabbages. Some of these are not a million miles from North London. Some lie around Birmingham, others around the Northern industrial towns...
>
> I take the view that the playing of golf matters not a tinker's curse in wartime. The game will live on in our minds as a hibernating animal lives on through its long winter sleep. So, if we can grow carrots on Carnoustie, turnips on Turnberry, and sprouts at St And—- (no, there is a limit to sacrilege!), then by all means let us do so. Bellies before bogeys, say I.

Not that the anti-sport politicians needed any encouragement in this direction. As in the First World War there was the usual faddist clique, this time led by Manny Shinwell, the firebrand socialist member for Seaham, Durham, who described wartime race meetings as "these insane and unseemly spectacles" and argued that the daily 16lb oats ration (later cut to 9lb) for racehorses should be fed instead to hens.

Amid a general food-shortage hysteria which saw a woman prosecuted for putting crumbs on a bird table, Shinwell and his ilk were enthusiastically supported by large sections of the press. Just before the start of the 1941 Flat season, when the government stated there were about 2,200 horses in training that would consume 3,500 tons of corn a year; Meyrick Good highlighted the latest example of Fleet Street flummery.

Quoting a writer in the *Daily Express* who had likened the 32 entries for the Lincolnshire Handicap to "1,920 hens which might have laid 268,800 eggs," he surmised: "It is inconceivable that Ministers could be influenced by the tosh that has been written by many of the anti-racing zealots who have become ardent poultry fanciers."

The old chronicler was also critical of the churlish councillors of Cheltenham who refused to host the 1941 Grand National after it had been decided it was too risky to stage it at Aintree as Liverpool was being targeted by the Luftwaffe. The council's decision had the backing of the town's Tory MP, Daniel Lipson, and was upheld by the Home Secretary, Herbert Morrison, with the result that the National was not run again until 1946. In commenting on the news Good wrote:

> At Cheltenham last week I had first-hand evidence of the local opposition that was organised to

---

* In 1942, the Minister of Agriculture stated that out of a total of 2,359 acres held by the Jockey Club for racing and training purposes in the Newmarket area, 1,688 acres had been requisitioned for military purposes and 196 acres had been ploughed up for arable cultivation leaving 493 acres for gallops. Out of a total of 7,990 acres of grassland on stud farms in the same area, 2,910 acres had been put under plough and much of the remainder was used for grazing dairy herds.

resist the suggestion of the National Hunt Stewards that a substitute Grand National should be run at Prestbury Park. As a result of this agitation the Government have banned the Stewards' proposal, and for the first time since its inception in 1837 there will be no National.

Why Cheltenham folk should be opposed to the staging of the race in the vicinity of their town passes my comprehension. Over a period of many years racing has done Cheltenham an immense amount of good and brought a deal of money into the town, particularly the hotels. It also served to materially increase the circulation of the local evening papers, yet these journals strongly supported the campaign in opposition to the National.

The fact that Cheltenham went ahead with its NH Meeting that March (and also in 1942) was defended by its town clerk, R Owen Seacome, who responded to Good's criticism by claiming:

The transfer of a meeting of the magnitude of the Grand National to a smaller town would have been likely to disorganise and delay the delivery of food, coal and other essential supplies, and was therefore on a different footing to the National Hunt meeting.

This argument didn't wash with the NH community whose feelings were best summed up in a letter from 'Disgusted' of Erdington, Birmingham:

What undoubtedly should have been done was for the Cheltenham people to have grasped the opportunity with both hands and supported the stewards to stage a good race. The running should have been broadcast all over the world and particularly throughout Germany. By this means we would have been delivering a smashing blow at German morale. As for our friends across the seas they would have heard of the event with that admiration which makes us feel proud to be British. As matters have turned out, it is enough to make Fred Archer and other old Cheltonians renounce their native town.

Cheltenham at least escaped the fate of Newmarket that February when a lone raider dropped eight bombs on the town killing 27 people including George Groves, a former Sheffield United footballer and Notts County cricketer, who was the *Sporting Chronicle*'s local correspondent. After the bombing, which demolished the White Hart hotel, the bookmaker, Martin Benson, had an air-raid shelter built for his stallion, Nearco, at his Beech House Stud, Cheveley. The undefeated winner of 14 races, which included the 1938 Derby Italiano and the Grand Prix de Paris, was thus better protected than many in London where a bomb claimed the lives of Arthur Portman, proprietor and 'Audax' of the *Horse & Hound*, his wife and their seven servants.

Another victim of the blitz was Lord Glanely, affectionately known as 'Old Guts and Gaiters', who had spent vast fortunes on the Turf over the years and had been rewarded with victories in all the classics bar the One Thousand Guineas.

The toll was also mounting among racing men in the services. No fewer than four Grand National winning jockeys were to lose their lives during the war. The first and, in a way, most tragic casualty was Tommy Cullinan who had completed a unique treble when winning the Champion Hurdle (Brown Tony), the Cheltenham Gold Cup (Easter Hero) and the Grand National (Shaun Goilin) in 1930. The former jockey was based at an RAF station in Oxfordshire in the spring of 1940 when he was shot dead by a nervous sentry as he was returning to barracks after a night out on the town.

Four Grand National winning jockeys were killed on active service during WWII: a). Bob Everett DSO (1929 Gregalach) of the Fleet Air Arm, presumed lost at sea, February 1942; b). Tommy Cullinan (1930 Shaun Goilin) mistakenly shot dead, April 1940; c). Frank Furlong (1935 Reynoldstown) of the Royal Naval Volunteer Reserve, killed in a plane crash near Stockbridge, September 1944; d). Mervyn Jones (1940 Bogskar) of Bomber Command, shot down over Europe, April 1942. (In November 1944, his brother, Hywel Jones DFC, also lost his life on operations with Bomber Command. He had won the 1935 NH Chase on Rod and Gun amongst other races).
© [Rouch Wilmot Thoroughbred Racing Library] Thoroughbred Advertising.

Bob Everett, who rode Gregalach to victory in the 1929 National, joined the Fleet Air Arm at the outbreak of war and was awarded the DSO in September 1941 for "bravery, skill and tenacity in many hazardous operational flights in the protection of shipping," but five months later he was reported missing, presumed dead.

Frank Furlong, successful as an amateur on Reynoldstown in 1935, was killed in an air crash in 1944. He had taken part in the operation to sink the *Bismarck* in 1941 when he had to ditch in the North Atlantic and spend 48 hours adrift in a dingy before he was picked up.

Mervyn Jones, who won the 1940 National on Bogskar, failed to return from a sortie while serving with Bomber Command in April 1942 and two years later the war also claimed the life of his brother, Hywel – who had also ridden in the 1940 National – when his plane was shot down over Europe.

Many other famous sportsmen were lost to the war, but their names and deeds were too numerous to mention in a paper that had to be cut back to six pages in March 1941 when newsprint restrictions forced it to drop the columnists it had taken on ten months earlier. The alternative, it explained, would have been to maintain the size of the paper, but reduce its circulation, which "would have meant disappointment to many thousands of readers".

At the end of that year, when it was announced that the 55-day Santa Anita meeting in California had been abandoned as a result of Japan's attack on Pearl Harbor, the Ministry of Supply launched a drive to collect waste paper for the munition factories that were desperately short of raw material. When the target of 100,000 tons had not been reached by February 1942, the *Life* carried a reminder that more was needed:

> There are still many who have not combed out their bookshelves for old novels, directories, and other volumes they will never need again. Such people should do so at once, but there is one word of warning. Foreign directories, maps or guide books may be useful to the authorities. The Minister of Economic Warfare would like to receive such books for use of the Intelligence Staff, if found suitable. If not, they will be turned over for re-pulping.

Under the heading 'Paper Makes Munitions', a list of dubious calculations estimated:

> 1 Racecard = 8 cartridge wads; 1 Old Betting Book = 4 mine interior compartments; 6 Old Form Books = 1 mortar shell carrier; 5 Bookmakers' A/c Forms = 1 washer for a shell; 1 Greyhound Sale Catalogue = 1 box for rifle cartridges; 20 Large Cigarette Cartons = 1 outer shell container; 6 Bookmakers' Betting Lists = 8 aero engine gaskets; 20 Tote Tickets = 3 cartridge wads.

The year also saw the Jockey Club bring in regional racing by dividing England on a north-south basis with 80 days racing spread among just five courses. Newmarket was given its own enclave with 30 days; Pontefract and Stockton had 23 days for horses trained north of the Trent, and Salisbury and Windsor 27 days for the southern area (Ascot was added as a sixth course in 1943 when the number of days racing was reduced to just 67). With the exception of the classics and a handful of prestige 'open' races there was to be no raiding across the divides.

At the same time the transport of horses to race meetings (open races excepted) by rail was banned and limited to 45 miles (later extended to 50) by road; a restriction that was flouted with a deserved contempt for the bureaucracy that allowed a horse to be driven any distance provided a different horsebox was used for each 45-mile leg of the journey!

Sun Chariot and Gordon Richards are led in by George VI after winning the 1942 Oaks at Newmarket. Sun Chariot went on the complete the filly's Triple Crown by adding the St Leger to her 1,000 Guineas win and effectively silenced those calling for the suspension of racing.
© [Keystone]/[Hulton Archive] Getty Images

Despite these restrictions, the 1942 season was a memorable one highlighted by the performances of the King's flighty filly, Sun Chariot. This loopy, lop-eared daughter of Hyperion had been leased to George VI by the National Stud and had gone through 1941 unbeaten in four races to top the two-year-old Free Handicap, 1lb ahead of her stable companion, Big Game, who also carried the royal colours and had won all his five races.

Trained by Fred Darling at Beckhampton, these two horses did much to silence racing's critics and boost the nation's morale by winning four of the five classics to the accompaniment of triumphal headlines and much patriotic cheering.

Sun Chariot, so intractable at the start of her career that only a delayed export licence prevented her from being sent back to Ireland from whence she came, cast aside her wilful ways to win the fillies' Triple Crown – the One Thousand Guineas, Oaks and St Leger – while Big Game won the Two Thousand Guineas, but failed to see out the Derby trip although he later redeemed himself in the 10-furlong Champion Stakes.

While Flat racing revelled in these royal victories there was no joy for the jumpers even though hunting continued on a limited basis. The 1942-43 NH season was scrapped, and there was to be no more steeplechasing until January 1945 when the defeat of Germany was assured. The loss of the winter sport brought in many letters of protest to the *Life* and elicited a scornful editorial from Ben Clements who observed:

> The ban will effect some trifling saving in fodder, will slightly alleviate transport problems, may increase by an infinitesimal fraction the number of man-hours devoted to war work, and will unquestionably please the vociferous minority of kill-joys – if anything can be said to bring pleasure to that doleful section of the community who probably do more to clog the war effort than would a thousand race meetings.

Overall, the war situation was still grim, but as Churchill declared so memorably that November, the Eighth Army's successes at El Alamein and Tobruk marked the end of the beginning. The PM's cautious optimism was reflected at the Newmarket sales the following month when bloodstock prices reached their highest level for 12 years with 417 lots selling for an average of 390gns (£14,800) – 12 months earlier 404 lots had averaged just 185gns with many horses being knocked down to knacker men for 5gns (£200).

In occupied France, a Major Pulte of the Union Klub (German Jockey Club) did not have to pay a sou for the best bloodstock when he went on a shopping spree in the summer of 1940 and 'acquired' five stallions, 21 broodmares and 27 horses in training for the German Army stud at Altefeld. The majority of the horses belonged to Jews who had to rely on the French Government for compensation, while other owners were paid a flat rate of 30,000 Marks for stallions and 3,000 Marks for mares and horses in training.

Quoting from the *Frankfurter Zeitung* of 30 December 1941, the *Life* revealed that the unbeaten Pharis together with the stallions Brantôme, Mirza II, Bubbles and his son, Éclair au Chocolat, had been shipped off to Altefeld. At the same time, Joachim von Ribbentrop, Hitler's Foreign Minister, commandeered Baron Edouard de Rothschild's entire string of 118 horses to form his own private stud and racing stable.

Ribbentrop, in partnership with Christian Weber, president of the Munich Racing Club, raced many of the horses on the Parisian tracks, but he was not at Longchamp in April 1943 when an American air-raid took place just before the first race. The target was the Renault works two kilometres away, but a stick of 14 bombs hit the course leaving a line of craters from the Moulin to the Petit Bois.[2] Miraculously, only seven racegoers were killed and after a delay of half an hour the meeting went ahead, but it was the last to be held at Longchamp until July 1944 by which time the Allies were battling their way through Normandy.*

In keeping with its 'no war news' policy, the *Life* did not mention the D-Day landings, but eleven months later an exception was made when the paper, now a bi-weekly publishing on Mondays and Wednesdays, carried a front-page photo of Churchill together with the headline 'Prime Minister's VE Day Broadcast' and the text of his address to the nation on 8 May 1945. It was not one of the old man's most memorable speeches, but it was nonetheless welcome for all that:

---

* During fierce fighting in the Falaise Gap about 20 studs were left in ruins and many others badly damaged. Some 300 thoroughbreds were killed or disappeared including the famous mare Corrida, dual winner of the Arc de Triomphe (1936-37). Many were taken by the retreating Germans, but were later abandoned or eaten. Only about 160 horses of the 700 that had been taken by the Nazis were repatriated, but among them were Pharis and Brantôme. Other stallions such as the Arc winners Éclair au Chocolat and Mon Talisman; his son, Clairvoyant (Grand Prix de Paris and Prix de Jockey Club), and about 100 high-class broodmares were never recovered.

On Monday morning at 2.41 a.m. at General Eisenhower's H.Q. General Jodl, the representative of the German High Command and of Grand Admiral Donitz, the designated head of the German State, signed the act of unconditional surrender of all German land, sea and air forces in Europe to the Allied Expeditionary Forces and simultaneously to the Soviet High Command.

Hostilities will end officially one minute after midnight tonight, Tuesday, May 8 – but in the interest of saving lives the ceasefire began yesterday to be sounded all along the front, and our dear Channel Islands are also to be freed today ... We may allow ourselves a brief period of rejoicing, but let us not forget for a moment the toil and efforts that lie ahead.

Japan, with all her treachery and greed, remains unsubdued. The injury she has inflicted on Great Britain, the United States and other countries, and her detestable cruelties call for justice and retribution. We must now devote all our strength and resources to the completion of our task, both at home and abroad. Advance Britannia! Long live the cause of freedom! God save the King.

A NATION IN CRISIS

DAILY PUBLICATION of the *Sporting Life* was resumed for the start of the 1946 Flat season, but along with food, fuel, clothes and other essentials in post-war Britain, it was strictly rationed – in fact, it was like gold dust. In announcing its return to near-normality and an increase in price to 3d, it urged readers to confirm their order with newsagents "otherwise, owing to the exceptional demand for the paper and the impossibility at the moment of increasing supplies, they may find that there is not a copy of the new issue available for them". Worse still, "pending an increased paper ration, no additional readers, either through the trade or by postal subscription, can be supplied".

The restrictions on the supply of newsprint were to limit the size and circulation of the paper for the next ten years and the old journalistic cliché of 'news before views' was the ruling factor in what was normally no more than a six-page issue. Into this limited space Ben Clements managed to squeeze the returning war heroes Henry Longhurst (ex-Royal Artillery) and Tommy Wisdom, who emerged from the RAF as a fully-fledged Wing Commander cloaked in an aura of derring-do and 'special missions'.

In his first 'Golf Mixture' column since being so rudely interrupted by Herr Hitler, Longhurst filed a poignant piece fittingly entitled 'Links of the Past':

Turning up the records I find that I last wrote about golf in the *Sporting Life* in March 1941. Soon after that, my worldly possessions were touched off by a landmine and I joined His Majesty's Army as a driver. A great deal of water, as well as such other fluids as were obtainable, have flowed by since then – but for the moment we are only concerned with golf…

And how has the game survived? Uncommonly well, when you cast your mind back over the five intervening years. There are many fine fellows, though, who will never play again, and if I mention only one or two, it is not because I am unaware of the others. For six successive years, for instance, during which time we won it on five occasions, I shared a bedroom with Dale Bourn for the Halford-Hewitt tournament at Deal. A great-hearted player, and therefore a lucky one – for the two nearly always go together – Dale was the gay cavalier of golf. For all the outrageous things he sometimes did, everyone loved Dale Bourn. He was killed in an air smash.

So, too, was Pam Barton, who played better than any other woman in Britain and had not an enemy in the world. John Rowell, Ian Lyle, Kenneth Scott, John Lyon, Dick Twining – I remember Bernard Darwin, a man not usually given to emotion, reading out these and other names at the first reunion dinner of the Oxford and Cambridge Society, and being scarcely able to finish the list.

Courses, too, have suffered their casualties, though in all conscience the loss of them is trivial beside that of all the good fellows who did not live to play on them. Two were among my own particular favourites. If anyone had asked me just before the war where I would most like to spend a golfing holiday beside the sea, there would have been no hesitation in the answer – Turnberry.

Many a time in the days when my body was being taught 'turning at the 'alt' or how to slope arms by numbers, my spirit used to wander from the barrack square to more congenial surroundings of its own choosing. Often its choice would be Turnberry, and once again I would be sitting up on the terrace in the evening, watching the gannets flapping slowly along over the waters below and suddenly folding up their wings and diving like plummets into the sea for their supper.

The two lovely courses lay silent in the evening sun, the white lighthouse glistened on the distant point, and Ailsa Craig and the Western Isles shimmered vaguely in the background. And now the whole thing is one vast airfield.

Then again, nearer home ... though I was never so fond of it as some people, I had to acknowledge the qualities of Prince's, Sandwich, and, indeed, I have a certain sentimental affection for it, as I played (and won!) my first University match there.

Prince's became a target range. The famous cottages at Bloody Point, once the seaside home of the Duchess of Kent's children, turned into a heap of stones; the whole links went to wrack and ruin, and a friend of mine recently there was unable to detect the shape or even the general position, of the 18th green.*

There were also a lot of changes in racing. Among the courses that closed during the war, Gatwick, like Turnberry, had become 'one vast airfield' and many others never reopened. The *Life* had lost one of its most promising journalists in Basil Middleton, who was killed during flying operations with the RAF in 1942, and there was new man at Newmarket in Tom Nickalls who had taken on the 'Warren Hill' mantle following the death of Willie Standring in May 1945.

An Old Etonian with 22 years of soldiering behind him, Thomas Wentworth Nickalls was new to journalism, but at home with horses. Commissioned to the 17/21st Lancers after passing out of Sandhurst in 1923, he had ridden in point-to-points and also under Rules when stationed in India during the 1930s.

At the outbreak of war his regiment, the 'Death or Glory Boys', was mechanised and he was given command of a light tank squadron. Rising in the ranks from Captain to Lt-Colonel he was on the headquarters staff of the 2nd Army throughout the Normandy campaign before being invalided home from France in the autumn of 1944.

With no trade to fall back on, Nickalls pursued his instincts and Ben Clements with equal determination and was eventually rewarded with the Newmarket job. Anxious to prove himself, he charged into his new profession with all the ardour of a lancer at full gallop. His uninhibited style soon raised the hackles of the Establishment, but after a series of magnificent indiscretions that incurred the wrath of Lord Rosebery and earned him a 'red card' (later withdrawn) from the editor, he learnt to temper his views with a measure of diplomacy that did not dull the thrust of his criticisms.

It was clear his fearless, free-thinking approach, uncluttered by an over-familiarity with the racing scene, could be used to advantage on a broader scene than Newmarket and with Meyrick Good beginning to ease down at 70, Nickalls started to deputise for 'Man on the Spot' in 1947. A born campaigner, he was particularly outspoken in his condemnation of non-triers and felt the stewards should be more active in weeding them out. As his predecessor stated in his second volume of memoirs, *Lure of the Turf* (1954):

No one reading Tom Nickalls is left in any doubt whatever that here is a correspondent who has but one axe to grind, and that a large and sharp one destined for the necks of all, whatever their station, who tend to bring racing into disrepute.

---

* Even as Longhurst was writing these lines a new course, the Ailsa Craig, was being laid out at Turnberry, while Prince's (Lord Brabazon likened its use as a target range to "throwing darts at a Rembrandt"), was derequisitioned in 1949 and was redesigned and restored the following year.

Good's book, so much more readable than his first offering as it was ghosted by Len Scott, a mainstay of the *Life's* subs desk from 1932 to 1977 (less six years army service during the war), also gives a fine pen-portrait of Bill Munro, a feisty Aberdonian who replaced Nickalls as 'Warren Hill' in 1947. The description is redolent of Scott's purple prose which embellished many an excellent feature article during the winter months:

[*He*] is a Falstaff-like Scotsman with a crime reporting background and a vocabulary (both laudatory and abusive) which would have staggered Dr Johnson whom he in some way resembles. It has been said that folk who have never been racing and who do not know one side of a horse from the other, could read Munro with exquisite enjoyment, that is, if they appreciate the art of paradox, metaphor and the occasional, artfully-chosen, unfamiliar, yet telling phrase, which stands up in his articles like a rock.

Munro, analysing the Newmarket angle on a big race, goes to work like a Sherlock Holmes. One by one the inessentials are eliminated, one by one the doubtful horses are weeded out; the impression is that of a gigantic sieving operation. Only pure gold remains, and it is amazing how often it really is the genuine article.

There was also a new man in the north in Aubrey Renwick whose father and uncle had both trained with success in Yorkshire for many years and who was, himself, granted a licence to train under both codes at the age of 20 in 1932. Although he never had more than four horses in his Richmond stables at any one time, he sent out 17 winners in five years before he turned his hand to journalism in 1937.

This new blood was just what the *Life* needed at a time when there was a uniformity in racing news due to the extensive coverage given to the sport by the Press Association which had a large outside staff backed up by an ambitious (and therefore industrious) team of reporters in its Fleet Street offices.

With such masters of their craft as Peter O'Sullevan (later *Daily Express*); Lionel Cureton ('Templegate', *Daily Herald/Sun*); Julian Simcocks ('Captain Heath', *News Chronicle/Daily Mail*) and Dai Davies, who became the agency's chief reporter, all working for the PA in the immediate post-war years, the national press was spoon-fed with the best of racing stories.

The *Life* and *Sporting Chronicle* were also reliant on the PA for reports from the smaller meetings that were uneconomic for them to cover, as well as for race descriptions, a full results service, and lists of probable runners and riders. But while the PA's service was extensive, it lacked individuality; plain English and essential facts were what mattered and it was here that the *Life's* men scored by adding colour and pungent opinions to their copy at a time when post-war austerity was casting an unrelenting gloom over the whole nation.

The country was bankrupt, taxation had never been higher and the luxuries of life were to be found only on the black market. For relief, the working man once again turned to sport and, as in the aftermath of WWI, capacity crowds were seen at football grounds and racecourses that were not always capable of accommodating them safely.

At Worcester in October 1945, thousands of racegoers were left outside when the gates were closed after some 25,000 had passed through the turnstiles. Not to be denied, the excluded stormed into an already packed cheap enclosure and some climbed onto the roof of a Tote building to get a better view of the action. Others followed and eventually the roof caved in pitching all and sundry onto the staff below. Miraculously, no one was killed, but 25 had to be taken to hospital.

It was only a matter of time before a real tragedy occurred and it duly happened at Burnden Park in March 1946 when the *Life* reported:

The greatest disaster in the history of British sport occurred during the FA cup-tie between Bolton Wanderers and Stoke City at Bolton on Saturday when two steel crush barriers collapsed. Thirty-three people were trampled or crushed to death, three were seriously injured and 500 others slightly injured. The gates were closed when 65,419 people had been admitted to the ground, but thousands forced their way into the enclosure by climbing a 10 foot wall or swarming over a railway embankment.

The usual knee-jerk reactions followed. The FA Council held an emergency meeting to consider what safety measures could be taken; police inspected grounds throughout the country checking entrances and barriers, and the Home Secretary launched an inquiry. It had all happened before in 1923 when the first FA Cup Final was held at Wembley. Then a paying crowd of 126,047 was swollen by thousands of gatecrashers resulting in the biggest pitch invasion in history, but, remarkably, no deaths. By a grim coincidence, Bolton were also playing that day when they beat West Ham 2-0.

Cup Finals were made all-ticket affairs after 1923 and a similar restriction was placed on semi-finals following the Bolton disaster but, despite all the official inquiries, more catastrophes were to take place before clubs were forced to put safety before profit by doing away with terraces and converting to all-seat stadiums.*

Not unnaturally, the footballers of 1946 wanted a cut of what the clubs were raking in and there was the real threat of a strike as the new season got underway in August when the 2,000-strong Players' Union was demanding a weekly wage of £12 (£380) during the season and £10 in the summer. The Football Management Committee was only prepared to offer £11 and £9, so the dispute over £1 rumbled on throughout the season and it was not until April 1947 that the players won their case when it was settled by arbitration.

At the same time, racing was facing a crisis of a different kind. Stables had been left desperately short-staffed during the war and for the first time girls were taken on in numbers to fill the gaps. The situation did not improve with demobilisation when many stable lads who had served in the forces went into the factories as the drive to return to pre-war production pushed wages well above what they could hope to earn in racing.

In Newmarket the situation was made worse by the proximity of sugar beet factories in Bury St Edmonds and Ely, and with a nationwide housing shortage (a quarter of homes had been destroyed during the blitz) there was also the problem of accommodation for newcomers to the area. The final blow came in 1947 when racing was deprived of its annual intake of youngsters as the school-leaving age was raised from 14 to 15, while the lowering of height and weight regulations for National Service to 5ft and 100lb (7st 1lb) increased the drain on stable staff.

Bill Munro addressed all these factors in February 1947 when he reported that racing's workforce was about to undergo a radical change:

Renewing a slight wartime experiment several trainers completed arrangements this week for qualified young women to enter their establishments to take up riding-out work and general stable

---

* At a Rangers v Celtic game at Ibrox in 1971 66 died; the toll was only slightly less at Bradford (56 dead) in 1985, while 96 died at Hillsborough four years later.

duties as a career. More will be arriving immediately to begin probationary terms in other stables ... There is every indication that the large-scale employment of women will soon become common after the difficulty of providing suitable lodging has been overcome.

Most of those recruited in the last few days ... are girls of good family with high school education and some have had initial experience in hunting stables and riding academies ... Girls – mostly former members of the Women's Land Army – have also been accepted this month at a number of the principal studs...

Employment of women in racing stables even on the largest possible scale will by no means solve the labour menace to the sport ... I know that some trainers in their despair have been going much further than merely looking for competent female labour. They have gone so far as to inquire officially if relief can be forthcoming from among the 160,000 Poles in Britain, 45,000 of whom have registered for employment, or from the ranks of the displaced persons in Europe whose importation in large numbers is being considered by Mr George Isaacs, the Minister of Labour.

At the time this article appeared the country was in the grip of its worst winter in living memory. In the same week, a squad of 200 German POWs* was used to dig out a train that had been trapped in drifts at Loughborough for 12 hours; Halifax bombers dropped food supplies to villagers cut off in Staffordshire, and farmers in Lincolnshire reported that flocks of starving crows were pecking out the eyes of snow-bound sheep.

As temperatures plummeted to −16°F (−27°C), the Thames froze over at Windsor, Admiralty barges were used as ice breakers on the Medway, and on parts of the south coast small ice-floes extended for a mile out to sea. Worst of all, coal was not getting through to the power stations. Factories were forced to shut down; the use of domestic coal and gas fires was banned and electricity cuts became routine as the price of candles soared by 400%. When the publication of weekly journals was suspended for a fortnight, the *Life* stepped into the breach as it announced:

To be deprived of the *Racing Calendar* is an unprecedented happening to the racing industry and the public and one which would, in the course of a few weeks, produce a state of chaos in all that appertains to the sport ... In these circumstances we have afforded Messrs Weatherby the opportunity to use our columns to disseminate such notices as they consider essential, and they have been pleased to accept.

Thus the *Life,* once again, became a truly invaluable source of information, a fact Francis Weatherby was pleased to acknowledge in a letter to Ben Clements:

The stewards of the Jockey Club and National Hunt Committee wish to thank you on behalf of the racing community as a whole for your kindness in publishing in your columns so much of what would have been in the current *Racing Calendar*. This has made it possible to continue the machinery of racing. Your action has bridged over a most difficult time for all and the stewards are most grateful.

---

* At the end of the war the government held on to about 500,000 German POWs who were used as forced labour to help the depleted workforce in reconstruction projects; the last POWs were not sent home until November 1948, while some elected to stay on in Britain including the former Nazi paratrooper Bert Trautmann who overcame initial hostility to become a national hero playing in goal for Manchester City.

Throughout that last frozen February fortnight, the paper also carried columns of 'guest news' from the *Horse & Hound*, *Motorcycle*, *Autocar* and *The Racing Pigeon*. And at the end of the month more space become available when Clement Attlee's Labour government banned the use of electricity, and therefore racing, at greyhound tracks even though some of them had their own generators. The National Greyhound Racing Society protested:

> There is absolutely no justification for selecting greyhound racing out of all entertainments as a means of fuel economy. The Ministry has stated that the consumption of fuel at our meetings is comparatively negligible; power companies say that it is insignificant, and we say that a meeting represents a saving in domestic current in that a large percentage of the public attending the meeting would otherwise have been at home using fuel and electricity.

Eventually, Manny Shinwell, the Minster for Fuel & Power, admitted the main reason for his action was the perceived "psychological effect" dog racing might have on the general public when they saw "flaming lights" over the stadiums while the rest of the area was in semi-darkness. The ban lasted for a month before tracks were allowed to stage meetings on Saturdays when the period during which racing could take place and the number of races allowed was doubled to eight hours and 16 races. On the last Saturday in March, 13 of London's 16 tracks took advantage of the new regulations to hold both afternoon and evening meetings, while Stamford Bridge staged a marathon 16-race card which started at 6.15pm and finished at 10.50pm.

The crisis also brought restrictions to football and rugby. Under pressure from a government worried about absenteeism in the workplace due to mid-week sport, both the FA and the RFU instructed their clubs to stop playing on weekdays while at the same time and for the same reason the Grand National was switched to Saturday from its usual Friday spot and the Derby and St Leger were later moved from their traditional Wednesday dates to Saturday, but otherwise mid-week racing was not affected.

Bill Munro, in congratulating the Jockey Club and National Hunt stewards for persuading the government that racing was a high priority for weekday fixtures, added a nice vignette to his comments on the Grand National switch:

> Finally, a tender reaction from Eire. On every Grand National day for generations conspicuous companies in the County and Tattersalls ring stands have been composed of hundreds of Irish parish priests and curates, who, from year to year, save enough from their small stipends to cover the cost of travel, accommodation, admission and betting on the occasion of the Aintree festival…
>
> Until this year, the railway and steamer companies have always made it possible for them (holding back the Friday night packet boat as long as the tide permits) to be back in time for celebration of the dawn Mass on Sunday. That would not be possible this month with the Grand National put on to Saturday … [*but*] yesterday the bishops and chapters in different dioceses gave absence-dispensation for priests who had arranged to go to Liverpool, and provided reliefs for the Sunday services. Posterity should find that gesture in the chronicles of racing.

Meanwhile, the Arctic weather played its own part in curbing sporting fixtures. After several postponements, the Waterloo Cup was finally abandoned as was the NH meeting at Cheltenham, although the most important races were transferred to the April fixture. There was also a mass migration of horses to the seaside and from Ayr in Scotland to Minehead in Somerset, the foam-flecked beaches drummed to the beat of impetuous hooves. At the end of February more than 60 horses from Newmarket along with many from the Yorkshire training centres were working on the sands at Redcar.

"Never in the history of Redcar racecourse have so many horses been stabled there during the non-racing season," the *Life* reported as it noted the presence of such ante-post fancies as the 1946 Lincolnshire Handicap winner Langton Abbot and the Grand National hope Sheila's Cottage (who was to triumph in 1948), but on this occasion both horses might as well have stayed at home for all the good their seaside breezes did them.*

When racing finally resumed at Taunton on March 15 after seven blank weeks, Tom Nickalls was on hand to record the happy event. It was not a day he would forget in a hurry. Feeling more like Captain Oates; he reported:

> The paddock and enclosure quickly became a quagmire; with mud over the ankles it was very difficult to stand upright, while the snow obscured visibility at the far end of the racecourse, fogged one's race-glasses and, like the cold, penetrated everywhere. Surely never before can a meeting, which supposedly celebrated a return to more normal conditions and which meant so much to so many, have been held under more depressing and downright unpleasant circumstances.

When the thaw finally came so too did the floods. One hundred square miles of Fenland were submerged, two million sheep were drowned and the list of jumping days lost to the weather was extended to 67 as the weekly *Sporting Record* (which enjoyed a 300,000-plus circulation during the post-war boom) started a relief fund to help those hardest hit. In ten weeks it raised a remarkable £8,209-10s (£243,440) to give the country's 340 licensed jump jockeys a much-appreciated £24-3s (£716) each.

As the snow and ice finally disappeared at Newmarket, Bill Munro witnessed some rare sights on the blasted Heath:

> Under skies of placid blue enchantment, the clarion of the spring and the Flat produced a spectacle never seen before in this generation. For four hours daily, nearly 1,200 horses – daft with fire and rarin' to go after long incarceration – have made sheer pandemonium on the few narrow Heath strips which are in service. Greater liveliness occurs every other minute as a score or so of riderless ones detach themselves from the trotting or cantering strings and bound to the horizon pursued by the unseated boys.

He could have added 'and girls', but preferred to deliver more constructive views designed to prod the authorities into moving with the times. In an article entitled 'The State and the Turf', he implied that racing's autocratic rulers were not best suited to achieving a good working relationship with a Labour government that was overseeing the birth of the Welfare State and advising the electorate to combat meat rationing by dining on squirrel pie. He cautiously suggested:

---

* Both races were won by 100-1 shots. Jockey Treble, ridden by 18-year-old Manny Mercer (who was killed in a fall at Ascot in 1959), beat a record field of 46 runners in near waterlogged conditions at Lincoln, while Caughoo, successful in the last two Ulster Nationals, accounted for 56 rivals as he slogged through the Aintree mud to win the Grand National by 20 lengths.

To pace the changes, might it not be desirable for the Jockey Club, while maintaining the full government of racing, to agree to the establishment of a more representative, secondary and complementary body – more freely and democratically chosen.

Once again, here was a *Life* man giving the authorities a radical lead, but it was to be 46 years before the 'more representative' British Horseracing Board came into being. In the meantime, the Jockey Club declined to implement racing's most pressing need – to provide the public with accurate racecards and, in so doing, save reams of valuable newsprint and boost the takings of the Tote to the benefit of all involved in the industry.

Instead of insisting that intended runners should be declared the day before a race, the authorities published a statement in the *Racing Calendar* of 25 March 1948:

> The stewards of the Jockey Club notice that a very large number of horses are left in races but do not run. With the present shortage of paper, it is of great importance that the final programmes and cards be kept as small as possible. They hope that trainers will do their best to co-operate by striking out all horses which are certain not to run.

Some hope! The fact that trainers wilfully chose to ignore this feeble plea was graphically illustrated by a pointed editorial notice in the *Life* two months later:

> *The Sporting Life* is anxious to give racing the greatest possible coverage within the limits of its restricted space, but an already difficult situation is aggravated by the size of the racecards ... Of the 79 remaining in the Guernsey Produce Stakes at Birmingham today only 13 are expected to face the starter. How much more we – and others – could have done with the space!

The 79 five-day acceptors for that one race took up a full column in the *Life*, yet only ten of them ran! Despite this deplorable state of affairs racing's rulers remained obdurate on the matter and that December Ben Clements reported through gritted teeth:

> Yesterday's *Racing Calendar* states that at a meeting of the Jockey Club in London on Monday the Duke of Norfolk, the senior steward, gave the view of the stewards that overnight declarations were not desirable in this country. This had the unanimous agreement of the members present.
>
> Great Britain is the only country in the world in which runners are not declared overnight. In Eire and every other country, lists of runners are supplied to the Press at least 24 hours before the races take place, but in England the provision of a reasonably accurate list of probable runners and jockeys is left to the Press.[*]

'Unanimous agreement,' mark you!

---

[*] Ireland, as ever, had moved with the times and introduced a 24-hour declaration of runners system in 1930, while France brought in a staggered forfeit system in 1936 to provide an accurate list of runners.

ROUGH JUSTICE

OR MORE than two decades after the Second World War racing was plagued by an epidemic of doping that left the sport's image in tatters. Lives, too, were torn apart as innocent trainers were warned off under a catch-all system that automatically convicted them if any horse in their care tested positive for drugs. In wielding such autocratic powers that ignored the laws of natural justice, the Jockey Club relied solely on one analyst's suspect findings against which there was no appeal.

By the time the scourge was effectively tackled, one jockey had been killed in a fall on an allegedly doped horse and two dozen trainers had lost their livelihoods, some – though by no means all – through no fault of their own.

A few of those involved with the dopers also paid a high price. Three chose to commit suicide rather than face public exposure, while jail sentences amounting to 26 years were handed out to 11 others; but the vast majority escaped scot-free. It was the blackest period in the long and chequered history of the Turf and yet so much of the damage inflicted on individuals and the sport could have been avoided had the lessons of the first high-profile case been taken on board.

Doping had been outlawed in Britain since 1904, but it was not until 1930 that the first trainers were warned off because of it. During the interim, the practice was carried on with impunity and it was only after repeated reports of nobbling or of horses being doped to win that the Jockey Club was stirred into action.

In September 1930, David Taylor, a young Doncaster trainer and brother of a leading northern jockey, Joe Taylor, achieved the unenviable distinction of becoming the first person to be warned off under Rule 176 (i) which related to the doping of horses. Taylor denied any wrongdoing and announced he intended to appeal, but there was no procedure for appeal against the rulings of the Jockey Club. Its authority could only be challenged in open court, which is where Charles Chapman took his case after he was warned off a fortnight later when his consistent handicapper, Don Pat, tested positive for caffeine after winning a minor race at Kempton Park.

A former jumps jockey, Chapman trained a string of 30 horses at Lavant in Sussex for some notable owners including the ducal Jockey Club members, Norfolk and Richmond. No one who knew him believed he would ever dope a horse and there was immediate speculation in the *Life* that an injustice had been done.

In commenting on the case of "a man who has protested his innocence and who has the backing of people of position who are convinced of it," an editorial highlighted two salient points which, if acted upon at the time, would have prevented a lot of grief and injustice in the years to come:

> The possibility arises of an innocent man being the victim of unscrupulous conspirators if the powers adhere rigidly to the principle that the onus of proving by whose hand a horse is drugged is placed upon the trainer[*] … There is a strong feeling among trainers that when the saliva of a horse is examined to find out whether a stimulant has been administered, the owner of the horse or his representative should be given, in a sealed container, one of the swabs taken by the veterinary surgeon for an independent examination on his behalf.

---

[*] Even if a trainer was able to prove he had been a 'victim of unscrupulous conspirators' it did not necessarily mean he would be exonerated by the authorities as at least one subsequent case was to show

Common sense, perhaps, but it took the Jockey Club 31 years to address these issues and bring in more equitable regulations. Chapman could not afford to wait for reform and, in an effort to clear his name, he brought an action for libel against the stewards of the Jockey Club – Lords Rosebery, Harewood and Ellesmere – as well as Weatherbys, who published the warning off notice in the *Racing Calendar*, and *The Times* which, in common with the *Life* and other newspapers, reprinted it.

In singling out *The Times*, Chapman took into account a comment made by its racing correspondent, Bob Lyle, a week before he was banned. In his innocence, Lyle had written: "It is quite safe to assume that extreme measures will not be taken by the authorities unless they are very fully satisfied that the party punished is the offender."

The warning-off notice, typical of its kind, left little doubt as to who the offender was:

The Stewards of the Jockey Club … satisfied themselves that a drug had been administered to the horse for the purpose of the race in question. They disqualified the horse for this race and for all future races under their rules, and warned C Chapman, the trainer of the horse, off Newmarket Heath.

The case came before the courts in November 1931 when Sir Patrick Hastings, KC, representing the trainer, maintained that any person who read the notice would assume that Chapman had been warned off for doping Don Pat, not because he failed to prevent the horse from being doped. After describing his client as a man of the very highest character and "as straight a man as might be found on the Turf, not excluding the very distinguished gentlemen who are the stewards of the Jockey Club," Hastings continued:

"I am not going to suggest that any of the stewards have acted in any sense other than perfectly honestly. But I am going to suggest that these gentlemen, who have placed upon them an awful power, do not seem to have appreciated in the least the obligations which those powers carry, and do not seem to realise that before they stigmatise a man in the way they have done they must be very careful they do not commit a grave injustice."

For the defence it was argued that under the rules of racing the stewards were required to publish their findings in the *Racing Calendar* and since Chapman was bound by those rules he could have no cause for complaint. It was further submitted that in their ordinary meaning, the words of the notice were true.

In giving evidence, Lord Rosebery, the senior steward, said that a trainer was solely responsible for the safe custody of his horses and there was no provision in the rules to deal with a trainer who failed to prevent a horse from being doped. He did, however, concede that the warning off notice could have been better framed so as to indicate that Chapman had not been found guilty of doping, but rather of what Rosebery chose to call "a grave dereliction of his duty as a trainer".

Hastings then asked whether Chapman had prejudiced his chances of being reinstated by going to law. In view of subsequent events, Rosebery's response was less than honest. "Not in the slightest," he replied, adding that Chapman could reapply for his licence in the spring when his application would be considered on its merits.

In his summing up Justice Horridge declared: "It is one of the rules in libel … that when you write something about a person it does not matter what you intended to say; it is what you wrote, and the test is what any reasonable minded person would understand what you wrote to mean."

The jury put the notice to the test and decided it had, indeed, implied that Chapman had doped

Don Pat. They awarded him a total of £16,000 (£830,000) in damages, but an appeal was immediately lodged and three months later the verdict was overturned. The Law Lords ruled that the stewards of the Jockey Club and Weatherbys were protected since the warning off notice was the *bona fide* decision of a domestic tribunal and its publication in the *Racing Calendar* was privileged.

The ruling that 'privilege' did not extend to *The Times* (which settled out of court), was of scant consolation to Chapman, as was the fact that the private detectives hired by him eventually found a chemist who had supplied drugs to one of his stable lads, but by then the man in question had left racing and could not be traced.

The Appeal Court's judgement set a benchmark for all future challenges to the disciplinary rulings of the Jockey Club, while Sir Patrick Hastings was left to reflect: "There is somewhere a defect in our legal system when a completely innocent person may have to suffer from the public belief that he is guilty, [*and*] there exists no means of proving his innocence except by bringing an action which he cannot win."[1]

For Chapman there was no comeback even though the Jockey Club withdrew his warning-off notice in 1934. He reapplied for his licence then, but despite having the backing of the Duke of Richmond, he was turned down as he had been in 1932. He tried again after the war, this time with the Duke of Norfolk adding his support, but once again his application was rejected due the influence of one man – the 6th Earl of Rosebery.

> It was reported back to the applicant that he [*Rosebery*] had reacted by saying, in so many words, 'that man took us on – he shall not come back'.[2]

Such petty-minded vindictiveness was still in evidence when the Jockey Club came to dealing with a welter of post-war doping cases. From early on there were concerns over the criteria employed by the stewards and the Club's vets in selecting horses for testing, while there was also criticism of the way samples were taken as well as questions over the reliability of the analyst's findings.

The first major case concerned the Malton trainer, Cecil Ray, who was warned off in 1946 when his well-fancied Maranta tested positive after finishing a well-beaten fifth in a two-year-old race at York's big May meeting.

Ray had been an accomplished jockey in his time having made his name in South Africa where he rode some 700 winners before returning to England in 1926. It was while riding for Dick Dawson's Whatcombe stable that he completed a unique double when he won the Irish Derby and St Leger in 1933 and '34 on the full-brothers Harinero and Primero, but at the end of the 1934 season his career in the saddle came to an abrupt end in bizarre circumstances.

After being narrowly beaten by a horse of Lord Derby's at Liverpool that November he objected to the winner on the grounds of boring and crossing. Derby, who was officiating at the meeting, stood down for the inquiry at which his fellow stewards not only overruled the objection but, "being extremely dissatisfied with Ray's riding," referred the matter to the Jockey Club stewards who promptly withdrew the jockey's licence *sine die*.

Ray spent the next three years in the wilderness before he was granted a licence to train. With the backing of owners such as Phil Bull, founder of the world-famous *Timeform* publications, he built up his stable to become one of the leading trainers in the north only to be knocked down again by the actions of one of his own stable lads who was in the pay of a local bookmaker. After a private detective hired by the trainer had extracted a confession from the doper the Jockey Club was informed of the facts, but the stewards refused to restore Ray's licence although they did lift their warning-off notice. This was of little help to Ray who died two years later a broken and embittered man.

The next case to hit the headlines was that of Jim Russell who had an international training career of 40 years behind him. He had started out in his native Australia and went on to gain fame in South Africa where he won the prestigious Durban July Handicap four times in six years. Following a trial season in England in 1926 and short stints in America and France, he finally put down roots at Mablethorpe from where he sent out two winners of the Lincolnshire Handicap before he was warned off in 1947 when his Boston Boro failed a dope test after winning at the opening Lincoln meeting.

The following year Russell brought an action against the Jockey Club for breach of contract on the grounds that his licence had been wrongfully withdrawn and he had not been given a fair hearing. Despite having Geoffrey 'Khaki' Roberts, Britain's leading prosecuting counsel at the Nuremberg war crimes trials, acting for him it is debatable if the hearing he received before the Lord Chief Justice, Lord Goddard, was any fairer than the one he had obtained at 15 Cavendish Square, then the London offices of the Jockey Club.

Roberts, a former England rugby international and, incidentally, a nephew of the *Life's* former managing editor, Edward Dorling, wasted no time in challenging the analyst's findings. It transpired that Lt-Col J Bell, one of four vets employed by the Jockey Club, could have contaminated the swabs as he was not wearing gloves when he took the samples, while the analyst, Mrs Lilian Mundy, had failed to identify any specific drug; her report merely stated that the swabs had given a general reaction for alkaloids.

Roberts then called on the trainer's own vet, John Beaumont, to give evidence which would show the analyst's report contained no proof that any drug had been administered, but to his dismay Goddard, a controversial Establishment figure at the best of times, ruled that expert evidence on doping was not material to any matter the court had to try. Whether the analyst had reached the right or wrong decision was not in issue, what the jury had to decide was whether Russell had received a fair hearing before the stewards.

Beaumont was, however, able to shed some light on the affair when he implied that the stewards had been gunning for Russell because of some past misdemeanour. Boston Boro had been tested in his last two races in 1946 and it seemed more than a coincidence that he should have been singled out again from 149 runners at the Lincoln meeting.

There was also the fact that Russell had been refused duplicate swabs when he asked for them. At the time, Bell claimed he did not have enough swabs with him, while Lord Willoughby de Broke, one of the Jockey Club stewards who gave evidence, asserted that duplicate swabs were not given because in some cases the samples of saliva obtained were so small there was only enough for the Club's analyst to work on.

Having heard all the evidence that was allowed to be given, the jury retired, but after an hour's deliberation they failed to reach a verdict and were discharged by Goddard who then declared that there had been no case to go before the jury in the first place and dismissed the action with costs. Russell appealed but lost again, and the following year a sad postscript was added to his case when, at the age of 69, he appeared before the Grimsby bankruptcy court with liabilities of £2,917 (£80,000) and no assets.

The apparent injustice suffered by Russell prompted the highly respected Epsom vet, Major A E Carey-Foster (ex-Chindit), to write to the *Life* to point out the risks of analysts returning false positives by confusing tonics prescribed and administered under veterinary supervision with drugs given illegally to affect a horse's performance in a race. He also claimed that the testing procedures employed by the Club's vets were inadequate and outdated.

In describing the system employed in California, Foster referred indirectly to the Russell case when he stated that the presence of minute quantities of alkaloids in samples of sweat or saliva were not considered evidence that a horse had been doped and, therefore, it was essential to identify the drug used. He advised:

> From the legal point of view the ideal practice is to have three samples taken and sealed immediately, one of which is handed to the owner or trainer, the second examined by the racing authorities' analyst and the third retained by the clerk of the course pending any gross disagreement on the analytical findings.
>
> A quantitative analysis is essential because many vegetable drugs are employed in the course of everyday veterinary practice; for example belladonna in cough electuaries and nux vomica in tonics, and traces of the alkaloids of these drugs can be found many days after treatment has ceased.
>
> In this connection it is a physiological fact that urine or blood samples are by far the most reliable media for detecting drugs … When I was acting as a veterinary surgeon and judge to the Straits Racing Association in Malaya, and later working under Royal Calcutta Turf Club Rules, these American methods I have briefly outlined were meticulously employed with marked success when taking routine samples at random from at least two races per day.

Despite lagging so obviously behind the times, it was to be another 13 years before the Jockey Club even considered employing such methods and in the meantime more lives were ruined and one was tragically lost when Ray Cane died of injuries received when his mount, Woolpack, fell in a hurdle race at Doncaster in March 1948.

At the inquest on the 31-year-old jockey it was revealed that Woolpack had tested positive for the stimulant Benzedrine.* Woolpack's Malton trainer, Val Moore, was automatically warned off and, on the face of it, was lucky to escape a manslaughter charge. According to the racing authorities he was, at the very least, guilty of negligence in that he had failed to prevent the horse from being doped, but the jury and the coroner decided there was no evidence to show that Woolpack had fallen because he was doped.

But once again there was controversy over the analyst's findings. When Moore heard that Woolpack was to be officially tested he had asked the racecourse vet to take samples as well. These had proved negative, but the Jockey Club's analyst claimed to have found the drug in 1/50,000[th] of a grain extracted from a sweat sample.

Moore's solicitor, E Freeman, challenged the findings on two counts – contamination and quantity. In the first instance he cited the peat bedding in the box Woolpack was stabled in, and the fact that the Jockey Club's vet, Lt-Col Donald Gillmor was a regular smoker and he, again, was not wearing gloves when he took the samples.

The Club's analyst, Mrs Mundy, responded by stating that even if the swabs had nicotine on them they could not have given a reaction to Benzedrine. When asked how she made her tests Mundy

---

* Benzedrine, better known under its generic street name 'speed', was given to soldiers on both sides during WWII. It is estimated British troops got through some 72 million tablets, while large amounts went astray and were widely used in all fields of sport after the war.[3]

initially refused to give any details, but when pressed further she relented and gave a full account of the process, part of which involved testing some of the substance on her tongue!

Stunned by this illuminating insight into the cutting-edge of forensic technology, Freeman turned to the next imponderable: "Here is such a minute quantity, which I am instructed on the authority of three analysts could not be identified, and yet on the findings of this minute particle a man's livelihood has already been taken away."

Mundy replied that she had records of cases where one-twentieth of that amount had been identified, whereupon Freeman snapped: "We are not concerned with your records. We are concerned with British justice."

But British justice was not to be found in the corridors of 15 Cavendish Square, and in the circumstances Moore was remarkably philosophical about his banishment as he commented: "I have no cavil against the National Hunt Committee. They did only what they thought was their duty in the light of the facts. My conscience is perfectly clear. I only wish the inquest had brought out who had done the doping to clear me completely."

Before the year was out more rough justice was to be dispensed by racing's authorities. Even as the inquest on poor Cane was taking place another tragedy of almost equal dimensions was unfolding in deepest Hampshire.

In 1946, Capt. Bobby Petre, late of the Scots Guards and a former champion amateur rider, achieved what every jump jockey dreams of when he won the Grand National on Lovely Cottage, trained by his old-time mentor, Tommy Rayson. Shortly after his Aintree triumph Petre turned professional and at the same time started to train a small string near Basingstoke, but his riding career came to an end in March 1948 when he had to have his left leg amputated below the knee shortly after breaking it in a freak accident. At the time his wife was quoted as saying:

> You simply cannot understand what this terrible thing must mean to Bobby. Race riding was his life. His whole thoughts were centred on winning the Grand National on Lovely Cottage for the second time. You can take it for certain that Bobby's first interest in life will remain horses, and now that he cannot ride anything better than a hack, he will devote himself to training.

But that was not to be. Two months later Petre was warned off the Turf after Bray Star, a horse he had trained and ridden in a hurdle race at Plumpton that January, had tested positive after being pulled up in a distressed state. Bray Star returned home a sick horse and died shortly afterwards.

The fact that three and a half months had elapsed between the race and the warning off, seemed to indicate the stewards of the NH Committee had serious doubts about the case; doubts that must have increased when Petre's former amateur colleagues, Lord Mildmay and Peter Cazalet (who was to train the Queen Mother's horses for many years), sent in samples for analysis that had been taken from a couple of jumpers turned out at grass. The tests on both samples were returned as 'positive'![4]

That the situation had become a tragic farce was demonstrated by yet another case that year when, only a few weeks after being granted his training licence, John Petts had it taken away from him when his first runner – Mr Deans, a 6-1 chance who finished fifth of six in a hurdle race at Plumpton in September – failed a dope test. The question of why relatively minor trainers were being targeted while the authorities failed to test horses from stables patronised by influential owners, remained unasked as Petts lamented:

Lovely Cottage and Bobby Petre make their way through the crowd after their victory in the 1946 Grand National; the cruellest of fates was to overtake Petre two years later.
© [Keystone]/[Hulton Archive] Getty Images

I am a poor man, but would give a lot to know how it [*the drug*] got there. It is a complete mystery to me, I did not have a penny on Mr Deans; I can't afford to bet. The stewards gave me a very fair hearing and I have no complaints against them. The rules say that trainers are responsible. When something goes wrong we must take the blame.

George Allden was not so ready to take the blame when his plater, Luxuriant (a 100-6 chance carrying 3lb overweight), tested positive after winning a 16-runner seller at Pontefract in 1949. The Newmarket trainer had made a careful study of the rules and he became the first to challenge the Jockey Club's authority in public when, in a statement to the Press Association that December, he declared:

There is nothing in the rules of racing which implies that a trainer will be held responsible for any unlawful act committed without his knowledge on any horse under his care. Rule 17 does state that the Stewards of the Jockey Club have the power at their discretion to grant and withdraw licences to officials, trainers, and jockeys. However, in accepting this rule when applying for my licence I did so in the firm belief that it would not be used in an arbitrary and totalitarian manner, but in accordance with the accepted principles of British justice...

I intend to do all in my power to clear myself of any suggestion that I could in any way be held responsible for the doping of Luxuriant ... I believe that this will clear my name of any stigma attached to the publishing of the verdict in the *Racing Calendar* and will show that the 'doping' of Luxuriant may have been made possible by the negligence of the racing authorities themselves.

I believe that doping both for the purpose of winning or losing a race is being carried out by doping gangs on a large scale in both Newmarket and Epsom and possibly other training centres and that the racing world would have a shock if every case could be brought to light.

By accusing the authorities of negligence Allden must have known he was throwing away any remote chance he might have had of getting his licence back. His charge was based on the fact that many courses licensed by the Jockey Club had insufficient and/or unsuitable stabling; a point picked up by Bill Munro in his Warren Hill column a week later when he advocated the setting up of a secure racecourse stabling system:

If that measure entails the provision of an adequate amount of stabling on the course, then let it be provided. It is indeed an open invitation to wrongdoers that so many courses are outmoded to an extent that horses have still to be quartered in odd boxes at pokey establishments often two or three miles away.

Central stabling and central supervision would also frequently require the earlier despatch of horses from the training areas, so that they would be in the care of the course executive in such time that pre-doping would be futile. Better, however, that inconvenience be suffered by many trainers than that one of their number be wrongfully condemned merely because, by the terms of his licence, he has been compelled to assume technical responsibilities which nowadays cannot be properly discharged by even the most meticulous and vigilant trainer.

By now the situation was so serious it was raised in parliament where the Home Secretary was asked if legislation would be introduced to make the doping of racehorses an indictable offence. Chuter Ede replied that he had no reason to suspect that the practice was of such proportions as to justify adding a new offence to criminal law. The very next day the *Life* revealed that six greyhounds had been doped at an Altcar coursing meeting. The contagion was spreading beyond proportions the Home Secretary or the Jockey Club stewards could ever dream of in their worst nightmares.

The following year (1950) saw the usual quota of banishments as the Jockey Club plugged the gap in its rules that had been exposed by George Allden. A new clause added to Rule 102 read:

If in any case it shall be found that any drug or stimulant has been administered to a horse for the purpose of affecting its speed in a race, the licence of the trainer of the horse shall be withdrawn, and he shall be declared a disqualified person.

Even before the new rule came into effect, John Beary, who had trained for the Aga Khan before the war, was warned off after his plater, La Joyeuse – unplaced at 20-1 in an apprentice handicap at Lingfield that October – tested positive. The question here was not who had doped a 20-1 no-hoper in such a lottery of a race, but who, in their right mind, would believe such a 'doping' had taken place?

A few days later the *Life* led its front page with a letter from the trainer's brother, the jockey

Michael Beary, who highlighted the injustice of the situation as he argued:

> Through the new rule about doping, the stewards of the Jockey Club have their hands tied, and they
> stand on the report of the lady analyst who may or may not be right. Therefore my brother John can
> only regain his livelihood and honour by finding the man who doped La Joyeuse … If Scotland Yard
> and the Berkshire Police under such an able organiser as Sir Humphrey Legge, cannot find who
> doped her, how can John? My brother is ruined financially and socially, although innocent. He was
> automatically judged guilty before the hearing of the case, which is entirely contrary to natural
> justice.[*]

More letters followed including one from Samuel Edgedale, KC, who called the authorities'
handling of the affair "a travesty of justice" and cited the Greek historian Herodotus, who maintained
that every autocrat eventually suffers from hubris and when that time comes the only thing to do is to
get rid of them. He reasoned:

> It is obvious from the fact that they have seen fit to defy one of the most elementary Rules of Justice
> that those magnificent autocrats, the Jockey Club, are suffering from that complaint, and if racing
> is to go on their constitution must be changed.

Bill Munro, as a former crime reporter, was also well acquainted with the law and he made a
telling point when referring to the number of trainers that had been warned off:

> If there was any evidence that any of them had been guilty of, or been accomplices in, doping it
> would have been the bounden duty of the Jockey Club stewards to report the facts to the Director
> of Public Prosecutions with a view to proceedings in the criminal courts on a charge of attempting
> to obtain a share of a prize by fraud. As no such action has yet been taken, it has to be presumed that
> in none of the cases was it believed by the stewards that the trainer himself could be held culpable
> of malpractice.

Munro also reminded the Jockey Club that prevention was better than cure and that depriving
an increasing number of small, humble trainers of their living was no solution to the problem. But
even when the stewards were given the opportunity to take a more positive role in suppressing doping
they failed to act on it.

Just before Christmas 1950 the *Life* published a circular letter that had recently been sent to
trainers and owners by the infamous Peter Christian Barrie, a self-confessed doper and ringer of horses.[†]
In his letter Barrie had brazenly plugged a 'special tonic' he was selling for 25s (£32) a bottle, which

---

[*] In a rare instance of clemency, the Jockey Club restored Beary's licence in 1953. During the interim, Michael took over
training his brother's horses and sent out Ki Ming to win the 1951 Two Thousand Guineas, thus adding to his four classic
successes as a jockey: the 1937 Derby (Mid-day Sun), two St Legers (Trigo '29 & Ridge Wood '49) and the 1932 Oaks
(Udaipur).

[†] Barrie's activities had earned him a three-year jail sentence in 1920 after which he carved out a notorious career for himself
in America before he was deported back to England in 1934. Although warned off, he had continued to run doped horses
under various aliases or in other peoples' names up until WWII.

'works wonders for rogue horses when given three and a half hours before a race'.

To accompany the publication of the letter, the paper carried an interview Munro had with Barrie, who showed him a list of addresses to which he was sending some 300 bottles, and also a number of letters asking for repeat supplies.

Munro then asked Barrie: "Have you any information that the authorities are in possession of samples of your preparation?"

Barrie: "Oh yes. Men whom I knew to be representatives of the Jockey Club called upon me and asked for a quantity, which was willingly supplied."

Barrie went on to claim that a recent winner had tested negative after being given his 'harmless dynamite'. He stressed: "My tonic contains no pernicious drugs, even in the tiniest quantity. If administering it is a crime then I am an arch-villain and the public would expect to find me in the dock on a charge of conspiring to perpetrate a felony or, at least, being an accessory before the fact. But no such action will be taken. No one can find evidence on which to lay a charge."*

It was, of course, all a pack of lies and after the 'arch-villain' had stated he intended to send out 1,000 more circulars in the New Year, Munro concluded:

> Such, therefore, is the testimony of 'Ringer' Barrie and the plans for a large scale extension of his activities. It raises many issues, chief of them the growing peril to which innocent trainers will be defencelessly exposed.

The warning was plain enough and one would have thought it would have been endorsed by the authorities either through a statement denying the tonic was harmless or by cautioning trainers against using it. They did neither, but there was a response of sorts. In his circular Barrie had claimed that Lord Rosebery was present in a racecourse bar when he bought a horse, which subsequently won thanks to his tonic. The following day a single column box on the *Life's* front page announced:

> Lord Rosebery wishes it to be clearly understood that there is no truth in the statement implied in 'Ringer' Barrie's circular letter, quoted in yesterday's *Sporting Life*, to the effect that he, Lord Rosebery, was ever 'present in the cocktail bar' in Barrie's company.

Well, that's all right then – problem solved! Really, the insularity and incompetence of racing's rulers was breathtaking.

Meanwhile, the cull continued. Two more trainers – Mark Collins (Blewbury) and Joe Thwaites (Malton) – were warned off that December and in October 1951 a fourth Malton trainer, Ernie Street, suffered the same fate when Rock Star failed a dope test after finishing third in the Clarence House Stakes at Ascot.

Rock Star, the 2-1 second favourite, was an ideal target for nobblers in what was virtually a two-horse race since his 'removal' (he would have won but for swerving all over the course inside the final furlong) cleared the way for the 6-4 favourite to win.

Rock Star was one of the best two-year-olds in the country, but under Jockey Club rules he was

---

* Following Munro's interview, Barrie sold his story to *The People* and soon afterwards disappeared from the scene when the Sunday paper revealed his 'harmless dynamite' was in fact a potent and "cunningly devised dope" containing quantities of potassium bromide, caffeine and alcohol.[5]

automatically barred from racing again;* a double injustice that left his owner, Alick Barnett, feeling bitter and disenchanted as he commented:

> This is terribly unfair to me and my trainer as we are absolutely innocent. Rock Star is by far the best horse I have owned … I am very upset by the whole business as it is obviously the work of some crooks and I shall now give up owning horses.

Barnett's decision reflected the growing disillusionment with racing that was being expressed in all quarters. Trainers lived in fear of their horses being got at and now that the worst had happened to him, Street could only hope for a miracle. He explained:

> The stewards allege that the test on the horse showed that opium and one of the belladonna group of drugs were present in the saliva. My vet is of the opinion that if the horse was got at it must have been within two hours of running and administered at Ascot. The horse may have been tampered with in his stable at Ascot where there are three entrances to the yard, but only one policeman on duty.
> I am told the drug is used to prevent a horse winning. We backed the horse that day and if he was tampered with it must have been the work of an outsider. The Malton police have been working on the case for me and they are still trying to obtain evidence which I hope will help me to clear myself.

Just over a month later, Street must have felt he had been thrown a lifeline when Lord Rosebery sensationally announced that a private test taken on one of his horses had shown it had been nobbled and that he was offering a £1,000 reward for any information that would lead to identifying the dopers.

Every trainer who had been warned off after their horse had tested positive for a 'stopping' drug must have taken heart from this unexpected development. Surely, they reasoned, this proved what they had long maintained; gangs of dopers were at work and not even Lord Rosebery's trainer, Jack Jarvis, could stop them.†

The *Life's* editor, Ben Clements, was just one of many who believed their cases should be reviewed and he applauded Rosebery for bringing the matter into the open:

> We may assume that this is Lord Rosebery's forthright way of urging upon the stewards and his fellow members of the Jockey Club the necessity of revising their ill-conceived rule which came into effect on January 1, 1951 … If the private veterinary examination to which Lord Rosebery refers had been an official enquiry, then by the rigid terms of this rule, Jack Jarvis would today be a disqualified person. That would be a miscarriage of justice which would have revolted every follower of the Turf.
> Trainers of less renown may have suffered this injustice. From the time that the rule was first mooted

---

* Rock Star was retired to stud in 1953 and despite covering only 39 mares in his first five years, he sired some smart sprinters with 14 of his first 15 runners winning a total of 60 races, but he became infertile and was put down in 1962, the year after his full-brother, Rockavon, had won the Two Thousand Guineas.

† The horse in question was the two-year-old filly, Snap, a half-sister to Rosebery's 1944 Derby winner, Ocean Swell. A winner at Newmarket in October, Snap was well beaten when 5-2 favourite to follow up over the same course four weeks later. However, in his autobiography, Sir Jack (as he later became) Jarvis says: "There was a certain lapse of time before the test was taken … and personally I always entertained doubts as to whether in fact she was really nobbled."[6]

we have pointed out its dangers and consistently condemned its tyranny. Lord Rosebery's frank statement is a vindication of our campaign. We look for a prompt amendment of the rule, a reconsideration of some sentences passed under its terms and a more flexible approach to the problem in future.

But Clements looked in vain. He was not to know it had been Rosebery who had blocked Charles Chapman's renewed applications for a trainer's licence, and neither the 6th Earl nor the acting stewards were in any hurry to reconsider the cases of 'trainers of less renown' just because one of his horses had been got at.

What did happen was that security at racecourse stables was tightened up and stable lads were issued with identity cards. For the 1952 Craven meeting a high wire fence was erected around the 102-box stable block, the gate was manned on a 24-hour basis and the whole yard was floodlit at night.

At last it seemed as if the authorities were beginning to listen to their critics, but there was still no relief for the condemned trainers. As there was no redress against the Jockey Club in open court, George Allden (who had been reduced to working as a store clerk in a London factory), and Ernie Street petitioned the Queen for an independent tribunal to be set up to investigate their cases. On 1 December 1952, the *Life* announced:

> The petition declares that the Jockey Club and National Hunt anti-doping rules are unsound and unjust in construction, are very unfair in application and do nothing to prevent doping. It also declares that the rules under which they were penalised were carried out without the delivery of justice in the accustomed manner of the law courts, as no legal representation was allowed to the accused trainers.

Street was quoted as saying: "All we want is a fair hearing ... The disqualification imposed on us operates all over the world. At the moment we only get medieval justice. We have been branded as rogues although we have never been convicted of any offence."

The story was published on the same day as the Jockey Club held its annual winter meeting in London, but if the petitioners thought this might help their cause, they were sadly mistaken. Showing up the authorities in this way was the worst move they could have made and their action ensured they would never be reinstated.*

In addressing members of the Club that day, the senior steward, Major Reginald Macdonald-Buchanan, announced that a review of the doping situation together with the 22 positive cases that had come to light over the past seven years had been considered by the stewards at a meeting in November. The review had produced "no evidence of the existence of alleged doping gangs" and he

---

* Allden was to spend most of his life's savings trying to clear his name, while Street's wife, Lillian, even wrote to the Queen pleading 'as one woman owner to another' but it was all to no avail. At the start of the 1962 Flat season, the *Life* reported the Jockey Club had refused to restore Street's licence for the tenth successive year. His wife was quoted as saying: "This is enough to break my husband's heart. Since he lost his licence he has gone from job to job – office, factory... he cannot settle. His life is racing. I don't know what he will do now." Street, then 53, revealed he had tried to get clearance to train in Ireland or Rhodesia, but it had been withheld by the Jockey Club. He said: "The stewards have refused to meet me to explain why I am still blacklisted so many years after the incident. They gave no reason for refusing to grant me a licence. I have been moved behind a curtain, yet there is nothing in my life on the turf for which I could not give a satisfactory explanation." The report ended with a cursory quote from the senior steward, Lord Crathorne: "The decision of the stewards' is based on certain facts about the incident which we are not prepared to discuss in public." Whatever the 'facts' were, they could not have been too damning otherwise, as Munro had pointed out, the stewards would have been duty bound to pass them on to the DPP.

hoped that: "Members will feel able to support the view that the main policy of the Club needs no alteration and that Rule 102 (ii) is proving a satisfactory deterrent which is keeping the practice of doping in check."*

It was reported the Club unanimously supported the stewards' motion to pursue their policy. Not one member of that august and privileged body had the balls to stand up and declare the policy was *not* working and that it was a rank injustice to honest men.

---

* The Jockey Club could not have it both ways. From 1946 to 1951 just 39 official tests had been taken on horses and of these 20 had proved positive.[7] On this count either half the horses running under Rules were doped or their analyst was finding dope where there was none.

THE NOBBLERS

WHILE the stewards talked tough on doping, their resolution to pursue their policy evaporated in the wake of Lord Rosebery's revelation and the growing evidence that there was a major question mark hanging over the findings of their analyst. For the remainder of the 1950s, racecourse stewards were reluctant to order dope tests knowing full well what the consequences would be if they proved positive, while trainers who suspected their horses had been got at had them privately tested and kept the findings to themselves.

With no exchange of information between the two camps, the dopers were able to continue their work unhindered and rumours of foul play were rife as the last minute withdrawal of fancied horses from races often indicated a case of nobbling. Then, in the spring of 1960, the whole festering carbuncle was lanced by the blast from a .410 shotgun.

The previous year Sir Gordon Richards, then training a string of 60 horses at Ogbourne Maisey on the Wiltshire Downs, had called in the Flying Squad after he had been tipped-off that his horses were being doped. Enquiries led the police to the door of a pretty thatched cottage in Compton, Berks, where they searched the room of the resident lodger, Bertie 'Bandy' Rogers, a 66-year-old former stable lad.

Some powder and a box of incriminating letters were found and Rogers, a "kindly, genial little man" according to one detective,[1] was taken away to be interviewed. After 'helping police with their enquiries', he returned to his lodgings where, early the following morning, he walked outside the back door and blew out his brains.

Following the suicide of their chief suspect the police intensified their enquiries. They found that Rogers had been questioned ten years earlier in connection with doping activities and again in 1954 when he was working in stables in the Wetherby area. On that occasion, his accomplice was a chemist's assistant in Harrogate, but he too had committed suicide before charges could be brought. The Yorkshire police did, however, find evidence of doping and the ringing of horses. Two bookmakers and a professional punter were suspected of being behind the operation, but the DPP decided the evidence was not strong enough to stand up in court and so no charges were ever brought.

This time the police had their evidence in black and white. On 5 July 1960, they swooped and arrested Bert Woodage, who rode as second jockey for Sir Gordon Richards; three stable lads connected with other stables, and Harry Tuck, a chemist's dispenser in Hednesford, Staffs. All five were charged with administering drugs to horses between 1 January 1958 and 31 December 1959.

Tuck admitted he had sent batches of caffeine to Rogers who passed them on to stable lads to give to the horses. When asked if he had supplied any other people with caffeine (then available without a prescription) Tuck replied: "It's been going on for years up here. When I was a lad in the shop, trainers used to come in and my old governor, who is dead now, used to supply them."[2]

As Tuck had worked at the chemist's for close on 40 years, the amount of doping to win going on in his area alone must have been extensive. The trainers concerned would have known how to administer the drug effectively, but it soon became clear during their trial at Gloucester Assizes in October 1960 that Rogers' gang were a bunch of amateurs.

Caffeine acts as a stimulant only if given up to two hours before a race, but it can have the opposite effect if administered earlier as the horse would become hyperactive and expend its excess energy by walking its box. In most of the cases quoted, the caffeine had been given at least six hours before the race so it would have had a detrimental effect or none at all.

Among the letters Rogers received from his accomplices telling him which horses they had doped, Woodage named eight trained by Richards, but their performances in such top class races as the King George V Stakes at Ascot and the Chesterfield Cup at Goodwood were unexceptional. Humphrey Cottrill, Jack Colling and Dick Hern were other trainers whose horses were named as having been doped.

Woodage and Tuck were both sentenced to 18 months imprisonment and two of the stable lads received lesser sentences, but while they were serving their time a more professional and ruthless gang was wreaking havoc in stables throughout the country as they nobbled short-priced favourites with sedatives that worked only too well.

In the meantime, the reliability of dope tests had again been brought into question in sensational circumstances. In May 1960, Ireland's champion trainer, Vincent O'Brien, was warned off when his colt, Chamour, tested positive after landing the odds of 4-6 in a maiden plate at the Curragh.

Since taking out a licence in 1944, O'Brien had trained three successive winners of the Grand National; had sent out Cottage Rake and Hatton's Grace to complete hat tricks in the Cheltenham Gold Cup and Champion Hurdle, and had won a St Leger and an Arc de Triomphe. He was hardly likely to dope a horse to win a piddling race worth just £202.

The Irish stewards knew this well enough, but they were compelled to act on a report from the Jockey Club's analysts,[*] which was similar to the one that had condemned Jim Russell to his lonely exile 13 years earlier. The report merely stated that 1/10,000th of a grain of an amphetamine derivative resembling methylamphetamine had been found in the saliva sample taken from Chamour.

A disbelieving O'Brien sought out the most eminent experts in the field to get their opinion on the findings and their verdict was unequivocal: "(1) No identification of a drug was made. (2) Only approximate amounts of a derivative resembling something were found. (3) It appeared that the amounts purported to have been found were outside the scientific limits available with the most up-to-date techniques."[3]

And this was 12 years *after* Mrs Mundy maintained she had found 1/50,000th of a grain of Benzedrine in Woolpack's sample!

The experts, who ranged from the director of the police laboratories at Scotland Yard to a former president of the German chemical industry, confirmed what many already suspected, namely: "The secretions of animals contain a large number of substances, some of which are related chemically to materials of the nature of amphetamine."[4]

The Turf Club, which had carried out an investigation into all aspects of doping at the beginning of the year, accepted these findings, but told O'Brien that if they admitted their mistake their authority would be undermined to the detriment of racing. However, by way of an apology, they lopped six months off the trainer's original 18-month ban.

Autocratic they may have been, but the Irish authorities had already shown they were more flexible than their English counterparts by imposing a limited sentence on the trainer; by not banning Chamour from racing, and by allowing A S 'Phonsie' O'Brien, Vincent's younger brother, to take over training the 70 horses at Ballydoyle.

It was left to Chamour to exonerate his former trainer from the slur of doping when he returned

---

* Since 1956 samples had been double-checked by Mrs Mundy in London and a Dr Schwabe in Germany.

to the Curragh on June 22 and, amid "the most thunderous cheers that have ever been heard at an Irish Derby meeting" beat the 1-3 favourite, Alcaeus, to win Ireland's premier classic.

The man himself spent the day quietly casting a fly on his favourite stretch of the Blackwater in Co. Meath; he knew he had bigger fish to land – six Epsom Derbys among them – when he returned from exile to fulfil his role as Ireland's greatest trainer.*

It had been a landmark case from which lessons were learnt in Dublin if not in London. The Irish Turf Club already operated a random system of testing at least one winner a day, the race being decided by ballot, and that autumn it went a step further by testing all winners, with the samples of saliva and urine (not sweat) being sent to the pharmacology department of Trinity College, Dublin, instead of the Jockey Club's analysts.

Yet the mandarins in Cavendish Square still refused to acknowledge that somewhere along the line of swabs, sweat and saliva, something was seriously wrong. Confirmation that the British system needed a radical overhaul came less than a month after the O'Brien case, when the Cheltenham trainer Phil Doherty was warned off after his 11-year-old gelding Précipité, a 20-1 chance having only his second race in two years, tested positive after being pulled up in a handicap chase at Newton Abbot.

As he emerged from the subsequent inquiry with his career in ruins, a distraught Doherty was quoted as saying: "The horse travelled with my young stable boy, Richard Pitman, and the driver on the day before racing and did not stop on the way to Newton Abbot. The horse was stabled overnight at the racecourse stables. I have no plans for the future; my livelihood has gone after a lifetime with horses."

Having dealt with the press, Doherty turned away and broke down in tears.

In the same week, Bill Munro indicated one likely reason for all the inexplicable test results in an article headed 'Medicine Or Dope – Do We Blunder?' Referring to the fact that the American authorities had recently set up a committee of research chemists, vets, racing legislators, lawyers, trainers and breeders to investigate the whole question of drugs in racehorses, he suggested the Jockey Club should hold a similar top-level inquiry in the light of the O'Brien and Doherty cases:

> Throughout racing a doubt is growing if these and the preceding cases involving condemnation of trainers had anything at all to do with doping. Is it not more likely, it is being asked, that they were due entirely to the delayed action of highly-sponsored medical preparations, which have a definite place in the veterinary field and which were trustingly used in the best of faith?
>
> The American inquiry has been sparked by the public fear that a grave injustice had been done to a number of trainers suspended lately; that the findings were … based largely on the theory 'If it can be detected, it is wrong'; that false positive indications could be produced from innumerable drugs and chemicals, none of which are stimulants and practically all of which are harmless if properly used under veterinary supervision.

The publicity given to the two cases was largely responsible for breaking down the taboo that surrounded any mention of doping in racing circles and, one by one, trainers began to come forward with evidence of foul play. That summer, the Newmarket trainer Jack Watts found his star sprinter, Sing

---

* There was no happy ending for Chamour who died in freak circumstances the following February after he had cast himself in his box. In struggling to right himself, his rug became twisted around his neck and the buckle pin on the breast straps was forced open and pierced his jugular vein.

Sing, in a dazed condition in his box a few hours before he was due to met his northern rival, Tin Whistle, in a match for the July Cup. Sing Sing was withdrawn and after a private urine test on the colt had proved positive 'Warren Hill' disclosed:

> There have been reports in Newmarket of similar cases, as yet not officially confirmed. Current opinion among Newmarket trainers is that this serious problem has reached a critical stage and there must be immediate and drastic action.

This was asking a bit much of the Jockey Club, but things were bustled along nicely the following month when the former senior steward, the Duke of Norfolk, revealed that two of his horses, Skymaster and Red Letter, had been nobbled. They had been ideal targets for the dopers, hot favourites in small fields; those in the know could afford to lay them with impunity and back the second favourite.

Skymaster was in a three-runner race at Ascot and the writing was on the wall for all to see after he had opened up at 1-2 and drifted out to evens as the second favourite was backed in to 11-10. Skymaster was beaten five lengths with the 10-1 outsider tailed off. And it was the same with Red Letter, an uneasy 7-4 favourite when a well-beaten fourth of five at Kempton the following week.

Three days later, the Bob Read-trained Silver Kumar (evens), trailed in last of six under Lester Piggott at Hurst Park. Once again a private test proved positive, and finally the Jockey Club began to get its act together. On August 25, a *Life* editorial revealed:

> A complete change of attitude to trainers by the stewards of the Jockey Club on the question of the doping of horses became evident yesterday when all license holders received the following notice:
>
> "The Stewards wish to draw the attention of trainers to the notice published in the *Racing Calendar* of August 18: 'It would be helpful to the Stewards under the present circumstances if trainers who are in a position to give any information to the Stewards as a result of their own enquiries at any time would communicate immediately with the secretary of the Jockey Club'."
>
> The cheering fact in the new situation is that the Jockey Club are at last seeking the help of trainers on this dope question rather than using the 'big stick' which they have wielded from time immemorial.

The depressing fact was that the authorities were still not prepared to approach the people who could really help them – the bookmakers; the men who could trace the source of 'inspired' money in suspect races and point to those who were repeatedly laying the hot favourites that were being nobbled.

As early as 1951, Dan Summers, the secretary of the National Bookmakers Protection Association (NBPA), had declared: "We are desperately anxious to co-operate with the authorities in helping to clear up this blot on racing. We invite the stewards of the Jockey Club to seek our co-operation at the earliest possible moment and we can assure them it will be readily given. Unless racing is kept clean and this canker removed from our national sport we shall all be put out of business."[5]

That offer was never taken up and it was to be another 11 years before the stewards were publicly shamed into liaising with the layers. In the meantime, the Jockey Club announced at its 1960 winter meeting in London that a three-man committee had been set up under the Duke of Norfolk to inquire into the efficiency of dope detecting methods and the effectiveness of the Club's rules on the matter.

In commendably quick time the tribunal* took evidence from 95 representatives of the racing industry and published its findings the following May. The *Life's* three-deck headline summed up the report in a nutshell: 'Duke of Norfolk's Committee urges revolutionary changes / Daily Dope Tests – And New Deal For Trainers / No warning-off for innocent men'.

In truth, the changes were only revolutionary to Britain. They had been implemented by the Irish authorities the previous year and had been in use in other countries for many years. Significantly, the 23-page report incorporated many of the recommendations that had been put forward by various experts – most notably by the vet, Carey-Foster (now Sir Winston Churchill's racing manager) – and columnists in the *Life* over the past 30 years.

Routine and random testing; no life-bans for doped horses; no sweat samples; triplicate samples of saliva and urine; no medication for horses within 72 hours of a race, and, most important of all, where a drug – stimulant or sedative – was detected, provided the stewards were satisfied the trainer had taken all reasonable precautions to protect the horse his licence would not be withdrawn.

The establishment of a research laboratory to carry out tests and monitor new drugs was also recommended along with the setting up of an advisory council, made up of a vet, chemist and pharmacologist, to assist the stewards in interpreting analysts' reports. All in all, the Norfolk report represented a victory for common sense, and in 1961 common sense was desperately needed in the face of a wave of audacious dopings that was sweeping the country.

At the time the report came out a horse called Pinturischio was a firm 6-1 favourite for the 1961 Derby. Unraced as a two-year-old, the Noel Murless-trained colt had long been the subject of rave reports from the gallops and when he made a winning debut in the Wood Ditton Stakes at Newmarket in April, the front page of the *Life* carried a collage of superlatives lifted from Tom Nickalls' report:

A magnificent specimen of horseflesh … his girth is terrific and his quarters massive … he has the disposition of a real gentleman and a kind, intelligent eye … his action is faultless … he sailed in on a tight rein looking wonderfully impressive.

This hype took a knock when Pinturischio could finish only fourth to the 66-1 winner, Rockavon, in the Two Thousand Guineas, but he still retained his position at the head of the Derby market. It was felt he would be better suited by the longer trip and confidence in him grew as he sparkled in his work with his stable companion Petite Etoile, the outstanding filly of 1959 and 1960.

But the nobblers were waiting in the wings. Two days before Pinturischio was due to run in the Dante Stakes at York, the lock on his stable door was picked and he was given a physic of the kind vets used as a purgative for elephants. At first the news that the colt had been 'got at' was hushed up and on the day of the Dante it was reported he would miss the race because he had a stomach upset and was running a temperature.

Remarkably, 'Pinto' recovered so well he was back on course for the Derby within a week although bookmakers fielded against him at the Victoria Club call-over on May 19 when he was pushed out to 9-1. The following night he was nobbled again and this time it finished him for good even though his participation at Epsom remained in the balance up until Lester Piggott rode him in a workout on the 27th, four days before the Derby.

---

* The other committee members were Sir Laurence Byrne, a former High Court judge who had presided over the celebrated 'Lady Chatterley' obscene publication case, and Dr Walter Wooldridge, chairman, scientific director and founder of the Animal Health Trust.

Sir Victor Sassoon's colt was taken out of the race later that morning and never ran again. By this time it had been widely reported he had been nobbled and although the perpetrator was never publicly named he was known well-enough in Newmarket:

> The inside man proved to Lester's and everyone's disgust to be one of the best lads in the stable. He had cared for one great horse and at the same time ruined another. He had taken the owner's compliments and thanks and cynically robbed Sir Victor Sassoon behind his back not only of another possible Derby, but of the colt's future at stud.[6]

That a Derby favourite could be got at so easily, not just once but twice, was a shattering blow to racing's image. The motive was obvious. The bookmakers made a killing – an estimated £250,000 (£4.3m) was netted in ante-post bets – but only a few of them knew who was behind the doping; the rest strongly resented the aspersions that were inevitably cast on their profession, particularly as their previous offers of help had been spurned by the authorities.

Racing was still reeling from the effects of the 'Pinto' blow when it was hit again by the 'Pando' nobbling. In July, Pandofell, winner of the previous month's Ascot Gold Cup, was found dazed and bleeding in his box on the morning of the Sunninghill Park Stakes at Ascot for which he was expected to start a hot favourite to beat his three rivals. This time, however, the gang blundered by overdosing the horse with phenobarbitone. There was no ante-post betting on the event and so no money was made out of it when Pandofell was withdrawn from the race.

As the Norfolk report had noted: "often the doping agent is given inexpertly, either in inappropriate quantity or at a time misjudged in relation to the time of the race."

Unlike Pinturischio, Pandofell recovered to end his season by winning the Doncaster Cup. Other horses did not fare so well. Indian Melody (also phenobarbitone) never regained her form after finishing last of four in the Newmarket Oaks that October. Once again the outcome was reflected in the betting as the Epsom-trained filly opened at 6-4 and went out to 5-2, while the winner was backed down to 11-8 from 5-2.

In the wake of this latest nobbling the *Life* received an anonymous phone call from a man who said he 'wanted to see justice done'. He gave the editor, Ossie Fletcher (who had taken over from Ben Clements in 1959), the name of a bookmaker he claimed was the ringleader of the gang, and identified other members including a mysterious 'French girl' who posed as a prospective owner when spying out stables for the dopers to target.

It was a major breakthrough. When Fletcher passed on the information to the Jockey Club and Scotland Yard it transpired that CID officers already had some of the suspects under surveillance, but more information was needed and as a spate of new doping cases was reported, the *Life* had to be careful not to prejudice any prosecutions that might arise from its own or police investigations.

When the forecast favourite Caca Dora was withdrawn from her race at Plumpton in November after the Chris Nesfield-trained mare showed signs of being doped, the paper had to play dumb as it asked:

> Who is the woman – reputedly French – who has visited stables in all parts of Britain recently and about whom all trainers have been warned in a letter from the racing authorities? … The almost certain doping of Caca Dora could be the work of a gang associated with her … She visited Chris Nesfield's stable while he was at the last Fontwell Park meeting two weeks ago … The woman also

visited Major Verly Bewicke's stable on the Scottish border and three of his recent runners are now suspected of being doped.

Three days later, more of anonymous caller's information was carefully blended in with a statement from Cavendish Square when it was reported:

A well-known London gambler was last night identified as the man who accompanied a 'French woman' to the stables of a northern trainer last Saturday. A Jockey Club spokesman said 'We know this man and his confederates. They include another London gambler and a Manchester bookmaker.' … The man who accompanied the woman to the stable last Saturday was earlier seen in Newcastle an hour before racing talking to a representative of a bookmaking firm in the lounge of the Royal Station Hotel.

The following day, Ossie Fletcher used his Saturday 'Talking Points' column to urge bookmakers to come forward with their information:

When a horse is doped somebody makes a lot of money out of it. Some bookmakers, somewhere, cannot help but have a shrewd idea who it is. It is their duty to their calling as well as to the community as a whole to pass their knowledge on. It may not be important. They may have drawn the wrong conclusion. But it is only by the pooling of information that a pattern can emerge which would be helpful to the authorities.

On Monday the paper revealed that Fresh Winds, a forecast 1-2 favourite when withdrawn from a steeplechase at Uttoxeter eleven days earlier, was the sixteenth horse known to have been doped in the past few months. Fresh Winds was trained by Roy Whiston whose Wollerton, Salop, stables had twice been visited by the 'French woman'.

Whiston gave a chilling insight into the dangers jockeys were facing as he described the condition in which he found his horse on the morning of the race:

He could not stand. His legs were paralysed. It was not a nice sight and I don't think he was the only one got at. At least two more of my horses were doped too. Unfortunately it was not until after they had raced that I discovered it. Both surprisingly drifted in the betting when I thought they would have been at much shorter prices. Both finished well down the course. They were staggering all over the place and when they returned to the unsaddling enclosure they looked as if they were drunk.

On Tuesday the threat to human life was further emphasised when it emerged that Verly Bewicke's Bronze Warrior was drugged with phenobarbitone when he ran in a chase at Kelso the previous month. The 6-4 favourite had crashed through the first few fences and fell as he rounded the first bend – his jockey was lucky to escape injury.

On Wednesday it was confirmed that Caca Dora had been nobbled. The drug this time was chlorobutol which had long been used as a sedative for dogs prone to car-sickness, and in large doses caused symptoms similar to those described by Whiston. Something had to be done before another jockey was killed.

On the same day, Ossie Fletcher had a meeting with Colonel Neville Blair, the Jockey Club's chief security officer, and on Saturday morning trainers throughout the country choked on their cornflakes as they picked up their *Life* to see a front-page picture of 'Glamorous West End beautician Micheline Emilienne Lugeon' who was none other than the prospective owner they had recently shown around their yard.

There was no 'Wanted Dead or Alive' notice slapped across Mlle Lugeon's shapely bosom as the reason for the appearance of the photo – taken a month earlier following the anonymous tip-off – was cloaked in a caption story that reported she had recently bought a horse in France to race in England.

The publication of the photo brought in a flood of phone calls from alarmed trainers, foremost amongst them were Neville Crump and Fred Rimell, respectively responsible for the last two Grand National winners, Merryman II and Nicolaus Silver.

Crump said he had shown Lugeon around his Middleham yard only a few months earlier, while Rimell revealed that Nicolaus Silver had a narrow escape after Lugeon visited his Kinnersley stables shortly before the National that March. He recalled she had taken a particular interest in the grey, but he had later spotted her at Stratford races in the company of some "highly undesirable characters".

Rimell reported the matter to the authorities before he went home and moved Nicolaus Silver out of his box and replaced him with another grey in his yard. "Sure enough the dopers broke in and got at the other horse, but Nicolaus was safe."[7]

A fortnight after the photo of the 'glamorous West End beautician' had caused such a stir in the racing world, the great and the good met in York for the annual Gimcrack Club dinner when the traditional speeches, unsurprisingly, centred on the crisis. For the first time the Jockey Club took the opportunity to ask the bookmakers for help, for while the identities of most of the gang were known, more evidence was needed. In referring to the dopers, the senior steward, Sir Randle Feilden, declared:

> They nobble because there is cash in it – cash is paid for information. The man who buys this information is one of the links in the mist at the moment. Will he come forward and reveal to the authorities the source of the offer? Make no mistake, our investigations to date show us that there are a few who know much and many who know a little, and they are connected with the betting ring … I divulge these facts in particular to the betting profession and would ask bookmakers to suggest how such transactions and the passing of such information might be tracked … I would say to all interested in the prosperity of racing in this country that before many months are passed we shall know those who assisted to eliminate this menace and there will remain those who will regret their lack of help and some who will be exposed. There is no time for delay.

Mark those words 'There is no time for delay' for they brought a damning response from the country's biggest bookmaker, William Hill. In offering a £10,000 (£170,000) reward for information leading to the conviction of the nobblers, Hill revealed:

> The Bookmakers Protection Association wrote to the Jockey Club in June offering the fullest co-operation in an endeavour to track down the doping culprits to protect the good name of the bookmaking profession. Up to now the offer has not been taken up. The Jockey Club cannot expect the bookmakers to make out their case for them, but if their detectives have any questions that they want to ask bookmakers, then the bookmakers will gladly supply the answers. Believe me, if bookmakers knew who the dopers were, they would be the first to report them.

Micheline Lugeon as she appeared on the front-page of the *Life* in December 1961.
© [Mirror Syndication International]Mirrorpix.

This public rebuke resulted in the stewards hastily arranging a meeting with Archie Scott and Bill Yeadon, two of the foremost figures in the bookmaking world, but, as future events were to show, it was merely a cosmetic exercise.

Meanwhile, as a result of the publicity given to Lugeon and a general tightening up of stable security, which had been woefully lax in many jumping yards, the dopers kept a low profile until the prospect of rich pickings brought them out again just before the 1962 NH Meeting at Cheltenham in March. On the eve of the Champion Hurdle an attempt was made to nobble the hot favourite Another Flash at Arthur Thomas' Warwick stables. Two intruders picked the lock to the main stable block, but fled off into the night when confronted by stable lads guarding the horse who, as it turned out, was narrowly beaten the following day.

A week later, the *Life* was able to give a first-hand account of a particularly shocking case of skulduggery. The question mark at the end of the 72pt block-capital headline 'The Finn A Dope Victim?' was hardly necessary in the light of Tom Nickalls' report:

The Finn, 7-4 favourite for Saturday's Monaveen Chase at Hurst Park, was almost certainly 'got at'. He behaved as if he were blind ... Racegoers saw The Finn hit the first fence, making no attempt to jump it, and dislodge his rider-trainer Derek Ancil.

The horse picked himself up on the far side, galloped on riderless and did exactly the same thing at the next fence. Again The Finn went on and galloped straight into the open ditch. He came out of this, galloped in the opposite direction and crashed through some rails as though he did not see them … What happened to The Finn? Here is the story as Derek Ancil told it to me.

"The Finn is normally a very jaunty horse, so I was worried when I went to saddle him up and found him dull and listless. So dull, in fact, that he walked straight into the partition between the saddling stalls as though he did not see it. I immediately sent for the racecourse vet who tested his heart and said 'This is very bad. I must have a second opinion.'

"A second vet was sent for who also tested The Finn's heart and reported it as very intermittent. However, he said this could be caused by chronic indigestion. At that moment the horse passed some dung. 'That may have sorted out the trouble,' said the vet. They told me they thought the horse should run, but that if he did not appear to be going well I ought to pull him up … Just as I was mounting him in the parade ring he passed some more dung and the owner noticed amongst it what she thought to be a worm. This was investigated and found to be no less than seven rubber bands."*

Amazingly, after all this the horse was still allowed to take its chance. Not surprisingly Nickalls concluded: "I cannot help feeling that if a vet has the slightest suspicion that a chaser is not absolutely a hundred per cent, he should forbid the horse to run, certainly in cases where the heart appears to have been affected in some way."

Because Ancil had guard dogs loose in his yard at night, the suspicion was that it had been an inside job and this proved to be the case when one of his lads later confessed to the crime. The Finn, who had been a top-class juvenile hurdler and had promised to be just as good over fences, lost his confidence as a result of his experience and was killed in a first fence fall at Wetherby later that year.

And so it went on: Twice Over at Newbury and Persian Crest at Royal Ascot in June, and Henry's Choice at Ascot (yet again) in July. In the case of Henry's Choice, his Malton (yet again) trainer, Rufus Beasley, revealed it was the second time the horse had been nobbled in two years.

But in their greed, the gang began to get careless and in August 1962 they left a trail a blind man could follow when a major off-course coup was landed in a three-horse race at Lewes. Shortly before the race – in which Countess, a 4-11 shot, trailed in last – betting shops in London were inundated with straight forecast bets on the other two runners (Lucky Seven at 11-4 and Dear Joe, 20-1) which paid 33s 2d, just over 7-1.

The whole scenario screamed 'dope' especially as Countess's owner reported she had looked "half asleep" in the paddock and had shown "complete indifference" when blinkers were fitted on her. After the race, the last on the card, the owner had tried to get the filly tested, but the vet had already left the course and it was not until her Epsom trainer, Dick Thrale, had returned home from racing at Warwick that samples were taken by a vet who noted the filly was unsteady of her legs and lacked co-ordination.

Due to the lapse of time, the test proved inconclusive, but there was plenty of evidence in the betting shops and the *Life's* star columnist, Gus Dalrymple, was soon on the trail. Dalrymple had been in the bookmaking business before joining the *Life* and he quickly obtained the name of one of the men who had placed the bets. He also found a bookmaker who had taken a substantial win bet on Lucky Seven and "a surprisingly large forecast wager" on the winning combination from a commission agent

---

* When a horse was nobbled the night before a race, a bolus of crushed sedatives wrapped in tissue and bound with adhesive tape and rubber bands was used. The action of the dope would be delayed for up to 12 hours before the tape was dissolved by the horse's digestive juices and the dope released into its system.

who had phoned his office just before the race. The bookie added that the same man also had large bets on Lucky Seven and the forecast with at least two other big firms at the last moment.

Leads aplenty, but was the Jockey Club interested? Not according to Dalrymple who reported:

I attempted to contact Col Neville Blair, the Jockey Club's security advisor. I was told he was on his holidays. Who was deputising for him? Col H B McNally. He was at lunch. I left a message asking him to telephone me. An hour later – not having heard – I telephoned again. I was told Colonel McNally had gone to the races.

When I told a woman I understood to be his secretary that I could disclose the identity of one of the backers who had invested heavily on Lucky Seven she said, 'Why not write in about it?' She went on to say 'this was Mr Thrale's own private inquiry … apparently racecourse officials didn't see anything wrong with the race.'

Late last night [*Thursday*] the bookmaker who offered on Tuesday to help the authorities by revealing the name of the trade firm who placed a heavy bet on Lucky Seven and the forecast, told me, 'Another day has come and gone. I have not heard a word from the authorities. Apparently they don't want my help.'

This was typical. Despite the information the stewards had already received from the *Life*, the Jockey Club viewed press investigations into such matters as an unwelcome intrusion upon its territory. Eventually, however, the leads were followed up and they only confirmed what the police, the Jockey Club and the *Life* already knew – their chief suspect was a London bookmaker called Bill Roper.

Finally, on 12 November 1962, three of the gang – Richard McGee, Ted Smith and Len Steward – were arrested and charged with doping horses between 1 April 1957 and 9 August 1962. At the committal proceedings it emerged that McGee and Smith had worked for a pharmaceutical firm in Surrey and had been supplying stable lads and apprentices with drugs to dope horses since 1953. They operated through a bookmaker, Bernard Howard, who paid Smith £25 (£470) every time a doped favourite lost.

Howard had fled the country before he could be arrested and spent the rest of his life soaking up the Mediterranean sun, but the rest of his gang joined up with Roper when he took over operations in 1959. They were made up of a motley collection of bookmakers, stable lads, habitual criminals and a heavy-handed thug called Charlie Mitchell, a racecourse tic-tac man who regularly beat up anyone – man or woman – who upset him.

On New Year's Day 1963, the trial got off to a sensational start when the court was told that Smith, appropriately known as the 'Witch Doctor', had 'fallen' from a balcony in Lewes prison the previous day and was in a coma (he died six weeks later without regaining consciousness and an inquest recorded a verdict of suicide).

The jury heard that McGee, by then working as an assistant manager in a Newcastle laboratory, had supplied Smith with enough drugs to dope between 600 and 900 horses. McGee pleaded guilty to stealing drugs and conspiracy, but Steward, a former apprentice who quit racing in 1959 to work for Roper, denied all charges of doping even though the evidence given against him by a former accomplice was overwhelming.

It was no surprise when Steward was found guilty and sentenced to four years corrective training,[*] while McGee was jailed for two years. In passing sentence, the recorder, Charles Doughty, QC, accepted

---

[*] In July 1963, Steward had his conviction quashed and was discharged after the Court of Appeal ruled that some of the evidence given against him had been inadmissible.

that Steward was "only a tool in a highly organised business" and that there was "a person or people – who must be bookmakers – who are behind all this and organise it and profit from it."

Over the next few months the rest of the gang were rounded up and in October they went on trial at Lewes Assizes. Apart from Bill Roper, 58, and his Swiss (not French) girlfriend Micheline Lugeon who came to England in 1955 as a 19-year-old *au pair* to work for Roper's mother, the seven accused included Joe Lowry, a stallholder from Forest Gate in London; a former bookmaker, Edward 'Jackie' Dyer, and his nephew Charlie Mitchell.

For 20 days the court heard evidence from 121 prosecution witnesses and 'frightened accomplices', during which time it emerged that the gang had attempted to have Sir Victor Sassoon's 1960 Derby winner, St Paddy, doped before the race.

Owen Stable, QC, the prosecuting counsel, quoting evidence from three Newmarket stable lads who had turned Queen's Evidence, did not disclose their real names but said that the one called 'Snuffy' had looked after St Paddy and although he had allegedly doped other horses in Noel Murless's yard he had drawn the line at nobbling his own particular favourite when it came to the Derby.

Later 'Snuffy', one Philip Lawler, was offered £500 (£9,000) to give St Paddy a physic ball (which would have caused severe purging) before the St Leger, but he again refused, allowing the horse to romp home in the Doncaster classic. But because of a deal struck between the prosecution and Lawler, the nobbling of Pinturischio the following year was not mentioned during the trial.

The appropriately named Stable also produced evidence to show that Lugeon had visited 21 racing stables from Kent to Roxburghshire in 47 days during the autumn of 1961, and five of them suffered an outbreak of doping involving 12 horses shortly after her visit. "Doping followed her about like some evil spirit," he said.

On the fourteenth day of the trial, Roper fairly put the cat among the pigeons when giving his evidence. A former military policeman with the RAF, he had joined Max Parker's bookmaking firm after the war and worked for them on the racecourse until the end of 1959 when he left to become a professional punter and run his own commission agency, which he set up in Covent Garden in 1961.

During his time with Parker (né Stein), Roper mixed with many of the top names in racing and now he claimed: "I knew everybody who was anybody at the races. I put money on for as high as Lord and Lady Rosebery down to the paper boy."

'I Put Bets On For Lord Rosebery' echoed the *Life's* headline the following day. Surely this was not the same Lord Rosebery who had repeatedly blocked Charles Chapman's applications to have his licence restored and who had accused that trainer of a 'grave dereliction of duty' in failing to prevent Don Pat from being doped in 1930?

Surely not the Lord Rosebery who declared he had every confidence in his trainer, Jack Jarvis, when one of his own horses was doped in 1951? It couldn't be the same noble lord who, during his second term as a steward of the Jockey Club (1946-48), had condemned Cecil Ray and Jim Russell to their lonely exile; not the Rosebery who denied he was in the bar with 'Ringer' Barrie – but indeed it was the very same 6th Earl himself.*

---

*Albert Edward Harry Meyer Archibald Primrose (1882-1974) had many fine attributes. A first-class sportsman – he captained the Surrey XI from 1905-7 – with a distinguished military record, he did much good work in the public sector as well as for racing, but he had his blind spots. Bill Roper, a man known to the stewards of the Jockey Club as a suspect doper for at least two years, appears to have been one of them. After the trial Rosebery told the *Life*: "I had never heard of the man until I saw my name in the headlines of *The Sporting Life* … It may well be that I placed commissions with the man Roper, but as far as I am aware all my bets were with the Parker firm."

The 'anesthetised' French colt Relko demolishes his rivals in the 1963 Derby in much the same way as he demolished the suspect findings of the Jockey Club's analysts over the past 18 years

In the light of this revelation the rest of the trial paled into insignificance and in his summing up Justice Melford Stevenson got it just about right when he addressed the jury with the observation: "It would not be a surprise if any respect or sympathy you feel in this case were strictly confined to the horses." All seven defendants were found guilty. Of the principals, 'Roper the Doper' got three years; Mitchell,* Lowry and Dyer two years each, and Lugeon 12 months.

Worryingly for the Jockey Club, it emerged during the trial that some of the horses the gang claimed to have doped had returned negative test results. It seemed as if the analysts had gone from one extreme to the other, and their credibility was further undermined by the Relko case which occurred during that torrid summer of 1963 when the nation was hooked on a much juicier affair involving politicians, prostitutes and Russian spies (the John Profumo-Christine Keeler scandal).

---

* Mitchell had his conviction quashed on appeal. Two years later he was charged with doping greyhounds, but was found 'not guilty' although two other men were each jailed for five years. In the same week, Len Steward and Joe Lowry, together with John Barnham, a former professional boxer, were found guilty of attempting to nobble Spare Filly at Bob Read's Lambourn yard. This time there was no let off for Steward who, together with Barnham, was sent down for four years, while Lowry got five years. Of course, doping didn't end with the conviction of the Roper gang. The last known case of wholesale doping was committed by one man, the former champion amateur jump jockey, Dermot Browne, who admitted to nobbling 23 horses during a seven-week period in 1990 when he claimed to be working for the professional punter, Brian Wright. Browne, who was a trainer at the time, was warned off for 10 years in 1992 for passing information to a bookmaker and, following his doping confessions to the police in 2000, his sentence was extended by a further 20 years.

To summarise: the French-trained Relko had hacked up in that year's Derby, but six weeks later the Jockey Club announced that routine tests taken on seven horses, including Relko, had proved positive. An inquiry followed, attended by the trainers of the horses involved along with three expert witnesses – a biochemist and two vets – representing Relko's connections.

The Jockey Club's evidence was shaky from the start in Relko's case as its analysts had produced conflicting findings; one found butacaine, the other benzocaine in the urine samples, but both agreed the saliva tests were negative.

The defence's witnesses were able to show that a racehorse's urine normally contains several grams of benzoic acid, which was very similar to benzocaine, and that the minute amount found in Relko's urine (one gram) could not possibly have acted as a stimulant, in fact, benzocaine was an anaesthetic! As *Timeform's Racehorses of 1963* so succinctly put it: "What a commentary upon the quality of the best three-year-old colts in England that they should have been trounced by a horse who had been anaesthetized before the race."

The outcome of the inquiry was that Relko and the other horses, four of which were also winners, were allowed to keep their races, no action was taken against their trainers and an official statement on the findings noted: "The experience of these and previous cases has pointed to the necessity for further research into drugs and their effects."

Well, what do you know! Ossie Fletcher summed up the embarrassing saga by observing:

Thus everybody connected with each of the only seven horses to have given a positive reaction to dope in tests since mid-April have been exonerated from any culpability. And it has also been established that it is possible for what has hitherto been regarded as dope to be present in a horse without anyone apparently having administered it and without its having, in any event, any real effect upon a horse's performance.

'Tis a pity Jim Russell, Ernie Street, George Allden, *et al* did not have the financial resources of Relko's connections to challenge the analyst's findings. Perhaps, even now, it is not too late for the authorities to grant these gentlemen a posthumous pardon.

A LICENCE TO PRINT MONEY

IN SEPTEMBER 1959, Ben Clements eased himself towards retirement by vacating the chair to become consultant editor of the *Life's* associated publications, the weekly *Sporting Life Guide* and that hardy annual, *Ruffs Guide to the Turf*, which Odhams had acquired along with the *Sportsman* in 1924. Eighteen months later, following IPC's takeover of Odhams Press, he took his leave of Fleet Street to spend his twilight years in contented retirement at Colyton in Devon, where he died at the age of 79 in 1976. In paying tribute to his former editor, the *Life's* Len Scott painted a portrait of an avuncular man who was…

> a considerable judge of personality and spotter of hidden talent. He never bore grudges, was unstinting in his praise of good work – and scathing in his denunciation of anything he considered less than worthy of the paper. His temperament was normally sunny and he liked to express it by exercising a pleasing baritone voice around the office – usually something from Gilbert and Sullivan. And when he deserted the Savoy Operas for 'Oh What A Beautiful Morning!' the *Life* staff knew that all would be set fair for that day at least![1]

During his 22 years as editor, Clements developed a close relationship – many would say, too close – with the bookmaking fraternity and in 1944 he became the first chairman of the grandly styled Advertising Bookmakers Investigation Committee, a fairly toothless body which was set up to ensure that only *bona-fide* firms advertised in the press.

Throughout the stringent post-war years, when he was working to an extremely tight budget and reliant on the advertising revenue bookmakers brought in, the charge that the *Life* had become a 'bookmakers' paper' was uncomfortably close to the truth. The accusation gained added weight in 1951 when, after yet another Royal Commission on Gambling had recommended the establishment of licensed betting offices, Clements sided with the large credit firms that were opposed to them.

Under the influence of his Birmingham compatriot, William Hill, who memorably described betting shops as "a cancer upon society," the editor even expressed his hostility to them in a letter to *The Times* in which he took the extraordinarily pedantic view that, "Aesthetically, betting shops are abhorrent. They are the saddest places in Ireland."[2]

The big firms were understandably frightened of losing business to the shops and Clements felt that as they helped to keep the *Life* solvent (the paper carried no fewer than 39 bookmakers' adverts on the opening day of the 1951 Flat season) it was his duty to back them to the detriment of the ordinary punter.

This was a rank betrayal of everything the *Life* had stood for since Harry Feist first advocated the licensing of betting shops in 1859 and there must have been a fearful subterranean whirring in West Croydon cemetery in April 1951 when his old paper reported the Royal Commission's findings in a negative, one-sided manner.

Remarkably, there was no editorial comment on this most important of all reports; instead, the antis were allowed a free rein to express their views. They were typified by Alfred Cope, vice-chairman of the NBPA, who declared his Association would oppose any legislation which sought to establish betting shops since it believed them to be undesirable and unnecessary.

A Douglas Stuart spokesman was even quoted as saying: "It will be a sad day in the life of this country if betting shops are introduced here unless the hours of operation are drastically limited. The betting shop attracts the addict who stays there all day long trying to recover his early losses and often with his children at the door."

In the light of such rhetoric, the church's ever-vocal Council on Gambling must have felt strangely redundant especially when the Archbishop of Canterbury, Dr Geoffrey Fisher, came out in favour of giving betting shops a try.

But as with the 1932 Royal Commission, which recommended the legalisation of cash betting and the licensing of bookmakers, the advice of the latest body was ignored by the very politicians responsible for setting it up. Finally, with a general election looming in September 1959, the *Life* reported: "Betting law reform, a famous non-starter in politics, is in the running once again," as it revealed that both the Labour and Conservative parties had pledged to legalise off-course cash betting after the election. A 'political correspondent' went on to explain:

> A blueprint for reform is already at hand for Britain's next Home Secretary – the report of the Royal Commission on Gambling. It was set up by a Labour Government in 1949 with Mr (now Sir Henry) Willink, Master of Magdalene College, Cambridge, as its chairman. Two years later, after holding 42 meetings and hearing the evidence of 141 witnesses, it issued its report. For most of Britain's newspapers it was the story of the day. It seemed that betting shops – which the Commission recommended – were just around the corner. But nothing happened.
>
> Four years later, Sir Henry Willink complained in a letter to *The Times* about the way his Commission's findings had been neglected. For at the time the report had never even been discussed in the Commons. Eventually the Conservative Government revealed its hand. And in 1956 a Front Bench spokesman said a Bill was being prepared to implement the main lines of the Commission's recommendations on off-the-course betting. It would be introduced, he said, at the earliest practicable opportunity.
>
> As we know it was an 'opportunity' that never presented itself. When the move does come it will be controversial and bitterly fought, not only in Westminster but in the country. The politicians are aware of this.

The article had been written by the *Life's* new editor, 38-year-old Oswald William Fletcher, formerly chief sub-editor and night editor of the *Daily Mirror*. Ossie, as he was always known, did not pretend to have a profound knowledge of racing – he was a newspaper man first and foremost – but he was politically astute and, unlike his predecessor, he was able to view the approaching changes with an impartial eye.

He could see the racing industry was on the cusp of the most important development in its history as the legalisation of betting shops would enabled it to derive an income from off-course bookmakers and it would also help his paper.

At the time the *Sporting Chronicle* was outselling the *Life* by 2 to 1 with daily sales of over 100,000, partly due to the fact that virtually every illegal betting shop in the midlands and the north had the *Chronicle* pinned up on its walls for form students to study. In the more affluent south, where most betting was conducted through credit firms or street bookmakers, betting shops were few and far between, but Fletcher realised that if they were legalised they would offer a new outlet for sales of the *Life*.

On October 8 the country went to the polls and returned the Conservatives to power under Harold Macmillan and, for once, a manifesto pledge was promptly honoured when R A 'Rab' Butler, introduced his Betting and Gaming Bill on November 2. At the same time the reforming Home Secretary announced that the government was considering imposing a levy on bookmakers. This was outside the scope of his bill, but it was not altogether unexpected since the Jockey Club had been in consultation with the Home Office in 1956 over ways in which off-course betting could be made to contribute to a racing industry that was then labouring under a 24 per cent entertainments tax.[*]

Few bookmakers were willing to concede that the Jockey Club had a case, but increasing calls for a Tote monopoly prompted a re-think and in January 1957 the *Life* carried a front-page letter from the rails bookmaker Laurie Wallis in which he argued that as on-course layers subscribed heavily to racing though entrance fees and betting badges, office bookmakers, who made far greater profits, should do the same.

Grudgingly, the NBPA formed the Racecourse Amenities Fund in 1958 to raise money on a voluntary basis from off-course bookmakers. This sop to the racing authorities produced £61,563 for improving racecourse facilities, a sum that paled into insignificance when, in April 1960, a government appointed committee under Sir Leslie Peppiatt, a former president of the Law Society, recommended a levy on off-course bookmakers to produce £1.25m (£22m) a year for racing. Even this was less than half of what the Jockey Club had hoped for, but in an authoritative editorial Fletcher showed the equitable qualities that were to stand him in good stead for the next 25 years as he commented:

> The Peppiatt Committee have produced a most competent survey and a set of recommendations that are both balanced and workable ... By and large the bookmakers seem quite happy about the Committee's recommendations. That being so, it follows logically that the Jockey Club are – again, by and large – unhappy.
>
> A torpedo has been fired into their years' old argument that racing would be in peril of extinction if it did not receive a yearly contribution of at least £3,000,000 from off-course betting. They have been politely rapped over the knuckles for asking for a sum which the Committee feel is both an unrealistic assessment of what is needed and, at the same time, more than the bookmakers could reasonably be expected to provide.

After going on to naively ponder over whether the bookmakers would pass the levy on to punters in the form of a tax, Fletcher ended on a controversial note:

> All these issues, however, are insignificant compared with the main one that will face MPs when Parliament considers the Peppiatt report. It is this: 'Is it morally right to intervene BY LEGISLATION to enforce a payment by one group of people for the benefit of other groups – in this case people who speculate in the luxury of owning, racing and breeding bloodstock, and people who invest in the shares of commercial racecourse companies?'
>
> If the answer is 'yes,' then surely greyhound racing interests will be entitled to a levy from

---

[*] The tax had been imposed on all forms of entertainment in 1916 and had been gradually increased from its initial 10 per cent to peak at 84 per cent during WWII. Its removal in 1957 gave the country's cash-strapped racecourses some much-needed relief.

bookmakers. So will the Football Association and the Football League[*]... The Peppiatt Committee claim there are precedents for the levy they propose, and one example they cite is the levy on cinema takings for the benefit of British film production.

We wonder if MPs will see the connection.

It was a valid point, but as the Betting Bill and then the Levy Bill made their way through parliament during the first and second half of 1960, this subtle observation became lost under a welter of debate much of which reflected the arguments that had been voiced over the Tote Bill in 1928.

The usual concerns were expressed on moral grounds, especially over the issue of bookmakers' permits when it emerged that preference was to be given to those who were able to prove they had been operating in their locality for at least a year. This was sound in principle as it provided a safeguard against welshers moving into the area and it also gave the small man a certain amount of protection against being swamped by the big firms, but it was also seen as a reward for those who had been operating illegally and who regarded their betting convictions as 'honourable scars'.

But the betting laws had been such a farce for so long it would have been absurd to deny reputable street bookmakers the chance to go legit especially as Charles Longbottom, MP for York, pointed out that there were some 40 to 50 shops in his constituency that were tolerated by the police and had not been raided since 1938.

The Street Bookmakers Federation underlined how widespread illegal betting was when it claimed that of the 76,000 pubs in the country, 61,000 had a bookmaker or his agent doing business on the premises, largely with police knowledge and concurrence. Enforcement of the law varied from town to town, but the Federation estimated that 15,000 to 16,000 street bookmakers paid some £200,000 (£3.5m) in fines every year.

To accompany these statistics, some extraordinary statements were made by MPs in debate. In referring to the prevalence of illegal betting in Scotland, George Wigg (Lab. Dudley), then a government appointed member of the RBCB, upheld his reputation for outspokenness when he said: "So far as I can see, not a single policeman or magistrate in Scotland has not been 'straightened' in some way or other."

Reginald Paget (Lab. Northampton), a lawyer by profession, was presumably referring to the few English police who had not been 'straightened' when he commented on the lengths they were prepared to go to in order to obtain betting convictions: "The police – not occasionally, but continually as a matter of practice – go into court and tell a pack of lies. All who practice in the courts know that."

No wonder Rab Butler wanted to get betting off the streets! Eventually, on 11 May 1960 after 88 hours had been spent discussing its measures, the bill was given a third reading by 211 votes to 42 and it passed into law that July. The Levy Bill was not far behind and received the Queen's Assent the following March.

In between these two epoch-making events the Jockey Club announced that a 24-hour declaration of runners system would be introduced in 1961. It was not before time. In August 1959, inspired by the earlier High Court judgement on the Football League's fixture list, the Club had attempted to issue a list of runners on which it could claim copyright.

---

* In May 1959, the High Court ruled that the fixtures list as used by the pools firms was the copyright of the Football League. As a result the pools operators agreed to pay 0.5% of the stake money – some £275,000 a year – to the League for the next 10 years, since when the terms have been revised and extended.

For some perverse reason the authorities decided on a three-day forfeit system which imposed fines on horses that were declared at that stage but did not run. Not only was the scheme foisted on owners and trainers without consultation, but insult was added to injury by withholding the lists of declared runners from the press for 24 hours. This move was to prevent the *Life* from publishing its 'advanced cards', which gave readers an idea of the likely runners for the following day – a guide that was particularly important to owners and trainers – not that the declared runners in the latter half of 1959 bore any resemblance to the actual fields.

The hard ground, which lasted late into the autumn, resulted in wholesale and costly withdrawals and when, to general disbelief, the system was retained in 1960, a coughing epidemic caused more long lists of non-runners. Even by Jockey Club standards it was a shambles of epic proportions, so it was a great relief to all when the *Life* announced on 29 September 1960:

> It's a fact that we shall have overnight declaration of runners on the Flat next season. This was made clear in a statement at Newmarket last night following a meeting of the Jockey Club attended by 26 members. A resolution by the Stewards of the Jockey Club 'that a scheme to produce an accurate list of runners next season shall be overnight declarations' was adopted unanimously.
>
> We believe that the Jockey Club's decision will now meet with universal approval, for the opposition to overnight declarations has been receding as the failure of the three-day forfeit scheme became more apparent, month by month. It has long been our view that an accurate list of runners in the Press day by day was the best possible advertisement for racing.
>
> With the advent of the new Betting and Gaming Act and the attempt to get off-course money into the Totalisator it has become even more important to keep the public well informed ... Britain is now coming into line with every other major racing country. It remains to be seen whether everybody will be as happy about it this time next year. We believe they will.

At a press conference in London two days later the senior steward, Maj-Gen Sir Randle Feilden, did not attempt to hide the reason why the Jockey Club had finally brought in 24-hour declarations. Without a blush he said the Club felt the public was entitled to the best possible information now that the money bet with bookmakers would help racing.

Unfortunately, he then spoilt this image of enlightenment by going on to state that there was no question of the draw being made the day before racing, nor would trainers be required to declare their jockeys overnight. He also had the gall to express his regret that the new scheme "will restrict the freedom of action of the owner to decide whether to run or not right up until the last minute," ignoring the fact that for more than a year the Club had been demanding they should do so 72 hours before a race.

But these were petty quibbles compared with the great leap forward that had been made and on the eve of the 1961 Flat season Ossie Fletcher was full of the joys of spring as he predicted "the most momentous of years":

> First of all it will see the introduction at long last of overnight declarations. Surprise runners will be a thing of the past. Surprise non-runners, we have every reason to suppose, will be the rare exception. Then in May, ready-cash off-the-course betting will become legal. The bookmaker will no longer be 'a man of furtive activities and mysterious comings and goings', but an officially recognised businessman. His client will no longer be aiding and abetting the breaking of the law every time he hands over a bob each-way.

There is going to be far less hypocrisy and far more down-to-earth realism about racing and betting. That is good.

And it got better when the paper announced that of the 246 horses that had been declared for the three meetings that Monday – Lincoln, Ayr and Folkestone – only one did not turn out and that was because it had a sick note in the form of a vet's certificate.

Meanwhile, local licensing authorities were being deluged with applications for betting permits at a cost of £100 (£1,750) each. From October 1960 the *Life* had carried column after column of statutory notices containing details of each bookmaker's application. Those who wished to oppose the applicants had two weeks in which to lodge their grounds for an objection. Confusion often followed in their wake.

In January 1961, Bernard Clark, chairman of the Lincoln licensing committee, voiced a reservation held by other like-minded bureaucrats when he declared:

The [*Betting*] Act requires the application to be advertised in a newspaper circulating in the authorities' area. With some reluctance we think it is arguable that *The Sporting Life* satisfies that condition and we accept it on this occasion. At the same time we should like it to be known that we regard the use of that paper as not fulfilling the spirit of the Act. It is important that the advertisement should be seen not merely by the limited readership of the paper in question, but by the residents of the district generally who are most likely to be affected. We hope these remarks will be borne in mind by future applicants.

This was a slight on the *Life* Fletcher was not prepared to tolerate. In reply, he put Clark to rights as he addressed him directly in a 'We ARE a newspaper' editorial:

If we fulfil the requirements of the law today, we shall still fulfil them tomorrow, and you have no right to differentiate between one of our advertisers and another simply because their applications are made at different times. And we would point out that, in the opinion of leading counsel whom we have consulted, we DO fulfil the requirements of the Act.

In the main, the licensing authorities were ignorant of betting matters and granted permits *carte blanche* irrespective of whether the applicant was 'a fit and proper person' to hold one. Objections to bookmakers who had been warned off as defaulters and even to those who were habitual criminals were often dismissed.

In February 1961, the Newington licensing committee granted permits to all 41 applications it received including one from a man who had convictions for at least eight counts of welshing, and also for assaulting the police, stealing, and, horror of horrors, selling stockings without clothing coupons. The chairman of the bench said that despite the applicant's bad record they did not wish to take his living away!

At the other extreme, Wilfred Sherman, chairman of the Licensed Bookmakers' Federation, was refused a betting shop licence in Caldicot because "the premises are on a busy main road and children might get pushed into the road by people using the shop".

In Somerset, the Long Ashton magistrates ordered nine clergymen to pay costs of one guinea each for lodging a frivolous objection to an applicant, while an East Suffolk committee approved a betting office application for the village of Sizewell so it could be used by the workers building the nearby power station.

In Doncaster, many back-street shops that had operated illegally in the past failed to pass muster with Sydney Firth, chairman of the local licensing committee, who declared that converted hen houses and air-raid shelters would no longer be tolerated as betting offices. From 100 applications, he said only a quarter of the shops met the minimum standard required. Too often they were dilapidated, dirty, poorly ventilated, badly lit and heated. Eight bookmakers had been ordered to close their shops before the Betting Act became law on May 1, while others were given a year to clean up their premises.

When the great day finally arrived, the *Life* dispatched its roving reporter, David Hedges, to record his impressions of a historic May Day. Hedges, who had joined the paper three years earlier after stints with the Press Association and the *Evening Standard*, was destined to make a major impact on the global racing scene when he founded the International Racing Bureau in 1970, but here he was on his own doorstep as he dropped into Jack Swift's shop in fashionable Mayfair:

> The chief impression was one of sheepish customers sidling in, not quite sure of the right procedure. It was unfamiliar ground for most of them, though some might have visited the betting shops in the Midlands and North, which have been following a well-trodden if illegal path for years...
>
> The first shop I visited yesterday was right in the heart of London. Part of the Dover Street offices of a well known SP bookmaker has been converted into a betting shop within a stone's throw of the Ritz Hotel. There was a fascinating mixture of clients.
>
> Military looking gentlemen with bowlers, umbrellas and carnations in button holes were placing bets alongside working men from the Hyde Park Corner road improvement site, messengers, doormen from the big hotels and chauffeurs ... Procedure was much the same as in any other betting shop. There was a blackboard for results and betting fluctuations, a counter for taking and paying out bets and a loud speaker, with somewhat nasal tone, churning out race descriptions and betting shows.

As more and more shops opened, the demand for top-class settlers who could calculate speedily and accurately the amount to be paid on winning bets became acute and wages spiralled. At first a good settler could expect to earn £15 (£255) a week, but by the start of the 1962 Flat season, when the paper was carrying adverts for settling courses, the going rate was £25 (£410) for a five-day week with three weeks' holiday.

In November 1961, a government white paper disclosed that of the 10,142 applications for bookmakers' permits in England, Scotland and Wales only 83 were refused. Glasgow (pop 1,054,913) headed the list with 407 shops, 26 per cent more than London (pop 3,194,480) with 301. Birmingham had 286 and Manchester 241.

Despite the fact that there were no bookmakers in Orkney, Shetland or Sutherland, Scotland, with 1,506 shops, had almost twice as many per head of population (2.91 to every 10,000) than England with its 6,647 (1.54). Explaining the imbalance a Scottish bookie said: "Betting shops existed here long before they became law because the Scots instinctively rebel when told not to do things." Especially, one assumes, when they're told by the English!

It was another Scottish layer, the colourful and controversial Glaswegian, John Banks, who described bookmakers' permits as 'a licence to print money' and betting shops as 'gold mines'. And by 1968 a record 15,782 'mines' were tapping into a rich seam of expendable income, but they were dour places compared with their illegal predecessors, many of which had televisions and stayed open for evening racing.

The government's policy had been to make the shops as inhospitable as possible to discourage loitering, and while betting shows and commentaries were allowed, it was laid down there was to be 'no television, radio, music, dancing or refreshments on the premises'.*

It was not long before nit-picking policemen (sorely missing their bungs from the old street bookies) were ferreting around the shops looking for any infringement of the regulations, and they were prepared to go to any lengths to secure a conviction. In the summer of 1962, Gus Dalrymple reported that an East End layer was in danger of being prosecuted for having a mynah bird called Percy on his premises.

The bookmaker, Bill White, related: "The other day a police officer came into the shop and told us that Percy's presence was contravening Home Office regulations as laid down in the Betting and Gaming Act. Apparently he considered that Percy is an 'entertainer' within the meaning of the Act and also, because Percy shouts 'I say, I say, let's have a bet' as soon as a punter comes in, that he constitutes an inducement to bet."

The matter was referred to the NBPA whose secretary, Charles Wiseman, advised that Percy should be left where he was and if the police brought a case against White, the Association would engage the finest legal advisers to fight it.

No more was heard of the matter.

---

* The absurd spectacle of punters trooping out of betting shops to watch races in nearby television shops lasted until 1986 when TVs were finally allowed in Licensed Betting Offices. The following year Satellite Information Services (SIS) started to supply shops with a full coverage of racing, but it was not until 1993 that LBOs were allowed to stay open for evening racing during the summer months.

OSSIE'S SIGNINGS

OSSIE FLETCHER was faced with a formidable task when he took over the chair at the *Life* in 1959. With an average daily circulation of 48,941 for the first half of that year, sales were about as low as they had ever been in peacetime and it needed something special to turn the paper around; something to catch the reader's attention – and hold it.

It was decided that the 1960 Grand National edition would provide that magic ingredient. After weeks of planning and trials, the front-page splash headlines that day trumpeted 'IT'S A 'NATIONAL' SCOOP! / The Life brings you brilliant colour pictures to mark a Red Letter Day in Sport'. Below, a preening announcement expanded:

To celebrate the first TV Grand National, *The Sporting Life* is proud to present today, for the first time in a national daily newspaper, editorial features in full colour gravure. On This Page are the racing colours of leading entries – and wearing them are the jockeys engaged at the time the pictures were prepared. On Page Three is a magnificent souvenir painting that captures all the drama of the great occasion.

And on page 2, an editorial stressed the significance of the 'breakthrough':

The technical achievement is one of considerable magnitude and there was keen competition among the great newspaper houses to see who would first put the process into production. Our pride at winning the race is tinged with only one regret – that it was necessary to send the pictures to press before we knew the probable runners.

And that was the problem; the photogravure process was such a lengthy and complex operation it was used only for magazines and was not suitable for a daily paper. Of the 16 jockeys featured on the front page, seven no longer had a ride in the race; while Gerry Scott who was on the favourite and, as sod's law would have it, the eventual winner, Merryman II, was not included.

Similarly, the Lionel Edwards painting which had been completed a month before the race, depicted four horses – the leading fancies at the time the work was commissioned – jumping Becher's on the second circuit, but, again, two of them were non-runners.

It was all rather embarrassing, but nothing compared with what happened on the night of the big print run – as Monday's paper apologetically reported: "Unfortunately after 42,000 copies had been printed, unforeseeable technical troubles developed and it became necessary to switch entirely to black and white production."

The monochrome copies were at least in keeping with the televised coverage of the race for which BBC TV's genial head of Outside Broadcasting, Peter Dimmock, had finally won a three-year contract from Aintree's formidable *grande dame*, Mirabel Topham, after eight fraught years of negotiations.

For Fletcher the whole experiment was an unmitigated disaster – the *Life* had simply been used as a guinea pig for the *Daily Herald* which was toying with the idea of using colour to boost its flagging sales – and a year later he had more to worry about when IPC, publishers of his old paper, the *Daily Mirror*, took control of Odhams.

Under Odhams, the *Life* had enjoyed a privileged existence. Any losses it incurred were absorbed by the profits that flowed from the company's increasing fleet of diverse publications, which included trade and technical journals, film and musical reviews and popular colour magazines such as *Today* (formerly *John Bull*) and *Woman's Own* with its circulation of over two million.

As a subsidiary of the *Mirror* group, Odhams continued to publish the *Daily Herald* (re-launched as *The Sun* in broadsheet form in 1964), *The People* (which boasted a circulation of 5.4m) and the *Life*, but Fletcher was now under increased pressure to make his paper a viable concern. It was a massive challenge at a time when the national dailies were able to extend their coverage of racing thanks to the introduction of overnight declarations, while sales of the *Sporting Chronicle* had soared to even greater heights with the boom in betting shops.

In August 1964 the *Chronicle's* circulation peaked at 127,295 compared with the *Life's* 85,184 which, nevertheless, represented a huge increase on the 1959 figures and was a ringing endorsement of Fletcher's editorial policy:

> I knew that if the *Life* was to go up we had to take sales from the *Chronicle* and gradually we did. I set about producing the kind of racing paper that I, as a potential reader, would want. I put myself in the position of the man in the street, bearing in mind that as a specialists' paper we had to cater for minorities.[1]

To this end Ossie encouraged the writers he already had by giving them more space for feature articles and individual columns, while he also brought in new blood from outside to cater for the needs of a new and rapidly expanding betting market.

One of the first of the many talented writers he was to sign up was Gus Dalrymple who joined the staff as a bookmakers' gossip columnist in the spring of 1962. A charismatic, bespectacled, 6ft 4in giant, Dalrymple had started out working for William Hill in his Park Lane office in 1945 and after a stint at running a book in the cheap ring at Walthamstow dogs during the '50s, he became manager of Jack Swift's credit office in Piccadilly before overseeing the betting shop side of that business in 1961.

He was, therefore, well qualified to portray the Runyonesque characters of the betting world and despite his lack of journalistic experience – or perhaps because of it – his light, humorous, off-beat style was an immediate hit with readers and the trade alike.

To cover the more technical side of the business, Jack Chenery, secretary of the Association of Rails Bookmakers, was engaged to write a weekly 'Mainly For Layers' column, which was taken over by the Brummie bookie, Laurie Wyles ('Michael Rolfe'), in 1965 and continued for another 20 years under the title of 'Calling All Bookmakers'.

The policy of recruiting specialist writers was extended in 1965 when the Newmarket-based vet, Peter Rossdale, became the paper's veterinary correspondent. Rossdale's lucid prose made a highly scientific subject fascinating reading for the layman and in 1967 a selection of his weekly articles was published in book form under the title *Your Horse*.

But of all Ossie's signings during his first decade, the most significant was the former Home Office minister Sir David Llewellyn who was taken on as a regular columnist in 1968. Llewellyn, who entered parliament as Conservative MP for Cardiff North in 1950 and was knighted on leaving politics ten years later, was a brother of Colonel Harry Llewellyn, the 1952 Olympic gold medallist showjumper of Foxhunter fame.

Sir David had written for papers ranging from the *Los Angeles Examiner* to homely Welsh provincials before he started to contribute the occasional article to the *Life* under his own name in 1959. Shortly afterwards he adopted the *nom de plume* of 'A Skinner' and also wrote book reviews as 'John Bliss', but it was as the Friday columnist 'Jack Logan' that he made an indelible mark on racing journalism.

To quote from his obituary (written, with unabashed conceit, by himself), which appeared in the *Life* on 10 August 1992, a month after he had filed his last column:

> Many were the causes he embraced, including a minimum wage for stable boys and the replacement of concrete posts with plastic ones on courses to lessen the danger to jockeys. He campaigned for the wearing of hard hats when out riding and firmly rebuked the Queen whenever she opted for a headscarf. He even started a movement after the Falklands war to help restart racing at Port Stanley.
>
> The column which took particular delight in sniping at the Jockey Club was not without its critics who complained that 'Logan' often sounded like a dog gnawing at a bone. But Llewellyn, unperturbed, described his style as 'the repetition of unpalatable truths' – and held it to be an effective way of getting things moving.
>
> His behaviour reflected what he wrote in that he preferred the company of the underdog. He shunned the members' enclosure and the press box, avoided all the more fashionable race meetings and never turned up at official dinners if he could help it. He preferred the quieter backwaters of British racing, mingling with farmers in Shropshire or in Devon or enjoying the smoky camaraderie of the betting shop – though he never gambled seriously himself.
>
> Although the column noticeably declined in recent years, his copy was always meticulous and on time. When finally he retired in July, the paper devoted a page of tributes to him and announced that 'Jack Logan' would die with him.

Whatever one thinks of a man who writes his own obituary, his column was essential reading. Always challenging and controversial, it blended wit with wisdom as it gave an opinionated digest of the racing press's coverage of the issues of the day, while an accompanying 'Sayings of the Week' compilation added spice to the page.

To counterbalance Logan's penchant for 'sniping at the Jockey Club', Fletcher enlisted Tony Fairbairn, the director of the Racing Information Bureau, to write an 'Around Portman Square' column under the pseudonym of 'Charles Croft'.

The RIB had taken on the job of representing the Turf authorities when the Jockey Club and the National Hunt Committee amalgamated in 1969, and while Fairbairn's pen was not as sharp as his adversary's he nevertheless provided the Establishment with a valuable outlet to defend itself against the charges of its critics.

But not all of Fletcher's signings turned out to be the assets he thought they would be. In 1970 he took on that notorious skater on thin ice, Jeffrey Bernard, as a bi-weekly columnist. The itinerant scribbler was a gifted and witty writer whose unrestrained, self-deprecating style and unerring eye for the absurd was tailor-made to portray the eclectic characters of the racing world of which he himself was one, but he had his weaknesses – Smirnoff vodka, loose women and a partiality for all-day sessions at the Coach & Horses in Soho, figured prominently among them.

As his binges with the sport's renowned drinkers became more frequent and prolonged, the line 'Jeffrey Bernard is ill'* began to appear where his article should have been and after a year his stint on

---

* This was later amended to 'unwell' when he started writing what was once described as 'A suicide note in weekly instalments' for *The Spectator* in 1978. The line 'Jeffrey Bernard is Unwell' became the title of a hit West End play based chiefly upon his drinking exploits and marital (four times) experiences.

the paper ended with a spectacular vino-collapso at the Kensington Close Hotel in London.

Most unwisely, he had been chosen as guest speaker for the annual point-to-point dinner at which the *Life* presented a cup to the season's leading female rider. Seeking inspiration for a suitable subject with which to entertain his audience, Bernard had started out at daybreak with a few jars in an all-night Smithfield market pub in the company of Albert Bright, a celebrated member of the paper's greyhound staff.

After Bright had regaled his drinking companion with the lurid tale of how he had lost his virginity while fire-watching on the roof of the *Greyhound Express* building during an air-raid in 1941, the two inebriates moved on to the *Life's* local watering hole, the White Hart – better known as 'the Stab' (in the back) because of all the inter-office character assassinations that took place in its narrow, photo-lined bar.

Bright was a privileged before-time drinker at the Stab where he would be supplied with a floor brush along with his early morning pint so he could be passed off as the cleaner if 'plod' paid a call. On this occasion Bernard proved an enthusiastic apprentice with a feather duster and by mid-afternoon he was trawling his way through his Soho haunts without the hint of a speech.

The wonder was that he made it to the hotel on time, but thus far, no further. After he had tried to molest Sue Aston, to whom he was supposed to present the *Sporting Life* Cup, he flaked out in the hotel lobby and was finally carried upstairs and put to bed. In his 12 months with the *Life*, Bernard had made the effortless transition from hardened drinker to hopeless alcoholic and it was the final straw for the long-suffering Fletcher who wrote to inform his angst-ridden columnist:

> It will come as no surprise to you that following your unpardonable exhibition at the point-to-point dinner which you attended as a representative of the paper on Friday evening, it is no longer possible for you to continue in our employ. This was not, you will agree, the first time your behaviour has compromised us and to protect myself and all connected with *The Sporting Life* from further embarrassment, I have no alternative but to terminate your engagement forthwith.

As Bernard's 'exhibitions' had included vomiting into the flowerbed beneath the Royal Box at Ascot and fornicating in the open ditch at Sandown, Fletcher felt he was better served by the more conventional columnists he had inherited.

Foremost amongst them was the amazingly prolific Jack Fairfax-Blakeborough, the author of 107 books (he once wrote 13 racing novels in the space of a year), who furnished the *Life* with a wealth of information on paddock personalities and general Turf history up until the day he died (New Year's Day) at the age of 92 in 1976.

No one could match the Yorkshire sage in pen-power, but Michael Williams did his best when he started to cover the point-to-point scene, which had previously been ignored by the paper, in 1953. Through his weekly reports he introduced a whole generation of urbanites to 'the sport between the flags', while he also wrote extended features on the principal horse shows and showjumping competitions throughout the year.

There was also John Hislop who had joined the paper as its breeding correspondent in 1954 when he was still ruling the roost as an amateur rider having won the first of his 13 Flat championships in 1938 before serving with the SAS during the war when he was awarded the Military Cross (as was Fairfax-Blakeborough in WWI).

On being demobbed, Hislop resumed his riding career to maintain his hold on the Flat

A 1971 promotional poster of Lester Piggott studying the *Life* – the balloon was added later by Jeffrey Bernard after a session in 'the Stab'.

championship until 1956 (sharing the title on three occasions) with a remarkable 49 per cent strike rate of 87 winners from 177 mounts, while he also notched up 18 winners from exactly 100 post-war rides over jumps.

His dry but precise style of writing did not appeal to everyone, but he knew what he was talking about as he showed when he bred Brigadier Gerard who carried his wife's colours to victory in the 1971 Two Thousand Guineas and 16 of his 17 other races. By that time he had left the *Life*, but he was still able to supply the paper with exclusive information on 'the Brigadier' throughout the colt's racing career.

Tommy Wisdom, the John Hislop of motor racing, was coming to the end of his 32-year association with the paper, but he was still as competitive as ever. In 1961 he was invested with the 'Order of Sport' by Prince Rainier of Monaco after taking part in his 18th Monte Carlo Rally – an event that had contributed a remarkable episode to his colourful career two years earlier. On 23 January 1959, he had reported:

> The most fantastic pile-up of all-time saved me and my partner, Douglas Johns, from the strangest mishap in a life not exactly free of them.
>
> On a treacherous corner, covered in the dread black ice beside the high banks of the River Paillon, some 20 miles in the mountains behind Monte Carlo, it all began. Number One starter, a Citroen driven from Lisbon by Frenchman Gilbert Lafabrie, went over the edge but was stopped by a tree from hurtling into the river below.
>
> Then the Sunbeam, driven by Roy Evans and Edward Stephens, was the next to pile on top of the Citroen. They had almost manhandled their car back on to the road when a Peugeot arrived, slid into it, knocked it back into the ravine and landed almost on top of them.
>
> By now, the three-car pile of banked cars was at the level of the road – all held up there by that same spindly little tree. Our Healey Sprite arrived at speed, slid out of control, and the front wheels went over the edge to land on the back of the French car. It held there. We reversed the car back on to the road and went on to the end.* Not a member of the pile-up car crews was even scratched.

Sadly, not everyone had been so lucky that day. The same edition of the *Life* carried a front-page report on the death of Mike Hawthorn, written by Wisdom who had been told the news while filing his copy from Monte Carlo. It was a deeply personal tribute:

> Mike Hawthorn, who had taken every possible driving risk over all the world, was killed yesterday on an English road. The world champion racing driver was 29 and had already announced his retirement from the sport.
>
> The accident took place on the Guildford by-pass. Hawthorn, driving his Jaguar, skidded 100 yards on the wet surface, grazed a lorry travelling in the opposite direction, overturned and crashed into a tree. He was killed instantly and the car completely wrecked. The crash occurred shortly after noon, Hawthorn being on his way to a lunch appointment in London. It is ironic now to remember Mike telling me how much more dangerous it was to drive on British roads than in Grand Prix motor racing.

---

* They eventually finished 58th of the 119 (from 322 starters) that completed. Wisdom's daughter, Ann, fared better. She had partnered Pat Moss, the 24-year-old sister of Stirling Moss, to win the 1958 European Ladies Championship and this time, driving an Austin A40, they won the Ladies Cup and finished tenth overall, the highest position attained by an all-women crew in the Rally that was first held in 1911.

So the gay, debonair, don't-give-a-damn Mike followed his friend, Peter Collins, to his death. In a few months two of the three great stars of motor-racing have been killed. Only lonely Stirling Moss is left.

It was in Germany last autumn that Mike said, 'Uncle Tommy, try my car and tell me if it isn't the fastest saloon in the world.' The car was his very special Jaguar, built by Sir William Lyons – and it was this he was driving yesterday.

Mike's decision to retire from motor-racing last month was a result of the advice of his father Leslie – killed in a road accident in 1954. 'Get into motor-racing', said his father. 'Put your heart into it. Get to the top and then get out.'

It was before the war, at Brooklands, that I was introduced to a serious, blond schoolboy who was driven round the famous concrete saucer by Brooklands ace Freddy Dixon. That small boy was to win his first race with a Freddy Dixon Riley. In 1949 Mike's father, a famous motor-cyclist, tuned the old Riley for the son who was one day to become a champion.

Remarkable for his vivid blond hair, his great height and yet to become famous bow tie, Hawthorn went rapidly to the forefront in club meetings at Goodwood. He gained a trial with Ferrari and showed that great man of motor racing, Enzo Ferrari, what he could do by beating the great Juan Manuel Fangio, five times world champion, in the French Grand Prix of 1953.

Mike was made, but disaster followed. His father was killed. Mike was unfairly blamed for the Le Mans disaster in which so many spectators were killed;[*] the Germans refused to allow him to drive in the Nürburgring race the following year. He thought about giving up racing and going abroad, but his friends persuaded him against it.

After he gained the world championship he decided to retire. He was going to settle down, run his Farnham garage and do some flying. He was deeply in love with a London model, Jean Howarth, whom he wanted to marry last November. 'But she won't have me,' he told me. That was true. Jean said racing drivers were in a dangerous business and they should not marry. Mike forlornly agreed she was right.

So we shall see no more the gay, pipe-smoking Mike on the race track and join with him in his great zest for life. Racing men all over the world will mourn the loss of a brilliant driver who brought great prestige to Britain. Mike was one who, from the sidelines, would have been of great help in training the racing drivers of the future. He was also a loved friend of one he was pleased to call 'Uncle Tommy'.

When Wisdom retired from journalism – but not from rallying – at the end of 1961 he was replaced by Barry Gill who was to chronicle the Grand Prix triumphs of a succession of British world champions starting with Graham Hill in 1962, Jim Clark in '63, John Surtees '64, Clark again in '65, Hill again in '68 and Jackie Stewart in 1969, '71 and '73, but by the time James Hunt took the title in 1976, the motoring column had been dropped.

Fletcher decided there was nothing to be gained from trying to rival the specialist motoring journals and instead he concentrated on making the coverage of horse and greyhound racing better than it had ever been. To this end he took on Archie Newhouse, former editor of the *Greyhound Express*,

* In 1955, in the worst disaster in motor racing history, Pierre Levegh's Mercedes hit the back of another car and somersaulted into the crowd killing Levegh and 82 spectators. Hawthorn went on to win the race in a Jaguar and became the first British driver to win the world championship when he beat Stirling Moss by one point in the final race of the 1958 season, the Morocco Grand Prix.

The author, signed up by Ossie Fletcher in 1974, gets his information straight from the horse's mouth.

to head a strong team on the dog desk and in 1970 he enlisted a rare talent in the private handicapper Dick Whitford. Here was someone who could give readers what they wanted most of all – winners, big-priced winners by the score, winners galore.

Whitford, now the acknowledged father of modern handicapping, was the first man to compile a universal handicap by allotting every horse a rating expressed in pounds and based on a fixed scale which enabled horses of different generations to be compared. He was the man who put the 'form' in *Timeform* when he joined up with Phil Bull in 1948 and allied his form ratings with the Halifax guru's time figures. That partnership didn't last long, but for the next 20 years he managed the horses owned by Jack Gerber and Jack Scott, and advised the South African high-rollers on their betting investments.

It proved an outstandingly successful set-up with Whitford taking full advantage of the fact that there were up to ten Jockey Club handicappers each working on an individual basis, covering different areas of the country and different categories of horses – sprinters, middle distance, stayers and two-year-olds. There were often considerable variations in how horses were handicapped at different meetings and the art of 'placing' them where they were 'best in' was all-important. The partnerships' principal trainer, Sam Armstrong, used to say it would take him three months to improve a horse 7lb, but Whitford could do it with one copy of the *Racing Calendar*.

Handicaps such as the Cesarewitch, Ebor, Royal Hunt Cup, Stewards Cup and Portland Plate fell to their horses, while among the top two-year-old races to be farmed by the team were the Gimcrack, Cheveley Park, Champagne and National Breeders' Stakes.

In announcing 'a fantastic FREE EXTRA' for readers at the start of the 1970 Flat season the *Life* carried a preface by Whitford who described the thoroughbred as:

> …that most rare of living creatures – one of a specialised species, at once consistent, measurable and predictable … What they have done once they are likely to do again and again. Perhaps not every time they run but often enough, and exactly enough, to make a sound assessment of their past performances by far the best guide to what they may do in the future.
>
> The form book contains all the data about these past performances. What I as a handicapper do is to translate this data in respect of each horse into a series of figures, the best of which indicate the summit of that horse's ability … With ratings at hand readers will appreciate more fully the task a horse is set to do; how well he has run; how near he is to his peak; how much he has progressed, and how he now stands with his rivals.

The ratings, which appeared on the page-2 marker-sheet (a page specifically laid out for the benefit of betting office settlers and brought in by Ben Clements in 1957), soon gained a tremendous following and that June the paper's sales topped the 100,000 mark for the first time as it finally overhauled the *Sporting Chronicle* in their circulation battle.

Headlines such as 'Win With Whitford' and 'Wonderful Whitford' started to appear with remarkable regularity and in July 1976 he was hailed as 'The 2,090-1 Wizard' when all his five selections won at Ascot on Diamond Day, and 48 hours later he went through the card at Newcastle. "Bookmakers fear him, his followers swear by him. You can't afford to ignore our form man when he's in form," crowed the paper.

Combined with his own low-profile brand of leadership, O W Fletcher had brought together all the special ingredients he needed to ensure the future success of the *Life*, but there were troubled times ahead.

A TRIER ON NON-TRIERS

HROUGHOUT the Swinging Sixties as racing began to benefit from the levy that was being generated by punters through betting shops and the Tote, the *Life* continued to press for further reforms in the face of typical Jockey Club intransigence. Ossie Fletcher led the way as he called for the draw for starting positions to be made at the Registry Office and released to the press along with the declared runners.

It was particularly important for the public to have this information as the draw was often a decisive factor at certain courses, yet it was available only to racegoers after the jockeys had been weighed out half an hour or so before a race. Not only did this system restrict the betting turnover on many major races and therefore diminish the levy, but it made a lottery of the ante-post market as Fletcher pointed out in 1961 when he cited the Lincolnshire Handicap as an example:

In races like the Lincoln the betting market before the draw bears little relation to the market afterwards. Honeymoor, for instance, was an 11 to 1 chance on Tuesday night, but drifted to 20 to 1 once the draw was known[*] ... All bookmakers and all punters would certainly be happier if the draw were known overnight. Owners would probably be glad to be put out of suspense that much earlier. The Clerk of the Scales would hardly object to having one job less. So act now, Jockey Club! Here is one issue on which you can so easily please *all* the people and upset none!

But the authorities were not in the business of pleasing people and they put up a series of feeble arguments against informing the off-course punter who, through the levy, was supplying owners with some 16 per cent of their prize money.

In 1967 the former senior steward, Tom Blackwell, listed three reasons why the Jockey Club was continuing to resist the demands for an overnight draw. He maintained: (1) It would only lead to more non-triers; (2) many owners and trainers would happily pay a fine to withdraw a badly drawn horse; (3) It would help the dopers. To which Sir David Llewellyn, in the guise of 'A Skinner', responded:

Why connections should be less inclined to have a go if they know of a bad draw overnight, instead of half an hour or so before the race, I cannot fathom. As for these affluent owners and trainers who, we are asked to believe, would be so ready to pay fines ... that's a matter of fixing the right scale. If a pony is chicken feed to the average owner, fine him a century. And how on earth could overnight declarations help dopers? To imagine that a gang will rush out to buy the evening paper, find a well-drawn favourite and fix it within 24 hours, belongs more in the realm of fiction rather than fact.

In the face of such logic the Jockey Club capitulated before the year was out and finally adopted the suggestion Meyrick Good had first proposed in 1934. Moreover, there was no increase in the number of doped horses or non-triers; rather the reverse in fact. Doping had already been greatly reduced by increased security measures, while local stewards had begun to clamp down on the racecourse cheats.

---

[*] Honeymoor, the ante-post favourite, was allotted the number one draw which was considered the kiss of death over Lincoln's straight mile, but he ran the race of his life to finish third of the 37 runners.

This was not before time. It had taken a long and courageous campaign by the *Life's* Len Thomas and a few other journalists to galvanise the stewards into action. Too often the racing scribe will opt for an easy life and turn a blind eye to the horses he sees being hooked up or given a quiet run. He will not risk upsetting the trainers and jockeys he relies on for information on a daily basis, particularly if they are also his friends.

Those who are prepared to speak out against such practices are a rare breed. They are also worth their weight in gold to their sport and their paper. Len Thomas was such a man. Ever helpful and kindly, he was also a formidable foe to those who operated on the six Ws principle as conveyed in the race-reader's apocryphal close-up 'waited with, will win when wanted' no matter how well established or high up racing's social scale they might be.

He had, after all, faced far worse things in life than the wrath of a self-important trainer, having served with the 27th Armoured Division during the war. After many adventures which saw him emerge shaken but unscathed from sunken amphibious tanks, the D-Day landings and the Battle of the Bulge, Major Thomas ended up in Hanover as part of a holding force. By chance he found himself quartered in a military riding school along with 20 thoroughbreds the Germans had acquired as a *prix de guerre* in France.

It was too good an opportunity to miss for a keen racing man. After VE Day he and an amateur rider started to train the horses and race them at a nearby course where they achieved some notable successes with an animal that had been named Luftgangster by the locals after it had been found running loose in the streets following an Allied air-raid.

On being demobbed at the end of 1946, 'The Major' tried his hand as a professional punter for a few years, but, with a young family to support, a run of bad luck persuaded him to find a more reliable income so he joined the Press Association in 1950 and, after an invaluable grounding on its racing staff, moved on to the *Life* in 1955.

No cheap sensationalist or scandal monger, he had the full backing of his editor when he began his crusade against racing's rogues in August 1963. In a forceful front-page introduction headed 'The non-triers at Windsor', Fletcher declared:

> Len Thomas is an experienced and responsible member of *The Sporting Life's* race reporting staff. He is at the races, watching the races, every day of his working life. He is a man not given to exaggeration. Yet today he has felt impelled to say: '<u>During the past two days at Windsor I have seen more non-triers than I care to number.</u>'
>
> Turn to page 7 for Len Thomas's straight-from-the-shoulder comments on a disease that is far more prevalent than doping, and for that reason even more harmful to racing. A disease that racing's rulers could and should stamp out with a few salutary punishments.

In his report, Thomas maintained that some of the non-triers were horses with obvious winning chances and belonged to "some of the more fashionable circles". He concluded:

> Committees and sub-committees have been formed to explore ways and means of encouraging people back into racing. While flagrant disregard of the rules is allowed, this extra work is worthless … The remedy lies with local stewards and their stipendiaries. Vigilance, stricter control and harsher penalties for offenders is the answer.

Len Thomas, ably backed by Ossie Fletcher (right) , waged a relentless campaign
against non-triers during the 1960s.

The accusation that 'fashionable circles' were defrauding the public was repeated even more
forcefully two years later following a two-day meeting at Bath when the far-from-doubting Thomas saw
similar "gross contraventions of the rules":

> How so many trainers get a licence to give their horses an 'airing' at this particular meeting is beyond
> my comprehension. Such actions destroy public confidence and bring an immense amount of harm
> to the sport. In the majority of cases the horses concerned were from fashionable stables and ridden
> by top class jockeys. The pity of it all is that had the horses been able to do their level best they
> would probably have won…
>
> The fashionable trainer who thinks he has a licence to do as he pleases simply because he trains
> for someone in authority must quickly be brought into line. In the same way severe penalties must
> be meted out to offending jockeys. It is no good just to give them a heavy fine … The thing that
> really does hurt is for a jockey to be stood down. One month's suspension should be the minimum.

Such outspoken comments were hardly calculated to make 'The Major' the most popular man
on the racecourse. The stewards didn't like being shown up any more than the guilty trainers and
jockeys, while there was a self-righteous clique of Establishment hacks who sat on the fence and
muttered darkly about the *Life's* man who was rocking the boat.

When two trainers accused Thomas of bringing racing into disrepute, he retorted with typical
bluntness by saying that if he had managed to prick their consciences then he had done nothing but
good. It was a long time before either trainer spoke to him again.

But the message was beginning to filter through and in July 1965 the Winchester trainer Les Hall
and his jockey Tony Jones lost their licences over the running of the two-year-old filly, Littleton Queen,
at Salisbury. A former pony-racing trainer, Hall had a reputation for laying horses out for major
gambles, but on this occasion the stewards picked on the wrong horse. Littleton Queen, who was having
her second race and started at 20-1, had never looked remotely capable of winning, and she never did.

In three subsequent outings for another trainer, she finished nearer last than first and before the end of the season she was sold for 280gns, by which time the Jockey Club, in a tacit acknowledgement that a mistake had been made, had restored the licences of both trainer and jockey.

In the same week that the Littleton Queen story broke, the *Life* published a letter from a Bradford bookmaker who had a novel idea for cutting the cost of the Levy Board's anti-doping precautions:

> As a bookmaker who is helping to foot the bill for the newly-inaugurated Securicor guard on horses stabled at racecourses, I would like to propose, in the interests of economy, that the said horses be split into two groups, triers and non-triers. I cannot see the logic in trying to prevent horses being 'got at' when the persons responsible for them have not the slightest intention of letting them win … It would, I estimate, cut the Securicor bill by about 70 per cent.

A slight exaggeration, perhaps! But the authorities were starting to get serious and the following day the paper announced: "The Jockey Club are taking action to eliminate non-triers in two-year-old races. It means that the practice of giving a juvenile 'an easy' on its first outing, which has become almost customary, must end."

The move came from Lord Allendale, the senior executive steward, who instructed local stewards to make better use of the camera patrol film which had been introduced in 1960. At first coverage had been restricted to the last furlong and a half of a race and the film was used simply to help stewards sort out objections and cases of interference, but as the camera's range was extended and mobile 'Scout' cameras were brought in, it became an invaluable aid in spotting non-triers.

But despite this new technology and Lord Allendale's urgings, there were still times when Len Thomas felt the racecourse stewards were asleep on the job and in 1966 he delivered his most scathing criticism yet after he had focused his 10 x 50s on certain horses running at a mixed (NH and Flat) meeting at Ascot.

On October 28 a banner headline demanded: 'Our Man on the Spot wants to know why no action was taken about – THE NON-TRIERS AT ASCOT'. And Fletcher added weight to the charge by declaring:

> *The Sporting Life* prints this report in good faith and with due regard to the seriousness of the accusations it contains. It does so in discharge of its first duty as a newspaper: to tell the public as much of what it believes to be true as Britain's heavily-weighted libel laws will allow. The writer is a professional race-watcher of many years' experience in whose judgement, integrity and eyesight *The Sporting Life* has complete faith.

By Len Thomas –

During the past two days at Ascot, I have seen several cases of horses not being allowed to 'run on their merits'. In short, blatant non-triers.

Such incidents have become prevalent at provincial tracks during the recent weeks, especially under National Hunt Rules. Now it has spread to the Royal Heath, we can only hope that the authorities will take appropriate action.

One incident at Ascot was so blatant that a colleague, one of the most experienced race-readers in the country, remarked to me: 'Do you think we shall ever see trainer ——- on a racecourse again?' Yet the authorities took no official action, which suggests they either did not see this gross contravention of the rules or turned a blind eye. I cannot for one moment believe it was the latter.

Horses are not machines. We are bound to see upsets in form. But to stand and watch a horse being virtually strangled to prevent him from winning is a totally different matter. It was incidents such as this that brought about the downfall of pony racing in this country. I have also noticed a number of horses under National Hunt Rules being brought to a racecourse in an unfit state to race. Many would not have looked out of place as broodmares, except for the fact that they were geldings.

In both cases the remedy is simple. Let's hope the authorities will take the appropriate action – and quickly, too.

The report was featured on the BBC's radio programme 'Today's Papers' and was backed up the next day by the former trainer, Tim Fitzgeorge-Parker, writing in the *Daily Mail*: "More than £50,000 a year is provided by the Betting Levy Board for the camera patrol services. It appears that local stewards and their paid secretaries are either frightened to use it properly or powerless to act upon the evidence it provides."

For the record, the Ascot stewards were Lord Derby, Gen. Sir Miles Dempsey and H J 'Jim' Joel. To assist them there were no fewer than three stipes; the senior stewards' secretary Brig. C B 'Roscoe' Harvey, Lt-Col. J M Christian and A J Marsham. Twelve eyes, six pairs of binoculars, a battery of cameras and not a non-trier in sight!

Could a general, a brigadier and a lieutenant-colonel have failed to see what had been so glaringly obvious to 'The Major'? And if they did see these breaches of the rules why did they not arraign the guilty parties before them? Frightened or powerless?

Fortunately for racing there were some stewards who were not so short-sighted or faint-hearted. At the beginning of July 1970 the Salisbury stewards – and let their names be carved with pride – Lord Tryon, Lord Margadale and C L 'Larch' Lloyd, enquired into the running and riding of the Duke of Norfolk's two-year-old filly, Skyway.

This was no Littleton Queen affair. Skyway, having her first race, had opened up at 5-2 before drifting out to 9-2. To quote Len Thomas: "Skyway certainly showed promise. After being prominent in the early stages, she lost her place after a couple of furlongs, but then came along with a great run to be beaten a neck and a length and a half."

The stewards interviewed John Dunlop and Ron Hutchinson, the trainer and rider of the horse, and referred the matter to the stewards of the Jockey Club because they were "not entirely satisfied with the explanations offered". Neither were the Jockey Club stewards when they held their inquiry a week later. They were, however, satisfied that Hutchinson "after a good break, failed to persevere in the first part of the race so that he prejudiced his chances of winning." Moreover, they considered the instructions which Dunlop gave for the riding of his two-year-olds were "contrary to the requirements of Rule 151 and so were contributory to Hutchinson's riding in the race."

Rule 151 laid down that every horse must run on its merits and that its rider should ensure it was given every opportunity to win or obtain the best possible placing.

Dunlop was fined a maximum £500 (£5,870) and Hutchinson suspended for 14 days. The Duke of Norfolk, who attended the inquiry, refused to comment at the time, but the following day he gave a lengthy interview to Guy Rais, the *Daily Telegraph's* distinguished reporter. In it he claimed he had been made a scapegoat by the Jockey Club stewards who had "made a grave error of judgement" and that he was the victim of "a sort of witch hunt" inspired, he suggested, by jealousy arising out of his stable's success.

In a petulant outburst he declared he would never run another horse at Salisbury and that it was an unwritten law that stewards did not hold inquiries into the running of two-year-olds first time out unless it was "a diabolical case". He asked: "If local stewards are going to initiate inquiries on the running of some two-year-olds, where will it all end?"*

In commenting on the case in an editorial headed 'Justice on the Turf', Fletcher wrote:

Understandably the Duke will feel aggrieved: whatever the dispute and whoever arbitrates, no one ever likes the verdict to go against him, and resentment is likely to be enhanced in one who himself has often sat in judgement. But the public will view the findings differently: for them it will have the tremendously important effect of restoring confidence in the impartiality of Turf justice. Rightly or wrongly the feeling has persisted that little people have felt the full weight of discipline while the eminent have always escaped.

The Sporting Life applauds the Jockey Club for finally dispelling this suspicion. And having itself called for stricter enforcement of discipline, it does not intend now to cavil, as some sections of the Press have done, at the stewards handling of a specific case. On this issue it does not run with the hare and hunt with the hounds...

At the end of this historic week we put on record our opinion that there is now little fundamentally wrong with Turf justice. We now have impartiality and we no longer have indeterminate sentences. We have legal representation. We also have the camera patrol. Certainly there should cease to be 'unwritten laws.' Either they should be forgotten or, if deemed worthy of retention, be written into the code.

The repercussions of the Duke's comments dominated the gossip columns in the national press and rumbled on into the highest echelons of society where it was well known that Lavinia, the Duchess of Norfolk, was the real governor of the Arundel stables and had been so for many years.

In commenting on what had now become a *cause célèbre*, Sir David Llewellyn, in his 'Jack Logan' column, called on the Duke to apologise to the stewards:

In his interview he gave to the *Daily Telegraph* he announced 'I am not going to run my horses any differently as a result of what has happened.' This is the language of defiance, not defence, of the authority upon which he could once fairly be called the Defender of the Faith in its membership and its methods ... The Duke must now decide which Duke of Norfolk he is – the rebel Duke storming the citadel of which he is part, or the steady Duke, calling for moderation and goodwill.

If he is wise he will even now express his public regret to colleagues whom he has injured however inadvertently: he will by his example reinforce the authority of the body which he has served so well: and within it he will work for changes which his own bitter experience has shown him to be due.

---

* This was an interesting insight into the mindset of a man who, as senior steward at Ascot in October 1953, was responsible for reporting to the Jockey Club stewards the 'improvement in form' of the Paddy Prendergast-trained two-year-old, Blue Sail, who was beaten a neck after starting a well-backed 5-2 favourite for the Cornwallis Stakes. As a result of a subsequent inquiry, the Jockey Club refused to accept entries from the Irish champion trainer for ten months, although the Irish Turf Club held their own inquiry into the matter and cleared Prendergast of any wrong doing.

And apologise he did, but only after the Queen had intervened and persuaded 'Uncle Bernard' (as she always called him), to patch up his differences with the stewards.*

In a statement issued through the Racing Information Bureau ten days after the *Telegraph* interview had appeared, Bernard Marmaduke FitzAlan-Howard, 16th Duke of Norfolk, Earl of Arundel, Baron Maltravers, Earl of Surrey, Baron Herries, Baron FitzAlan, Clun and Oswaldestre, Earl of Norfolk, Earl Marshal and Hereditary Marshal and Chief Butler of England, Premier Duke and Earl, said:

"It has become clear to me during the past few days that my remarks which were published in the *Daily Telegraph* on Friday July 10, have given offence in certain quarters. I made those remarks in good faith to defend the names of my trainer, John Dunlop, and my jockey, Ron Hutchinson, in both of whom I have complete confidence. If, however, I caused offence to anyone concerned in the Skyway case I unreservedly withdraw such remarks and offer an apology."

Today, non-triers are still with us, but they are not as easy to spot or as numerous. It is thanks to men of integrity such as the Salisbury stewards, the Jockey Club stewards who judged the Skyway case and journalists like Len Thomas that this is so.

---

* The Queen was particularly keen that Norfolk should make his peace with Lord Tryon as both men were members of her Royal Victorian Order although this was about the only thing they had in common. Charlie Tryon was the exact opposite of the Duke; fun-loving and ever courteous, he abhorred any form of snobbery or pomposity and deplored the manners of some of the older order of Jockey Club members.

THE LAST BASTION

S O MUCH was achieved during the sixties – the legalisation of betting and the suppression of doping; overnight declaration of runners and draw; the introduction of camera patrols and starting stalls (in 1965) and a betting levy – it seemed, at last, as if the industry had hauled itself into line with all the other major (and minor) racing countries. But there remained one last great bastion of Jockey Club conservatism – the refusal to recognise the rights of women to train horses and ride them in races.

There was but one exception; the historic Newmarket Town Plate confined to amateur riders of either sex. In October 1961, the day after Lester Piggott's wife, Susan, had ridden the winner of the Plate (run over three and three-quarter miles of Jockey Club land), the stewards of that august body imposed a set of petty restrictions on Miss Norah Wilmot, one of the country's most respected and longest established trainers – except she wasn't a trainer in the eyes of the Jockey Club.

The story was carried in the *Life* without comment; that followed later – in volumes:

Miss Norah Wilmot, who has been training horses for 30 years with a head lad holding the licence, was told at Newmarket yesterday by the stewards that she will not be allowed to supervise the saddling and unsaddling of her horses on the racecourse or superintend them in the stable block. This must be done by R Greenhill, who has held the licence on her behalf for a number of years.

Miss Wilmot, who is 72 years of age and acted as assistant trainer to her father from 1911 to 1931, was very upset by the decision. She said: "I am a most unhappy woman. In the eyes of the Jockey Club stewards I am nothing, after all these years in a training stable." She applied for a trainer's licence on the death of her father in 1931, but the Jockey Club decided that she was 'not a person' within the meaning of their rules. She stated that the Club has told her that to grant a licence would create a precedent.

In her younger days Norah Wilmot had been an experienced work-rider and even rode in gallops at Beckhampton for that renowned martinet, Fred Darling, the trainer of seven Derby winners. After taking over from her father, Sir Robert Wilmot, she sent out such pre-war winners as Loosestrife (Newbury Autumn Cup and Goodwood Cup) and Haulfryn (Doncaster Cup) from the small string she trained at her Binfield Grove stables near Bracknell in Berkshire. In 1961, her star performer was the three-year-old No Fiddling who was shortly to win his fifth race for her in memorable circumstances.

The stewards' action incensed almost everyone in racing. If anything was designed to illustrate the Jockey Club's nit-picking hypocrisy this was surely it and it resulted in some indignant letters appearing in the *Life* with one from another long-established trainer, Florence Nagle, being given front-page prominence:

This year has been remarkable for the great success of women owners in the classics – the One Thousand Guineas, the Oaks, the first three in the Derby, the first four in the St Leger. The Jockey Club have celebrated these successes in the most extraordinary – although characteristic – way by virtually debarring Miss Norah Wilmot, our oldest woman trainer, from exercising any supervision whatsoever over her horses.

For over 30 years they have been well aware that she trained her horses, although the licence has been held by her head lad ... There are few professions in the world today not open to women, but the sex phobia of the Jockey Club has to be felt to be believed, and I suppose that this latest touch is their method of eliminating any who have dared to open even a tiny chink in the barred door.

Autocratic bodies who govern sport and are self-elected should take great care to govern justly, and I feel that in this case justice has not been done and that Miss Wilmot has been put in an impossible position after thirty years' service to racing.

These views were supported in a letter from Renee Castello, owner of that year's One Thousand Guineas and Oaks heroine, Sweet Solera, who had kept her first broodmare at Miss Wilmot's stud, while racegoers expressed their feelings on the matter the following week when cheering home Jimmy Lindley on No Fiddling. Tom Nickalls reported:

There can be no doubt about what the public thinks of the Jockey Club's recent edict placing restrictions on Miss Wilmot. Their opinion was voiced in no uncertain manner as Lindley brought No Fiddling back to unsaddle after winning the Windsor Castle Handicap at Kempton yesterday. It was an ovation such as only classic winners receive.

This was not a case of the public speaking through their pockets – No Fiddling was favourite – but a spontaneous demonstration of the respect in which Miss Norah Wilmot, the colt's 'trainer,' is held by all racegoers. Cheers soon developed into shouts for 'Norah!' and these reached a crescendo as Capt. Charles Moore, the Queen's racing manager and a steward of the meeting, took Miss Wilmot into the unsaddling ring to stand by her winner ... Miss Wilmot said, 'I am absolutely overwhelmed by Captain Moore's gesture and the wonderful reception the crowd gave me.'

The very next day Nickalls witnessed a scene at the headquarters of racing that exposed the farce and folly of the clubmen's edict:

After all the passions aroused by the Stewards' warnings to Miss Wilmot, I could hardly believe my eyes at Newmarket yesterday as I saw Mrs ———-* carrying a saddle from the precincts of the weighing room right across the paddock in full view of everyone to the saddling boxes, obviously with the intention of saddling a runner. If the Stewards are so concerned to tighten up their regulations, are these regulations meant to apply only to Miss Wilmot?

On the same day Ossie Fletcher had his say in his 'Talking Points' column:

The cold-blooded way in which the Stewards of the Jockey Club have handled the Miss Wilmot affair has left them almost devoid of public sympathy. Nearly everybody who has commented on the matter, whether in the Press or on TV has been 'for' Miss Wilmot and 'agin' them ... Then, last Monday, *The Times* weighed in with a piece, the introduction to which was so phrased that we could

---

* This was Rosemary Lomax whose husband, Ian, held the licence. After training licences were finally granted to women, she became the first of her sex to gain a major success when she sent out Precipice Wood to win the 1970 Ascot Gold Cup. Fourteen years earlier, Helen Johnson Houghton, the widow of former Blewbury trainer Gordon Johnson Houghton, became the first woman to train a classic winner when Gilles de Retz won the 2,000 Guineas, although her achievement was not officially recognised.

not help thinking it had been dictated not in Printing House but in Cavendish Square.

It appeared that The Establishment in racing had chosen the traditional Establishment organ to leak their reply to correspondence which, naturally enough, had been running in the Top Racing People's paper. And what was the reply? It amounted to this: 'We can recognise only the licensed trainer, and we cannot give licences to women because the profession is already overcrowded.'

The actual phrase used in *The Times* was: "The situation would be economically worse if the gates were thrown open to the host of women who would like to take up training." Now, no one suggests that trainers' licences should be granted to 'a host of women'. But this column shares the opinion of the vast majority that they **should** be granted to those women who, over the years, have given every proof of their integrity and their ability to compete on equal terms with men.

Referring to the reception No Fiddling had received at Kempton, Fletcher concluded with the observation that as Charles Moore was the Queen's racing manager and also a member of the Jockey Club that had so recently slighted Miss Wilmot, "the thought did occur that perhaps someone more richly endowed with humanity than the Jockey Club had dropped a gracious hint."

Meanwhile, the *Life* kept readers informed on how women trainers were faring in more enlightened lands. Sweden's leading trainer, Miss B Strokirk, had, for instance, won three Scandinavian Derbys, five St Legers (from six runners) and four Oaks (from five runners) since taking out a licence in 1954.

For his part, Jack Fairfax-Blakeborough drew on his archives to disprove the stewards' assertion that they would be setting a precedent if they issued a licence to Miss Wilmot. He pointed out that in 1886, Ellen Chaloner, the sister of the famous Middleham jockey cum trainer John Osborne, had been given a licence to train at Newmarket on the death of her husband, the classic winning jockey Tom Chaloner.

The Jockey Club's position was clearly untenable, but with typical stubbornness the stewards refused to acknowledge the fact even when Miss Wilmot sent out the Queen's filly, Don't Tell, to win a small race at Folkestone in 1964. In the same year the Club blocked an attempt by Florence Nagle to challenge their policy in the High Court, but the West Sussex trainer was no quitter and in July 1965 she was reported as saying:

> I think the stage has now been reached when I must instruct my legal representatives to issue a writ on the Stewards to ask them to show cause why they have failed to issue trainers' licences to women. The Stewards are not running a private men's club. It has to be borne in mind that racing is now existing on public money and it should not, therefore, debar women from full participation in the sport.

Mrs Nagle had been training her own horses since 1938, having narrowly failed to win the previous year's Derby with her 100-1 chance, Sandsprite, a fast-finishing second to Mid-day Sun. After the war, with her head lad holding the licence, she sent out a succession of home-bred winners from her Westerlands Stud at Petworth, although her best horse, Elf-Arrow, the winner of eight races including the 1959 Liverpool St Leger, had been bought as a foal.

In January 1966, Mrs Nagle had her case against the Jockey Club struck out by a High Court judge, but she appealed and the following month the Law Lords gave her leave to proceed with her action as, one by one, they spelt out the obvious.

Lord Denning, the Master of the Rolls, could not have put it more plainly: "If Mrs Nagle is to carry on her trade without stooping to subterfuge, she has to have a training licence." Lord Salmon declared the Club's stand was "as capricious as refusing a man a licence simply because of the colour of his hair," while Lord Danckwerts condemned the practice of the head lad holding the licence as "a childish subterfuge without any merit and quite unworthy of the importance of the matter."

There was now no question as to what the High Court's judgement would be and that summer, after a five-minute hearing, Mr Justice Sachs found for the plaintiff. Even then, the Jockey Club still tried to have the last word by declaring that Mrs Nagle could have her licence *provided* she acknowledged it was granted "in the exercise of the stewards' absolute and unfettered discretion".

Racing's Emily Pankhurst had no problem with that. Tired but happy, the 72-year-old great-grandmother said: "It is the end of a long fight. I hope this means an end to the sex bar in racing – at least as far as trainers' licences are concerned."

And a week later the headline 'Winner Trained By Miss N Wilmot' announced that the 77-year-old *grande dame* of British racing had become the first licensed woman trainer to send out a winner when her filly, Pat, gained a hugely popular victory in the South Coast Stakes at Brighton.

The pressure was now on the Jockey Club to grant jockeys' licences to women. As early as 1960 Fletcher had forecast the inevitable when commenting on the news that the French were to stage races for women riders:

> However much Man resists it, the forward march of Women continues in all spheres of life. Racing will surely be the last bastion to fall. But fall one day it will … Let us hope that when the battle is joined it will not be too bloody, and we shall not be treated to the spectacle of girls in riding breeches chained to the railings of Cavendish Square.

The following year a trickle of girls – Sally Hall, niece of northern trainer Sam Hall, and Diane Smyth, daughter of Epsom trainer Ron Smyth, among them – started to cross the Channel to ride in women's races such as the Grand Prix des Dames at Ostend and the Preis der Perlenkette (pearl necklace) at Neuss in Germany. While, on the home front, alderman Albert Cammidge, chairman of Doncaster's race committee, tried (and failed) to get clearance from the Jockey Club to stage a ladies race at the 1962 St Leger meeting.

But women riders were hardly a new topic. In 1930, a certain Jean Sanday made the headlines when she mounted her father's horse, The Beezer, to complete the course after its jockey had been injured when it fell at the final fence in a two-horse race at Haydock. The Beezer was placed second by the judge and Miss Sanday was duly weighed as correct (at 11st 9lb) by the clerk of the scales.

The racecourse stewards were then left to ponder over Rule 170 which stated: "in the event of a rider being disabled, his horse may be ridden home by any person of sufficient weight provided he be qualified according to the conditions of the race."

Insofar as amateurs did not require a permit to ride in a race until they had ridden ten winners, Miss Sanday was qualified, but when the matter was referred to the National Hunt Committee the stewards latched onto the words 'provided *he* be qualified' and ruled that the horse should not have been placed second. Shortly afterwards Rule 170 was amended to prevent horses being ridden home by a person other than the jockey.

The Beezer incident prompted Mrs Arthur Heald, a successful point-to-point rider, to apply to Weatherbys for a permit to ride under Rules, but she was summarily rebuffed and the issue faded away until girls became an important part of racing's labour force after the Second World War, although even then, their calls for equality were muted.

Florence Nagle's victory over the Jockey Club changed all that. On the same day as the *Life* carried the news of her breakthrough, Fairfax-Blakeborough looked further ahead than most commentators when he asked:

> Will jockeys' licences be granted to girls to ride on the Flat and are women members of the Jockey Club in the offing? … In these days when women are taking an ever increasing part in racing, training and breeding, and when many of them have practical experience and skill equal to most men, it is not surprising that they should agitate for more active participation – and some say administration.

And, again, he delved into his archives to show that female jockeys would be no new phenomenon. He quoted from a letter John Hutton, the breeder of Marske, the sire of Eclipse, wrote to his brother Matthew (who became Archbishop of Canterbury in 1757) in 1723: "We went to Ripon races to see eight women ride for a £12 plate. They all rid astride in jockey dresses. Two or three of 'em fell off, but got up again no worse."

JF-B also cited the famous match at York in 1805 between 'Mrs Thornton' (Alicia Meynell, the mistress of a noted local sportsman, Colonel Thornton), and the champion jockey, Frank Buckle. Described by a contemporary as somewhat lacking in "pretty virginities" in her "purple silk cap and waistcoat, nankeen skirt, purple shoes and embroidered stockings," young Alicia rode her paramour's mare, Louisa, side-saddle, and took full advantage of the 4st she was getting from Buckle's mount to win by half a neck.

As for officials, the old quill-driver (he always wrote with a quill pen) found that there was once a female clerk of the scales at Blandford races in Dorset. In 1831 a writer in the *Sporting Magazine* reported: "I could not help thinking it rather outré to see a fair lady weighing jockeys … They stood as cool as cucumbers before the fair maid, with breeches all unbuttoned."

Meanwhile, the girls continued to make the best of their only chance to take part in a Flat race on British soil. The Newmarket Town Plate had been instituted by Charles II in 1665 when he ordered the race "to be rid yearly, the seconde Thursday in October, for euer," and so it was until it was interrupted by the Second World War.

The post-war revivals came to be dominated by women and in 1971, Marie Tinkler, a former top-class show jumper and a successful point-to-point rider, won the race for the second year running thanks, in part, to her 12-year-old son, Nigel, who rode the pacemaker for her horse, Ocean Sailor. Also riding in the race that year was Judy Goodhew, who finished fourth on Pindon; a horse her permit-trainer husband had sent out to win the Meyrick Good Handicap Hurdle at Fontwell the previous year.

As she returned from unsaddling Pindon, Mrs Goodhew received a well-meant "never mind, better luck next year, eh!" consolation from an official that fired her determination to tackle the Jockey Club. She reasoned: "Why should I, because of my sex, have to wait twelve months to ride in a race again?"[1] and that evening she posted off her application for a licence to ride under National Hunt rules.

A fortnight later, the *Life's* Sue Wreford, who had also ridden in that year's Town Plate, reported that Mrs Goodhew had received a curt reply from Weatherbys which stated: "the stewards of the Jockey Club do not issue licences for lady riders."

Petite, gritty, chirpy and attractive, the 31-year-old mother of three was not one to take 'no' for an answer. She was quoted as saying: "I shall keep applying for a licence and am thinking of legal action. The refusal is blatant sex discrimination. That is ridiculous because women put money into racing, they school over fences at home and there are many who are capable of race-riding."

Wreford, herself something of a pioneer in the male-dominated world of racing journalism, ended her article by disclosing that Mrs G had already asked the stewards to reconsider their decision and they would be holding a meeting to discuss the matter in four days' time.

That the stewards should even consider holding such a meeting as a result of a request from an unknown housewife in Kent showed how much their position had changed since their age-old bias against women had been undermined by Mrs Nagle, and it took just one blast of the Goodhew trumpet for the last bastion of Jockey Club defiance to come tumbling down. On 2 November 1971, Wreford reported:

> We may soon be seeing women riders racing under rules. The stewards of the Jockey Club met in London yesterday and although they have clearly shut their eyes for the time being to the possibility of mixed races, they agreed to look into the question of introducing women-only races for amateur riders. The stewards, who included Sir Randle Feilden, Lords Allendale and Leverhulme and the man who looks after licensing, Jakey Astor, decided to seek the views of various racing organisations … The next general meeting of the Club, which meets quarterly, is on December 13.

Three days later 'Jack Logan' put his shoulder to the wheel under the headline 'Why shouldn't our girls have the chance of riding a Derby winner?' as he cited the case of the Dutch rider, Ina Schwarzkächel, who, in 1966, was the first girl to ride as a professional in Europe and had recently become the first of her sex to ride a Derby winner when she partnered Cleopatra to success in the Netherlands Derby.

Llewellyn, never afraid to snatch the crusading torch from other hands and claim it as his own, concluded:

> Today I give the racing journalists of Britain a lead. I stand up and am counted as an advocate of equal rights for women, including their right to ride under rules. Do they want our Ina Schwarzkächels ever to have the chance to win an English Derby or not? As Britain goes forward into Europe, let them come off the fence and show once and for all whether they are on the side of the apes or the angels.

And right on cue, that night the Sportswriters Association voted Princess Anne as Sportswoman of the Year for her win on Doublet in the European 3-day-event championship at Burghley. The following month, the Princess also won BBC TV's Sports Personality of the Year award by beating George Best, who was runner-up, with Barry John, the Welsh rugby international and British Lions star, in third.

Throughout November the debate rolled on around the country. At a Midlands racing forum, Sue Wreford reported that from a 14-strong panel only the Jockey Club's senior handicapper, Dan Sheppard, was against the idea whereas his brother, Gay, was keen to stage the first woman's race at Stratford where he was clerk of the course.

The panel was chaired by the former senior steward and noted racing administrator, Lord Willoughby de Broke who was all in favour of allowing a limited number of races on the Flat for women. The 1969 Grand National winning jockey Eddie Harty, sitting next to his weighing room colleague, David Nicholson, shared that view but drew the line on mixed races. "It's one thing to trample over David; it'd be another thing to trample over David's missus," he quipped.

During the discussion Tony Fairbairn of the RIB provided a rare nugget of gossip from the Jockey Club meeting that had considered the question when he revealed: "One steward said that apart from changing rooms we'd have to double up on many other things including first-aid rooms and ambulances. Then another steward said with a perfectly deadpan face: 'It wouldn't matter if they shared an ambulance if both were unconscious!'"

In the same week, the *Life* reported that Italy's first professional female jockey, Tiziana Sozzi, had opened her account by beating the likes of the reigning champion Gianfranco Dettori (father of Frankie) in Milan, while in America, where women had been riding professionally since 1969, Robyn Smith was steadily racking up her total and was to end the year with 40 winners from 353 rides.

The letters' column also brought in some interesting opinions from the girls. Gillian Kelleway, a successful point-to-point rider and wife of leading NH jockey Paul, maintained: "Jump racing is far too tough a sport for women – we are not really equipped for the job … I, for one, want to remain a *female* female. So let us leave it to the men. They are so much better at it. Don't let us women lower the tone of NH racing."

Jocelyn Reavey, wife of trainer Eddie Reavey, took a different view as she observed: "It does seem wrong that half the talent in the country should be excluded just because their physical conformation makes riding a horse more comfortable!" But it was the voice of experience that offered the best advice to the Jockey Club when Florence Nagle wrote in to say: "Women riders will come eventually and how much better to give way gracefully than to be forced to agree."

And give way they did. At their meeting on December 13 the stewards gave the go-ahead for a series of Flat races for women amateurs in 1972. The first of 12 such races, run at Kempton on May 6 and sponsored by the perfume company, Goya, attracted a host of entries which resulted in 12 horses having to be balloted out at the overnight stage leaving 21 to face the starter.

As a spectacle the event went down well with the crowd, but it proved even more popular with the bookmakers as the winner was the 50-1 shot, Scorched Earth. The successful rider, Meriel Tufnell, rode a remarkably cool race and explained later: "The reason I wasn't really nervous was because everyone expected us to be last."

Judy Goodhew, who had brought about the Jockey Club's *volte-face*, finished unplaced along with Mrs Kelleway who was typically outspoken in her pre and post-race comments; a fact picked up by 'Jack Logan' in his review of the week's papers:

> Gillian Kelleway told Claude Duval bluntly in *The Sun*: "Sadly, the best horses in the race are ridden by the worst jockeys … I think some of them will end up in the Silver Ring." Many more comments of this character and the traditional camaraderie of the changing room will not survive for long in the women's caravan...
>
> One girl's bitchiness is, of course, another's candour, but as I'm too gallant – and frightened – to take sides between women exchanging verbal felicities, I'm not going to tell you in what category I put Gillian Kelleway's birds-eye view of the race as revealed to Tim Fitzgeorge-Parker in *The Sun*: "It was pathetic to see these girls who know nothing about racing flopping about in front of me."

Ah, yes! but they were *in front* of her, and with increased race-riding opportunities standards improved enormously. In 1974, women were able to ride against men in amateur races on the Flat and the following year girls were allowed to become apprentices and could ride in mixed apprentice races.

When the Sex Discrimination Act came into force midway through the 1975-76 jumping season, they also received clearance to ride over fences and in 1978 women professionals competed against men on equal terms, since when the march of the great sisterhood has been relentless. They have competed in the Derby and the Grand National; ridden winners at the great festival meetings of Cheltenham, Aintree and Royal Ascot, and, in 2005, 22-year-old Hayley Turner tied with Saleem Golam as champion apprentice with 44 winners, and three years later became the first British woman to ride 100 winners in a calendar year.

The advance of women trainers – chiefly over jumps – has been even more impressive. Jenny Pitman led the way in the 1980s when, within the space of a year, she became the first woman to win the Grand National (Corbierre in '83) and then the Cheltenham Gold Cup (Burrough Hill Lad, '84) – winning both races again with Royal Athlete ('95) and Garrison Savannah ('91) – while Henrietta Knight sent out Best Mate to win three successive Cheltenham Gold Cups (2002-4) and Venetia Williams stunned the pundits with her 100-1 Grand National winner, Mon Mome, in 2009.

On the Flat, Lady Anne Herries, numbered the 1995 French Derby (Celtic Swing) among her successes and Pam Sly became the first woman to officially train an English classic winner when Speciosa landed the 2006 One Thousand Guineas, while Mary Reveley became the first of her sex to train 1,000 winners on the Flat and over jumps.

In fact, for many years now women have played a major role in every sphere of racing. They act as stewards, judges, racecourse managers and clerks of the course. They are prominent in the media with former *Sporting Life* journalists Sue Montgomery (*The Independent* and *Independent on Sunday*) and the peripatetic Lydia Hislop providing top class copy and informed comment. And way back in 1977 they were even ELECTED TO THE JOCKEY CLUB.

Truly, there hadn't been such a thunderous crash of collapsing masonry since the walls of Jericho came atumbling down.

WAR ON WYATT

ONE OF THE most important and successful campaigns ever waged by the *Life* was its exposure of the way those who had control of the Tote were shamelessly ripping off punters in their attempts to restore financial stability to the machine.* The first indication that the oft derided Nanny Goat had suddenly developed a more rapacious appetite came when Snow Knight stunned the Epsom crowd with a 50-1 victory in the 1974 Derby. The few clairvoyants who had backed the colt on the Tote anticipated a bumper payout, but were dismayed to receive odds of just 29-1.

This was not the way pool betting was supposed to work. Ever since the Tote was first set up in 1929, it had always paid much better than SP on outsiders. The Derby dividend seemed as inexplicable as the race result, but there had to be an explanation and three weeks later it was provided by the *Life*. An exclusive report headed 'Scandal Of Secret Tote Deductions' revealed that a massive 45 per cent rake-off had been taken from the win pool before the dividend was calculated:

> The deduction was in accordance with a sliding scale adopted by the Tote Board earlier this year whereby the percentage deduction increased as the percentage of winning units decreased. Had the percentage of tickets on Snow Knight been slightly less than it was, the percentage deduction from the pool would have risen to the maximum – a staggering FIFTY FIVE PERCENT.
>
> The *Sporting Life* learned of the scale of deductions only this week – and then unofficially. And more than a week after it had been abandoned in favour of another scale, this time a little less punitive to backers of outsiders. The maximum deduction is now 39 per cent.

The information had been fed to the *Life* by Lord Wigg, a former Tote Board member (1958-64) and Levy Board chairman (1967-72), who was currently chairman of the Betting Office Licensees' Association (BOLA). Ossie Fletcher had formed a close and valuable friendship with Labour's ex-Paymaster General who would often use the *Life* as a conduit to further his various campaigns for the good of racing and its labour force.

The Tote, then under the chairmanship of Lord Mancroft, a former Conservative minister in Harold Macmillan's government, excused its failure to inform the public of its new scale of deductions by claiming they were for an experimental period only and that its main aim was to produce a gross revenue from pool betting of 19 per cent. To this Fletcher had no objection, but he declared:

> What is not tenable is that the board should experiment with fresh scales of deduction which could have a profound effect on dividends without letting the public, who are its guinea pigs, know.

---

* In 1970 the Tote was broke and owed the Levy Board some £700,000 (£7.5m). What had once been heralded as racing's golden goose had been done to death by a succession of taxes – a grossly inequitable, albeit voluntary, Levy contribution (27.5% of the Board's total revenue from 1961-70), the betting tax (re-introduced by Harold Wilson's Labour government in 1966), a selective employment tax and a short-lived rateable value tax. Ineffective part-time management and the boom in betting shops had not helped. In order to save the Tote from bankruptcy the Home Secretary, Reginald Maudling, introduced a Bill (the Horserace Totalisator and Betting Levy Boards Act of 1972), to enable it to operate as a bookmaker and charge its rivals a fee for the right to accept bets at Tote odds. This 'if you can't beat 'em, join 'em' policy made a mockery of the Tote's *raison d'être* – to provide pool betting – but it saved the organisation, although it probably would have done just as well if it had been given a franchise to sell hamburgers (as the Royal Commission on Gambling so succinctly remarked in 1978).

No wonder backers of outsiders this year have felt cheated! No wonder SP has been beating the Tote in areas where hitherto the bookmaker couldn't compete! Such business methods would be reprehensible whoever was responsible: when it is a board appointed by the Home Secretary, and thus carrying the seal of Government approval, they are altogether unacceptable.

Home Secretary Roy Jenkins must ensure that full details of changes in deductions are published *before* they are implemented – even if only on an experimental basis – and that deductions are never again altered surreptitiously.

Roy Jenkins did neither but, to the dismay of many, he did ensure the recently appointed Tote Board member and former Labour MP, Woodrow Wyatt, succeeded Mancroft as chairman in May 1976.

A flamboyant and controversial journalist who made his name on BBC TV's Panorama programme, which he started with Richard Dimbleby in 1955, Wyatt did at least have an interest in racing in contrast to many of his predecessors. He had owned a few horses in his time and liked a bet, but he also epitomised the public's perception of all that is rotten in a politician – self-serving, arrogant, unprincipled, slippery and untrustworthy.

He had entered parliament in 1945 as member for the Aston division of Birmingham but lost his seat in a boundaries reshuffle in 1955. He returned four years later as MP for Bosworth, Leics., but lost that seat in 1970 and later became a sycophantic admirer of Margaret Thatcher much to the disgust of his former colleagues on the Labour benches.

The *Life* greeted his appointment as Tote supremo with the guarded observation:

Mr Wyatt will no doubt regret some of the things he has said on betting. In 1975 he advocated a 25 per cent deduction on turnover. Perhaps he has learned more about the mathematics of the business since joining the Tote.

And perhaps not! Within six weeks of taking office, the 58-year-old chairman secretly introduced a fiendishly complicated formula for calculating dividends that had little to do with pool betting and everything to do with drastically reducing Tote payouts. This time the scandal was exposed by the *Sporting Chronicle* and was followed up by the *Life* the next day under the headline 'The Tote doctor their dividends'. When contacted by the paper, a Tote spokesman explained: "We are experimenting, as we always do, with the object of reducing operating costs and improving dividends."

O W Fletcher was not to be fobbed off by such twaddle. Citing the example of a 25-1 winner at Pontefract that day, which had paid just over 7-1 on the Tote, he fired off a three-point condemnation of the practice:

WE SAY it is monstrous that a state monopoly which exists to promote pool betting on horseracing should so arrange its affairs that it has virtually abandoned that function and for practical purposes is operating as a bookmaker.

WE SAY that by allowing the public to believe their investments are going into a pool when clearly not all of them are, the Tote are taking money under false pretences.

WE SAY – as we did two years ago – that the public have a right to know at all times how Tote pools are operated and what the deductions are. And the Tote Board have a duty to tell them.

The next day with the help of a leaked Tote memo, the editor published a detailed account of how the dividends were being calculated and how the new formulae could deprive punters of anything up to 80 per cent of their rightful winnings.

These revelations were followed by the news that BOLA, many of whose members offered punters the facility of betting at Tote odds, was investigating the probability that the Tote was in breach of the Betting, Gaming and Lotteries Act of 1963 which laid down the procedure for pool deductions and the distribution of winnings.

Wyatt, initially 'unavailable for comment', finally responded a week after the story had broken with a statement that began by referring to "a campaign conducted in the sporting press and by racing correspondents designed to show that Tote dividends are worse than starting prices."

He quite rightly stated that on a number of recent occasions Tote dividends had beaten the SP, although the instances he quoted curiously dated from the day after the scandal had been exposed. As ever, when cornered, he sought to justify his actions with a mixture of bombast and baloney, which Fletcher eloquently countered point by point. To quote just one of the exchanges:

WW: "The Tote does not mind reasonable criticism of its activities, but it does expect tolerable standards of fact-finding amongst journalists before they launch into attacks designed to denigrate the Tote and promote the interests of bookmakers."

OWF: "We leave readers to judge whose standards have been tolerable in this affair – ours or the Tote's. As for Mr Wyatt's cheap and unoriginal innuendo that we are promoting the interests of bookmakers – what's he complaining about? The Tote ARE bookmakers – nationalised bookmakers. And that's half the trouble: if they were NOT bookmakers their pools would have to be pools, and not the basis for artificially contrived prices, which is all they are now."

And that, indeed, was the crux of the matter. The Tote's off-course cash betting subsidiary, Tote Bookmakers Ltd, already had more than 100 high street shops which accounted for 29 per cent of the organisation's turnover and it was a side of the business Wyatt was determined to build up with the help of Bill Balshaw, a former chairman of the William Hill organisation who had joined the Tote as a consultant in 1973.

As a result of the press revelations and BOLA's protestations, the latest 'experiment' in calculating dividends was scrapped within a month. At the same time Dr Geoffrey Ardron, the director-general of the Tote Board, was given the push. His was the first of many heads to roll under a sacrificial regime Wyatt employed to keep himself in power at the cost of his fellow executives' jobs. In reporting the climb-down Fletcher commented:

> As the *Life* understands the present position, pools are again being operated on a basis that is reasonable, even though many would still prefer a uniform rate of deduction rather than one that fluctuates according to the percentage of winning units. And always provided – it should go without saying – that any off-course money sent for the pool by Tote HQ is committed before the result is known.

The very suggestion! How could a responsible editor of the nation's leading racing paper imply it could be otherwise? It was surely unthinkable – wasn't it?

At the end of the year, Wyatt caused more controversy with his submission to the latest Royal Commission on Gambling. In it he suggested that the Tote should take over all betting shops, close down 6,000 of them and form an off-course monopoly with the remaining 8,300. The following month, Tote Bookmakers brazenly applied to join BOLA, which represented 4,200 of those shops! Unsurprisingly, its application was rejected and its £1,650 membership fee returned.

Five months later, in May 1977, things took an unexpected turn for the better when the *Life* announced:

> The Tote have seen the light. From next Saturday they will make a uniform deduction of 20 per cent from the win pool whatever horse wins instead of the present sliding scale which ranges from four percent when a hot-pot wins to a massive 39 per cent for a rank outsider … *The Sporting Life*, so often critical of the Tote Board in the past, now applauds them for doing the right thing. It has always been our contention that the percentage deduction from pools should be constant, irrespective of the number of winning units.

Wyatt, in explaining the change, said that a fixed-rate deduction would "more nearly match the popular conception of what a pool is intended to be." The trouble was that Wyatt's idea of pool betting did not tally with the popular conception. This became apparent a week later when Fletcher had cause to criticise the organisation's oldest subsidiary, Tote Investors Ltd (soon to become Tote Credit Ltd), for failing to transmit off-course bets on the Daily Tote Double and Tote Treble to the racecourse pools. In two recent instances at Bangor and Hexham this had resulted in dividends being declared on the first leg only even though some off-course Tote clients had selected all the winners.

Once again, punters were being robbed of their rightful winnings. Under the headline 'Oh what a tangled web they weave…' the editor commented:

> The Bangor and the Hexham cases serve to illustrate the complications that can arise now that the Tote Board are bookmakers as well as pool operators with absolute discretion as to what bets they stick and which go into the pool … The *Sporting Life* says it is idiotic that the law should allow the Tote this discretion. The Tote's pool operating function and bookmaking function should be totally separate.
>
> Every client has a right to know when he places a bet whether it is or isn't going into the relevant pool. At present only on-course backers can be certain. If the Tote prefer to confine pool betting to the course and stick off-course bets in their role of gilt-edged bookmakers, so be it – but let it be on an all or nothing basis; not the present mishmash which leaves everyone wondering exactly what game is being played.

That summer, a select committee on nationalised industries declared the Tote must never again change its methods of computing dividends without informing the public, but dividends continued to fluctuate wildly over the next two years giving rise to speculation that whatever game was being played by the Tote, it certainly wasn't cricket. At the same time Wyatt continued to incense his critics by the high-handed manner in which he conducted the Tote's affairs, but his nemesis was waiting just around the corner in the enlarged form of his alter ego, John McCririck.

The *Life's* award-winning reporter reflected many of Wyatt's traits even down to the large Havana cigars he liked to pose with. An unabashed self-publicist and a slavish disciple of Margaret Thatcher, his bombastic opinions on everything from how racing should be run to the alleged failings of his supposedly 'supine' fellow hacks – as he liked to call them – were deliberately calculated to cause controversy.

Unsurprisingly unpopular in racecourse pressrooms, he was barely tolerated in the office. Seen by many as a pseudo-eccentric who tricycled to work in a deerstalker hat and sunglasses; his loud-mouthed bluster and near pathological craving for attention, often drove his long-suffering colleagues to breaking point. Usually it was the normally undemonstrative sub-editor cum race-reporter, Mick Connaughton, who cracked first. Fired up by a few lunchtime pints in 'the Stab', he would advance on 'the Screaming Sofa' with his right index finger furiously slicing the air as he read the Riot Act.

It was an awesome sight as the little man's dark, beady eyes bored into the pallid, quivering features of his adversary who would deflate like a pricked balloon under the blistering onslaught. For a few hours peace and order would be restored, but then McCririck would gradually pump himself up again and return to full volume. Yet in the entire history of the *Sporting Life* no other journalist ever matched his ability to hunt down stories on such a regular basis. During the 13 years he wrote for the paper (1972-84), first as a freelance coursing correspondent and then as a reporter working on the editorial desk, he came up with some truly sensational exclusives.

Tenacious and resourceful, he pursued his leads with the unflagging enthusiasm of a terrier on a ratting expedition. In 1978 he won the British Press Award for Specialist Writer of the Year and 12 months later he was voted Campaigning Journalist of the Year. It was a unique double for someone attached to a sporting journal.

The latter award was in recognition of his work in exposing the illicit dealings of the Tote.* It was on 4 July 1979 that the latest in a long line of 'freak' dividends sparked McCririck's interest when a dual forecast on the 11-1 winner Shine On coupled with Tina's Gold (20-1) paid just 45p to a 10p stake in an 18-runner handicap at Carlisle.

Initial inquiries to Tote House were brushed aside by the organisation's PRO, the former *Sporting Life* sub-editor Geoff Webster, who dismissed the dividend as 'inexplicable', but as McCririck pursued the matter over the next few days Webster became more and more evasive and it soon became obvious he had something to hide.

Still, after five days of routing around, McCririck was no nearer to uncovering the truth when he got the break all journalists need. An anonymous phone call to the *Life* supplied the all-important information: Tote HQ had sent £50 to Carlisle for the winning forecast *after the result was known*; the on-course pool had amounted to some £200; there were two winning tickets before the extra £50 arrived to swamp the pool and crush the dividend; there had been an error in transmission, only £5 was supposed to be sent.

The caller, obviously a Tote employee, concluded: "It's been going on for years, usually in dual forecasts. A few bets are sent down after the race and almost always the winning combination is amongst them. Mainly it's for £5 units. I'm sickened by what's going on. Something's got to be done."

If true, this was fraud on a grand scale, but confirmation was needed. The key man was so blindingly obvious he had been overlooked in the initial enquiries. He was the *Life's* own northern SP reporter, John Broadway, who had once worked for the Tote.

Broadway had been at Carlisle on the day in question and had discussed the 'inexplicable' dividend with his friend Bill Baxter, the Tote's northern racecourse manager. What Baxter had told him had been in confidence, but now McCririck had the story he felt free to confirm everything the anonymous caller had said and more.

The two winning on-course tickets were for £1 and 50p; Baxter had already calculated the

---

* Ironically, McCririck received his award from his idol, Margaret Thatcher, whose favourite minister, Home Secretary Willie Whitelaw, did his level best to cover up everything 'Mac' had uncovered!

dividend at £13.46 to a 10p stake before he was told that a £50 bet on the winning forecast had just come in from London. Baxter "couldn't believe it and was very annoyed," ditto the winning punters.

The next move was to confront the Tote chairman with the evidence, but as usual when things became too hot for him, Wyatt had gone to ground. Repeated calls to his secretary failed to flush him out and finally she was told the *Life* would be running the story whether or not her boss spoke to them.

It was not long before McCririck received the anticipated call. Wyatt was at his unctuous best as he wheedled: "Hello old boy, it's about that Carlisle dividend isn't it? Well, to be perfectly honest, it was a monumental cock-up – as simple as that. There was a stupid mix-up, but I'll tell you what we'll do. If the punters come forward we'll pay them the full dividend. Now could we be fairer than that?"

McCririck told him he could, and the tone of the conversation changed. Interspersed by increasingly longer pauses at Wyatt's end of the line, it went something like this:

WW: "Naturally we have to collate all the bets laid in our 230 shops and those on credit. This takes time. Indeed bets can be put into the pool up to five minutes after the result is known."

JMcC: "How can you justify anyone, anywhere, being able to place bets after time?"

WW: "As we take pool bets right up to the off it is part of procedure to send our hedging commissions down after time. Nothing other than *bona-fide* bets from punters are ever transmitted to the course. I give you my word on that."

JMcC: "But how can you Mr Wyatt? How do you personally know what is happening at any given time in the transmission room?"

Answer came there none, instead a new voice came on the line, the unmistakable Glaswegian growl of Bill Balshaw, now managing director of Tote Bookmakers.

"Now look here, John, you're making very serious accusations and you'd better be very careful indeed. There are courts which deal with this kind of situation. It is mischievous and malicious to insinuate this was anything more than a coincidence."

JMcC: "Bill, are bets placed in racecourse pools by Tote Bookmakers after-time? One former employee has assured me they are."

BB: "Untrue. It doesn't happen and there is no question of impropriety by Tote Credit or Tote Bookmakers employees. We've offered to pay those involved in the wrong dividend at Carlisle. What more do you want?"

Quite a lot actually. But McCririck had enough to be getting on with. Wyatt had admitted that bets were being placed in racecourse pools after the result was known. Balshaw's snarling denial only served to emphasise their guilt.

On Friday July 13 – unlucky for some – the headlines drove the first nails into what should have been the Tote chairman's coffin: 'Woodrow Wyatt calls it 'the Carlisle cock-up' / How After-Time Bets Get Into The Tote Pool'.

To accompany McCririck's revelations, the editor penned an 'Opinion' piece in which he accused the Tote Board of "an irresponsible disregard for the interests of its clients and dereliction of its duty to the public in general" as he spelt out the full implications of what its chairman was happy to dismiss as 'a cock-up'.

> If the consensus of bets taken by the Tote as bookmakers are losers, they can be 'stuck' so that the stakes profit the bookmaking subsidiary concerned. If they are winners, they *can* be passed to the pool, so that the bookmaking subsidiary's losses are recouped at the expense of *bona-fide* winners on the racecourse … Is it in the public interest that any firm of bookmakers – least of all the

nation's bookmakers – should be in a position to put money into a pool, after the result of a race is known?

The question was answered by next day's headline 'Resign! The Tote Boss Must Go Call By MP'. The call came from the Labour member for Walsall South, Bruce George, who had little time for a man he regarded as a shameless turncoat.

George was quoted as saying: "I find it amazing that the chairman should condone betting after the results of races are known. The Tote must be the only organisation in the world that allows this. The potential for abuse is unlimited. I am seeking an emergency debate on the whole internal workings of the Tote and meanwhile Mr Wyatt, who has admitted knowledge of this scandalous affair, ought to resign at once."

The same edition of the *Life* also carried an extract from a letter it had published a year earlier from Geoff Webster in response to the charge that the Tote might be placing bets after time. The PRO's reply was unambiguous: "Tote Credit and the Tote's on-course cash division are two separate operations and the suggestion that they could or would collude to put money into the pool 'after time' has no foundation in fact and is an unwarranted slur on those concerned."

This paragraph appeared as a 'tear-out' between the headlines 'This is what they said a year ago –' '– but it isn't what they are saying today!' underneath which was a press statement from Woodrow Wyatt. In a petulant attack on the paper, its editor and chief reporter, the Tote boss declared:

> The loss-making *Sporting Life*, which could not survive without bookmakers' advertisements, devotes much of its space to violent attacks on imaginary defects in Tote procedures but is very gentle in its criticisms of the real defects of the procedures of the big bookmakers. John McCririck and the editor in Friday's *Sporting Life* pretend to be shocked that Tote Headquarters transmits to the pools on-course bets which have been struck *before* the start of the race *after* the off.

Wyatt went on to employ his usual tactic of sowing disinformation in an attempt to justify the indefensible, but Fletcher was having none of it. In dissecting "Mr Wyatt's blustering and condescending attempts at self-justification," he dismissed the chairman's "snide opening gambit" by referring to the criticism the *Life* had levelled against the big bookmaking chains that were refusing to pay out over the Rochester greyhound coup.* He continued:

> Next he talks of 'imaginary' defects in Tote procedures. They are clearly imaginary to him. But they are not to those of us who've progressed beyond the kindergarten stage in betting education.

---

* On 27 May 1978, the Rochester track staged a bizarre 'Long and Short Trip Stakes' with two heats run over 277 metres and the final over 901 metres. The first heat was won by Leysdown Pleasure at 33-1 and the second by Leysdown Fun at 4-1; both dogs were trained privately by Jack Purvis and had been heavily backed off-course in the heats to win more than £300,000, ('Fun' was withdrawn from the final and 'Pleasure' finished last). BOLA advised its members to withhold payment, the police were called in and a report submitted to the DPP who decided to take no action. Meanwhile, the stewards of the NGRC held an inquiry into the races and were satisfied no rules had been broken. It appeared a legitimate coup had been landed, but the 'Big Four' bookmakers and some others still refused to pay up. As a result, the coup organisers began a campaign against them by super-gluing the locks on some 800 betting shop doors. Eventually, an arbitrator was appointed and in 1985 Leonard Caplan QC ruled that the bookmakers were not liable to pay as the races had been deliberately framed to discourage other dogs from entering and the Leysdown pair had been running in trials that would not reveal their true form.

At *The Sporting Life* we don't *pretend* to be shocked. We *are* shocked. Shocked not only at what has gone on, but even more at Wyatt's attempts to justify it. Shocked at the conflict between what he says now and what his PRO said last year.

He makes great play of the fact that bets are allowed up to the off in the Tote's 230 betting shops and their credit offices and speaks as though all bets have to be collated and sent down to the course.

This is unadulterated balderdash. Every bet placed at an off-course Tote office is placed not with the pool, but with one or other of their bookmaking subsidiaries. That's what we've repeatedly been told. None of the bets *has* to go to the course.

The Tote accepts them just as any other bookmaker would do. If any other bookmaker wants subsequently to get any of his Tote-odds commitments into the pool, he must do something about it before the race. Tote Bookmakers and Tote Credit Ltd should do likewise – not wait till they're in a position to know which bets will cost them and which, if retained, will swell their profits.

The paper also noted that in a 'World at One' interview on Radio 4, Wyatt was asked if it would not be possible for a Tote employee to place a bet after time. The chairman was indignant: "No employee is allowed to bet," he snapped. "There is no conceivable way an employee could insert a bet into the pool after the race."*

Over the following week McCririck dug out more information on the scandal. On Monday July 16, he obtained quotes from four former Tote executives covering the period 1959-72 who all refuted Wyatt's claim that it had been a regular practice for hedging bets to be placed in racecourse pools after the result of a race was known.

On Tuesday, acting on information received from a long-serving racecourse employee of the Tote, he produced another bombshell as he revealed:

Tote racecourse managers have been under instructions to telephone Tote Credit Ltd in London when there are only one or two winners of the dual forecast at the course. And usually they are told to add at least ten units (£1), and often more, on to the successful combination.

His source maintained that the after-time 'selective bets' system had been introduced about three years ago, just when Wyatt took over as chairman. "Before then there was no problem," the informant added.

On the same day, Fletcher delivered his most forceful editorial yet as he declared:

It will be a major scandal if Woodrow Wyatt survives as chairman of the Horserace Totalisator Board. Out of his own mouth he has demonstrated that in this role he is either an incompetent ass or an opportunist with little regard for the truth ... It is all too easy for him to sneer at *The Sporting Life*: the first defence of any politician without a case is to belittle his opponent.

What we and the betting public would prefer to hear from him, and what we have a right to know, is how many other 'freak' dividends can be explained in this way ... How many times all told have trusting punters on the course had their pay-outs reduced with a consequential increase in Tote Board profits?

---

* Ten months later the Tote sacked two of its on-course staff at Wolverhampton for putting a £5 bet on the winner, Strawman, after time. The bet reduced the win dividend from 91p to 74p.

How many times have punters in Tote Bookmakers betting shops been similar sacrificial victims? … Wyatt has never shrunk from claiming credit for the increase in Tote profits since he became chairman. The Home Secretary should now order a thorough inquiry to determine whether improper procedures have contributed to it.

And right on cue that day the Tote rushed out figures to show a massive 42 per cent increase in pre-tax profits of £2.32m for the year ended 31 March 1979.

On Wednesday the headline 'The Tote Climb Down – No More After-Time Betting' signalled the *Life* had won the first round in what was to be a long and bitter battle. The text of the Board's statement could have been drafted by only one man:

In view of the attacks made by *The Sporting Life* on its Chairman, Mr Woodrow Wyatt, the Horserace Totalisator Board at its meeting today affirmed its total confidence in Mr Wyatt. The Board reviewed the procedures for transmission of off-course bets to the racecourse pool. It is entirely satisfied that there is no impropriety in these procedures … The Board recognises, however, that such procedures, although perfectly proper, are open to malicious misinterpretation.

To ensure that misrepresentation of this kind can no longer occur, the Board decided that, starting from today, all off-course bets which it is desired to include in the Win, Place, Dual Forecast, Daily Double and Daily Treble pools will be transmitted to the relevant racecourse pool before the off.

By now, Bruce George had carried the fight into the Commons by asking Margaret Thatcher if she would order a public inquiry into the affair. With the glib quip: "I am not very expert at betting," Mrs T passed the buck to Willie Whitelaw who also dodged the issue as he informed George: "The activities of the Horserace Totalisator Board were exhaustively examined by the Select Committee on Nationalised Industries in July 1977. On the information available to me I see no need for a further inquiry."

As George ruefully remarked: "The PM may not know about betting, but even she knows it wasn't possible to back the Tories after the election! But serious allegations of financial mismanagement by a nationalised company should concern her."

On the same day Fletcher received a hand-delivered letter from Wyatt's solicitors informing him that their client was taking 'urgent advice' on the content of the *Life's* stories and that: "We think it right that you should take this fact into account when determining your own future course of action."

Wyatt was clearly rattled, but with only 12 days to go until parliament's summer recess it seemed as if he had been thrown a lifeline by his Tory friends. More pressure was needed to force the issue and to this end McCririck enlisted the help of Sir Timothy Kitson and Bob Mellish, respectively chairman and vice-chairman of the All-Party Parliamentary Racing Committee.

On Thursday, the indefatigable reporter revealed that the Tote Board, most of whose members claimed to have been unaware of the practice of after-time betting, had initiated a full-scale internal inquiry into the affair.

On Friday, he disclosed that in the autumn of 1976 "a ferocious internal struggle" for control of the Tote had taken place between Wyatt and Balshaw on one side and the pool traditionalists on the other. The old guard was routed; there were many redundancies and the transmission of off-course bets to racecourse pools was "ruthlessly downgraded".

On Saturday, a former senior management employee of the Tote, Dennis Savage, revealed that evidence of exactly what had been going on was available to any would-be investigator in the field sheets that recorded bets phoned through to racecourses from Tote HQ. Savage, who had been with the Tote for 32 years before resigning earlier that year, was branch secretary of the Association of Clerical, Technical and Supervisory Staffs (ACTSS, the white collar section of the TGWU) and was speaking out on behalf of his union's members.

He said that ever since the system of transmitting selected bets was introduced in 1976 it was "uncanny" how often winners were included in the after-time 'reads' sent from London: "All union members of the Tote have a right to an independent inquiry at once if only to clear their names. And I will be prepared to give evidence on what has gone on."

Now Whitelaw had to act. With the rest of the press taking up the call for an inquiry and renewed pressure from MPs in the House, the *Life* was able to announce on July 25: 'Tote: Whitelaw Calls An Inquiry – Wyatt Calls In Police'.

Despite all his efforts to dismiss the *Life's* accusations, to belittle the paper and to resist calls for an outside inquiry, Wyatt was presented as the instigator of the action in a Home Ofice statement, part of which read: "Mr Wyatt has informed the Home Secretary that he is calling in the police to investigate whether criminal offences have been committed. He has also asked the Home Secretary to hold an independent inquiry into the Tote's procedures for the inclusion in their on-course pool of bets made off the course."

There was no mention of 'malicious misinterpretation of perfectly proper procedures' this time. Round 2 to McCririck and the *Life*.

Over the next few days it emerged that Jeff Wells, the managing director of Tote Credit, had been suspended on full pay; that Wyatt's much vaunted promise to recompense backers of the Carlisle forecast did not extend to punters who had the bet with other bookmakers, and that the Crown Court recorder, Francis Aglionby, was to head the inquiry.

Aglionby announced his findings the following February, and as with most Home Office instigated inquiries they were predictable. It was a Whitehall whitewash in the finest tradition. The *Life* gave up the whole of its front page to it under the headline: 'The Tote Found Guilty – But Minnows Take The Rap'.

The inquiry had found that the procedure of sending selected bets into racecourse pools after-time had been in operation since 1 September 1977 and since September 1978 Tote Credit employees had transferred to pools "bets which bore no relation to the bets received from clients and which were intended to reduce artificially the dividend."

Astonishingly, despite this damning evidence, Aglionby found that "there was no breach of any statutory provision or of the common law;" and even seemed surprised that "some bets transmitted … after the result of the race was known embodied genuine forecasts." But the most incredulous statement was contained in his conclusion:

> The abuses arose out of misplaced enthusiasm by some employees of Tote Credit Limited who took improper advantages of opportunities presented to them believing that it was in the Tote's interests to depress dividends … The chairman of the Board of the Tote, the members of the Board, the Chief Executive and other senior officials were ignorant of these abuses.

It is little wonder that Ossie Fletcher found his credibility "taxed to the limit" by the findings. He wrote:

If, as Mr Aglionby asserts, Mr Wyatt knew nothing of the malpractices until *The Sporting Life* exposed them, it serves only to endorse our previously expressed view: that in that event he was incompetent. And it poses inevitably the question: What degree of incompetence is regarded as acceptable in the chairman of a nationalised industry?

When customers are shown to have been cheated of their rightful dues over a long period without the chairman, the rest of the board, or any senior executive knowing anything about it, one is entitled to ask – what the hell were they all doing? What are they there for? Simply to rush out periodic statements about greatly improved Tote profits which many people will now regard more cynically as ill-gotten gains? *

There were other findings that taxed credibility to the limit. Despite the selective bets procedure having allegedly been in operation since September 1977 (the rigging of the Tote Double and Treble pools at Bangor and Hexham in May 1977 showed it had been operating earlier), the inquiry's auditors, Messrs Deloitte, Haskins and Sell, only examined forecast pools from September 1978 and of the 697 investigated they found just 15 that had been "certainly affected" and whose dividends had been reduced by "a very large amount".

Further, the list of the doctored dividends released by the accountants only dated from 19 March 1979. Each one carried a revised dividend and the discrepancies were enormous: £62.86 instead of £5.77 in one case; £137.76 against £23.01 in another.

The total amount of money by which punters had been defrauded ran into thousands of pounds on these 15 forecasts alone, but they were only the tip of the iceberg according to Mark Elks, a former Tote Credit racing manager who had been sacked in October for sending a late bet into a racecourse pool after the procedure had been abandoned.

Speaking to John McCririck, Elks claimed he had been made a scapegoat by the inquiry and maintained: "The instructions on how we operated came from above and the abuses stemmed directly from these orders … The pools were altered daily. I could give you dozens of examples."

The Tote Board's offer to recompense anyone who could *prove* they had a bet on the doctored forecasts appeared as hollow as their previous defence of the scandal; their subsequent threat to dismiss any employee who talked to the press about it, was not.

Lord Wigg echoed the views of many when he said: "I am sickened but not surprised to read the report … Mr Aglionby uses the words 'malpractice', 'improper', 'abuses', almost as terms of endearment! The conditions of pool betting are laid down in the Horserace Betting, Gaming and Lotteries Act, 1963. If money has either been selectively withheld from the pool or added to it this must constitute a breach of the Tote's statutory responsibility."

Bruce George renewed his demand for Wyatt's dismissal and pointed out that had the *Life* not exposed the scandal punters would still be being swindled, while Sir Timothy Kitson asked: "Who authorised the introduction of the system on September 1, 1977? It cannot have been at a lower level of management. This is the crucial question to be answered." (Wyatt answered the question at the 1980 Tote luncheon when he brazenly claimed *credit* for introducing the system in May 1977).

---

* For the record, the Board members were Dame Elizabeth Ackroyd, a former civil servant and head of the Patients Association; the Duke of Devonshire, a Jockey Club member, racehorse owner and breeder; Tony Stratton-Smith, racehorse owner and boss of Charisma Records; Sir Alexander Glen, chairman of the British Tourist Authority; Frank Chapple, electricians trade union leader; Nigel Broackes, chairman of Trafalgar House, a construction and shipping conglomerate, and chief executive Geoffrey Rae-Smith, former chairman of Bryant & May (matches).

All these queries and allegations made a mockery of Aglionby's so-called inquiry and more criticism was heaped on Wyatt when it emerged that, true to form, he had scuttled off on holiday to Italy just before the findings were published.

On his return, the discredited chairman shed a few crocodile tears in his *Sunday Mirror* column, describing the Aglionby findings as "very shocking," but immediately went on the defensive by claiming that senior Tote officials had no suspicion anything was wrong because even after the dual forecasts had been artificially reduced "they still paid better than the bookmakers' equivalent computer straight forecasts bet".

This was yet another example of Wyatt deliberately distorting the truth. On aggregate the 15 doctored forecasts did indeed pay more than the CSFs (£262.10 to £108.74), but not individually; in five instances they paid less, considerably so in four cases.

Meanwhile, rumours circulating at Westminster led McCririck to pursue a new line of inquiry and on February 8 the headlines above his latest scoop announced: 'New Tote sensation: Employee tells of Woodrow's instructions once he knew the SP / Wyatt Ordered Royal Ascot Dividends To Be Altered'.

In referring to the 1976 Ascot meeting, a Tote employee alleged: "At least half a dozen races were affected. Usually the win dividend was altered, occasionally a place dividend. I felt highly indignant and joined with several of my colleagues in protest. I felt punters were being swindled when the dividends were cut."

A few days later Wyatt's solicitors served a writ on Mirror Group Newspapers, claiming damages for libel in the *Life*.

In the meantime the paper consulted counsel on the Aglionby report and was able to announce that in the barrister's opinion there had been a conspiracy to defraud the public, it also revealed that Jeff Wells, the MD of Tote Credit who had been under temporary suspension, had 'resigned', and that Bruce George had demanded that Deloittes should audit the remaining forecast pools – all 3,658 of them – in the period under investigation.

The MP pointed out that the 697 pools examined represented only 16 per cent of the total and even the law of averages suggested about 80 other forecasts would have been reduced by 'a very large amount'.* He said: "It is outrageous that a nationalised industry, having swindled the public out of their rightful dues, does not reveal the full extent of the fraud. Why the cover-up?"

Why indeed! Political cronyism; Home Office embarrassment; contempt for the punter; disdain for the *Life*, or just the usual disregard for ministerial responsibility?

On February 21 the scandal was debated in the House of Lords where the Tote Board was accused of a "lamentable and distressing lack of vigilance" by Lord Airedale who said that had similar malpractices gone on in the commercial world without being spotted the board would have been prosecuted.

On the 29th, under the headline 'The Day 'Dr' Wyatt Rigged The Win Dividend', Ossie Fletcher, disclosed that the Tote boss had admitted to Whitelaw that he had altered a dividend for a race at Royal Ascot in 1976 – but he had raised it *not* lowered it.

In a written reply to John Golding, Labour MP for Newcastle-under-Lyme, the Home Secretary stretched credulity like a rubber band as he maintained that Wyatt had asked to be told of the Tote

---

* Only pools in which 10 per cent or more of the winning stakes had been transmitted from head office were investigated. Wyatt claimed that anything less than 10 per cent of off-course winning stakes would have had only "a minute effect on the dividend".

dividends before they were declared because "he had only recently taken over as chairman and wished to be fully in touch with the Tote's arrangements."

Wyatt, he said, had raised the win dividend (from 41p to 47p) on the appropriately named Marquis de Sade (6-1) in the King Edward VII Stakes because "following the withdrawal of the favourite and the need to repay punters who had backed the favourite, the dividend was lower than it would otherwise have been."

At a time when the Tote's furtive formulae for calculating dividends had been reducing payouts across the board, this was indeed a surprising act of benevolence from the chairman. Furthermore, Whitelaw said that Mr Wyatt had assured him that this was the only dividend he had altered – just as Mr Wyatt had assured Mr McCririck that only *bona-fide* bets went into the racecourse pools, no doubt!

Whatever the truth of the matter, the fact remained that Wyatt had altered a dividend and by doing so he had defrauded the bookmakers who took bets at Tote odds. How could he possibly remain in office after this, people asked?

The man himself provided the answer at the annual Tote luncheon the following week. With his bosom buddy, Willie Whitelaw, seated on his right as guest of honour (the two men were pictured chortling away like errant schoolboys as they taunted their critics), Wyatt smugly declared: "Over many years as a politician and journalist I have often recommended those who have incurred my displeasure to resign. I have observed they never take the slightest notice. I propose to follow their example."

Cue all-round sycophantic laughter and Establishment cheers. Round 3 to Wyatt.

Two days later there were more damaging revelations. This time Whitelaw was in the dock as McCririck reported:

> Fears that evidence given in confidence to the Home Office inquiry into the Tote had become known to the chairman, Woodrow Wyatt, were confirmed last night. In reply to a written question from Lord Wigg, the Home Office minister, Lord Belstead, said: "The Home Secretary sent a copy of Mr Aglionby's report to the chairman of the Horserace Totalisator Board at whose request the inquiry was set up."

An appalled Dennis Savage, the former Tote employee and union representative who had given evidence to the inquiry, was quoted as saying: "This means a direct pledge has been broken. No one on the Tote would have dared speak to Mr Aglionby if they thought the chairman would find out what they had said. Promotion prospects have been ruined – careers are in jeopardy. How can anyone ever again trust the word of the Home Office?"

How could the Home Office wriggle out of this one, readers wondered? Easily. The next day an editorial headed 'How Ministers Twist Words' revealed:

> Yesterday Lord Wigg received by hand a letter from Lord Belstead. It said: 'I understand that you are concerned that my written answer about the Aglionby report means that the chairman of the Tote knows of the evidence given to Mr Aglionby and the identities of those who gave it. This is not so. While the report is based on evidence given to Mr Aglionby in confidence it does not list the persons who gave evidence. The evidence does not form part of the report and it has not been and will not be sent to the chairman or anyone else at the Tote.'

In view of the fact that an earlier request for the report to be published had been turned down by Whitelaw on the basis that it was confidential, Fletcher countered: "If the report contains neither evidence nor names, the Home Secretary's argument for non-publication disappears and he should let everyone know as much as he has let Mr Wyatt know. Mr Wyatt didn't ask for the inquiry until he was pushed – so why should he alone be favoured? The Tote belongs to us all."

But Whitelaw remained obdurate. He refused to publish the report, or to dismiss Wyatt or to refer the Aglionby findings to the DPP despite evidence that there had been breaches of both statutory requirements and the common law; he failed to insist that every Tote forecast dividend during the period under investigation be examined; he would not comment on the Tote Board's threat to dismiss any employee who spoke to the press (even though it was only through the actions of a whistleblower that the frauds had been exposed), and he refused to amend the 1972 Horserace Totalisator Act to prevent Tote Board members from betting with their own organisation.*

In view of the fact that Whitelaw also refused to condemn the Tote Board for their 'lamentable and distressing lack of vigilance' Fletcher asked: "Do they still enjoy his confidence – and if so, ought he still to enjoy ours?"

It was a question that was to acquire even more relevance eight months later when, once again, John McCririck broke an incredible story after a high-stakes gambler had won a record £199,039 for a £100 each-way yankee with the Tote on the Cambridgeshire winner Baronet (22-1) along with Earthstopper (6-1), Decorative (6-4) and Ardross (5-6).

It emerged that the client, Alan Spence, a Surrey businessman and racehorse owner whose identity was withheld by the *Life*, had only a £1,000 credit rating with the Tote, but at one stage during that summer he had owed the organisation more than £225,000 and was still £178,000 in the red when he landed his 'get-out' bet.

With his mole at Tote House tunnelling away in grand style, McCririck was able to follow up his exclusive the next day with the news that the Tote had charged its privileged client the on-course rate of 4% tax on at least £87,000 worth of bets that had been placed off-course when they would normally have been taxed at 9% − 7½% of which should have been paid to HM Customs and Excise.

The fact that the bets were recorded as being placed with the Tote's on-course rails representatives on days when the Tote was not represented on any racecourse showed that another mighty fraud had been uncovered although this time it was the Treasury that was being ripped off rather than the punter.

Remarkably, this was not the first time the Tote had been in trouble on this score. Four months earlier Tote Credit had received a letter from Bob Lyne, senior officer of Customs and Excise, informing them they owed £35,580 in duty on racecourse bets. Lyne had added: "May I remind you of the serious nature of this underpayment and your continuing need to ensure that all betting duty is fully and correctly accounted for."

Yet, within days of this censure, bets taken by representatives of Tote Credit were being entered on field sheets as if they were on-course bets when they were not.

The revelations inevitably resulted in Whitelaw and Wyatt again coming under fire. Clement Freud, Liberal MP for the Isle of Ely, demanded an immediate inquiry into the affair and described the Tote's policy of giving unlimited credit as "commercial lunacy," while Bob Mellish (Lab. Bermondsey)

---

* In 1979, Wyatt had boasted he had backed the Derby winner, Troy, ante-post at 50-1 the previous year. As 25-1 was the best price on offer at the time he claimed to have had the bet, it was assumed he had indulged in a bit of insider dealing with Tote Bookmakers Ltd.

declared it was "an absolute bloody scandal" adding, somewhat unnecessarily, "Clearly there has been an appalling lack of control."

Lord Wigg, who had been in correspondence with the Home Secretary and the Attorney General over his conviction that Tote was in breach of statutory provisions in the after-time bets affair, fired off another letter to Whitelaw. Among the points raised, he claimed that if the Tote was prepared to allow clients unlimited credit it must follow that the possibility existed of unlimited winnings. In which case, he asked, would the Home Office pick up the tab if the Tote was unable to meet its obligations?

At the end of October, while Custom and Excise officers were investigating the Tote's books,* Whitelaw turned down demands for an independent inquiry into the latest scandal and, in his reply to Lord Wigg's letter, he reiterated that the government had accepted in full the findings of the Aglionby report and that the police had found no grounds for a criminal investigation.

The fact that he skirted around other questions Wigg had asked drew a stinging rebuke from the Labour peer who told the *Life*: "Never, in nearly 40 years as a member of the House of Commons and the House of Lords, have I received a letter from a Minister which is so unsatisfactory."

Matters did not improve in November when it emerged that the Tote had written off £816,903 (£2.7m) of public money on a 'mechanisation project' designed to bring racecourse betting into the computer age, in addition some £325,000 (£1.07m) in 'authority fees' had been lost that April when virtually every bookmaker stopped accepting bets at Tote odds.

The month ended with the announcement that Bill Balshaw was to take "an extended holiday" before retiring at the end of March 1981. At the same time the Tote stated it would no longer be represented on the rails at racecourses, an operation Balshaw had set up in 1977.

Three days later, McCririck reported that Bob Cooper, general manager of Tote Credit Ltd and former personal assistant to Balshaw, had been fired for 'gross insubordination' following a "flaming row" with Wyatt. At the same time Bruce George wrote to Margaret Thatcher listing all the scandals that had taken place at the Tote under the stewardship of its chairman as he called for the name of Woodrow Wyatt to be added to the growing list of unemployed at Tote House.

The PM's reply surprised no one: "Under the present chairman the Tote's contribution to racing has increased from £409,000 in 1976-77 to almost £1.5 million in the last financial year. I see no justification for your suggestion that he should resign."

Ripping off the poor punter and tax evasion were, it seemed, perfectly in order if it helped to subsidise wealthy racehorse owners, no matter that much of the profit was, according to George, "in spite of Mr Wyatt not because of him. Betting shops are largely responsible for the improvement and Mr Balshaw masterminded that side of it."

Round 4 to Wyatt, and the bell had hardly sounded for the fifth before the wily campaigner scored a technical knockout. At the end of January 1981, the *Life* was required to apologise publicly to him for "a grave injustice" as the paper accepted that the allegation that he had lowered Tote dividends at

---

* After Customs and Exercise had spent hundreds of hours investigating the Tote's operations and thousands of pounds in preparing a case, the Tote's former rails representatives Neville Berry and his son, were summoned over the alleged evasion of betting duty. Following a three-day hearing at Guildhall in November 1981, the magistrate, Edwin Phipps, made no secret of the contempt he felt for the Tote's management as he observed: "It is unfortunate other people are not standing before us in this court. I feel very strongly about it." His remark was not surprising as the Berrys had nothing to do with paying betting duty, which was the responsibility of officials at Tote House, but the case was still referred on to the Old Bailey where both men were cleared of all charges during a nine-minute hearing when the commissioners for Customs and Excise decided not to proceed with the case. In the meantime, the Tote paid the outstanding duty in addition to a sum to compound the offences. Neither sum was disclosed, nor were the 'other people' referred to by Phipps ever charged.

Royal Ascot in 1976 was without foundation. Mirror Group Newspapers had to pay him "a suitable sum in damages".

The fact that Wyatt had written for MGN since 1965* was the least of the ironies that accompanied his victory. While he survived all the calls for his dismissal and had his term as Tote chairman extended by Whitelaw in 1982, it was McCririck who got the sack from the *Life* two years later, when he refused to deny newspaper reports that he was heavily in debt to bookmakers.

This was one thing Fletcher would not tolerate: "You can murder your grandmother, but you can't owe bookmakers money because they've got you if you do," he told McCririck as he demanded his star reporter publish a denial in the *Life*. But while McCririck maintained the stories were untrue, he refused point-blank to deny them in print or to sue the newspaper concerned, claiming "Hacks don't sue hacks." He then took a leaf out of his old adversary's book and went AWOL for three weeks.

The day of reckoning came on 5 March 1984 when the *Daily Star* splashed the story, 'Punters' pal owes us a packet, says bookie', across its front page. The paper quoted Tom Jenkins, boss of the John Power chain of betting shops, as saying that McCririck had large gambling debts with his firm and he didn't expect the part-time TV pundit to pay them off. "All I know is that I'm going to get the firm's name mentioned on the telly by John now and again," he said.

The *Star* also quoted Fletcher as saying: "You can't harm *Sporting Life* staff any worse than to say they owe large sums of money to bookmakers. There have been three cases in recent years of staff being dismissed for the very same reason. It is a very precarious position and there is quite a lot of bad feeling in the office about this."

McCririck, for his part, claimed he had been placing bets for other people: "It definitely wasn't my own money although the account was in my name."

The upshot of it all was that two days later the Campaigning Journalist of 1979 was fired from the *Life*. He subsequently changed his mind about 'hacks not suing hacks' and in 1986 won substantial damages from the *Star*, since when he has not looked back.

Woodrow Wyatt's star was also in the ascendant as honours were heaped on him. As a reward for his support of her policies, Margaret Thatcher put him in for a knighthood in 1983 and then for a life peerage four years later, and it was as Lord Wyatt of Weeford that he served out his final ten years as Tote supremo.†

Few of those years passed without controversy. The ermine chairman took a perverse delight in going out of his way to antagonize his opponents and he relished their impotent rage as much as he did the plaudits of his political patrons. When Michael Howard became the last Home Secretary to extend Wyatt's £95,000-a-year, part-time job for a further two years in 1995, Jack Straw, Labour's Home Affairs spokesman, described it as "a favour too far and an unacceptable reward for services rendered to the Tory party."

Wyatt made his final bow as Tote chairman in July 1997 when he announced profits were up 21 per cent to £12.8m with record contributions to racing of £7.9m. At the end of that month he handed

---

* In 1983, Wyatt was sacked by the *Sunday Mirror* because of his continued backing for Thatcher's regime, after which he was warmly embraced by Rupert Murdoch for whom he wrote a 'Voice of Reason' column in the *News of the World* and fortnightly articles for *The Times*.

† To show that some semblance of merit remained in the honours system, Ossie Fletcher was awarded an OBE in 1982 for his services to racing and in the same year the Royal Coat of Arms was added to the paper's masthead.

over the reins to Peter Jones, former president of the Racehorse Owners Association and director of the British Horseracing Board (BHB).*

Having defied all his critics to the end, the self-proclaimed 'saviour of the Tote' died suddenly five months later. Despite his acknowledged 'foibles', the tributes to "a terrific political operator" were many and generous.

---

* By this time 'freak' dividends were a thing of the past as the Tote had become fully computerised and, with Tote Direct outlets already installed in more than half the nation's betting shops, all off-course bets meant for racecourse pools went directly into them. In 2003 the uniform deductions from win and place pools were cut to 13.5% and 18% respectively – and they have remained at that rate ever since.

ANARCHY

T HE MID-1980s saw the *Life* rocked to its foundations by a series of seismic shocks. In the space of two years the paper acquired a new proprietor in the pugnacious publisher and consummate crook, Robert Maxwell; it underwent two changes of editor; endured a two-week shutdown; made the transition from hot-metal printing to computer typesetting; moved offices, and faced the challenge of a vibrant new rival in the form of the Arab-backed *Racing Post*.

During this traumatic period the paper teetered between life and death as it was used as a pawn by Maxwell in his battle with the print unions that had held Fleet Street to ransom for so long. It had not faced such a crisis since the newspaper strike of 1955 when 700 maintenance men and electricians stopped the production of London's evening and national papers for 26 days.[*]

The first day of that notorious dispute cost the *Life* its biggest issue of the year as it coincided with the Grand National, the Boat Race and the semi-finals of the FA Cup; it also set the trend for the next three decades when production of the paper was to be increasingly disrupted by the militant malcontents of the machine room.

Most stoppages were caused by the unofficial actions of the shop-floor chapels (office branches) of the three big print unions – the National Graphical Association (NGA), the National Society of Operative Printers and Assistants (Natsopa) and the Society of Graphical and Allied Trades (Sogat). There were also ten other unions and some 73 chapels within the *Mirror* group that were ever ready to withdraw their labour as they ratcheted up their demands for more money.

There were days when the *Life* did not appear because members of the Amalgamated Engineering Union and the Electrical Trades Union "refused to turn on the power for the presses".[1] Other days were lost due to an "unofficial stoppage by electricians, plumbers and heating engineers."[2] One week distribution would be severely curtailed because of an unofficial overtime ban by the National Union of Printing, Bookbinding and Paper Workers;[3] another week by a dispute involving 1,700 Sogat members, packers and van drivers.[4] Demands for pay increases of 40 per cent or more were not unheard of.

While the group's mass-circulation titles were able to weather these wildcat strikes, a specialist publication such as the *Life* was particularly vulnerable and matters were not improved in July 1971 when the paper moved from its Long Acre base in Covent Garden to Orbit House in New Fetter Lane, just across the road from the *Mirror's* headquarters at Holborn Circus where it was to be printed.

When the Holborn building had opened ten years earlier, the *Mirror* boasted that it housed machinery capable of producing newspapers at the rate of 1,600,000 copies an hour. But the best machines in the world were of little use if the men who operated them were hell-bent on stopping the paper from coming out in pursuit of their latest pay claim.

The London print unions were made up almost exclusively of white East-Enders who ran the

---

[*] The Communist-backed *Daily Worker* managed to be back on the streets after just 12 days when its racing correspondent, Alf Rubin (famous for napping Russian Hero, the 66-1 winner of the 1949 Grand National) gained a host of new readers as sales of the paper soared – even the Duke of Norfolk was seen with a copy, holding it, *Time* magazine reported, "as if it were a week-old fish". Provincial papers were also in great demand and every morning long queues formed outside their Fleet Street offices for the limited number of copies available. By the third day of the strike, privately published newssheets containing football and racing results and the cards for the following day's meetings were selling at 3d or more a copy; later on the big bookmaking firms, whose turnover was badly hit, issued lists of probable runners to their clients.

show pretty much as they pleased while supine managements tolerated absurd overmanning levels and abuses in order to keep their papers on the street.

Sunday papers, in particular, were ruthlessly exploited. On Saturday nights casual shift workers – most of them on the dole – would sign on under two or more names to receive extra wages. There was no attempt to disguise the fraud; 'Mickey Mouse' and 'Donald Duck' were favourites with the MGN men who would spend the night watching blue movies, playing cards or drinking in 'the Stab' or the Printer's Devil. At the end of a shift some were too drunk to remember the names they had registered under and it was not unknown for pay packets to remain unclaimed.*

Others operated a lucrative trade in stolen goods and at times the basement of the *Mirror* building resembled a Savile Row outfitters as the latest consignment of top quality shirts, coats and jackets were laid out for prospective buyers who, it has to be said, often included *Sporting Life* journalists.

But the printers' days were numbered and they knew it. The writing had been on the wall for years. The first photocomposing machine had been designed in 1894, but it was not until after WWII that the process began to be developed along commercial lines. By the 1960s the technology was being coupled to computers and with the advent of the microchip in the early '70s, a revolution in printing techniques became inevitable.

As with the Linotype machine 80 years earlier, it was the provincials that led the way in embracing the new technology and many county papers were using it long before the first tentative steps were made towards modernisation in Fleet Street.

When the Queen visited the *Life's* offices in 1976, Ossie Fletcher proudly showed her the paper's newly installed computer which could update and print out horses' form as it appeared in the paper at 1,100 lines a minute. But it was not until two years later that MGN struck a £3,000-extra-per-man (£13,000) deal with the print unions to have its popular weekly, *Reveille*, set by photocomposition.

The plan was to introduce the process gradually throughout the group, but from the start it was bedevilled by a demarcation dispute between the NGA and Natsopa. A hardcore of 21 once-a-week machine minders defied NGA orders to work normally and for four months they disrupted production of the journal, which lost its entire print run of 520,000 copies on three occasions before a settlement was finally reached.†

In the light of this disruption it appeared long odds against the technology being successfully applied to the *Life* when it was tried that May. There was a world of difference between typesetting a weekly tabloid by computer and using the process to produce a daily broadsheet with its pages of complex form and racecards, yet the *Mirror* management wouldn't even hear of a trial run.

---

* In 1978, PAYE (Pay As Your Earn) tax inspectors found 57 names on the MGN roster that could not be traced to their nominated address, they included 'Sir Gordon Richards of Tattenham Corner' and 'Percy Roberts of Ross-on-Wye' (Roberts was chairman of MGN from 1977-80). When the Conservative MP Nicholas Ridley introduced a Ghost Workers (Abolition) Bill in 1979, he quoted an Inland Revenue estimate that some 3,000 print workers were receiving wages under 10,000 aliases. But the Bill was successfully opposed by Jim Callaghan's Labour government with such left-wing luminaries as Michael Foot, Roy Hattersley and the Employment Secretary, Albert Booth, voting against it.

† The machine minders, who were in overall charge of the presses, agreed to a 'no compulsory redundancies – no automatic replacement of labour' deal, but the following year the same men demanded a replacement for a 78-year-old colleague who had died, even though his job had disappeared with the introduction of the new technology. This time, production of *Reveille* was halted for three weeks before it was closed down for good. Launched in 1940 as a free, light-entertainment paper for the Forces, the *Reveille* was bought by Mirror Newspapers in 1947 and its 80,000 circulation soared to peak at 3.7m in 1953 when it was famous for its double-page pin-ups that were the forerunners of the *Sun*'s page 3 girls.

Graham Taylor, then deputy editor of the *Life*, recalled: "There was a bumptious bloke from the *Mirror* in charge of it all and he was adamant it would work. 'We'll go in at the deep end,' he said, but he didn't have a clue and it was absolute chaos. The NGA insisted on its men doing what the new technology [*Natsopa*] people did and type in lines of form which was ridiculous because most of them had never typed in their lives.

"I was in at 7 o'clock on Sunday morning to get all the copy down because we didn't want any excuses from the unions saying it was our fault, but the first person I met was our head printer who told me we had no chance of getting a paper out. He'd had his men in overnight and they couldn't handle it. Then the computers had a brainstorm and started spewing out form, pages and pages of it, and that was all that was coming out. By midnight we realised it was hopeless – we couldn't even get one page out."

Despite all the evidence to the contrary, the abortive trial was continued for the next five days before the management and the unions reached a mutual agreement to revert to hot-metal. The anguish contained in Fletcher's front-page notice of Monday 15 May 1978 was all too evident:

> *The Sporting Life* apologises to readers, advertisers, wholesalers and newsagents for its non-appearance last week. To attempt to explain why would involve what is known in the trade as intrusion into private grief, in this case ours. Suffice it to say we hope never again to encounter a predicament as ghastly as that in which we found ourselves.

It was a forlorn hope. The extent of the disruption convulsing Fleet Street was brought home that December when the Thomson Organisation suspended publication of *The Times* and the *Sunday Times* indefinitely. In the first quarter of that year the titles had lost 7.7m copies, 20% of their normal output, through strikes and restrictive practices, while Fleet Street as a whole had lost a staggering 130 million copies in 1977 and things were getting worse. Someone had to make a stand.

The shutdown lasted for almost a year and was to prove a crippling blow to the *Life's* only rival, the *Sporting Chronicle*. As part of the Thomson group, the Manchester paper relied on Times Newspapers for its distribution in London and the Home Counties, but for the duration of the dispute it was blacked by the unions in the south.

Circulation slumped by 26%, from 58,835 copies in the first half of 1978 to 43,690 for the last half of 1979 and it was never able to recover the lost ground. When it finally succumbed to the combination of rising production costs and falling sales (under 30,000) on 23 July 1983, its editor, Tom Kelly, expressed the hope that the demise of his paper would "bring some stability to our friends at the *Life*."

It was a nice thought and for a short time things did improve. The paper picked up some 10,000 in sales from the departure of its old rival, while it also brought out the *Weekender* in opposition to the long-established weekly *Handicap Book* which had been taken over by *Raceform* publications when the *Chronicle* folded.

Perversely, the *Weekender* was produced by photocomposition while the *Life* struggled on with the last surviving relative of Johann Gutenberg's movable type. First edition costs were enormous as Linotype operators made an 'error' every two or three lines and were then paid exorbitant London rates for correcting them.

Then, in July 1984, the picture changed dramatically when Robert Maxwell arrived on the scene with all guns blazing. The Mirror Group's parent company, the sprawling pulp-to-print publishing conglomerate Reed International, had been proposing to float MGN as a separate company on the stock exchange, but, in typical style, Maxwell bulldozed his way in with a £113.4m offer – double what the floatation was expected to realise.

The Reed board had no option but to sell even though they shared the grave misgivings of the unions about a man who had been described in a 1971 Department of Trade and Industry report as "not a person who can be relied on to exercise proper stewardship of a publicly quoted company."

This slap on the wrist would hardly have troubled the former Labour MP for Buckingham (1964-70) who had come a long way since he escaped the Nazi holocaust that all but wiped out his impoverished Jewish family in Czechoslovakia. His metamorphosis from the fleeing refugee Jan Ludvik Hoch to Ian Robert Maxwell was made after he joined the British Army's Pioneer Corps as a 16-year-old private in 1940.

Brave and resourceful, he ended the war as a captain in army intelligence with a Military Cross (presented to him by Field Marshal Montgomery) and a reputation as a shrewd wheeler-dealer that was to stand him in good stead in the post-war years. During the 1950s he acted as a part-time information gatherer for MI6 and flirted with the KGB while he liaised with Russian publishing houses as he built up his Pergamon Press company to become a major publisher of international trade and scientific journals.

His formidable business brain, tireless energy and unshakable self-belief saw his fortunes grow during the '60s, but his shady deals and creative accountancy prompted the DTI inquiry into Pergamon in 1969 when he lost control of the company and was also beaten by Rupert Murdoch in his bid to buy the *News of the World* and *The Sun*. The following year he suffered another bitter reverse when he lost his seat in parliament.

The mercurial Maxwell was down but not out, and the Second Coming of 'the bouncing Czech' was even more impressive than the first. In 1974 he regained control of Pergamon and six years later bought the ailing British Printing Corporation. In 1982 he relieved Reed International of its loss-making Odhams Press plant in Watford together with 23 acres of land, a print order worth £30m and a £7.5m interest-free loan from Reeds. The whole package cost him just £1.5m. He then proceeded to make 1,400 workers redundant and sell off much of the site for a massive profit.

Together with Pergamon's record £54m profit in 1984, his dealings in BPC, whose shares had rocketed from 12p to 214p in the four years since his takeover, and his acquisition of MGN, he seemed poised to achieve his ambition of matching Murdoch as an international media tycoon, but first of all he had to sort out the print unions. To this end he selected the *Sporting Life* as his main bargaining chip.

By the beginning of 1985 it was apparent that his massive investment in the *Mirror* was not yielding the returns he had expected. A succession of gimmicks that included a £1m 'Who Dares Wins' bingo competition, and his penchant for moulding front-page stories around himself to boost his bloated ego did nothing for the paper. To add to his disenchantment, the *Life* was continuing to lose money despite having the field to itself.

In a letter to MGN employees that January, he announced that he was taking over the £200m pension fund assets from Reeds to enable "MGN's own trustees to manage our excellent and very beneficial pension scheme" (beneficial to whom? was a question that had yet to be asked). He also described the *Life* as "an unbearable financial burden" and said that a task force would be brought in to cut costs. The 'Maxwellgram', as his frequent missives to staff became known, inevitably sparked speculation in the press that the future of the *Life* was in jeopardy.

This, undoubtedly, would have been the case had it been any other paper, but the fact that it enjoyed a privileged place on the breakfast table at 'Buck House' protected it from the Maxwell axe.

The last thing he was going to do was deprive the royal family of their favourite reading and he responded to the rumours with a statement in the *Life*:

> *The Sporting Life* is a national institution and there is no question of it closing down. But with a daily circulation of only 70,000 it continues to be an unbearable financial burden on Mirror Group Newspapers. The title is losing £3 million per year.
>
> I intend to have urgent discussions with management and workforce about the steps necessary to bring the title back into profitability. It is in everyone's interest to cut costs and I am sure that agreement can be reached quickly. If early agreement cannot be reached, then the paper may have to be produced outside Holborn…

The threat to take the paper out of Holborn was aimed directly at the print unions that had an age-old agreement with management that no national daily would be produced outside central London, but Maxwell knew that if he could set a precedent with the *Life* it would make it easier for him to move all his titles out of Fleet Street.

Shortly after this declaration of intent, the need to escape the clutches of the unions became even greater when it was announced that a new seven-day-week, full-colour, national paper was to be produced by new technology outside London. The man behind this potential rival to the *Mirror* was Eddy Shah, the owner of a chain of free, through-the-letterbox, papers based in Warrington, Cheshire.

Shah, a distant cousin of the Aga Khan, had come to prominence in 1983 when he took on the mighty NGA (dubbed the 'No Go Area' union because of its eternal demarcation disputes) over its closed shop policy. It had resulted in a bitter seven-month battle with the union during which he became the first person to invoke Margaret Thatcher's newly introduced industrial laws to curb secondary picketing.

Despite death threats, which included the delivery of five coffins (two adult-sized, three for the kids) to his home, Shah stuck it out and eventually defeated the 100,000-strong union which lost £1m in the courts for taking unlawful action against his papers.

Now Shah had negotiated a no-strike, no-restrictive practices, single-union deal with the electricians that would allow his new paper (*Today*) to be brought out by a small, flexible staff of journalists. Copy would be typed into the computers by reporters (direct input), while other journalists would set the stories into pages on VDU screens and then, at the touch of a button, send the completed pages off to press. As the need for typesetters and other print workers would be dispensed with, Shah optimistically estimated he could cut production costs by 80 per cent.

The labour pendulum was about to start its long swing back from overmanning to understaffing.

There was also news of a new rival to the *Life* to spur on Maxwell. In June, Sir Gordon Brunton, former chief executive of the Thomson Organisation, announced that Graham Rock, one-time chief correspondent of the *Sporting Chronicle*, had been appointed editor of an embryo *Racing Post*. The paper was being backed by the oil-rich rulers of Dubai, the Maktoum brothers, who had made a huge impact on British racing in recent years.

Brunton, as chairman of the *Post*, revealed it would be produced by new technology outside London and that the Maktoums were sinking enough money into the venture to ensure the paper would survive for at least three years.

It was obvious that the *Life* was going to have a fight on its hands, but Maxwell was up for it and warned "any would-be rivals who aim to take on the Queen's favourite newspaper" that: "There's no

The Queen at breakfast with her favourite newspaper, as portrayed by *Spitting Image*.

room for two such publications, the *Life* has been tops for 126 years, and I am prepared to spend whatever is required to keep it there." He added that he planned to move the paper to a more modern plant in London so it could be produced in colour and ended by saying he had already received several offers to buy the *Life*, but his reply was always the same: "It's not for sale."

By now Maxwell had installed the latest computer typesetting system at the *Mirror* and, by using the threat of the 'Daily Shah' to force concessions from the unions, he was able to bring it in at the end of June 1985 although he was not allowed to use it to its full potential. The NGA insisted on its members' right to type editorial copy into the computers which produced photographic proofs (bromides) of the text. Other printers then cut the proofs to size by hand and pasted them onto a page make-up for the press stage. It was an unnecessarily protracted process, but it was progress of a kind – *if it had worked*, but once again efforts to produce the *Life* by this method were a shambles.

The first attempt was a disaster. Despite the printers having all of Saturday night and Sunday to set the racing results, Monday's paper was missing the returns from Newmarket, Longchamp and the Curragh, while regular features also failed to appear because of 'production difficulties'. And things did not improve.

In the daily aftermath of late or missed editions, Graham Taylor, who had taken over from Ossie Fletcher as editor three months earlier,* had to pen a series of contrite front-page notices such as: "We hope to remedy these problems as soon as possible. Meanwhile, our profuse apologies, and please bear with us a little longer." (July 2); or: "Once again many of our regular readers, particularly in the North and in Ireland, were unable to get a copy of the paper on Saturday. We again apologise for the problems in our production department." (July 8).

It was a nightmare for the mild-mannered, easy-going Londoner who shuddered as he recalled: "I was in despair because the paper was a disgrace. The printers couldn't have cared less whether we came out or not. We were lucky to get any sort of paper out at all, and eventually we reverted to a sort of hybrid system with some pages produced by hot-metal and some by new technology."

The bloody-mindedness of the printers only served the exacerbate the situation and when the NGA's Tony Dubbins claimed in the *Sunday Times* that "Our record of co-operation with change in the printing and newspaper industry is second to none,"[5] it drew a blistering response from Fletcher in a letter to that paper:

> As an ex-newspaper editor who opted for early retirement because he simply couldn't stand any more NGA-induced frustrations, I marvel at the effrontery of NGA secretary Tony Dubbins.
>
> The whole purpose of new technology is to make possible direct input of copy by anyone who can type, which at once renders NGA compositors as such redundant. But will they accept they are yesterday's men? Of course not. As long as they can get away with it, they will continue to insist on re-keying copy that needs no re-keying, frequently introducing error where none existed, and ironically being paid more for doing so than those who originated the work.
>
> Mr Dubbins is proud of what industrial muscle has achieved for his members. But how many papers have died because of it? How many, indeed, have never been born? Some might think every two-bit protection racketeer has more to be proud of. At least such people don't operate behind a screen of righteousness and shield of legality.[6]

---

* It was as the longest serving editor of a national daily in Fleet Street that Fletcher took his well-earned retirement on Grand National day, 1985. He had given 26 years of his life to the paper and when he died in August 1993 the tributes to him were many and sincere. Graham Taylor recalled that when Fletcher became editor: "Almost overnight the *Life* changed from a dry-as-dust racing-sheet into a newspaper that proved a by-word for authority, in-depth reporting and understanding of the betting world. It was Ossie who gave truth to the *Life*'s slogan 'The Paper the Professionals Read'."

Sir David Llewellyn, who predeceased his old friend by a year to the day bar one, left a posthumous tribute to "a gentle man of courage, a loyal friend and a steadfast companion of the sport he served ... when the fur started to fly, he was magnificent in defence of his writers, cool, calm, determined, not merely to save the paper money, but to protect those who were taking the flak. He had high standards. Not only did he expect the *Life*'s servants to write well and to produce a good paper, but to behave well ... Although a very private man, he was a most cheerful companion and he laughed easily."

Archie Newhouse, the *Life*'s greyhound editor for 21 years before becoming chief executive of the National Greyhound Racing Club, remembered: "A man of great dignity, kindness and understanding who got all the staff working for him ... He had owned a share in the 1976 Greyhound Derby winner Mutts Silver, and became a valued steward for the NGRC. His sense of justice and knowledge made him ideal."

Ron Allen, a talented member of the editorial staff, contrasted Fletcher's obsession for accuracy with his engaging absent-mindedness: "When the *Life*'s famous (infamous?) football team played a bookmakers' side from Newcastle, Ossie stood on the touch-line to lend his support and asked another fan if he had enjoyed his trip down from Tyneside. 'Er, I work for you,' was the reply. Ben Clements, Ossie's predecessor, made the same sort of gaffe with somebody who had been his secretary only a month earlier. Perhaps that vagueness on matters physical is the hallmark of those who sink their devotion into a calling, as Ossie immersed his into making the *Life* the voice of racing."

By this time Maxwell was holding talks with the NGA over the future of the *Life* and on August 21 he struck a deal with Dubbins, which allowed the paper to be moved out of Holborn to be printed by a subsidiary of Pergamon that was not bound by Fleet Street restrictions. But the agreement counted for nothing because at Holborn the union's FoC (Father of the Chapel) refused to accept it and called a mandatory chapel meeting that resulted in the *Mirror* losing 750,000 of its 3.1m copies.

Maxwell, his patience exhausted, retaliated the following day by suspending London production of the *Mirror* and the *Life* (he had intended that the *Mirror* would continue to be published in Manchester, but the NGA put a stop to that). Extreme as it was, the move was welcomed by the group's editors who expressed their support for their chairman in a letter to *The Times*. Signed by Graham Taylor, Mike Molloy (*Daily Mirror*), Richard Stott (*Sunday People*) and Peter Thompson (*Sunday Mirror*), it was headed 'Matter of life and death in Holborn':

> It is a truism in Fleet Street that an editor's first duty is to make sure that he is not the last editor of his paper. Equally, it is the management's duty to run newspapers efficiently to safeguard their future ... *The Sporting Life* is an excellent newspaper, a national institution, but it loses £3m a year. Nearly 250 production staff are employed, many earning, with benefits, over £500 [£1,150] for a 32-hour week.
>
> Some months ago the typesetting and composition of the paper was transferred to so-called new technology. (It has, in fact, been successfully used for years in the provinces). No newspaper can survive indefinitely if deadlines and editions are missed and if printing standards decline below the quality required. Regrettably, this is what has happened since new technology was introduced on *The Sporting Life*.
>
> Even with first rate production the paper would still lose a fortune at our plant. Clearly *The Sporting Life* either has to close down, or be transferred to a printing plant more suitable for an average sale of 80,239. What our company is trying to do is to save *The Sporting Life*, because manifestly it cannot continue as it is, and bring some sanity and order into our neck of Fleet Street.[7]

As the shutdown entered its second week, a free emergency edition of the *Life* was cobbled together by two of its brightest young stars, Neil Cook and Alastair Down. Cook, after an apprenticeship on the *Worthing Gazette*, had joined the Orbit House team as a casual sub in 1981 and in four meteoric years had risen to become assistant editor to Graham Taylor. Down had also been taken on as a sub in 1981 – "They wanted me to join in mid-March. I said I couldn't possibly do that, but I'd come the week after Cheltenham" – and his progress through the ranks bore all the hallmarks of 'future editor'.

The two friends worked well together as they drew on their production skills to bring out an eight-page, tabloid-sized paper that was distributed to betting shops in London, Birmingham and Manchester and at racecourses wherever possible.

Down recalls: "There wasn't much of it, to be fair, but it was pretty tough work getting it out. There was always some debate about where we would be producing it each day. Mostly we put it together at a printer's in Camden, and for a few days at Maxwell's home at Headington Hill Hall in Oxford."

On the same day (August 29) as the first emergency edition appeared, Maxwell issued a press statement in which he explained that an agreement had been reached with Dubbins on four NGA principles that would have allowed all the MGN titles to resume publication, but once again it was unacceptable to the committee of the NGA chapel at Holborn. It was the last straw, and in a messianic message to the nation he declared:

The Sporting Life

33,113   FRIDAY, SEPTEMBER 6, 1985

FREE EMERGENCY EDITION

Slip Anchor can return in triumph

By GEORGE ENNOR

SLIP ANCHOR can make a triumphant return to action by winning the September Stakes at Kempton today.

He has been off the course since the Derby but has fully recovered from the injury which kept him out of Ascot's King George six weeks ago.

All the reports from Newmarket indicate he has been giving every satisfaction in his work and it will be a major surprise if he is beaten.

His Derby defeat of Law Society and Damister was a performance of authority and the subsequent runs of the two placed colts have done the form no harm.

Though he is dropping back a furlong in distance from his Epsom and Lingfield victories, Slip Anchor should find neither that, nor the ground, nor this

Shernazar, not that far off the top last term, has won his only two starts this year at Goodwood and Newbury. He beat Spicy Story decisively at Newbury last time and before that accounted for his own stablemate Shardari at Goodwood.

Shardari went on to beat Damister at York, only to lose the race in the stewards' room, but a line through those two three-year-old's suggests that Slip Anchor should beat Shernazar on terms only 4lb worse than weight-for-age.

Circus Plume won the Oaks last year and showed high-class form throughout the season, winning the Yorkshire Oaks as well as being runner-up in the

LIFE YANKEE

LYRIC WAY (2.0 Kempton),
TUFUH (3.5 Kempton),
CAPO DI MONTE (4.10

Irish and in the Prix Vermeille.

She was most disappointing on her only run this term, back in the spring, but though her stable has emerged from the doldrums it remains to be seen whether Circus Plume has maintained her ability. At her best she would be a most interesting rival for the Derby winner.

Supreme Leader was more than 13 lengths behind Slip Anchor when fourth in the Derby and has been beaten twice since.

He was not disgraced in either race and was earlier an excellent third in the Two Thousand Guineas but he is now only 7lbs better off with Slip Anchor and clearly has a major task trying to reverse the Epsom form.

Southern Dynasty has shown much improved form this year, winning four times from five starts. She is clearly useful in her class but this

PUBLISHER'S STATEMENT

AS IS well known, following some "local difficulties" at Mirror Group Newspapers' headquarters at Holborn Circus, which so rudely interrupted our publication, agreement has now been reached with the printing trade unions to cease production of The Sporting Life at Holborn Circus.

As from tomorrow we shall be reverting to our previous broadsheet format and hope to make available a sufficient number of copies to satisfy all our readers' needs.

Please accept my sincere apologies, dear readers, for the inconvenience and annoyance caused you.

ROBERT MAXWELL

Little London looks capital

NEWS SUMMARY
Layers on Run from punters

COMMANCHE RUN has come in for strong support with virtually every layer for Sunday's IR£261,500 Phoenix Champion Stakes and is now best priced at 6-4.

Michael Jarvis is still trying to contact Antonio Balzarini in the States to agree on a jockey for Bob Back but riding arrangements for the other ten runners have been finalised as follows:

Baillamont (Cash Asmussen), Commanche Run (Lester Piggott), Damister (Steve Cauthen), Leading Counsel (Pat Eddery), Reprint (Danny Murphy), Scottish Reel (Walter Swinburn), Theatrical (Michael Kinane), Vice Admiral (Declan Gillespie), Helen Street (Willie Carson) and Triptych (Christie Roche).

Sean Graham goes: 11-8 Commanche Run, 4 Leading Counsel, 8 Damister, Theatrical, Helen Street, Scottish Reel, 12 Triptych, 20 Bob Back and Baillamont, 200

An emergency edition of the *Life* brought out after Robert Maxwell had suspended its publication during his battle with the print unions in 1985.

This anarchy can have only one result. The first consequence is that MGN will never publish the *Sporting Life* again. It is now for sale. When I became publisher of MGN a little over 13 months ago I believed I could change a floundering enterprise into a flourishing one. Regrettably, I must admit failure so far. The events of the past nine days have shown the impossibility of what I had hoped to do.

For generations the print unions, and particularly their London branches and chapels, have had a firm grip upon Fleet Street. Their monopoly of labour has meant that they have controlled the recruitment of all employees – including most managers – the numbers employed, the conditions of employment and, in effect, the wages and salaries paid to them. Management has ceased to manage. Indeed, they surrendered the right a long time ago ... my determination to restore that right has led to the present situation. It is impossible to build success on anarchy. It seems equally impossible to be rid of that anarchy so deeply entrenched has it become ... The choice facing Fleet Street and its unions is to change or perish.

Stirring stuff, and it was not all rhetoric. Maxwell saw it as his mission to bring about a revolution in Fleet Street and to set his own house in order before Shah's *Today* emerged to challenge the *Mirror*.

To show he meant business he sent out dismissal notices (later suspended) to the group's 4,500 production employees and finally even the NGA chapel at Holborn began to get the message.*

The *Mirror* resumed publication on September 3 and on the 7th the *Life* returned to its broadsheet format published by Odhams Newspapers (a cosmetic change from MGN). In a 'We're Back' message, Maxwell appeared to confirm the suspicion that he had no intention of selling the paper when he stated that anyone wishing to buy it "must be beyond reproach and acceptable to our senior editorial and management staff".

This declaration provided him with ample scope to reject bids or raise the asking price far beyond any reasonable offer that was made as, indeed, proved to be the case later that month when he was approached by Sir Gordon Brunton, acting for the Maktoums. Their meeting was but brief. In a statement afterwards Brunton said: "The value ascribed to the titles by both parties is so far apart that it was agreed that there was no point in continuing discussions." (Maxwell was said to be asking for £20m for the *Life* and *Weekender*, while the initial cost of setting up the *Racing Post* was put at £6m).

If Brunton could not buy the paper for the Maktoums, the next best thing was to buy up the *Life's* top men. With so much uncertainly surrounding the future of the paper and with staff morale at an all-time low, it was like picking plums. Among those who were enticed away were George Ennor, who had succeeded Len Thomas as chief racing reporter in 1984; Tony Morris, who was not only a gifted writer and racing historian but was recognised as one of the world's foremost authorities on bloodstock breeding; Melvin Day who had a big following with his 'Form' tips, and Mike Palmer from the greyhound staff, while the *Weekender* lost its main tipster, Adrian Cook, and its acting editor, Francis Kelly.

Tim Richards, a former Derby-award winning 'Racing Journalist of the Year', was poached from the *Mirror* to become the *Post's* chief correspondent, while MGN's operations director, Jeremy Thompson, was signed up as chief executive, and the group's senior circulation manager, Alan Thompson (no relation), also switched camps.

At the same time Brunton announced an impressive list of board appointments headed by the 'voice of racing' Peter O'Sullevan as well as Nick Clarke, managing director of the International Racing Bureau; former RCA chairman Air Commodore 'Brookie' Brooks, and the *Sunday Times* columnist and ITV racing presenter Brough Scott who had first suggested to Sheikh Mohammed al Maktoum that he should set up a new racing daily.

It was a formidable line-up and Brunton, himself, had been well chosen. Not only did he have an in-depth knowledge of the media world, but he had been a keen follower of racing for many years and, as a small-scale owner-breeder, was eventually to hit the big time when his mare, Indian Queen, won the 1991 Ascot Gold Cup.

It seemed as if nothing could stop the new publication from becoming a success as soon as it hit the streets particularly as the *Life* remained in dire straits. The paper was now being typeset at various sites scattered around London as no one company could take it on (at one stage as many as five firms were setting various sections of the paper). It's survival hung by a thread as it relied upon a shuttle service of motorcycle couriers to ferry editorial copy from Orbit House to the typesetters and then the made-up page plates to its new printers in the East End.

---

* By the end of the year Maxwell had achieved much of what he wanted. Restrictive practices were ended and overmanning reduced by 1,600 redundancies in London and 500 in Manchester with settlement payments funded from the £75m surplus in their pension fund. Britain's woefully lax company laws allowed Maxwell to do this and he took full advantage of them to buy up companies such as BPC and Odhams that were struggling but had large pension surpluses which he used to fund redundancies. In this latest instance he was also saving himself some £40m a year in salary payments.

The deadline for copy had been brought forward to 7pm, but the paper was not going to press until 11.30, two hours later than normal and, inevitably, distribution was badly affected. For a month there was only a skeleton results service with just the 1, 2, 3, SPs and Tote returns; regular features were dropped and apologies were as numerous as ever.

There was just one glimpse of what the future held when, on St Leger day, the front page carried its first high-quality colour pictures; one a fine study of Lester Piggott who was looking for his 30th classic win on Lanfranco, the other of Sheikh Mohammed's Oh So Sharp, odds-on to complete the filly's Triple Crown which she duly did – just.

But gradually the old paper did pick up and it was almost back to normal when, in January 1986, it made the move to new offices in Alexander House, Farringdon Road, to the north of Holborn Circus. The half-mile flit was completed just a few days before Rupert Murdoch made his famous 'dash for freedom' with his four News International titles – *The Times*, *Sunday Times*, *Sun* and *News of the World* – to his new £100m printing plant at a razor-wired 'fortress Wapping' in London's docklands.

The *Life's* move was not so dramatic, but it was eventful enough. In the middle of it a dispatch rider lost a page of the paper on his way to the printers. The next day readers were presented with a page of adverts where the Wincanton racecard should have been. The lights on the *Life's* switchboard had never flashed so furiously; the phones never answered more reluctantly.

Yet again it fell to a war-weary Taylor to pen an abject apology as he explained: "In the upheaval of changing offices and typesetters the page plate went missing and by the time the clanger was noticed, it was too late to do anything about it."

Maxwell was, to say the least, not best pleased, but it only served to stoke up his determination to see off his Arab rivals. In formally opening the new offices he took the opportunity to deliver one of his more macabre metaphors as he declared: "If the Maktoums wish to squander their oil money by starting a price war against *The Life* with their plans for the *Racing Post*, then so be it … [it] will give them about as much pleasure as they would get from chewing frozen concrete."

And by March the *Post* was looming large on the horizon. In an effort to steal its thunder the *Life* attempted to cover the Cheltenham Festival in colour, but it ended in monochrome misery on the first day with the loss of more copies and another apology, which was partly offset by 'Augur' (Bob Toseland) tipping River Ceiriog, the 40-1 (94-1 on the Tote) winner of the opening race.

The following week saw the start of the Flat at Doncaster where the *Post* was sponsoring a race on each of the three days, but it failed to make an appearance as it encountered its own production problems. At the same time the *Life* prepared to meet the challenge by slashing its cover price from 40p to 25p (60p to 35p in Ireland).

In proclaiming 'The bargain of a Life-time' following "the abandonment of many of the old restrictive practices which bedevilled the established papers," it announced: "For years we have been forced to pass on the high production costs of Fleet Street to readers. Now we are in the happier position of being able to reverse that trend and, instead, pass on the benefits of our new typesetting and printing arrangements."

The tide had finally turned and much of the credit belonged to George White, former editor of the *Weekender*, who was all set to join the *Post* when Maxwell, acting on the advice of Graham Taylor, offered him a substantial pay rise and the title of managing director of Odhams Newspapers, i.e. the *Life* and *Weekender*.

White knew more about new technology than anyone else on the editorial staff and had been responsible for keeping the paper going on a life-support system of typesetting companies and contract printers when it moved out of Holborn, but there were still major problems to overcome. The first was that the paper was now limited to a maximum of 20 pages because the presses at its new plant in Leyton E10 were designed for tabloid printing.

In order to fit in all the features and racecards on Saturdays and for the big mid-week meetings adjustments had to be made to the machines as the paper was s-t-r-e-t-c-h-e-d to nine columns. The innovation possibly made the *Life* the broadest broadsheet in the world. Reading it was like exercising with a chest expander and decidedly anti-social when travelling on public transport. Inevitably, the cumbersome format would give the new racing tabloid another big advantage – if it ever appeared.

At the beginning of April, the launch of the *Post* was again postponed, while the line 'The independent voice of racing' was added in red under the *Life's* title, but a fortnight later the phoney war was over. The Sheikhs' paper finally made its appearance on the opening day of the Craven meeting when its front page carried an attractive colour shot of Sonic Lady, Adrian Cook's winning tip for the Nell Gwyn Stakes. Battle had commenced.

Before the end of the month it was announced that Monty Court, racing editor of the *Sunday Mirror*, had been appointed editor of the *Life* as Graham Taylor was taking early retirement. Taylor had joined the *Life* on leaving school in 1945 and a year later started to cover football matches and act as assistant to the paper's much-respected boxing writer, Joe Bromley, who became his mentor and friend.

A born enthusiast, the avuncular Taylor developed into a fine journalist with a knack for seeing an angle to a story that was not apparent to anyone else; people worked well with him and for 40 years he enjoyed every minute of his time on the paper, but his last 13 months as editor had been a nightmare.

Not only did he have to deal with the unions and the switch to computer typesetting, but he had the dreaded 'Max factor' to contend with. Maxwell's drive to cut costs was understandable when it came to curbing union abuses and profligacy among his own executives, but he would also refuse to sanction trivial expenses much to the chagrin of Taylor who recalled: "When someone who was known to us died, the *Life* would always send a wreath as a mark of respect, but then the florists suddenly refused to take our order because Maxwell never paid the bills.

"There were also the impossible demands he would make on us. He used to ring me at home at 11 o'clock at night and say 'I've just been to dinner with such and such an owner who had a winner today, get his picture in the paper tonight'. It was absolute hell; I couldn't wait to get out."

Monty Court, fresh, vigorous and competitive, couldn't wait to get in an' at 'em.

COURTING SUCCESS

AS THE *Sporting Life* squared up to the *Racing Post* for what many predicted would be a fight to the death it could not have had a better man in its corner than Monty Court. The new editor had been around the block a few times on the newspaper circuit and was a hardened street fighter who was not prepared to accept second best at any price. What's more, the 58-year-old son of a Royal Artillery sergeant major had a thorough knowledge of racing and was in the happy position of being able to exercise an editorial freedom that had been denied to his immediate predecessors.

Union tyranny had broken the once innovative Ossie Fletcher who became a virtual recluse in his own office long before he took his leave. The only indication staff had of his presence on the editorial floor were the rasping coughing fits that emanated from behind his closed door as he puffed his way through a succession of small but bulky continental cigars that would eventually kill him.

Similarly, while Graham Taylor had worked wonders to hold the paper together during the worst of the troubles, he never really had the opportunity to make his mark on it before he left. But now the shackles of the print unions had been cast off, Court was able to inject new life into the *Life* and give its staff the lift they so badly needed.

The challenge of the task also rejuvenated the new incumbent who had been treading water as racing editor "in charge of myself" on the *Sunday Mirror* for the past 13 years and was beginning to feel unfulfilled and even – when his services had not been sought by the *Racing Post* – unappreciated.

He had, after all, much to offer. He had been drawn to racing during his early days as a reporter on the *Evening Advertiser* in Swindon where his beat took in Lambourn and the surrounding area. With his boyish enthusiasm and gregarious nature, he was soon rubbing shoulders with the locals as he started to build up what was to become a wealth of influential contacts in the racing world.

But Court was a newspaper man first and foremost and after three years on the *Advertiser* he joined the *Birmingham Gazette* as chief reporter in 1951. Two years later the lure of Fleet Street took him to the *Evening News* where he spent four years as a general reporter. A short stint on the ailing *News Chronicle* followed before he moved on to the *Daily Mail* where life was sweet for eight years as he worked his way up to become news editor before he had a major fall-out with the editor in 1964 and was awarded the 'DCM' – Don't Come in on Monday.

It was then on to the *Sunday Mirror* where he was installed as investigations editor and feature writer under Mike Christiansen, "a smashing editor, son of the great Arthur Christiansen of the *Daily Express*," and three years later he was made news editor to complete a national Daily-Sunday double in that post.

Working for a Sunday paper gave Court more time to follow the horses and when the chance came for him to become racing editor he jumped at it. The post seemed tailor-made for him, but it wasn't all he had imagined: "I didn't really enjoy my time there because the paper wasn't remotely interested in racing, but the marvellous thing about it was that I could go and stay with my trainer friends for a few days during the week."

It was in his last year with the *Sunday Mirror* that he began to write a cathartic column for the *Weekender* and when that paper's former editor, George White, approached him in the spring of 1986 to ask if he would be interested in the editorship of the *Life*, he didn't have to think twice. But his first thought was a profound one since it centred on the man he would be working for.

He'd had no contact with Maxwell when he was on the *Sunday Mirror*, but with the *Life* he knew things would be different, yet it was a chance he was prepared to take: "I told Maxwell I was only interested in doing the job for five years because I'd been with the *Mirror* group for 20 years and with another five I would be qualified for a pension – of course, at the time, I didn't know he was going to piss off with it, but that was my strength with him if I had one; in effect I'd given him notice.

"He wanted to know what I would do with the paper and I told him there were so many things wrong with it, it was just not true. It was a paper that never got started. If there was nothing happening in racing, it would often lead on some race at Harringay dogs; page 2 was the bookmakers' marker-sheet and page 3 was often taken up by an advert for some stud or other. It had totally lost its way, and although it had come back to what it was, it still wasn't punching its weight and it hadn't done for years."

That seems a harsh judgement, particularly as it was only a short time since John McCririck and Brian Radford were delivering major front-page stories on a daily basis. Radford had been imported from the *Western Mail* by Ossie Fletcher in 1978 and was a good investigative journalist. He got some excellent exclusives, particularly through his West Country contacts, but he always seemed to focus on the negative aspects of racing and eventually his constant knocking pieces became wearisome and Graham Taylor was quite happy to see him move on to *The People* at the end of 1985.

The role of chief reporter was then filled by Mark Popham, formerly of the *Sporting Chronicle*, who had joined the *Weekender* when it was set up in 1983. By a curious coincidence Popham had been at York University at the same time as Alastair Down and Tony Elves, who graduated through *Timeform* and Weatherbys to join the *Weekender* in 1986 before he eventually took over as 'Warren Hill' in 1990.

What this says about the tuition to be had at York Uni is debatable, but as Down points out he only chose to read politics and philosophy at that particular seat of learning because he could get to any one of six racecourses in 45 minutes – a genuine 45-minute claim that obviously suited his fellow students as well.

The resourceful Popham had his work cut out to fill the void left by the departure of McCririck and Radford, but he had the valuable backing of Sue Montgomery, a fine features writer and all-round journalist, while Court beefed up the news reporting side soon after he took over by signing on Jon Freeman as a three-day-a-week casual.

Formerly a race reporter with the *Sporting Chronicle*, Freeman was muddling through as a freelance at the time writing a northern column for the *Weekender* and feature articles and close-up reports for the *Life*. A talented and respected journalist, he had been surprisingly passed over by his old colleague, Graham Rock, for the position of northern correspondent on the *Post*.

Court could sympathise with any grievance Freeman might have felt on that score since his own ego had been sorely bruised when he was not offered the chance of joining the new paper. He readily admits: "I was miffed, although if I had been asked I doubt if I would have gone because of the years I had invested in the *Mirror* group, but the truth is I would like to have been asked. Anyway, I wasn't so maybe I was the ideal person to lead the Dad's Army of other rejects in a fight the *Post* genuinely thought would be a pushover.

"Their attitude was 'now we are going to show you how to do it', but the *Life* had some terrific operators working for it and they were all nice people, good people, which is why there was no fallout of staff when I went there. There was a tremendous atmosphere and a great enthusiasm for the paper. In World War One terms they would have gone over the top for the *Sporting Life*, but they didn't have a leader. Nobody had taught them how to play newspapers. All they needed was a bit of encouragement and they responded magnificently."

He had a fair team to draw on; they included such long-serving stalwarts as Dave Cox who had lived for the *Life* since he joined it as a 15-year-old messenger boy on the same day as another school-leaver, Chris Gundry, in 1961. The two men became firm friends and avid students of the Form Book as they strove to improve the lot of the punter (and themselves) which was, after all, what the paper was all about.

By 1986 Cox was editing the increasingly weighty tome that was *Ruff's Guide* and also acting as a one-man statistical department, working all hours in between R and R visits to the Rheingold Club off Oxford Street where Henry Zeisel, part-owner of the 1973 Arc de Triomphe winner after which his club was named, was always on hand to welcome a regular troupe of toilers from the *Life* who brought him the latest edition hot off the press.

A low-profile man, but tall of stature and beloved by all, Coxie epitomised the spirit of the paper and his work-hard, play-hard ethic was shared by other 'Lifers' such as the innovative Bob Betts who had joined in 1960 and worked his way up to become greyhound editor following the departure of Archie Newhouse in 1986.

On the general sports side there was Danny Garrett, who had taken over as boxing correspondent on the death of Joe Bromley in 1967. The whipcord-fit reporter also covered the Wimbledon tennis championships with the authority of one who played the game on a daily basis, while he was backed up on the boxing side by Malcolm Hanover who had joined the paper as a sub-editor from the *Greyhound Express* in 1965.

Football was the province of Derrick Shaw, a 1961 veteran and regular winner of the Xperts draw-forecasting competition, while the paper had a shrewd golfing correspondent in its deputy editor, Jeremy Chapman, who had a happy knack for picking out long-priced winners as well as being a valuable layout man designing pages along with assistant editor Ernie Dymock who had come from the *Barnsley Chronicle* in 1960.

The outside team was particularly strong, headed as it was by Geoff Lester, a 1964 copy boy graduate who had taken over as chief racing reporter when George Ennor left to join the *Post*. Nominated 'Racing Journalist of the Year' in 1988, Lester was at his best when covering the big meetings whether at home or abroad and had his own colourful style of prose that tended towards hyperbole. It landed him in trouble on occasions, but he could never be accused of being dull or sitting on the fence.

He was supported in the south by Steve Taylor, a fast and informed operator who kept his finger on racing's pulse through his close contacts with trainers and jockeys many of whom he numbered as his friends. There was also the resident Lambourn correspondent and roving racecourse reporter John Santer, a brother of the then Bishop of Birmingham, and one-time assistant to the great Clive Graham ('The Scout') of the *Daily Express*.

The mainstay in the midlands was the ever-dependable Ted Allen who forayed south and north when the need arose, while the peripatetic Mike Roberts, who was later to join the *Daily Telegraph*, covered every racecourse in England bar Sedgefield during the four years he was on the outside rota.

In the north the author was ably supported by freelancers such as the paper's former northern correspondent Joe Rowntree, Jon Freeman and former *Raceform* race-reader Steve Boggett, the only man to ever include a dead bird in the close-up comments that describe how each horse performs in a race – "swerved to avoid dead seagull".

Heading the team of SP reporters was Doug Newton, who joined the *Life* on leaving school in 1948 and worked his way up from tea boy to take over from Geoffrey Hamlyn when that venerable compiler of odds retired in 1975. John Stubbs, just a year behind Newton in length of service, had won the 1958 NH naps table as 'Solon' "with a consistency that has rarely, if ever been equalled" and a profit of £39 from 33 winners and just 39 losers. In addition to returning SPs, Stubbs also contributed snippets of news and gossip from the betting ring in his weekly 'Ringlets' column.

To complement the regulars, there were the *Weekender* lads who would go racing on their days off to report on meetings that could not be covered by the outside staff. Foremost among them were Mick Connaughton, a jump-racing aficionado, and Simon Holt, who fell into the role he is now best known for when he stood in for a racecourse commentator who failed to turn up at Worcester one day.

Both Connaughton and Holt also weighed in with regular feature articles along with their *Weekender* colleagues Mike Cattermole, formerly a comment writer for *Timeform*, and Trevor Halling, a one-time trombonist in his own dance band who was one of the best connected men on the racecourse yet least known to the public as only his initials ever appeared at the end of his articles.

After almost four years of touring the country profiling trainers and running the rule over their most prominent horses in his two-page 'Straight from the Stable' series, T.H. had built up a string of useful contacts and was getting some top class inside information which he used to start a 'Hot Gossip' column in the *Weekender*.

This mix of humorous titbits, wicked whispers and valuable pointers, did not even carry his initials as he felt he had to protect his sources, as he did when he began a weekly 'Ahead of the Game' column in the *Life*, which highlighted dark horses to keep an eye on. Written under the pseudonym 'Haruspex', he was, in Etruscan terms, a stable companion to 'Augur' in that a haruspex would foretell future events by studying the entrails of an animal offered in sacrifice (i.e. a non-trier), whereas an augur relied on the flight and cries of birds to arrive at his predictions.

In addition to the *Weekender* team, a variety of freelancers contributed to Alastair Down's burgeoning feature pages. The north had been sadly neglected by the paper for many years, but was now as well covered as the south with such enthusiasts as Roy Briggs and John Budden providing regular profiles on trainers and jockeys with the former being particularly hot at scouting out news stories.

Budden, who eventually took over the weekly 'View from the North' column after a trio of Yorkshire-based worthies had turns at writing it over the years, was in the unusual position of being a school teacher based on the south coast of Kent when he first started to submit articles on the northern scene. He had made his contacts during a ten-year spell (1964-73) of teaching near Carlisle where he began to write for the local paper and do part-time work for Border Television. On returning to his native Kent he continued to cover the north for the slimline weeklies, *Racing and Football Outlook* and the *Racing Specialist*, before he joined the racecourse commentators' team and returned to Cumbria in 1987 to become a full-time journalist.

Michael Tanner, MA (Hons), was another school teacher whose byline became familiar to readers along with the eminent Turf historian and author, Richard 'Dickie' Onslow, and *The Times*' cricket correspondent Alan Lee whose increasing fascination with racing eventually persuaded him to transfer his allegiance from the pitch to the paddock.

Then there were the regular columnists. Joe Hirsch, who had reported on the American scene since 1961, and Michael Clower, who took over as Irish correspondent from the legendary Michael O'Hehir in 1983, both supplied weekly round-ups, as did Tony Jakobson, 'Warren Hill' since 1965, and John Santer, who started 'Lambourn Life' in 1985 but handed over to Nick Deacon two years later.

A son of Fulke Walwyn's famous head lad, Darkie Deacon, Nick was better informed than most in the Valley and won the 1987-88 winter naps table at his first attempt before repeating the feat for the 1989 summer competition – a remarkable achievement.

Andrew Caulfield, a former comment writer for *Timeform* and editor of *The Thoroughbred Breeder*, was the paper's bloodstock correspondent; Tom Kelly, director-general of BOLA, wrote a bookmakers' column, and in a lighter vein Julian Armfield reported on the social activities – those that were printable – of the jockeys, while Gerald Delamere, a one-time MFH of the Westmeath, provided a ten-year statistical analysis and summary of televised races for the big meetings.

Just as important as the wordsmiths were the photographers. The *Life's* regular lensmen included the jolly, rotund figure of Ron Hammond; Wimbledon FC's official photographer Phil Smith, and Pat Larkin, a marvellously laid-back Irishman with a fascinating repertoire in homespun philosophy.

Another son of Erin, the leprechaun-like Ed Byrne, began supplying the *Life* with photos in the early '70s when he was a bus conductor on the No. 25 route which took him past Holborn Circus where his double-decker stopped just long enough for him to sprint into the *Mirror* building to drop off his latest batch of prints. It was his 1973 photo of the dual King George VI Chase winner Pendil taking off from outside the wings at Kempton that made his name. Captioned 'Poetry in Motion', the shot captured the power and the beauty of a steeplechaser in full flight and, after the *Life* had featured it on its front page, his phone hardly stopped ringing as the rest of Fleet Street and the world beyond clamoured for copies.

In the north the paper relied on Alec Russell who became hooked on racing as a 13-year-old when he went to York's second post-war meeting in 1945 and saw George VI's Kingstone (Doug Smith up) land the odds in the Yorkshire Cup. The following year he attended his first Ebor meeting armed with a box Brownie camera that led on to a hobby he turned into a full-time profession in 1970 when he quit his job as a computer programmer with the Darlington Corporation.

Court also made good use of the *Mirror's* cameramen: "Maxwell agreed to let me have any photos in the group that weren't wanted. The *Mirror* would send five photographers to the Derby, but would use only one or two pictures. I would hoof it up Farringdon Road to get all their over-matter and we would have a page of pictures. They helped to transform the paper; they made it look brighter and read tighter."

This was one great advantage a broadsheet had over a tabloid; it was able to use a spread of big pictures to great effect, and when archive photos were dug out to record the passing of some famous jockey or trainer they made the *Life* a real collectors' item as was the number that recorded the death of Sir Gordon Richards in November 1986.

Four photos of the 'Pocket Genius Who Rewrote The Record Book' accompanied Sue Montgomery's front-page report and racing's tributes to a man who rode 4,870 winners, was champion 26 times, topped the 200 mark on 12 occasions (with a record 269 winners in 1947), and who rode 12 successive winners over three days in 1933.

Inside, a two-page spread headed 'Farewell and thanks for the memories' carried another nine marvellous photos dating from the 1930s to go with a detailed account of Sir Gordon's career written by Dickie Onslow, who noted that the only jockey ever to be knighted was most remarkable not for having won so many races, but for having lost so few he should have won. But above all:

At a time when the integrity of many of the leading riders was a long way from compatible with their brilliance in the saddle, he was quite untouched by scandal. His name was a byword for honesty, and the example he set was deeply appreciated by all those with the good of British racing at heart.

In addition to his use of pictures, Court brought in many other improvements such as 'the finest daily weather service presented by any newspaper', which he introduced shortly after becoming editor. "The weather report used to be dismissed in one or two lines, but the most important thing in racing is the going," he reasoned. "I had three days of meetings with the Met Office people and got a contract going that would hopefully give us as reliable a forecast as the farmers had."

It was certainly comprehensive. It detailed the amount of rainfall in 11 regions over the past week and 28 days, while two maps showed the outlook at midday and mid-afternoon, and another provided a general forecast for 29 regions ranging from the Channel Islands where there was racing to the Shetlands where there wasn't.

The forecast for Derby-day 1986 was bright and sunny, which seemed to reflect the future of the *Life* as it produced a bumper edition which included a free 32-page colour magazine put together by Neil Cook. It included articles by the esteemed Roger Mortimer, formerly of the *Sunday Times*, on the most impressive Derby winner he had seen: "Sea Bird II swept past I Say like a Rolls-Royce passing a tinker's cart" and by Sir David Llewellyn on the two men who had saved the Derby – Lord Wigg and Stanley Wootton – as well as a Sue Montgomery interview with Lord Howard de Walden, owner of the 1985 winner, Slip Anchor, and contributions from other *Life* regulars.

All this as well as the main paper with its features by Charles Benson (ex-'The Scout' of the *Daily Express*) and the professional punter Alex Bird; little wonder Monty Court's old friend, the classic-winning trainer Guy Harwood, shouted across to him: "You bastard! I've been meaning to cancel that paper of yours for three years; and now I can't."

The colour magazine was to become a regular feature of the Derby and Grand National issues for the next three years until Cook and George White left for America to run the *Racing Times* which Maxwell brought out to rival the long-established *Daily Racing Form*. It was an ill-fated venture that cost the *Life* dear in the loss of two good men.

Court, meanwhile, had completed his transformation of the *Life* by revitalising its Saturday issue. This all-important day had been left devoid of stimulating editorial matter when it lost Tony Morris's 'As I See It' column, which had regularly slaughtered the sport's most sacred cows with a blend of impish mischief and cold logic.

On one memorable occasion Morris accused the "pig-ignorant media of misinforming the public with incredibly irresponsible propaganda about a superannuated chaser" who just happened to be the nation's heart-throb, the 13-year-old, three-time Grand National winner Red Rum. The howls or retribution knew no bounds as an avalanche of letters – most very rude, while some even threatened violence – engulfed the Morris household.

The editor now stepped into the breach with his 'Court Circular' column which was to stir up similar indignation from various quarters as he addressed the topical issues of the day, while his provocative views were accompanied by amusing 'Williams' cartoons drawn by his old golfing friend, Bill Martin, a former art editor of the *Sunday Express*.

Another inspired addition to Saturday's paper was the 'Lifestyles' column introduced in 1988. Designed to give a quick, easy-to-read insight into the lives of prominent racing people, it posed a series of questions that allowed them to air their views on the sport, what they would do to improve it, their pet hates and heroes, best and worst moments in racing, etc.

Mark Popham initially compiled the column and one of his first interviewees was the Newmarket trainer Tom Jones, whose 'Funniest Racing Moment' was:

> Standing outside the ambulance room at Fakenham with Sally Hindley, waiting for the wreckage of her husband of a few months to be delivered after a hideous fall, and seeing only an ambulance man on a stretcher with his leg in a splint emerging. Jeremy had left the saddle like an Excocet and scored a direct hit on the unfortunate man breaking his leg in the process. I suppose it was relief that made us laugh like a pair of idiots. Certainly the head ambulance man made it clear that he didn't think it at all funny.

Although Court frowned upon some of the more flippant and clichéd replies jockeys gave to certain questions (e.g. 'Hobbies': "Bird watching"), he enjoyed the wry humour of seven times champion John Francome: 'Pet hates': "Dogs that find my leg sexually attractive." 'Favourite clothes': "Women's when they're on the bedroom floor." 'Superstitious?': "Yes, I never walk under buses."

'Lifestyles' provided a perfect balance to the 'Court Circular' column that raised as many hackles in the royal palaces of Dubai as it did at 42 Portman Square W1 (the then headquarters of the Jockey Club), since its author could not resist the temptation of having a go at "racing's minority newspaper".

The *Racing Post* had suffered a shaky start when the machines at its printers in Burgess Hill, Sussex, failed to cope with its first 56-page number and a planned 160,000-copy launch was reduced by a third. There were also major problems at its offices in the south-west London suburb of Raynes Park where, on a glorious summer's day in 1891, the Sporting Life XI beat the Rodney Road Police XI by 145 runs and one wicket.

The Maktoums' paper may have had one of the most advanced computer typesetting plants in Europe, but while the *Life's* printers worked away with scissors and a pot of paste, the *Post's* expensive fax machine, which transmitted the pages for its northern edition to Eddy Shah's Warrington plant, kept on breaking down.

Graham Rock was often reduced to hiring a helicopter to fly the page plates to Warrington and as his paper approached its hundredth issue, the break-even point of 40,000 copies he had hoped to achieve was looking more and more like a pipedream.

At the beginning of August 1986, 'Court Circular' asked its readers "What do you think of it so far?" as it cited the on-course sales at Ascot on King George VI & Queen Elizabeth-day when 2,100 copies of the *Life* were sold compared to 375 of the *Post*, a pattern that was repeated at Goodwood over the first three days when the figures were 3,763 and 650 respectively. Court's chortle was almost audible as he calculated:

> If applied nationwide these kinds of figures make my estimate of its circulation in the office sweep look over-generous. I have gone for 25,500.[*] Whatever the figure, the piles of unsold copies in newsagents must make a depressing sight to the men who have sunk millions in the enterprise. It is not popular with punters or with the large majority of professionals. And advertisers, unless based in paddocks thousands of miles away, don't want to know. They weren't kidding in one of their pre-

---

[*] Court lost the sweep, but the July-December half yearly figures were a clear 2 to 1 in favour of the *Life* with average daily sales of 79,291 against 38,091, a ratio that remained much the same for the next few years with the old paper returning a record monthly figure of 103,291 for July 1988 against the *Post's* 48,338, as both titles were boosted by bulk sales at discounted prices.

launch advertisements. It read: 'What's the betting there's only one racing paper worth reading tomorrow?'

To rub salt into the wounds, the advertising department began to promote the *Life* with an opportune photo taken by one of Monty's merry men that captured Sheikh Hamdan al Maktoum pouring over 'Racing's Greatest Daily', while mischievous slogans such as 'First past the Post' and 'Don't get left at the Post' were used at every opportunity.

Crisis meetings at the *Post* became the order of the day as its management was forced to reduce a print-order that had been calculated on the basis that two-thirds of the *Life's* circulation was there for the taking. Soon a trickle of executives began to take their leave. Before the year was out, the advertising sales director, John Trickett, and chief executive, Jeremy Thompson, both quit with the latter's return to the *Mirror* fold leaving a beleaguered Graham Rock to double up on his duties.

Poor Rocky grafted on for another five months before a replacement for Thompson was found in Bryan Hope who "had some success publishing specialist magazines, but suffered from pathological anal retention".[1] Hope's appointment signalled the end for Rock: "early in 1988 I was summoned to his office. He told me I should relinquish my post, leave immediately, and return on Saturday when the building was closed to clear my desk … the manner of the dismissal was wilfully brutal."[2]

Meanwhile, back at Alexander House, Court was enjoying the novel experience of working with printers who were not directly descended from Genghis Khan: "I was a able to go into the composing room and say 'I don't like that headline' and take it out; if I had done that at the *Mirror* they would have walked out."

Not that everything in the garden was rosy. "For the first year or so we were dealing with a series of very curious print shops in east London and they were bloody awful, you would pick up the *Life* and have more ink on your hands than was on the paper. I used to get phone calls from readers threatening to send in cleaning bills for their clothes which had been ruined by the ink.

"There were also problems with our distribution because we had to get the paper across from the East End to hitch a lift on the *Mirror* vans and sometimes Ireland missed out because we didn't get to Luton in time for the regular flights. Geoff Hubbard, the permit trainer who had a lot of success with jumpers like Shady Deal, Gee-A and Sibton Abbey, helped us out for a time. He ran a small airline from Luton and promised the *Life* would never be left behind provided it got there in reasonable time, but then there were problems over refuelling the plane in Dublin for the return flight."

But while these snags were frustrating, they were far outweighed by the continued improvements in the paper which stole a major march on its rival in 1987 when Brian Beel and Jonathan Neesom began to supply a comprehensive results service for the point-to-point season. For the first time close-up comments were included and all races were indexed and laid out in quarter-page segments so they could be cut out and pasted into an A4-sized folder to enable readers to build up their own form book.

Subscribers to the weekly index (£20 for the season), which included a merit rating for each horse, were therefore able to trace past performances at a glance. The innovation provided the *Life* with a key selling point which it promoted by sponsoring the first two point-to-point classics of the season – the four-mile Lord Ashton of Hyde's Cup at the Heythrop and the Lady Dudley Cup at Worcester.

Then, on the eve of the 1987 Grand National, the paper was given a mighty boost by one of its most loyal readers. During a television documentary on the Queen Mother's horses, the former champion NH jockey, Terry Biddlecombe, asked jumping's favourite owner if she read 'Racing's Greatest Daily'. HRH gave her inquisitor an almost pitying smile that he should even have asked such a question and replied sweetly: "Of course I read *The Sporting Life* to get my day-to-day news and a little gossip which is always great fun. One likes to keep in touch."

Indeed one does! Court seized upon the remark and passed it on to the advertising department with the result that the paper was soon carrying adverts for T-shirts (at £4.99) with the quote "Of course I read *The Sporting Life*" emblazoned in green across the chest. The intrepid editor even tried to go a step further: "I actually asked Sir Martin Gilliatt, her private secretary, if I dared put 'The Queen Mother' in much smaller type underneath. '*You dare!*' he said.

"But the Queen Mother was marvellous; my greatest ally. Whenever she saw Maxwell at some charity do or other she would always make a point of saying 'what a very good paper the *Sporting Life* is these days, Mr Maxwell'. She never missed the chance. These royal plugs were reported to me not only by a preening Maxwell, but also by his aides who told me of the extraordinary effect they had on him; transforming a tiger into a pussycat, although his moods were never guaranteed to last for long. But it all helped when pleading for more money to improve the paper."

Court's ring-craft often helped him to outmanoeuvre his capricious employer when it mattered most: "I soon found from bitter experience that it was pointless merely to get him to agree to do something, because he either forgot to send the appropriate instruction to the department concerned or he didn't bother. The only way to get action was the have the authorisation already typed out, as though it had been written by him, so after he had agreed to something like the placing of TV advertisements, sponsorships or, most importantly, across-the-board NUJ pay increases, I could say 'to save any problems, I just happen to have the necessary authorisation here for you to sign'."

In addition to sparring with Cap'n Bob, Court waged a continuous and contentious war on the Maktoums as he accused them of driving small men out of the game and stifling competition with their weight of money and saturation ownership. In the summer of 1988, he started to build up a head of steam in what appeared to be a personal vendetta against the rulers of Dubai. When Sheikh Mohammed bought the unraced two-year-old filly, Kerrera, on the strength of some sparkling home gallops, Court considered the prospect of her going on to win the One Thousand Guineas (she finished second):

> Human nature would have to undergo a remarkable change if the racing public saw a classic win for
> Kerrera as anything other than just another successful exercise in indulgence by the man who has
> everything. Beautiful and talented though Kerrera is, when she passed out of the ownership of Simon
> Fraser and Sonia Rogers the other day she became less of a racehorse and more of a collector's item.

Coincidently, the article appeared on the day 'the man who has everything' fielded two runners for the Irish Oaks which was being sponsored for the first time by his Kildangan Stud. The outcome? His Epsom Oaks winner Diminuendo and his Italian Oaks winner Melodist dead-heated for first place!

Two weeks later, 'Court Circular' was on the attack again after Kerrera had destroyed her rivals in the Cherry Hinton Stakes (Gp 3) at Newmarket's July meeting where her owner also won the July Cup (Gp 1) with Soviet Star, while his brother Hamdan took the Princess of Wales's Stakes (Gp 2) with Unfuwain.

> With the same names and same faces crowding into the winner's enclosure after every big race there
> is a marked lack of atmosphere and fun. The juggernaut effect of the Maktoum racing mammoth
> is in very serious danger of flattening everything in sight just as it would if every big winner came in
> wearing the colours of The Queen, Lord Howard de Walden or Uncle Tom Cobley.

Almost inevitably, Court was accused of "envy and sour grapes"[3] in criticising the Sheikhs simply because they owned the *Racing Post*, a charge he vigorously denied as his campaign reached its climax that November when he published a Special Report cleverly entitled 'Racing's gulf crisis'.

The front page was dominated by a head and shoulders photo-montage of the four brothers accompanied by the caption 'The Maktoums: The men who seek to dominate British racing'. Inside, an editorial prefaced three pages of tabulated figures detailing the winners each brother had on a course-by-course basis, as well as their group winners, their breeding empire of studs,* stallions and mares and their 1988 yearling buys.

Alongside a list of the season's top nine owners that included all four brothers headed by Sheikh Mohammed (122 races won worth £1,143,343) and Sheikh Hamdan (112 races worth £724,742), Court presented the case for the prosecution:

> It does not require a detailed analysis of the 1988 Flat and Sales season to reveal that British racing has reached a state of crisis … old and established owners, trainers too, are being driven away because they can no longer compete. After eight short years, the Maktoum family factor is in danger of dominating and destroying the very fabric of the greatest racing in the world…
>
> Yet there was a time when it all looked so different and so very promising. This low-profile family from Dubai looked as though they might be the saviours of a bloodstock industry that had been starved of capital investment. Unfortunately, they never know when to stop spending – and the damage they are now inflicting on the game is beginning to outweigh the massive amount of early good when they helped retrieve lost bloodlines and provide employment on a variety of studs and stables.
>
> They and their advisors have failed totally to appreciate the responsibility and duties imposed on them by their staggering wealth. They have swamped the world's yearling markets with astonishing sums of money, knocking any real sense of values sideways.

Court went on to ask a series of 'Can it be good for racing' questions, the principal one hinging on the fact that the Maktoums had won 39% of Group 1 races and roughly 32% of Group 2 and Group 3 races. He also accused them of having "a rapacious appetite for success, however modest," and declared that anyone who could study the accompanying pages of facts and figures "and still say the scale of the Maktoum operation is a good thing for racing, is either on the gravy train – or incapable of balanced judgement."

Predictably, the report brought in a flood of letters from readers who did not believe they were 'incapable of balanced judgement' as they pointed out that racing had always been dominated by the super-rich which was why it was called 'the Sport of Kings'. The Maktoums, they claimed, were just filling the void left by the demise of the old aristocratic owner-breeders by maintaining and cultivating the breed at the highest level; they bought yearlings at prices many could afford (their pony-sized dual Oaks winner, Diminuendo, cost $125,000); their horses were always trying, and if it was not for them many of the horses listed in the report would be racing in France or America.

On the other hand it was contended that the family were running Derby horses in donkey races

---

* Before the month was out, it was announced that Sheikh Hamdan had bought the Ballygoran Stud in Co. Kildare, while Sheikh Mohammed was in the process of buying Meg Mullion's Ragusa Stud to add to those they already owned in Ireland: the Woodpark, Kildangan and Derrinstown studs.

by farming maiden races with million-dollar horses (the north, in particular, suffered from such raids), while they were also in the habit of buying up some of the best of the opposition during the course of a season to remove competition.

It was, as with most things in racing, all a matter of opinion.

Apart from the stack of letters the 'gulf' report bought in, its immediate effect was to get the *Life* banned in Dubai by the country's censors (the ban was lifted after a few days on the orders of Sheikh Mohammed), otherwise it was business as usual and business was good. With each passing month Court was able to post up soaring sales figures, while his policy of making news happen led to other 'Special Reports'.

In January 1987, he sent out questionnaires to all the senior jump jockeys regarding conditions at Britain's 44 NH courses. Most welcomed the opportunity to air some long-held grievances and under the heading 'Life survey exposes Britain's weighing-room slums' Sue Montgomery listed their main complaints. These ranged from having to stand on saddle pads on bare concrete floors to keep their feet warm and dry, to having only cold water and a single sink to wash in at the end of the day.

It was claimed that very few courses had saunas (although facilities were better at dual purpose courses); that "changing rooms on all except a few tracks are still the same as they were half a century ago" that "most courses tend to treat jockeys as a necessary evil" and the surest way to get a shower at Towcester was to "flush the overhead loos".

On day two, the focus was on safety standards. Newbury easily came out on top as the best and fairest test for a horse, while the last fence at Hereford was voted the worst sited in Britain and the bends at Sedgefield were likened to a motorcycle scramble track, although the course was praised for having first-aid attendants at every jump.

But while the volunteers from the St John Ambulance Brigade and the Red Cross were appreciated, it was felt that "with the amount of money generated by the racing industry, one or two paramedic teams should be provided" particularly as not all volunteers were trained to deal with spinal injuries. One jockey reported seeing an injured colleague dragged from beneath a dead horse, while another noted "there are still too many concrete posts and, on some tracks, wire round the inside of the running rail."

Two years later Court felt it necessary to run a 'News Special' headed 'Post Haste For Safety / Concrete evidence of the need to speed use of plastic running rails'. The survey was conducted by Gary Nutting, a new and enthusiastic member of the editorial staff who rang up every clerk of the course to check on the progress that was being made in removing the hazard of concrete posts supporting sturdy wooden running rails.

Apart from Richard Merton (Devon & Exeter and Taunton) who refused to comment, most clerks willingly co-operated. Twelve of Britain's 59 courses were concrete-free and while the inside running rail had been replaced by plastic at most courses, others were waiting for more Levy Board money to finish the job, and a few had sections of concrete supported rails they had no intention of removing since they acted as crowd barriers or because "horses don't run near them".

Court also provided a platform for the movers and shakers in racing to express their views by inviting them to deputise for 'Jack Logan' when he was on holiday. These guest columnists provided a veritable think tank of inspiration for the Jockey Club to draw on and one of the most enlightened contributions came from Henrietta Tavistock.

The Woburn Abbey owner-breeder of Pushy (Queen Mary and Cornwallis Stakes), Precocious (Norfolk, Gimcrack and Molecomb Stakes) and Jupiter Island (two St Simon Stakes, an Ebor Handicap and, most gloriously, the Japan Cup) all out of her 2,100gns buy, Mrs Moss, placed the welfare of racehorses at the top of her priorities:

> Surely the days of shooting horses on racecourses before injuries have been properly diagnosed should be over ... all racecourses should have appropriate equipment to return a horse to a properly equipped medical box at the racecourse stables. The inadequate trailers now in operation should be replaced by custom-designed ones with padded clamps to hold a horse so it does not have to support its own weight ... [*each trailer*] would cost in the region of £12,000. If that is too much and the racecourse cannot afford it then, in my opinion, racing should not be allowed to take place there.

Among other suggestions, she advocated a return to the old system of entering yearlings for the Derby: "This would generate far, far more money than it used to, for 50-60 per cent of the cream of the USA crop of thoroughbreds sold come here to race. All those yearlings, in order to find buyers, would have to be nominated ... so let the breeder be the first to pay."[*] She also called for better hygiene in racecourse stables which were "some of the biggest spreaders of diseases".

The campaigning editor, always ready to capitalise on any good idea or pinch it from the *Racing Post* if needs be, wasted no time in launching a survey into conditions at racecourse stables and hostels for stable staff, some of which the straight-talking Marchioness had described as "positively Dickensian".

Conducted among the most experienced travelling head lads in 40 leading yards, the findings were again presented by the industrious Ms Montgomery who, in between conducting high-profile interviews with such as the Queen's racing manager, Lord Porchester, and Lavinia, the Duchess of Norfolk, revealed a catalogue of "squalor, danger and indignities suffered by valuable horses and those who look after them":

> The same names crop up time after time. The lads CONDEMNED the stables at Wolverhampton, BRANDED the yard at Windsor as a possible fire hazard, and said Folkestone should be BOMBED.

The list of complaints included filthy, poorly ventilated boxes; unguarded glass windows and flintstone walls; dusty, dirty bedding for horses; damp, dirty bedding for stable staff who, in extreme cases, had to put up with overcrowding, bad food and insanitary washing facilities. In reviewing the findings 'Court Circular' observed:

> Racing is lucky to be dealing with such a long-suffering labour force. The same conditions in any other industry would have resulted in a walkout years ago ... The Jockey Club must re-examine the job being done on its behalf by the men who carry out examinations of all racecourse stables and accommodation. The business of inspecting by appointment must be scrapped ... Spot checks during the hurly-burly of race-days must be introduced ... The Levy Board must review any funds made payable to courses which fail to observe acceptable standards of hygiene and accommodation.

---

* A yearling entry stage closing in December was introduced for the 1993 Derby when it drew in 634 nominations at £200 a head (under the old system, when three-year-olds were entered in March, the 1992 Derby had attracted just 118 entries). Originally, Epsom had planned an April entry with the object of tapping into the American sales market as suggested, but this was dropped following opposition from the Thoroughbred Breeders Association. As a compromise, breeders were offered prize money incentives totalling £40,000 to enter their yearlings before the sales, but this attracted only 64 entries.

The royal trainer, Ian Balding, one of a consortium in the process of buying Windsor racecourse, wrote in to promise that the course would get a major facelift and applauded the *Life's* survey as "the best thing that could have happened. If there is anything that makes racecourse managements act quickly it is bad publicity."

In many cases, plans for improvements were already in place as soon as money became available from the £20m five-year deal the Racecourse Association had negotiated with Satellite Information Services who were about to start beaming live television coverage of racing into the nation's betting shops. Together with a reallocation of Levy Board cash and constant prodding from the *Life's* team of campaigners, the influx of funds was to bring about considerable improvements over the next few years.

And if any editor led by example it was Court who, a month after his paper broke through the six-figure barrier with an average daily sale of 101,472 in June 1987, interviewed the Princess Royal (Princess Anne) shortly after she had ridden Ten No Trumps to victory in the Dresden Ladies Diamond Stakes at Ascot.

In an exclusive two-page 'Questions and Answers' session conducted in the Princess's apartment at Buckingham Palace, he elicited some interesting insights into the equestrian life of his "briskly efficient" subject who was not in the best of moods having just had a brush with the paparazzi who had invaded the grounds of her Cotswolds home.

After a series of monosyllabic answers, HRH gradually thawed out as Court steered her onto the subject of race-riding which, she revealed, had come about purely by chance. Being master of the Worshipful Company of Farriers in the year they organised a charity race at Epsom to raise funds for Riding for the Disabled of which she was president, she felt she had no option but to take part. She chose David Nicholson as her tutor because she knew he would not be afraid to tell her if she was "doing it wrong".

During the course of the interview Court asked the Princess her views on the use of medication in eventing and was somewhat disappointed when she didn't go along with the idea of a blanket ban, but suggested that a small dose of Bute would be acceptable to relieve competing horses of their aches and pains.

The question was put at a time when there had been a spate of disqualifications in racing due to contaminated feedstuffs which involved minute traces of theobromine. In many cases the amount involved was as little as one part in 50 million, less than would be produced by one chocolate Smartie never mind a Mars Bar as had happened in the celebrated case of the horse, No Bombs.

The Irish 'winners' of the 1980 Cheltenham Gold Cup and Two-Mile Champion Chase, Tied Cottage and Chinrullah, had been early victims of the Jockey Club's strict rules governing doping (No.53 and 180) which knew no half-measures, and as the cases mounted up the editor accused the authorities of employing double standards.

He maintained it was hypocritical of them to disqualify horses for having minute traces of theobromine that "wouldn't inspire a gnat" and yet sanction the participation of British horses in the 1986 Breeders' Cup at Santa Anita where 33 per cent of the runners were 'doped' with Lasix, which not only aids horses with a tendency to break blood vessels, but is a powerful diuretic that eases their breathing and can mask other drugs. As the use of Lasix was banned in Britain and almost every other racing country, he asked why our horses were allowed to compete in such races:

> The reason surely cannot be that British racing, through the European Breeders' Fund, last year received $800,000 from the American Breeders' Cup. The fact the almighty dollar has caused US racing to swallow its principles, should not mean that the same thing can happen here.

If the Jockey Club can and does declare a man involved in flapping as a 'disqualified person' are the stewards not failing in their duty if they do not declare that anyone who races at meetings where doping is permitted should be similarly treated?

An ultimatum in the same straight language as Rules 53 and 180 should be sent to the American Breeders' Cup committee stating that unless medication is outlawed, the Breeders' Cup shall be regarded as an unlicensed event, carrying the same penalties for those who take part. Any other attitude must indicate that Portman Square presumes doping to be acceptable, providing the prize money is big enough.

And 18 months later, in August 1988, he returned to the fray when he derided as a "vapid offering" a speech Lord Hartington gave at a conference in New York on 'The Position of the Jockey Club of Great Britain in Drug Testing and Quality Assurance':

[*This*] was a time for views straight from the shoulder on doping problems that are a menace to the whole idea of international racing. It was not a time for a pussyfooting history lesson on what steps have been taken in Europe to clean up our act … Lord Hartington would have done the cause of world racing a much needed service had he spelt out the plummeting prestige of US racing in Europe because of their use of drugs.

He should have challenged them to achieve nationwide agreement on the use of Lasix and other 'medications' instead of the hotchpotch of regulations which vary from State to State. He should have dared them to start by making all Group One races – especially the Breeders' Cup – medication free and warned them that if they pursue their present perverted course they will become a nation totally lacking any integrity on the international scene.

The argument was irrefutable and two months later it resulted in the senior steward, Lord Fairhaven, persuading Henry Cecil to abandon his plans to run Sheikh Mohammed's French Oaks and Champion Stakes winner Indian Skimmer on Bute in the Breeders' Cup Turf at Churchill Downs where she was subsequently beaten just over a length into third place.

While America still maintains her proud tradition of flouting international opinion by allowing horses to run on 'medication' (not to mention more crucial world concerns) and Britain shamefully kowtows to her on this matter (not to mention more crucial world concerns), Court's campaigns continued to bear fruit on other fronts.

Safety was the overriding factor in his calls for a 1lb weight allowance for jockeys wearing body protectors; for crash helmets to be made compulsory for *all*, and for fences to be omitted when injured jockeys or horses were being attended to on the landing side. All common sense procedures one would have thought, yet the Jockey Club continued to drag its feet on all three issues even after near-fatal incidents involving the jockey Chris Grant and trainer Susan Piggott.

For years Sir David Llewellyn had been banging on about how the Jockey Club should compel trainers to wear riding helmets (he had finally persuaded the Club to make them compulsory for stable staff in 1976) and when Susan Piggott's life was saved by one in a skull-fracturing fall on the Newmarket gallops in August 1988, Court took up the cause.

Bewildered by the "Portman Square cocktail of obduracy with dashes of lunacy that insists that everyone but trainers, wives and friends must wear riding helmets on Newmarket Heath," he asked:

Is it too much to hope that, in the aftermath of 'The Susan Piggott Affair', the Jockey Club will now see fit to take positive action and review their instructions to trainers concerning helmets? What are they waiting for? A fatality?

In reply, the Jockey Club's PRO, David Pipe, stated:

The stewards expect all trainers to act responsibly and set a good example to the riding public by wearing an approved skull cap whenever they are on a horse … It shouldn't be necessary for the Jockey Club to bring in a rule to cover this.

A week later Court was up with the lark at Newmarket and counted at least a dozen unprotected heads on the gallops, which forced him to conclude:

To a certain extent I agree with David Pipe. It *shouldn't* be necessary for the Jockey Club to bring in a rule compelling trainers to wear helmets. But, alas, it is.

A month later another vital concern was brought to the fore when Chris Grant, who had broken a leg in a first-circuit fall at Market Rasen, had the same leg clipped by one of the three remaining runners as they jumped the fence second time round even though warning markers had been set up to show where he was lying.

Had the horses bypassed the fence, the race would have been declared void as had happened at Stratford the previous season, when a doctor waved the runners around a fence where an injured jockey was being attended to, after which the stewards ruled that by missing out the fence the horses had failed to complete the proper course.

When subsequent appeals for the rules to be made more flexible were rejected by the Jockey Club, Court was prompted to ask why stewards could allow jumps to be bypassed when ground conditions were bad or when a setting sun might blind horses and jockeys, but could not make similar exceptions when a jockey's life was in danger. He quoted Mark Dwyer, the northern jockeys' safety officer, who, in referring to the Grant incident, had asked: "What if there had been 16 jumping the fence instead of three? And what if one of them had landed on his head instead of his leg?"

The consequences didn't bear thinking about and, following an approach from the Jockeys' Association, the Jockey Club reconvened its working party into racecourse safety. Court, ever anxious to help, advised them to consider the Health and Safety at Work Act of 1974 when reviewing the latest incident: "The fact that horses were allowed to jump the fence close to, or on to, the stricken Grant clearly suggests a breach of the Act might have occurred at Market Rasen."

Within a few weeks a measure was brought in to give racecourse doctors the authority to stop a race in such circumstances, while motorway cones would be used to mark off part of an obstacle not to be jumped, but the proposal to miss out jumps was once again rejected because, it was claimed, only seven of the 44 NH courses had the necessary room to bypass all their fences.*

With regard to body protectors Court felt the case for a 1lb allowance had been won when the

---

* It took seven years before the necessary alterations were made to allow all jumps to be bypassed on all courses. In the meantime, injured jockeys' lives continued to be put at risk along with the medical staff attending them, by horses jumping fences or hurdles that had been partly and/or inadequately dolled off.

In dangerous company: Monty Court is flanked by Robert Maxwell and Lord Wyatt of Weeford at his retirement party in 1990 – what is it about men who wear bow ties?

Jockey Club announced on the eve of the 1988 Grand National that they had agreed to it in principle and that "clerks of the scales are now considering a number of suggestions on how the weight allowance might be implemented … [*and*] will present their comments to the stewards by the end of April."

In July, the Club announced that the wearing of body protectors would be compulsory from the start of the jumping season, but: "No weight allowance will be made for it until such time as the stewards have monitored weights of riders from the start of the new season and also completed a study of international weighing out procedures."

Court was furious. He accused the Club of going back on the apparent pledge it had made on "this vital safety reform" and declared:

> Many saw this statement at the end of three months of procrastination as nothing less than a double-cross. In any other walk of life resignations would not have been out of order for such dilatory behaviour … Meanwhile, as the Jockey Club agonises over a simple solution of resetting scales, one is left to ponder: Do they really care?

But 'Say not the struggle naught availeth'; that November the headlines trumpeted: 'Jockey Club heeds two Sporting Life safety campaigns / Jump jockeys get one-pound allowance for body shields / New safety helmet rule for trainers', while Peter Scudamore, the reigning champion jockey and vice-president of the Jockeys' Association, was quoted as saying: "We all owe a big thank you to *The Sporting Life* for campaigning on our behalf."

The icing on the cake was added the same day when it was announced that the Club had asked the Levy Board for £240,000 to provide racecourses with modern horse ambulances. In the stately Georgian pile that is Woburn Abbey, the Marchioness of Tavistock gave a dainty little curtsey.

And so Court continued to chivvy and harry the Jockey Club into implementing other reforms until the day came when they hosted a dinner for him to mark his retirement from the *Life* at the beginning of November 1990. It was a unique and magnanimous gesture by the clubmen and demonstrated a remarkable change in attitude from the days when their forefathers barely deigned to recognise the existence of the press, but if they thought they had heard the last of their dogged tormenter they were in for a nasty shock.

As part of his retirement package the editor had arranged with his employer that he would continue his 'Court Circular' column for as long as needs be, which, as things turned out, was a lot longer than Bob Maxwell was to be around and was long enough to see the *Life* to the end of the road.

MAN OVERBOARD

WHEN Monty Court took his leave of the paper he had served so well he did so as its outgoing editor-in-chief, a position he attained in the summer of 1989 when his second-in-command, Mike Gallemore, succeeded to the chair. A small, prematurely grey-haired man hot-wired to a world of fantasy in which he was the principal player, the new editor had been born and brought up in Manchester where he followed his father into journalism by joining the *Daily Mirror* as an ambitious 19-year-old in 1964.

As he grafted his way up as a sub-editor he took an increasingly active part in union affairs and was elected FoC of the *Mirror's* NUJ chapel at Withy Grove in 1978. He quickly made his mark as a shrewd negotiator and six years later was made the union's divisional convenor. It was in this role, when acting for the journalists made redundant in the sweeping staff cuts of 1985, that he inadvertently enhanced his career prospects.

At the time, Maxwell was trying to buy the Manchester plant from its Canadian owner, Lord Thomson of Fleet, but negotiations had broken down and Lord Marsh, the chairman of the Newspaper Publishers Association, stepped in to act as an intermediary. With Gallemore pleading the cause of the journalists who would be thrown out of work if, as seemed possible, Withy Grove was to close down, a deal was finally done whereby Maxwell got the plant and its prime-site car parks for a knock-down price.

For playing his part in the negotiations, Gallemore became a favoured son of Cap'n Bob and when, early in 1987, an agreement was finally reached with the NGA for direct input, he was given the job of co-ordinating a team of hi-tech experts who had moved into Withy Grove to install the latest computer systems and train up the local journalists.

It was a steep but rewarding learning curve for the tubby Mancunian who recalled: "The great advantage of having some of the best technical people and sub-editors on the team was that if somebody we were instructing froze in the middle of doing the work we could go in and finish the job. We just produced the paper that night and went back to the teaching job the next day until they got it right."

But no sooner had the Withy Grove journalists 'got it right' than they were out of a job when most of them were made redundant in the early summer of 1988 as Maxwell prepared to close down the plant and move to a new site at Oldham where he had installed six of the 21 vastly expensive colour presses he had bought from Germany.

Shortly afterwards, Gallemore took up his Maxwell-appointed position of managing editor at the *Life* where his initial task was to improve profitability by ensuring regular distribution and reducing the amount of returns (of unsold papers) which were unacceptably high particularly during the winter months when everything was frozen off or flooded out. The advent of all-weather racing in 1989 helped to stabilise things but, with a publication sold on a 'sale or return' basis, Gallemore found that getting the right number of copies into the nation's newsagents was still a delicate balancing act.

"One of the difficulties in reducing returns is that you automatically reduce your sales because you are denying casual readers the chance of buying the paper, but our circulation reps did a fantastic job. If you can get your returns down then, obviously, most of the copies you are printing are being sold so it brings down all your other costs; newsprint, transport, production, everything.

"But the first thing we had to get right was our off-stone times. If we were late, we would miss the pick-up and once they had got the *Mirror* into the delivery vans they wouldn't wait for us and we would have to do a separate run which cost the earth. Even then there was no guarantee the wholesalers would get the papers on time. People would say we got the paper out, which was fine if you lived in London, but if you were in the north, in Ireland or elsewhere you weren't going to get your *Life*."

Gradually, with its return to the *Mirror* fold in 1988* when the paper started to be printed at the old *Reveille* plant in Stamford Street, together with the aid of new technology – principally page-facsimile transmissions to the various print sites – production picked up and distribution improved, no more so than in Ireland where, at the beginning of 1989, the *Life* started to be printed in Belfast.

"Once we got into Ireland we saturated the country with the paper and soon overtook the *Post* which had been able to establish a big lead there because of our hit-and-miss distribution. Michael Clower, our Irish correspondent, was a great help then. He was highly respected and knew everybody, as well as being a good operator and writer."

That summer the *Life* also started to appear in colour when it joined the group's other titles that were being printed on the new presses Maxwell had installed at the old Odhams plant in Watford. First editions of the paper were also being run off in Oldham to offset the advantage the *Post* had enjoyed by having its northern editions printed in Warrington.

At the same time work began on devising a system to carry jockeys' (owners') colours on the paper's racecards. Much of the technology involved had to be created from scratch and it took the group's technical director, Gerald Mowbray, and his team of experts the best part of nine months to get the operation up and running.

The colours first appeared on a special back-page spread for the Ladbroke Hurdle at Leopardstown in January 1990, but the gremlins that had cut short the colour run for the 1960 Grand National issue once again got into the works. This time, however, a little ingenuity and Mike Gallemore's experience of working on the *Mirror's* art desk in Manchester some 20 years earlier saved the day.

"I sent out my secretary to an art studio to get some paints and ended up colouring in the outlines of the jockeys' jackets by hand. Some of the cross-belts and stripes were a bit shaky, but we got the paper out on time. It was quite a milestone."

It took two more months of trials to iron out the glitches before the colours were brought in on a permanent basis for the first day of the Cheltenham Festival. Maxwell hailed them as part of his 'rainbow revolution' and described the racecards as: "The greatest advance ever in serving our readers … an enormous benefit for racegoers and viewers alike."

It was a great coup for the *Life*. The innovation was acclaimed in betting shops, which had been receiving live SIS coverage for the past three years, while the paper's on-course sales were boosted as many punters shared the opinion of the Cheltenham racegoer who was quoted as saying: "The colours are so good nobody will need to buy a racecard again."

At the same time, Monty Court took great satisfaction in getting Brough Scott's Channel 4 team-mate, John Francome, to promote the colours in a TV commercial. Scottie Rough was not best pleased. "It caused a hell of a row," chuckles Court with a wicked smile. More to the point, it took the *Racing Post* three whole years to catch up.

---

* In September 1988 the editorial department moved back to Orbit House much to the relief of Monty Court: "The office accommodation was a vast improvement on Alexander House and we had the production department virtually on the premises. The whole thing was infinitely more convenient with the *Mirror* library just across the road to say nothing of 'the Stab' downstairs!"

It was a good start for Gallemore in his first year as editor, but there were stormy times ahead. That autumn the country slid into a major recession that was to hit the racing and newspaper industries hard and then, in November, Maxwell appointed Charles Wilson, former editor of *The Times*, as the paper's new editor-in-chief and managing director. Wilson could not believe his luck at being given the chance to combine the two great passions in his life – newspapers and horseracing. Gallemore was less happy. He knew the abrasive Scot by repute and it was "bad, all bad".

The Glasgow-born son of a miner turned steelworker, Wilson had started out in Fleet Street as a 16-year-old office boy on *The People* in 1951 and, after National Service with the Royal Marines, he progressed through provincials in Melton Mowbray and Bristol to become West Country correspondent for the *News Chronicle* in 1959.

That post lasted barely a year before the *News Chronicle* was absorbed by the *Daily Mail* whose deputy news editor just happened to be Monty Court: "Charlie was top of our shopping list. He was a bloody good reporter and because I knew he was mad keen on racing we sent him to Cambridge with a special brief to keep an eye on Newmarket."

During his time on the *Mail* (1960-74) Wilson graduated from reporter to take over Court's old job on the news desk before going on to become sports editor and then deputy northern editor in Manchester. As he climbed the journalistic ladder so his reputation for being a hard man grew, and by the time he finished a seven-year stint on his home patch as editor of the Glasgow *Evening Times*, the *Herald* and the short-lived *Sunday Standard*, he was portrayed as a fully-fledged terror.

His return to London as executive editor of *The Times* in 1982 proved a massive culture shock to the literati of Gray's Inn Road and it was not long before *Private Eye's* 'Street of Shame' column was gleefully relaying reports of eruptions involving 'Charlie Gorbals'. Mike Gallemore, no shrinking violet himself, was better equipped than most to handle the new editor-in-chief when he arrived at the *Life,* but that didn't stop some heated exchanges from taking place: "Charlie tried to put the fear of God into some people and that was one of the main causes of the rows I had with him because he wasn't doing the place any good. It wasn't the way to get the best out of people."

In his well-cushioned retirement, a mellowed Wilson refutes the charge although he does so with a twinkle in his eye: "It's a fairly common cliché for people to say I was a bully; they said that about me everywhere I went in newspapers, but I'm not big enough to be a bully. I'm a forceful character; the reason I don't hold back is because I'm very passionate about what I do. I was as passionate about wanting the *Life* to succeed as I was about *The Times* and every other newspaper I've worked for."

But however passionate he was about serving his new paper, Wilson quickly found that Maxwell had imported him primarily as a trophy from the Murdoch empire – the *Life* just happened to be a convenient place to park him until he was needed for more important assignments elsewhere, and there was no shortage of them.

In March 1991 he was required to stand in as editor of the *Daily Mirror* for two weeks to bridge the gap between Maxwell replacing one editor (Roy Greenslade) with another (Richard Stott) who had been fired the previous year. Days later he was off to America with Maxwell to negotiate with the trade unions over the media mogul's latest acquisition, the *New York Daily News*. Deals done, Wilson just had time to snatch a couple of days at the Cheltenham Festival on his return before he was dispatched to New York again to get the *Racing Times* up and running.

His role as chief *aide-de-camp* took precedence over everything else and even when he was at the *Life* he had to be ready to be put on display: "It became very clear soon after I joined that Maxwell didn't want me to run the *Life*, he just wanted to show me off. I'd often get a call to go and see him when he was entertaining the ambassador from an East European country or some such personage and when I walked in he would say 'Oh, this is Charles Wilson, the former editor of *The Times*'."

When he was allowed to fulfil his appointed role, Wilson chose to work through Alastair Down rather than Gallemore: "There were two reasons why I used Alastair. Firstly, he was a better journalist than Mike Gallemore, but the main reason was that Gallemore was never in the office early enough. His insistence on commuting from Macclesfield every day, at the mercy of late-running trains, meant he wouldn't get in until 10.30 or later and was often absent when he should have been at the helm of the paper."

By this time Down had moved on from features to become news editor, and the fact that he also found himself acting as deputy editor, didn't entirely displease him since he had already set his sights in that direction; the pressure, however, was something else.

"I used to see Charlie Wilson at 9 o'clock every morning before anyone else was in the office. He would have gone through every newspaper and torn out bits he wanted looked at for possible stories; there would be about a dozen of those and then I would give him a list of things I had thought of. It would take about half an hour and once he had set me off I wouldn't normally see him again until the following morning although he'd ring me three or four times during the day to see how things were going.

"He set the agenda for the day through me and it was my fault if it didn't get carried through even though I wasn't in charge. It was a really difficult position to be in. He expected me to make everyone else come round to his way of thinking; if it didn't happen it was my fault and if it did it was 'well done him'. He was very clever and he didn't take the answer 'no' or 'it's not possible', *ever*. He was a nightmare and a bully, you had to stand up to him or you would die.

"He also changed the whole climate of things on the paper; news stories became the number one priority because he was a *news*paper man. He said we needed news, news and more news, but he overdid it and we got bogged down in a lot of industry stuff which was hardly of any interest to anyone in the office let alone to people outside it.

"But on the days when we had to invent the news ourselves it was quite fun. We were expected to produce a major story every day and if we hadn't got one by about 7 o'clock I would chose a small paragraph that had come in as a filler from the PA and make it our lead. We'd turn an item like 'Mrs Briggs has horseshoe stolen off mantelpiece' into something approaching the Great Train Robbery by the time the paper landed on people's breakfast tables the next day. We had a great team with reporters like David Ashforth, Colin Vickers, Nick Reeves and Gary Nutting – they were masters of invention."

Down takes a quiet pride in having 'discovered' Ashforth who started to submit feature articles on spec in 1988. It was immediately apparent to him that the one-time Ladbrokes board-man, who had attained a doctorate in philosophy at Cambridge and afterwards lectured in history and economics, had something special to offer.

"When we interviewed David for the job neither Monty Court nor Mike Gallemore wanted him because they thought he was an academic not a journalist, but I persuaded them to give him a go and if I hadn't he might have given up the idea of writing on racing. I think he is a great writer, very amusing and incredibly disciplined; after he joined us he raised the whole tone of our coverage of the racing industry material."

As the news columns expanded so too did the paper which began to bulge with supplements Gallemore and Court put together for bank holidays and big-race weekends. Their first and most important collaboration was achieved with Bob Betts, when they brought out the *Greyhound Life* in November 1988. The eight-page pull-out section incorporated the bookmakers' page-2 marker-sheet and freed up more space for news stories in the main paper, while readers who did not follow the dogs developed the irreverent habit of filleting their *Life* on purchase and binning the unwanted section in the nearest convenient receptacle.

Pull-out sections were also introduced for big sporting occasions such as the Open golf tournament and big fights, while Andrew Caulfield's annual 16-page Stallion Guide for the Flat and another for National Hunt brought in valuable advertising revenue.

Operating on the principle that "Supplements work so long as you've got something strong enough to warrant the section going on its own," Gallemore introduced a Saturday *Sportslife* in 1991. The four-page section focused on the sports-betting market and was continued in a condensed form in the main paper during the week adding an extra dimension the editor was eager to develop: "I wanted to turn the *Life* into a sports-betting paper because it was obvious the betting industry was already moving that way, but I didn't want to diminish the racing coverage one little bit.

"At the same time I was keen to have more entertaining articles in the paper because most of it was not what you would call easy-reading although it was informative and well-written." To this end he was happy to welcome Michael Pope as a contributor after Court, in his role as consultant to the *Life* (another bonus of his retirement package), had encouraged the former president of the National Trainers Federation to put pen to paper.

Pope had been around long enough to have seen Lord Derby's bonny little chestnut, Hyperion, romp home in the 1933 Derby. He had served with the North Irish Horse in North Africa and Italy during the war (winning a Military Cross in the process), and had started training in the Thames Valley village of Streatley in 1947 before moving on to Blewbury where his former brother officer, Dick Hern, joined him as his assistant.

A born raconteur with a wealth of stories to draw on, Pope's *joie de vivre* infused his writing. The articles, often laced with a dash of chicanery (whisky for faint-hearted horses; electric spurs for lazy ones, were all part of the game), read like a cross between Dick Francis and James Herriot. On one occasion, Pope and his stud groom, "a wonderful character and a broad Scot called Frank Horne," assisted the stallion Blason in the rape of a well-named filly called Frigid Flower. After the reluctant bride had shown she had no intention of being deflowered, the trainer was summoned to the scene:

When I arrived at the barn there was this poor wretched article trussed up like a chicken. One foreleg was strapped up, a twitch on her nose, another on her ear and hobbles on her pasterns. I said: 'You're not taking any chances with her, Mr Horne?' He replied: 'No, and I haven't finished yet. I'll blindfold the poor wee lass.'

With that he slipped out of his jacket, put it over her head, and tied the sleeves under her jowl ... Handing me the reins of the bridle and the two twitch handles, he said: 'Keep her head tight up against the boards 'cos she's sure to plunge forward when the 'oss gets across her.' Then off he went to fetch the stallion from his pen.

You could hear Blason coming some way off, shouting and hollering, clearly in the mood for love. As they entered the barn Horne shouts: 'Hang on man and keep those twitches going.' With that, Blason bounded on top of the mare and amid screams of unwillingness to lose her virginity the poor beast tried to leap forward.

On three legs and helpless, she collapsed onto her knees knocking me arse over head. I was now wedged against the wall in a sitting position with one of her knees in my crotch. Horne shouts: 'Come on out from under there, man, the 'oss is nearly done.' 'Nearly done,' I thought to myself; he's not the only bugger! With that the horse slid off and somehow I extracted myself and scrambled to my feet.

Having relieved poor Frigid Flower of all the paraphernalia, old Horne said: 'If that mare's in foal I'm Fred Archer. Just as well the ladies are not as reluctant as that!'

But the covering was successful and three years later Pope found himself landed with the result, "a pathetic-looking article, very small, narrow, no bone and light in condition". The plan was to give the horse, Blazing Scent by name, a few runs in sellers before trying to pick up a nursery with him. Ridden by Greville Starkey on his debut at Nottingham:

Blazing Scent was soon in arrears, with Greville booting and scrubbing but going nowhere. With only a few hundred yards left to run, as a last resort, he gave him one slap. Whoosh! The horse took off and flew past the field as if they were standing still to win going away by two lengths.

At the auction, a shell-shocked Pope let his winner go to a bid of 700gns. This was a mistake. Trained by George Todd, the 'pathetic-looking article' proved a game and consistent performer winning ten more races and landing some tidy gambles in the process as well as the 1964 Victoria Cup at the rewarding odds of 25-1.

Mike Pope's marvellous stories ran, intermittently, for several years during which time Gallemore indulged himself in his own form of light entertainment. A keen rider to hounds in the High Peak district of Derbyshire, he took part in a series of 'Golden Oldie' charity races featuring an assortment of retired jockeys and 'personalities' that were staged at various courses around the country.

His exploits in the saddle were not uneventful. In 1991 at Uttoxeter he put up 13lb overweight at 12st 9lb on the Jack Berry-trained Miami Bear who shot off in front like a scalded cat before staging an equally rapid retreat to finish an exhausted last. The following year he partnered the Martin Pipe-trained Tom Clapton to an effortless 'win' at Warwick, but was disqualified for missing out a hurdle, and in 1993 he finished third in a race at Haydock on the 33-1 chance Mo Ichi Do, but because the gelding did not wear the blinkers he was declared with the matter was referred to the Jockey Club.

But by that time, life at the *Life* and throughout the *Mirror* group had changed forever. It was on the 5th of November – a date to remember – 1991 that Bob Maxwell took his notorious early-morning plunge from his 430-ton yacht, *Lady Ghislaine*, as she cruised off the Canary Islands. On the day of his death, the *Mirror* mogul was due to fly back to London to face his bankers who were demanding more collateral on loans totalling hundreds of millions of pounds – collateral he no longer had after the payments on his 1988 $2.6bn purchase of the giant American publishing house, Macmillan, had finally exhausted his and his employees' coffers.

Six months earlier he had floated 49 per cent of MGN on the stock market and sold off Pergamon Press for £446m in a bid to raise the necessary funds to keep his creditors at bay. But even plundering over £420m from the pension funds was not enough to prevent his empire from collapsing around him under the weight of debt and deceit. On the day he took his fateful dive, he knew the game was up. The Serious Fraud Office was about to launch an investigation into his operations and it was only a matter of time before his embezzlements from the pension funds were exposed.

No sooner had his 22-stone (308lb) body been found in the sea off Grand Canary than an orgy of speculation swept Fleet Street and the world beyond. Did he jump or was he pushed? Circumstantial evidence pointed to suicide. An inveterate bully, he delighted in humiliating his underlings, so how then could he himself face being humiliated?

Medical evidence, as revealed in a 40-page autopsy report, stated he had died from heart failure (there was not enough water in his lungs for him to have drowned). But, as always, the conspiracy theorists held sway. There were claims that he had been involved in arms deals on Israel's behalf; that he had links with Mossad and had tipped off its agents when the Israeli nuclear technician, Mordecai Vanunu, was about to expose his country's nuclear programme in the *Sunday Times*.*

Certainly, his burial on Judaism's sacred Mount of Olives showed he had been much more than just a good friend to Israel. He was given what amounted to a state funeral attended by the President, Chaim Herzog, the Prime Minister, Yitzhak Shamir, and nearly every other member of the Israeli cabinet. In a remarkable graveside eulogy Herzog described Maxwell as "a figure of almost mythological stature" and paid tribute to his commitment to and involvement in "many facets of our struggle for economic independence … and for the security of our country".[1]

The late publisher's flagship newspaper was no less effusive in its praise of 'The Man Who Saved The Mirror' and devoted 11 pages to him. Charlie Wilson, who had been appointed spokesman for the company, dismissed all talk of suicide as he declared:

> He thrived on what you and I would call pressure. He thrived on criticism. I cannot imagine he would get himself into any state where he would consider taking his own life. He had too much arrogance of his own abilities to conceive such a thing.[2]

Mike Gallemore was of the same mind but, with his vivid imagination, he has come to believe it was a state-sponsored assassination: "What I've since heard from various people whose opinion I respect is that some of the crew on his yacht were Mossad agents. The theory is that Maxwell was getting desperate and went to the Israelis for help because he had done a lot of deals for them in the past. He said he needed bailing out, but they weren't interested.

"I think what happened then was that he said 'in that case I'm going to blow the lid on all you've been doing' and the Israelis thought 'there's only one way to stop this and that's to shut him up for good'. The whole thing about Maxwell was that he had no fear and no morals. Life was a game as far as he was concerned and money was just chips to play with. Position and power was what turned him on; he certainly wasn't a suicide candidate."

The *Mirror's* hierarchy were still in mourning for their 'saviour' when Sir David Llewellyn rocked the boat as it were, by sending in a quote taken from a *Guardian* obituary for inclusion in his 'Sayings of the Week' selection. It related that after Maxwell had given a dinner at his Oxford home for some influential guests he said goodnight to them in some of the nine languages he professed to speak fluently. When it came to Lady Coutts, she answered him in Swahili leaving her host completely flummoxed. Her graceful: '*Kwaheri ashante sana sitaki kukuona tena*' translated as 'Goodbye. Thank you very much. I don't wish to see you again.'

Alastair Down recalls: "I got into terrible trouble for letting that quote go in. All hell broke loose.

---

* In 1986, Vanunu offered the information to the *Sunday Mirror*, but when Maxwell turned him down he went to the *Sunday Times*, which splashed the story under the headline 'Revealed: The Secrets of Israel's Nuclear Arsenal' by which time Vanunu had been lured to Rome by a female Mossad agent. There he was drugged and smuggled out of the country to Israel where he spent 18 years in jail – 11 of them in solitary.

There were dire threats of dismissals and that sort of thing, but a week or two later, when it became clear that Maxwell had had his fingers in the pie, there was no more talk of dismissals."*

Instead, it was Gallemore who took the flak. As a trustee of the pension fund, he was accused of failing in his responsibilities by ignoring the danger signs especially after a fellow trustee, the *Daily Record*'s Harry Templeton, smelt a large fat rat and started to ask questions about the fund's investments. This was not what Maxwell expected from trustees and Templeton was promptly given his marching orders.

Yet, for years, there had been a growing unease about how the pension fund was being managed and the print union, Sogat, was due to see Maxwell in court over the matter the week he died. There were also plenty of MGN executives who knew Maxwell was on the fiddle and had even colluded with him. Among those named and shamed in a DTI report that was published ten years after spoof Fleet Street headlines had reported 'Fat Man Falls Overboard – Not Many Dead' were Maxwell's sons Kevin and Ian, the Labour peer Lord Donoughue, head of one of Maxwell's private companies that had control of the pension funds, and a heap of other supine directors who had either been bought off for their silence or who were too terrified of the mighty mogul to challenge him.

Kevin and Ian Maxwell (both on legal aid) actually stood trial for fraud, but were cleared after a 32-week lawyers' bonanza that cost the taxpayer £20m.

The fact that the regulatory authorities had, once again, fallen down on the job, forced Norman Lamont, the Chancellor of the Exchequer, to fumble in his word-bag of worthless phrases and come out with the usual cliché that the government was "determined that all the lessons of the Maxwell affair must be learned and implemented".[3] Yet, it took the politicians with their gilt-edged pensions 15 years to set up a barely adequate protection fund for less privileged mortals during which time thousand were robbed of a secure retirement after the companies they worked for had gone bankrupt taking their pension money with them.†

Gallemore, like everyone else within the *Mirror* group, was still trying to come to terms with the scandal almost a year later when it was announced that David Montgomery had been appointed chief executive of MGN. To those who had witnessed the rise to power of the ruthlessly ambitious Ulsterman, it was almost as if Cap'n Bob had risen from the grave and returned to haunt them in an altogether different guise.

Dour and puritanical with a Presbyterian upbringing that had instilled a philosophy of 'You're not here to enjoy yourself, you're here to work and die', Montgomery was returning to his journalistic roots having started out on the *Mirror's* training scheme for young journalists in Plymouth some 22 years earlier.

---

* When the financial circumstances surrounding Maxwell's death came to light, Charlie Wilson was one of many who changed their mind and opted for the suicide theory: "A few weeks after I had gone on television and radio to say what a great loss to British journalism, society and the world at large Maxwell was, the accountants discovered a very large hole in the group's finances and I was going on the same television and radio programmes saying what a swine the man was. There were a lot of us with red faces at the time. Maxwell was massively ego-driven and that's why he died. Some men would have fronted it out, but he couldn't have stood the ignominy of the exposure. I've not the slightest doubt he committed suicide."

† It should be recorded that not a single MGN pensioner lost a penny of their entitlement thanks to the efforts of the Association of Mirror Pensioners led by Tony Boram and a sub-committee of the pension fund trustees headed by Charlie Wilson. Wilson was appointed a trustee after it was found that the fund had been looted by Maxwell and, in a series of typically forceful, one-to-one negotiations with representatives of the banks that had accepted the fund's shares as collateral for their loans to Maxwell, he recovered a large portion of the plundered assets. Subsequently, the government-appointed Sir John Cuckney put together a 'Global Settlement' which fully reimbursed the fund.

In the interim he had become editor of the *News of the World* and then *Today* after he had persuaded Rupert Murdoch to buy that paper in 1987. Along the way he had acquired the nickname 'Rommel' after one disgruntled journo had quipped 'I thought Montgomery was supposed to be on our side'.

The *Life's* editor had got to know Montgomery when the combative but quietly spoken loner joined the *Mirror's* subs desk in Manchester in the early 1970s. Not one to mix with the lads, the new man stood out as a thick-skinned, workaholic dedicated to cultivating the favours of anyone he thought might be able to help him advance his career.

Recalling those days, Gallemore says: "I gave him my Friday night news-subbing shift on the *Sunday Mirror* because he was struggling to make ends meet at the time, but he never even bought me a pint afterwards. When I heard he had been appointed chief executive I went out and got pissed. I was absolutely dumbstruck."*

He was not the only one. When Montgomery took up his appointment on 23 October 1992, journalists at the *Mirror* stopped work in protest. The new CEO coaxed them back with three written assurances: (1) "I have definitely got no plans for job cuts in editorial departments." – three weeks later nearly 100 casual journalists were sacked without explanation; (2) "The editors of all titles remain in their positions." – 19 days later Bill Hagerty, editor of *The People*, was sacked along with Cathy Galvin, editor of that paper's colour magazine; four days later Richard Stott, editor of the *Mirror*, was sacked; (3) "Union recognition will continue." – the NUJ house agreement that stated all sackings must be discussed with union officials was ignored as were the approaches of union representatives.[4]

Other high-ranking journalists left for their own reasons, among them were columnist Anne Robinson (formerly married to Charlie Wilson), who later found fame as the dominatrix quiz mistress on the television game show *Weakest Link*, and the *Mirror's* political editor Alastair Campbell who, ten years on as Tony Blair's head of communications, was to infamously spin the case for war in Iraq.

The purge even reached the *Life* after departmental heads were told to assess their staff and cull any 'surplus to requirements'. One of those Gallemore selected was his admin manager, Carolyn Cluskey, who had served three previous editors in Ossie Fletcher, Graham Taylor and Monty Court. Court had rated Cluskey as highly as his predecessors: "Carolyn could be contrary at times, but she was utterly invaluable, an absolute rock."

Late in 1992, the 'absolute rock' was shattered: "Gallemore called me into his office with a 'can I have a word'; there was no preamble, he just said 'They're making you redundant'. It was a terrible shock. After more than 20 years, my career was just chucked out of the window on a whim."

The cull extended to other long-serving members of staff before, as in all the bloodiest purges, the executioner was himself executed. On 7 April 1993, Gallemore was summoned to Wilson's office: "It was the same day we received record profit figures. I remember going through them with the general manager, Peter Robins, and we were slapping each other on the back; they were fantastic. I'd put in for a staff bonus if we hit the figures I expected, and when I was called in to see Charlie Wilson and David Montgomery I thought I was going to get the go-ahead to pay it.

---

* Montgomery was backed by a consortium of banks that effectively owned the Mirror group through the MGN shares (legitimately owned by Maxwell) they had taken as collateral security. His brief was to bring the MGN share price back to a point where the banks could bail out. As the shares had fallen to 49p after Maxwell's death, Montgomery had his work cut out to bring them back to their initial floatation price of 125p, the minimum exit price for the banks. He could only achieve this by across-the-board savings on all titles and drastic cuts in personnel. Within a year of his taking over, the share price had risen to 186p and while he succeeded in bringing the company out of administration, by the time he left with a £1.35m pay-off in January 1999, the circulation of the *Mirror* had fallen by around 500,000 and the *Life* had ceased to exist.

"I was absolutely dumbfounded when they said 'that's it'. They didn't explain their reasons; they just said something along the lines of 'We can't go on like this. We're going to have to terminate your employment as of now.' I just said 'fine' and walked out. I got back to the office still in a state of shock, made a short announcement saying I'd been relieved of my post, wished everybody luck for the future and left."

The irony was that Gallemore had piloted the paper through a recession that had seen the circulation of other titles in the group slump by as much as 14 per cent (in the case of the *Mirror*) yet only the previous month the *Life* had achieved a sale of 136,000 (from a print run of 200,000) for the first day of the Cheltenham Festival. To those in the know, however, the sacking did not come as a surprise. Three months earlier, Tom Clarke had been replaced as sports editor of *The Times*, a job he owed to his good friend Mr Wilson.

Two days after Gallemore's departure Wilson announced that his old buddy was to be the new editor of the *Life*, but he denies there was any cronyism in the appointment: "The idea that I would put anyone into a job because he was a mate is a non sequitur. I hired Clarke onto the *Life* because we needed a good editor and I thought he would certainly make a better editor than Mike Gallemore."

Events were to prove otherwise.

A NEW BROOM

T HE THIRTEENTH and last editor of the *Sporting Life* arrived at Orbit House on a high. The previous week, Tom Clarke had received a special award from the Sports Writers' Association for his "outstanding services to sports journalism". There was every reason to believe the 53-year-old Londoner deserved the accolade. He had 22 years of sports editorship behind him, having graduated through the usual run of provincials and, more unusually, from a four-year stint in Africa where he worked on newspapers in Southern Rhodesia (Zimbabwe) and Kenya.

On his return to England, he had four years of subbing on the *Daily Express* and then two years on the fashion magazine, *Queen*. It was after a similar period working on the women's feature pages of the London *Evening Standard* that he found favour with the editor, Charles Wintour, who promoted him to sports editor in 1971.

Three years later, he moved on to the *Daily Mail* where he had the privilege of working with the outstanding sports writer Ian Wooldridge and the irrepressible Jim Stanford, racing newshound extraordinaire. Finally, in 1986, he was recruited onto *The Times* by Wilson, and then served under Simon Jenkins, who took over the chair in 1990, before he was one of some 20 journalists who were either sacked or resigned after Peter Stothard became the paper's third editor in as many years.

Stothard went on to push the circulation of Rupert Murdoch's flagship newspaper to new highs of 800,000 plus and was knighted for his services to journalism in 2003. Sadly, his erstwhile sports editor achieved somewhat less impressive results for his new paper despite his determination "to emphasise the *Life's* pre-eminence in its field" as he informed readers on his first day in office.

"We will be enhancing the quality of our news coverage, our writing, our pictures and our presentation," he promised. That was a lot of enhancing by any standards and by the already high standards of the *Life* his rhetoric left its band of dedicated toilers bemused and not a little sceptical. To a great extent, Court and Gallemore had set up the paper for the new editor, all he had to do was to steer it along the course they had so successfully charted, but, as with any new incumbent, it was only natural he should want to make his mark and this he did in no uncertain manner. Initially, he focused his attention on sorting out the "anarchic" working practices of the editorial staff.

Having come from one of the biggest newspaper operations in the world where everything was highly regulated and planned down to the last detail, the fastidious Clarke was dismayed by the easy-going ambience of the *Life's* office. He recalled: "Sloppy leadership, both editorially and in management, is what I inherited. There was no sense of discipline in the place. It was a disorganised paper and in many ways it was anarchic; the lunatics were running the asylum.

"Some of the subs were taking holidays far longer than the six-and-a-half-week norm; they were meant to be working a nine-day fortnight, but were on a four-day week, and others were claiming expenses for going racing when they never went racing.* I told Charlie Wilson I was going to 'clean out the stables' and make the place work properly and I did. I'm very proud of that although, obviously, I didn't make many friends in doing it."

---

* This was a carry-over from an in-house agreement negotiated between the NUJ and the management in 1978 when under-the-table arrangements of this kind were common throughout Fleet Street as increasingly militant union branches secured deals that would get around the Labour government's social contract with the unions to limit wage rises at a time when inflation was running into double figures.

Perhaps this was because he had likened the *Life* to 'a snake pit' during an early meeting with senior staff on working arrangements, yet those he branded as 'asylum lunatics' were the same people who had impressed Monty Court as the sort 'who would have gone over the top for the *Sporting Life*'. Admittedly, there had been some shuffling of the pack in the interim. Mark Popham had left in 1988 to start up his own *Racenews* agency, but his name was as prominent as ever in the paper as he kept it supplied with news stories right up to the end.

Sue Montgomery had, providentially for her, bailed out before her ex-husband made his appearance as MGN chief executive. A gifted writer, but a contrary madam at times, she made the bold decision to go freelance in 1989 after a final fall-out with the pedantic chief sub, Noel Blunt, who threw a wire in-tray at her and missed. Two years later, Blunt retired on health grounds, while several others joined what became known as the 'Britvic Club' by opting to take early retirement after journalists aged 55 and over were encouraged to take advantage of a new severance scheme brought in by Maxwell.

The loss of Dave Cox – the heartbeat of the paper – to cancer at the tragically early age of 45 in 1992 had left a huge gap in the ranks, while in the same year Sir David Llewellyn penned his last article – his own obituary. In paying tribute to 'Jack Logan', the Queen's former trainer, Dick Hern, gave a brief but weighty endorsement to the 'Court Circular' column that moved in to fill Llewellyn's traditional Friday spot: "Monty Court can be trusted to look after the interests of the small men," he declared.

The multi-talented David Ashforth took over Court's Saturday slot with his witty, idiosyncratic blend of irreverent observations and lucid comments on the latest contentious issues. On the same day, the jockey Richard Fox (through his agent, John Karter of the *Sunday Times*) gave readers a humorous insight into the lives of his weighing room colleagues and his own incident-packed career which had come to a jarring halt when he shattered a thigh in a fall at Salisbury in 1992.

Other regular columnists included Tony Fairbairn who, freed from his obligation to his former masters at Portman Square in his previous incarnation as 'Charles Croft', started the week with an enlightened critique on the topics of the day from which the Jockey Club was not spared – 'Jack Logan' would have been proud of him.

On Tuesday, Sir Clement Freud, grandson of Sigmund; former apprentice chef at the Dorchester; ex-dog food advertiser and Liberal MP, supplied a gossipy piece on his latest adventures (often gastronomic and gratis) that was usually sautéed with his dry, dejected wit, but occasionally as rambling and stale as a dissertation on British Rail sandwiches that once took up so much space, a report from York's Ebor meeting had to be cut by half.

Wednesday was the turn of John Sexton, racing editor of the *Wolverhampton Express and Star*, with his mix of amusing anecdotes and in-depth analysis of current affairs, while in the *Greyhound Life*, the popular Harry Lloyd supplied "a fearless and witty offering which not only stood up for the grass-roots workers in the industry, but also pulled the rug away from the authorities whenever he felt it appropriate."[1]

Ian Carnaby, the Damon Runyon of the *Life*, was a Thursday delight. His highly individualistic column, often hilarious and brimming with homespun philosophy, was full of weird and wonderful tales gleaned from the landlords, rustics and gamblers he met in pubs, at racecourses or on the 4.25am from Paddington when returning home after an appalling/exhilarating night on the casino tables.

Much of his writing was done on his train journeys to and from Bristol Temple Meads when he would often punctuate his advice to fellow commuters and punters with incisive little anecdotes as he did in the space of a few paragraphs in May 1996:

Incidentally, if you are of a mind to get down to some hard graft on the rattler and need plenty of space, I recommend carrying a few empty miniatures of Smirnoff vodka. Spread them around on one of those foldaway tables, dangle your binoculars from the little red knob in front and you will find that no one takes the seat alongside you. Even on very busy mornings…

At Swindon, a black man in a black hat got on. He had black hair, a black suit, black shirt and black tie. When the trolley came along, he asked for a black coffee. And the girl said: 'No, really?' Which went totally unremarked by the other passengers, but I thought it was great…

When it rains in the South and West, and Goodwood and Salisbury race on the same day, you could lose everything, I suppose. Especially if you knew nothing about the draw. Official form publications fall short in terms of emphasis, I feel. 'When the going is soft, low numbers may have an advantage'. May? MAY? When the going is soft, rest assured the little chaps in brightly-coloured clothing will piss off over to the stands side and do their level best from there. Tell it like it is.

Carnaby could always be relied on to 'tell it like it is'. A former trainee with the Jockey Club before becoming a wines and spirits salesman in London during the 1970s, he also wrote the occasional feature article and compiled a valuable four-page review of Turf events at the end of each year as well as contributing a column on spread betting when that form of high-risk, intoxicating gambling came into vogue in 1994.

In addition to the weekly line-up of columnists who included all the usual regional and foreign reporters (Alan Shuback had, by now, taken over from Joe Hirsch as American correspondent), the paper also carried its full quota of lively and informative interviews and profiles.

New contributors included Malcolm Heyhoe of the *Weekender* and Andrew Sim who was to develop into an intrepid investigative reporter for the *Life* as he exposed such unsavoury characters as Ron Dawson, who ripped off thousands of racing enthusiasts with his ill-starred Classic Bloodstock owners' club, before he was warned off by the Jockey Club and eventually jailed for fraud. Freelancers such as Colin Cameron and Colin Fleetwood-Jones, late of the *Daily Star* and *Daily Sketch*, also weighed in with an abundance of colourful feature articles.

It was difficult to see how Tom Clarke was going to improve on such a line-up particularly as he had a limited knowledge of racing, but this didn't stop him sending out a stream of memos couched in a fussy, schoolmasterly style that was hardly designed to win him the respect of seasoned journalists who knew the game, and the paper, inside out.

His initial missive – "From time to time, I will be issuing instructions on style to help us improve the quality and consistency of our writing" – contained a list of finical dos and don'ts along the lines of: "Don't waste words. 'Golden Bear Jack Nicklaus rose from his slumbers to grab a share of the early lead…' is wrong on two counts: 'Golden Bear' is unnecessary; and 'take' would have been better than 'grab'."

A month later, staff were instructed to use the third person singular when referring to bodies such as the Jockey Club, Channel 4, etc, but to "follow normal usage in other areas: 'Manchester is the birthplace of Fred Bloggs', but 'Manchester United are the champions'." Which was useful to know!

As the memos became progressively more bizarre, reporters were assigned the task of assessing racecourses on the state of their toilets. "I'd like you to have a look at the loos in Members', in Tatts, and in the cheapest enclosure. Give each loo stars out of five: five for excellent, four for good, three for adequate, two for bad, and one for (if you'll pardon the expression) piss poor!"

This was all good and well when it came to inspecting the gents, but for an all-male outside staff it posed some decidedly tricky problems in checking out the ladies!

Perhaps fortunately, the stars never appeared because, as with many of his directives, Clarke never followed them up, while his desire to 'improve the quality and consistency of our writing' was consistently undermined under his very nose.

One particular sub-editor routinely destroyed the flow and sense of reports by rewriting them in a form of ungrammatical English only he understood. No matter how many complaints were made to the 'chair' or the chief sub, they brought only a temporary respite before the offender was allowed to lapse back into his old habits. Yet, despite alienating staff with his supercilious ways, Tom Clarke confounded his critics by doing exactly what he said he would do – during his first three years, he *did* improve the paper.

His claim that the *Life* was "a very tired newspaper" when he joined it may not have said much for its news-driven editor-in-chief or Alastair Down's team of inspired reporters, but there was no denying his commitment to the task at hand. He was in at 10 o'clock every morning and saw the first edition away at 9 o'clock at night; a work schedule that put his predecessor in the shade.

Astonished to find that neither Gallemore nor Court had held editorial conferences, he introduced them on a twice-daily basis: "We met every morning to talk about what we were going to do and then in late afternoon to discuss what had happened during the day so that departmental heads and their deputies had a clear outline of the paper we were producing and what we were planning for the days ahead."

Clarke was also strong on layouts. He prided himself at having redesigned the racing pages at the *Mail* "to make them more sensible" and the racecards at *The Times* "to make it a proper racing page". He reintroduced Graham Taylor's innovation of splitting race reports into two parts. This benefited readers and reporters alike as a meeting would often throw up more than one story that was capable of standing on its own, although there were times – chiefly at northern Flat meetings – when a succession of Arab-owned, Newmarket-trained winners accompanied only by their lads made the task of making bricks without straw seem like child's play.

The serialisation of extracts from new books was also high on his agenda. In his first year no fewer than five books were featured including *Horsetrader*, the story of the escalating duel between the Robert Sangster-John Magnier-Vincent O'Brien triumvirate and the Sheikhs for the world's best bloodstock. The extracts ran over seven days after their appearance in the paper had been advertised on TV at considerable cost to MGN.

But above all, Clarke's grand passion was for columnists and in his first year he pulled off a major coup when he signed up the then five times champion NH trainer Martin Pipe to write a Saturday column (with David Ashforth) during the winter, and when the Flat season started in 1994, he enlisted Henry Cecil (with Tony Elves) and Mark Johnston (with his own laptop) to air their views on alternate Saturdays.

The columns were an education and provided readers with an insight into each man's training methods, a running diary on the myriad problems they and their horses faced, and the opportunity to glean first hand information on the chances of their runners – straight from the horse's mouth, as it were.

For the trainers, it was an opportunity to have their say on matters they felt were important to racing and their profession, and there was plenty of constructive criticism on such contentious issues as the Jockey Club's clampdown on the use (or misuse) of the whip and an increasingly overcrowded fixture list.

While Pipe and Johnston remained regular contributors to the bitter end with the latter, in particular, relishing the chance of getting on his soapbox to cut through bureaucratic nonsense with a laser-like logic, other members of the profession flitted in and out of the *Life* with their thought-provoking observations as the editor extended seasonal invitations to such as Paul Nicholls, Kim Bailey and Gay Kelleway.

In the space of three weeks during the spring of 1995, five more new columnists made their appearance – the Newmarket and Lambourn trainers Michael Bell and John Hills; Jason Weaver, "Britain's brightest young jockey with the inside stories" (as told to his agent, *Life* journalist Terry Norman); Graham Cunningham (who had recently joined the paper from *Timeform*), with his 'Running Report', "which puts the most significant performances of the week under the spotlight", and the BBC radio and TV presenter Clare Balding with her Sunday 'Racegoers Guide', a light-hearted column designed to enlighten novices on the terminology and workings of the Turf.

In 1996, the shrewd racing brain and business intellect of Peter Savill was harnessed to the team. A man with radical views, Savill had incensed traditionalists the previous year when he bypassed the Derby with his Celtic Swing and went instead for the Prix du Jockey Club. Tony Morris in the *Racing Post* famously condemned the decision under the headline 'Sad, Mad, Bad' yet it proved to be precisely the right one.

Unknown to anyone at the time, Celtic Swing was already on the verge of breaking down when he won the French race. Epsom's roller-coaster crucible would almost certainly have finished him as it did his Guineas conqueror, Pennekamp, but as it was he lasted out to the Irish Derby, which effectively ended his racing career.

Savill, an owner since 1975, had 50 horses cannily spread among 16 trainers when he introduced himself to readers with the declaration: "I shall be touching on issues of topical interest as well as expressing my views on some of the more fundamental problems which confront the racing industry." And this he did with some force, as when he argued for a late-entry stage for *all* the top English races:

> The French, Irish and Germans all have a consistent system of supplementary entries which allow a horse to be entered within three to six days of the race at a fee that approximates to the prize-money on offer for fourth place. What is the British system? There is no system. You can supplement for the St Leger and the Oaks, but not for the Derby, the Two Thousand Guineas or the One Thousand Guineas; for the Epsom Oaks but not the Yorkshire Oaks; for the Champion Stakes and the Eclipse but not for the Juddmonte, the Coronation Cup or the King George VI and Queen Elizabeth Stakes; for the July Cup but not the King's Stand, the Nunthorpe or the Haydock Sprint Cup...

And so on for another ten races before he lamented: "If ever anyone wanted ammunition to say the right hand doesn't appear to know what the left hand is doing in British racing, they need to look no further than this mess." The solution, he concluded, was simple – adopt the Irish system.*

Savill used his column to good effect and quickly became a motive force in racing after he was first elected president of the ROA in 1997 and then as chairman of the BHB on the very day the *Life* appeared for the last time.

While the proliferation of big-name columnists approached overkill, some talented youngsters

---

* A uniform system of supplementary entries was eventually introduced for all Group 1 races in 2004, but it is still left to individual racecourses to decide whether to allow a late entry stage for their Group 2 races.

were also recruited onto the paper such as Chris McGrath who, shortly after joining as a news reporter cum feature writer in 1993, won the Martin Wills award for the best racing article written by an under 26-year-old.

Another to make an immediate impact was Mark Winstanley who devised his 'Beat the Book' column with one purpose in mind – "to take the bookies' trousers down as often as possible". Written in a uniquely demotic style with a liberal sprinkling of rhyming slang – 'Fanny Cradock' = paddock; 'Rod Laver' = saver; 'Wilson Pickett' = ticket; 'eau de cologne' = phone, etc. – the column pinpointed the value-for-money bet at the five-day stage of ante-post races and was followed up on Saturdays and during televised mid-week meetings with selections for two or three other races.

His debut selection for the 1993 Cesarewitch: "Aahsaylad cannot be out of the first four and five points each way at 14-1 is the recommended stake" duly obliged, and two weeks later he announced: "The Tote have given us an early Christmas present by offering 20-1 about Triple Witching," for that firm's sponsored handicap hurdle at Chepstow.

His selection sparked a nationwide gamble on the gelding who, having his first race for 18 months, came home a comfortable 17-2 winner to put 'The Couch' (as in potato) 213 points up, and four months later he had more than doubled that profit as he continued to debag the bookies with indecent enthusiasm.

On the same day – 19 February 1994 – as Winstanley increased his profit to an amazing 436 points, the *Life* bade a fond farewell to Orbit House and 'the Stab' as it and the group's other titles moved into One Canada Square; the 800ft, 50-storey Canary Wharf Tower on the Isle of Dogs in the heart of London's docklands.

The bright, airy offices on the 23rd floor, which the paper shared with *The People*, offered an impressive view of the city and fitted in well with Tom Clarke's vision of the future: "Our great plus there was that we could take advantage of all the state-of-the-art technology the *Mirror* had invested in; it was one of the benefits of working within a big organisation, which we wouldn't have had as a single paper."

On the minus side, state-of-the-art technology didn't fit in with the *Life's* extensive news cuttings library at Orbit House and on the eve of the move a large amount of valuable archive material dating back to the early 1920s was thrown into skips in a *Mirror*-orchestrated clear-out that was akin to book-burning. It was a sign of the times, and the times they were a-changing both at the *Life* and in racing.

Soon after the move to Canary Wharf, the popular general manager, Peter Robins, retired and was replaced by the equally unpopular David Annat. Robins, who had joined the *Life* from Odhams book division, had the respect of everyone and had been highly regarded by such as Mike Gallemore: "Peter was the best manager any paper could possibly have. He did a fantastic job and came up with ideas for books, supplements, promotional stuff and things we could do with the bookmakers."

David Annat, who had a background in marketing kitchen-appliances and electrical goods, knew little about racing and even less about newspapers although Clarke considers this was an advantage: "He brought in a breath of fresh air, a more dynamic style and new thinking. He had quite good commercial ideas like getting more copies into the motorway service stations."

Alastair Down, who had by this time finally been persuaded that his future lay in writing not editing, provides a different take on the man and one more in line with the consensus of the office: "I thought David Annat had an amazingly damaging and destabilising influence on the place because he neither understood nor cared; he particularly didn't care about the people working there. A frightful man, out of his depth and thoroughly unpleasant with it; he had the distinction of having the respect of nobody."*

The move to Docklands seemed to epitomise the changing world for Down: "The *Life* used to be an enjoyable and stimulating place to work; it was the era of the enlightened amateur who did his work in a professional way, but the joy drained out of it somewhere along the line. The atmosphere at Canary Wharf was much more fraught and it all got messy and recriminatory in the end. One of the problems was that you were spending a lot of your time guarding your back; time you should have been putting into the paper was spent on office politics and that was diversionary and difficult."

There had been political changes in racing too. The summer of 1993 had seen the end to almost 250 years of Jockey Club rule when it handed over most of its powers to the new and more representative British Horseracing Board that had been set up under the chairmanship of the senior steward, Lord Hartington.

One of the first responsibilities taken on by the new authority was to tailor the ever-expanding fixture list to the needs of the betting shops which, from April that year, were allowed to stay open for evening racing. By December, Wolverhampton was racing under floodlights and in 1994 the Commons voted by an overwhelming majority of 101 (290 to 189) to allow betting on Sundays and so paved the way for the first Sunday meetings with on and off-course betting to be held the following year.

It was a momentous breakthrough, but coupled with the introduction of a summer jumping programme in 1995, the glut of non-stop racing had become what that noted racehorse owner, Sir Winston Churchill, would have called 'animated roulette' and what 'Augur' had warned against when he wrote:

> The Jockey Club may some day find it necessary to introduce a measure limiting the number of meetings which shall be held within the space of one week. At the present moment no one can doubt that racing is dreadfully overdone in all parts of the country. Even the most popular of pastimes must suffer or languish when there is such a plethora of sport. Since Monday there have been twelve days of racing crammed into five, and all have suffered more or less, as the insignificant fields and scanty attendances prove.

That, of course, was Harry Feist writing in July 1872. A more recent shot across the bows had come from Tony Fairbairn in March 1994 when he produced a special report to show that the policy of the race-planning department was in danger of killing the goose that laid the golden eggs – if it had not already done so. With an accompanying graph to illustrate the dramatic fall in racecourse attendances as the number of meetings had increased to provide cannon fodder for the betting shops, he declared:

> The fixture list is the key to racing's prosperity, and the shambles which has been allowed to develop over the past decade or more has been responsible for more profligate spending of racing's limited financial resources than anything else.

* To be fair, Annat's input extended to the development of the *Sporting Life*'s hugely successful internet site launched in conjunction with the Press Association at the end of 1996. The biggest database of sports and betting information in Europe, it quickly became the No. 1 sports site in the UK and the second most popular site overall with almost 20 million hits in June 1997 and 3 million pages accessed.

The initial scheme to maximise the Levy through a balanced fixture list of at least two meetings a day had helped to restore racing's fortunes in the 1970s, but things had got hopelessly out of hand since then and now there were plans for two meetings a night together with a welter of afternoon fixtures. As Phil Bull argued *ad nauseam* there is only a finite amount of money available for betting and once that is exhausted no amount of additional fixtures – which inevitably spread the Levy Board's prize money allocation ever thinner – will bring any more money into the betting shops or racing.

There had to be a sensible balance between the needs of the racing and betting industries and as a record number of 1,175 meetings began to take its toll in 1996, an exasperated Henry Cecil used his column to rebuke David Oldrey, the chairman of the race-planning committee, for sacrificing racing to the demands of the bookmakers.

> The powers-that-be fail to take notice of other professionals in the industry and they seem to be blind to the damage they are causing with their programme. A leading handicapper told me at Goodwood this week that he felt there was too much racing and too many low-grade handicaps for horses who, in his opinion, should not be racing…
>
> The authorities are gradually weakening and bringing down our industry. It's about time they opened their eyes and got their act together … *There is so much racing that a number of jockeys admit they are travelling and riding so much they are permanently tired and near exhaustion. What a dreadful state of affairs. Something must be done before we lose so much.*[2] *

This *cri de coeur* prompted Tom Clarke to instigate a survey on the subject and after Roy Briggs and David Lawrence had polled 60 Flat trainers, the results showed that 53% of them sided with Cecil against 37% who felt the race-planning department was doing a good job, while 10% had no opinion either way.

The Lambourn trainer Barry Hills, who had resigned from the NTF over the issue in 1995, was unambiguous:

> There is far too much racing, especially bad racing, and it all seems to have been put on because the bookmakers wanted it … I am not alone in my views, but what is so ridiculous is that no one in authority appears to be listening. If we are continually ignored I dread to think how it will all end.

But up north where life was hard, Chris Thornton contended:

> There cannot be too many opportunities to exploit, and trainers who say David Oldrey is not doing a good job are off their trolley … Trainers as a body are the last people to take notice of, they have a terrible track record. Just look at some of the innovations they fought tooth and nail against in the past.

Citing starting stalls and the five-day entry system which replaced three-week entries as examples,

---

* There are none so blind as those who will not see. It was not until 2008, when the number of fixtures had soared to 1,504, that the authorities (the BHB had by then become the Horseracing Regulatory Authority) finally took steps to curb the situation they had created. Races for horses rated 45 and below were limited, while jockeys were restricted to riding at a maximum of nine meetings a week, but by then racing *had* lost so much.

Thornton had his supporters in the south, most notably Peter Walwyn who was typically outspoken:

> I've read more rubbish about race planning recently than I've seen in the last 35 years ... I'm afraid that 80 per cent of the horses are very ordinary and you cannot help that. In the old days you could sell bad horses abroad, but you can't sell them now. You can't give them away so they will go on winning races in their class.

What was undeniable was that more racing equalled more mediocrity and more mediocrity meant a gradual drift of punter-interest into other sports. To accommodate this growing trend, Clarke bolstered the sports-betting section by signing up the 1975 England international, Chelsea, Arsenal and Stoke City midfielder, Alan Hudson to air his forthright views on the game from the start of the 1995/96 season.*

Not that the *Life's* editorial staff needed outside help to pick the winners. Jeremy Chapman was, as ever, in cracking form on the world's golfing circuit. In one weekend in April 1994, his recommended each-way bets on Ben Crenshaw (40-1) and Jose-Maria Olazabal (20-1) for the Freeport-McMoRan Classic in New Orleans, saw Crenshaw winning by three shots from Olazabal, while at the same time he picked out Stephen Ames at 66-1 to win the Lyon Open.

A year later his staking plans included Mark James, the 25-1 winner of the Morocco Open, on the same weekend as he went for Mark O'Meara (50-1) to land the Honda Classic in Florida. And he headlined O'Meara again at 40-1 when the American won the Mercedes Golf Championship in January 1996. Little wonder the legendary Hugh McIlvanney wrote of Chapman: "[He] has had enough extraordinary success in the game's betting market to make most of the other professional forecasters seem the equivalent of municipal course hackers."[3]

Sports betting had come a long way since Chapman's early days on the *Life* when he persuaded Ossie Fletcher to have the paper on sale at the Open Championship. It proved a salutary lesson for both men when only one copy was sold. Now the medium was a major part of the betting market. In April 1996 a puff for some of the previous autumn's headline tips that had recently hit the jackpot included: '66-1 Sri Lanka a massive price' for the Cricket World Cup; 'Sunderland too good to miss at 33-1' for the First Division championship, and '16-1 Villa can be Cola kings', for the Coca-Cola Cup.

These bookie-busters were matched on the racing side with Jon Freeman ('Northern View') winning the winter naps table in 1995 and Nigel Shields (NH 'Form'), following up two years later, while Frank Carter ('Augur'), Howard Parker (Flat 'Form') and Dave Edwards ('Stop Watch') regularly sifted out long-priced winners. But despite all the tipping successes, the mass of columnists and some of the best writers and reporters in the business, the paper was gradually losing ground to the *Racing Post*.

As many of the *Life's* old readers drifted off to the graveyard, Clarke tried to attract a younger audience by launching a Fantasy Racing competition with the prize of owning a two-year-old for the season, but it only covered a six-week period each year and was no match for the *Post's* Tote-sponsored Ten-to-Follow competitions which ran throughout the year taking in both the Flat and jump seasons and offering prizes of up to £250,000.

---

* In December 1997, Hudson was seriously injured when knocked down by a car, but he battled his way back from the brink with the tenacity of a man who had already overcome alcoholism and bankruptcy and resumed his column three months later, writing it from his hospital bed.

The editor also tried to tap into a new generation of racegoers by staging on-course *Sporting Life* Road Shows on Sundays when a prominent trainer and jockey would run through the card with the reporter covering the meeting, but it was all to no avail and in the end the irony was that he tried too hard.

As the *Life's* circulation slipped from the low 70,000s into the 60,000s as the *Post's* crept up from the mid-40,000s into the 50,000s, he and Charlie Wilson decided to reformat the paper. It was to prove a classic example of the road to hell being paved with good intentions or, in this case, a lamentable lack of foresight.

THE FINAL NAIL

THE FIRST SIGN of the impending doom that was to overtake the *Life* appeared on 28 May 1996 when a cryptic front-page flyer announced "Watch out for RF Day in *The Sporting Life* next week". Readers were none the wiser the following day when they were informed "It's a week to RF Day in *The Sporting Life*".

The countdown continued with "It's just 6 days to RF Day in *The Sporting Life* – the day you've been asking for," and so on up to the fateful "It's RF Day" issue of June 5 when it transpired that RF stood for 'Reader-Friendly' as the paper proclaimed:

> It's the day when racing's greatest daily has a new reader-friendly layout – whether you're reading your *Life* at home, in the betting shop or on the racecourse. We are confident you will give it the thumbs-up, as it will take you a lot less time to find exactly what you're looking for.
>
> Each racecard will have its form, analysis and statistics on consecutive pages ... Every day the paper will have two equal sections; the principal race meeting will always be in the middle of Section I; the No. 2 meeting will always be in the middle of Section II. *The Greyhound Life*, complete with cards and reports, will always be at the back of Section II. Sports Betting will always be at the back of Section I. The Marker Sheet will be on page 2 of Section II. Augur (Frank Carter), our flagship tipster, will be on page one of Section II.
>
> We believe the changes make racing's biggest-selling paper the best laid-out, as well as the best informed. Enjoy Reader Friendly Day and judge for yourself.

All that was missing was a map and a compass! Racing folk are a conservative lot by nature and had become used to the idiosyncratic layout of the paper. They might have moaned about it, but in the main they were prepared to tolerate it and, significantly, not one letter praising the new RF format ever appeared in the paper, but the scrapping of the *Greyhound Life* pull-out section was condemned by all.

Its editor, Bob Betts, who had argued vehemently against the changes, recalls the office was inundated with angry phone calls from both readers and bookmakers: "The phones never stopped ringing. Geoff Ballard and his messengers spent all day, and for many days afterwards, fielding a torrent of complaints, some of them pretty abusive."

Bookmakers, in particular, were outraged by the changes. It was immediately apparent to them that whatever else the RF *Life* was, it most assuredly was not a BF *Life* unless the initials applied to the men who had thought it up. Up until that fateful Wednesday the layout of the paper had catered for the needs of the bookmakers whose betting shops accounted for about a third of its sales.

Whenever possible, racecards and form were designed to run across the same sheet of newsprint so they could be pinned up on the walls of the country's 8,700 betting shops for the benefit of punters. If this was not possible, cards and form would be on consecutive pages provided they did not back onto each other.

This format became increasingly difficult to achieve as the fixture list grew year-by-year, but with careful planning the layout could usually be tailored so that form for an afternoon meeting would back onto that for an evening meeting and all the betting shop staff had to do was reverse the pages once the afternoon racing had finished.

The so-called 'Reader-Friendly' *Life* changed all that overnight as the tried and tested layout that had served the paper well enough since the legalisation of betting shops in 1961, was discarded at a stroke. Shop managers found the new design bad enough during the week, but on Saturdays, with six or seven meetings to deal with, it took them up to an hour to slice up the multiple copies of the paper they needed, cut out the adverts of rival firms and pin up the whole complex jigsaw of pages on the walls.

The idea of restructuring the paper had come from Charlie Wilson whose Mirror Group responsibilities had increased with each succeeding year as his considerable energies were diverted away from the parochial world of the *Sporting Life*. In 1991 he had been made editorial director of the group and its managing director the following year.

His workload was further increased in November 1995 when he was appointed editor of *The Independent* (then part-owned by MGN) for a finite period of six months during which time he selected the paper's former political correspondent, Andrew Marr, to succeed him when he returned to his duties as MD of MGN.

By now his role as editor-in-chief of the *Life* was largely a nominal one, yet it was during this period that he implemented his plans for the radical redesign of the paper, a move he defends to this day: "When I joined the *Sporting Life* I thought its architecture, the way it was put together, was not very reader-friendly. Its layout showed that the first and most important person was the bookmaker. The form was often a long way away from the racecard, it dodged around; there was no sense of continuity.

"In any decent newspaper there are certain things that are anchored, but the only thing that was anchored on the *Life* was the mid-spread racecard – the principal meeting of the day – and I objected to bookmakers telling publishers how they should run their newspapers."

Any concession to the layers went against the grain of Wilson's combative nature. An enthusiastic punter, he didn't like losing money to them any more than he did having them tell him how he should plan his paper, and Clarke backed him to the hilt on this issue: "We had been under enormous pressure from the bookmakers – William Hill in particular – to provide special pages for betting shop display. Heavyweight missions had been round to the office at Orbit House and to Canary Wharf. They wanted something they could pin up on their walls without having to buy multiple copies of the paper, but our readers had to come first and one of my key missions was to go out and meet them at the races.

"Their great criticism of the *Life* was that they couldn't find their way around it. They wanted the paper in better order, something I had been concerned about from the beginning. The bookmakers did provide most of our advertising revenue, but the *Life* shouldn't have been hanging on their coat tails and I'm very proud to say we didn't although we respected them and their importance to the newspaper."

For those who believed in omens – bad ones – the first issue of the redesigned *Life* proved a portent of things to come. For one, it carried an advertisement for what was to prove the last edition of *Ruff's Guide to the Turf* (est. 1842) which had become a weighty and expensive £40 tome containing "1,472 pages full of Facts, Features, Statistics and Bloodstock. Including *The Sporting Life* Who's Who In Racing."

The paper also had a picture of a sad-faced Michael Williams being honoured at a function where he received a cheque from appreciative bookmakers in recognition of all he had done to promote point-to-point racing. Williams had been reporting on the sport for over 40 years for the *Life*, but at the start of that season he had been unceremoniously demoted by Clarke, who just happened to be standing besides him grinning broadly and Blairishly.

Michael Williams is honoured at the Point-to-Point Owners & Riders Association luncheon at Stratford in 1996 – a few months after he had been demoted by Tom Clarke (on his left).

In truth, he had little to smile about. He had just presided over a move that would see the *Life's* sales plunge by 30 per cent over the next 12 months, while his treatment of Michael Williams was well known at the gathering (the Point-to-point Owners & Riders Association awards luncheon) and was generally deplored.

Jonathan Neesom, who had started to cover Sunday point-to-points for the *Life* when they were introduced in 1995, had been told by Alastair Down that summer that Clarke wanted him to take over as chief correspondent the following season, but Williams was left in the dark about it all, a fact that still rankles Neesom, who was accused by some of effecting a coup when he hadn't.

"Clarke treated Williams disgracefully by not telling him he was being sidelined until a week before the 1996 season started, and then telling him by way of a three-line letter saying, in effect, 'as from this year you will be required to report on only one meeting a week'. For months he had been promising to break it to him gently by taking him out to lunch and telling him what a marvellous job he had done for the *Life*, but he never did."

Even Down, who got on well with Clarke and defended him against his critics, drew the line at this point: "I thought Michael Williams was shamefully treated. He was an institution in the point-to-point world and a fascinating man, a lovely human being, one of the old school. Given his length of service and his devotion to the *Life* he was treated with monumental shabbiness and he was deeply hurt."

Clarke, however, is unrepentant: "Michael Williams could have been doing the job for 50 or 60 years, the time was there for a change. Dismissing somebody is always brutal. I've done it very rarely, but it has to be. It's a tough life."

Things were certainly about to get tough for the *Sporting Life*. The bookmakers were up in arms and John Brown, managing director of William Hills, was the first to demand a meeting with the editor, but his pleas for mutual co-operation fell on deaf ears: "Tom Clarke did say he would make some changes to the new layout, but they were cosmetic, they really didn't do anything – the general message was take it or leave it, if you don't like it you will have to put up with it."

In the leafy suburbs of Purley, south London, Monty Court was dismayed by the new format: "The *Life's* pages were always designed to be taken apart and pinned up on betting shop walls. Unfortunately it was a prisoner of that situation, but you could still produce a bloody good newspaper and accommodate the bookmakers' needs, and that was what we had been doing – you don't have to chuck out the baby and the bathwater."

For a time there was talk of the bookmakers bringing out their own paper as in the days of old, but in the event they didn't need to. The Reader-Friendly *Life* had at once astonished and delighted the management at the *Racing Post*. Its chief executive, Michael Harris, and director Brough Scott could not believe their eyes, or their luck.

They immediately realised that in alienating the bookmakers the *Life* had thrown away its trump card and left the door open for them to take advantage of a monumental blunder. From the start their paper had been racking up huge losses – up to that point it was estimated it had cost Sheikh Mohammed £40m – but now it seemed as if Allah had served up their rival's head on a plate.

Work quickly started on designing a one-sided, broadsheet betting shop edition containing just racecards and form, and a few weeks later Harris was able to take a mock-up of it to show John Brown at Hills. It was exactly what Brown had always wanted and with his backing Harris then took his prototype to Ladbrokes and Corals where it was received with equal enthusiasm.

Meanwhile, as news of the *Post's* outflanking manoeuvre began to filter through to a stupefied management at the *Life*, hurried plans were now made to accommodate the bookmakers' every wish, but by then their horse had bolted to the greener pastures of Raynes Park where a three-year contract was signed between the 'Big Three' and the *Post*. It was a contract that was to prove a death warrant for the *Life*.

Harris, who had built up the *Pacemaker* magazine into a publication of international renown during the 1970s before taking over from Graham Rock as editor of the *Post* in 1988, felt he had pulled off the publishing coup of a lifetime. "The deal was done on the basis that each betting shop that took our display sheet had also to take a *Racing Post* and almost overnight we were able to turn around our 40/60 market share with the *Life*.

"The fact that the display sheet was hugely expensive to produce and distribute was not a primary concern. We had never been given any directive to save money and we initially launched it as a loss-leader because we knew it would change the market and drive the *Sporting Life* to the negotiating table, but the final outcome was not what we had anticipated."

It was on Thursday, 16 January 1997, that both papers announced the forthcoming launch of their betting shop editions. In promoting its "tailor-made paper for easy and exciting display in the shops," the *Life* patronisingly addressed the people it had outraged eight months earlier:

Calling All Bookmakers and Betting Shop Managers! Introducing TODAY *The Sporting Life* Betting Shop Edition! Yes! Your OWN paper, exclusively for you … Inside today's issue of *The Sporting Life* is a live example of the Betting Shop Edition – a pullout with all *The Life's* cards, colours, form and selections for SIS racing and greyhounds, plus the Marker Sheet, and it's printed on one side only for trouble-free presentation in the shops.

See how today's Betting Shop Edition covers the racing at Lingfield (printed twice because it's the main betting meeting), Ludlow and Taunton and the dogs at Crayford and Wimbledon – and we're confident you'll be looking forward to the start of the daily service next Monday.

On launch day, the *Post*, in seeking a feedback from the betting shops for its £1 edition, could not resist having a dig at its rival as it commented: "Unlike some recent converts to the idea of helping shop managers, the *Racing Post* is ALWAYS ready to listen and learn from its customers."

The *Life*, for its part, plugged its edition relentlessly for the next three weeks as it canvassed the views of more than 40 bookmakers or their representatives. Not surprisingly, after months of struggling with the RF *Life*, they were delighted with the special edition which was voted "a big improvement … well thought out, much needed and much appreciated" and even "absolutely marvellous – it is exactly what bookmakers have been screaming out for, for years".

More's the pity then that Messrs Clarke and Wilson had cocked a deaf 'un for all those years!

But as "staff and punters chorused their approval" of the *Life's* BSE there was one snag – the approval was coming from only the independent shops. The big three chains had, of course, the *Post's* edition on display and as they owned almost half of Britain's 8,700 shops there was much discontent among their punters who were used to studying the *Life's* form which was presented differently to the tabulated style favoured by its rival.

It was not long before the *Life* was running a 'Power to the Punters' campaign. "Is your shop Lifeless?" it asked. "If you're a punter, tell the manager you want to see *The Sporting Life* Betting Shop Edition on display – and remind him or her it's 35p a day cheaper than the rival paper." And under the heading 'Give us back our Life!' a succession of punters voiced their anger at having the *Post's* BSE foisted upon them.

David Willis, a regular at Ladbrokes' Westahope shop in Newcastle, had sent a 121-strong petition to that firm's head office. He protested: "Ladbrokes just sprang the situation of taking down *The Life* on us – there was no warning to punters, no consultation. I will not bet in the shop again until *The Life* is put back up on the walls. It's absolutely outrageous that customers are being overlooked. What other business would deny the customers what they want?"

Harry Shaw, a patron of Hills' branch in White Inch, Glasgow, was another petitioner who declared: "We all need *The Sporting Life* in order to stand any chance in this game and I am disgusted Hills are not displaying it. The form is more legible than anywhere else. Man on the Spot is more reliable than anyone else and the betting forecasts are the most accurate there are."

Barrister's clerk, Lee Kyprian, and a dozen other regulars even formed a picket outside Ladbrokes' Mile End Road branch in London, while an anonymous and harassed manager of a Hills' shop reported: "I have been swamped with complaints from punters because they don't have access to *The Life* in our shops. All I could tell them is that I don't know what is going on and how the situation happened in the first place."

There were, of course, people high up in the ivory tower of Canary Wharf, who knew full well 'how the situation happened', but their paper affected an air of surprise at the "astonishing decision to replace *The Life* with an unfamiliar and inferior (but more expensive) paper". To others in the know, the whole 'Power to the Punters' campaign reeked of hypocrisy and an attempt to cover up past incompetence.

During the first week of the BSEs, *The Times* carried a report by former *Sporting Life* journalist Julian Muscat on the battle between the two titles in which Tom Clarke was quoted as saying: "The *Post* has broken into territory we are proud of and prepared to fight for. In the short term they will gain some market share, it will be modest, but not substantial. In the long term our readers will have the final say. If enough of them complain the Big Three will have to act."[2]

He went on to describe Michael Harris's estimate that the *Life* could lose as many as 8,000 copies as a "worst-case scenario". In fact, the paper was to lose more than 20,000 copies as its average daily sales plummeted from the previous year's 67,751 to just 47,647 in 1997 – a massive 30 per cent fall.

By February, in the first full month of the BSEs, the circulation of the *Life* had dropped to 51,936 and four months later, for the first time in its relatively short history, the *Post* took over as market leader with sales of 52,418 compared to the *Life*'s 51,431. Then a remarkable further drop took place. Having seemingly stabilised at around 52,000 for the first half of the year, the *Life*'s circulation for July suddenly slumped to just 43,810.

This was an extraordinary fall-off in what had always been a high-peak month and while the *Post*'s sales also dropped to 48,385, its lead over its rival had increased from 1,000 copies to 4,500 copies.* But long before these disastrous figures came to light, Brigadier Michael Barclay, Sheikh Mohammed's corporate advisor in the UK, had entered into secret negations with David Montgomery over a possible merger.

Some years earlier Charlie Wilson, frustrated by the *Post*'s unwillingness to join with the *Life* in presenting a united front to the bookmakers, decided the way forward lay in either buying the Sheikh's paper or coming to some sort of arrangement with them.

"I went to see Sir Gordon Brunton, the chairman of the *Racing Post*, and we spent the day sounding each other out. They wanted to buy us and we wanted to buy them and it became clear at that stage, with the depthless wealth of the Arabs, they weren't interested in selling. They had started the paper so why the hell should they sell it?"

The situation in 1997 was very different. The *Life* had thrown away the one big advantage it had held over the *Post* – its dominance of the bookmakers' market – and the *Post* was now the top-selling paper, but while the Sheikh wanted out, he was fiercely proud of his newspaper and demanded that its title should be the one to survive. In the end an agreement was reached whereby MGN bought the *Post* for the less-than-princely sum of £1 with the all-important proviso that they would guarantee its publication for ten years and pay for the redundancies on both papers.

News of the deal shocked the board of the *Racing Post* who had been kept entirely in the dark during the negotiations, but so it was that on December 6 it was announced that the *Post* would become the principal racing paper and the *Life* would be developed as a general sports paper "to meet the demands of the ever-increasing public interest in sport".

This arrangement, it was added, "will protect and improve the economic viability of both the *Life* and the *Post*". Well, not quite! While it certainly improved the finances of the *Post*, it did not do much for the *Life*, which limped along for another five months before the *coup de grâce* was finally administered.

In the meantime, Charlie Wilson took his leave of the *Mirror* group in January 1998 – "Montgomery suggested I went," he says flatly – with a £608,000 pay-off plus a £38,000 bonus, an

---

* MGN's subsequent purchase of the *Racing Post* was subject to formal approval by the Board of Trade. This was given in February 1998 when the DTI ruled the acquisition did not have to go before the Monopolies and Mergers commission because the *Post*'s circulation was below 50,000, as it had been ever since June 1997, but the very next month, boosted by the Cheltenham Festival, it shot back up to 55,229.

award of 20,485 shares worth £49,574, and £79,500 paid into his pension scheme as a reward for having played a leading role in rebuilding that fund.[3]

Altogether a nice little earner that enabled him to concentrate on maintaining his country squire lifestyle in Leicestershire where he rode, yoicks, tally-ho, to hounds, while he devoted his energies to furthering the cause of the Countryside Alliance and attending meetings of the Jockey Club, to which he had been elected in 1993.

To this day he robustly denies the disastrous consequences of his decision to reformat the *Life* contributed to the paper's demise: "It was bugger all to do with the circulation of the *Life*, the figures could have been treble what they were and it wouldn't have made any difference. It was purely a commercial decision to keep the *Post* as the main racing paper and turn the *Life* to general sports.

"To Montgomery it didn't matter whether it was the *Racing Post*, the *Sporting Life* or the *Horseracing Gazette*, the title meant nothing, it was the monopoly that was the goal and what the profit for the next ten years would be from that monopoly. The only way Sheikh Mohammed and his organisation would concede a monopoly to us was that the *Racing Post* had to have it.*

"The cost of achieving the monopoly was the title of the *Sporting Life* and I was very sad about that because I thought the *Life* was a vocation. The people who worked on it loved the work they did; it was rather like the people who work in the National Health Service or for charities like the World Wildlife Fund. They work for lower wages than they could get elsewhere and that was massively true about the people on the *Life*.

"There was a huge amount of sentiment involved in the paper, more sentiment than any other publication I've had anything to do with. They'd fought a battle with the *Racing Post* for years, and it was a daily battle, and in the end they saw it as a defeat because one day the *Post* came out and the *Life* didn't so they had to look for a reason for that defeat.

"To say that I was the architect of its downfall is a terrible suggestion; didn't the editor of the paper have anything to do with it? It's the same as when our troops lost battles in the First World War, they always blamed the generals."

Ah yes! *That* War again, what was it they said about lions being led by donkeys?

---

* MGN, which merged with the Trinity Provincial group in 1999 to become Trinity Mirror, made the most out of the monopoly before selling on the *Racing Post* in October 2007 to FL Partners, an Irish investment group, for £170m (£10m of which went to racing charities at the request of Sheikh Mohammed who still owned the paper's title).

WHO'S A LIAR THEN?

AS THE *Life* teetered towards its sad but inevitable end it had one last battle left to fight. This time principles were at stake as it defended its right to expose what it saw as a fraud upon the public just as it had done so many years before when it was a fledgling penny journal struggling to make its mark in the sporting world.

In February 1860, the paper won 'The Great Libel Case' that had been brought against it by the notorious swindler 'Captain Barry'. In February 1998 it was 'The Great Top Cees Libel Case' that dominated the headlines after it had accused the north Yorkshire training team of Lynda and Jack Ramsden and their jockey, Kieren Fallon, of cheating.

There was an uncanny symmetry to the two cases and the articles written 138 years apart by the paper's editor Harry Feist and its associate editor Alastair Down. One appeared within the paper's first year of publication, the other in its last year; both were written with the aim of protecting the punter from unscrupulous dodges.

There had been other cases in between, of course. One of the biggest was decided in 1963 when the paper successfully defended itself against the great Australian jockey, Scobie Breasley; a lesser case in 1980 was lost to the Newmarket trainer Jeremy Hindley and his jockey, Tony Kimberley.

A libel action can result from a few careless words dashed off by a reporter struggling to meet his deadline or from a carefully considered article written in the knowledge that a law suit is likely to follow. Such was the comment piece 'Contempt for the punter' penned by Down after Top Cees, trained by Lynda Ramsden and shrewdly placed by her husband, Jack, won the 1995 Chester Cup in the hands of Kieren Fallon.

At the time, the performances of the Ramsdens' horses had been catching the eye not only of *Sporting Life* journalists, but also of the racecourse stewards and there had been several high-profile inquiries, two of which had resulted in Mrs Ramsden being fined over the running of her horses, Rafferty's Rules and Captain Carat.

Prior to his Chester Cup victory, Top Cees had been the subject of two such inquiries. The first, in December 1994 when he finished third in a handicap hurdle at Edinburgh ridden by Russ Garritty, had resulted in the local stewards referring the matter to the Jockey Club stewards who cleared both trainer and jockey at their subsequent inquiry.

Four months later, the running of Top Cees was questioned again after he had finished fifth in the Swaffham Handicap at Newmarket. On that occasion the stewards accepted the explanation that the horse had to be held up and Fallon could not get a clear run when he wanted it. The following day, the jockey admitted in a Channel 4 TV interview that he had ridden a poor race and had overdone the waiting tactics.

Three weeks later, Fallon gave Top Cees a much more positive ride to win the Chester Cup in decisive fashion. The race had been watched on television in the *Life's* offices by Alastair Down and Tom Clarke and, as one, they decided the time had come to speak out, and this the former did to some effect in a comment piece that began:

Pity the poor punters. If proof were ever needed that their interests are still treated with contempt, it came yesterday with the seedy and deeply unpopular victory of Top Cees in the Chester Cup …

It was one of those rare occasions on a British racecourse when the stench of being short-changed was so palpable that it goaded even the poor put-upon British punter into a genuine display of anger.

In referring to the horse's previous run in the Swaffham Handicap, Down dispensed with such woolly euphemisms as 'tenderly handled' by stating: "It was perceived by virtually all observers that the horse was 'not off' or, to put it in plain English, cheating." He went on to criticise the Chester stewards for not holding an inquiry into the horse's improved performance and concluded:

Will someone please tell those in authority in this game that the inaction over Top Cees is sending punters pretty scantily clad into the betting shop and that those who have caught a cold may not want to return for a dose of pneumonia.

The writ that followed took its time. Jack Ramsden spent ten weeks weighing up the pros and cons of exposure in open court before he instructed his solicitors to act, and it was a further two and a half years before the case was heard. In that time the Ramsdens had shrewdly obtained the services of Patrick Milmo QC to represent them and Fallon.

Milmo was a keen follower of racing and had acted for the Jockey Club on several occasions, most notably when defending its right to disqualify the Aga Khan's 1989 Oaks winner, Aliysa, after she had failed a dope test. He had also been hired by the Club to question those involved in a so-called jockeys' strike at Haydock in October 1996 when 21 jockeys refused to ride in a race after complaining the course was unsafe.

In commenting on the Haydock case, the prescient Monty Court had observed that Milmo had "an impressive record against some doughty opponents in a variety of high-profile civil and libel cases ranging from allegations of cheating on golf courses to cases involving commercial giants."

On 3 February 1998, Milmo set out to add to that record as he delivered his opening address before the Hon. Mr Justice Morland and a jury of seven men and five women at the High Courts of Justice in the Strand. His clients, he said, claimed substantial damages for being branded 'cheats' by the *Sporting Life*. They had been "ferociously attacked" and subjected to a "savage verbal onslaught" in the article 'Contempt for the punter', which "was full of venom and emotive language aimed at arousing maximum public hostility towards the Ramsdens and Fallon."

Richard Hartley, QC for the defence, said that Mirror Group Newspapers denied libel and claimed the article was true in substance and fact, or fair comment on a matter of public interest.

Naturally, the case was given extensive coverage in the *Life* and for the 18 days it lasted David Ashforth excelled as a court observer, lacing his amusing, off-beat comments on the proceedings, with penetrating descriptions of the main characters in the drama. Take his pen-portraits of the two QCs; of Hartley:

A short figure, a touch impish, white hair beneath his well-worn wig, glasses on his round, light pink face. The Pickwickian look of a kindly-hearted man. A metallic tang rings through his voice, sometimes an aggrieved whine, sometimes an expressed disbelief.

And of Milmo:

Taller, slimmer, steel grey of hair and manner, strikingly large ears. At times, Mr Milmo takes his glasses off; at times, he puts his hands in his pockets. He speaks in a measured way, his sentences full of pauses, sometimes metronomic, but fluent. Mr Milmo has an impressive command of his material; it is structured, and organised, and delivered in a well-considered sequence. Mr Milmo is, it must be conceded, a fine advocate.

On the third day, the reporter's clipped, perceptive prose described the duel between the elegantly attired trainer (a different outfit every day) and the defence counsel:

Today, red tunic, black blouse. This is a cross-examination to test a witness's wardrobe to the limit. Lynda Ramsden and Richard Hartley QC have settled into a routine. Mrs Ramsden appears resentful, veering towards crossness; Mr Hartley is resolute, tending to frustration. Mrs Ramsden's 'yes' is a barometer of her mood. Today the mercury has edged a little further up the tube. 'Yep, yep, yep …yes.' 'Yesss,' she hisses.

On the fourth day the focus was on her husband:

There he is, at last. A near mystical figure, Jack Ramsden. We imagine him quietly making his plans, bookmakers nervously watching, waiting for him to move, bluff and double bluff. What is fact and what fiction? A clever man, people say, Jack Ramsden.

Smart-suited, straight-backed, slightly military. And a good witness, undeniably a good witness. His 'yes' is crisp; his answers direct, concise, confident, self-assured. People are right. He is clever when he talks about a race, about a ride, he is precise. He says what he means: no less, no more, no elaboration.

Kieren Fallon presented a very different picture:

Mr Fallon is slightly round-shouldered, slightly crouched, head slightly tilted but, above all, not animated. He is quiet, full of pauses, strangely distant, as if a spectator rather than a participant. Occasionally, he smiles, at unexpected moments.

As the case progressed the jury learnt that Fallon had received a cautioning letter from the Jockey Club's disciplinary committee following the Swaffham Handicap. It informed him that although the stewards had decided to take no action he should not assume they were satisfied with his riding. It explained:

In reaching their decision they had particular regard to the problems you encountered in running prior to the furlong pole. However, they considered that once the gaps appeared you failed to ride Top Cees with sufficient effort and therefore, in similar circumstances, an offence under Rule 151 must be a likely outcome.

Armed with this information, Hartley accused Lynda Ramsden of being economical with the truth by not disclosing that she had been sent a copy of the letter by the Jockey Club and for claiming that Fallon had been "completely cleared" by the stewards. Mrs R responded by saying she had thrown the letter away and forgotten about it: "There seemed to be no reason to keep the letter. What was I supposed to do with it? Frame it?"

In his evidence, Fallon claimed the gaps had "closed as quickly as they opened … I was travelling so well I thought the race was mine, but when the gaps came he didn't pick up for me, he just plugged on at one pace." But later, when confronted with the Jockey Club's letter, he appeared to contradict himself, saying: "I wasn't satisfied with my riding either. I went for the wrong gaps. If I'd gone for the right ones, I'd probably have won."

As the video of the Swaffham was replayed to the jury for the umpteenth time on the sixth day, Ashforth was in Tennyson mode:

> This is a day full of gaps; split-second gaps, seven-second gaps, gaps opening and closing. Gaps to the left of Kieren Fallon, gaps to the right of Kieren Fallon. On, on, into the seven-second gap he rode. At least, that's what Mr Fallon says: Mr Richard Hartley QC begs to differ … On this day of gaps, few are larger than the ones between Mr Hartley's questions and Mr Fallon's answers.
>
> The champion jockey sets the pace, and it is a slow one. He has a curious manner; dreamy, wide-eyed, as if bemused … We move on, fitfully, to the equally contentious issue of the vigour displayed by Fallon in addressing the gap. 'As soon as the gap appeared, I ask my horse to quicken,' says Fallon. 'I'm down behind my horse, I'm lower than most of the other jockeys, I'm asking.' 'No you're not,' insists Mr Hartley.

And to round off his report, the court chronicler concluded: "Mrs Ramsden and her pink outfit leave Court 13 for the day. I make my way to the Underground. 'Please mind the gap'." It was award-winning stuff, and the pace quickened when Jim McGrath, a director of *Timeform* and a Channel 4 Racing pundit, was called as an expert witness for the defence on day eight. Ashforth again:

> Jim McGrath stands in the witness box and 20 feet away, Jack Ramsden leans on his elbow, strokes his chin, tilts his head back. The case is suddenly about two men who never speak to each other. "Is it true you have a low opinion of Mr Ramsden?" Mr Patrick Milmo QC asks McGrath. "Low opinion of him? I don't speak to him. I don't speak to him over a racing incident which happened many years ago, which made me feel he was someone I wanted to steer clear of." And the court is gripped.

Once again the Swaffham video was played through in an effort to determine whether Fallon's claim that Top Cees was "flat to the boards" held water. McGrath thought not.

> "Was he flat to the boards?" Mr Hartley asks. "Palpably not. Visibly not. The horse isn't at the back of the field because he's outpaced." Mr Ramsden chews a Polo. Mr McGrath does not consider that Top Cees met with significant interference. The problem was not obstruction, but lack of effort. "In my opinion, that's a feeble effort, that's a cosmetic smack. It was all cosmetic, all to make a show. He twirls the whip, he doesn't actually use it. He moves the reins – yes, better do that."
>
> The videotape rolls on. "A gap opens up and he doesn't try to take it. Amazingly, he switches inside. Look at Top Cees' head. Is it extended like the others? The overriding impression of the ride is that it was non-competitive … Even when a gap appeared, he still did virtually nothing. Top Cees could have and should have won." Contrast the Chester Cup: "A copybook ride. Easing to the outside, doing what he does so well, splendid riding."

Under cross-examination, McGrath conceded that remarks he had made on television amounted to a suggestion that the Ramsdens' explanations at stewards' enquiries were 'dishonest'; he also acknowledged inaccuracies in some specific statements he had made, after which Milmo questioned his right to be regarded as an 'independent' expert. But it was shown that McGrath had awarded best-turned-out prizes to the Ramsdens' horses on four occasions and had defended Mrs Ramsden and her daughter, Emma, when he felt the stewards had acted wrongly in taking action against them.

On his second day in the witness box, McGrath was pressed by Hartley to reveal the origin of his dislike of Jack Ramsden, but he demurred:

> "I came here in good faith," he says, pugnaciously, passionately. "I am not prepared to go into it." People's names would be mentioned without them having the opportunity to respond. The judge invites Mr McGrath to indicate 'the nature of this problem,' without mentioning names. "It relates to a race," Mr McGrath states. Asked for a year – 1982. But that is as far as he is prepared to go, unless the judge insists. The judge does not. "I am not biased in any professional sense," says Mr McGrath. "I feel I've got integrity. I do understand that the jury may choose not to believe me. That is their prerogative."

By this time the jury had learnt that Lynda Ramsden believed two of the stewards' secretaries, William Nunneley and Rachel Tonks, were reacting to the "rubbish whipped up about us in the newspapers" and were conducting a witch hunt against them. "We have friends who are stewards, and they tell us that Nunneley and Tonks almost plead with them to inquire into the running of our horses and swear that they will see us lose our licences if it is the last thing they do," she claimed.

Unsurprisingly, the trainer was not enamoured with the racing press: "By and large they are a bunch of failed punters and tipsters who seem to resent success," she said, pointing out John McCririck as an example of "a failed punter and bookmaker". When Hartley asked her if she saw her job as getting horses handicapped as low as possible so they would win races, she replied: "Yes, that is the whole idea, but it does not mean you are cheating. We are not doing anything wrong by getting a horse handicapped."

Jack Ramsden told the court he made between £50,000 and £100,000 from gambling in a good year. Ladbrokes, Hills and Corals had closed his accounts, but he used his son, owners and friends such as Robert Sangster to place bets for him and was paid a retainer of £5,000 a year to supply the racecourse bookmaker, Colin Webster, with 'inside information'. Webster had a half share with Mrs Ramsden in their horse, Captain Carat.

Ramsden said he hadn't backed Top Cees at Newmarket because "he was trying a new distance and I wasn't confident" and he didn't back the horse in the Chester Cup for the same reason. Instead he backed his other horse Harlestone Brook (who finished second), because "I thought he represented better value".

On the eleventh day Tom Clarke defended his decision to publish the offending article: "I felt that the Jockey Club, by not pursuing the Top Cees case more thoroughly, had not satisfied the natural public demand for a proper inquiry ... Here was something which had obviously caused great concern to the racing public at Chester and it had been a simmering issue since the Swaffham Handicap. There was obviously only one course for us to take, and that was to offer an opinion about it."

By that time, Geoff Lester's Chester Cup report in the *Life* which claimed that "angry punters jammed the racecourse phone lines" after the race, had been shown to be well wide of the mark when two switchboard operators testified that they had received only one or two calls and they had not been abusive. Milmo also had fun in ridiculing the reporter's closing line "the talk in all the Chester pubs last night was how the Ramsdens had pulled off the coup of the season."

Now the barrister played on the fact that Clarke was a member of the Press Complaints Commission as he threw its Code of Conduct (which warned of the need to distinguish between comment, conjecture and fact) at the editor. What evidence did he have that Top Cees' victory was 'deeply unpopular'? How was this unpopularity manifested? How many punters did Geoff Lester speak to? Were racegoers 'shaking their heads in disbelief'? Was Top Cees' victory 'the talk in all the Chester pubs last night'?

Clarke parried the first two questions by stating his office had received at least a dozen phone calls after the Chester Cup and seven or eight letters criticising Fallon's riding in the Swaffham. He placed Lester's more flowery expressions under the heading of 'hyperbole' and agreed the reporter would not have gone on a pub crawl after racing, "I did not take it literally," he said. "It was a graphic impression of the mood at Chester."

He added that the *Life* published about twenty comment pieces a year and its accusation of cheating had embraced the Ramsdens because in his view Fallon would not have ridden Top Cees in the way he had at Newmarket "of his own volition". He admitted he couldn't understand what the motive might have been. He had eliminated the possibility of a betting coup, but implied that although Jack Ramsden said *he* hadn't backed Top Cees in the Chester Cup he could have used his friends to back the horse for him.

On day 12, Alastair Down spoke the truth as he saw it: "I thought the way the horse had been run at Newmarket was a disgrace and that, in a sense, the racing public had their noses rubbed in it by the completely different approach at Chester. It confirmed all my worst fears about what had been done at Newmarket. Our overwhelming feeling was that punters had to be stood up for; that their interests had not been looked after at Newmarket – quite the reverse, and that a line had to be drawn."

Of his comment piece, he said: "They are very strong words and they gave me absolutely no pleasure to write," but the Ramsdens and Fallon "had caused a great offence to be done to the racing public and to the integrity of racing. It was in many ways the most depressing day's work I can remember in racing."

The following day the jury were excused duty while the opposing counsels argued over fresh evidence introduced by the defence which had subpoenaed Channel 4 Racing presenter, Derek Thompson, as a surprise witness. Two days later Thompson's impact on the case was hammered home by the *Life's* dramatic banner headlines:

THOMPSON   **Mr Fallon told me he stopped Top Cees**
FALLON   **No. That is a lie. Mr Thompson's inventing it**

And under the heading 'Who's a liar, then?' David Ashforth wrote:

Lying lies at the heart of day 14, for the truth and lies are brought bluntly face to face. Mr Thompson and Mr Fallon have both sworn under oath to tell the truth, but one of them is lying.

In courtroom dramas, there is the familiar shock of the unexpected. Derek Thompson is an unlikely figure to provide it – and a reluctant one. He did not want to come ... It was the evening of April 18, 1995, the day etched in the court's mind as the day of the Swaffham. Mr Thompson was having dinner at the Old Plough at Ashley, near Newmarket. Mr Fallon was having a drink with a friend. Mr Fallon set off from the bar in search of the toilet and, on the way, exchanged words with Mr Thompson. There, agreement ends. According to Mr Thompson: "I was asking what happened with Top Cees because I thought it would win and Kieren Fallon said 'I thought the horse would win too, but when I got on in the paddock Jack told me to stop it'."

In 14 long days, there has not been a line to match the hushing impact of Mr Thompson's low, slow, explosive revelation. 'Jack told me to stop it.'

Thompson, who had been commentating on races in Dubai when he was subpoenaed, said in evidence that he had mentioned the conversation to two of his colleagues at a Channel 4 Racing meeting the following morning and in the afternoon had interviewed Fallon on television about the race after reassuring him that what had been said in the Plough would not come out.

Fallon, for his part, could not remember exactly what he had said to Thompson but thought he might have told him that Top Cees had been unlucky. He said it was terrible for someone to invent such a lie especially as it could jeopardise his career. He couldn't remember what instructions he had been given, but supposed they would have been the usual 'hold him up and take your time'. "I was never told to stop any horse by Mr or Mrs Ramsden, let alone Top Cees," he said, adding that the Swaffham was a £10,000 handicap and certainly worth winning.

When Jack Ramsden was recalled to the witness box, he said that Thompson's allegations were totally untrue and he had been "horrified" and "appalled" when he heard them. He had given Fallon his riding instructions in the paddock in the presence of the horse's owner, Allan Leonard, and his daughter. Lynda Ramsden said her husband could not have given instructions without her hearing them.

In their closing speeches both QCs described Thompson as the crucial witness. Hartley, quoting Sir Walter Scott, said that the plaintiffs could well have been in the author's mind when he wrote 'Oh, what a tangled web we weave when first we practice to deceive' and dismissed Milmo's suggestion that Thompson had come to the court to save his Channel 4 job as "grotesque". On the contrary: "He came here in the certain knowledge that his evidence would actively harm his career. What conceivable reason could there be for Mr Thompson to come here and lie? Absolutely none."

Milmo argued that Thompson had been "trapped by his own conceit" in that having told his colleagues a tall tale to impress them, he either had "to put his hand up and say to his Channel 4 chums that the story he told was untrue … or to stick to his story whatever might be the consequences to Mr Fallon or the Ramsdens … the moral is that if you start lying you must continue to lie."

Which was, more or less, what Hartley had said about the plaintiffs.

With regard to the article 'Contempt for the punter', Milmo maintained that Down's fondness for "flamboyant phraseology" had led him astray; that the Life's coverage of the affair amounted to "irresponsible and reckless journalism" and its assertion that it was acting in the interests of the punter was "an over-righteous attitude and humbug".

In summing up on day 17, Justice Morland revealed there were inconsistencies in Derek Thompson's statements. In a gist notice in which the Mirror Group's solicitors laid out the basis of the evidence their witness intended to give, Thompson quoted Fallon as saying that Ramsden had told him: "We have missed the price. Today is not the day." But as he had not mentioned this in his testament to the court, the judge advised the jury that it "throws serious doubt on the reliability of what Mr Thompson has said".

Morland went on to tell the jury that one of the main issues to consider was the right of a newspaper to publish what it saw as fair comment on a matter of public interest and whether the defence had established that "Top Cees was deliberately and dishonestly ridden by Mr Fallon … on the Ramsdens' deliberate and dishonest instructions".

If the jury were not satisfied the *Sporting Life* had proved the truth of its accusations they had to move on to its second line of defence which was 'fair comment'. If the comments made were fair, then it was a defence to libel, but to succeed the newspaper had to show that what it said was a comment not a statement of fact and establish, on a balance of probabilities, that the comment was justified.

Faced with these conundrums it was hardly surprising the jury failed to reach a verdict by the end of the afternoon and so the case stretched on into another day when, after more than five hours of deliberation, they unanimously cleared Lynda Ramsden of all charges and returned a majority decision of 10-2 that the allegations of cheating were neither justified nor fair comment in the case of Jack Ramsden and Kieren Fallon.

The plaintiffs were awarded damages totalling £195,000 with costs of some £160,000. Outside the court Jack Ramsden told reporters: "This sends out a message that our horses are trying their best for their owners and that betting is secondary. I think Lynda has probably won the case for us, basically, because I think it is very hard for anyone to imagine that she does anything other than tell the truth." He also took the opportunity to complain of a "trial by media and television" and describe Derek Thompson's testimony as "utterly contemptible".

An aggrieved Thompson declared: "I am annoyed about the way that the judge rubbished my evidence in his summing up. I made that gist statement to my solicitors, who only gave the Mirror Group's solicitors a rough guide of what I said. The only time I had a chance actually to say what I had been told on that day was in court and I stand by those words. It was the truth, the whole truth and nothing but the truth."

The *Life's* report was accompanied by a front-page statement from Tom Clarke:

> We have to accept the jury's verdict – and we do. We are bitterly disappointed. The jury accepted that
> we honestly believed in the truth of our allegations which were not lightly made. The case was fought
> on a matter of principle by *The Sporting Life* in our capacity as a guardian of the punter's interests.
> We think it is a sad day for racing, but we do not regret this action for one moment.

Alastair Down, whose original comment piece went some way towards earning him the Horserace Writers 'Journalist of the Year' award in 1995, wrote:

> We hope that this defeat will not deter us and others in racing journalism and broadcasting from
> standing up and crying 'Foul' – or worse – whenever we see something we honestly regard as being
> not in the best interests of the sport, particularly the best interests of the punter. As racing slides little
> by little down the scale of punter interest, it is more important than ever that the Jockey Club hardens
> its resolve to impose the rules with firmness, consistency and openness. It is not enough to slap wrists
> in private and send confidential letters of caution.

In his Saturday column, David Ashforth wrapped up his outstanding coverage of the trial – for trial it was for all concerned – by observing:

The word 'cheating' is unlikely to be seen on the racing pages for a while but, despite losing the libel action, *The Sporting Life* may yet have made life more difficult for non-triers. It depends on the Jockey Club. It is inconceivable that erring jockeys will be able to cite the precedent of Kieren Fallon's riding of Top Cees in the Swaffham as an example of an acceptable level of effort. If they can, racing is lost.

And he concluded, controversially but succinctly:

Under the English legal system, trials are not about the pursuit of truth but about selling a particular case to judge and, more especially, jury. Patrick Milmo is an excellent salesman.

It was left to the racing public to add a tidy postscript to the saga when, three weeks later, Top Cees won the three-mile Coral Cup Handicap Hurdle at Cheltenham and received a reception that was far removed from the sullen quiet that had greeted him at Chester in 1995.

Never before nor since had booing been heard for a winner at that great National Hunt Festival. Some of it may have been because the horse had finished down the field in his three previous races over an inadequate two-mile trip, but mostly it showed that the outcome of the recent case still rankled with many (fair comment or statement of fact?).

The boos accompanied Top Cees as he returned to the winners' enclosure, but they were more of the ribbing kind than ugly, and jeers were mixed with ironic cheers when Derek Thompson turned his back on the Ramsdens and walked out of the enclosure, microphone in hand. There was to be no television interview this time.*

The libel verdict also generated a record post bag for the *Life*. From the hundreds of letters received, the paper published just 17 of them. Twelve for, five agin.

Richard Coe, of Sydenham, London SE26, could not believe the jury had ignored the evidence of their own eyes and that of experts when shown replays of the Swaffham:

The High Court judgement is a sickening attack on the competence, skill and integrity of experienced race-readers (apparently every race-reader in the land was wrong) … Forget the Derek Thompson evidence, the evidence of race-readers Jim McGrath and Alan Amies should have been the deciding factor.

Paul Loewenthal, of Morden, Surrey, queried how an inexperienced jury – even one led by expert witnesses – could be expected to interpret the subtleties of race-riding:

If the Jockey Club had acted swiftly and decisively in the first place over the Swaffham Handicap in April 1995, this sad and sorry case would have been avoided. If racing stewards and those who run the game couldn't work it out, is it any surprise that a jury of lay people should fail to find otherwise?

Andrew Simpson, of Pewsey, Wilts, felt that journalists and TV commentators were not in a

---

* A few months later, Jack Ramsden announced that he and Lynda were calling it a day after 12 years of training in England. The couple went to live in France for two years, but returned to resume operations at their old yard at Sandhutton, near Thirsk, in 2001. However, they were never able to achieve their previous level of success and eventually retired from training in 2005.

position to pass judgement on others. Citing Brough Scott and John McCririck of Channel 4 Racing (and by implication Alastair Down and the *Sporting Life*) he wrote:

> They are not the conscience of racing, nor do they wield moral authority over the sport, nor are they the champions of the public. They are simply tele-journalists grubbing away at earning a living just like the rest of the human race. For all their professional identification with racing, it is significant that on pay day they cease to be luminaries of the turf and reveal themselves as media men pure and simple. The fact that their association with the sport is therefore largely parasitic is another reason for finding their moral posturings mildly ludicrous.

Andrew Hamilton 'and others' from Edinburgh took the opposite view:

> We have always thought *The Sporting Life* has been fair to the myriad characters who make up racing, a paper which doesn't get caught up in tittle-tattle, innuendo, half-truths and gossip, concentrating, instead, on the deeds of our racing heroes. Equally, where you perceive that an injustice has been committed, you don't pretend it hasn't happened, you have the courage to stand up and write about it. We do hope that despite this setback, you will continue to do so.

And the *Life* did just that for the few remaining weeks of its existence.

THE WAKE

TUESDAY, 12 MAY 1998, was, quite literally, the last day of your *Life*; it was also a grand day for a wake if you happened to be in central London. The early summer sun bathed the city with a warmth that was singularly inappropriate for the occasion, for this was a day of cold hearts and bitter feelings.

An almost tangible sense of anger hung in the air as the close-knit family of mourners made their way in dribs and drabs along the lunchtime bustling pavements of Long Acre towards the Freemasons Arms in Covent Garden. The question "How could it have been allowed to happen?" was asked over and over again. "How could the actions of a few 'here today, gone tomorrow' men destroy the work of generations of journalists who had built up a modest penny paper into a British institution? How could 139 years of history be torn up and thrown carelessly away, regardless of public, or even royal, opinion?"

To those who had spent their entire working life on the *Life* it seemed a rank betrayal that was inherently rotten and unforgivable. To the Mirror Group management it was simply a question of basic economics. Loyalty and tradition didn't figure in their calculations when performance bonuses and the interests of their shareholders came first.

At the time of its closure, the paper had seldom been better staffed with an array of top-class reporters and award-winning journalists whose professionalism put to shame those they had served so well. Many of them, knowing they would be without a job in a few weeks' time, could have been forgiven had they given up in disgust, but instead they raised their game and worked on to the last. It was testimony to what the *Sporting Life* meant to them, yet, in truth, it was only a newspaper that had been killed off and a few jobs lost (about 70 were shed in the final 12 months), but the blow was still as deeply felt as a personal bereavement.

The Freemasons Arms had been the favoured watering hole for many of the *Life's* team during the 45 years (1927-1971) the paper had its offices at 93 Long Acre. Now, the pub was to serve as a maudlin chapel of remembrance for the last generation of 'Lifers'. Bob Betts, the newly redundant editor of the *Greyhound Life*, was first to arrive at the bar of his misspent youth. As organiser of the wake he brought with him £300 donated by his late employer to form the basis of a short-lived kitty for food and drink. He also carried a letter from David Montgomery. Dated 23 April 1998, it informed him:

> In purchasing the *Racing Post*, Mirror Group gave certain undertakings to the vendors relating to the title. One of those undertakings was that the editor, Alan Byrne, would be given complete freedom to chose the team of his choice for the merged title … in consultation with Tom Clarke and David Annat he considered fully all members of the *Sporting Life* team taking into account his requirements for the coverage of different sports … You certainly will not be leaving the paper with a black mark against your name, and speaking personally I respect the significant service that you have given to the title and to the Mirror Group.

It was a fair acknowledgement of the 38 years' work Betts had put into the paper and was a decided improvement on the stereotyped letter, signed in facsimile by Tom Clarke, sent to another long-serving journalist. Dated 8 May 1998, it explained that the *Life* was being merged with the *Post* because "the market for racing newspapers is not large enough to support two titles and that the racing public will be better served by one paper with a secure future".

The outgoing editor, who had spent the preceding weeks vainly trying to persuade several publishers to launch a new racing daily to challenge the *Post*'s newly acquired monopoly, went on to inform the reporter that the first four editions of the merged title would be on sale at a special trial price of 50p. He signed off:

> I've attached your own personalised 50p coupon which you can use on the first four days for a free copy, or after that until May 30, 1998 for a half-price copy. Thank you for your loyalty over the years. I do hope that you will try the new *Racing Post* and enjoy it as much as you have enjoyed *The Sporting Life*.

It was close on midday when the first of the elite began to drift in. True to form, Chris Gundry led the field. His 'CKG' initials had appeared at the bottom of countless 'Man on the Spot' race-preview columns, as had Len Poole's, another early arrival who had spent all his working life on the *Life* having joined in 1957, the year that saw the retirement of Meyrick Good who had penned his first 'Man on the Spot' article in 1897.

Two men linked by a century of columns during which time the increase in race fixtures had seen 'Man on the Spot' cloned into half a dozen itinerant tipsters (deceptively off the spot in the office) headed by Poole who had been 'through the card' five times in his principal role. Other members of his team to join the muster included Steve Barnes who used to glean some useful inside information through riding out for the shrewd Greystoke trainer, Gordon Richards, on his weekends off.

The first pint had just been pulled when an old toiler wandered in from out of the sun to ask if he was in the right place for the *Life*'s 'do'. Len Sibley had worked on the paper from 1932 to 1974; from the days of Golden Miller and the infamous 'body-line' tour of Australia through to the 'Rumble in the Jungle' in Zaire where Muhammad Ali regained the heavyweight championship from George Foreman. A lifetime of sporting memories.

Julian Armfield, the freelance contributor of a jockeys' gossip column for almost 20 years, was warmly welcomed as he brought with him £500 to swell the kitty. The money had been generously donated by the PR company, Market Racing Agency, the racecourse caterers Ring & Brymer and the World of Racing Exhibition, "in appreciation for all that the *Life*'s loyal staff have contributed to racing over the years".

Gradually the trickle of arrivals became a steady stream. The quietly efficient Terry McGovern and the affable Vic Woodman, two of the best subs on the racing desk came with their chief, the unflappable Bryan Pugh and his equally flappable deputy, the enthusiastic but sycophantic Alan Smith.

The tall, bearded figure of Dave Atkinson did not have the length of service (just 12 years) as some, but as a representative of the Staff Association he had taken a leading role in the fight to keep the paper going and had even written to the Queen Mother to ask if there was anything she could do to help save the *Life*. He received a courteous reply from Clarence House which informed him that Her Majesty had read his letter 'with great sadness' but regretted she could not interfere in the matter. The mere acknowledgement of what had been a decidedly presumptuous appeal had given the demoralised staff a much-needed fillip, but that was all.

The last day of your *Life* as the paper goes on sale outside York racecourse - 12 May 1998.
© [Julian Herbert]/[Allsport]/Getty Images.

Stalwarts from the greyhound desk included Mark Sullivan who, on 21 December 1990, gave the paper its greatest success with a 12-race through-the-card, 256,279-1 accumulator at Wimbledon that gained him a coveted place in the *Guinness Book of Records* under the title of 'Topmost Tipster'.

Steve Delve was among the outside staff in attendance. In his 33 years with the paper he had worked his way through most jobs in the office, from the drudgery of typing out returns to compiling betting forecasts, before becoming a full-time SP reporter and small-time racehorse owner. His four-time winner, Mon Amie, had been owned in partnership with his *bon amie*, Stuart Oliver, who overcame brittle bone disease and a machinegun-like stammer to start work in the *Life's* form room in 1966 before moving on to join the copy-takers under Mick Malone (1964-98), a fearsome tackler in his days with the *Life's* all-stars football team.

Malone's band of unsung heroes, the saviours of at least one dyslexic outside reporter in pre-computer days, turned up in force. They included the perma-tanned Alan Watkins (1962-98), the ever-cheerful Cockney, John McGhee (1972-98) and Des McKeogh (1986-97) whose lightning typing speed and long acquaintance with racing phrases often enabled him to finish off a reporter's sentence before it had been uttered.

Former employees were also well represented in the congregation. Ron Allen, of dry wit and sadly redundant pen, had written an incisive Turf Topics column in the late 1960s before leaving to become press officer to the ebullient Glaswegian bookmaker, John Banks, in 1971. He rejoined the paper after a year and eventually became FoC of the *Life's* NUJ chapel, fighting many a worthy battle for better wages and conditions.

Ernie Dymock (1960-96), whose unswerving dedication to the paper and the pressures he was put under when assistant editor caused him to have a nervous breakdown in 1994, had to leave the gathering early as he was still troubled by ill health. Other 'old boys' included many of those who had lost their jobs in a savage cull a year earlier and a few representatives of the 1991 Britvic Club.

Monty Court was on hand to deliver a few well-chosen words on the shabby way the closure had been handled (a shining exception being the group's personnel manager, Graham Curtis, who sent out the redundancy notices with a message of genuine regret and ensured the recipients got their maximum entitlement of compensation).

Mike Gallemore also had his say. In a stirring speech he made a point of emphasising that at the time he was sacked in 1993, the paper was making an annual profit of £2.2m for MGN – a profit that disappeared overnight with the introduction of the so-called Reader-Friendly *Life*.

Speeches over, attention switched to the big-screen television that was showing the first day of York's Dante meeting. Cheers rang out as Kieren Fallon got Augur's 9-2 nap, Largesse, home in the opener – Harry Feist could not have wished for better.

As the day wore on, third and fourth-generation readers of the *Life* drifted in seeking autographs from the assembled scribes. Bob Betts signed pages of the *Greyhound Life* that carried tributes from a score of the sport's most prominent figures; among them were John Nicholson, senior steward of the NGRC: "The relationship between the NGRC and the *Greyhound Life* team has not always been one of agreement, but one of fairness and sound judgement with a balance of humour and good journalistic banter."

Geoffrey Thomas, CEO of the British Greyhound Racing Board: "The commitment and dedication shown by both past and present *Life* journalists for over half a century has enabled greyhound racing to be amongst the best-reported sports in Britain and has done much to contribute to the continued popularity and success of greyhound racing."

Michael Field, chairman of Ireland's Bord na gCon: "*The Sporting Life* has been part of our lives and we are very sorry to see it go. Over the years it has given a great service to our industry and always maintained an excellent level of journalism, presentation and photography."

Geoff DeMulder, the trainer of two Greyhound Derby winners, described the *Life* as: "One of the greatest newspapers ever published in Britain. It's always printed the truth and I have never been afraid to talk to any person from the *Greyhound Life*."

Tributes in the national press were no less generous. Peter Oborne's column in *The (Daily) Express*, headed 'Her Majesty regrets the tragic loss of a national treasure', featured a tear-out section of the Queen Mother's reply to Dave Atkinson along with a photo of a teenage Lester Piggott studying a copy of the *Life*. Oborne wrote:

> For a century and a half the paper has been deeply entrenched in our national consciousness. The 'rub down with *The Sporting Life*' is as English as hot tea, warm beer, wet summers and the Changing of the Guard. It is one of those curious national monuments that belongs to all of us and extends far beyond the few that know and love racing. Unlike so many English things, the attraction of *The Sporting Life* has nothing whatever to do with class.
>
> It may be the Queen Mother's favourite paper – and for that matter the Queen's … but you can walk into the roughest Glasgow pub with *The Sporting Life* under your arm and immediately get involved in a conversation rather than a fight … The closure of *The Sporting Life* counts as a barbarous act of destruction. All of us will be the losers.

In Scotland, Martin Hannan, aka 'Bob Magill', devoted his whole column in *The Herald* to the closure, describing it as "a tragedy for British racing":

572 THE STORY OF YOUR LIFE

For nearly 140 years the newspaper has chronicled the turf with unique insight, and its reporting has often been of the highest order, particularly recently when the *Racing Post* came along as a rival … The Green Seal service for settling disputes between punter and bookmaker is one of many marvellous innovations which the *Life* provided. Its form analysis was second to none over the years, and its chronicling of the activities of racing's leaders was admirably impartial … Racing will continue without the *Life*, but the quality of our sport and our lives will be the poorer for its passing.

And as the sun set over the Freemasons Arms, the bitter inquests on the closure gave way to nostalgic reminiscences dating back to the immediate post-war years in Long Acre where costermongers' carts still plied their trade outside the office as the Odhams doormen in their gold-braided, burgundy livery stood to attention and saluted the then Viscount Southwood (as Elias became in 1946) and Ben Clements as they walked in.

Tales were told of how the Odhams chairman would distribute white fivers to all the staff at Christmas-time while 'Clem' loaded the festive hampers his bookmaker friends had sent him into taxis to take to Victoria station and thence by train to his West Sussex smallholding at Storrington. And of how Southwood used to leave messages at the office for the editor who would stroll in at 10 o'clock singing 'Oh, What a beautiful morning' and request a minion: "Would you do me a kindness? Would you tell Lord Southwood's secretary that I can be reached up until 12 o'clock and then I shall be going to lunch, but I'll be back about three and shall be here until five."

The stories moved on to Holborn and the after-hours sessions around the piano in 'the Stab', but Canary Wharf held few fond memories and gradually the assembly began to break up and make their way home to start new lives. There were hangovers aplenty the following morning, but none as bad as the one David Montgomery had been left with as he and his new managing director, former *Sun* editor Kelvin MacKenzie, struggled to bring out the new general-sports paper that was to carry the *Sporting Life* title.

Few outside Bedlam believed the project would succeed. The public were already well-catered for by the excellent sports sections in the national dailies, while production problems and the unsubtle antics of the combustible MacKenzie had already resulted in the departure of the new editor. The launch date was then postponed until the autumn, but in August the 70 journalists who had been signed up learnt the paper would not be coming out until the spring of 1999.

Meanwhile, old Fleet Street looked on with wry amusement as the tragic-comedy was played out. Alan English's 'Whistle Blower' column in the *Sunday Times* drew a parallel between what was not happening at Canary Wharf and *Waiting for Godot* – "Surreal scenes worthy of Samuel Beckett at the *Sporting Life*, the newspaper where nothing happens every day"[1] – as Montgomery, Mirror Group's cost-cutter general, was shelling out £150,000 a month to staff a paper that didn't come out.

In September, another pre-launch editor was sacked and in January Montgomery was forced out after losing the support of the company's new chairman, Sir Victor Blank, and its directors. He did not leave empty-handed, pocketing a £1,125,000 pay-off and share options worth £105,500 plus a bonus of £123,750.[2]

Finally, after ten months of costly and abortive trials, the inevitable was accepted and the *Life's* title was finally laid to rest on 5 March 1999. It was left to the *Daily Telegraph's* gifted sports columnist, Robert Philip, to write the obituary of 'Racing's Greatest Daily' under the headline 'The Life's last breath':

The Sporting Life expired quietly at home in Canary Wharf, London EC14, after a prolonged and brave struggle against corporate strangulation.

Forgive me, if you will, this moment of personal mourning to mark the tragic death of one of Fleet Street's most noble names.

The Sporting Life, which ceased publication as horse racing's bible last year, has been officially declared dead and buried.

Any lingering hopes that it would reappear on the news stands this summer as a daily general sports paper were brutally dashed on Wednesday night when the staff were informed that it would never again roll off the presses.

For those of us employed in the industry, the demise of any newspaper title is always a sad occasion as we grieve for our colleagues whose families have been suddenly threatened with an uncertain future. This is especially so in the case of *The Sporting Life* which, for a century and more, was prescribed reading for kings and queens, plumbers and plasterers.

To the workers, my deepest condolences; to the management at the offices of Mirror Group Newspapers, shame on you.

The Sporting Life RIP.

As the great James Cameron wrote on the demise of the *News Chronicle* in 1960, the autopsy report revealed the *Life* had died of "a simple thrombosis, defined as when an active circulation is impeded by clots".[3]

SOURCES, BIBLIOGRAPHY,
GLOSSARY, INDEX
AND CHRONOLOGY
OF IMPORTANT DATES

SOURCES

Unless otherwise indicated all extracts have been taken from the *Sporting Life*; only where there is no indication as to when such extracts or quotes appeared have they been given an index number.

Introduction (Page 3)
1.   Charles Dickens, 'The Rough's Guide', *All the Year Round*, 16 December 1865, pp492-96; *Sporting Life* 16 December 1865

Chapter 1 – 'In the Beginning' (Page 5)
1.   Quoted by William Acton, *Prostitution, considered in its Moral, Social & Sanitary Aspects*, 1857, p16
2.   *Morning Advertiser*, 12 March 1859
3.   *Baily's Magazine*, May 1864, p60
4.   J B Booth, *Bits of Character*, 1936, p45

Chapter 2 – 'The Penny Press' (Page 9)
1.   Curtis on Manhood, quoted in *Sporting Life* adverts, 1859
2.   James D Symon, *The Press and its Story*, 1914, p93
3.   The Druid, *Post and Paddock*, 1856, Revised edition, p175
4.   *Sporting Life*, 10 November 1903
5.   Quoted by Kennedy Jones, *Fleet Street and Downing Street*, 1920, p89
6.   Quoted by Derek Hudson, *British Journalists and Newspapers*, 1945, p27
7.   J B Booth, *Old Pink 'Un Days*, 1924, p381

Chapter 4 – 'Bankrupt and Beeton' (Page 21)
The quoted extracts from Sam Beeton's letters are taken from *The Times*' extensive reports (some 30 in number) of the case and also from his affidavits held at the National Archives.
1.   *The Times*, 14 January 1862
2.   *Sporting Magazine,* March 1860
3.   *Sporting Life*, 21 December 1859
4.   *The Times*, 31 March 1860
5.   E E Dorling, *Epsom and the Dorlings*, 1939, p21
6.   Sarah Freeman, *Isabella and Sam*, 1977, p235
7.   Kathryn Hughes, *The Short Life & Long Times of Mrs Beeton*, 2005, p184

Chapter 5 – 'Betting in Bride Lane' (Page 30)
1.   Quoted by Vincent Orchard, *Tattersalls*, 1953, p162
2.   Ralph Nevill, *Light Come, Light Go,* 1909, p99
3.   The Druid, *op. cit.* p60
4.   *Hansard*, 3rd series, Vol. 129, 11 July 1853
5.   *Sporting Life*, 25 October 1865
6.   J Rice, *The History of the British Turf,* Vol 2, 1879, p275

Chapter 6 – 'Scribes and Touts' (Page 42)
1.   Charles Adolph Voigt, *Famous Gentleman Riders at home and abroad*, 1925, p251
2.   Voigt *op. cit.* p86
3.   Quoted in the *Sporting Life*, 21 March 1959
4.   J B Booth, *Bits of Character*, 1936, p38
5.   Rules and Orders of the Jockey Club, *Racing Calendar*, 1821, p xxxvii
6.   John Porter, *Kingsclere*, 1896, p245
7.   *The Times*, 8 May 1876

Chapter 7 – 'Welshers and Dead 'Uns' (Page 57)
1.   The Druid, *op. cit.* p56

Chapter 8 – 'The Tarragona Affair' (Page 66)
1.   T H Bird, *Admiral Rous and the English Turf*, 1939, p190
2.   *The Standard*, 16 March 1829
3.   *The Times*, 23 March 1829
4.   Elizabeth Longford, *Pillar of State*, 1975, p237

Chapter 9 – 'Campaigns and Consumption' (Page 78)
1.   Bird, *op. cit.* p82
2.   Dorling, *op. cit.* pp75-6
3.   Alexander Scott, *Turf Memories of Sixty Years*, 1925, p27
4.   *The Times*, 9 November 1865
5.   Rules and Orders of the Jockey Club, *Racing Calendar*, 1869, p lv

Chapter 10 – 'The Rules of the Game' (Page 88)
1.   *Sporting Life*, 1 January 1870
2.   John Arlott (ed), *The Oxford Companion to Sports and Games*, 1975, p335
3.   R G Graham, 'The Early History of the FA', *Badminton Magazine,* Vol 8, June 1899, p75
4.   Geoffrey Green, *The History of the Football Association*, 1953, p29
5.   *Ibid.*
6.   Titley & McWhirter, *Centenary History of the Rugby Football Union*, 1970, p75

Chapter 11 – 'A Transatlantic Challenge' (Page 99)
1.   Victor Dowling, *Fistiana*, 1846, pp100-2

Chapter 12 – 'Fisticuffs At Farnborough' (Page 107)
1.   Quoted by Iain Manson, *The Lion and the Eagle*, 2008, p242
2.   R P Watson, *Memoirs of Robert Patrick Watson*, 1899, p31

Chapter 13 – 'Competition' (Page 117)
1.   *op. cit. Waterloo Directory of English Newspapers and Periodicals 1800-1900*
2.   *Sporting Mirror*, January 1882, p202

Chapter 14 – 'An Exodus of Bookmakers' (Page 122)
1.   *Sporting Times*, 11 February 1865
2.   J B Booth, *Bits of Character*, 1936, p272
3.   J Peddie, *Racing For Gold*, 1891, p5
4.   *Ibid.*

Chapter 15 – 'On Dogs, Rats and Songbirds' (Page 130)
1.   W H Langley, *Sporting Times*, 12 December 1903

Chapter 16 – 'No New Thing' (Page 142)
1.   J B Booth, *Old Pink 'Un Days*, 1924, p48
2.   *Ibid.* p49
3.   *Sporting Magazine*, March 1870, p154
4.   Porter, *op. cit.* p71

Chapter 18 – 'A Vet in the Chair' (Page 165)
1.   Martin Cobbett, *Racing Life and Racing Characters,* 1903, p319
2.   Dorling, *op. cit.* p94
3.   Quoted in the *Bloodstock Breeders Review*, 1915, p133
4.   J B Booth, *Sporting Times, The Pink 'Un World*, 1938, p6
5.   J B Booth, *Old Pink 'Un Days*, 1924, p55
6.   H R Fox-Bourne, *English Newspapers*, Vol 2, 1887, p278
7.   *Sporting Life*, 'Racing and the Telegraphs', 31 January 1872

Chapter 19 – 'Captain Webb's Channel Trip' (Page 172)
1.   Watson, *op. cit.* p32
2.   Frederic Boase, *Modern English Biography*, Vol IV (2nd ed, 1965) pp334-5
3.   Watson *op. cit.* p113
4.   *Ibid.* p114
5   *Ibid.* p115
6.   Parliamentary paper issued 12 November 1878, quoted in *The Times*

Chapter 20 – 'Wobble Weston's Walkabout' (Page 180)
1.   *Sporting Life*, 16 October 1907
2.   *Sporting Life*, 25 April 1906

Chapter 21 – 'Blake's Daily Balderdash' (Page 189)
1.   Edward Spencer, *The Great Game*, 1903, p220
2.   *Sporting Life*, 17 May 1881
3.   *Sporting Gazette*, 27 October 1866

Chapter 22 – 'The SP Wars' (Page 196)
1.   J B Booth, *Old Pink 'Un Days*, 1924, p207
2.   Watson, *op. cit.* p343

3.   *Bell's Life*, 7 February 1880
4.   Joseph Hatton, *Journalistic London*, 1882, p207
5.   Meyrick Good, *Good Days*, 1941, p27
6.   The Guildhall Library, MS No.23038, 9 January 1912
7.   *National Sporting League Journal*, May 1925, p69

Chapter 23 – 'Tragedy and Scandal' (Page 207)
1.   E M Humphris, *The Life of Mathew Dawson*, 1928, p113
2.   *Sporting Times*, 13 November 1886
3.   Richard Marsh, *A Trainer to Two Kings*, 1925, p317
4.   *Sporting Times*, 13 November 1886
5.   *Racing Calendar*, 1884, p lxvii
6.   *Bloodstock Breeders Review*, 1917, p21
7.   Sir George Chetwynd, *Racing Reminiscences, Vol I*, 1891, p viii
8.   Sir George Chetwynd, *Racing Reminiscences, Vol II*, 1891, pp142 & 146

Chapter 24 – 'The Irish Connection' (Page 222)
1.   Watson, *op. cit.* p113
2.   Quoted from the *Manuel de la Boxe Francais et Anglaise*, *Sporting Life*, 10 March 1888
3.   John L Sullivan, *Life and Reminiscences of a Nineteenth Century Gladiator*, 1892, p241
4.   Good, *op. cit.* p22
5.   Guy Williams and Francis Hyland, *The Irish Derby*, 1980, p120
6.   *Sporting Life*, 7 March 1883

Chapter 25 – 'The Trodmore Coup' (Page 231)
1.   *Sell's Dictionary of the World's Press*, 1892, p44
2.   Good, *op. cit.* p33

Chapter 27 – 'The American Invasion' (Page 245)
1.   'The American Jockey Invasion', *Badminton Magazine*, Vol 24, April 1907, p429
2.   Tod Sloan, *Tod Sloan*, 1915, p49
3.   George Lambton, *Men and Horses I Have Known*, 1924, p242
4.   *Sporting Life*, 22 December 1933

Chapter 28 – 'A Lethal Legacy' (Page 259)
1.   *Sporting Gazette*, 29 October 1864, p850
2.   *Sporting Life*, 23 August 1871
3.   Sir John Astley, *Fifty Years of My Life, Vol II*, 1895, p201
4.   Sir George Chetwynd, *Racing Reminiscences, Vol I*, 1891, p240
5.   Edward Spencer, *Dopes*, 1901, pp48-9
6.   *Sporting Life*, 24 October 1900
7.   *Bloodstock Breeders Review*, 1943, p212
8.   Lambton, *op. cit.* p254

Chapter 29 – 'The Scottish Reformation' (Page 264)
1.   Christopher Martin-Jenkins, *The Complete Who's Who of Test Cricketers*, 1980, p35

Chapter 31 – 'The Fight Against the Faddists' (Page 282)
1.   Cobbett, *op. cit.* p249
2.   *Sporting Life*, 9 August 1894
3.   *National Sporting League Journal*, August 1912

Chapter 32 – 'Football Bandits' (Page 290)
1.   *The Times*, 19 September 1911
2.   *Sporting Life*, 23 January 1914

Chapter 33 – 'Prepare for the Horrors' (Page 296)
1.   C E Cole-Hamilton Burton, 'Touchstone' of the *Daily Mail*, 'The Sportsmen', quoted by Fred
      W Ward in *The 23rd (Service) Battalion Royal Fusiliers*, 1920, p3
2.   *The History of the Times* Vol IV, 1952, p780
3.   *Bloodstock Breeders Review*, 1914, p274
4.   *Bloodstock Breeders Review*, 1917, p177
5.   Ward, *op. cit.* p12

Chapter 37 – 'The Race Gang Wars' (Page 341)
1.   *Daily Telegraph*, 22 August 1898
2.   William Bebbington, *Rogues Go Racing*, 1947, p17

Chapter 38 – 'Churchill's Iniquitous Levy' (Page 346)
1.   *Sporting Life*, 'Police For Trial', 19 January 1928

Chapter 40 – 'A New Life' (Page 362)
1.   Adair Dighton, *My Sporting Life*, 1934, p157
2.   Good, *op. cit.* p170

Chapter 41 – 'Going to the Dogs' (Page 371)
1.   Good, *op. cit.* p 30
2.   A C Critchley, *Critch! The Memoirs of Brig-Gen A C Critchley*, 1961, pp145-6

Chapter 43 – 'Battling Against the Old Guard' (Page 388)
1.   *Racing Calendar*, 1922, p lxxxi
2.   Sidney Galtrey, *Memoirs of a Racing Journalist*, 1937, p17

Chapter 44 – 'A Staff of Experts' (Page 394)
1.   Roger Mortimer, *The Turf*, 1979, p261
2.   *Sporting Life*, 28 May 1945
3.   *Sporting Life*, 10 August 1927
4.   *Sporting Chronicle*, 4 January 1938

Chapter 45 – 'A Wartime Weekly' (Page 403)
1.   Geoffrey Hamlyn, *My Sixty Years in the Ring*, 1994, p130
2.   Arthur Fitzgerald, *The Arc*, 1997, p65

Chapter 47 – 'Rough Justice' (Page 426)
1.   H Montgomery Hyde, *Sir Patrick Hastings: his life and cases*, 1960, p236
2.   Peter O'Sullevan, *Calling the Horses*, 1989, p310
3.   Les Woodland, *Dope: The Use of Drugs in Sport*, 1980, p19
4.   Roger Mortimer, 'Stewards Asleep On Dope', *Pacemaker International*, February 1985
5.   *The People*, 25 February 1951; David Ashforth, *Ringers & Rascals*, 2003, pp98-102
6.   Jack Jarvis, *They're Off*, 1969, p98
7.   Ashforth, *op. cit*. p97

Chapter 48 – 'The Nobblers' (Page 439)
1.   Norman Lucas and Bernard Scarlett, *The Flying Squad*, 1968, p150
2.   *Sporting Life*, 26 October 1960
3.   Raymond Smith, *Vincent O'Brien: Master of Ballydoyle*, 1990, p190
4.   *Ibid.*
5.   *Sporting Life*, 13 December 1951
6.   Dick Francis, *Lester: The Official Biography*, 1986, p84
7.   Fred and Mercy Rimell, *Aintree Iron*, 1977, p92

Chapter 49 – 'A Licence to Print Money' (Page 453)
1.   *Sporting Life*, 30 January 1976
2.   *The Times*, 24 April 1951
3.   *Sporting Life*, 3 May 1960

Chapter 50 – 'Ossie's Signings' (Page 461)
1.   Howard Wright, 'Chronicle Dead: Life in Danger', *Pacemaker International*, March 1984

Chapter 52 – 'The Last Bastion' (Page 477)
1.   George Duncan, 'Judy Goodhew – Housewife Extraordinaire', *Pacemaker*, March 1972

Chapter 54 – 'Anarchy' (Page 502)
1.   *Sporting Life*, 5 October 1967
2.   *Sporting Life*, 25 September 1969
3.   *Sporting Life*, 13 February 1964
4.   *Sporting Life*, 21 September 1970
5.   *Sunday Times*, 28 July 1985
6.   *The Times*, 28 August 1985
7.   *The Times*, 30 September 1985

Chapter 55 – 'Courting Success' (Page 514)
1. *The Observer*, 18 November 2001
2. *Ibid.*
3. *Sporting Life*, 30 July 1988, letter from John Ciechanowski, former French correspondent for the *Life* and later trainer to Sheikh Mohammed in Dubai and Lambourn

Chapter 56 – 'Man Overboard' (Page 531)
1. *The Times*, 11 November 1991
2. *Daily Mirror*, 6 November 1991
3. *The Times*, 5 November 1992
4. Paul Foot, *UK Press Gazette*, 5 April 1993

Chapter 57 – 'A New Broom' (Page 541)
1. *Racing Post*, 19 April 2001
2. *Sporting Life*, 3 August 1996
3. *The Observer*, 23 July 2006

Chapter 58 – 'The Final Nail' (Page 551)
1. *The Times*, 23 January 1997
2. Mirror Group PLC, *Report & Accounts*, 1998, p62

Chapter 60 – 'The Wake' (Page 568)
1. *Sunday Times*, 13 September 1998
2. Mirror Group PLC, *Report & Accounts*, 1998, p62
3. James Cameron, *Point of Departure*, 2006 ed., p282

PERIODICALS AND ANNUALS CONSULTED

All the Year Round; Badminton Magazine; Baily's Magazine; Bloodstock Breeders Review; British Journal of Sports History; British Journalism Review; Cope's Racegoers Encyclopaedia; Directory of the Turf; Fistionar; Illustrated Sporting and Dramatic News; London Gazette; National Association of Bookmakers file 1955; National Sporting League Journal; The Newspaper Owner; Pacemaker, Pacemaker International; Racing Calendar (weekly and annual volumes); Racing Review; Ruff's Guide to the Turf; Sell's Dictionary of the World's Press; Sporting Mirror; Sporting Record; Sporting Magazine, Stud & Stable; Timeform annuals; UK Press Gazette; Waterloo Directory of English Newspapers and Periodicals 1800-1900; Who's Who.

NEWSPAPERS

Aberdeen Evening Express; Bell's Life in London; Burton Daily Mail; Daily Express, Daily Herald, Daily Mail; Daily Mirror; Daily News; Daily Star; Daily Telegraph; Daily Worker (Morning Star); Irish Field; London Evening News; Manchester Guardian (The Guardian); Morning Advertiser; Morning Post; News of the World; Racing Post; Reading Mercury; Sporting Chronicle; Sporting Gazette; Sporting Telegraph; Sporting Times; The Sportsman; Sunday Mirror, Sunday Times; The Herald; The Observer; The People (Sunday People); The Standard; The Star; The Times; Yorkshire Post.

BIBLIOGRAPHY

A Lounger in the Courts, *Pen and Ink Sketches In Chancery* No 3 (William Ames, 1867)

Acton, William, *Prostitution* (John Churchill, 1857)

Arlott, John (ed.), *The Oxford Companion to Sports and Games* (Oxford University Press, 1975)

Ashforth, David, *Ringers & Rascals* (Highdown, Newbury, 2003)

Ashworth, John, *Strange Tales from Humble Life* (Tubbs and Brook, 1867)

Astley, Sir John, *Fifty Years of My Life* 2 Vols. (Hurst and Blackett, 1895)

Bebbington, W, *Rogues Go Racing* (Good & Betts, 1947)

Bird, T H, *Admiral Rous and the English Turf* (Putnam, 1939)

Boase, Frederic, *Modern English Biography* 6 Vols. (2nd ed Frank Cass, 1965)

Booth, J B, *Bits of Character: A Life of Henry Hall Dixon, 'The Druid'* (Hutchinson, 1936)

Booth, J B, *Old Pink 'Un Days* (Grant Richards, 1924)

Booth, J B, *Sporting Times, The Pink 'Un World* (T Werner Laurie, 1938)

Booth, Keith, *The Father of Modern Sport: The Life and Times of Charles W Alcock*, (Parrs Wood Press, Manchester, 2002)

Bourne, H R Fox, *English Newspapers* 2 Vols. (Chatto & Windus, 1887)

Bower, Tom, *Maxwell The Outsider* (Arum Press, 1988)

Bower, Tom, *Maxwell The Final Verdict* (HarperCollins, 1995)

Chesney, Kellow, *The Victorian Underworld* (Harmondsworth: Penguin, 1972)

Chetwynd, Sir George, *Racing Reminiscences* 2 Vols. (Longmans, Green, 1891)

Chinn, Carl, *Better Betting with a Decent Feller* (Harvester Wheatsheaf, 1991)

Cobbett, Martin, *Racing Life and Racing Characters* (Sands, 1903)

Cobbett, Martin, *The Man on the March* (Bliss, Sands, 1896)

Cook, Theodore Andrea, *A History of the English Turf* 2 vols. (Virtue, 1901)

Corsan, James, *For Poulton and England* (Matador, 2009)

Critchley, A C, *Critch! The Memoirs of Brig-Gen A C Critchley* (Hutchinson, 1961)

Curzon, Louis Henry, *A Mirror on the Turf* (Chapman Hall, 1892)

Custance, Henry, *Riding Recollections and Turf Stories* (Edward Arnold, 1894)

Davies, Nicholas, *The Unknown Maxwell* (Sidgwick & Jackson, 1992)

Davies, Russell, *Foreign Body: The Secret Life of Robert Maxwell* (Bloomsbury, 1995)

Dighton, Adair, *My Sporting Life* (Richards Press, 1934)

Dorling, E E, *Epsom and the Dorlings* (Stanley Paul, 1939)

Fitzgeorge-Parker, Tim, *The Guv'nor: A Biography of Sir Noel Murless* (Collins, 1980)

Fitzgerald, Arthur, *The Arc* (Genesis, 1997)

Francis, Dick, *Lester: The Official Biography* (Michael Joseph, 1986)

Freeman, Sarah, *Isabella and Sam* (Gollancz, 1977)

Galtrey, Sidney, *Memoirs of a Racing Journalist* (Hutchinson, 1934)

Good, Meyrick, *Good Days* (Hutchinson, 1941)

Good, Meyrick, *Lure of the Turf* (Odhams Press, 1957)

Green, Geoffrey, *The History of the Football Association*, (Naldrett Press, 1953)

Greenslade, Roy, *Press Gang* (Macmillan, 2003)

Gubbins, Nathanial, (pseudo. Edward Spencer), *Dopes* (R A Everett, 1901)

Hamlyn, Geoffrey, *My Sixty Years in the Ring* (Sporting Garland Press, 1994)

Hatton, Joseph, *Journalistic London* (Sampson Low, 1882)

Hawke, John, *A Blot on the Queen's Reign* (Elliot Stock, 1893)

Hodgman, George, *Sixty Years on the Turf* (Grant Richards, 1901)

Hudson, Derek, *British Journalists and Newspapers* (Collins, 1945)

Hughes, Kathryn, *The Short Life & Long Times of Mrs Beeton* (Fourth Estate, 2005)

Humphris, E M, *The Life of Mathew Dawson* (H F & G Witherby, 1928)

Hyde, H Montgomery, *Mr and Mrs Beeton* (George G Harrap, 1951)

Hyde, H Montgomery, *Sir Patrick Hastings: His Life and Cases* (Heinemann, 1960)

Jarvis, Jack, *They're Off* (Michael Joseph, 1969)

Jones, Kennedy, *Fleet Street & Downing Street* (Hutchinson, 1919)

Kaye, Richard, with Ray Poskett, *The Ladbrokes Story* (Pelham Books, 1969)

Lambton, The Hon. George, *Men and Horses I Have Known* (Thornton Butterworth, 1924)

Lawley, Francis, *The Life and Times of The Druid* (Vinton, 1895)

Longford, Elizabeth, *Wellington: Pillar of State* (Panther Books Ltd., St Albans, 1975)

Lucas, Norman and Bernard Scarlett, *The Flying Squad* (Arthur Barker, 1968)

Manson, Iain, *The Lion and the Eagle* (SportsBooks Ltd., 2008)

Marr, Andrew, *My Trade: A Short History of British Journalism* (Macmillan, 2004)

Marsh, Richard, *A Trainer to Two Kings* (Cassell, 1925)

Martin-Jenkins, Christopher, *The Complete Who's Who of Test Cricketers* (Orbis Publications, 1980)

Moorhouse, Edward, *The History and Romance of the Derby* 2 Vols. (Biographical Press, 1911)

Morison, Stanley, *The English Newspaper* (Cambridge University Press, 1932)

Mortimer, Roger, Richard Onslow, and Peter Willett, *Biographical Encyclopaedia of British Flat Racing* (Macdonald and Jane's, 1978)

Mortimer, Roger, *The Turf* (George Allen & Unwin, 1979)

Neville, Ralph, *Light Come, Light Go* (Macmillan, 1909)

O'Sullevan, Peter, *Calling the Horses* (Stanley Paul, 1989)

Orchard, Vincent, *Tattersalls: Two Hundred Years of Sporting History* (Hutchinson, 1953)

Peddie, James, *Racing For Gold* (Messrs. Fores, 1891)

Pitt, Chris, *A Long Time Gone* (Portway Press, 1996)

Porter, John, *Kingsclere* (Chatto & Windus, 1896)

Rice, James, *History of the British Turf* 2 Vols. (Sampson Low, Marston, Searle & Rivington, 1879)

Richardson, John Maunsell and Finch Mason, *Gentleman Riders Past and Present* (Vinton, 1909)

Rickman, Eric, *Come Racing With Me* (Chatto & Windus, 1951)

Rickman, Eric, *On and Off the Racecourse* (George Routledge, 1937)

Rimell, Fred and Mercy, *Aintree Iron*, (W H Allen, 1977)

Saville, John, *Insane and Unseemly*, (Matador, 2009)

Scott, Alexander, *Turf Memories of Sixty Years* (Hutchinson, 1925)

Scott, George, *Reporter Anonymous: The Story of the Press Association* (Hutchinson, 1968)

Seth-Smith, Michael and Peter Willett, Roger Mortimer and John Lawrence, *The History of Steeplechasing* (Michael Joseph, 1966)

Simonis, H, *The Street of Ink* (Cassell, 1917)

Sloan, Tod, *Tod Sloan by Himself* (Grant Richards, 1915)

Smith, Raymond, *Vincent O'Brien: The Master of Ballydoyle* (Virgin Books, 1990)

Spencer, Edward, *The Great Game, and how it is played* (Grant Richards, 1903)

Stoddard, T L, *Master of Manhattan* (Longmans, New York, Toronto, 1931)

Sullivan, John L, *Life and Reminiscences of a Nineteenth Century Gladiator* (G Routledge, 1892)

Symon, James D, *The Press and its Story* (Seeley, Service, 1914)

The Druid, *Post and Paddock* (Frederick Warne, 1856)

The history of the Times Vol IV (The Times, 1952)

Titley, U A and Ross McWhirter, *Centenary History of the Rugby Football Union* (Rugby Football Union, 1970)

Vamplew, Wray, *The Turf* (Allen Lane, Penguin Books, 1976)

Voigt, Charles Adolph, *Famous Gentleman Riders at Home and Abroad* (Hutchinson, 1925)

Ward, Fred W, *The 23rd (Service) Battalion Royal Fusiliers* (Sidgwick & Jackson, 1920)

Watson, Alfred E T (ed.), *The Racing World and its Inhabitants* (Macmillan, 1904)

Watson, R P, *Memoirs of Robert Patrick Watson* (Smith, Ainslee, 1899)

Webb, Arthur, *The Clean Sweep* (George G Harrap, 1968)

Welcome, John, *Fred Archer his Life & Times* (Faber & Faber, 1967)

Williams, Guy St. John and Francis P M Hyland, *The Irish Derby 1866-1979* (J A Allen, 1980)

Woodland, Les, *Dope: The Use of Drugs in Sport* (David & Charles, Newton Abbot, 1980)

Wright, Howard, *Bull: the Biography* (Timeform, Halifax, 1995)

GLOSSARY

ABBREVIATIONS
BDRA – Betting Duty Reform Association
BHB – British Horseracing Board
BOLA – Betting Office Licensees' Association
NAB – National Association of Bookmakers
NBPA – National Bookmakers Protection Association
NSL – National Sporting League
NTF – National Trainers Federation
NUJ – National Union of Journalists
RBCB – Racecourse Betting Control Board
RCA – Racecourse Association
RCVS – Royal College of Veterinary Surgeons
RIB – Racing Information Bureau
ROA – Racehorse Owners Association
RSPCA – Royal Society for the Prevention of Cruelty to Animals
SIS – Satellite Information Services
TBA – Thoroughbred Breeders Association
TUC – Trades Union Congress

JOURNALISTIC/PRINTING TERMS
Many of the words relating to the printing process are from the days of hot-metal and although now made obsolete by computer technology they are still used in the trade.

Block – the surface from which an illustration is printed.

Box – a border enclosing a news item.

Brief – a short news item.

Copy – editorial matter sent for printing, journalists used to make carbon copies of their typed articles for sub-editors and readers to check against page proofs.

Crosshead – a centred heading placed in text to break up the solid appearance of a column.

Filler – a brief used to fill the gap left when a main article falls short of the space allotted to it.

Flyer – a short announcement, usually given prominence on the front page.

FoC – Father of the Chapel, the head of an office branch of a printers' or journalists' union.

Hot metal – printing type made from molten metal; the process of printing by such means.

Layout – a page design with regard to the position and size of headlines, stories and pictures.

Make-up – the arrangement of type and items into columns or pages.

Masthead – now most commonly used to describe the front page title-line.

Page proof – an impression taken of a page of type used for correcting printing errors.

Returns – of racing results, comprising the order of finish and SPs. Also used to describe a newsagent's return of unsold newspapers.

Specials – an all-embracing term for special correspondents.

Spike – a metal spike on which unused copy is filed.

Stone – originally a slab of slate on which compositors made up the pages; the 'off-stone time' is when the completed pages are sent to the printers.

Stringer – a locally based freelance correspondent paid for part-time work.

Sub – an abbreviated term for a sub-editor, or the act of sub-editing.

Tear-out – a section of text from a previous article or another publication, reproduced to emphasise a point.

RACING/BETTING TERMINOLOGY

Betting show – the latest on-course betting movements as relayed into betting shops.

Board-man – before the advent of SIS transmissions to betting shops, a board-man used to chalk up betting shows and race results on a large blackboard.

Flapping meeting – unlicensed race meeting held outside the jurisdiction of the Jockey Club.

Flash bet – a fictitious bet made for the purpose of misleading bookmakers and others.

Forfeit list – a list of defaulters printed in the *Racing Calendar*, so long as an owner's name is on the list they are unable to run their horses.

Milking (a horse) – when an owner or bookmaker lays against a horse knowing it has no chance of winning or, perhaps, even running.

Nap selection – a racing correspondent's idea of the best bet of the day.

Nursery – a handicap race for two-year-olds; the nursery season starts in July.

Penciller or layer – a bookmaker.

Rails bookmaker – an on-course bookmaker who has his pitch alongside the rails that divide the main betting ring (Tattersalls) from the members enclosure.

Recall flagman – a starter's assistant who is positioned some 150 yards down the course from the start so he can signal a false start if necessary.

Rope or pull – the act of restraining a horse to stop it from winning.

Rubbing house – a hut or shelter where horses were rubbed down and dried off after exercise.

Scratch – to withdraw a horse from its engagement before a declaration stage.

Tic-tac – a bookmakers' telegraphy system similar to semaphore where arm and hand signals are used to indicate changing prices across the betting ring.

Warned off – racing's ultimate disciplinary sanction against wrongdoers. Initially the stewards' powers extended only to banishing miscreants from Newmarket Heath, but during the 19th century their authority was extended to cover any racecourse which raced under Jockey Club rules.

Weight-for-age scale – a sliding scale of weights to be carried by horses of different ages running against each other over different distances at different times of the year.

COURSING

Puppy – a first season dog not yet 2 years old.

Puss – a hare, as in the genus *Lepus*.

PRE-DECIMAL CURRENCY

1 farthing = $^1/_4$ of a penny; 1 penny = 0.416p; 1 shilling (12 pennies) = 5p; half-a-crown = 12½p; crown = 25p; 1 guinea = £1.05; (slang) 'a pony' = £25

INDEX

When a reference frequently occurs such as Newmarket or the Jockey Club, minor mentions have been omitted. 'i' adjoining a page number indicates an illustration

CHRONOLOGY OF IMPORTANT DATES IN THE LIFE OF THE *LIFE*

1859 - March 9-11: Forthcoming launch is advertised in the *Morning Advertiser* and other papers.
March 16: Registered as a newspaper.
March 24: *The Penny Bell's Life and Sporting News* appears a day late, published as a bi-weekly (Wednesday and Saturday), at 1 Crane Court, Fleet Street.
April 26: The proprietors of *Bell's Life in London* are granted an injunction against the 'penny imitator' using its title.
April 30: First published as *The Sporting Life*.
June 1: Moves offices to 148 Fleet Street.

1860 - April: Sale of the Sayers v Heenan big-fight special edition is put at 367,000.
August: 'Augur' (Harry Feist) 'joins' the *Life*.

1861 - January: John Shipley, joint-proprietor, is made bankrupt and the manager, William Stephens, flees to Scotland to seek bankruptcy.
March: Sam Beeton buys Shipley's half share in the paper and brings in his brother-in-law, Edward Jonathan Dorling, as manager and publisher.

1862 - October: French correspondent H L Dillon is killed in a duel.

1863 - Sales of the Heenan v King big-fight issues for the week ending December 12, total 550,878.

1865 - August: A two-page supplement is issued containing "a mass of Cricket and Aquatic Intelligence".
December: Sam Beeton sells his share in the *Life* to John Hutton and William McFarlane after losing a two-year court battle for outright ownership.

1870 - March: Henry Hall Dixon, leader writer and famous as 'The Druid', dies.

1873 - May: Edward Dorling leaves following the death of his father, Epsom racecourse manager and clerk of the course, Henry Dorling.

1874 - December: Henry Mort Feist, founding editor and Augur, dies.

1875 - January: Charles William Blake becomes editor and Augur.

1877 - October: First sponsorship of a sporting event – a 50-mile bicycle race for the *Sporting Life* Cup at London's Lillie Bridge stadium.

1881 - March: Publication is extended to four times a week.
May: A telegram racing results service is launched and the paper begins returning its own starting prices through its 'Man in the Ring' (Martin Cobbett).
December: Sponsors a weekly series of pedestrian handicap sprint races and swimming events.

1883 - March: Published as a daily when the annual postal subscription is 39s (£175) = cover price of 26s plus 13s postage @ ½d.

1886 - May: Takes over of *Bell's Life in London* (est. 1822).

1891 - June: Charles Blake dies and George Shortland Lowe becomes editor.

1903 – December (?): William Will takes over as editor. He transforms the paper with the help of William Smith Morley-Brown, who joins as news editor in March 1904.

1904 - June: Editorial offices move to 27 St Bride Street off Ludgate Circus.

1905 - February: Linotype machines are finally installed, 15 years after they were first used in Scotland

1907 - October: William McFarlane dies and the paper is taken over by his widow, Eleanor.

1909 - Eleanor McFarlane marries managing editor Walter Elliot Broomfield.
May: The 4ft 6in, £500 (£45,000) *Sporting Life* Challenge Trophy is presented to the winner of the first Windsor-London marathon.

1911 - March: William Will leaves and William Lints Smith takes over as editor.

1914 - July: Lints Smith moves to *The Times* and W S Morley-Brown takes over.

1915 - May: Friedrich Becker, the German-born bloodstock correspondent, is interned on the Isle of Man.

1918 - March: After 59 years of holding its price at a penny it takes a world war to force an increase to 2d.
November 12: A single sheet edition reports the end of the Great War.

1920 - January: After 60 years, the *Life* moves out of 148 Fleet Street when publishing and advertising transfer to nearby 10 Shoe Lane.

July: Following the death of his wife, Walter Broomfield sells the *Life* to Odhams Ltd.

1924 - November: Takes over of *The Sportsman*; the title is changed to *Sporting Life and Sportsman* until it reverts to *The Sporting Life* in May 1927.

1925 - November: After a series of SP wars which saw different papers carrying different sets of starting prices, agreement is reached with the *Sporting Chronicle* for a unified set of returns.

1927 - March: Morley-Brown leaves and Chris Towler becomes editor.
May: Offices move to Odhams headquarters at 93 Long Acre and a 'new' *Life* is born.

1932 - May-October: A daily campaign is run to raise £10,000 (£527,000) for the Royal Veterinary College Appeal – the King responds and the target is reached to the grateful thanks of Sir Frederick Hobday.

1938 - January: Jimmy Milne, the athletics editor, wins the famous Powderhall sprint; Towler dies and A B 'Ben' Clements becomes editor.

1939 - September: Published as a weekly for the first three weeks of the war, then reverts to daily status before becoming a weekly again in June 1940.

1944 - October: Publication stepped up to twice a week on Mondays and Wednesdays.

1945 - May: End of war in Europe sees the addition of a Saturday edition.

1946 - March: Returns to daily publication with its price increased to 3d, but sales and pagination are restricted by newsprint rationing for the next ten years.

1949 - March: The *Life* hosts a luncheon for 300 guests at the Savoy "to honour the stewards and members of the Jockey Club and NH Committee for their conduct of our sport". Duke of Edinburgh, Lords Rosebery, Norfolk, *et al*, attend. The luncheon is held again in 1950 and 1951.

1955 – March-April: In common with other national newspapers, the *Life* does not appear for almost a month because of a strike by maintenance electricians and engineers.

1957 - March: Clements introduces the page-2 marker-sheet for the benefit of bookmakers.

1959 - September: Clements steps down and Ossie Fletcher becomes editor.

1960 - March: The *Life* becomes first national daily to carry colour (for one day only in its Grand National issue).

1961 - March: Odhams and the *Life* are taken over by the International Publishing Corporation, publishers of the *Daily Mirror*.
December: A front-page photo of Micheline Lugeon alerts trainers throughout the country to a key member of Bill Roper's gang of dopers.

1971 - July: Moves offices from Long Acre to Orbit House, New Fetter Lane, opposite the *Mirror* building at Holborn Circus.

1976 - February: The Queen and the Duke of Edinburgh visit the *Life's* offices.

1978 - May: An attempt at computer typesetting results in the loss of a week's production and a return to hot-metal printing.

1979 - July: In a series of scoops under the general heading of 'The Carlisle cock-up' the *Life's* star reporter John McCririck reveals how the Tote, under the chairmanship of Woodrow Wyatt, was placing fictitious bets in Tote pools after the result of races was known. Despite incontrovertible evidence of fraud and tax evasion, no one was ever prosecuted for one of the biggest ever racing scandals.

1982 - October: The Royal Coat of Arms is added to the paper's masthead.

1983 - July: *The Sporting Life Weekender* is launched to rival the *Handicap Book* which is taken over by *Raceform* following the closure of the *Sporting Chronicle*.

1984 - July: Robert Maxwell buys Mirror Group Newspapers from Reed International.

1985 - March: Fletcher retires and his deputy Graham Taylor is appointed editor by Maxwell.
August 23: Maxwell closes down the *Life* and the *Mirror* for two weeks in his continuing battle with the print unions. A free emergency edition of the *Life* is issued before the paper returns to normal on September 7.

1986 - January: Offices move to Alexander House, Farringdon Road, as the paper is typeset and printed by various contract firms spread across London.
April: Taylor takes early retirement and Monty Court takes over.

1988 - July: Maxwell appoints Mike Gallemore from the *Daily Mirror*, Manchester, as managing editor.
September: The paper moves back to Orbit House.
November: *The Greyhound Life* is launched with Bob Betts as editor.

1989 - January: Starts to be printed by Thomson Regional Newspapers in Belfast.
July: Starts to be printed in colour and is also printed in Oldham.

July: Gallemore takes over as editor and Court becomes editor-in-chief.

1990 - March: Jockeys' (owners') colours are printed on the paper's racecards.
     November: Court retires and Maxwell brings in Charlie Wilson as managing director and editor-in-chief.

1991 - August: *Sportslife*, a four-page Saturday supplement aimed at the sports-betting market is launched; it is continued in reduced form in the main paper on weekdays.
     November: Maxwell goes overboard.

1992 - October: David Montgomery becomes chief executive of MGN.

1993 - April: Gallemore is sacked and Tom Clarke takes over.

1994 - February: Offices move to One Canada Square (Canary Wharf tower).

1995 - May 7: A Sunday edition on "a historic day for British racing" as Newmarket and Salisbury stage the first Sunday racing with on-course betting.

1996 - June: The paper is issued in two sections as its page-layout, especially formatted for betting shop display, is redesigned as 'The Reader-Friendly Life'. Bookmakers are not happy.
     December: Launch of PA/Sporting Life sports internet website.

1997 - February: A specially designed Betting Shop Edition is produced to rival the *Racing Post's*, but too late to stop the big three bookmaking chains signing up with the *Post*.
     June: The *Life* loses its market lead to the *Post* after a 25% slump in sales over the past 12 months.
     December: MGN buy the *Racing Post* for £1 and announce that it will be the main racing paper, while the *Sporting Life* is to be developed as a general sports paper.

1998 - February: The *Life* (MGN) has to pay £195,000 damages plus costs to Lynda and Jack Ramsden and Kieren Fallon after losing the Top Cees libel case.
     May 12: Closedown.